Camerapix Publishers International
NAIROBI

Spectrum Guide to South Africa

First published 1996 by
Camerapix Publishers International
P.O. Box 45048,
Nairobi, Kenya

ISBN 1-874041-86-5

This book was designed and produced by
Camerapix Publishers International,
P.O. Box 45048,
Nairobi, Kenya

The **Spectrum Guides** series provides a comprehensive and detailed description of each country it covers, together with all the essential data that tourists, business visitors, or potential investors are likely to require.

Spectrum Guides in print:
African Wildlife Safaris
Ethiopia
Jordan
Kenya
Maldives
Mauritius
Namibia
Pakistan
Seychelles
South Africa
Tanzania
Zambia
Zimbabwe

Printed and bound by Tien Wah Press Singapore.

Publisher and Chief Executive:
Mohamed Amin
Editor: David Barritt
Picture Editor: Duncan Willetts
Associate Editors: Caroline Jones
and Jan Hemsing
Photographic Research: Storm Stanley
Editorial Assistant: Sophie Brown

Editorial Board

South Africa is a huge, fascinating and complex country. Two years of work have gone into the preparation of the Spectrum Guide to South Africa, and it is certainly the latest and most exhaustive guide available.

South African writer and publisher **David Barritt** co-ordinated the research and served as editorial director. Barritt says he owes a South African-sized debt of gratitude to his editorial team, particularly to the two Sarahs — **Sarah Brown** and **Sarah Scarth** who chivvied contributors, checked facts and begged for more time from merciless publisher **Mohamed Amin**.

Sarah Brown researched and wrote parts one, four and most of six, and was responsible for the organization of much of the rest, before departing to give birth to Molly. Sarah Scarth took over where Sarah Brown left off.

Claire Ward, a South African journalist, contributed the sections on what was the Transvaal — Northern Province and Mpumalanga — and Free State.

Alf Wannenburgh, a well-known Cape Town-based writer and author of many books on aspects of South Africa, wrote the Eastern Cape, Western Cape and Northern Cape sections.

John Maytham contributed the bird section. A journalist and keen bird watcher, John is a member of the Vulture Study Group monitoring population growths and security of the six vulture species in the country, and is also involved in the southern African bird atlas project.

Sonia Learmont painstakingly researched the abundant flora.

Grant Brewer, who contributed the section on the economy, is studying at the University of the Witwatersrand in Johannesburg.

Journalist **Shelagh McLoughlin**, chief sub-editor of the *Natal Witness* newspaper, wrote the KwaZulu-Natal section.

Caroline Jones did sterling work sourcing pictures, research and editing. **Patricia Czakan** subbed, edited and captioned.

Above: The Cape sugar bird belongs to the only bird family that is unique to South Africa.

TABLE OF CONTENTS

IN BRIEF

LISTINGS

MAPS

Half title: Elephants — South Africa's magnificent natural heritage. Title page: Sunset at Milnerton in Cape Town. Pages 8–9: Kirstenbosch Gardens at Kenilworth, Cape Town. Pages 10–11: White Rhino grazing in the famous Mala Mala Game Reserve: the two species, black and white, are endangered.

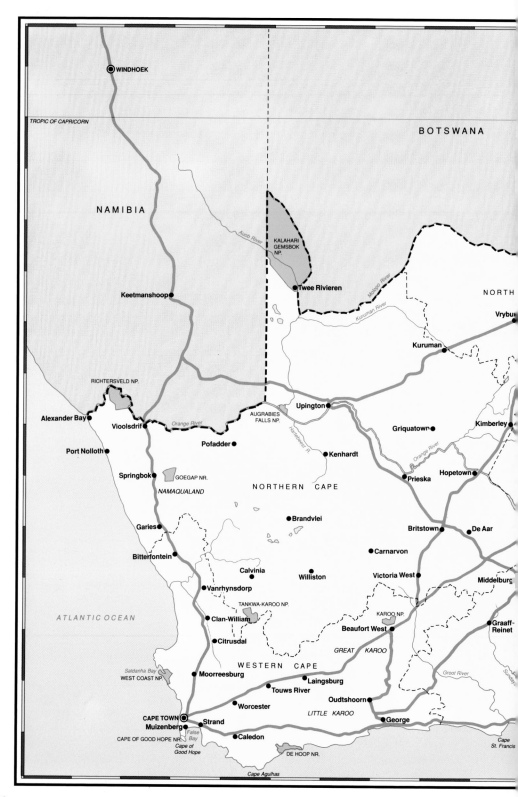

WINDHOEK

TROPIC OF CAPRICORN

BOTSWANA

NAMIBIA

Auob River

KALAHARI
GEMSBOK
NP.

Keetmanshoop

Twee Rivieren

Malopo River

Kuruman River

NORTH

Vrybur

Kuruman

RICHTERSVELD NP.

Alexander Bay

Vioolsdrif

Orange River

AUGRABIES
FALLS NP.

Upington

Griquatown

Kimberley

Port Nolloth

Pofadder

Hartebeest R.

Kenhardt

Orange River

Springbok

GOEGAP NR.

NAMAQUALAND

NORTHERN CAPE

Prieska

Hopetown

Garies

Brandvlei

Britstown

De Aar

Bitterfontein

Carnarvon

Calvinia

Williston

Victoria West

Middelburg

Vanrhynsdorp

TANKWA-KAROO NP.

ATLANTIC OCEAN

KAROO NP.

Clan-William

Beaufort West

Graaff-
Reinet

Citrusdal

GREAT   KAROO

Saldanha Bay
WEST COAST NP.

Moorreesburg

Laingsburg

Groot River

Sunday

Touws River

Oudtshoorn

Worcester

LITTLE KAROO

WESTERN CAPE

CAPE TOWN

George

Muizenberg

Strand

CAPE OF GOOD HOPE NR.

False
Bay

Caledon

Cape
St. Francis

Cape of
Good Hope

DE HOOP NR.

Cape Agulhas

12

South Africa

ZIMBABWE
Beit Bridge
Messina

VENDA
Louis Trichardt
Thohoyandou

MOZAMBIQUE

NORTHERN PROVINCE

Ellisras

Pietersburg
Tzaneen
Phalaborwa

KRUGER
NATIONAL

PARK

Potgietersrus

Olifants R.

Limpopo River

Gaborone
Thabazimbi
Nylstroom

Warmbad

BLYDE
RIVER
CANYON NR.
Lydenburg

BOPHUTHATSWANA
PILANESBERG NP.

Crocodile R.

Komatipoort

Sun City

Rustenburg
PRETORIA
Witbank
Nelspruit

Mmabatho
GAUTENG
MPUMALANGA

Maputo

Mafikeng

Lichtenburg
Krugersdorp
JOHANNESBURG

Mbabane

WEST

Potchefstroom
Vereeniging

SWAZILAND

Klerksdorp
Vaal River

Standerton
Piet Retief
Lavumisa

Frankfort
Volksrust

MKUZI GR.

Wilge R.
Pongola River

ITALA NR.

Kroonstad
Newcastle
Vryheid

GREATER ST. LUCIA
WETLAND PARK

Christiana
Welkom
HLUHLUWE/UMFOLOZI
PARK

Bethlehem
Dundee

Winburg
Harrismith
KWAZULU-NATAL

GOLDEN GATE
HIGHLANDS NP.

FREE STATE
Ladysmith

Modder R.
Caledon River
ROYAL
NATAL NP.
Tugela River

BLOEMFONTEIN
Greytown
Richards Bay

Maseru
NATAL
DRAKENSBERG
PARK
Stanger

LESOTHO
Pietermaritzburg
DURBAN

lippolis

INDIAN OCEAN

Aliwal-North

Port Edward

Elliot
TRANSKEI
MKAMBATI NR.

EASTERN CAPE
Umtata

Queenstown
Coffee Bay

Cradock
Gt. Kei River

W I L D   C O A S T

King
William's
Town

CISKEI

Gt. Fish R.

JRBERG
NP.
East London

Grahamstown

Port Alfred

PORT ELIZABETH

| 0 | 100 | 200 | 300 | 400 | 500 km |
| 0 | 100 | | 200 | | 300 miles |

The South African Experience

The 'New South Africa' is the latest international tourist destination, offering the African experience combined with the comfort of a westernized nation. That's why South Africa is dubbed 'Africa without the hassle'.

South Africa is an extraordinarily beautiful country — its climate is good, the scenery magnificent, its beaches unspoiled and, unlike most of Africa, there is a sophisticated infrastructure including a first-rate road system, good air links between all major centres and good telephone communications. Health care is of high quality and is inexpensive by world standards. Hotels are good and relatively cheap. South Africa is one of the world's best kept secrets and now, for the first time, the rest of the world is free to enjoy it.

The political changes that have taken place in South Africa since 1989 were completely inconceivable only a few years previously. The country's nascent democracy has been applauded by the international community, and South Africa's long years of isolation are over. Economic, cultural and sporting boycotts have ended as South Africa regains its place on the world stage.

And these changes have also returned South Africa to the tourist map for those eager for new experiences at reasonable prices. The rand, South Africa's currency unit, is bought cheaply on international foreign exchanges, allowing visitors to live at high standards for little cost.

Travel to the famous Kruger National Park, one of the largest game reserves in the world, where Africa's wild animals roam through the bush. Or spot the birds and animals in seventeen other national parks throughout the country. Approximately 6.6 million hectares (16.3 million acres) are presently under protection in South Africa. There are also a large number of private game reserves, some of which offer trophy hunting, although this particular form of tourism raises the ire of the country's increasingly vocal conservation lobby.

The country's economy grew from wealth generated by its mineral deposits; gold and diamonds being only the most famous of a wide range of mining concerns from kaolin to coal. In modern times, its industrial and financial sectors have become the most sophisticated in Africa.

Peer into the Great Hole of Kimberley, the world's largest man-made hole, where a mountain was first levelled, then the ground beneath excavated in the search for diamonds. Descend into a no longer working gold mine at Johannesburg's Gold Reef City to see how the wealth of the nation is prised from the ground.

Water is scarce throughout the central highland plateau of the country where cattle and maize are the main agricultural products. But on the wetter coastal plains a vast array of produce can be grown. On the sub-tropical eastern lowlands bananas and mangoes thrive, while the temperate climate of the Cape Province is perfect for apples and vines.

Tour the wine routes, visiting the verdant vineyards nestling in the foothills and valleys of the mountains near Cape Town. Experience South Africa's celebrated wines in their home territory, accompanied by excellent, traditional Cape fare.

The country's turbulent history records the great variety of peoples and cultures who have settled in South Africa from prehistoric hominids to the mixture of races and tribes who today call South Africa home. Explore the rocks and caves of the imposing Drakensberg mountains, where San tribespeople etched and painted the mountainsides with depictions of their lives and beliefs. 'Bushmen' art follows the gradually changing lifestyle of this ancient tribe from about 20,000 years ago to the last century.

Opposite: South Africa's ethnic peoples: a rainbow of colour.

Above: Hex River Valley in the Cape Province.

Stay in a Zulu beehive hut at Shakaland and see tribespeople making handiwork and ancient rituals being carried out, or visit the San tribespeople of the Kamma Kagga or the Venda of Northern Province.

Discover the history of Cape Town, the Mother City. Visit the Afrikaner Monument, and travel back in time to the Great Trek days and the foundations of the 'white tribe of Africa' — the Afrikaners.

For the tourist interested in nature, there is a wealth of wildlife, over ten per cent of the world's avifauna, a unique flora and breathtaking scenery.

Hike along the Wild Coast, up dramatic cliffs and along silent stretches of deserted beach. Trek through the Karoo mountains surrounded by herds of zebra and wildebeest.

Immerse yourself in the flowery landscape of the Cape, one of the six floral kingdoms of the world. See the desert bloom every spring in Namaqualand.

Go on safari to the sand dunes of the Kalahari, where wildlife of all kinds have specially adapted to the arid conditions.

Swim with leatherback turtles among the brilliant corals of the northern Natal coastline, or surf at Jeffrey's Bay, South Africa's surfing capital.

Drive along the garden route, see primeval cycads, pockets of indigenous forest and visit ostrich farms along the way.

For those more interested in the spicier side of life, there are plenty of thrills to be found. Journey to Sun City, and there in the splendour of the wild Pilanesberg mountains, try your luck at gaming tables and slot machines. Wander through the jungle of The Lost City, a massive African theme park which also boasts one of the world's finest hotels.

Thrill to the nightlife of metropolitan Johannesburg; sunbathe on Durban's golden beaches and stroll down streets purple-canopied by jacaranda trees in the capital city of Pretoria.

South Africa is a vast country with something for everyone. Its wealth of flora and fauna, its huge horizons and stunning scenery combined with its year-round sunshine, make it a dream destination.

Welcome.

Travel Brief and Social Advisory

Some do's and don'ts to make your visit more enjoyable.

Under South Africa's veneer of Western civilization you can find the wonder of Africa. The mixture allows you to travel and stay in comfort while experiencing the thrills of the wildlife, scenery and cultures of this diverse country.

This peculiar combination of First and Third World can be amusing and sometimes irritating. Just when you expect First World treatment, something will happen to remind you that you're in Africa. Yet just when you expect the worst, lo and behold, all the trappings of the First World will be at your feet. Sit back and enjoy this unique blend of experiences.

Getting There

By air

South Africa is well serviced by many major airlines. South African Airways, the national carrier, flies regularly between South Africa and the United States of America, the United Kingdom, Europe, South America, Hong Kong, Bangkok, Singapore, Taipei, Bombay, Australia, Dubai, Tel Aviv and to several African countries.

Flights can be heavily booked, particularly at peak holiday seasons, so book early if possible.

By sea

Although the grand old days of travelling in luxury by mailboat are over, and South African ports cater almost exclusively for cargo ships, there is the occasional cruise ship that docks at Cape Town or Durban. The RM *St Helena* docks at Cape Town, arriving from Britain via Ascension and St Helena islands, and the *Symphony* calls in at both Cape Town and Durban. Safmarine's giant container liners have five luxury cabins available for passengers cruising between Cape Town and Europe.

By road

You can drive into South Africa from all its neighbouring countries. Large car rental firms will issue you with letters of transit if you want to drive between South Africa and most neighbours, but check first.

By rail

There are rail links with Namibia, Botswana, Zimbabwe and Mozambique, but local air services are generally much more convenient and reasonably priced.

Getting Around

By air

South African Airways, Comair, Phoenix Airways and Sun Air have regular, inexpensive domestic flights to main cities. There are several independent airlines which fly to smaller centres, and there are safe and reliable charter services.

By road

South Africa's roads are of excellent standard, with about 84,000 kilometres (52,200 miles) of tarred roads, and a further 163,000 kilometres (101,300 miles) of well-tended, untarred roads, only the remotest of which may become impassable in wet weather. The standard of South African driving does not match the quality of its roads, and visitors should be aware that basic road courtesy and highway codes are frequently ignored.

South African drivers have a lethal combination of powerful cars, bad driving habits and macho aggression. Driving on the freeways can be particularly hair-raising. Matters are made worse because many drivers have never passed a driving test, having simply bought a licence on the black market.

Driving is on the left and the general speed limits are sixty kilometres (37 miles) an hour in town, 100 kilometres (62 miles)

Above: South African Airways, frequently voted the best airline in Africa, has regular, inexpensive domestic flights to main cities. SAA also operates 40 international destinations.

on rural roads and 120 kilometres (75 miles) on freeways and major roads. There are special traffic squads that impose heavy fines if you are caught violating traffic laws (speeding, drunk-driving or not wearing your seatbelt, etc). Automatic cameras to catch speedsters are also sited at the side of some roads. South Africans often paint information on their roads in both Afrikaans and English. You are warned of traffic lights by the word 'Robot' (South African for 'traffic light') painted on each lane before it.

Car rental is cheap, and rental cars are of a high standard. The cost of an air-conditioned car with all trimmings is about the same price as for a standard model in Europe. There is no extra charge from major companies for dropping a car off at a different destination from where you picked it up. Petrol is cheap by European standards, and petrol stations are found all over the country. Diesel is usually available. Many petrol stations are open 24 hours.

In large cities there are standard taxis which have meters — but check that the driver turns the meter on, or negotiate a price before you start. Taxis don't cruise the streets. You must either go to a taxi rank or phone for one. These taxis can also be expensive.

'Black taxis' are also available. These are minibuses which follow a designated route and are basically small, private buses. They were developed by black South Africans as a cheap way of getting about in the face of inefficient and inadequate bus services provided by municipalities. Services are frequent and cover many more areas than municipal buses which only cover town centres. There is a flat fee for however far you travel. Anyone can take advantage of these communal taxis.

To catch a black taxi stand at the side of a main road — there are no bus stops — raise your arm and stick out your index finger. Routes are not marked on the taxi, and you'll have to ask for help to get to your destination. Black taxis will also travel intercity. For further information phone the South African Black Taxi Association (SABTA) Tel: (012) 325 1570.

Municipal double-decker buses service all main city centres, but services are infrequent and unreliable. Coaches are a cheap and popular mode of transport for intercity travel, and also for tours both around cities and through the South African countryside. Greyhound and other local coach services offer regular services between towns. Transnet — the once state-owned bus and train service — and several tour operators offer a variety of coach tours, including week-long trips along the beautiful Garden Route, trips to game parks and half-day visits to townships or diamond mines.

By Train

Passenger trains operate between main towns and on many small branch lines throughout the country but services are generally slow, inefficient and of a poor standard.

The exception is South Africa's luxury express, the Blue Train. Here, comfort and service are of a high standard. It is rather like a modern Orient Express with a viewing lounge, cocktail bars and adequate food. There are four classes of cabins from basic (toilet facilities shared), to rooms with showers or baths to private suites. The train runs between Pretoria, Johannesburg and Cape Town, one to three times a week depending on the season. The Blue Train also operates a winter service, running to the Mpumalanga lowveld — a bonus for visitors going to the Kruger National Park. The train runs from Pretoria to Nelspruit. Booking well in advance is essential.

Express trains, which run between most main towns, have dining cars and three classes of accommodation. Long distance trains have sleeping berths included in the price of first and second class tickets. Buy a bedding ticket when you make your reservation or obtain it on the train, and give it to the bedding attendant who will make up your bunk.

On several lines you can experience the gentle art of steam travel. Some engines pull special tourist trains. (See Part Four).

By Foot

Hiking is very popular in South Africa, with many trails created in government-proclaimed nature reserves, and others on private land. There are beautiful trails for the fit and the not-so-fit from two-hour walks to a fortnight's hike, in vast plains, mountainous scenery or along the seashore. Many hikes take you through conservation areas where you can stroll among zebras, look at cycads and appreciate eagles soaring above you.

That said, walking in non-designated areas can be a problem since most private land is fenced off, and trespassing laws are strictly enforced. Many trails, especially those with cabin accommodation along the route, are fully-booked far in advance during school holidays.

The People

South Africans pride themselves on giving visitors a warm welcome, but because of the isolation they have experienced for the last few decades, they are unused to having to explain their culture or language to those not in the know. You may well find yourself invited to a 'braai' — the South African national pastime — without being told that you're going to a barbeque.

Similarly, the South African tourism industry is geared to the local tourist, so people in all areas of the industry will assume you have a far higher level of knowledge about the country and how it works than you are likely to possess. Try not to get angry if things are not fully explained, tell them that you are a foreigner and need more information.

As in most western civilizations, you are unlikely to make new friends unless you make a special effort. Sure, you'll see the Zulu dancers, or chat to the tour guide at the vineyard, but actually getting to know new people takes time and energy. People will get on with their private lives unless you show a special interest.

The race issue is still noticeable in South Africa, though now more from a socio-economic viewpoint. You will still find some whites passionately supporting colonial domination of the blacks, and some blacks believing that all whites should leave the country. The issue is a complex one, as you will be bound to discover. A white

Above: Donkey carts are still found in small rural towns.

family which has had roots in South Africa since the seventeenth century believes itself as South African as the blacks of the subcontinent. Keep an open mind, listen to differing views and you will be surprised.

There are ten different tribal groupings in South Africa, and within the black population all is not roses. Internecine fighting between supporters of different tribes or political groups can be very common.

There are two main white groupings: those speaking English and those speaking Afrikaans as a first language. Animosity between the two groups can be intense. The Afrikaners regard themselves as true white people of Africa who fought and struggled to win a living on the harsh subcontinent. The Boer — Afrikaans for 'farmer' — sees the English-speakers as latter-day colonialists. The English-speakers, in turn, generally perceive themselves as more liberal, forward-thinking and in tune with world-wide policies than Afrikaners.

There are also many Indians, coloured (mixed race), Chinese, Portuguese and other ethnic minorities in South Africa.

Safety

City crime rates are high and rising. Certain areas of Johannesburg, Cape Town and Durban are prime areas for muggers. Ask at your hotel if it's safe to walk around at night. Don't advertise that you're a tourist — don't walk around with a camera round your neck, check where you're going before you set out and try not to consult maps en route. Wear a money belt if it makes you feel more secure, and only carry as much money as you need. Keep valuable items out of sight, handbags closed and held tightly to the body, lock your car, don't fall for conmen offering bargains on the street. Thefts from cars are common, so lock anything valuable out of sight in the boot.

Hotels in South Africa are not responsible for thefts from your hotel room, so make sure you keep your valuables in the safety deposit boxes which are provided by most hotels. In the national parks there are no locks on any accommodation, so lock valuables in the boot of your car.

You are obliged by law to carry your driver's licence with you when driving.

You will need a passport to change foreign currency into rands.

Clothing

South Africa has several different climates so dress requirements can vary widely. One good tip is that if you intend to be outdoors for any length of time, wear a hat for protection against the sun.

In the winter, although the sun shines almost every day, it can get very cold in the evenings — temperatures as low as minus 12 degrees Celsius have been recorded in Johannesburg — so bring warm clothing as well as something lighter for the relatively mild — around 17 degrees Celsius — days. At the coast and in the lowveld regions the evenings are not so cold, but there is light rain in the winter months.

In the summertime, lightweight cotton clothing is a must with daytime temperatures commonly around 25–30 degrees Celsius. On the inland plateau there is often an afternoon or evening thunderstorm, which cools things down considerably, but because the rain can be heavy, some waterproof clothing is advisable. In the evenings the heat lessens and a light jacket or sweater is all that is required.

In Cape Town all year round, and in Johannesburg in the winter, a chill wind can whip through you even as the sun beats down, so bring wind-proof clothes to protect yourself.

In the malarial areas — the Mpumalanga lowveld, the Kruger National Park and Zululand in KwaZulu-Natal — it's wise to take light clothes that cover the body to don at dusk against the dreaded mosquito.

There are a few topless and nude beaches in South Africa but bear in mind that South Africa is a conservative society and that nudity is generally frowned upon.

South Africa is also an informal country, so there is very little need for smart clothes or ties except at the smartest restaurants and grandest of occasions.

What to take

All western consumer goods are readily available in South Africa, though some imported goods are quite expensive.

Optical goods are costly in South Africa so bring cameras, binoculars etc., as required.

Good bookshops are thin on the ground, and books are expensive, so bring reading matter except for field guides which you can readily buy in South Africa.

Health

If you arrive at Johannesburg, remember you are 1,800 metres (6,000 feet) above sea level. The slighty rarified atmosphere at this altitude will make anyone not used to it feel drowsy for the first couple of days, and some people experience nose bleeds, so take it easy until you become acclimatized.

Apart from the risk of malaria in some areas, mosquito bites can be troublesome everywhere in South Africa. Use repellents, and spray your bedroom at nightfall.

Bilharzia (schistosomiasis) is endemic, so don't drink from or swim in lakes, lagoons, dams or stagnant water unless you are officially told that the water is safe. If you get wet from contaminated water, dry yourself off vigorously as soon as possible as the bilharzia parasite can penetrate the skin within minutes.

The water is safe to drink in all main towns, but in rural areas it is best to drink bottled water.

The tsetse fly has been exterminated so sleeping sickness is not a concern.

In summer months beware of the heat of the sun, make sure you are adequately protected and drink plenty of liquid.

Should you fall ill you will have to pay for the use of private medical facilities, so make sure you insure yourself before arriving in South Africa. Private medical services are excellent and widely available.

If you intend to spend long periods in rural areas, take an emergency medical kit. There are poisonous scorpions, spiders and snakes in South Africa, but most are very shy and will flee before you even see them.

If you're trekking, be alert to the possibility of coming across dangerous animals and use your common sense. Don't turn over rocks — disturbed spiders and snakes may bite in self-defence.

When trekking wear long trousers and boots to prevent bites by scorpions etc., while pushing through long grass. Ticks

can carry seventy different viruses including tick fever and Crimean-Congo haemorrhagic fever. After hiking check yourself for ticks, and if any have attached themselves to your skin burn them off with a cigarette or suffocate them with vaseline or alcohol. Do not try to pull a tick off as the head will more than likely be left behind under your skin.

There are sharks in the oceans surrounding South Africa, but public beaches are well protected by shark nets, which are checked regularly by the district shark board. If you are swimming on an unprotected beach, be alert, and avoid swimming at dusk. Also be warned that the ocean currents can be fierce and unpredictable.

Photography

Film and processing facilities are readily available throughout the country. It is forbidden to photograph military installations, prisons and inside police stations.

When to go

South Africa's climate allows for a sunny holiday at any time of the year. Some visitors prefer to visit the Kruger National Park in the dryer, cooler winter months. With low to non-existent rainfall at this time animals tend to congregate around waterholes making them easier to find, and the shorter grass makes them easier to see. However, this is the time when the park is at its busiest, so those who appreciate the quiet of the bush might prefer other seasons, when the game is just as prolific but slightly harder to find.

Visitors interested in South Africa's unique flora should come for the magnificent spring flowerings from September to November. For bird-watchers the summer months are most profitable because the influx of summer migrants greatly increases the species to view.

Where to stay

Hotel standards range from the sublime to the not-to-be-recommended, but the relative prices are low in international terms. Some good chains are Southern Sun, Holiday Inn, Sun International, City Lodge, Protea and Karos.

Visitors travelling to South Africa should get advice from travel agents on the type of accomodation they require, or get a copy of the informative and comprehensive *Where to Stay* issued annually by the South African Tourist Board (SATOUR). See Listings for Hotels, SATOUR offices abroad, etc.

Alternative accommodation is available throughout the country in guest houses and bed and breakfast establishments. There are also youth hostels and YMCAs for those wanting a reasonable but cheap night's sleep, and there are many camp and caravan sites throughout the country.

In national parks, private game reserves and on hiking trails, self-catering accommodation can usually be booked. The National Parks Board provides two types of accommodation, some fully equipped and others where you provide your own crockery, utensils, etc. Bedding, but not towels, is provided in all national park accomodation, as are fridges. In private reserves you should check what is provided and what you need to bring.

During the South African school holidays you should book accomodation well in advance. School holidays are during December-January, July-August and March-April.

Communications

Letters vary in the time they take to come and go overseas. Within South Africa, door-to-door postal delivery occurs only in city centres. Almost all mail is delivered to post office boxes. Post offices are open between 08.30–13.00 and 14.00–16.30 on weekdays and 08.00–12.00 on Saturday, except for main post offices which may stay open during lunchtime.

Except in remote rural districts, you can telephone most countries in the world direct. Public phone boxes are available. Telex and telegraph services are available from most post offices, and South Africa is linked to the Tymnet data system.

Opposite: Spectacular flowers adorn a hillside in Postberg, Western Cape.

Unrest

If you want to visit any of the townships, for example Soweto or Alexandria in Johannesburg, make sure that the areas are calm. The townships are normally quite safe, but please check first.

If you go in a hired car check whether you're insured for entering township areas — chances are you won't be. You can also ask for a police escort into the townships.

Do not under any circumstances go into areas of potential danger alone or after dark. Visitors are strongly advised not to travel by train into the townships as this can be exceedingly dangerous.

National Anthems

South Africa has two national anthems -- *Die Stem* written by C.J. Lagenhoven, music composed by Marthinus Lourens de Villiers and *Nkosi Sikelel' iAfrica*, (God Bless Africa) a hymn written by Enoch Sontonga in 1897.

Nkosi Sikelel'iAfrika
(Xhosa)
Nkosi sikelel' iAfrika
Maluphakamisw' udumo lwayo
Yiva imithandazo yethu
Nkosi Sikelela
Thina lusapho lwayo (x2)
Chorus:
Yihla moya, yihla moya
Yihla moya oyiNgcwele
Makubenjalo makubenjalo
Kude kube nguna phakade
Kude kube nguna phakade
(Sotho)
Morena boloka sechaba saheso
Ofedise dintoa lematshoenyeho (x2)
Oseboloke
Oseboloke morena
Oseboloke sechaba
Sechaba saheso
Sechaba saheso
English translation
Lord, bless Africa
May her horn rise high up
Hear Thou our prayers
And bless us.
Chorus:
Descend, O Spirit
Descend O Holy Spirit.

Descend O Spirit
Descend O Holy Spirit.

Bless our chiefs
May they remember their Creator,
Fear Him and revere Him,
That He may bless them.

Bless the public man
Bless also the youth
That they may carry the land with patience
And that Thou may bless them.

Bless the wives
And also all the young women
Lift up all the young girls
And bless them.

Bless agriculture and stock raising
Banish all famine and disease
Fill the land with good health
And bless it.

Bless our efforts
Of union and self-upliftment
Of education and mutual understanding
And bless them.

Lord, bless Africa
Blot out all its wickedness
And its transgressions and sins
And bless it.

Die Stem van Suid-Afrika
Uit die blou van onse hemel, uit die diepte van
    ons see,
Oor ons ewige gebergtes waar die kranse
    antwoord gee, Deur ons ver verlate vlaktes
    met die kreun van ossewa —
Ruis die stem van ons geliefde, van ons land
    Suid-Afrika.
Ons sal antwoord op jou roepstem, ons sal offer
    wat jy vra:
Ons sal lewe, ons sal sterwe — ons vir jou,
    Suid-Afrika.
In die merg van ons gemeente, in ons hart en
    siel en gees,
In ons roem op ons verlede, in ons hoop op wat
    sal wees,
In ons wil en werk en wandel, van ons wief tot
    aan ons graf —
Deel geen ander land ons liefde, trek geen ander
    trou ons af.

*Vaderland! ons sal die adel van jou naam met
  ere dra;*
*Waar en trou, as Afrikaners — kinders van
  Suid-Afrika.*
*In die songloed van ons somer, in ons
  winternag se kou,*
*In die lente van ons liefde, in die langer van ons
  rou,*
*By die klink van huw'liks-klokkies, by die
  kluitklap op die kis —*
*Streel jou stem ons nooit verniet nie, weet jy
  waar jou kinders is.*
*Op jou roep seg ons nooit nee nie, seg ons
  altyd, altyd ja;*
*Om te lewe, om te sterwe — ja, ons kom, Suid-
  Afrika.*
*Op u Almag vas vertrouend het ons vadere
  gebou:*
*Skenk ook ons die krag, o Here, om te handhaaf
  en te hou —*
*Dat die erwe can ons vaad're vir ons kinders
  erwe bly:*
*Knegte van die Allerhoogste, teen die hele
  wereld vry.*
*Soos ons vadere vertrou het, leer ook ons
  vertrou, o Heer —*
*Met ons land et met ons nasie sal dit wel wees,
  God Regeer.*

The English translation, authorized in 1952:

The Call of South Africa
*Ringing out from our blue heavens, from our
  deep seas breaking round;*
*Over everlasting mountains where the echoing
  crags resound;*
*From our plains where creaking wagons cut
  their trails into the earth —*
*Calls the spirit of our country, the land that
  gave us birth.*
*At thy call we shall not falter, firm and
  steadfast shall we stand,*
*At thy will to live or perish, O South Africa,
  dear land.*
*In our body and our spirit, in our inmost heart
  held fast;*
*In the promise of our future, and the glory of
  our past;*
*In our will, our work, our striving, from the
  cradle to the grave —*
*There's no land that shares our loving, and no
  bond that can enslave.*
*Thou hast borne us and we know thee, may our
  deeds to all proclaim*

*Our enduring love and service to thy honour
  and thy name.*
*In the golden warmth of summer, in the chill of
  winter's air,*
*In the surging life of springtime, in the autumn
  of despair;*
*When the wedding bells are chiming or when
  those we love depart,*
*Thou dost know us for thy children and dost take
  us to thy heart.*
*Loudly peals the answering chrous: we are thine
  and we shall stand,*
*Be it life or death, to answer to thy call, beloved
  land.*
*In Thy power, Almighty, trusting, did our
  fathers build of old;*
*Strengthen them, O Lord, their children to
  defend, to love, to hold —*
*That the heritage they gave us for our children
  yet may be,*
*Bondsmen only to the Highest and before the
  whole world free.*
*As our fathers trusted humbly, teach us, Lord,
  to trust Thee still;*
*Guard our land and guide our people in Thy
  way to do Thy will.*

National Flower

The protea is the national flower of South
Africa.

PART ONE: HISTORY, GEOGRAPHY AND PEOPLE

Above: The camelthorn tree which is a common sight in semi-arid areas of South Africa.

Opposite: Chapman's Peak overlooking Hout Bay in Cape Town. The narrow road was built by Italian prisoners during World War II.

History

From pre-history to the Boer Wars

Fossils of primitive microscopic algae and bacteria have been found in South African rocks more than three billion years old. Fossils of some small marine vertebrates date back to the Precambrian period, more than 600 million years ago.

The most significant fossil evidence found is an ancient group of fossilized part-mammal, part-reptile creatures — possible 'missing links' in the evolution of mammalian animals. The creatures lived 250 to 200 million years ago while South Africa was still a part of the massive super-continent, Gondwanaland. They show features of both classes of animals, reptile and mammal.

The fossils are found in the rocks of the Karoo sequence, named after the semi-arid area where the exposed geological strata were first described. These beds form a broad-sweep form the south-west to the north-east of the country. Fossils were preserved in rocks formed from layers of mud, sand and clay deposits in the swamps and plains that were the animals' habitat.

The earliest specimens have predominantly reptilian anatomy, with small brains and loosely-knit skulls. But 250 million years ago, many creatures had mammalian characteristics such as stronger, larger skulls, and jawbones made from fewer parts.

Later, the reptilian forerunners of dinosaurs evolved and began to dominate, while other species evolved from proto-mammals into some of the first recorded mammals. The tiny, hairy Megazostrodon, which probably lived a nocturnal existence, is one of the earliest mammals yet discovered on earth.

About 190 million years ago, great volcanic activity in the area either forced the animals to migrate northwards or wiped them out completely.

Floral fossils

Fossil records of the cycad show that the plant has hardly evolved in the last 190 million years. This primitive, palm-like tree is much sought-after due to its rarity and has been declared a protected species.

Other plant evidence helps scientists reconstruct the climates of previous ages. Erica (heath), which is now only found in the Cape region, is found in fossil form in Northern Province, suggesting that a more temperate climate once prevailed there. Evidence of tropical evergreen forests or bushveld where they have not existed for thousands of years points to changes in altitude and even latitude.

Early man

Evidence of proto-human life is found in South Africa as early as three million years ago. It is hotly debated whether southern Africa was an independent birthplace of mankind, or whether early ape-man migrated there from East Africa. Fossils found in the earliest sites, Sterkfontein and Kromdraai, show similar evolutionary development at similar times to those in East Africa, strongly supporting the theory that man developed separately in South Africa.

Some of the best finds in South Africa have been in dolomite sinkholes, such as at Sterkfontein and Swartkrans in the Transvaal, and in caves at Taung in the Cape Province as well as Kromdraai and Makapansgat in the Transvaal.

The Makapansgat valley in Northern Province shows an unprecedented record of humanoid and human occupation spanning the past two-and-a-half million years. Fossils have been found in caves in a rocky, limestone cliff and in nearby, open sites.

The earliest fossils record the ape-man *Australopithecus africanus*, and many of his contemporary animals: sabre-toothed cats, musk-oxen, chalicotheres, giant porcupines and giant dassies (rock rabbits).

Above: The Khoikhoi preparing to move to greener pastures: living along the Orange River, they came to South Africa 2,000 years ago.

Stone artefacts from earlier, middle and later Stone Age man have been found in layers of calcified deposits in the Cave of Hearths at Makapansgat dating back between 100,000 and 200,000 years. Lying close by are mammal bones, some of which have been fashioned into tools by man. Fossil fragments of the Neanderthal-like *Homo sapiens rhodesiensis* have also been found in the cave.

In the uppermost levels of the cave there are relics from the Iron Age, and evidence of human occupation from many centuries later is found in the form of Voortrekker cartridges and brassware from the nineteenth century.

Other Iron Age remnants have been found at the nearby Ficus cave where a medieval settlement was located. Pottery making, iron-ore smelting and animal husbandry were all carried out in the settlement.

A famous skull

The most famous South African fossil, 'Mrs Ples', the cranium of an *Australopithecus africanus* adult, was found at Sterkfontein in the 1950s. The discovery thrust South Africa into the raging international debate on the 'missing link' between man and ape.

Ape-man

Fossils of *Australopithecus africanus* have been found in many places in South Africa, mainly in caves, near river banks and springs. Their diet was principally vegetarian — roots and nuts — supplemented by insects and leftovers of carnivore kills. They made use of naturally occurring sharp-edged stones and pointed sticks. Their inability to fashion weapons made them vulnerable to attack from sabre-toothed cats and other carnivorous animals.

The most recent discovery of a hominid site was made by Lee Berger in June 1992, near Krugersdorp in what is now Northern Province and Mpumalanga. There, bones of *Australopithecus africanus* were discovered along with the bones of giant horses, extinct antelope and giant carnivores. This rare site, which is more than two-and-a-half million years old, is one of a handful of rare hominid sites in southern Africa.

Developing later than *Australopithecus*

Above: Many rock paintings throughout South Africa show hunting scenes.

was *Homo habilis*, the first tool-maker, who made sharp, cutting edges and round, pounding instruments out of stones. One million years ago *Homo erectus* evolved. A relatively sophisticated hunter, *Homo erectus* could fashion cleavers and make axes with handles. They hunted the herbivores of their age — the three-toed horse, giant baboon, buck, buffalo and wild pig.

Almost a million years later — about 150,000 years ago during the Middle Stone Age — man's tools had become more refined and he invented a superior way of flaking stone.

Later Stone Age

A population explosion appears to have occurred 30,000–40,000 years ago in the Later Stone Age. Later Stone Age man invented the bow and arrow and perfected Stone Age tools. 'Flake' stone weapons and pottery have been uncovered at some 600 sites.

Rock paintings by medicine men in drug-induced trances tell far more about the daily lives of the people than the archaeological remains. Hunting is often depicted and

sheep are shown in abundance, but cattle very seldom. Anthropologists have argued that this suggests that animals were domesticated in southern Africa at a later stage than elsewhere.

The San, or Bushmen, are thought to have descended directly from these Stone Age people. The tools and weapons they were using in the fifteenth century, when Europeans colonized their lands, were virtually the same as those made 20,000 years ago by Later Stone Age tribes. San rock paintings, found extensively in South Africa, trace the evolution of the tribe from 20,000 years ago to the last century.

The origins of the Khoikhoi — called Hottentots by European explorers because of their sharp, click-sounding language — are the subject of debate. Some anthropologists argue that they arrived, with the first cattle, in the Cape region after migrating from eastern Africa about 2,000 years ago. Others believe the Khoikhoi evolved, with the San, from early man living in South Africa.

The Khoikhoi and the San are ethnically and culturally very similar although the San were principally hunter-gatherers, and the Khoikhoi mainly pastoralists. Collectively, the two tribes are called the Khoisan, a race of small, yellow-skinned people seemingly unrelated to other African races.

Until about 2,000 years ago, scattered groups of Khoisan people were the sole occupants of what is now South Africa. The Khoikhoi, nomadic herders, lived along the southern and south-western coastal hinterlands. The hunter-gatherer San lived in the interior mountains and plains.

The arrival of the Bantu

About 2,000 years ago, Iron Age settlers arrived in South Africa. Bantu-speaking agriculturists migrated down the east coast of Africa and first settled in Northern Province and KwaZulu-Natal. Pottery shards have been found at archaeological sites at Broederstroom and Silverleaves, as well as in various parts of KwaZulu-Natal and the Cape.

Waves of other Bantu peoples came to southern Africa over the centuries. The exact time of the migrations is unclear and subject to debate, but it has been established that there were four main groups of Bantu migrants. The largest was the Nguni-speaking group, which included the Xhosa and the Zulu tribes. The other groups consisted of Tsonga, Sotho-Tswana and Venda-speaking peoples. It is thought that the different language groups might relate to different migrations at different times. The Nguni were the first wave, travelling furthest south and west.

The Bantu were successful pastoralists and agriculturists. A relatively predictable food supply allowed for rapid increases in their numbers, developments in technology and better social organization. They grew bullrush, millet and later, maize. They built villages of mud and wattle huts, made pottery and basketware and crafted simple iron tools and weapons.

Some were attracted by the abundant deposits of copper and iron-ore in the region. A flourishing minerals industry had been established by the fifteenth century when the first Portuguese explorers arrived.

By the Late Iron Age, about 1,000 years ago, major cultural changes had occurred.

As the Bantus' produce and livestock increased so did the population and size and number of villages. Stone buildings began to appear and pottery styles became more localized. Social and political organization became more complex.

Trading centres such as those at Phalaborwa and Mapungubwe in the Transvaal, and Bambandyanalo on the Limpopo River and Great Zimbabwe in Zimbabwe, developed into large settlements with wide trading regions. In the 12th century AD Great Zimbabwe was a community of over 10,000 people. Remains of Persian and Ming pottery shards from that period have been excavated there, along with Islamic glass, demonstrating a great trading sphere long before the arrival of Europeans.

By the 13th century AD Bantu tribes were well established in the eastern interior and the eastern and south-eastern coastal plains, while the Khoisan still occupied the west and south-east.

European interest in Africa

In the 15th century Europeans were caught up in a cultural renaissance. They were obsessed with pushing back the boundaries of the known world. The desire to find a sea route to India and the far east was also strong. The legend that a Christian king called Prester John ruled somewhere in Africa had intrigued European courts for centuries. The Portuguese were particularly anxious to find the king and enter into a Christian alliance with him against Islam. And, of course, the explorers themselves were anxious to make their fortune, spurred on by tales of gold and spices in abundance.

By 1445 the Portuguese had reached the westernmost bulge of west Africa, Cape Verde. In 1487 Bartolomeu Diaz set out from Portugal in command of two caravels — small 100-ton, wooden-hulled vessels with a central rudder and several triangular, lateen sails — and a store ship. By Christmas he had reached what is present-day Luderitz in Namibia, where he set up a stone cross. In 1488 he circumnavigated the Cape and landed near Mossel Bay on the southern coast of Africa.

Above: Monument to Vasco da Gama, an early Portuguese explorer, who landed on Indian soil in 1498 via the Cape.

He sailed on until he reached the Great Fish River before turning back. Sixteen months after his departure he returned, not wealthier, but convinced he had rounded the tip of Africa and opened a sea route to the east. Diaz called the Cape 'Tormentoso', which means the 'Cape of Storms', but King Joao of Portugal, renamed it the Cape of Good Hope.

It was Vasco da Gama in 1498 who first landed on Indian soil via the Cape; the Portuguese royal fleets had found their route to riches.

The early Portuguese explorers quarrelled frequently with the Khoikhoi people they found on the coast. But no serious attempts to set up permanent settlements or explore the interior were made by the Portuguese. They set up stone crosses to act as navigational aids along the South African coast but were principally interested in breaking the Arab monopoly on the spice trade with India and the east.

Portugal kept its southern sea route a secret for almost a century before it was discovered by the Dutch.

The Dutch

In 1595 Cornelis de Houtman arrived in Mossel Bay from Texel, Holland, while searching for a passage to the east. He traded with the Khoikhoi and continued on his way, eventually getting as far as Java.

In 1602 the Dutch East India Company was formed and trade with the east increased. The English, too, had found the way round the southern tip of Africa and their vessels also plied the route.

Dutch and English ships established Table Bay as a stopping point on journeys east in the early 17th century. The station was basic — a place to repair ships, wait for other ships in a fleet and allow sick mariners to recover.

The first Europeans to live on South African soil were shipwrecked sailors who scavenged as best they could while they waited for rescue. In 1630 the *Sao Goncalo*, a Portuguese ship laden with pepper from the east, was shipwrecked in Plettenberg Bay. Its 100 survivors set up a community on the shore, even building a yellowwood church in which to celebrate mass. After eight months with no sign of rescue the men constructed two boats and set sail in search of civilization. One group drowned but the other reached Mozambique.

The first settlement

Fresh produce was difficult to obtain on the long voyage to the Indies, and scurvy was rife among the sailors. In 1652 Jan van Riebeeck was appointed by the Dutch East India Company to set up a permanent station at Table Bay to supply passing ships.

Van Riebeeck sailed from Texel, Holland, with ninety people to garrison the Cape outpost. On arrival at Table Bay he planted a hedge of wild almonds around a 2,430 hectare (6,000 acre) area and established a settlement for his people to grow vegetables for the outpost and passing ships.

The garrison's first forays into the interior were principally in search of cattle. The local

Khoikhoi initially traded cattle for iron, tobacco and copper. The Dutch soon banned the sale of iron on the grounds that it was being used to make weapons. The Khoikhoi began to demand higher prices for their meat and to offer sheep instead of cattle.

Van Riebeeck subsequently sent expeditions inland to find meat supplies for the outpost and its customers. In 1655 the first expedition found large herds of cattle near present-day Malmesbury, fifty kilometres (31 miles) north of Table Bay. Other parties explored the Cape hinterland throughout the 1660s and 1670s.

The company's aims were commercial, prosaic and limited. It needed the outpost to provide a hospital and fresh food for its ships. But in the early years the station was a net importer of produce, unable to support itself, let alone provide for others. The company did not intend that a settlement be established, but many of the Dutch staff wanted to live permanently in the Cape. In 1657 Jan van Riebeeck, in a practical move to try and increase agricultural production, released some men from his employ and granted them land.

The results were excellent. The settlement became self-sufficient within a year, and other free-burgher families arrived from Holland to take up the challenge of farming the new colony. With the increasing exploration of the interior, the settlement slowly spread out from the Cape itself. During the 1680s, farms were established in Paarl and Stellenbosch — idyllic, temperate locations surrounded by mountains roughly forty kilometres (25 miles) west of Table Bay. With surplus wheat already available, farmers attempted growing vines in the area with great success. Their efforts provided the basis for an industry which today employs tens of thousands of people, and produces wines which are becoming increasingly prized on the international market.

Slavery

Slaves were used in the Cape colony for almost 200 years. The first settlers were short of skilled and unskilled labour. The local Khoikhoi were thought 'too unreliable' and their goodwill was required

Above: Jan van Riebeeck commanded a new victualling station at the Cape in 1651.

for trading. The first slaves, imported from west and east Africa and south-east Asia, arrived in the 1660s. By 1710 there were 1,200 adult slaves in the colony, by the turn of that century there were more than 25,000.

Slavery was not as prevalent as plantation slavery in the West Indies or southern North America. Most farms had fewer than five slaves, very few had more than fifty and some had none at all. The relatively small number of slaves in the colony, and the inability to organize themselves, meant that rebellion was almost unheard of. Desertion did occur, and captured slaves were punished with flogging, branding or amputation.

Slaves had few rights. In exceptional cases they became craftsmen and could hire themselves out to earn money to buy their freedom.

Manumission was rare — less than two per 1,000 slaves per year. The cost of manumission was high; an owner had to pay fifty rixdollars (approximately R10) in

1783 to free a slave and guarantee that he would not be a burden on the state for fifty years. There was a free black community in the Cape but it was too small to impose any social or political weight on the running of the colony. Free blacks had all the rights of the white settlers. They could marry, white or black, run their own businesses and own slaves.

A shortage of white women in the colony meant that many men took black concubines or had sex with their slaves. The resulting offspring were called 'coloureds'. European fathers rarely manumitted their offspring by slave mothers, and the coloured community was of slave status.

The Khoisan

The indigenous Khoikhoi, and later the San too, were used as cheap labour or fled north and east as their lands were gradually taken from them by the Dutch. Had they been agriculturists it might have been more difficult to usurp their land, but the nomadic herders stood little chance of defending their pastures. The earliest settlers were sorely tempted to take the Khoikhoi as slaves and seize their cattle, but this was banned by the Dutch East India Company.

Bitter disputes broke out between the Khoikhoi and the settlers as thefts of livestock and property by both sides increased. The Dutch East India Company launched a military campaign against the Khoikhoi between 1673 and 1677 to punish them for assaults on settlers. By this time the Khoikhoi chiefs accepted that the Dutch East India Company had some right to adjudicate disputes between their clans. Many had become labourers for the settlers.

The Khoikhoi also faced unknown threats in the form of contagious diseases from abroad against which they had no resistance. In 1713 a smallpox epidemic devastated clans living on the south-west coastal plain near the Cape.

The Khoisan also faced encroachment on their eastern borders as Bantu settlers continued to expand westwards along the south coast in the 17th century. The Nguni — the Bantu group which had moved furthest south and west — had a warlike mentality and technology superior to that of the Khoisan. The Xhosa vanguard of the group easily defeated the Khoikhoi peoples on the coastal plains and the Zulu and the Xhosa forced the San off inland plains.

French settlers

Between 1688 and 1700, 225 French Huguenots came to the Cape to escape religious persecution in their own country. The Huguenots were a welcome boost to the Cape's population. Their strict Protestant work ethic and values strengthened the morale and morals of the settlers, some of whom had gone to seed in the frontier country. The Huguenots quickly integrated with the Dutch settlers and their Protestant movement. French or corrupted French names are as common today as Afrikaans surnames.

The first white Africans

The isolated European community was proud of its achievements and self-sufficiency. Its members called themselves Afrikaners and their language developed into a separate dialect of Dutch which they called Afrikaans. They developed their own sect of the Calvinist Dutch Reformed Church. Their interpretations of the Bible allowed them to believe themselves the lost 'Thirteenth tribe' of Israel, with a divine right to the country in which they had settled. This belief of superiority as the chosen race, combined with the subjugation of black slaves and the Khoikhoi, meant that by the time the British took over the colony in the early nineteenth century, the Cape had developed into a plural, colour-segregated society.

Culturally, the new colony had little to offer the Europeans. Primary schools for settler and slave children were established in the 18th century, but secondary schools were not introduced until the 1790s.

In the late 18th century, under the governorship of Ryk Tulbagh, the Cape began to develop its own styles of architecture and furniture. The gabled Dutch house took on a new aspect in the Cape, with thatched roofs and whitened walls.

Cape furniture was somewhat rococo,

Above: The Great Trek: Louis Tregardt, the first Afrikaner Voortrekker, with his wagon at Wit Rivier Poort.

styled in simple European fashion but usually made by Malay craftsmen. Many examples of these houses survive to this day and some of the more beautiful have been declared national monuments.

The pioneer farmers — farmer is 'Boer' in Afrikaans — gradually spread inland, taking land from the indigenous people. The Boers no longer regarded themselves as expatriates. Like the American Wild West pioneers in the New World they conceived themselves as carving a permanent home for themselves and their children on a new continent. Unlike the westerners, however, they relied heavily on slave labour rather than working the land themselves.

By 1750, Afrikaners had settled in an area of about 170,000 square kilometres, (65,600 square miles). In the 1770s, the Afrikaners met with their first real resistance as they pushed east to the Gamtoos River. There they met with the Bantu-speaking Xhosa tribe, who had been expanding west. They were not the pushover the Khoisan had been. They were an efficient military organization and defended their lands fiercely. This was the first of the so-called Bantu or Kaffir Wars.

The Afrikaners fought the Xhosa back to the Great Fish River but that boundary to the Cape colony was bitterly disputed for more than a century. No fewer than nine frontier wars were fought as the colony slowly expanded eastwards.

By the time the British annexed the Cape colony in 1795, the colony was divided into four districts. Explorers had gone inland as far as the Orange River and Cape Town itself was thriving with more than 2,000 houses and a busy harbour.

The frontier folk resented the economic and political orders passed down to them from the distant Cape Town authorities. In the 1790s two short-lived independent republics were declared along the colony's eastern boundary: Graaff-Reinet and Swellendam. The Dutch East India Company had virtually no control over the rugged individuals of the colony's fractious extremities.

British occupation

Admiral George Elphinstone landed in the Cape at Muizenberg with more than 1,600

Above: Shaka, the militant Zulu King, meets Lt Farewell in 1824.

men on 5 August 1795. The deputy commander of the Cape garrison, Carel Willem de Lille, led 900 armed men — garrison troops and Cape Town burghers — against the British. The colonists defended their territory weakly and with a further influx of 5,000 British troops in early September, the Dutch lost heart and surrendered on 16 September 1795.

The British enforced the Roman–Dutch legal system on the colony. They banned monopolies and attempted to stop corruption of officials. Their most difficult task was trying to control the unruly independent frontier folk who opposed any government from the Cape.

The First British Occupation was brief. With the Treaty of Amiens in 1803 between the British and the French, the Cape was handed over to the new Batavian Republic, as the Dutch United Netherlands became known.

The British were not absent for long. As Napoleon prepared for renewed war with them, the British returned to take control of the Cape. In 1806 the British, under General Sir David Baird, landed with a force of 6,700

troops at Blouberg, north of Cape Town. On 10 January, the Dutch surrendered but it was not until 1814 that the Dutch permanently ceded the Cape to Britain at the London Convention and it was officially given Crown Colony status at the Congress of Vienna.

The colony comprised 26,000 whites, 30,000 slaves and 20,000 Khoikhoi when the Earl of Caledon became the first governor of the colony in 1807, replacing military with civil rule. Caledon's new government faced severe problems. It was replacing an antiquated, ill-managed and tenuous system of law and order. The colony's financial situation was rocky following the slow demise of the Dutch East India Company in the 1790s; the governor's brief was to economize due to the huge British debt incurred during the Napoleonic wars.

Further problems included what to do about the slave community, the treatment of both blacks and the Khoikhoi by the Afrikaners, the constant border skirmishes with the Bantu on the colony's extremities and the increasing unrest among the predominantly non-British and fiercely independent white population.

Caledon established a new system of law, based on the English system. A circuit court was introduced to hear civil cases throughout the country. In Cape Town a Burgher Senate was established to administer municipal affairs.

Caledon's successor, Lieutenant-General Sir John Cradock, tried to solve some of the mounting problems of the fractious eastern frontier by recommending further settlement in the area. The garrisons of Grahamstown and Cradock were established in 1812 on the Cape's frontier and soon developed into nascent towns.

British rule led to the arrival of English-speaking settlers throughout the colony. British merchants arrived to trade in Cape Town. Most settlers were farmers anxious to get land, others were missionaries who denounced the Afrikaners' treatment of the black population.

British colonization

The colonization of the eastern frontiers received a massive boost in the 1820s. During the Fifth Frontier War the Xhosa, led by Makanda, attacked Grahamstown. The town's garrison managed to repel the offensive and drove the Xhosa out of the area between the Great Fish River and the Keiskamma River. The attack prompted the third governor of the Cape colony, Lord Charles Somerset, to renew efforts to stop the frontier wars. He created a neutral territory between the Great Fish and Keiskamma rivers and promoted a massive British immigration scheme to create a human buffer against the Xhosas along the Great Fish River. The immigration would also serve to slightly redress the imbalance between English-speaking and Afrikaner whites on the volatile border.

In 1820 Chapman landed in Algoa Bay bringing the first of some 4,500 British settlers to arrive over the next twelve months. More than 90,000 Britons applied to settle in the eastern Cape at this time. Those chosen were predominantly literate traders and farmers, though a few were from the British land-owning classes. Between 1837 and 1851 a further 9,000 British settled in the area.

The initial influx of settlers increased the white population of the border lands by ten per cent. For the first five years conditions were hard. Land allocations were too small to be viable. Water was scarce and drought not uncommon. Plagues of locusts destroyed carefully tended crops. There was a shortage of labour, exacerbated by a ban prohibiting the employment of slaves or Xhosa tribespeople. And there were still the occasional border skirmishes. Many settlers abandoned their allotments and congregated around border garrisons, creating towns.

By 1825 things were improving. The new settlers acclimatized to their new surroundings. Restrictions were relaxed and farms enlarged to manageable sizes. Sheep farming was successfully introduced and became the principal activity of the area.

Almost as important in British eyes was the effect of the settlers on the frontier community. The English-speaking community helped to bridge the gap between both the colonial and Bantu, and the colonial and frontier Boer societies.

The British settle in Natal

In 1824 white hunters landed on the eastern coast on territory belonging to King Shaka of the Zulus. Their purpose was to hunt for game and ivory on the fertile eastern coastal plain. They were tolerated by Shaka, who allowed them to set up a trading post at Port Natal and granted them land on a transient basis. The hunters were not colonists, merely passing through.

In 1835 missionary and magistrate Allen Gardiner arrived in Port Natal and inspired the small settlement to proclaim itself a township.

The Zulu Nation

On the eastern coast of South Africa, kingdoms and borders were in dispute. The Bantu-speaking tribes which had migrated in the Iron Age were fighting among themselves for land. At the beginning of the 19th century they were in a continuous state of war.

Known as the Difaqane ('crushing' in Sotho) or in Nguni as the Mfecane ('hammering'), the warring resulted in

Above: Zulu Mtimuni, a nephew of Shaka.

wholesale destruction in southern Africa. J D Cooper writes that it was 'one of the great formative events of African history... which positively dwarfs the Great Trek.'

Some tribes were annihilated, others decimated; some tribes were subjugated, or forced to migrate, others expanded. Repercussions were felt from the Cape to central and east Africa.

Competition for minerals and ivory trading may have been contributory causes, but severe drought is most likely to have sparked off the fighting. The heavily crowded area that is now Zululand could not sustain its population. This crisis resulted in a gathering of clans into large groups. The Hlubi, the Mthethwa, the Ndwandwe and the Ngwane were the largest, forming great armies which battled each other for the best land.

The Zulu tribe, led by the brutal military genius Shaka, profited most from the bloodshed. Shaka was a minor chief in the Mthethwa until 1819 when he absorbed the whole grouping into his own. The Zulu were great warriors. Forming themselves into military groups known as impis they were ruthless and disciplined. Shaka's army chased the Ngwane southwards from what is now northern Zululand. The Ngwane then turned upon the Hlubi and split them in two.

Half of the Hlubi joined the Xhosa bordering on the Cape colony along with other refugees from the Zulu expansion and together came to be known as the Mfengu. The other Hlubis fled north into the central plains of the highveld.

Further forced migrations of Ngwane, led by chief Matiwane, joined the Hlubis on the highveld in 1822 as Shaka continued his merciless war. These two groups of exiles fought with the chiefdom of Tlokwa and then together the three groups attacked the Sotho peoples of the highveld. Meanwhile the Zulu set upon the Bhaca, and the northern Thembu who in turn battled with the Mpondo.

In 1824, one of Shaka's rebel generals, Mzilikazi, crossed the Drakensberg mountains with his followers and attacked the Sotho of the Magaliesberg mountains. He was pursued by impis sent by Shaka and further terrible internecine fighting took place.

Refugees from the various wars streamed in all directions, many to the Cape colony, many to the mountainous kingdom of Moshesh who ruled an area of the Drakensberg now known as Lesotho.

Shaka — 'The Black Napoleon' — had set out to create a vast empire and succeeded. By 1828 he controlled an area stretching along the eastern coast of Africa from the Mbashe River in the south to beyond the Limpopo River in the north. Only the mountain kingdoms of the Swazi and King Moshesh held firm in the area.

The Zulu Wars, as they were called by the Afrikaners, raged for about twenty years. The general belief is that the wars were a direct result of the Zulu king's greed for more land. Contemporary accounts of the wars described Shaka in very brutal terms. Ellenberger, for example, wrote that cannibalism accounted for the deaths of about 300,000 people during the wars.

The theory that the wars had almost completely depopulated the Transvaal before 1834 was promulgated by the Afrikaners from the mid-19th century onwards. The idea was a useful one for them as it allowed them to claim that the Voortrekker white pioneers of the Great Trek settled empty lands. Theal published a map which showed almost the entire highveld interior of South Africa as 'almost depopulated by the Zulu War'.

The area was not as populous as before, but other contemporary accounts, such as that of Captain Cornwallis Harris, show that tribes were still living on the highveld.

Shaka was killed in 1828 by his half brothers, Dingaan and Mhlangana. Dingaan took the Zulu throne, but was defeated by the Boers at the battle of Blood River in 1838 and died in exile. The fighting and brutal bloodshed continued sporadically throughout the 19th century, diminishing as white settlers spread across the land.

Cape Town

In Cape Town the government was continuing its Anglicization of the colony. English gradually became the only language used in courts and legislature. English-speaking teachers were in demand and were paid more than their Afrikaans-speaking counterparts.

Scottish clergy were encouraged to immigrate in large numbers to preach in the Dutch Reformed Church. British traders captured the market and set up as shopkeepers, even in remote areas of the frontiers where the community was exclusively Boer.

The British settlers were also demanding a more representative government. In 1825 a Council of Advice was set up, and in 1834 a partly nominated Legislative Council was established. It would not be until 1854 that an elected Parliament was created. A fully responsible government was not in position until 1872.

Slaves freed

In 1807 the British Parliament made the slave trade illegal throughout the Empire.

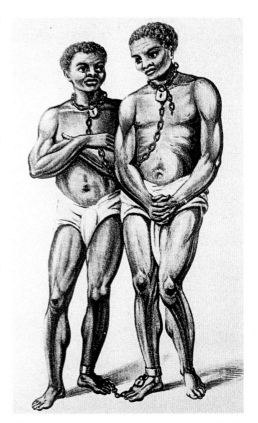

Above: Slaves chained together; there were 17,000 at the Cape by the end of the 18th century.

Though this law put an end to the importation of slaves, in practice it made little difference to the Cape colony. The increase in the number of slaves had been from natural local population expansion for many years, with little recourse to importing new stock. The principal result was that the prices of slaves doubled over the following twenty years. In practice the slaves, though nominally free, were indentured to their employers for fourteen years.

Anti-slavery campaigners considered the legislation against the slave trade insufficient. Manumission remained very low and a slave's children were still born into slavery. The demand for cheap labour increased. Both the Khoikhoi and free blacks were drafted into service in unsatisfactory working arrangements. These two groups of people became collectively known as the 'Cape Coloureds'

Above: Slave labour: diamond mining at Kimberley, 1875.

and in 1809 were required to carry passes to curb vagrancy.

The London Missionary Society sent Dr John Philip to the Cape in 1819 to investigate the situation for the indigenous Khoikhoi peoples. Philip's crusade resulted in the requirement of written contracts for Cape Coloureds to prevent debt servitude and other exploitation. In 1828 his efforts were rewarded by the passing of a new bill, Ordnance 50, which abolished passes for them and put them on an equal footing with the whites.

It was not until 1833 that a law was passed to free slaves, after an interim period of four to six years to lessen the owners' shock.

The Great Trek

The Great Trek — the migration of thousands of Afrikaner families from the Cape colonies — began in 1834. The movement was inspired by many factors. There was a general anti-British feeling among many Afrikaners for interference in their affairs. The language, culture, law and education were all alien impositions to the Afrikaner.

The Boers were proud of their heritage, independence and successful struggle to eke out a living in the new land. They felt stifled by British bureaucracy and indignant that the country they had conquered was being ruled in unfamiliar ways.

Most important perhaps, was that the eastern frontiersmen were tired of constant battles with the Xhosa and their inability to handle matters in their own way because of British laws designed to respect the rights of black people, which the Boers resented. The prospects of putting all their belongings into ox-wagons and setting off into the unknown became more attractive than staying in the Cape.

The route east was blocked by the inhospitable Xhosa. The road to freedom they chose was from the north-east of the Cape colony, over the Orange River and north. The migrants became known as the Voortrekkers — literally the 'trekkers ahead' or the 'first trekkers'.

The migration appeared to be spontaneous but was initially well organized, starting in a small way and gathering momentum as the decade went on. The first pioneering organizer, Piet Uys, had received some scanty information from early migrants — individual Boers who had, through the previous decades, set off in search of new pasture and farmland. These migrants told of great fertile plains in the highveld. More importantly, information filtered back that a lot of the land was de- or under-populated; the result of the Mfecane wars between the Bantu tribes.

Uys started his trek from Uitenhage in the eastern Cape, taking his party north and then east into the foothills of the Drakensberg mountains. His path, and that of further Voortrekkers, was fraught with difficulties. Not only were there deprivations and the physical effort of clearing a path through the thick bushveld, but heat, drought and disease took their toll. Battles with wild animals were common. But most dangerous of all were encounters with Bantu tribes who were still in the throes of the blood and carnage of the Mfecane wars.

In 1835, a party led by Louis Trichardt and Hans van Rensburg had reached Northern Province. Van Rensburg's party left Trichardt's and forged on over the Limpopo River and down into modern-day Mozambique. In 1838 they were all killed in a massacre in the Limpopo valley.

Trichardt's party set up a small settlement on the southern side of the Soutpansberg in Northern Province, but after a few years he tired of the harsh existence and led his people down to the eastern coast. In Delagoa Bay — now Maputo — Trichardt, his wife and many of his group contracted malaria and died. The remainder of the party sailed south to Durban.

Andries Potgieter set up a settlement at Thaba 'Nchu in lands occupied by the hospitable Barolong tribe. From there he ventured further north, crossing the Limpopo into present-day Zimbabwe as early as 1836. But he soon moved south again when news reached him that the Matabele, under the leadership of Shaka's rebel general Mzilikazi, had attacked and killed a number of Voortrekkers in a camp just south of the Vaal River. Potgieter fought the Matabele and pushed the tribe back over the Limpopo, claiming the area from the Vaal to the Soutpansberg for the Voortrekkers. He took a party into the north of the area and settled in Potchefstroom in 1838.

In 1837 Piet Retief, intending to settle at Port Natal, moved into Zululand. There, Retief bargained with Dingaan, Shaka's successor, to be allowed to settle on lands south of the Tugela River. After a dispute over stolen cattle, Retief and his pathfinder party of 100 moved into the area in 1838 where they were promptly killed by Dingaan. The Zulu then took the offensive and attacked several Voortrekker camps, killing 300 Voortrekkers and 250 of their coloured servants at Weenen.

After several attempts by Uys and Potgieter to quell the Zulu marauders, Andries Pretorius gathered a force of 500 men and pressed into Zululand to punish Dingaan. The army made camp on the Buffalo River on December 15, 1838 and spent a night in prayer, vowing to God that should He grant them victory they would build a church and henceforth treat December 16th as sacred. On the next day they engaged with the Zulu at the Battle of Blood River. The Zulu's spears and determination were no match for the Voortrekkers' rifles and more than 3,000 Zulu were killed without a single Afrikaner life being lost. The Voortrekkers then established the Republic of Natalia in the area, as they claimed had been earlier agreed with Dingaan. Fulfilling the promise to God, the Church of the Vow was built in Pietermaritzburg.

The end of the fighting led to further migrations from the Cape colony because it was now safe for farmers to settle the new lands. Between 1834 and 1840 about 15,000 Afrikaner people abandoned the volatile eastern frontier and joined the Great Trek northwards into the interior. With them they took thousands of black servants.

In South Africa the Great Trek is surrounded by myth and awe. The bravery and daring of the Voortrekker expeditions into the perceived 'Promised Land' added to the Afrikaner identity of independence and hardiness. The heroic saga succeeded in widening the gap between both the Afrikaner and the British, and the Afrikaner and the African.

Apologists for the Great Trek spread several stories about the 'virgin' land settled by the Voortrekkers. One argument has it that the Bantu themselves only arrived in southern Africa at the same time as the Afrikaners, and so neither had any more right to the land than the other. Another was that the highveld had been completely denuded of any people by the Mfecane wars, so again the land was empty for the Voortrekkers. The myths do not stand up to investigation, but even today are propounded in some circles.

The division of the land

The Great Trek left the Cape colony with under ninety per cent of its former inhabitants. In Natal the settlers demanded that some recognition of the lands they held be made; that is, they wanted legal title recognition from the British.

But the British refused to acknowledge the Boer Republic of Natalia. Instead, in 1842, they sent an expeditionary force to Port Natal — now Durban — to reinforce their interests in the east. The town was besieged by the Boers and the British received reinforcements at the last moment after a heroic 1,200-kilometre (745-mile) horse-back gallop for help by one Dick King to the garrison at Grahamstown. He was accompanied by his faithful servant, Ndongeni, who was forced to stop en route because of saddle sores.

The British defeated the Afrikaners and in 1843 Natal was formally recognized as a district of the Cape colony. Most of the Boer settlers of the area rejoined the Voortrekkers on their journeys northwards.

In 1856 Natal became an independent British colony separate from the Cape with limited powers of government. Durban at this time was a town of 8,000 settlers, but its population increased rapidly until, by the mid-1890s, the bustling port had more than 50,000 inhabitants.

In the 1860s the sugar farmers of Natal started to bring indentured labourers from India to work their fields; by 1886 the Indian population of Natal stood at 29,828.

In 1848, Cape governor, Sir Harry Smith, prompted by the lack of unity within the settler communities of the area, annexed the territory between the Orange and Vaal Rivers and the Drakensberg for the British, naming it the Orange River Sovereignty. The area had been one of dispute between Afrikaner settlers and black tribes.

Many of the Afrikaners who had been settled in the area headed north, crossing the Vaal into what was the Transvaal. Some who remained fought the new British regime, but were defeated in the Battle of Boomplaas. In February 1848, Bloemfontein was declared the administrative centre of the new territories. But the British had as little success as the Boers in stabilising the area.

In the 1850s the British decided against any further colonization in southern Africa. In agreements signed in 1852 and 1854, the British recognized the Afrikaner independent states of the Orange Free State, stretching between the Orange and Vaal Rivers, and the Transvaal, the land between the Vaal and the Limpopo.

Diamonds discovered

In 1867 diamonds were discovered north of the Cape colony in Griqualand, which prompted a change in attitude to the colony by the British. A hitherto unimportant, strife-ridden colony became potentially economically valuable with the result that the Cape Colony, Orange Free State and the local Griqua tribes all claimed the land as their own.

The first diamonds were discovered at Hopetown, but the largest and richest seam was found at Du Toit's Pan near Kimberley in 1870. A hill rich in diamonds was excavated to form the Big Hole of Kimberley, the largest man-made hole in the world. The town expanded dramatically, quickly overtaking Cape Town to become the largest in the colony. The boom town was characterized by lawlessness, gambling and bawdy behaviour as miners from all over the world flocked to the area to make their fortunes. Many made them, though

Above: Part of a diamond museum.

some lost their money again overnight on the turn of a card.

The British finally annexed the land for the Cape in 1871. Kimberley settled down to respectability, aided by the ministrations of a young Englishman, Cecil John Rhodes. Rhodes' company, De Beers, had taken control of the international diamond trade by the mid-1880s and Rhodes was well-placed to pursue his goal of empire building for England.

Transvaal annexed

In 1877 the British annexed the Republic of Transvaal. They said the independent state was unable to govern itself properly, or control the maurading tribes within its territories.

The Zulus rise again

Meanwhile, in Natal trouble was brewing again with the Zulus. The current king, Cetshwayo had restored Zulu military might to such an extent that both the British settlers in Natal and the Boers in the Transvaal feared Cetshwayo's rising power and the possibility of an invasion.

The British, anxious to appease the Boers in the Transvaal after their annexation of the republic, and also keen to protect their Natal lands, declared war on the Zulus in 1879. The resulting Anglo-Zulu War was extremely bloody, and certainly not the walk-over the British had anticipated. Underestimating the Zulus' power at Isandlawana, the British suffered one of the greatest defeats ever inflicted on a colonial army. On 23 January 1879, 24,000 Zulus attacked the main British camp and slaughtered 1,271 men. The British survivors fled to join a small camp at Rorke's Drift. There just over 100 men, under Lieutenant John Chard, repulsed a Zulu attack of 4,500 warriors. The battle cost seventeen British and 400 Zulu lives. Eleven Victoria Crosses were awarded to the defenders of Rorke's Drift.

In July of the same year the Zulus were finally defeated when Lord Frederick Chelmsford attacked the royal kraal and the Zulu capital at Ulundi. Cetshwayo was captured and Zululand divided into thirteen chiefdoms in an effort to decentralize power. Cetshwayo was given regency of one of the chiefdoms, but his quarrelsome nature led him to seek refuge under the British flag at Eshowe after a particularly messy local conflict. He died in 1884 and three years later the British annexed the Zulu lands and incorporated them into Natal.

First Boer War

The Boers of the Transvaal resented the annexation of their republic. On 16 December 1880, they declared war on the British. The British sustained heavy losses at Laingsnek and Skuinshoogte. Two months later the Boers regained their independence after the battle of Majuba Hill.

Gold and problems

Rich gold deposits were discovered in the Transvaal in 1886, altering once again the political importance of the Transvaal. The gold was found by a visiting Australian miner, George Harrison on the Witwatersrand (Ridge of White Waters) only fifty kilometres south of the republic's capital, Pretoria.

Again fortune hunters and prospectors from all over the world rushed to southern Africa to get a share of the wealth. A new town, Johannesburg, grew up rapidly along the ridge peopled by non-Boer immigrants, many of whom were British.

Paul Kruger had become President of the republic in 1882. His view of the 'uitlanders' (foreigners) was complex. Financially he welcomed the diggers, as the republic's treasury filled with revenues from the mines and from granting monopolies to suppliers of everything from beer to dynamite. But the foreigners also diluted the influence of the original Boer farmers of the state. Within ten years more than a third of the 200,000 inhabitants of the Transvaal were foreigners and had begun to demand citizenship and equal rights with the Boers.

The grievances of the Anglophobes was seized upon by the British as an excuse to retake the Transvaal and its mineral wealth for its empire. In 1895 the abortive Jameson Raid was carried out with the help of Rhodes, now Prime Minister of the Cape Colony.

Uitlanders were organized to rise up at the same time as a mounted party of 500 men invaded the Transvaal from the north (Rhodesia). The raid, led by Dr Leander Starr Jameson, misfired. Jameson and his men were routed by the Boers at Krugersdorp in January 1896.

Second Boer War becomes inevitable

The British High Commissioner at the Cape, Sir Alfred Milner, continued to demand from Kruger equal rights for the uitlanders in his territory. Kruger tried to avoid conflict by conceding to Milner's demands several times, only to find that further more stringent demands were made. Kruger became more and more convinced that Milner was after the Transvaal itself.

Meanwhile, Britain started sending troops to southern Africa early in 1898. On October 11, 1899, Kruger's ultimatum to stop British troop movements along the Transvaal borders expired. The Transvaal, joined by the Orange Free State, was at war with Britain. Britain deployed 450,000 troops in the war. The Boers never had more than 35,000 men. Both sides were augmented by fighters from Europe keen to show support for their chosen side. Irish, Russian and French soldiers all joined up for the war, the Boers benefiting most from these men because of a perception that they were underdogs against the might of the gold-grabbing British empire.

The war was widely expected to end in a few months, but lasted two years. Despite the small number and eventual defeat of Boer troops, the British suffered the worst losses in the history of their colonial wars. Although the conflict began as conventional warfare, after the first year, the Boers adopted guerilla tactics which proved very difficult for the British troops to counter. In retaliation, the British adopted a 'scorched earth' policy, burning Boer homes and incarcerating women and children.

The Boers had a successful start, attacking on three fronts. In Natal, under Commander Piet Joubert, they besieged the British military headquarters at Ladysmith. In the west, two British garrisons at Kimberley and Mafeking were besieged and the railway link from Cape Town was disrupted. In the south, commandos from the Orange Free State attacked British positions along the Orange River.

Trench warfare

The success of the relatively small numbers of Afrikaners was due in no small part to their invention of trench warfare. The Boers first used this tactic at the Battle of Modder River in November 1899. Eight thousand British troops marching towards Kimberley were fired upon by 3,000 Boers camouflaged and entrenched near the river banks. Five hundred British soldiers were killed at the cost of eighty Boer lives.

In December that year, the British forces suffered — in what became known as 'Black Week' — a series of humiliating defeats in which thousands of British soldiers were killed. At Stormberg and again at Colenso trench warfare was used against the unwary British with devastating effect.

The new military tactic was combined with camouflaged battledress. The British soldiers in uniform were an easy target for the Boers who hid in trenches.

By January, after further routs, the British were persuaded that stronger action must be taken. Field Marshall Lord Frederick Sleigh Roberts was appointed Commander-in-Chief, and General Horatio Kitchener his Chief-of-Staff.

In the first half of 1900, the British seemed to be well on the way to victory. The sieges of Ladysmith and Kimberley were relieved, Boer General Cronje and 4,000 of his men surrendered at Paardeberg. By March, Lord Roberts was in Bloemfontein, by May Johannesburg, and on 5 June he captured Transvaal's capital Pretoria.

The siege of Mafeking lasted seven months, and became the subject of daily headlines in the British press. Colonel Robert Baden-Powell, leader of the besieged British forces, became the hero of the hour. His was the last garrison to be relieved, on 17 May 1900.

By September, the remaining Boer troops had realized that they could not win the war in formal, set battles. They changed tactics, spreading out into small guerilla squads and struck at British com-

Above: Lord Kitchener, who after a successful campaign in Omdurman, was appointed Chief of Staff to Lord Roberts' forces in the Boer War.

munications, supply lines and small outlying garrisons.

Under such leaders as Louis Botha, Jan Smuts, Ben Viljoen and Christiaan de Wet, the raiding parties inflicted heavy casualties on the British. Some commando units struck deep into the heart of British territories. Generals such as Smuts and Wynand Malan took the guerilla war into the Cape colony itself.

Scorched earth and concentration camps

Kitchener succeeded Roberts as Commander-in-Chief of the British forces in November 1900 and decided to take a hard line against the frustrating tactics of the Boers. Thirty thousand farmhouses, their crops and fields were burned and some villages were also destroyed.

Afrikaner families and their black labourers were interned. The rationale, according to the British Secretary of State for the Colonies, Joseph Chamberlain, was that refugee camps were the only way to protect women and children left alone by their marauding menfolk. In practice the process left Boer guerillas demoralized and cut off their food supplies.

The camps were soon overcrowded and became unhygenic and riddled with disease. Half of the confined black farm labourers died — more than 14,000 people. Almost 28,000 Boers, most of them children under sixteen, also died in the camps — more than ten per cent of the white inhabitants of the republican states.

Kitchener also erected 8,000 blockhouses over the countryside and put up over 6,000 kilometres (3,728 miles) of barbed wire in an effort to stop the movements of the guerila groups.

Peace is negotiated

The policy split the freedom fighters in two. Some were all for continuing the fight but many wanted to negotiate peace to end the suffering of their families in the camps. The war continued for another year, into early 1902, before demoralized Boer leaders met to discuss a settlement.

On 31 May 1902 the Treaty of Vereeniging was signed in Pretoria between the British and the Boers of the Transvaal and the Orange Free State. The treaty gave all lands up to the British, but allowed the Boers to return to their land and have equal rights.

By the end of the war 7,000 Boers had been killed in action. The British lost 5,774 soldiers, and 20,000 Africans attached to their forces who were usually murdered by the Boers when captured.

The spectre of the scorched earth policy and the concentration camps linger in the minds of some Afrikaners to this day.

The Twentieth Century

British South Africa nominally comprised four separate colonies after the Boer war — Cape Province, Natal, Transvaal and the Orange Free State — though, effectively, they were ruled by Lord Milner, still in power in the Cape. Milner's first policies held two main themes: firstly to build the economy and secondly to Anglicize the colonies.

The Union of South Africa is created

On 31 May 1910, the four colonies united in the Act of Union. Britain soon granted dominion status to the new South Africa. Bechuanaland, Basutoland and Swaziland remained British protectorate states until they received full independence in the 1960s when they became Botswana, Lesotho and Swaziland.

With the Act of Union a new political system was introduced based on a Westminster-style government. Afrikaners dominated the Union's political life.

Black politics

Despite pleas from blacks and liberal whites, the black population of the country received no power-sharing in the new 'democracy'. They were to be represented in parliament by nominated whites — whites nominated by whites.

Some of the earliest protests against the suppression of the non-white peoples of South Africa were led by lawyer Mohandas Gandhi, later to become a pivotal political leader in India. Gandhi demanded rights for the Indian population. He had studied the pacifism of the Jain sect of Hinduism, and believed in non-violent, non-compliant protest — *satyagraha*. In this fashion he led campaigns against the Transvaal registration laws of 1906 which required Indians to carry passes.

Gandhi left South Africa soon after winning a temporary respite for the community. His campaigns have been called a failure, but his example of non-aggressive action made a big impact on non-white protest for several decades.

In 1923 Indians formed the South African Indian Congress to campaign for rights for their racial grouping.

In 1912 the South African Native National Congress (renamed the African National Congress in 1923) was launched in Bloemfontein. The ANC was formed to help create African unity and to fight for equal political rights. Its attitude until the 1950s was one of passive resistance, based on Gandhi's stance. Its appeals to the government were reactive rather than self-initiated. Its power base was weak, blacks being divided between many tribes and unwilling to join together under one united banner.

Whites strike over black employment

After the Boer War, unemployment became an important political issue. In the latter part of the 19th century, a gradual move to the towns by small-scale white farmers and squatters forced off the land by drought and changes in farming techniques had produced a class of urban 'poor whites'. Most of these people were Afrikaners. Thousands moved to shanty towns around main cities, competing unsuccessfully with blacks for jobs. By 1931 over 300,000 whites — a quarter of the Afrikaner population — were classed as 'very poor' out of a white population of 1.8 million.

Even to members of the white working class who did have employment there was a real threat of losing their jobs to blacks. Black labour was cheap — black miners earned two shillings and tuppence a day. It was estimated in the early 1920s that if fifty per cent of the white miners were replaced by blacks the mines would save one million pounds a year.

As early as 1913 white miners in the gold fields of the Witwatersrand had gone on strike in protest against the trend of employing black miners in skilled jobs. They argued that skilled jobs should be the exclusive right of the white man. The government had to use force to crush subsequent rioting.

The problem of the poor whites was partly solved in the 1930s by the introduction of legislation reserving some jobs for whites only and imposing artificial controls on other work. Black workers had no security of tenure nor any right to unionization until the 1980s.

Second World War

When war broke out in 1939, South Africa had to decide whether it would join forces with Britain. The country was divided between Britons eager to join the cause and Afrikaners still smarting after Kitchener's scorched earth policy. The government took South Africa into battle and South African troops fought against the Italians in

Above: Mohandas Gandhi, later the Mahatma, as a young barrister in Durban.

Abyssinia (now Ethiopia), in the western desert campaign and in Italy.

For South Africa the war was economically useful. The world clamoured for South Africa's minerals and, because the country was unable to import many goods, the local manufacturing industry was given an enormous boost. South Africa also became involved in producing armaments, today a major industry.

When the war ended in 1945 Jan Smuts, as Prime Minister of South Africa, was one of the signatories of the founding charter of the United Nations.

Apartheid rule

Smuts underestimated how much grass-roots support Malan's National Party (NP) had among the predominantly Afrikaner white population. The NP's policies of rigorous segregation between white and black — apartheid, literally 'apartness' in Afrikaans — won favour with increasing numbers of the white population while blacks, coloureds and Indians fiercely opposed it.

Above: Field-Marshal Jan Smuts: South Africa's war-time president.

In the 1948 general election, Smuts lost control to a coalition of the National Party and The Afrikaner Party. The government launched a policy of making colour segregation — which had informally been a large part of South Africa's culture since the 17th century — statutory law.

Laws were introduced which classified people into colour categories. These required non-whites to carry passes, restricted their freedom of movement and controlled where they lived and worked.

The new government also changed the concept of reserves for blacks to that of creating independent homelands. The homelands were effectively the native reserves created in the past, although the scattered areas were gradually consolidated into more coherent blocks of land. Every black South African would become a citizen of a homeland. Only blacks with work passes would be allowed to reside in 'white South Africa,' even then they would be officially classified as citizens of one of the homelands.

Most homelands refused to take independence, including KwaZulu-Natal (formerly Zululand). The Zulu leader, Chief Mangosuthu Buthelezi, maintained that it was more important to fight the South African regime from within than accept a hypocritical independence. In the 1970s he resurrected a Zulu cultural movement first founded in 1928, Inkatha — *Yenkululeko Yesizwe* — now known as the Inkatha Freedom Party (IFP). The IFP is now a political party with 43 seats in parliament, though its roots are based in the Zulu culture. The IFP advocates a federal system for South Africa.

Only four homelands out of ten chose to follow the path laid out for them by the South African government and became 'independent'. Transkei, Bophuthatswana, Venda and Ciskei became self-ruling in the 1970s and 1980s.

Areas around main cities were designated as black townships. The South Western Township — Soweto — was established in the 1940s. Regimented basic housing was built to accommodate people after mass clearances of black residential areas considered too close to the expanding white suburbs.

Hostility was engendered by the ever-spreading network of racially discriminatory laws which gained momentum over the years, until there was a network of legislation governing almost every move made by non-whites in South Africa.

Because of inevitable racial intermixing, absurd situations developed. Jac Rabie was a member of the coloured Chamber of Parliament in the 1980s. Under the Population Registration Act he was initially classified as Indian but later reclassified as coloured. His mother was classified white, then coloured. One of his brothers was officially black, another officially white. His three sons were each allocated to different sub-groups of coloureds. Two uncles were classified white and joined the pro-apartheid Conservative Party.

The Immorality Act outlawed marriage or sexual relationships between people of different colour classification. The Separate Amenities Act refused non-whites entrance to white facilities — toilets, restaurants, sporting facilities and bars. Blacks were prevented from sharing even the most basic amenities with whites. Today you can still occasionally find toilets with the words 'European' or 'Non-European' etched on them, although most of these signs have been removed by collectors.

In 1959 radical blacks broke away from the ANC to form the Pan Africanist Congress (PAC). Robert Sobukwe and his colleagues saw the only way forward as a South Africa with no white population at all. 'One settler, one bullet,' the slogan they adopted in the 1970s, remains their credo and still strikes fear into the hearts of whites.

When Hendrick Verwoerd, one of Malan's successors, applied for a republican South Africa to remain a Commonwealth member in 1961, it was clear that other African countries would leave it if he was successful, so he withdrew the application. Later that year South Africa declared itself an independent republic and left the Commonwealth.

Exile and imprisonment

The banning of black political movements forced them underground and into exile. The ANC created a military wing *Umkonto we Sizwe* ('Spear of the Nation'), to conduct a campaign of sabotage. Its policy was to attack government installations without causing loss of life. Training camps for guerrillas were set up in other African countries, principally Angola and Tanzania.

The PAC also formed a military wing called *Poqo* ('we go it alone'). This organization viewed soft targets as political fair game.

In 1966 Verwoerd was assassinated by a white parliamentary messenger, who was declared insane. John Vorster, previously Minister for Justice, took over the reins of power.

In 1974 the United Nations rejected South African delegates' credentials, effectively excluding the country from the organization. South Africa's status abroad deteriorated even further when, in 1975, the country intervened militarily in Angola.

By the late 1970s South Africa had diplomatic relationships with very few other nations and was closest to other isolated nations such as Israel, Paraguay and Taiwan.

Scandal erupted when it became clear that Vorster had been involved in the misuse of public funds, a situation which became known as the Information Scandal. The funds were used illegally to fund a covert worldwide pro-South African propaganda campaign. Vorster resigned as prime minister and the former Minister of Defence, P W Botha nicknamed 'The Big Crocodile' took over.

In 1977, the United Nations imposed a mandatory arms embargo on South Africa. Boycotts — economic, political and sporting — led to increasing isolation for the country.

Botha's reforms

Botha took over South Africa in its heyday of prosperity. Gold prices, which had been pegged at US$35 an ounce from the 1930s to 1970, were soaring. By early 1980 the price was US$850 an ounce and gold revenues to the treasury that year were R3,363 million.

Botha, as Vorster before him, realized that population growth was far surpassing any projections, and that industrialization on a grand scale was needed to employ the ever-expanding workforce. Two commissions, the Riekert Report and the Wiehahn Inquiry, recommended the abolition of all employment laws which reserved certain jobs for whites. These recommendations were accepted and the laws, which had in any case been naturally eroded as employers realized the impracticality of them, were abolished. Black workers were also allowed to establish unions and some of these quickly became strong and often political.

Further reforms

Botha was also talking about further reforms, including some form of power-sharing with the coloured and Indian populations. He argued that as these communities had no homelands in which to participate in politics, unlike the blacks, they should be given some rights. The argument led to a division in the National

Above: The late Oliver Tambo, first President of the ANC.

Party. In 1982, Dr Andries Treurnicht and other right-wing members of the National Party committed to white political domination split to form the Conservative Party.

This era of white right-wing discontent saw the creation of several extreme right-wing political groups, including the Afrikaner-Weerstands-beweging (AWB) — the Afrikaner Resistance Movement' — led by Eugene Terre' Blanche. This conservative resistance organization espouses a 'unitary state' whites-only, modelled on the original Boer republics.

A New Constitution

In 1983, Botha called a white referendum to institute a new constitution. The referendum agreed, by a two-thirds majority, to a new government in which coloured and Indian people had the right to elect representatives to their own legislatures. The new parliament was tri-cameral: the House of Assembly, representing whites, had 178 members, the House of Representatives, for coloureds, had 85 members and the House of Delegates,

representing the Indian population, 45 members. The ratio of members in the chambers accurately reflected the ratio of the different racial groups. The members for each house were largely elected by their separate ethnic groups.

The new parliament met for the first time in 1985 and began to repeal some apartheid laws, including those prohibiting sex between different race groups. In 1986 the pass laws were repealed, though a new system of identity documentation was introduced which allowed for some perpetuation of the status quo.

But the mid-1980s also saw a rapid decline in the country's economy. A sharp fall in the price of gold, inflation and government overspending led to a recession. The decline came at a time of increasing sanctions. A brain-drain of many of South Africa's best scientists, academics and industrialists, as well as members of the sporting and acting fraternities occurred.

Pressure by the public in western countries led to many multinational companies disinvesting in the country. The international media reported vigorously on the injustices in South Africa, and public awareness of the evils of apartheid increased rapidly. The United States imposed punitive additional taxes on companies with interests in South Africa. Many companies sold their South African subsidiaries at bargain-basement prices to local investors to stop consumer boycotts and prohibitive taxation abroad.

The economic decline, along with the relaxation of apartheid laws which included movement restrictions, coincided with a rise in black opposition to white rule.

The government declared a series of states of emergency throughout the 1980s as violence flared and subsided in the townships.

Pressure

By 1987 the need for more change was obvious and pressing. With South Africa's gold becoming more expensive as the cost of its extraction escalated, a rapidly increasing population, the departure of international companies (Mobil, Hewlett-Packard and others pulled out in 1989), the

Above: Nelson Mandela, soon after his release in 1990, with Winnie Mandela

country's economic future was looking bleak.

The result was a series of changes in international and local policies. South Africa ended its involvement in the Angolan civil war and stopped funding the rebel movement in Mozambique. Having been ruled by South Africa since 1919, Namibia was granted independence in 1990.

Domestic political reform took place throughout 1989. Thirty thousand people, mainly blacks, were released from prison during the year after being detained for varying lengths of time under security laws. The country also acquired a new, more moderate state president. Three weeks before a general election in late 1989, Botha resigned as State President and Frederick Willem de Klerk took over, both as head of the party and state president.

President de Klerk began talking with European leaders, notably Margaret Thatcher of Great Britain, about reforms. He talked of black/white power sharing and democracy. De Klerk promised to 'create a new South Africa,' within five years.

Mandela released

One of de Klerk's first actions was to release Nelson Mandela on 11 February, 1990. Mandela was seventy-one and had spent twenty-seven years in jail. To many blacks, Mandela had become a symbol of struggle, an almost godlike figure.

The year also saw the legalization of black political parties. The ANC and the government met to discuss the ground for beginning 'talks about talks about power sharing'. The ANC demanded that all apartheid laws be repealed before such talks could take place.

The five laws which formed the pillars of apartheid — the Population Registration Act, the Immorality Act, the Land Acts, the Group Areas Act and the Separate Amenities Act — were all repealed by June 1991. Within seventeen months of

Above: President Nelson Mandela with his Vice Presidents — Thabo Mbeki and F W de Klerk.
Opposite: Fireworks to celebrate the end of apartheid.

promising to abolish apartheid De Klerk had removed it from the statute book.

Other laws were also abolished or amended, including the stringent security laws.

Freedom

On 16 April, 1994, the first non-racial general election in South Africa's history took place, resulting in a landslide victory for the ANC. In 1994 a government of national unity was installed in which the ANC is dominant.

The ANC holds 252 seats in the national assembly, the National Party eighty-two seats, Inkatha Freedom Party forty-three seats, the Freedom Front nine seats, the Democratic Party seven seats, the Pan Africanist Congress five seats and the African Christian Democratic Party two seats.

The government is headed by President Nelson Mandela (ANC) and two vice presidents — Thabo Mbeki (ANC) and F W de Klerk (National Party).

The government is committed to national reconciliation and pledges upliftment of disadvantaged people and the creation of genuine democracy.

South Africa is currently experiencing unprecedented political and social freedom. Repressive laws have been dismantled, there is press freedom and extensive civil liberties. The country has been readmitted to the world community, the Commonwealth of Nations and the United Nations and has joined the Organization of African Unity (OAU).

The Land: Massive Country, a Geological Treasure House

South Africa is a massive country, five times bigger than Britain. In satellite images it is revealed as a shield-shaped sub-continent. The bulk of the sub-continent is a central plateau with a mountainous rim and an escarpment falling away to the sea, creating a narrow strip between mountain and coast.

The plateau is as low as 600 metres (2,000 feet) in the east, rising to more than 3,400 metres (11,100 feet) in the west, in the Drakensberg, or Dragon Mountains. But the highest point on the sub-continent is not part of South Africa. Thabana Ntlenyana, or Black Mountain, which rises to 3,482 metres (11,420 feet) is part of Lesotho, an independent nation surrounded by South Africa.

South Africa lies between latitudes 22–35° south. The north-east of the country is in the tropics, north of the Tropic of Capricorn. The country is over 1,127,000 square kilometres (435,130 square miles) in extent, divided into nine provinces — Gauteng, Northern Province, Mpumalanga, North-West, Free State, KwaZulu-Natal, Eastern Cape, Western Cape and Northern Cape. President Mandela's government has indicated that these names might change.

South Africa is a geological treasure house of ancient deposits. There are granite rocks in the Gauteng region which are almost four billion years old; others contain fossil micro-organisms dating back more than three billion years. The ancient rocks are rich in minerals including asbestos, antimony, beryllium, copper, diamonds, fluorspar, gold, iron, kaolin, lead, manganese, nickel, platinum, silver, tantalum, uranium, vanadium, wolfram and zinc. Younger strata contain major coal reserves and there is natural gas and oil offshore.

Some of the more recent strata are of great interest to the palaeontologist. South Africa is rich in fossils from the historical period, when dinosaurs were evolving into increasingly mammal-like forms.

South Africa is a dry country, with an average rainfall of only 502 millimetres (20 inches) a year compared with a world average of 857 millimetres (34 inches). There are no important lakes, and the inland plateau is drained by two river systems rising in the eastern mountains.

The Orange and its tributary, the Vaal, flow west into the south Atlantic. This mighty river basin drains forty-seven per cent of the plateau. The Limpopo River, which is the north-eastern frontier of the Republic, carries rainfall to the Indian Ocean. Shorter, fast-flowing rivers such as the Tugela, Kei, Sundays, Gamtoos and Berg drain the escarpment's coastal side.

The rivers are dependent on seasonal rainfall and many become entirely dry during the arid winter months. A meagre nine per cent of the rainfall reaches the rivers. The remainder soaks directly into the parched soil as it falls, or evaporates during the long hours of sunshine.

There is little or no rain on the west coast but rainfall figures rise as one travels east across the central plateau. The western desert, with an average annual rainfall as low as fifty-eight millimetres (two inches) in some places, gives way to semi-arid land where annual precipitation averages 250 millimetres (ten inches). This region yields to the highveld (grasslands) of the eastern Free State and what was Transvaal, where annual rainfall totals are in the 700–800 millimetres (28-32 inches) range, but evaporation rates are high.

This high interior gets rain in hot weather, mainly in the form of electric storms during the southern hemisphere summer. Thunderstorms occur up to eighty days a year and as much as ninety days in the high mountain rim of the eastern plateau. In Johannesburg, in a period of 100 years, lightning will strike more than six times per square kilometre. In winter the area gets little or no rain at all.

The southern and eastern coastal belts between mountains and sea get adequate

Above: The beautiful landscape of the Mpumalanga where most visitors go to see wild animals roaming as they once did throughout Africa.

rainfall for most of the year, with average annual rainfalls of 500 millimetres (20 inches) in the temperate south, and more than 1,000 millimetres (40 inches) in the lush eastern seaboard. Evaporation losses are reduced there by coastal humidity.

The west coast and Cape Town get winter rains of a more gentle and sustained variety than the torrential storms and flooding that follow prolonged droughts in the rest of the country.

Sixty-five per cent of the land gets less than 500 millimetres (20 inches) annual rainfall, the minimum considered necessary for successful crop farming.

Only one-tenth of South Africa's farming land can be cultivated without irrigation. It can be seen, therefore, that most of South Africa is arid and hardly suitable for human habitation — a point not generally well understood abroad.

Water management

Water is needed for agriculture, industry and the fast-growing population. South Africa boasts over 300 large dams.

Underground water sources are exploited and the drilling of over 500,000 boreholes has allowed people to farm in otherwise uninhabitable areas.

Oceans

With the Atlantic to the west and the Indian Ocean to the east, South Africa has more than 3,000 kilometres (1,800 miles) of coastline. The oceans, as well as providing excellent fishing, play a major role in the country's climate.

The warm Agulhas current flows from the equator southwards down the east coast of Africa, and then west along the southern coast until, at Cape Point, it meets with the cold Benguela current flowing from the Antarctic north along the country's west coast. The warm east coast currents account for the hotter summers and the heavier rain on that side of the subcontinent.

Vegetation

There are six main areas of climate and vegetation in South Africa.

The west coast is desert with sparse

Above: Farmland near Ceres in the Cape, an area famous for its deciduous forests.
Opposite: Table Mountain is one of South Africa's best-known landmarks. In this view it stretches towards Cape Point.

summer rain and fog along the coast. The semi-desert climate of the western interior is similar but less extreme. In these areas there are hardy perennial shrubs mixed with succulents, and wonderful spring flowerings after the first rains when 'the desert blooms.'

The south-western Cape area has a Mediterranean climate with cool wet winters and hot dry summers. The area is perfect for vineyards and its natural flora is unique and spectacular. Protea and other wild flowers as well as an abundance of evergreen shrubs have made the area one of six world floral kingdoms.

The southern coast has a temperate climate, with warm summers, cool winters and some rain throughout the year. The area is warmer than might be expected, for its latitude and vegetation is lusher because of the warm sea currents flowing along the southern coast.

The eastern coast is sub-tropical with hot humid summers and warm drier winters. This is the most productive farming area with tropical fruits grown in the north. Indigenous forests are found on the southern and eastern coasts where there is sufficient rainfall.

The sub-tropical lowveld of Mpumalanga has hot wet summers and warm dry winters. Lowveld vegetation is dry scrub interspersed with thorn trees, succulents and enormous baobab trees.

The central plateau has hot wet summers and cool dry winters, the rainfall increasing from west to east. The central 'highveld' of rolling grassy plains with few trees is replaced in the east by the true 'bushveld' — dry acacia savannah lands.

Natural resources

The mining sector accounts for about thirteen per cent of the country's gross domestic product. Eighty per cent of South Africa's exports are minerals, in raw or semi-processed forms. South Africa's main industry is gold mining which employs more than 650,000 people (though this has

been diminishing) and accounts for two-thirds of mineral exports.

South Africa has roughly forty per cent of the world's gold reserves. The metal is expensive to extract as the gold seams lie progressively deeper and very difficult to reach. The Western Deep Levels gold mine in the Gauteng goldfields (which means Place of Gold in Sotho) delves 3,800 metres (12,400 feet) — the deepest man has ever penetrated into the earth.

Despite being one of the oldest and most stable geological regions in the world, the Gauteng experiences regular earth tremors. More than 600 miners died in 1991, many of them in cave-ins triggered by seismic tremors.

South Africa mines over sixty minerals from some of the richest deposits in the world. Uranium, titanium, vanadium, coal, base metals, precious and semi-precious stones are all found in abundance in South Africa, mainly underground. Although this means there are very few unsightly open-cast mines, the extra costs of deep mining have become an increasing problem.

Diamonds

Diamonds were created by the heat and pressure of molten lava in volcanic vents. Kimberlite is the remains of ancient lava in which diamonds are found. Kimberlite 'pipes' are deposits filled with agglomerate clay, the so-called 'blue ground'. Hundreds of tons of clay must be mined and processed to obtain a single carat of gem diamonds.

Within a ten-kilometre (six mile) radius of Kimberley there are sixteen known kimberlite pipes, although only four are still being mined. In Kimberley none of the pipes were formed in a single event, but in multiple stages which resulted in separate columns of kimberlite within a single pipe. The diamond quality in each column varies.

The Orange River and its tributary, the Vaal, have yielded vast numbers of diamonds. The first found in South Africa was picked up by a boy on the banks of the Orange River at Hopetown in 1866. The river flows over and erodes volcanic agglomerations, releasing diamonds into the water. The gems are washed to the sea, then up and down the western coastline by longshore currents.

The diamond coast in Namibia provides the richest coastal deposits; in the early days diamonds could be picked out of the sand. In the largest earth-moving operation of its kind in the world, De Beers' Consolidated Diamond Mines (CDM) has pushed back the sea to mine the sea bed. Some divers still make a living by dredging the sea bed for diamonds. Using special machinery they suck up gravel from the ocean floor, and sift it to find the stones. These diamonds are often stronger than mined diamonds, having survived the buffeting of the ocean.

One of the most famous diamonds in the world, the Cullinan diamond, was discovered at Premier Diamond Mine in 1905. It weighed 3,106 carats — about 621.20 grammes — before it was cut into 105 stones, including the Star of Africa, which forms part of the British Crown Jewels.

Energy

South Africa has the seventh biggest coal reserves in the world — an estimated fifty-five billion tons, which should last for about 300 years. Ninety-seven per cent of the country's electricity is produced from coal; the rest is provided by hydroelectric power and one nuclear power station. Its small petroleum deposits being discovered only recently, South Africa has developed an oil-from-coal process which meets roughly twenty per cent of current liquid fuel requirements. The country relies heavily on oil imports from abroad.

South Africa is considered the economic superpower of sub-Saharan Africa, producing forty per cent of its industrial output, sixty-four per cent of its electricity, forty-five per cent of its minerals, forty per cent of its maize and sixty-five per cent of its steel.

South Africa covers a mere three per cent of Africa's land and contains five per cent of the continent's population. However, the country possesses forty-six per cent of all the cars in Africa and thirty-six per cent of the telephones.

Opposite: The ravine at Augrabies National Park extends for eighteen kilometres (11 miles).

People: 'The Rainbow Nation'

South Africa has one of the most diverse ethnic populations in the world. Of the eleven major tongues spoken on the subcontinent, there is no dominant majority language, with the possible exception of English.

In 1993, the estimated population was 32 million, broken down as follows: seventy per cent black, fifteen per cent white, thirteen per cent coloured (mixed race) and three per cent Asian.

The population has always been heterogeneous. The whites are mainly descendants of Dutch, French, German and British settlers. The early Cape was a melting pot of racial strains; the so-called coloureds have a rich mixture of genes, drawn mainly from Africa, Europe and South East Asia where the Dutch had colonies. The Indian population originated in 1860 when labourers were imported to work on sugar plantations.

The Khoisan

The aboriginal Khoisan peoples once had the subcontinent to themselves. The San (or Bushmen) lived in the interior and the Khoikhoi (or Hottentots) ranged along the coast.

Both these slender, yellow-skinned peoples stemmed from a culture of the later Stone Age, dating back more than 30,000 years. Khoikhoi and San spoke similar languages, rich in click sounds. The Khoikhoi (the name means 'men of men') were absorbed by miscegenation or wiped out by invaders, both black and white, but small numbers of San have survived.

San

Unlike their coastal cousins, these nomadic people never took up agriculture or herding. To this day the surviving San live in small bands as hunter-gatherers.

San art is world-famous. Their dreams, religious symbols, culture, customs and surroundings have been depicted in caves and rock overhangs and even engraved on rock faces near rivers. The finest examples are located in the mountains of the escarpment — in the north-eastern Cape and the KwaZulu-Natal Drakensberg. This amazing gallery accumulated works of art for 20,000 years until the San were squeezed between white colonists from the south and black migrants from the north-east.

The San were outnumbered. Some groups lived on as fugitives in remote mountain areas until the late-1800s. The majority of those who survived conquest or integration fled north-west to seek refuge in the arid Kalahari desert in present-day Botswana and Namibia, where the majority of the surviving 20,000 San live.

The Khoikhoi

Initially, the Khoikhoi population was dispersed along the Orange River and the coastal plain in the south and south-west. These sheep- and cattle-keeping nomads moved from one pasture to another with the seasons. Seafood was prominent in their diet as large shell-mounds testify.

In the beginning, the Khoikhoi traded with the Dutch, swapping cattle for tobacco. They also served as go-betweens in negotiations with black tribes. Although the Khoikhoi were never enslaved, they suffered considerable exploitation as a source of cheap labour. Colonial expansion ate into their territory, and imported diseases destroyed their herds.

Some survivors trekked to the interior and were absorbed by black tribes. The so-called Hottentots who remained at the Cape added their genes to the rich blend that was to become the coloured population. There are no 'pure' Khoikhoi left today, only distant relatives in the form of the Gqunukwebe, the Cape Nguni and Nama.

Bantu

A number of Bantu-speaking peoples migrated from the north and occupied the coastal regions in the south-east and east more than 2,000 years ago.

There are four broad ethnic groups:

Above: South Africa has one of the most diverse ethnic populations in the world.

Nguni, Sotho, Shangaan-Tsonga and Venda. Nguni and Sotho dominate an estimated black population of 23 million.

The map of South Africa was drawn by imperial cartographers with scant regard for cultural or ethnic realities. Their South Africa swallowed some tribal territories whole — like the areas that were home to the Xhosa and Zulu. Other borders bisected tribes such as the Tswana, Sotho and Swazi, leaving large ethnic populations cut off from their relatives outside the country.

Nguni

There are three main black language groups classified as Nguni — Zulu, Xhosa and Ndebele. Each group can be further sub-divided into smaller groups and local dialects.

Zulu: there are almost eight million Zulus in South Africa. Their ancestral homeland is in KwaZulu-Natal where constitutional monarch King Goodwill Zwelithini heads a hierarchy of tribal chiefs and headmen. There are many Zulus in urban areas, and the enclave of Kangwane on the border of Swaziland is home to more than one

million speakers of the closely related Swazi language.

Xhosa: three million people speak Xhosa including the Xhosa, Pondo, Pondomise, Hlangwini, Xesibe, Bomvana, Hlubi, Fingo, Bhaca and Ngqika tribes. Xhosa is sub-divided into many dialects; a grammar book was written as early as 1834. Xhosa was the name of the founding father of the group who lived some 500 years ago. Diverse Nguni tribes adopted the Xhosa label after their migration from north-eastern Africa.

They settled in the Eastern Cape after driving out the San and Khoikhoi and came into conflict with expansionist whites. To the Xhosa, cattle were capital. The hunger for cattle drove the Xhosa and the white newcomers to carry out cattle raids on each other. Between 1779 and 1852 there were eight so-called 'kaffir wars' between them.

In 1856 the prophetess Nongquose persuaded her people that the whites would be eliminated if the Xhosa destroyed all their cattle and grain. This great cattle killing was virtually national suicide, and the Xhosa never really recovered from the disaster.

Xhosa-speakers are to be found in urban

Above: Transkei woman smoking a pipe.

areas all over South Africa, as well as in their ancestral territories centred on the Kei river in the Eastern Cape.

South Ndebele: the northern branch of this people has been absorbed by the Sotho but the South Ndebele still preserve an identity in what was central Transvaal. This group includes the Mapoch, otherwise known as the Manala, and Ndundza peoples.

Sotho

Eight million Sotho speakers can be divided broadly into the North Sotho, the South Sotho and the Tswana.

The North Sotho are based in the Northern Province. Groups falling under this heading include the Pedi, Pulana, Pai, Kutswe, KgagaKone, Phalaborwa, Nareng, Tlou, Gananwa, Hlaloga, Kolobe and Lovedu.

The South Sotho comprises the Phokeng, Tlokwa, Kwena, Phetla, Phuti and Pulana groups. The South Sotho live in the kingdom of Lesotho and the Free State.

In South Africa the Tswanas live in the North West province and Gauteng. They are ethnically the same as the population of Botswana. The tribe was cut in half by a colonial border between the Transvaal and Botswana, then known as Bechuanaland.

White South Africans

English speakers: approximately 38.7 per cent of the five million whites in South Africa have English as their mother tongue. The first British occupation of the Cape in 1795 established a small English-speaking community, which was boosted in 1820 by settlers brought in to create a buffer zone on the eastern frontier. The discovery of mineral wealth in the mid-19th century brought many more English speakers to the interior and there was large-scale immigration from Europe following the Second World War.

Afrikaans speakers: approximately 57.5 per cent of whites are Afrikaans-speaking, having been in the country for fifteen generations. Afrikaans is also the mother tongue of the coloured community. Afrikaners are basically of Dutch descent but many have French names derived from the Huguenot refugees of the 17th century. 3.8 per cent of the population are of other genetic and cultural elements derived from German, English, Scottish and Portuguese sources.

The Afrikaner stereotype, fostered by colonial history and propaganda dating from the Boer War, is of a stolid, patriarchal farmer, with a bullwhip in one hand and the Old Testament in the other. Present day reality is far removed from this image. The lines between city-dwelling Englishmen and Boers tend to become increasingly blurred, and Afrikaner businessmen have carved out a significant sector of the industrial economy. Afrikaners do not see themselves as closely linked to the European nations, but tend rather to regard themselves as Africa's only white tribe.

There is a Portuguese-speaking community of more than 500,000 which was boosted by the collapse of Portugal's colonies in Angola and Mozambique. There are also immigrants from many European countries, including Holland, Scandinavia, Germany, France, Belgium, Spain, Italy, Poland, Hungary, Lebanon, Greece and Russia. The Chinese are a small group of growing importance. A prominent Jewish community has made an important impact on all spheres of South African life.

The coloured people

The coloureds are the third largest population group in the country. They live primarily in the Western Cape and sub-cultures exist within the broad grouping: Cape Coloureds, Griquas and Cape Malays.

The dominant Cape Coloureds are descended from several races — white, Khoisan, East Indian and Bantu. Approximately fifty per cent still live in the Western Cape. The Griquas, who have a strong sense of identity, live in the Northern Cape are descended from Khoikhoi and white ancestors who met 200 years ago.

The Cape Malays have Indian, Arab, Malagasy, Chinese and Malay blood, being the descendants of slaves owned by the Dutch East India Company. The Cape Malays are held together by their religion, Islam, and for the most part live in Cape Town.

Coloureds were traditionally fishermen, farm labourers and servants. Today, many still live on farms and in rural settlements, but a large number of this vibrant community have begun to take their rightful places in politics, commerce, industry, education and the arts. Coloured folklore and music is a bright strand woven into the cultural tapestry of South Africa.

The Asian community

Brought to Natal as indentured labour for the sugar plantations, the first Indians arrived in South Africa in 1860. At the end of their period of service, they could opt for repatriation or be settled on the land. KwaZulu-Natal remains an Indian stronghold but there are important

Above: An Asiatic: their ancestors came in the 1860s.

communities in urban centres throughout South Africa. Hindus make up seventy per cent of the population, with twenty-two per cent Muslims and a small percentage of Christians and Buddhists.

Hindus are divided into four language groups — Tamil, Telegu, Hindi and Gujarati while Muslims tend to speak Gujarati and Urdu. Almost all Indians can speak English, while fourteen per cent speak the other languages at home. South Africa's Indian culture is traditional and patriarchal.

The Chinese

Most of the Chinese speak English and have settled in Johannesburg and Gauteng. There are small communities in many other cities. There is also a Japanese community in Johannesburg.

PART TWO: PLACES AND TRAVEL

Above: Flamingoes at Fisherhaven in the Cape.
Opposite: Giant's Castle in the spectacular Drakensberg mountain range.

The Northern Provinces

The Northern provinces are richly endowed with scenic beauty and mineral wealth. They cover an area of 268,918 square kilometres (109,829 square miles) and are bordered by the Vaal River in the south and the Limpopo River to the north.

In the south and westerly regions the highveld plateau reaches an altitude of 2,000 metres (610 feet). Here the climate has average summer temperatures of 22 degrees Celsius and frequent afternoon thunderstorms. The highveld ends abruptly in a steep escarpment and there is a marked transition between this region and the lowveld areas to the north and north-east. On the lowveld, the daytime temperature can reach 38 degrees Celsius in the shade; it is here, in the game reserves of the north-east where one finds evidence of the teeming herds of game that once roamed the entire area.

Today, the Northern provinces still harbour great mineral treasures and the Gauteng region has become the hub of South African business. Johannesburg International Airport is situated between Pretoria and Johannesburg, and from it a number of airlines operate daily services to all major centres in South Africa and around the world. A service called Airport Link (Tel: 011 803-9474) operates a useful and relatively inexpensive door-to-door service between Johannesburg International Airport and points in Gauteng.

The train service is nowhere near as fast or as efficient as European metro rail systems. The Blue Train, one of the most luxurious trains in the world, makes regular trips between Johannesburg and Cape Town — an extremely comfortable way of seeing South Africa, if you can afford it.

National roads and highways connect the province with other major centres and most roads in the provinces are tarred. Conventional taxis do not cruise the province's roads, although minibuses provide a service to local populations. Nicknamed Zola Budd taxis, after a well-known South African athlete, the buses are usually packed to capacity and utilized primarily by the black population. Conventional taxis are expensive but can be arranged by telephone or via hotels. There are regular long distance coach services in the Transvaal.

Following the N1 north

The long road north to the country's border on the Limpopo River begins with the national N1 freeway, a large dual carriageway which starts in Johannesburg as the Ben Schoeman motorway. The N1 pushes through the Magaliesburg mountains, crosses the highveld and continues north to the plains and scenic mountain ranges of the Northern Province. The internationally famous Kruger National Park is the ultimate destination for many tourists, and the N1 leads directly to the northern regions of the park and a host of private game reserves. Here the 'big five' wander through the bushveld as they did hundreds of years ago; each year thousands of visitors journey to the Northern Province to appreciate Africa's big game in its natural habitat.

Northern Province

Besides being known for its wilderness areas, Northern Province boasts a number of hot springs. Many believe that their waters soothe a variety of maladies. A variety of holiday resorts have been developed around these mineral baths; perhaps the best known resort is at **Warmbad**, a small town which lies 100 kilometres (62 miles) to the north of Pretoria. A beautifully landscaped tourist and health complex has been established at Warmbad, with the hot springs at its centre. The waters are rich in salts such as sodium chloride and calcium carbonate which flow from a hot spring at a speed of approximately 22,000 litres (4,840 gallons) per hour. They are believed to have

Above: Tourists enjoy a game drive in the Kruger National Park watching as a lone leopard stalks its prey.

restorative powers for rheumatism sufferers, and a rheumatic pool forms part of the resort's health complex. Other facilities include a huge indoor swimming pool, a fully-equipped gymnasium, children's pools and a wave pool. There are self-contained, air-conditioned chalets for hire at the Warmbad resort, and a large campsite. In the town itself, accommodation is plentiful and the area has a number of holiday resorts and a game ranch. A private game reserve adjoining the spa provides protection for various game. Walking tours are permitted.

Sightseeing

A **bird park** and **tea garden** is located about five kilometres (three miles) from the Warmbad resort. The park has aviaries with some fine indigenous and exotic bird species. To reach the bird park, take the Rustenburg/Thabazimbi road from Warmbad and turn left at the first gravel road.

From Warmbad, the N1 passes through the towns of Nylstroom and Naboomspruit, both situated in the foothills of the Waterberg mountain range.

Nylstroom is regarded as the centre of the fertile Waterberg region, and was named by a group of Voortrekkers who, after their long journey north from the Cape, mistook the river that runs near the town for the Nile River — or Nylstroom as they called it.

The **Waterberg Mountains** which stretch for a distance of 150 kilometres (93 miles), from Thabazimbi in the west to the Lephalala River in the north-east, form a backdrop to the towns of Nylstroom and Naboomspruit. Aptly named because of the many streams and springs which flow through the range, the Waterberg mountains have been immortalized by the works of Eugene Marais, one of South Africa's best known poets and naturalists.

The mountain scenery of the southern Waterberg range is characterized by steep vertical cliffs and spectacular rock formations. The highest mountain in the north-western Transvaal is to be found in the **Kransberg** region of the range. It reaches a height of 2,100 metres (640 feet) above sea level. The northern slopes are less rugged and they descend gradually and merge with the vast plains below.

Nylstroom

The town of Nylstroom nestles in the southern foothills of the Waterberg Range. Buildings of historic interest include the residence of former South African Prime Minister, Advocate J G Strydom, and a church in Calvyn Street, which dates back to 1889. Advocate Strydom's house has been converted into a museum.

Where to stay and sightseeing

There are two holiday resorts in the Nylstroom area, each providing accommodation in the form of chalets and camp sites. Recreational facilities offered by the resorts include watersports, nature trails, swimming pools and tennis courts. In the vicinity of Nylstroom is the **Hans Strijdom Dam Nature Reserve**, a 4,654-hectare (11,500-acre) game reserve which is well signposted on the road from Nylstroom to Ellisras. The mountainous terrain of the reserve provides a sanctuary for the rare roan antelope and Sharpe's grysbok, both of which are indigenous to the Waterberg mountains. Game spotting is usually best in winter; during the summer months the Hans Strijdom Dam offers good fishing opportunities. The only roads in the reserve that are negotiable in conventional motor vehicles are the access roads. Game viewing is conducted on foot under the guidance of nature conservationists.

Lapalala is a scenic wilderness nestled in the Waterberg Mountains, about 125 kilometres (78 miles) from Nylstroom. Visitors to this 18,000-hectare (4,448-acre) sanctuary are transported to their camps by conservation officers and game viewing is on foot — no vehicles are permitted within the park. Both the Lephalala and Blocklands Rivers cut through the reserve, and accommodation is available in five bush camps, situated on the river banks. The camps are secluded and each has its own walks, trails and fishing spots. Canoes are available for hire and game viewing is excellent. Lapalala is a protected environment for the beautiful roan antelope, and a research project aimed at the preservation of this rare species is being carried out there. Wilderness trails are conducted by professional field officers.

Getting there

To reach Lapalala, follow the R517 from Nylstroom to Vaalwater. From there drive towards Melkwater. After forty kilometres (25 miles) there is a gravel road signposted Melkwater School. The entrance to Lapalala is twenty-five kilometres (16 miles) along this road. There is a landing strip in the sanctuary for visitors who wish to arrive by air.

Naboomspruit

Forty kilometres (25 miles) north of Nylstroom is **Naboomspruit**, a town which owes its existence to rich deposits of tin and fluorspar in the area. The minerals which were discovered at the beginning of the century, are still mined today. Naboomspruit is best known for its wide variety of holiday resorts, the majority of which have been built around mineral spas. Today the little town which grew up around a railway siding on the farm Naboomspruit, is also the centre of a thriving cattle and maize farming community.

The **Doorndraai Dam Nature Reserve** — situated fifty kilometres (31 miles) north of the town — boasts 7,000 hectares (17,297 acres) of typical Waterberg vegetation, including wild olive and wild syringa trees. The reserve specializes in the protection of rare antelope species such as the roan, sable and tsessebe. The Doorndraai irrigation dam is the focus of the reserve and fishing is excellent. Signposts on the N1, between Naboomspruit and Potgietersrus direct visitors to the sanctuary which offers no accommodation other than camping facilities. Many of the roads within the park can only be negotiated in a four-wheel-drive vehicle.

South of Naboomspruit, on the road to Nylstroom, is the **Nylsvlei Nature Reserve**, a game park situated on the sprawling floodplain of the Nyl River. Nylsvlei is used by South Africa's Council for Scientific and Industrial Research (CSIR) in its study of the savannah ecosystem of South Africa. It is also well-known for the more than 400 species of birds within its boundaries. They are attracted to both the savannah woodland that flanks the vlei and to the waters of the Nyl River. Visitors may only explore the reserve on foot and accommodation is limited to camping facilities.

Getting there

Follow the Nylstroom road south for thirteen kilometres (eight miles) and then take the Boekenhout turn-off. The entrance to Nylsvlei is on this road.

The road between Naboomspruit and the agricultural centre of Potgietersrus is steeped in the history of the early years of the Transvaal, as Northern Province and Mpumalanga were known. On the right of the N1, forty kilometres (25 miles) from Naboomspruit are two large camelthorn trees which mark the site where, in 1854, the Voortrekker parties under the leadership of Hermanus Potgieter were massacred by the local chief, Makapan. Today, the place is known as Moorddrif which means Murder Fort and a monument has been erected there.

In 1936 archaeological excavations began at **Makapansgat.** Workmen who were blasting in the area discovered a large limestone rockface which contained the fossilized remains of homonids — our near human ancestors. Makapansgat was such an important archaeological discovery that it was declared a national monument.

Potgietersrus

Within the town of **Potgietersrus** are a number of places of historical interest such as the camelthorn tree on the corner of Retief and Ruiter Roads where it is said the first school lesson north of the Vaal River was given. The **Arend Dieperink Museum** in Voortrekker Road exhibits historical photographs, documents, household and farm implements, some of which date back to the time of the Great Trek.

The missionary explorer, Dr David Livingstone, is believed to have camped beneath a clump of 'Apiesdoring' (monkey thorn — *Acacia albida*) trees on the road between Potgietersrus and Botswana. The eight trees are between five and seven metres (16 and 23 feet) high and can be found sixteen kilometres (ten miles) from Potgietersrus.

On the northern outskirts of the town is an interesting nature reserve and breeding centre which specializes in the propagation of rare animal species from all over the world, including the West African pygmy hippo, the Australian emu and South American llama. Among indigenous species to be seen at the reserve are white rhino, black rhino, Burchell's zebra and sable antelope. There is a dam within the reserve which has barbecue and picnic facilities on its banks. The reserve is open daily between 8.00 and 17.30 in winter and closes at 18.00 during the summer months.

Pietersburg

From Potgietersrus, the N1 follows a north-easterly path to **Pietersburg,** the commercial hub of Northern Province. Pietersburg is situated on the edge of the highveld plateau, at a height of 1,220 metres (4,000 feet) above sea level. It is known for its wide streets — which like Pretoria's are lined with jacaranda trees — a host of museums and places of historical interest.

Founded in 1886, the modern town of Pietersburg is the largest in Northern Province. The town's contemporary buildings provide a striking contrast to its older buildings in the city centre. The Victorian house, on the corner of Market and Vorster Streets, has been declared a national monument, as has the former home of Doel Zeederberg, a stage coach magnate who ran a passenger coach between Pietersburg and Zimbabwe in 1894. This can be viewed from Voortrekker Street.

Pietersburg's **Civic Centre** and **Civic Square** form the focus of the town. The complex has an impressive art collection, a conference centre and a conservatory with a magnificent array of exotic plants. The square, bounded by Landdros Mare, Vorster, Church and Bodenstein Streets, has

Above and opposite:
Pietersburg, the largest town in Northern Province, is a blend of old and modern architecture.

been enhanced by beautifully landscaped gardens. The Dutch Reformed Church, which was built in 1880, has been restored and now houses a photographic museum.

An open-air museum on Landdros Mare Street exhibits an old ore crusher, a steam locomotive and various agricultural implements. At the northern entrance to the town is a display of art created using discarded industrial materials. On the corner of Grobler and Hans van Rensburg Streets is a sculpture created from the remains of rifles confiscated from Chief Makgobo's tribe in 1895 after their defeat by forces of President Kruger's Zuid Afrikaanse Republiek.

A site of cultural interest is the **Bakone Malapa museum**, situated nine kilometres (five miles) south of Pietersburg on the Chuniespoort/Burgersford Road. Within the museum is a traditional Northern Sotho Bakone kraal, where tribesmen practise age-old crafts, archaeological remains, and rock paintings from the area which date back to 1,000 AD. Other

attractions include the remains of an Ndebele iron and copper smelting works, walking trails and picnic facilities.

The remains of a British fort, which was besieged for 105 days during the Anglo-Boer War may be viewed at Marabastad, about fourteen kilometres (nine miles) south of Pietersburg. Permission to view the **Fort Campbell memorial column** must be obtained from the owner of the farm.

A Voortrekker memorial on the N1, about six kilometres (four miles) from Pietersburg commemorates the trek of Louis Trichardt who journeyed to Delagoa Bay (now Maputo) in 1837.

Outdoor recreation facilities are offered at **Union Park**, five kilometres (three miles) south of the town. Angling is permitted and there is accommodation available in the municipal game reserve which adjoins the park. A large variety of game roam the beautiful grasslands of this 2,500-hectare reserve; springbok, eland, kudu, sable and white rhino may be sighted there.

The Letaba District

To leave the N1 at Pietersburg and journey into the mountain world of the eastern escarpment is to embark on one of southern Africa's most spectacular scenic drives. The **Letaba district**, to the east of Pietersburg, is a world of rugged mountains, ancient forests, trout streams and tropical fruit plantations. British novelist John Buchan called Letaba the 'land of the silver mists'.

Rain falls along the eastern escarpment during the summer months with about 178 centimetres recorded annually.

The climate of the Letaba district is ideally suited for tree cultivation and the area is heavily wooded by plantations and indigenous forests. Mist is common in the summer and snow falls occasionally during the winter months.

Tzaneen is the main town in the Letaba district. The R71 leads there via the grasslands of the Pietersburg plateau, across the Letaba River and through a beautiful mountain pass at **Magoebaskloof**. The first stop along the way is Haenertsburg, a small forestry town, best known for its well-stocked trout streams and annual Cherry Blossom and Azalea festival. The little village, only fifty-eight kilometres (36 miles) from Pietersburg, was founded in the 1890s when a prospector named C F Haenert started a gold rush to the area. Today one of its main attractions is a cherry and azalea farm situated near an old coach halt called 'Cheerio', on the outskirts of the town. For three or four weeks in October the trees are spectacularly in bloom. Because the timing is determined by rainfall, visitors are advised to check with local farmers to find out when the trees are expected to blossom.

At Haenertsburg the road to Tzaneen forks into a southern and a northern route. The southern route follows the R528 through **George's Valley**, along the slopes of the Wolkberg mountain range. The northern route winds its way through Magoebaskloof. Holidaymakers towing caravans and those driving heavy vehicles are advised to stick to the southern route which is slightly longer but not as steep.

This route offers good views of the thickly forested mountain slopes of the Wolkberg, and the farmlands of the Letaba valley which produce subtropical fruit and nuts. Six kilometres (four miles) along the R528 is a turn-off to the **Ebenezer Dam** which is situated among forestry plantations and offers watersports and picnic facilities.

The **Wolkberg Wilderness Area** is a 17,000-hectare (42,000-acre) nature reserve situated in the Drakensberg and Strydpoort mountains. It is accessible from the R71, along a signposted road, about forty kilometres (25 miles) from Pietersburg. The area consists of dense indigenous forest, high mountains and magnificent waterfalls. While leopard, brown hyena and caracal have been spotted here, game is generally scarce, but birdlife prolific. The **Thabina Falls** and **Mohlapitse River** potholes are among the attractions in the wilderness area. Fishing and hunting are not permitted but camping is allowed. Fires are prohibited in the forests so campers should bring gas cooking facilities.

One of the central features of the eastern escarpment is Magoebaskloof, a beautiful mountain region, steeped in history and legend. It was named after Makgobo, chief of the Tlou tribe who, in 1894, revolted against the taxes imposed on them by Paul Kruger's Suid Afrikaanse Republiek. Following its rebellion, the tribe fled into the Magoebaskloof mountains, seeking refuge in the steep ravines. Kruger sent a group of Swazi warriors to capture the errant Makgobo, who was eventually tracked down and beheaded. Legend has it that Makgobo's spirit became imprisoned in the trunk of a palm tree near Thabina. According to tribal elders, his spirit would only be released once a bulge in the tree's trunk reached the top of the tree. Unfortunately the palm tree was blown over in a storm before this happened.

The road through the Magoebaskloof drops 600 metres (183 feet) in under six kilometres (four miles), as it winds down the Drakensberg escarpment to the subtropical lowveld. It passes through some of the most impressive tracts of indigenous forest in South Africa which in some places is so dense as to be impenetrable. A number

Above: The beautiful Debegeni Falls are popular with swimmers and picknickers.

of small auxiliary roads branch off the main R71 and take scenic routes deep into the mountains and forestry regions of the Magoebaskloof. They are generally well sign-posted and usually link up again with a main road.

The **Magoebaskloof hiking trail** offers the opportunity to walk through the indigenous forests along the northern slopes of the Magoebaskloof. The Dokolewa section of the trail is a thirty-six-kilometre (22-mile) walk which begins at the De Hoek forest station. A twenty-eight-kilometre (17-mile) trail known as the Grootbosch section has the same starting point but ends at Christinarus, which is approximately seven kilometres from Duiwelskloof.

Five kilometres (three miles) from the turn-off to Ebenezer Dam is a gravel road which leads to the Woodbush State Forest and **Dap Naude Dam**. The twelve-kilometre (seven-mile) road runs along the edge of the escarpment and through the largest indigenous forest in Northern Province. The views of the lowveld are magnificent.

Still on the R71, but ten kilometres from the turn-off to Woodbush, is the entrance to the De Hoek State Forest. Within the boundaries of this plantation are the **Debegeni Falls**, a series of cascades which tumble eighty metres into a deep, pot-like pool — hence the name Debegeni which means, 'the place of the pot'. In days gone by, tribes believed their ancestral spirits lived in the pool and they would offer them gifts of food and drink there. Today the falls are a popular swimming and picnicking site. The area is open between 07.00 and 18.00 in summer. In the winter months, from April to August, it closes at 17.00.

Duiwelskloof is a picturesque village on the slopes of the escarpment, just eighteen kilometres (eleven miles) from the lowveld town of Tzaneen. The area surrounding Duiwelskloof is home to the Lovedu tribe and its rain-queen Modjadji, the legendary rain-queen who, according to her people, has mystical rain-making powers. She is said to be a direct descendant of the Karanga tribe who fled south from Zimbabwe in the 16th century and settled in the Molotutse valley near to Duiwelskloof.

Despite the heat, spring and summer are the best months in which to visit this region; this is when the town's bougainvillea, poinsettia and frangipani trees are in bloom. The high rainfall and subtropical climate of the area account for its prolific plant life and the abundance of tropical fruit such as pawpaws (papayas), bananas, avocados and mangoes.

There are a number of forest drives and walks in the vicinity of Duiwelskloof; one of the most popular excursions from the town is to the **Modjadji Nature Reserve**, situated some thirty kilometres (nineteen miles) from Duiwelskloof.

The most remarkable feature of the reserve is its cycad forest. Cycads belong to an ancient order, the Cycadales, which flourished on earth between fifty and sixty million years ago and are earth's most primitive seedbearing plants. Modjadji Nature Reserve has a variety of cycad species, including the largest concentration of a single cycad species in the world. This is a dense forest of Modjadji palms (*Encephalartos transvenosus*). These plants usually grow to a height of between five and eight metres, but in Modjadji, some of the oldest have surpassed twelve metres (40 feet) thanks to enjoying the special protection of generations of rain-queens. Cycads are protected by South African law and it is an offence to own one without a permit. A nursery situated approximately five kilometres (three miles) from the Modjadji reserve cultivates cycads and sells them to the public. It also arranges permits.

From Duiwelskloof the R71 continues east to Tzaneen — the capital of the Letaba District — into the lowveld areas. Tzaneen is situated at the foot of the Drakensberg mountains on the edge of the lowveld. The town marks the transition from the mountainous eastern escarpment to the sub-tropical regions of the lowveld. To the east of Tzaneen lies the Kruger National Park, the biggest game reserve in the southern hemisphere which, together with the private game parks which surround it, accounts for a substantial part of the lowveld. This is one of the most popular and spectacular of the tourist destinations in South Africa. The N4 is the main eastern route through the lowveld to the Kruger National Park.

North to the Limpopo

Sixty-one kilometres (38 miles) outside Pietersburg stands a stainless steel monument on a rocky outcrop. This marks the spot where the Tropic of Capricorn bisects the N1. Ahead lies the spectacular mountain scenery of the Soutpansberg, and to the west of the road the dry bushveld stretches north to the Limpopo River.

At **Louis Trichardt** the Soutpansberg Mountains rise up out of the flat bushveld, their heavily wooded foothills coming as something of a surprise because of their sharp contrast with the surrounding area. The town hosts a number of historically interesting places.

The town is named after a Voortrekker leader who camped in the area in 1836 before continuing his journey to Delagoa Bay (Maputo). A memorial in the town commemorates Trichardt's trek party's first encounter with the Shangaan and with the Portuguese in Mozambique.

Louis Trichardt's first settlement was established in 1847, when the town was named Zoutpansbergdorp after the mountains against which it nestles. The name was later changed to Schoemansdal and the settlement became a centre for ivory traders, cattle rustlers and hunters. Today Louis Trichardt serves a cattle and game ranching community. The subtropical climate provides the ideal environment for farming of citrus and subtropical fruit, ground nuts and vegetables.

The Soutpansberg mountain scenery surrounding the town provides a number of opportunities for outdoor activities. Game ranches offer photographic and hunting safaris.

The **Ben Lavin Nature Reserve** is situated twelve kilometres (seven miles) south east of the town. Giraffe, zebra and leopard may be spotted in the rolling grasslands of the reserve; you may catch a glimpse of the rare brown hyena or antbear.

Getting there

Travel south from Louis Trichardt and take the turn-off to Elim, three kilometres from the town. One-and-a-half kilometres further

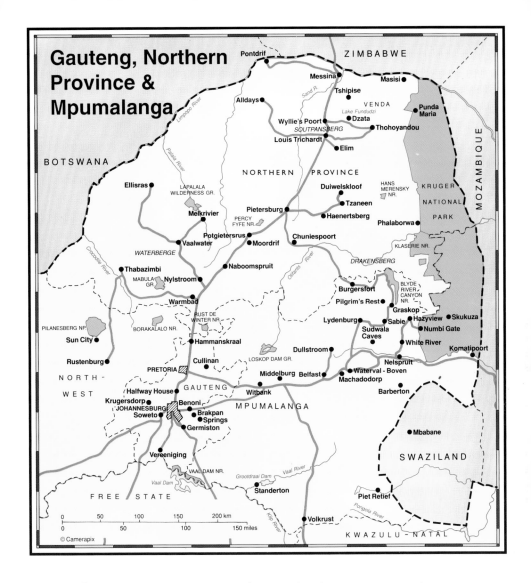

on, take the turning to Fort Edward. The entrance to Ben Lavin is situated five kilometres along this road. Also in the vicinity of Louis Trichardt is the **Langjan Nature Reserve**. The reserve was established in 1950 to provide a sanctuary for the only remaining herd of gemsbok in the Transvaal. Today it boasts large numbers of waterbuck, eland and zebra, and the rare civet cat is often seen there.

Getting there

Langjan Nature Reserve is situated ninety-four kilometres (58 miles) from Louis Trichardt on the road to Alldays.

The dramatic **Soutpansberg Mountains** form the great divide between the grasslands of the highveld plateau and the hot savannah plains of the northern bushveld. The range stretches for 130 kilometres (81 miles) west to east and takes its name from a large salt pan on its western edge — these are the salt-pan mountains. The high annual rainfall recorded in the Soutpansberg accounts for large tracts of both exotic and indigenous forests. Rare cycads, tree ferns, stinkwood and yellow wood trees are all common in the range. Bird life here is phenomenal, and the extremely timid Narina trogon may be

75

spotted in the forests. Species of game which are found in the mountains include klipspringer, bushbuck, and grey and red duiker.

The forests of the Soutpansberg Mountains provide some opportunities for walks and hikes.

A less energetic way to view the sights of the Soutpansberg is to take a scenic drive along the western summit of the mountain range. The route begins a little way out of Louis Trichardt and winds up the thickly forested southern slopes of the mountain range. At the summit, there is a small gravel road which is signposted Bluegumspoort. This is the start of a spectacular sixteen-kilometre (ten-mile) drive along the western side of the mountain.

From the top of the range, the N1 descends into the valleys of the Soutpansberg. At Wyllie's Poort pass, the road climbs again and for twenty-two kilometres (14 miles) it winds through mountains. Here the road is flanked by towering cliffs and at two points it burrows into the peaks. The tunnels in this section of the Soutpansberg are both named after Hendrick Verwoerd, a former South African Prime Minister and the 'father of apartheid'. The tunnel which leads to Messina is 381 metres (1,270 feet) long, the tunnel to Louis Trichardt is 290 metres (967 feet). At the entrance to each tunnel are viewing points which offer wonderful views of the richly forested slopes below.

The Home of the Vhavenda

The home of the Vhavenda people is a small area, covering a total area of 6,500 square kilometres (2,510 square miles). It juts into the Soutpansberg Mountains and lies between the N1 and the Kruger National Park, with a little island of land situated to the west of Louis Trichardt. This enclave is linked to the area's most important town, Thohoyandou, by a good tar road.

The Vhavenda people were granted quasi-independence from South Africa in 1979 as the state of Venda. In 1994 Venda was reincorporated into South Africa. The history of the Vhavenda people, however, stretches back more than 800 years to a time when their ancestors migrated south from the region surrounding the great lakes of Africa. They are the direct descendants of a chief called Dimbanyika who led his followers across the Limpopo River in the early 18th century. Dimbanyika and his people wandered up the valley of the Nzhelele River, and settled in the mountains near the river, naming their new home 'the pleasant place'. They established their kraal at Dzata and it was there that they encountered other clans who had migrated south from what is now Zimbabwe. They united under the great leader, Thohoyandou. The ancient ruins and sandstone caves where their forefathers lived bear witness to the Vhavenda's rich heritage; the past is an integral part of the Vhavenda's lifestyle, with almost every aspect of their existence steeped in legend, superstition and folklore. The 'land of legend' as the area is known, is an enchanting tourist destination, with many places of interest regarded as sacred by the people. For this reason it may be advisable to enlist the services of an experienced guide when visiting, to ensure that the beliefs and traditions of this ancient culture are respected and that the people who still honour age-old customs are not offended.

At the heart of Vhavenda legend and mysticism is **Fundudzi**, the holy lake, situated in the south west. Fundudzi is a fresh water lake about two kilometres (one mile) long, with an average depth of five metres (15 feet). It is believed to have been formed by the crumbling of surrounding hills which blocked the natural flow of the Mutale River. The lake is regarded as a spirit world by the Vhavenda and it is the focal point of a number of their beliefs. The Vhavenda say that its waters will never mix with anything. Rocks thrown into the lake will pass right through it, as will rain and surface water. The Mutale River which flows into Fundudzi is believed to pass through the lake and out into an underground opening, never mixing with the holy waters. So strong is the legend which surrounds Fundudzi, that its waters may not be used for domestic purposes.

Above: Young Vhavenda girls dance to the python god of fertility.

According to the legend which surrounds it, any container used for this purpose will burst open a short distance from the lake.

The python god of fertility is said to live in Lake Fundudzi, and young girls who are preparing for marriage perform an ancient and intricate python dance in homage to the deity. The sensuous and rhythmic dance is called the Domba and is performed to the beat of the powerful domba drum. The girls dance in single file, with their hands clasped to the forearms of the girl in front of them, rocking in a long, snakeline line.

Although Lake Fundudzi can be clearly seen from the road that winds through the surrounding hills, it may only be visited with the permission of the local chief or the priestess of the lake. Permits may be obtained from tourism authorities in Thohoyandou, who will also provide information about guided tours of the area. The highland, 'land of legend' tour is conducted in air-conditioned, four-wheel-drive vehicles, and takes tourists to the lake, the sacred Thathe Vondo Forests, the Duthuni potters, the Tshivhase tea estates and the Phiphidi waterfall.

Twenty kilometres (13 miles) from Thohoyandou, on the Wyllie's Poort road, is the entrance to the **Thathe Vondo** forest plantation. The plantation has both indigenous and exotic forests, and is criss-crossed with picturesque rivers, streams and spectacular waterfalls. Tree ferns, creepers and the pre-historic cycad are prolific in the forests of Thathe Vondo. There is a popular viewpoint within the plantation which affords breathtaking views. This is located only 300 metres (300 yards) from the road, 3.6 kilometres (two miles) from the entrance to the plantation — watch for the signpost.

At the centre of the forestry plantations is the **Mukumbani Dam** where fishing and recreation opportunities are excellent. A scenic drive around the dam leads to the beautiful Mahovhohovho waterfall. The Mutale River — which eventually flows into the holy Lake Fundudzi — rushes over a spectacular waterfall in the north-eastern region of the plantations. There are swimming and picnic facilities available at the Mutale Waterfall.

Thathe Vondo also features the **Holy**

Forest, realm of the Vhavenda's ancestral spirits. Visitors are allowed to drive through the Holy Forest and even stop to admire the splendour of the mysterious woods, but walking in the forests is not allowed; even the Vhavenda are forbidden to venture into these mysterious recesses for fear of angering the spirits.

The forests are said to protect the burial place of the chiefs of the Thathe clan and legend has it that a white lion prowls the forests keeping guard over their graves. The lion is believed to be the spirit of Nethathe, an important chief who had the power to turn himself into various animals in order to keep watch over his people. Today, members of the Tshidzivhe communities continue to make sacrifices to the white lion of the holy forest. The produce of their fields is only enjoyed once a portion of it has been offered to Nethathe.

The Ndadzi, or lightning bird, is another creature said to live in the Holy Forest. Ndadzi carries the rain in its beak and takes its name from its eyes which are said to flash like lightning. The Vhavenda believe that when Ndadzi drops its egg at the foot of a tree, the tree will burn immediately, leaving no trace of fire.

Getting there

From Thohoyandou, follow the Wyllie's Poort/Makhado road in a westerly direction. The entrance to the Thathe Vondo forest plantation is located twenty kilometres from Sibasa. The Holy Forest, Mutale waterfall and Lake Fundudzi are all accessible from within the plantation. A more direct route by which to view Fundudzi is to take a turn-off on the Wyllie's Poort/Makhado road, thirty-four kilometres (21 miles) from Thohoyandou. This follows a scenic route through the Soutpansberg mountains and then back towards the forestry plantations. The Fundudzi lookout is located 300 metres (328 yards) from the road.

The legends and folklore that surround Fundudzi spill over into other aspects of the Vhavenda's lives. For instance, water sprites called Zwidutwane are said to live in Fundudzi and other watery places, and it is necessary to appease them by offering gifts like beer, ornaments or a tuft of hair when passing their residential pools. According to legend, the Zwidutwane are small creatures with only one eye, one arm and one leg and should be avoided by humans. Above the Phiphidi Waterfall, near the Thathe Vondo Forest, are some large, hollowed-out stones. The Vhavenda believe these are the water sprites receptacles for gifts of beer and food.

Clearly visible to the west of Thohoyandou is **Lwamondo Hill** which rises out of the Soutpansberg Mountains. The hillock takes its name from the Lwamondo people who used it as a stronghold during tribal wars, and is best known for the troop of sacred baboons that are said to keep watch over the mountain slopes. In the past, the baboons would warn the Lwamondo people when their enemies approached their village. The enemy would then be dispersed by a shower of rocks and arrows. Vhavenda elders still talk of an attack by a group of Swazis which was repelled in this way.

Thohoyandou, which means the 'head of the elephant', is located a short distance from Louis Trichardt on the main route R524. It is named after a 19th-century leader who was responsible for uniting the Vhavenda nation. The old administrative centre of **Sibasa** is situated a little way out of Thohoyandou, and the older town is abuzz with activity centred around hundreds of market stalls.

Thohoyandou on the other hand is a growing urban area which features modern shopping complexes, a university and **The Venda Sun**, a hotel and casino.

Acacia Park is situated alongside the main Louis Trichardt/Kruger National Park road, about three kilometres (two miles) from the centre of Thohoyandou. The resort has sixteen fully-serviced chalets, a campsite and offers facilities for self-catering holidays. There are twenty-four-hour security.

One of the most attractive places to visit within Thohoyandou is the **Ditike Craft Shop and Tourism Centre**. About 3,700 men and women in Northern Transvaal are economically active in the craft industry.

Above: The Thathe Vondo forest is an area of breathtaking beauty.

They make hand-woven baskets and mats, wood carvings and pottery. The Ditike craft market is where the majority of items that are created in outlying areas are sold. Also to be found at Ditike is a small fine-art gallery which displays works of contemporary Vhavenda artists, sculptors and metal workers. The craft centre is situated on the road from Louis Trichardt, before the turn-off to the city's industrial area.

Pottery is traditionally practised by Vhavenda women, many of whom still make their own cooking pots from natural materials. At **Tshimbupfe** in the south east is a cottage industry in which clay pots are produced and sold to the public. Pots are also made at **Mashamba** in the **Tshitale** district. A rough clay is used by potters who shape the pots with their hands.

Traditional cooking pots are hemispherical in shape and have a thick band of graphite burnishing just below the lip. Beer pots are of a similar shape but have a decoration etched into the clay on the upper half. These decorations are mainly geometrical and are separated from the bottom half of the pot by an incised line

which runs around the pot's circumference. Decorations are coloured by graphite which is applied after the pots are fired.

The Vhavenda are renowned for their exquisite weaving of baskets and mats. These are fashioned from reeds and grasses and are often patterned by black wefts. In the past, the Vhavenda people made their baskets really big for storage purposes — a basket filled with grain could be exchanged for a number of cattle.

A sleeping mat is known as a *thovo*, and there are a variety of woven and knotted mats to be purchased at Ditike. The **Roman Catholic Mission** at **Tshakhum** is well-known for its wool and cotton mats, and **The Tshimbupfe Sisal project** sells sisal mats to the public. In the Masisi area, mats are crafted from reeds obtained from the Limpopo River.

Wood carving is traditionally practised by Vhavenda men who make everything from wooden bowls to walking sticks, but specialize in the crafting of drums which have great significance in Vhavenda culture. Drums are used during initiation ceremonies and a domba drum is a prized possession. Generations of wood workers have kept the art of carving ornate domba drums alive. A piece of leather is tightly stretched across the opening of the drum to ensure the sound that emerges from it is rich and powerful. An open-air workshop near Mutale allows visitors to observe how the Vhavenda create their drums; the products of their labours are displayed for the public in an adjoining showroom. The drums that are crafted here range in shape from the round *ngoma* to large hemispherical objects, almost two metres (six feet) high. Most drums have handles and are beautifully decorated.

Seventy-five kilometres (47 miles) north of Thohoyandou, in the thickly-wooded foothills of the Soutpansberg Mountains, is the **Nwanedi National Park**. Nwanedi which extends over an area of 12,600 hectares (31,135 acres), is well stocked with game. White rhino and a variety of antelope species live in the park, including nyala, klipspringer and impala. Giraffe, blue wildebeest and zebra are also common.

The dirt road to Nwanedi from Thohoyandou winds through the mountains and valleys of the Soutpansberg. An easier way to reach the game reserve is via Tshepedi. This route has only seventeen kilometres (11 miles) of gravel road, the rest is tarred.

Makuya National Park borders the Kruger National Park. Makuya boasts a spectacular gorge formed by the **Luvuvhu River** and features the 'big five': lion, leopard, buffalo, rhino and elephant.

Within easy reach of **Nwanedi National Park**, in the north is the village of **Sagole** where a herbalist and diviner may be consulted. There is also a natural **hot spring**, around which a holiday resort has been built. There are two fully-equipped cottages and six rondavels (cottages) at the Sagole spa.

Nearby is the largest known baobab tree in southern Africa, with a circumference of forty-three metres (47 yards). Places of historical interest in this northern region include the **Tshiungane fortress ruins and sandstone caves** in which there are rock paintings made by early inhabitants of the region. Attractive walks can be undertaken in the **Dambale hills**.

A tour of the western region of the former republic should include a visit to the **prehistoric footprints** at **Kokwane**, the **Mandadzi waterfalls** and indigenous forests and the **Dzata** ruins. This trip also incorporates a drive through the **Thathe Vondo Forest**, tea estates and the **Phiphidi Waterfall**.

The southern tour is most suited to those with an interest in traditional arts and crafts. It includes a visit to Noria Mabasa, an artist who models typical Vhavenda characters in clay and who is also a skilled carpenter. The tour also includes a trip to an old iron smelting furnace at **Tshimbupfe**, the **Twananani Batik printers** and the **Mukhondeni potters**.

Weekend package tours are available to Venda Sun and the Kruger National Park. Enquiries can be made through Sun International Central Reservations. Phone: 011- 780-7444.

Getting there

Thohoyandou is 520 kilometres (323 miles) from Johannesburg on a good tar road. There are routes via the lowveld and the Kruger National Park, but the most direct drive is to follow the N1 through Naboomspruit, Pietersburg and Louis Trichardt.

Inter-Air operates charter flights between Johannesburg and Thohoyandou from Monday to Friday. Air Link flies between Johannesburg and Pietersburg from Monday to Friday. Tel: 011-659-1574 for Inter-Air and 011-394-2430 for Air Link.

Air-conditioned coaches leave Johannesburg daily for Northern Province. Phone Transnet: 011-774-7662, or Lebowa Transport which operates coaches as far as Louis Trichardt: 01 551-911867.

Thohoyandou is located in an area where malaria is endemic and suitable prophylactics should be taken prior to a visit. Dams and rivers in the low lying areas may be infested with bilharzia and crocodiles so swimming should be avoided in these waters. Mountain streams and pools are generally considered safe.

Above: The distinctive baobab tree stores water in its thick trunk. It can live for thousands of years.

The Far North

Beyond the magnificent Soutpansberg Mountains lies the arid bushveld of far Northern Province, an extension of the Kalahari sandveld. The strangest tree in Africa, the wrinkled baobab dominates the dusty northern landscape where hardy Afrikaans farmers run cattle ranches and farm maize and cotton.

The baobab is instantly recognizable because its looks as if it is growing upside down. It is grey-barked and has a massive trunk, with comparatively slim root-like branches. Acacia thorn bushes and mopane trees form the other typical vegetation of this area.

This is hot, arid country and most visitors are tempted to pass through it as quickly as possible; but there are some worthwhile excursions in the area. One is to **Tshipise** which, at an altitude of 525 metres (1,675 feet) above sea level, is an oasis in the bushveld. Warm winter weather is guaranteed there while dense foliage cools the hot dry summers. Tshipise has a mineral spa which maintains a natural temperature of 65 degrees Celsius and is said to have medicinal properties. A resort has been built around the spa and its waters attract people from various parts of Northern province.

Messina is the northernmost town in South Africa. Situated only fifteen kilometres (nine miles) from the Zimbabwe border on the Limpopo River, it owes its existence to rich mineral deposits found in the area. Copper was first mined in Messina in prehistoric times by members of the Musina tribe. It was rediscovered by prospectors at the turn of the century. Other minerals mined near Messina include, coal, iron ore, graphite, asbestos and semi-precious stones.

Messina is well-known for its baobab trees. A particularly impressive specimen, called 'Elephant's trunk', so named because of the shape of one of its branches, grows on the outskirts of the town on the road to Malala Drift. The **Messina Nature Reserve** was established to protect the region's baobabs and there are more than 100 specimens within its borders. Game in the

Above: Giraffe squats for a drink.

reserve includes giraffe, kudu and wildebeest. Permission to visit the baobab reserve may be obtained from the officer in charge.

Messina is also the centre of far Northern Province's game farming industry. Evidence of this fast growing enterprise can be found in the number of auxiliary industries which have sprung up in the town; a biltong factory, a leather works and a number of taxidermy services. The game ranches in the area cater for both foreign and local hunters and offer a variety of big game.

About sixty-five kilometres (40 miles) west of Messina is a flat-topped sandstone hillock known as **Mapungupwe** — 'place of the jackal', which is situated in the **Vhembe Nature Reserve** at the confluence of the Shasi and Limpopo Rivers.

It is one of the most important archaeological sites in South Africa. Mapungupwe provided a natural fortress for the Mapungupwe culture between 950 and 1200 AD.

The hillock has been held in awe by local African tribes for centuries, but it was only in 1933 that its secrets were discovered. A party of farmers climbed the seemingly inaccessible slopes of Mapungupwe after being given a clue as to where to find a hidden pathway which led to the summit.

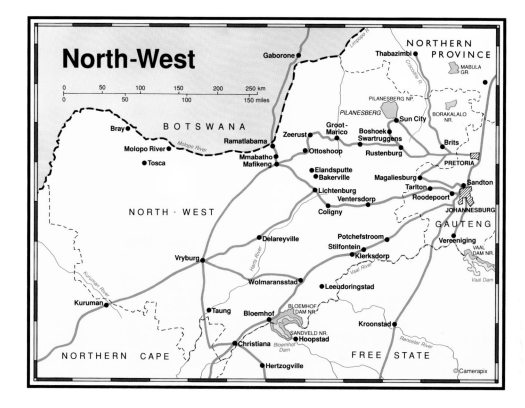

North-West

 map showing North-West province with labels: North-West, BOTSWANA, NORTHERN PROVINCE, Gaborone, Thabazimbi, MABULA GR., Limpopo R, Crocodile R, PILANESBERG NP, PILANESBERG, Sun City, BORAKALALO NR., Bray, Ramatlamabama, Zeerust, Groot-Marico, Boshoek, Swartruggens, Brits, Molopo River, Ottoshoop, Rustenburg, PRETORIA, Tosca, Mmabatho, Mafikeng, Elandsputte, Bakerville, Magaliesburg, Tarlton, Sandton, Lichtenburg, Roodepoort, Ventersdorp, JOHANNESBURG, Coligny, GAUTENG, NORTH - WEST, Delareyville, Potchefstroom, Vereeniging, Stilfontein, VAAL DAM NR., Vryburg, Klerksdorp, Harts River, Vaal River, Vaal Dam, Kuruman River, Wolmaransstad, Leeudoringstad, Kuruman, Taung, Bloemhof, BLOEMHOF DAM NR., Kroonstad, Renoster River, SANDVELD NR., Christiana, Bloemhof Dam, Hoopstad, NORTHERN CAPE, FREE STATE, Hertzogville, ©Camerapix

When they reached the top they found, to their amazement, that a storm had uncovered a burial site, revealing a skeleton adorned with gold jewellery.

It has been established that the people who inhabited the hill used it as a fort, even covering its surface with several tons of soil, dragged from the valley below. Their gold ornaments and finely crafted pottery bear testimony to the tribe's great skill. Mapungupwe provided the biggest hoard of wrought gold found in Africa since Tutankhamen's tomb was opened in Egypt.

More information and a permit to visit Mapungupwe may be obtained from the Department of Archaeology at Pretoria University, Tel: 012-420-9111. To reach the site take the Pontdrif turn-off which is situated two kilometres north of Messina. This tar road will lead you to the Vhembe Nature Reserve where accommodation is available.

North-West

The North-West province is populated mainly by the Batswana peoples of South Africa. North-West provides an ideal destination for day trips from both Johannesburg and Pretoria. This is farming country and the roads pass endless fields of maize and sunflowers. The region is within reach of both cities and a variety of holiday resorts set in scenic locations cater for those who wish to get away from the pace of city life and enjoy the peace and tranquility of a rural farming area. The region is charming and offers many outdoor activities.

Rustenburg

Rustenburg is situated 105 kilometres (65 miles) from Pretoria and 112 kilometres (70 miles) from Johannesburg. Rustenburg and its surrounding areas receive a large number of holidaymakers and tourists

Above: The north-west is farming country and the roads are bordered with endless fields of flowers.

every year. Many are attracted by **Sun City,** a casino resort complex nearby. But the town has its own tourist attractions, including dams, nature reserves and parks.

Rustenburg is the centre of a prosperous mining and agricultural community. The **Rustenburg Platinum Mine** is the largest single producer of platinum in the world. On the outskirts of the town are chromium, asbestos and lead mines and there are large granite quarries in the area. The Rustenburg region is well known for citrus estates and peaches, mangoes and watermelons are readily available at farm stalls during the summer months.

Tobacco is produced in great quantities and the city boasts the largest tobacco handling unit in South Africa.

An average of 187 million kilogrammes of tobacco are cultivated in the area every year. An event which draws farmers from far and wide to Rustenburg is the annual agricultural show, held each May.

Sightseeing

Places of interest within the town include a museum and a memorial in **Church Street,** where a replica of a tree stump marks the site where Paul Kruger and a group of followers established the 'Reformed Church' in 1859.

The nearby Magaliesburg Mountains provide opportunities for long, scenic walks and hikes. The Rustenburg trail is a twenty-two-kilometre (14-mile) hike which takes two days to complete, and which rambles through the Magaliesburg Mountains in an area protected by the **Rustenburg Nature Reserve**. The reserve has abundant birdlife. There is a breeding colony of the endangered Cape vulture within its boundaries, and the majestic martial eagle and very rare black eagle are both common there.

Good angling and watersport activities can be enjoyed at the **Bospoort** and **Olifantsnek Dams,** both of which are situated on the outskirts of Rustenburg. Olifantsnek, on the south side of the city, offers scenic views of the Olifantsnek Pass.

President Paul Kruger had a farm in the Rustenburg area and it was from there that he went into exile in 1902 after his Transvaal Republic lost the Anglo-Boer war. The statesman's homestead is situated approximately twenty-five kilometres (fifteen miles) from Rustenburg, near the little town of Boshoek.

How to get there

Take the R565, the road to Sun City, and look out for a signpost on the left of the road which reads 'Krugerhuis'.

Where to stay

Rustenburg Kloof is a popular holiday resort in the Rustenburg area. It is set in the Magaliesburg Mountains and offers scenic walks and resort facilities, including swimming pools and sports facilities. The kloof is situated on the western boundary of the town and may be reached from Malan Street. Picnic and camping facilities are available.

North-West Province incorporates the former independent homeland of Bophuthatswana which gained independence from South Africa in December 1977 and was reincorporated into South Africa in 1994.

The countryside of the province is flat to undulating, with altitudes varying between 900 and 1,830 metres (3,000–6,000 feet) above sea level. Summers are hot and dry with average daytime temperatures of around thirty degrees Celsius between the months of October and April. Overnight temperatures drop to about eighteen degrees Celsius in summer. Winters are pleasantly warm; in most regions of the country daytime temperatures average around fifteen degrees Celsius. Temperatures often plummet overnight during winter.

Mining is the main source of income in the region. The second largest producer of platinum in the western world, the area also has large deposits of vanadium, chrome, gold, salt, iron ore, diamonds, lead, copper and manganese. Apart from its mining potential, which is believed to be one of the highest in the world, the region produces a variety of agricultural products including maize, sorghum, wheat, sunflower seeds, beef, poultry and vegetables.

Tourism is also a major industry, largely thanks to flourishing casino resort enterprises. Sun International, a South African-based multi-national company, has developed several gambling resorts in the region, one of which is Sun City, Africa's most famous resort. Visitors come from throughout southern Africa and further afield to try their luck on slot machines and table games such as roulette and punto banco. The resort also offers a wide range of other recreational facilities including two golf courses at the Lost City, an African fantasy theme resort.

Getting there

Excellent tarred roads link the North-West province with Botswana and Zimbabwe. Sun Air has daily flights between Johannesburg International Airport and major towns and there are also regular flights between Durban and Mmabatho, Johannesburg and Durban and Durban and Sun City. Furthermore, there are daily flights between Grand Central Airport near Johannesburg and Pilanesberg Airport near Sun City. Charter flights may also be arranged through Sun Air.

There are rail links between Zimbabwe and Botswana. A luxury coach service operates daily between Johannesburg and Sun City, and Johannesburg and Mmabatho. There is a similar coach service from Pretoria to Sun City at weekends.

Mmabatho

Mmabatho was the former capital of Bophuthatswana. Its name means 'mother of the people' and the city is situated adjacent to the town of Mafikeng. Mmabatho offers striking examples of contemporary architecture in which traditional Botswana designs and craftsmanship have been cleverly combined with modern construction. Perhaps the best example of this is **Ga-Rona,** the government buildings in Mmabatho which are situated in the central business district of the city. Ga-Rona was designed around the concept of a Kgotla, the traditional meeting place in a Batswana village.

Above: The Speckled Weaver — South Africa has a scintillating array of bird life.

While in the central area of Mmabatho, look for **Mega City** which is one of the most modern and attractively designed shopping complexes in South Africa.

Two Sun International casino resort hotels, the **Molopo Sun** and the **Mmabatho Sun**, are situated on the edge of Mmabatho, a short distance from Mega City.

If you are looking for quieter 'home-away-from-home' accommodation, try the **Protea Hotel** on the corner of Martin Street and Station Road in the nearby town of Mafikeng. The hotel restaurant has a wide selection of wines which are housed in a cellar which dates back to 1875. (See Hotel Listings.)

Mafikeng — Siege City

The city of Mafikeng, or Mafeking as it was once known, became famous during the Second Boer War of 1899–1902. During the war, the inhabitants of the town and the British soldiers who had made Mafeking their headquarters were besieged by Boer forces for 214 days.

The most colourful character to emerge during the siege was Colonel Robert Baden-Powell whose defence of the town made him a hero in Britain. Baden-Powell used cadet corps of young boys to carry out military duties including surveillance, reconnaissance, and message and ammunition bearing, thus laying the foundations for the present day Boy Scout and Girl Guide movements. The building which served as Baden-Powell's head-quarters during the siege is Number 18 Shippard Street which today houses the University Book Shop.

There is a superb array of documents and relics from the time of the Mafeking siege on display at the museum in Martin Street. The museum also houses relics from prominent periods in Botswana history and a tourist information office.

Getting there

Mmabatho and Mafikeng are situated in the Molopo region of the North-West, close to the Botswana border. From Johannesburg follow the Roodepoort highway (N3) west and take the 14th Street off-ramp. At the four-way stop turn right, and then right again at the traffic lights. Continue along Route 47 until you reach Tarlton. At Tarlton bear left, following the signs to Ventersdorp. Drive through Ventersdorp to Coligny and then to Lichtenburg. At Lichtenburg take Route 52 straight through to Mmabatho. The trip from Johannesburg to Mmabatho is approximately 275 kilometres (171 miles).

From Pretoria, the recommended route follows the R27 over the Hartbeespoort Dam wall and on to Rustenburg. After driving through the town, follow the same road to Swartruggens, Groot Marico and Zeerust. From Zeerust follow the R27 for another sixty-five kilometres (40 miles). The road passes through Mafikeng before reaching Mmabatho. This route is approximately 300 kilometres (186 miles).

On the Vryburg road out of Mafikeng (Route 27), are **Warren's Weir** and **Warren's Fort.** The fort originally served as headquarters for the Warren expedition, a company of British soldiers who, from 1884, were responsible for laying out the town of Mafikeng. They constructed barracks, sank wells and generated a water supply for the frontier town.

From Warren's Fort drive south along the Vryburg road for four kilometres (3.5 miles) and you will find the **Lotlamoreng Dam Nature Reserve.** Lotlamoreng is an excellent venue for a day of outdoor activities. The reserve provides a sanctuary for a wide variety of plants and birds, and the dam provides excellent fishing. Good catches of barbel, yellow fish and carp have been recorded there. On the banks of the dam is a recreation area with a children's play park, spacious lawns, thatched umbrellas for shade and neatly laid out barbeque areas. A kiosk sells beverages, snacks and firewood.

A walk in the aviary allows visitors to view a number of species of indigenous birds at close range. There are weavers, hornbills, lilac-breasted rollers, starlings, sunbirds and many others. The aviary provides excellent photo opportunities because the birds are hand-reared and tame.

In the heart of the nature reserve is the **Lotlamoreng Cultural Village,** the creation of Credo Mutwa, a sculptor and well-known author who writes imaginatively about African cultural traditions. At Lotlamoreng the customs and rituals of ancient African civilizations come to life. There are three Batswana villages represented, the main one dominated by the King's Hut, a large, thatched structure which is guarded by brightly decorated models of a lion and a cow. This hut is flanked on both sides by the traditionally decorated and furnished huts of the king's two wives. The Tswana guide who shows you around the village will take you to the home of the king's doctor, a bushman whose function it was to consult with the ancestral spirits and then advise the Tswana king.

Traditional healers (*sangomas* and *mangomas)* live and practice their ancient crafts in the village, divining, using herbs and communicating with spirits. Today, the inhabitants are predominantly Christian, but the Botswana people have combined the religion with their rich ancestral history. In many parts of the region there still exists a strong belief in the power of the ancestors. According to Batswana belief, a spirit angered in any way may retaliate by causing illness or environmental disasters like floods, drought or crop failure. Bone throwing and divining is as much a part of modern life as is the worship of 'modimo' — the Christian God.

There are village dancers who perform the steps of traditional rain ceremonies, pottery makers and those who weave messages with beads and work with iron. A traditional grave has also been prepared in the village and the guide explains how the deceased were wrapped in skins and buried with food and water containers. This was to ensure that their spirits would not go thirsty or hungry.

A settlement of the Barolong tribe is located close to the main Botswana village. The Barolong are, by tradition, metal workers and fine examples of their craft are exhibited at Lotlamoreng.

Visitors can also learn about the ancient customs of other tribes such as the Ndebele, the South-Sotho, the Xhosa and the Zulu.

Above: Colourfully dressed Ndebele women.

The **Ndebele Village,** with its distinctive beehive-shaped huts, is marked by colourful decorations which are traditionally applied to the exterior of the tribe's buildings. The women of this village create exquisite bead work.

Phalaborwa Village at Lotlamoreng is a replica of an ancient mining village similar to those found in Zimbabwe. It is surrounded by high walls and is dominated by a sun tower, a large and quite spectacular creation of Credo Mutwa's.

Only thirty kilometres (19 miles) north of Mmabatho and Mafikeng, on the Ramatlhabana road (take Route 52) is the **Botsalano Game Reserve.** Botsalano has magnificent rolling grasslands and the opportunity for excellent sighting of rhino and a wide variety of antelope species. Visitors can expect to see hartebeest, giraffe, springbok, impala, eland, gemsbok and zebra.

A network of good dirt roads links the corners of the 6,000 hectare (15,000 acre) reserve and facilities include picnic sites, a campsite and a safari camp.

On Saturday and Sunday the reserve opens at 06:30. and closes at 18:30. Day visitors are permitted to remain in the reserve until 16:00. On weekdays Botsalano opens at 07:30 and closes at 17:00. Reservations for accommodation can be made through the park warden: Botsalano Game Reserve, Private Bag X2078, Mafikeng 8670 (0140) 895156.

Also in the Mmabatho area is the privately-owned **Manyane Game Lodge.** Just twelve kilometres (eight miles) from the capital city and situated on the road to Zeerust (follow Route 27), Manyane is one of the only two parks in the North-West region where visitors have the opportunity to see lions.

The lodge is frequented by big game hunters. Manyane provides all facilities for the hunt: licences, trackers, back-up vehicles, gunbearers, camping equipment and food. After the hunt, fully equipped butcheries have facilities to prepare trophies which are sent to a taxidermist for curing and mounting. For further information: Manyane Game Lodge, PO Box 287, Mafikeng, 8670.

Above: Zulu, the largest ethnic community in South Africa.

Taung region

To reach the internationally-famous Taung district, it is advisable to travel back towards Bloemfontein on the R64, and then follow the same road north to Dealesville, Herzogville and Christiana. The journey cuts through the western region of the Free State, and traverses flat, dry sheep farming country. At Christiana you cross the Vaal River into the Northern Cape province. Following the R506 in a westerly direction and then the R47 north, the vegetation changes to a type of veld described as eastern grass and bushveld. It consists of bush-thickets and open grasslands with scattered trees and shrubs. Acacia thorn trees are the most prolific type of vegetation in this area; hence the veld type's scientific name — Acacia-Grewia.

'Taung' means the 'place of the Tau' — the Setswana word for lion. It is pronounced t-ow-ung ('ow' as in 'that hurt' and 'ung' like the philosopher Carl Jung).

Taung was originally named after chief Tau whose Bataung or Leghoya people settled in the area in the middle of the 18th century. The town of Taung was literally placed on the world map in 1924 with the discovery of the now internationally famous **Taung skull.** The skull was discovered in the Buxton Limeworks quarry about ten kilometres (six miles) south-west of Taung in November 1924. Professor Raymond Dart identified it as belonging to a five year old child who lived in the area over three million years ago. The Taung skull is believed to belong to the species *Australopithecus africanus*. Taung is the most southerly and most westerly of the sixteen African sites known to have harboured fossil ape men of the genus *Australopithecus.*

The marble quarries in the Taung area are also internationally renowned. About twenty million years ago, high temperatures deep within the earth's crust created a durable and beautiful marble which is today used around the world in both its rough and polished form. The material has been used extensively in the interior design of **Taung Sun,** a Sun International casino resort situated on the main road north to Mmabatho. A pale, honey-

Above: The entrance to the luxurious Palace Hotel at Sun City's Lost City.

coloured marble has been used to good effect to give the entrance foyer a cool and airy feel — in the sweltering summer heat this is very welcoming.

Taung Sun is located nearly halfway between the diamond fields of Kimberley and the town of Vryburg which lies to the north. The hotel offers accommodation and casino facilities, with the added attraction of a small nature reserve situated adjacent named **Boipelo**, which means 'Our Pride'.

Small as it, Boipelo is a beautiful tract of land and well worth a visit. It is situated at the meeting place of highveld and lowveld terrain, thus providing the ideal environment for certain species of game to co-habitate. In South Africa it is uncommon for springbok and impala to live in the same area, but at Boipelo the two species exist in harmony.

Boipelo provides a safe environment for a number of different bird species. The extremely rare olive tree warbler was resident in the reserve during the summer of 1990–1991; this bird has been sighted in southern Africa less than twenty times in the last thirty years.

Pilanesberg region

Sun City was mentioned earlier on in this description of North-West; the resort is one of southern Africa's main tourist attractions. Situated in the lovely Pilanesberg area, Sun City is a unique hotel and casino complex.

It has four luxury hotels, the **Cascades**, the **Sun City Hotel**, the **Cabanas** and **The Palace** reputed to be among the finest in the world. It has a stunning theme area called **The Lost City,** which has the most advanced water theme park in the world. One of the attractions is the **Valley of Waves** which boasts a surf-pool the size of a rugby field on which two-metre-high surfing waves are generated. Another is the **Temple of Courage** a seventy-metre (210-foot) high water slide. The **Superbowl** in the resort's **Entertainment Centre** has played host to a number of international stars — Frank Sinatra, Rod Stewart, Bryan Adams, Sting and Elton John among them. The **Cascades Hotel** at Sun City features some beautiful gardens.

Above: The Monkey Plaza and the Bridge of Time at Sun City.

Within the Sun City complex is the **Kwena Gardens Crocodile Farm.** A unique series of dams, ponds, waterfalls and streams provide a sanctuary for crocodiles from just a few weeks to more than a hundred years old.

Sun City's man-made lake **'Waterworld'** caters for watersport enthusiasts. Windsurfers, ski boats, jet skis and canoes are available for hire, and you can parasail and waterski too.

A host of restaurants, action bars, cinemas and live shows provide the night life at Sun City, and many of the resort's visitors like to take advantage of the extensive casino facilities. These include more than a thousand slot machines and numerous American roulette, punto banco, blackjack and dice tables. The restaurants cater for all tastes and budgets and the bars feature live music. There is a nightclub adjacent to the casino area.

The Lost City, an African fantasy world consists of twenty-six hectares of exotic jungle and the largest man-made waterscapes ever created. The jungle features more than a million plants and trees and is threaded with water courses and walkways. In the Valley of Waves, more adventurous visitors are able to choose between five waterslides, the most exciting of which is called the 'Temple of Courage' and features an astonishing vertical drop the height of a three-storey building.

The 350-room **The Palace** is one of the very finest hotels in the world with superb cuisine and outstanding accommodation. It is a must for any traveller not on a shoestring budget.

The **Pilanesberg National Park** is the third largest game reserve south of the Limpopo River and covers an area of 500 square kilometres (193 square miles). It was opened in 1979 and since then more than 8,000 large animals of twenty different species have been introduced.

The creation of the Pilanesberg National Park was one of the most ambitious conservation projects ever undertaken in South Africa. 'Operation Genesis' as it was dubbed, involved moving the cattle farmers who populated the area to new homes and game fencing the entire area. Today the park accommodates almost every mammal

Above: The endangered cheetah is found in open woodland and savannah areas in South Africa.

in southern Africa; including the 'Big Five'.

The countryside is spectacular. The unique geology of the Pilanesberg is the direct result of devastating volcanic activity that rocked the area over twelve million years ago. The hills of the Pilanesberg are actually the crumbling foundations of an ancient volcanic crater, the centre of which has been transformed into the beautiful **Mankwe Lake.**

Vegetation of the Pilanesberg is typical of the North-West bushveld. There are thickly wooded river banks, extraordinary granite outcrops and rolling grasslands. Game viewing is best in the cooler hours of the early morning and is generally better in winter when animals stay close to water holes. After the first rains of the year, around September, October and November, the land begins to recover from the long dry winter months. The brilliant green expanses of grassland are a real feast for the visitor's eyes.

Visitors to the Pilanesberg National Park have a wide variety of accommodation choices. Many of the park's visitors stay at Sun City and take advantage of daily game drives which are conducted from the Sun City Hotel. It is possible, however, to stay overnight in the reserve, and accommodation facilities in the Pilanesberg National Park include luxury hotel resorts, tented safari camps and a caravan park.

The Pilanesberg National Park is open between 05:30 and 19:00 during the winter months, and from 05:00 and 20:00 between August and April. Within the park there are a number of gravel roads with five scenic drives. The **Kedibone** and **Ratlhogo Hides** overlook waterholes and both hides are well worth a visit, and the game viewing is excellent.

Most evidence of human habitation has been removed from the Pilanesberg National Park, but the building which previously housed the **Pilanesberg Magi-strates' Court** has been preserved. It now serves as the park's information centre. There is a curio shop within the centre which also sells refreshments. During the hot summer months a visit to this historical building is very welcome — the thick stone walls of the structure provide relief from the heat of the day and a large map of the national park helps to place your visit into perspective.

Reservations can be made with the Reservations Officer: Pilanesberg National Park, PO Box 1201, Mogwase, 0302; tel: (01465) 55356/7/8/9; fax : (01465) 55356.

Getting there

To reach the Pilanesberg National Park and Sun City complex from Johannesburg, travel north along William Nichol Drive to the Fourways intersection with Witkoppen Road.

Assume a zero speedometer reading at this intersection. Turn left into Witkoppen Road towards Lanseria/Roodepoort.

At 6.3 kilometres turn right at intersection with Hans Strijdom Extension on the road towards Lanseria.

At 12.7 kilometres you cross over the Muldersdrift/Diepsloot Road, continue with the R512 towards Broederstroom and Lanseria.

At 14.3 kilometres you cross the bridge over the R28 Krugersdorp/Pretoria highway. At 19.2 kilometres you pass the Lanseria turnoff and carry on straight past.

At 37.3 kilometres you encounter a T-junction. Turn left on R512 to Magaliesburg. At 47.1 kilometres turn right on the R512 to Brits, cross the railway line and within three kilometres you cross a bridge over the Hartebeespoort Dam.

At 52.4 kilometres you encounter another T-junction and turn right on the R512 towards Brits.

The next intersection is a major four-way stop. The R513 to Pretoria North straight ahead, R27 to Pretoria via the tunnel bridge to the right and R512/R27 to the left for Brits and Rustenburg. Turn left.

At 58.5 kilometres you bypass the first Brits turn-off on the right. At 62.1 kilometres you turn right on the R27 signposted to Rustenburg/Brits.

At 62.8 kilometres keep left on the R27 signposted to Rustenburg/Brits.

At 67.6 kilometres take the slipway left, towards Rustenburg. The R27 becomes the new N4 highway.

At 75.8 kilometres, a sign indicates Pilanesberg to the left on Route 91.

Above: Lilac-brested roller in the Borakalalo National Park.

Above: Leopard takes a kill up a tree.

A further sign indicates the route to Sun City. Exit left off the highway and at 76.3 kilometres turn right across the bridge and travel 74 kilometres (46 miles) to Sun City.

Borakalalo

Less than half the size of the Pilanesberg National Park, but a significant wildlife reserve nonetheless, the **Borakalalo National Park** is situated in Odi 1 district, which is not far from Pretoria and Johannesburg. Borakalalo translates as 'the place where people rest' and consists of 15,000 hectares (37,000 acres) of gently rolling bushveld. The main attraction of the park is the ten-kilometre-long **Klipvoor Dam** which offers excellent fishing opportunities.

Fisherman may purchase a 24-hour fishing licence for R5 at the park gate. Kurper, carp and barbel are common and a five-kilogramme (11-pound) kurper caught in the Klipvoor Dam holds the official South African angling record for this species. Good catches of yellow fish and

other species have also been recorded at Klipvoor.

Borakalalo has been stocked with a variety of game including kudu, red hartebeest, zebra, sable, bushbuck and waterbuck. In addition to these, about 300 species of birds have been identified here.

Visitors who wish to spot game from their cars may take advantage of the network of good gravel roads which criss-cross the southern section of Borakalalo. An area of 7,000 hectares (17,297 acres) has been set aside in the northern section of the park for wilderness trails. Advance booking assures a guide for the day. There are picnic sites situated throughout the park and camp sites or permanent tents to hire.

Between October and March, Borakalalo is open from 05:00 to 20:00. In the winter months the reserve opens 06:00 and closes again at 19:00. Reservations can be made with the Reservations Officer: Borakalalo National Park, PO Box 240, Jericho, 0264.

Getting there

To reach Borakalalo National Park, travel north from Johannesburg and Pretoria to Brits. From there the suggested route follows the road to Thabazimbi. Drive for fifty kilometres (31 miles) along this road and then take a right turn on a gravel road signposted Assen. Five kilometres (three miles) along this road is the signpost for Klipvoor Dam. Turn right there and after twenty-two kilometres (14 miles) you will reach a T-junction. The Borakalalo signpost is on the left side of the road, four kilometres (just over a mile) from this junction.

From central Johannesburg the journey takes about two hours; from Pretoria the trip is ninety minutes.

Moretele region

Two casino resorts, **Morula Sun** and **The Carousel Casino and Entertainment World** are both close to Pretoria in the Moretele region. The Morula Sun is a small luxurious hotel with a variety of restaurants and a big casino. The emphasis of the complex is on gaming and this is not the place to go for a relaxing weekend in the country.

The Carousel Entertainment World is a giant complex which houses the biggest casino in the southern hemisphere. There are a variety of bars which feature bands, comedians and dancers.

Restaurant facilities at The Carousel are diverse. These include a number of fast food outlets, a coffee shop, an à la carte restaurant and a residents lounge which serves breakfast in addition to some light snacks.

Children's entertainment is provided by video games, a children's theatre and daily cartoon film shows. A fully operational carousel is situated in the centre of the complex and children have free access to the sixteen horses on the roundabout.

There is a variety of shops at The Carousel and visitors can browse in a book shop, a jewellers' and a toy shop.

Waners trading store sells authentic American clothes and other western trappings and Papatso Curios sells African art treasures. The Carousel Hotel has 57 rooms.

Getting there

Both Morula Sun and The Carousel Entertainment World are situated to the north of Johannesburg and Pretoria. A highway leads to The Carousel from Johannesburg, the journey taking an hour. Take the N1 highway north, following the signs to Warmbaths. Take the Maubane off-ramp (you can see The Carousel from the freeway) and turn left at The Carousel sign. Parking costs R5 per car, and entrance to the casino is R3 per person.

Morula Sun is more difficult to find. Take the Ben Schoeman highway from Johannesburg, into Pretoria on Potgieter Street and turn left into Church Street. Turn right into D F Malan Street and after five kilometres turn left at the Maubane sign. After thirteen kilometres (eight miles) turn left at the Rosslyn sign and after a further sixteen kilometres (ten miles) turn right at the Maubane sign. Morula Sun is situated on the left side of the road, three kilometres from this intersection.

Above: The Red Bishop.

Marico district

From Swartruggens the road to Botswana winds through the heart of the Marico countryside, an area of thick undulating bushveld, which has become familiar to many South Africans through the enchanting stories of South African author Herman Charles Bosman. The Marico district stretches from the town of Groot Marico in the east, to Botswana in the west, and incorporates the towns of Zeerust, and Ottoshoop. For generations the local people have been distilling a potent alcoholic brew known as 'mampoer', and it is this mampoer culture which Bosman captures in his stories.

Sightseeing

Capitalizing on the publicity Bosman's tales have brought the district, the people of Marico recently established a 'Mampoer Route', a fascinating tour designed to introduce visitors to the unique character of the region. The sixty-kilometre (37-mile) route begins in **Zeerust** and includes a visit

Above: Flamingoes wading through the Barberspan lake.

to a trout farm, a game farm and, naturally, a mampoer still. Mampoer is brewed from a variety of fruits, including peaches, apricots and, occasionally, the fruit of the morula tree. It may only be brewed under licence. Enquiries about the Mampoer Route may be made with the town clerk of Zeerust. Phone: (01428) 23713.

At the heart of Herman Charles Bosman's stories is the little town of **Groot Marico** which is situated in the fertile valley of the Marico River, about thirty-one kilometres (19 miles) from Swartruggens. The **Marico Bushveld Nature Reserve** on the outskirts of the town preserves vegetation that is typical of the Marico district. A wide variety of indigenous trees such as the wild olive, red syringa and tambotie trees flourish there, attracting a wealth of birdlife. The Marico reserve is adjacent to the **Riekerts Dam** which provides watersport opportunities.

Zeerust serves a large farming and mining community. It is the home of the annual **Mampoer Festival** and also the starting point of the Mampoer Route. The **Klein Maricospoort Dam,** located about

five kilometres (three miles) from the town offers excellent fishing.

Lichtenburg

Lichtenburg, situated some eighty kilometres (50 miles) from Zeerust, on the main route between Johannesburg and Mmabatho, like Zeerust, serves a large farming community. Its history is closely tied to the Anglo Boer War, and one of the famous characters of this conflict, General Jacobus Hercules De la Rey, once lived there. A museum on De la Rey Square is devoted largely to documenting his life. There is an art gallery in Melville Street which houses some valuable South African paintings.

Sightseeing

In 1926 the biggest diamond rush in South Africa took place on the farm Elandsputte, twenty kilometres (12 miles) from Lichtenburg. More than 100,000 hopefuls from all over the world rushed to a dried-up river bed on the farm to stake their claim on the new diggings. The diamonds were of good quality but it didn't take long to exhaust the deposits. Within ten years the diggings were deserted. Today, a few hardened diggers still try their luck, particularly in an area known as **Bakerville.** The prospectors live in simple corrugated iron homes and sort through the diamond-bearing gravel exactly as was done 100 years ago. To find the diggers, turn off the R505 at Bakerville.

The Barberspan Nature Reserve, eighty-one kilometres (50 miles) south-west of Lichtenburg and twenty-one kilometres (13 miles) north-east of **Delareyville** is a bird sanctuary with a large freshwater lake at its centre. The lake attracts vast numbers of waterfowl to its shores. A hide has been created for those who wish to view the birds at close range. One of the biggest attractions of the reserve is the chance to see flamingoes which visit the lake. Watersports and fishing are permitted and there is a campsite situated on the banks of the pan.

Delareyville itself is characterized by a number of **saltpans** which also attract flamingoes and there are **bushman paintings** in the vicinity of the town.

Potchefstroom

Potchefstroom is one of the oldest towns in South Africa, having been established on the banks of the Mooi River in 1838. It is situated 119 kilometres (74 miles) from Johannesburg and was the first capital of the Zuid Afrikaanse Republiek ruled by Paul Kruger. Later, Kruger transferred his government to Pretoria. Potchefstroom was the first town to be established north of the Vaal River, and has many buildings of historical interest. Some of the older streets still have irrigation furrows on either side.

Sightseeing

The Potchefstroom Museum on the corner of Wolmarans and Gouws Streets in the city centre contains exhibits of great historical significance, including one of the ox-wagons that was used to form the laager (circular enclosure) at the famous Battle of

Blood River in 1838, when the Boers decisively defeated the Zulus. The oldest **church** north of the Vaal River is situated in front of the town hall, and the remains of an **old fort** may be seen on the road to Klerksdorp. The fort was besieged by Boer forces in the Transvaal war of independence in 1881.

On the same road is one of the town's oldest buildings, a **powder magazine** which dates back to 1857. This was used during the Transvaal war of independence and the Anglo-Boer war of 1899–1902.

Klerksdorp

Klerksdorp is in an important gold and uranium mining area. It is located fifty kilometres (31 miles) from Potchefstroom and is older than its neighbour, having been established in 1837. Klerksdorp began as an agricultural town, but changed virtually overnight into a raucous shanty town when gold was discovered in 1885, a year before the discovery of the Witwatersrand goldfields. Its years as a gold-rush town were short-lived, however, as by the 1890s production costs had made mining unprofitable.

New life was breathed into Klerksdorp's gold mining industry after the second world war, when improved technology allowed ore to be removed from the mines at a reasonable price. The town has maintained its status as an agricultural centre and today it is the headquarters of one of the largest grain co-operatives in the southern hemisphere.

The oldest street in Klerksdorp is **Hendrik Potgieter Road** on the western banks of the **Schoonspruit River,** where the Voortrekkers settled in 1837. Most of the houses in Hendrik Potgieter Road date back to the last century and, although they are not open to the public, they are fascinating to look at, varying as they do from small, humble homes to large dwellings.

Sightseeing

Klerksdorp's **museum,** on the corner of Lombaard and Magaretha Prinsloo Streets, was built in 1891 and was used as a prison

Above: Vaal River, where several nature reserves and holiday resorts offer good facilities.

until 1973. There are fascinating cultural, archaeological and geographical exhibits in the museum which is open daily, except on religious holidays.

Prehistoric rock engravings from the late Stone Age, can be found on a hill at Bosworth, some sixteen kilometres (10 miles) from Klerksdorp, on the road to Ventersdorp.

Many old mine shafts may be seen on the road to Stilfontein; dating back to the 1880s, some of these have engravings made by British soldiers who camped in the shafts during the Anglo-Boer war.

The **Faan Meintjes Nature Reserve** and **Johan Neser Dam** are both situated on the outskirts of the town and have recreation facilities. The reserve is a sanctuary for a large variety of game, including giraffe, buffalo and white rhino. The dam is a popular venue for angling and watersports.

The Vaal River

A number of nature reserves and holiday resorts have been created along the banks of the Vaal River, the southern boundary of the Transvaal.

The **Wolwespruit Nature Reserve** is a popular angling resort, situated about twenty kilometres, (12 miles) from the small agricultural centre of Leeudoringstad. The 2,500-hectare (6,177-acre) reserve provides a sanctuary for several species of game, including wildebeest and zebra, in an attractive riverine setting. Camping is permitted in the reserve (tel: 01813 705).

The **Bloemhof Dam Nature Reserve** is much bigger than the Wolwespruit reserve, covering an area of 14,000 hectare (34,594 acres). It is situated on the banks of the

Bloemhof Dam and excellent catches of barbel, carp and yellow fish have been recorded there.

There are three entrances to the reserve, the main one at **Hoopstad Bridge,** approximately five kilometres from Bloemhof on the R34. Although most visitors to the reserve are keen anglers, Bloemhof has a variety of large game including white rhino and eland.

The **S A Lombard Nature Reserve** is situated some seventeen kilometres (ten miles) outside Bloemhof on the R34. The reserve is small, consisting of 3,660 hectares (9,044 acres) of flat grassland and a large pan which attracts waterfowl. It is used primarily for the breeding of highveld game species.

Mpumalanga

One of South Africa's favourite tourist destinations, the lowveld of Mpumalanga — formerly Eastern Transvaal — is a showcase for the country's wildlife. Dominating the area is the internationally-famous **Kruger National Park** and some of the largest and most exclusive private game reserves in the world. In this wonderland, Africa's 'big five' — lion, leopard, buffalo, elephant and rhino — live exactly as they did hundreds of years ago. In addition to splendid game viewing opportunities, Mpumalanga has other scenic attractions, including the spectacular 'summit route' — an area renowned for its magnificent landscapes, large tracts of indigenous forests and cascading waterfalls. The area is also rich in history. The splendour of the eastern region can be appreciated from the comfort of one's car, or on foot. A good network of tarred roads exists, and a variety of hiking trails criss-cross the eastern landscape.

The N4 is the main road east. From Johannesburg it leads to **Nelspruit,** the centre of the lowveld region and a well-known stop-over for tourists en route to the southern Kruger National Park. The road cuts across the farmlands of the highveld until it reaches **Witbank.**

Situated in the centre of Mpumalanga's

Above: Female waterbuck cools off during midday heat.

coal production area, Witbank is an industrial town surrounded by a number of nature reserves. The best known is the 26,000 hectare (64,246 acres) **Loskop Dam Game Reserve** which lies in the foothills of the Waterberg Mountain range, alongside the picturesque **Loskop Dam.** Game abounds and fishing is permitted in the dam. The reserve has accommodation, a restaurant and swimming pool.

The next town on the N4's route is the modern industrial town of **Middelburg,** established in the early 1890s. The town's past is closely linked to the Suid Afrikaanse Republiek in South Africa's history and reminders from this period include the old railway station and **Meyers Bridge.**

In the area surrounding Middelburg there are a number of hiking trails, many of which may be completed in a day. Huts for overnight stays are available.

Forty-five kilometres (28 miles) east of Middelburg is **Belfast,** a small agricultural centre which was named by an unknown immigrant after the capital of Northern Ireland in 1890. Today it is the centre of a thriving sheep farming industry. The surrounding district is well-known for its wood, granite and the cultivation of bulbs, especially tulips. Trout fishing is excellent in the Belfast region and the neighbouring town of **Dullstroom** has one of South Africa's most famous trout fishing lodges, **The Critchley Hackle.**

Dullstroom was named after a Dutch immigrant, Wolterus Dull. The town is situated on the edge of the escarpment at a height of 2,379 metres (724 feet) above sea level and has the highest railway station in southern Africa.

Near **Machadodorp,** which is the next stop along the N4, there are good trout fishing opportunities. Further east, the R36 branches off the main road and heads for Lydenburg and the popular 'summit route'. From this junction the N4 continues in an easterly direction, winds through the **Elandsberg Pass,** and arrives at the little town of **Waterval-Boven.** Further east is **Waterval-Onder** where President Paul Kruger spent his last days as president of the Zuid Afrikaanse Republiek.

A hiking trail leads between the two towns and takes between one and two days to complete. A short from way Waterval-Boven, the Elands River flows over a rocky outcrop, creating a beautiful waterfall. Another interesting feature in the area is a 122-metre-long (390-foot) tunnel which was created in 1892 by the railway company of the **Suid Afrikaanse Republiek.** The tunnel was built as part of the eastern line that linked Pretoria with Mozambique.

A more scenic way to approach Nelspruit — for those who have the time — is to follow the R36 to **Schoemanskloof** and then take the R539 to the **Montrose Pass.** Look out for the signs to the **Sudwala Caves** located to the north-west, these are well worth a visit. The most impressive feature of the caves is the huge **P R Owen Cavern,** a natural underground amphitheatre, sixty-seven metres (220 feet) wide and thirty-seven metres (121.5 feet) high. The acoustics in the cave are so good that it is often used as a venue for music concerts.

Nobody knows how far the catacombs extend into the dolomite rock of the **Mankelekele Mountains,** but the series of caves so far discovered are an important source of scientific data, as well as one of Eastern Transvaal's major tourist attractions. Guided tours of the Sudwala Caves are conducted daily.

Situated on a hill next door to the caves is the unique **Dinosaur Park complex.** The park displays life-size replicas of a variety of dinosaurs and other prehistoric reptiles in gardens which have been designed with a prehistoric ambience.

Nelspruit is situated at the junction of the Sabie and White River railway lines in the **Crocodile River valley**. It is the commercial and administrative centre of the lowveld region and one of the richest agricultural districts in South Africa. Citrus fruit and tropical fruit like litchis, bananas and avocado pears are farmed there. Nearly one third of South Africa's export quality oranges are produced in the Nelspruit area.

For many tourists, Nelspruit is a stepping stone on the road to the southern **Kruger National Park**, and a pleasant place to stretch one's legs and stock up on provisions at one of the many farm stalls that are common on the roads surrounding the town. The **Lowveld Botanical Gardens,** on the northern border of Nelspruit, provide an ideal place to escape from the sometimes oppressive summer heat. The gardens are affiliated to the famous botanical gardens at Kirstenbosch in Cape Town and display a variety of plants that are indigenous to the lowveld. There are walks within the gardens, one of which winds along the banks of the Crocodile River for two kilometres. The gardens are open to the public at all times.

Opposite: The waterbuck is found near rivers and marshes.

Above: The Sabie river.

White River is a picturesque little town, twenty kilometres (twelve miles) outside Nelspruit on the R40. Further north is **Hazyview,** the last town on the road to the **Kruger National Park's Numbi Gate.** Both of these lowveld towns are surrounded by some of the most fertile farmland in South Africa, and are well-known for the quality of their fruit, vegetables and wood. From Hazyview there is access to a number of private game reserves as well as the Paul Kruger Gate, close to the Skukuza rest camp in the Kruger National Park.

From Nelspruit the N4 continues on its eastern journey past the southern edge of the Kruger National Park. There are entrances to the game reserve at **Malelane** and **Crocodile Bridge** and at Komatipoort the road crosses the Mozambique border.

The Summit Route

Situated at the summit of the Drakensberg escarpment, this is an area of unsurpassed beauty and is a tourist 'must' for those visiting Mpumalanga. Accessible via a number of roads, the most popular way to travel the summit route is to begin at Lydenburg and follow the R37 over **Mount Anderson** — the second highest peak in the Transvaal — down the spectacular **Long Tom Pass** to the little town of **Sabie.** A highlight en route is the **Gustav Klingbiel Nature Reserve**, a 2,200-hectare (5,436-acre) sanctuary, best known for its abundant bird life and lovely nature trails and picnic spots.

The Long Tom Pass is the second highest mountain pass in South Africa. At some points it reaches a height of 2,150 metres (7,054 feet) above sea level and provides breathtaking views of the surrounding areas. It was named during the Anglo-Boer war, after the Long Tom guns that the Boer forces mounted on the heights of the escarpment. Near the summit of Long Tom pass, at a site called 'The Devil's Knuckles', is where the last of these cannons was fired against British forces. A replica of a Long Tom cannon is in place here to commemorate the event.

Nestling in the foothills of the Drakensberg, at the base of the Long Tom

Above: The Mac Mac waterfalls.

Pass is Sabie, a small agricultural town in the centre of the world's largest tree plantation. **Sabie** is known for its waterfalls — there are twelve within easy reach of the town, the closest of which is the **Horseshoe Waterfall**, only eight kilometres away. It was there that one of South Africa's first sawmills was established.

A little further west of Sabie is the twenty-one-metre (sixty-eight-foot) **Lone Creek Waterfall** which is accessible from the tar road. A brisk ten minute walk through indigenous forest will lead you to the **Bridal Veil Waterfall**; the **Sabie Waterfall** is located on the other side of town, near to an old bridge which was built in 1915 by Italian prisoners of war. The popular **Fanie Botha hiking trail** begins at the forestry station on the road to the Bridal Veil Waterfall. Enquiries and reservations can be made with the Director, Mpumalanga Forestry Division, Private Bag X503, Sabie, 1260. Phone: 01315 - 41058.

Within the town of Sabie there are numerous places of historical interest; the **Forestry Museum** in Ford Street exhibits different aspects of the South African wood and paper industries. Outside the First National Bank building is a commemorative plaque — one of many in Eastern Transvaal — which honours **Jock of the Bushveld,** the dog who was immortalized by his owner Sir Percy FitzPatrick, in the classic story of *Jock of the Bushveld.* Jock and Sir Percy camped in Sabie's market square in 1885. Across the street is **St Peter's Anglican Church,**

Above: The Forest Falls are one of a series of picturesque waterfalls between Sabie and Graskop.

designed in 1913 by Sir Herbert Baker, the architect responsible for Pretoria's impressive Union Buildings.

A number of scenic drives lead from Sabie to other areas of Mpumalanga. Many of these wind through forestry plantations and provide spectacular views of the lowveld from high mountain peaks. The summit route follows the R532 through open grasslands to the town of **Graskop**. Tourist attractions along the way include the **Mac Mac Pools and Waterfall.**

The Mac Mac area was named in 1873 by Thomas Burgers who was then president of the South African Republic. He observed that many of the prospectors who were working claims in the region came from Scotland or Ireland, and that their names more often than not began with Mac or Mc. He laughingly declared that he would refer to the area between Sabie and Graskop as Mac Mac, and the name stuck.

The Mac Mac Pools may be found eleven kilometres (seven miles) from Sabie, approximately one kilometre's walk from the road. Swimming is permitted and picnic areas surround the crystal clear waters. The Mac Mac falls are situated in a thickly wooded area, a little further north. The double streams of the falls were created by early gold prospectors who discovered the precious metal in the cliff over which the Mac Mac river runs, and blasted it away.

Other picturesque waterfalls on the road to Graskop include the **Maria Shires Waterfall** — named after a forester who began to utilize Mpumalanga's forestry resources as early as 1876 — and the **Forest Falls**. There are some charming picnic spots at the base of this waterfall which also marks the end of the three kilometre-long (two-mile) Forest Falls walking trail.

Outdoor enthusiasts who wish to cover longer distances on foot may be interested in the five-day **Prospectors' hiking trail**, a sixty-nine-kilometre (43-mile) trail that begins at the Mac Mac forest station and winds through some of the most spectacular scenery that Mpumalanga has to offer. Enquiries and reservations may be made with The

Above: Many of the old buildings in Pilgrim's Rest have been restored to their original appearance when the town was created during a gold rush.

Director, Mpumalanga Forestry Division, Private Bag X503, Sabie, 1260. Phone: 01315 - 41058.

Graskop itself is the centre of an important wood producing region and one of the town's main attractions is an outlying tract of indigenous forest which has been nicknamed 'Fairyland'. **Kowyn's Pass** lies to the east of the town, and there are spectacular views from this road which leads to the lowveld regions of Mpumalanga.

The mining village of **Pilgrim's Rest** was established in 1873 when a prospector called 'Wheelbarrow' Patterson (who carried his worldly belongings in a wheelbarrow) discovered gold deposits in the stream that flows past the town. Another prospector, William Trafford, named the town Pilgrim's Rest because he was convinced that the new-found gold deposits signalled the end of his life-long search for wealth.

The gold deposits at Pilgrim's Rest brought fortune seekers from far and wide and, before long, there were 1,400 diggers panning for gold near the town. By 1881 the alluvial deposits were depleted, but in just eight years, some R80-million in nuggets had been taken from the river.

In 1974 the former Transvaal Provincial Administration bought the entire village, and today it is preserved as a living museum and a reminder of South Africa's gold mining heritage. Many of Pilgrim's Rest's original houses have been restored and the town has a romantic ambience.

The most interesting buildings in Pilgrim's Rest line the town's main street, at the heart of which is the Royal Hotel. Inside this establishment is the most famous bar in the Transvaal which began life — believe it or not — as a Catholic chapel in Maputo, the capital of Mozambique. In 1882 the chapel was dismantled and transported to Pilgrim's Rest where it was reassembled. One of the bar's seats is an old pew. On display in the bar are lanterns, shovels, prospectors' pans and big chunks of 'fool's gold' (iron pyrites).

The town's graveyard is situated on a hill above the village and there are fascinating inscriptions on many of the

Above: A spectacular view of the Drakensberg — the name means 'Dragon's Mountain'.
Opposite: Dramatic views of the spectacular Blyde River Canyon.

gravestones. The 'robber's grave' is particularly interesting. Unlike the other graves, it faces north and the robber remains unnamed. Legend has it that the unfortunate man made the mistake of robbing a claim and was murdered by four diggers.

To the west of Pilgrim's Rest, on the R533, is the **Mount Sheba Nature Reserve**, a 1,500-hectare (3,706-acre) sanctuary set amid a forest of indigenous yellowwood trees. Mount Sheba has thickly wooded ravines and impressive waterfalls. The reserve is well stocked with antelope and is home to more than 100 bird species. There are a number of nature trails within the reserve, the most popular of which is the walk to Sheba's Lookout which provides a magnificent view of the summit route and lowveld areas.

From Pilgrim's Rest the R532 continues in a northerly direction to the **Blyde River Canyon**, undoubtedly one of South Africa's finest attractions. The twenty-six kilometre-long ravine was formed over millions of years by the Blyde River which flows north to the point where it joins the Olifants River. It cuts into the Drakensberg escarpment and forms the most spectacular valley in South Africa.

There are a number of tourist attractions along the route. At **God's Window**, one can appreciate one of the most spectacular views in Mpumalanga, while the picnic site next to the magnificent **Lisbon Waterfall** provides a perfect place to stretch one's legs. **The Pinnacle** is a lone chunk of granite which rises out of a thickly wooded ravine and forms part of the **Blyde River Canyon Nature Reserve** and is inhabited by a number of species of tropical birds, baboons and leopards. Two hiking trails begin at **Bourke's Luck potholes**, situated at the confluence of the Treur and Blyde Rivers. The potholes are the result of prolonged erosion. They are easily accessible via a suspension bridge and footpaths. An information centre near the potholes provides extensive information on the natural history of the area and on hiking trails.

The Kruger National Park

Dominating the lowveld regions is the magnificent Kruger National Park. Founded in 1926, the park is the second largest game reserve in Africa and a tourist mecca for South Africa's visitors. The Kruger Park, as South Africans usually call it, covers 19,000 square kilometres (7,336 square miles) — the same size as Wales. It shares an eastern boundary with Mozambique and extends from the Crocodile River in the south to the country's northern border on the Limpopo River.

The game reserve's history stretches back to a time when vast herds of game roamed the northern areas of South Africa. They lived a relatively undisturbed existence until the late 19th century when white settlers began to move into the area. The pioneers influence was devastating, it is estimated that over two million animal hides were exported to Europe before the end of the 1870s. Buffalo, wildebeest and other antelope species were hunted for their meat, their hides and for pleasure. Indiscriminate game slaughter often took place, leaving the plains scattered with unutilized carcasses.

It was President Paul Kruger who first perceived the catastrophic effects that uncontrolled plunder could have on the country's game populations. Kruger began to expound on the necessity for conservation and in the 1850s the Transvaal Volksraad passed an act which prohibited hunters from killing more game than they could use. In 1870 snares and pit-traps were banned and in the 1890s Kruger began the creation of wildlife sanctuaries. Towards the end of his presidency he proclaimed the tract of land between the Crocodile and Sabie Rivers a protected area and named the area the Sabie Game Reserve.

After the Boer War, James Stevenson-Hamilton, a former major in the British

Opposite top: Lioness and her cubs at a waterhole.
Opposite: Springbok with new born calf.

Kruger National Park

Above: Londolozi Game Reserve is one of South Africa's private reserves where it is easily possible to see the 'big five' — lion, leopard, elephant, rhino and buffalo.

army, was appointed as South Africa's first game warden. Together with a few other dedicated men, Stephenson-Hamilton shaped what is today the Kruger National Park; he controlled the populations of predators like lion and leopard, patrolled the reserve's borders and prosecuted poachers. In 1903 he coordinated the extension of the Sabie's border to the Olifants River. Shortly afterwards a second reserve, called Shingwedzi, was proclaimed and between them the two reserves provided a sanctuary for 7,000 impala, 250 buffalo and 25 elephant.

Stephenson-Hamilton knew that the game reserves' survival depended on their usefulness as a tourist attraction and so he canvassed for the creation of a public national park. The park was to be modelled along the lines of those in the United States and Canada. Having mustered some influential political support for his idea, Stephenson-Hamilton managed to persuade the South African parliament to pass the National Parks Act in 1926. Not long afterwards the Sabie and Shingwedzi

reserves were consolidated and the huge tract of land that was created by the merger became known as the Kruger National Park. Appropriately it was named in honour of the country's first conservationist, President Paul Kruger.

Today the Kruger National Park supports the greatest variety of animal species in Africa with 137 mammal species and more than 450 species of birds. The Kruger Park protects large numbers of the 'big five'. Lion, rhino, leopard, buffalo and elephant may all be sighted in the park.

Each corner of its nearly two million acres is easily accessible to visitors; there are 1,880 kilometres (1,168 miles) of tarred and gravel roads and fifteen rest camps which provide a variety of accommodation choice. In one day the Kruger Park is capable of catering for 3,000 visitors but even at peak capacity, the size of the reserve ensures that tourists are able to experience Africa at its wildest.

The Kruger National Park falls within South Africa's summer rainfall region and so the countryside is at its greenest between

Above: Serval kitten in the safe environment of Timbavati Game Reserve.

the months of October and April. Game viewing is best in winter when the bush is less thick. Entry to the park and travel within it is restricted to the daylight hours and speed limits are fifty kilometres per hour (30 mph) on tar and forty kilometres per hour (25 mph) on gravel roads. Open cars and motorcycles are forbidden as is getting out of your car in unprotected areas.

The Kruger National Park lies in a malaria area and it is advisable to take tablets before making a visit. Malaria precautions are especially important when touring in the north of the park.

Entrance to the southern Kruger Park is via four gates. There are two in the south, at Malelane and Crocodile Bridge and two which may be approached from the south-west — the Paul Kruger and the Numbi Gates. The Malelane and Crocodile Bridge rest camps at the southern entrances and the two south-western gates are situated near to the Skukuza and Pretoriuskop camps.

The central area of the Kruger National Park is accessible via the Orpen and Phalaborwa Gates. Special attractions in the central area include the **Masorini Museum** and a view point to the west of the Olifants rest camp. This is a worthwhile stop as it provides panoramic views of the Olifants River valley. The museum is situated to the east of Phalaborwa; one of its most impressive exhibits is that of an **Iron Age village**.

Vegetation is dense in the north of the Kruger Park, which is home to large elephant herds. Access to the region is via Phalaborwa Gate or the Punda Maria Gate in the north-west. There are two rest camps — at Shingwedzi and Punda Maria. The Pafuri Gate serves the extreme north.

Accommodation options in the Kruger National Park vary from basic camping and caravaning facilities to luxurious hotel-style accommodation. At most camps there is a choice between family accommodation in self-contained chalets and huts with communal ablution blocks. Each hut is furnished and bedding and cooking utensils are provided. Certain private camps, like Nwanedzi and Roodewal in the central Kruger, are hired to tour groups as a unit.

Above: Mala Mala is famous for night drives: here, headlights capture a leopard drinking.
Overleaf: Nesting cormorants silhouetted against a golden sunset in Kruger National Park.

Shops at the camps are stocked with food, alcohol, curios and books. Reservations for accommodation should be made many months in advance — especially for peak holiday periods.

It is possible to see some of the Kruger National Park on foot. Four **wilderness trails** have been established in recent years. Three-day walking safaris are conducted by game rangers and many consider them to be the ideal way to experience the bush.

Food, accommodation and washing facilities are provided and trailists walk without backpacks. The trails are limited to people between twelve and sixty years of age and reservations are essential. These should be made months in advance.

Getting there

The Kruger National Park is five hours' drive from Johannesburg. Access to the four southern gates is from Nelspruit and White River. Comair operates daily scheduled flights between Skukuza, Phalaborwa and Johannesburg and weekly flights linking the park with Durban. Both Skukuza and Phalaborwa have car hire facilities. Travel agents will arrange fly-in safaris. Luxury coach tours operate from Johannesburg, Durban and Nelspruit. Travel agents have details about the tours.

Information and reservations

Detailed information about the Kruger National Park is available in a variety of books and travel brochures, most of which are available at bookshops and travel agencies.

For reservations contact: The Chief Director, National Parks Board, PO Box 787, Pretoria 0001; tel: (012) 343-1991. This office is situated in Leyds Street, Muckleneuk, Pretoria.

The address of the Parks Board's Cape

Town office is: The Reservations Officer, National Parks Board, PO Box 7400, Roggebaai 8012; tel: (021) 22-2810.

Private Game Reserves

Beyond the western boundary of the Kruger National Park lie a number of private game reserves. The private reserves offer game drives with experienced rangers in open safari vehicles, guided hiking trails, luxury accommodation and personal service. Private vehicles are not permitted for game viewing purposes and a number of the reserves request payment in foreign currencies.

Klaserie, **Sabie Sand** and **Timbavati** are three of the largest private game sanctuaries in the world. Created by the consolidation of a number of individual game farms, the reserves together have one of the highest concentrations of game in South Africa.

The **Sabie Sand Nature Reserve** has more than 60,000 hectares (148,260 acres) of rolling grassland, bushveld and riverine forest and offers a choice of eight private lodges operated by three different companies: Londolozi, Rattray Reserves and Sabi Sabi. Which of the reserves is best is fiercely argued; there is a variety of accommodation choice, including Inyanti which can accommodate only eight people, and Mala Mala, which has the reputation of being the most luxurious game reserve in the world.

Londolozi means 'protector of living things' in Zulu and since its creation in 1970, conservation has been the watchword of this reserve. The 30,000 hectares (74,130 acres) of bushveld that make up the Rattray Reserves is best known for **Mala Mala** which over the years hosted some of the world's most famous people. Mala Mala prides itself on the quality of its accommodation and service and for the almost guaranteed sighting of the 'big five'.

The 10,000-hectare (24,710-acre) **Sabi Sabi Game Reserve** adjoins Mala Mala and provides accommodation at two lodges, the Bush and River lodges situated nine kilometres apart. River Lodge is set on the banks of the Sabie River. Excellent sightings

of game have been recorded and hippo and elephant visit the camp periodically. There are game viewing hides overlooking a waterhole.

The **Timbavati** private nature reserve is famous for its 'white' lions, but the 80,000-hectare.(197,680-acre) reserve is also a good example of how co-operation can ensure the survival of Africa's wildlife. In the 1950s a land owner called Peter Mostert convinced his neighbours to help create a private game reserve for their own use. Today Timbavati is owned by thirty different farmers who have banned hunting and introduced a number of endangered species like rhino and sable. There are two game lodges in the Timbavati, the **Ngala** and **Tanda Tula** lodges. Ngala — the Shangaan word for lion — can accommodate up to twenty people.

Walking trails are conducted from the camp which overlooks a river and waterhole. The **Tanda Tula Game Lodge** is small and exclusive. Three resident rangers structure daily programmes to cater for their guests' personal needs. A maximum of twelve people can be accommodated.

Possibly the least known of the Transvaal's 'big three' private nature reserves is **Klaserie,** a 64,000 hectare (158,144-acre) reserve which takes its name from the river which bisects it. Klaserie is owned by a hundred shareholders and is not open to the public.

A non-profit organization called the Wildernis Trust of Southern Africa does, however, operate walking trails in the reserve. Food, accommodation and other equipment are provided for trailists who are accompanied by a trained game ranger. Phone: 011-453 7645/6/7. Fax: 011-453 7649.

Getting there

All of the private game lodges listed above are in easy reach of Johannesburg and Pretoria. Travel time from the cities is approximately six hours.

Regular scheduled flights ferry guests from Johannesburg, Durban and Nelspruit to the private game farms and some lodges offer special fly-in packages. Travel agents will have further details.

The Free State

The vast flatlands of the Free State form the heart of South Africa. They stretch from the province's northern boundary on the Vaal River, south to the Orange River, where they merge with the semi desert 'thirstlands' of the Karoo. The mountain kingdom of Lesotho lies to the east, and it is in the east that many of the Free State's greatest tourist attractions lie.

The Free State is farming country; its landscape is dominated by seemingly endless fields of maize and extensive tracts of grasslands. Its appeal may not be immediately obvious to those who travel across its vast plains, but the province has a character all of its own — an allure that is intricately tied to the lifestyles of the hardy Afrikaner who first settled in the interior of South Africa, and the farmers who continue to carve out a life for themselves on the hot, dry plains of the savannah.

The Voortrekkers crossed the Orange River in 1836 and discovered that beyond the boundaries of the British-ruled Cape Province lay vast tracts of unsettled land, ideal for stock farming. Pioneers settled in the area, erected homesteads and began to cultivate the land. Before long they had claimed the territory between the Vaal and Orange Rivers as their own. Technically, however, the Voortrekkers were still subjects of the Cape Colony; they continued to clash with the British authorities until the Orange Free State was granted independence in 1854.

The Orange Free State lost its independence after the Anglo-Boer War, but when the Union of South Africa was created in 1910, the province regained its former status. Bloemfontein became the judicial capital of South Africa and was officially recognized as the capital city of the Orange Free State.

In 1946 gold was discovered on a farm near Welkom, and the character of the northern Free State changed dramatically. Towns sprang up around the new gold fields, and what was previously agri–cultural land began to support one of the richest gold mining industries in the world. Gold brought wealth to the Free State and today the province prospers from both agriculture and industry.

The Northern Free State and the Gold Fields

The Vaal River forms the Free State's northern boundary and provides a wealth of leisure and watersport activities. The river begins its journey in Swaziland and flows west to a point where it meets the Harts River, on the western border of the Free State. Its waters flow into the **Vaal Dam** which provides water for the Gauteng region and, when full, covers an area of 300 square kilometres (116 square miles).

The **Jim Fouche holiday resort** is situated on the southern banks of the dam and provides camping, picnic and barbeque facilities for holidaymakers. There are horses for hire, swimming pools, tennis courts and a water surface of about thirty-two square kilometres (12 square miles) which is suitable for watersports.

Sasolburg is an industrial town which owes its existence to the establishment of the South African Oil, Coal and Gas Corporation (SASOL), a massive project which manufactures petroleum products from low grade coal. It is an interesting town because it was designed to provide extensive recreational facilities for the employees of the fuel company, and the town comprises a number of linked parks and green belts. A total of 71,000 trees, including fourteen different species of oak have been planted, and the green belts have bicycle and walking lanes that lead to central and suburban shopping centres.

At **Parys** the Vaal River divides into hundreds of little streams which meander past the town, creating a number of quaint hideaways for holiday-makers and fishing enthusiasts. Parys takes its name from Paris, France, and is perhaps a rather

Above: Zastron area in the Free State.

fanciful name for this little Free State town which, unlike its namesake, is unsophisticated and an agricultural rather than an industrial centre. It is, however, popular with watersport enthusiasts who use the waters of the Vaal River for fishing, water skiing, boating and swimming.

Situated on the outskirts of Parys is the **Bloemhof Dam**, a five-kilometre stretch of water which is one of the longest dams in South Africa. Adjacent to the dam is a well-known nature reserve covering an area of 14,000 hectares (34,594 acres) and featuring game including eland, springbok and zebra. Three gates provide access to the **Bloemhof Dam Nature Reserve**, the waters of which provide excellent fishing opportunities. Right next door to this reserve is the **Sandveld Nature Reserve** which is widely regarded as one of the Free State's most important game reserves. The reserve is unique because its vegetation and flat terrain bear a striking resemblance to the sandy landscape of the Kalahari desert and this is one of the few places in the Free State where this type of countryside occurs.

The town of **Kroonstad** is situated on the national N1, about 90 kilometres south of Parys, and it is here that the industrial part of the Free State's economy becomes evident; the road leads to the gold fields of Welkom, Odendaalsrus and Virginia and the horizon is dotted with mine dumps. Kroonstad lies next to the Vals River and is one of the most picturesque towns in the northern Free State.

When in Kroonstad, keep an eye open for people playing a traditional South African game called **jukskei** which is played by pitching wooden yoke pins at a peg. Kroonstad is the centre of the national jukskei league and tournaments are an annual event in the town.

The city of **Welkom** owes its existence entirely to the discovery of gold. The third richest gold fields in South Africa were discovered outside the town in 1946 and in less than twenty years, Welkom was transformed into an industrial centre. Today, Welkom forms the heart of the Free State's gold fields and the bustling town is one of the most prosperous in the country; its residents have the highest per capita income in South Africa.

Above: Rhino cooling down — poaching has made these creatures among the most endangered species in the world, but South Africa has a successful breeding programme.

Should you visit the town on the second Saturday of the month, look out for a bustling **flea market** which takes place at **Central Park**. Here you will be able to buy anything from hand-crafted pottery to traditional South African fare like *koeksusters* (syrup-drenched twisted dough) and be entertained by a variety of musicians and other performers.

The **Welkom Publicity Association** is the authority to contact if a visit to a gold mine appeals to you. These excursions take a full day and advance arrangements should be made with the association. The tour includes a trip underground to the working face of a mine, a demonstration of gold pouring and traditional mine dancing.

One of the most popular nature reserves in the Free State is the **Willem Pretorius Game Reserve** which is located on the N1 between Ventersburg and Winburg. The reserve encompasses the **Allemanskraal Dam** and features a variety of typical Free State game including white rhino, giraffe and black wildebeest. The scenery is

spectacular and varies from rocky ridges to thickly wooded gorges. A holiday resort is situated on top of a hill overlooking a lake below. Facilities include chalets, a supermarket and restaurant, swimming pool and watersport opportunities.

The small towns of **Heilbron, Frankfort** and **Villiers** in the north-eastern Free State provide services for the region's farming communities. During the summer months, between December and April, the little towns burst into colour from the fields of flowers that surround them. The towns in the 'Canna Circle' as the region has been named, decided to brighten up their environment by cultivating fields of colourful flowers. They chose to grow a different colour of canna around each town with the result that the north-eastern region of the Free State is a spectacular sight to behold when the flowers start to bloom. Frankfort and **Vrede** are two of the main centres in the Canna Circle; both towns are situated on the R34. You will pass the towns of Heilbron and **Reitz** on the R26 which also passes through the Canna Circle.

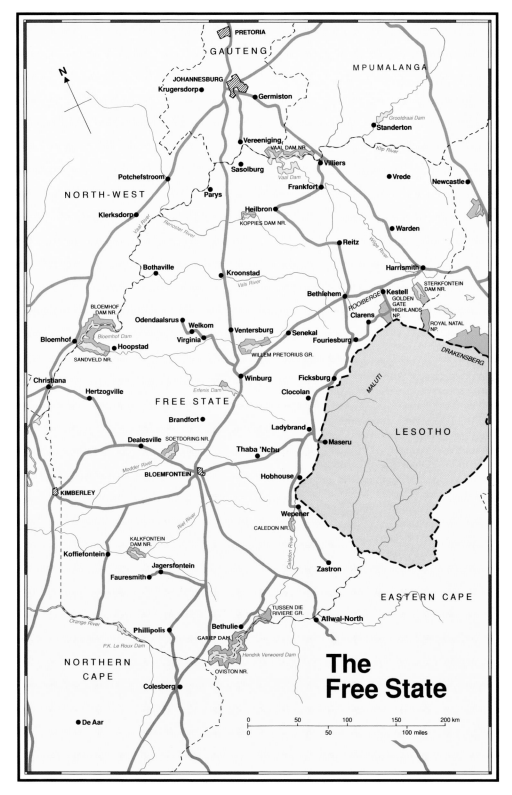

The Free State

119

Thaba 'Nchu district

Thaba 'Nchu is situated very close to the 'mountain kingdom' of Lesotho. The district takes its name from **Thaba 'Nchu**, the 'Black Mountain', a beautiful mountain which is steeped in African legend and tradition. An energetic climb up Thaba 'Nchu affords spectacular views over the surrounding countryside which has been the scene of fascinating historical events.

A Sun International casino resort/hotel complex called the **Naledi Sun** can be found in Thaba 'Nchu.

About fifteen kilometres (nine miles) from the Thaba 'Nchu central business district and five kilometres (three miles) from Thaba 'Nchu Mountain is an area called **Rakgokgo Farm,** which was a frequent camping site for Voortrekkers. The Barolong named the area Rakgokgo after the sound that the Voortrekkers' wagon wheels made when passing over rough terrain; a grating 'kg...kg...kg...'. Today Rakgogo Farm is owned by Dr Moroka, one of the first black men to qualify as a medical doctor in South Africa.

Ten kilometres (six miles) from the town of Thaba 'Nchu and only seventy kilometres (43 miles) from Bloemfontein — the capital city of the Free State — is the **Maria Moroka National Park,** named after the late Maria Moipane Moroka, mother of the reigning chief and regent to the chieftaincy for many years.

The nature reserve is situated in a natural amphitheatre formed by the Thaba 'Nchu mountain. Small hills of grasslands which fan out from the foothills of Thaba 'Nchu provide an ideal environment for more than 1,000 head of typical highveld game.

Visitors can expect to see springbok, blesbok, zebra, red haartebeest and eland and a variety of small mammals which are indigenous to the area; the clawless otter, mongoose and ground squirrel.

The game reserve extends over 3,400 hectares (8,400 acres). The grasslands of Maria Moroka are a bird-watcher's paradise. In the rainy season (September to April) the **Moutloatse Setlogelo Dam** covers an area of 240 hectares (593 acres), providing a haven for a large number of waterfowl including heron, cormorants, kingfishers, and a variety of duck and geese.

Khoraans are among the most common species in the reserve. The long-legged birds may be spotted feeding in long grass together with the ungainly secretary bird and bald ibis which are also indigenous to the area.

Exquisite birds of prey, such as the rare black eagle and the gently soaring jackal buzzard are common sights. Fish eagles may be sighted near the dam.

Inhabitants of the Thaba 'Nchu district fondly refer to the region as 'big sky country', and gazing over the grasslands of Maria Moroka National Park you can see why. The skies are clear and blue all year round and the grasslands that stretch out before the black mountain seem to go on for ever.

One of the unique aspects of Maria Moroka National Park is that visitors to the reserve, whether game viewing, hiking or angling, must enter the park on foot — unless they are on a conducted game drive. The only vehicles permitted to enter the park are those of the National Parks Board and the safari company that operates game drives in the reserve.

Visitors are asked to observe a few reasonable rules when walking in the reserve and viewing game. They must refrain from feeding, injuring or disturbing any kind of wildlife and to refrain from damaging, uprooting or disfiguring any tree or plant in the area.

Located next to the Maria Moroka National Park is the **Thaba 'Nchu Sun** Hotel, which has a casino.

Getting there

Good tar roads lead from Bloemfontein directly to Thaba 'Nchu. Follow Route 64 out of the city for sixty-three kilometres (39 miles). A signpost on the edge of the town of Thaba 'Nchu indicates a left turn to the central area and a right turn to Thaba 'Nchu Sun and the Maria Moroka Game Reserve. The entrance to the hotel complex is twelve kilometres from this turn-off.

Above: The Orange River.

The Southern Free State

One of the most impressive features of the flat, dry countryside which makes up the southern region of the Free State is the **Gariep Dam,** which dams South Africa's largest river, the Orange. On its way east from the mountains of Lesotho to the Indian Ocean, the Orange and its tributaries drain two thirds of South Africa. A drive across its ninety-metre-high (290-foot) wall gives one a fair indication of the dam's size; it covers an area of 374 square kilometres (144 square miles) when full. This massive expanse of water forms part of the **Orange River Development Scheme**, the most ambitious water supply system in Africa.

Its waters have been used for the production of hydroelectric power since 1972, and they are also vital for the irrigation of agricultural land in the southern Free State. From the Gariep Dam, water is channelled into the **Vanderkloof Dam** and from there it flows into the **Orange-Fish tunnel**, the longest tunnel in

the world. The tunnel carries water south, towards the Indian Ocean and the hot, dry Karoo where it is used for irrigation, industry and hydroelectric power.

The largest springbok population in South Africa is protected by the **Gariep Dam Nature Reserve**, which is situated on the northern banks of the dam. Among other game in the reserve are red hartebeest, black wildebeest and ostrich. The dam has also become a favourite spot for watersport enthusiasts. There is a holiday resort on the shores of the dam which provides a variety of accommodation choice, including caravan and camping sites as well as fully equipped chalets.

Also on the northern banks of the dam is the little town of **Bethulie**, situated on the R701. One of the Free State's oldest nature reserves is located near Bethulie: the **Mynhardt Game Reserve** boasts springbok and impala — two species which do not commonly occur in the same area.

Twenty kilometres (13 miles) south-east of Bethulie is the **Tussen-Die-Riviere game farm**. The Orange and Caledon Rivers converge in the western section of the farm

— hence the name, which means 'between the rivers'. During winter simple accommodation is provided for hunters who usually stay at the farm for a period of two days. Applications to hunt at Tussen-Die-Riviere are received from around the world, but the farm can only accommodate 300 hunters a year.

From the Gariep Dam, the waters of the Orange River flow into the Vanderkloof Dam which boasts the highest dam wall in South Africa, and two nature reserves. On the south eastern banks of P K Le Roux is the **Doornkloof Nature Reserve,** the **Rolfontein Reserve** is located to the southwest. Both feature grassy plateaus and mountain ridges with vegetation typical of the southern Free State — sweet thorn and karee trees are common and there are more than forty species of grass on the flatlands. Animal species which occur in the parks include eland, zebra, red hartebeest and white rhino. Hiking is permitted in the Rolfontein Reserve.

Tourists who visit the southern Free State during winter should enquire about the **National Endurance Ride** which takes place in **Fauresmith** each year. The endurance ride is a three-day horse race which attracts participants from around South Africa. The festivities surrounding the race give visitors an opportunity to sample traditional Afrikaner hospitality.

Fauresmith, which is situated on the R704, is also famous for a railway line which runs alongside its main street.

The southern Free State is diamond mining country and the little town of **Jagersfontein** — located on the R704 — is well-known for the size and quality of its diamonds. Prior to the discovery of the Cullinan diamond in 1905, Jagersfontein was the home of the biggest diamond in the world which was discovered near the town in 1883. Jagersfontein's other claim to fame is that the notorious American gangster Al Capone once wore one of the town's diamonds on his finger — or so legend has it.

Also famous for its diamonds is the little town of **Koffiefontein**, situated on the R48. A settlement sprang up there in the 19th century, around a site where transport riders would unsaddle their horses and stop for a coffee break — Koffiefontein means 'coffee spring'. In 1870 a transport rider picked up a diamond near Koffiefontein and thousands of fortune seekers rushed to the site. Today the precious stones are still mined in the area by the diamond mining company. Its open diamond mine may be viewed from a nearby tower.

The oldest town in the Free State is **Phillipolis**, located on the R717. It was founded in 1823 and there are a number of buildings within its boundaries which are of historical interest. These include the library buildings and the **Nederduitse Gereformeerde Kerk**.

The Eastern Highlands

As mentioned previously, many of the Free State's most impressive tourist attractions lie in the eastern region of the province. Here, the countryside is dominated by the magnificent mountains that surround Lesotho and there are ample opportunities for nature lovers and outdoor enthusiasts to appreciate the spectacular mountain scenery in the east. An ideal way to experience what this region has to offer is by following the popular 'highland route' which begins in Harrismith, near the Natal border, and ends in Zastron in the south. It has never been mapped but is identified by the towns and tourist attractions that are situated along the route.

Harrismith is the first stop. Founded in 1846, this little town is situated near the foothills of the Drakensberg mountain range, and is a centre point on the busy N3 which runs between Johannesburg and Durban. It was created as a military outpost and was named after a former governor of the Province of Queen Adelaide, Sir Harry Smith. During the Anglo Boer War, Harrismith became a site of military importance and the town still has many reminders from this period in its history.

At the foot of the **Platberg** are the **Drakensberg Botanical Gardens** — a showcase for flora that occurs naturally in

Above: Blue wildebeest are common throughout the Kalahari Gemsbok National Park, one of South Africa's most remote areas.

the Drakensberg mountain range. There is a picnic area in the gardens and a blockhouse which was erected during the Boer war to protect Harrismith's water supply. This is now a national monument.

The Mount Everest Game Reserve is also located on the outskirts of Harrismith; the 1,000-hectare (2,471-acre) reserve provides sanctuary for twenty-two species of game. The rolling hills and spectacular mountain scenery within Mount Everest are a favourite with hikers and mountain climbers who are free to roam the reserve unescorted. Visitors are warned to keep an eye out for rhino and ostriches. Horses and four-wheel-drive vehicles may be hired from the park authorities.

Twenty-five kilometres (15 miles) south-west of Harrismith is the **Sterkfontein Dam**, the crystal clear waters of which provide excellent trout fishing opportunities. The dam is surrounded by the hills of the

Above: The Golden Gate National Park is 11,600 hectares of nature trails and spectacular scenery.

Drakensberg. Guests can stay at the Kwantane or at the Mount Everest Game Lodge being erected here.

The village of **Clarens**, situated between Harrismith and Bethlehem on the road to the **Golden Gate Highlands National Park**, is commonly referred to as the gem of the Free State. Set in the Caledon valley, Clarens has a breathtaking view of Lesotho's Maluti mountains and in spring, when the fruit trees bloom, it is surrounded by a haze of pink blossoms. The beauty of the valley can be appreciated from a vantage point about one kilometre off the R711. Follow the Clarens-Fouriesburg Road for ten kilometres and turn on to a gravel road which leads to the top of a hill. The view from this road is stunning.

An important archaeological site is located near Clarens, and some well-known bushman paintings may be viewed on the farm **Shaapplaats**. In 1976 Dr Kitching, a researcher from the Bernard Price Institute for Palaeontology, discovered five fossil dinosaur eggs in a stream near Clarens. When he split them open, he found the embryos were so well preserved that minute teeth could be detected in the tiny jaws of the fossil creatures. This was the first time that fossils of this kind had been discovered in the Triassic beds and Dr Kitching's find excited archaeologists around the world.

The magnificent **Golden Gate Highlands National Park** is situated in the foothills of the Maluti mountains and it takes its name from the rich shades of gold that the sun casts on the sandstone cliffs at sunset. The most scenic route to the Golden Gate is via the little town of **Kestell**.

The Golden Gate Park comprises 11,600 hectares (28,652 acres) of land, situated at a height of 1,892 metres (6,207 feet) above sea level. Its landscape is dominated by outcrops of yellow and red striated cliffs. The vegetation is typically highland and consists of sour grasses and a variety of bulbs and herbs.

The reserve provides a sanctuary for numerous species of game, including zebra, buffalo, eland and springbok. In winter, temperatures in the region often fall below zero, but the summers are mild and warm. A hiking trail through the spectacular mountain scenery of the Golden Gate is an ideal way to experience the beauty of the area. The Rhebuck trail takes two days to complete and accommodation is provided in an overnight hut. Good accommodation and caravan as well as camping facilities are available at the Golden Gate National Park As its name suggests, the Free State town of **Bethlehem** was named after Christ's birthplace — by a group of Voortrekkers who settled on a farm called Pretoriuskloof in 1864. Today the quaint town situated on the **Jordan River**, is the agricultural and industrial centre of the region. It is known for its fine sandstone houses and one rather peculiar feature: Bethlehem has a nature reserve in the centre of town. The **Pretoriuskloof Nature Reserve** is surrounded by Bethlehem's bustling central business district. The small patch of land contains a variety of indigenous birds and small game. There are paths which follow the Jordan River and the short walks provide an ideal opportunity to enjoy the fauna and flora of the area without having to venture too far from the comfort of town.

Places of historical interest in Bethlehem include the **Cultural Museum** and the **A B Baartman Wagon House**. Displays include an old steam engine, agricultural equipment and horse carriages.

The **Wolhuterskop hiking trail** starts and finishes at the **Loch Athlone holiday resort** outside Bethlehem. It is a two-day trail which offers easy walking and excellent game viewing opportunities. Horse riding is permitted in the **Wolhuterskop Reserve**; stables are located on the R26, about two kilometres (one mile) past the entrance to the Loch Athlone resort.

Fouriesburg is the next stop along the Highland Route. This little town is located on the R26 and is known mainly for the **Brandwater Hiking Trail**, a five-day, sixty-kilometre (37-mile) route which follows a path through the high ravines and spectacular valleys of the **Maluti, Rooi** and **Witteberg Mountains**. Vegetation along the route is amazingly diverse, and the trail passes beautiful sandstone farm houses, some of which date back to the

Boer war. The largest sandstone cave in the southern hemisphere, **Salpeterkrans**, is on the way and there are good examples of rock art to be seen. The Brandwater trail begins and ends at the **Meiringskloof Caravan Park**. Further information about the hike is available from the Fouriesburg tourist information centre.

Ficksburg is a much larger town, best known for its annual **Cherry Festival** which takes place in November. Ninety per cent of South Africa's cherries are grown in the district surrounding Ficksburg and the town is a beautiful sight to behold when the cherry trees blossom in spring. Information about coach tours which, from mid-September, take visitors to view the cherry blossoms, may be obtained from the Ficksburg municipality.

Ficksburg, situated on the Lesotho border, is an important industrial and agricultural centre for the eastern Free State. The town also plays a key role in the multi-million-rand **Lesotho Highlands Water Scheme** which is jointly sponsored by Lesotho and South Africa and provides water and hydroelectric power for both countries. Like Bethlehem, Ficksburg boasts a number of impressive sandstone buildings, the best known of which is the **General J I J Fick Museum** on the town square. Other sandstone buildings include the **Town Hall**, the **Dutch Reformed Church** and the old **Post Office**. The museum has a display on Ficksburg's sandstone architectural culture.

A variety of outdoor recreation activities are offered in the district surrounding Ficksburg. These include the **Imperani Hiking Trail** which starts at the **Meulspruit Dam**, located on the Clocolan Road, five kilometres (three miles) from Ficksburg. The dam stretches ten kilometres (six miles) along the Imperani kloof, and the trail follows a circular route for twenty-three kilometres (14 miles) over the top of the **Imperani Mountains**. Along the route there are rock paintings, sandstone caves and breathtaking views of the Maluti mountains.

Hoekfontein game farm, thirteen kilometres (8 miles) from Ficksburg on the Fouriesburg Road, has the only hippos in the Free State. Other species of game on the farm include white rhino, blue and black wildebeest and zebra.

Clocolan is a picturesque little town with a view of the Maluti Mountains and an abundance of cherry blossoms in spring. There are two dams in the vicinity, the **Steunmekaar Dam**, approximately a kilometre (just over half a mile) from the centre of town and the **Lucretia Dam**, a little further out. Angling is permitted on both dams but a licence is required.

The next stop along the Highland Route is **Ladybrand**, located just off the main road from Bloemfontein. The town was established in 1867 as a border post for the region north of the Caledon River and its history is closely linked to the Basotho Wars of the 19th century.

Ladybrand has some excellent examples of sandstone architecture. The **Anglican** and **Dutch Reformed** churches are particularly impressive, as are the **municipal offices** and **Ladybrand Secondary School**. **The Catharina Brand Museum** houses an archaeological display which includes Stone Age instruments and a replica of a fossil found in a quarry near the town.

The fossil is of the diathrognatus-protozoon which is important because it constitutes an evolutionary link between mammals and reptiles. Another important archaeological discovery was made at **Rose Cottage Cave** near Ladybrand where the ashes from a fire hearth are estimated to be over 50,000 years old.

Zastron is the last town on the Highland Route. From Ladybrand the R26 follows a route close to the Lesotho border and passes through the little towns of **Hobhouse** and **Wepener**. Wepener features a number of historical monuments and a small game reserve.

The **Aasvoelberg** ('vulture mountain') marks the highest point in the Free State and forms a backdrop to the town of **Zastron**. The **Eye of Zastron** is a famous nine-metre-wide (29-foot) hole located in a cliff outside the town, and there are some excellent examples of Bushman art in the caves near the town. **Seekoei** ('hippo') **Cave** and **Hoffman Cave** harbour the most famous of these.

KwaZulu-Natal Drakensberg

The Drakensberg mountain range is part of the great escarpment of South Africa which, like a step, separates the narrow coastal range from the plateau of the interior.

There are various theories about the source of the name 'Drakensberg' or 'Dragon mountain': that it came from the San, the first inhabitants of the area whose mythology included giant serpent-like creatures; that their paintings of such creatures on rocky cave walls convinced other black tribes visiting the area of these beasts' existence and they in turn told the Boers about these 'dragons'; or that the name was derived from a peak called 'Drakensberg' or 'Dragon's Rock' near Matatiele. Whatever the origins of the name, it is certainly evocative of the range's spiky peaks which resemble a dragon's back, as is the name given to it by the Zulus — 'uKhahlamba' or 'a barrier of uplifted spears'.

These 'spears' or peaks are the remains of what was once a crust of basalt lava, spewed up when great fissures opened in the Lesotho area about 190 million years ago. Natural erosion has worn away much of the basalt and the sandstone which lay underneath, creating a dramatic landscape of deep ravines and spurs, Gothic peaks and heart-stopping overhangs. To Natalians, the Drakensberg is a special place because it contrasts so dramatically with the rest of the province; barely a few hours away from the balmy fecundity of the coast or the lush midlands, this region is both fragile and forbidding. The weather here can be treacherous, with rain, mist or snow coming on quickly and catching hikers by surprise. Because of the altitude, it can also be extreme, with sub-zero temperatures (Celsius) common in winter, especially at night.

The vegetation of these mountains is generally hardy, although part of a delicately balanced ecosystem. There are three distinct zones. In the lower gorges and slopes you find protea savannah — grassy areas where two types of proteas grow — and forests of mainly yellowwood, mountain hard pear, assegai wood, Cape holly and white stinkwood. From the tops of the forested gorges to the basalt walls of the escarpment, the grassland of the sub-alpine zone is found. Watsonias and irises are among many wild flowers which enliven these grassy plains in spring. In the sheltered areas *fynbos* grows. In the highly stressed alpine zone above the base of the walls of the escarpment all plant life is limited to less than one metre high.

For climbing and hiking enthusiasts the mountains beckon, but be sure to follow safety guidelines for many have lost their lives here. Weather conditions can change with frightening rapidity, and thick cloud can quickly obscure safe routes down. Access to all wilderness areas is by permit only. These can be obtained by making a written or telephonic booking with the controlling body or on arrival at the access point, provided the number of people in the area doesn't exceed the limit.

The detailed description of the different areas of the Drakensberg which follows describes various scenic landmarks and gives a taste of hiking trails in those areas. There are literally hundreds of trails throughout the Drakensberg, which range from gentle walks to difficult climbs. For a more detailed description of possible routes, consult David Bristow's *Drakensberg Walks* which lists more than a hundred and grades them according to difficulty. The booking offices are also a good place to find out about walks in those areas.

For the active person there is also swimming and trout fishing in the rivers as well as horse riding. Most Drakensberg hotels also offer a wide range of sporting facilities and other types of entertainment.

Where to stay

The Drakensberg offers everything from the razzmatazz of resort hotels to cosy cottages, mountain huts, campsites and solitary caves where San families may have once sheltered. (It is not permissible to stay

KwaZulu-Natal

overnight or make fires in caves where there is rock art.) To find out about accommodation in private homes and farmhouses (self-catering or bed and breakfast), contact Underberg Hideaways, tel: (0331) 443505.

How to get there

There is no reliable public transport to this area so you will need a car. Car hire facilities are available in most major centres. If staying in a hotel, it may be worth inquiring if they run any kind of shuttle service to nearby centres.

When to go

This really depends on your preference in terms of temperature. Rain falls in summer in this region, when temperatures vary from mild to hot. Winters are dry with some snow, but are mostly made up of cold nights and mild to warm sunny days. Bear in mind that the weather is variable here and that snowfalls are even possible in November, which is well into the South African summer. Check weather reports and pack wisely.

San paintings

San paintings adorn rock shelters and caves throughout the southern end of the African continent. The earliest, found in a cave in Namibia, dates back 27,000 years and is an indication that the San were the first inhabitants of the subcontinent. The most recent are less than 200 years old. The San were prolific rock artists and it is estimated that there are about 15,000 art sites scattered throughout the subcontinent.

In the Drakensberg, archaeological evidence suggests that the San were living in the mountains for thousands of years before the arrival of the first Nguni people. Excavations in south-eastern Lesotho have provided evidence of Middle Stone Age man as far back as 43,000 BP (before present). Later Stone Age material found here dates back to 1430 BC.

The materials the artists used were skillfully made. Brushes were fashioned from animal hairs, plant fibres or feathers. Most of the colours were produced by mineral oxides found in the earth — iron oxides for red, brown and yellow, manganese for black and zinc oxides for white. Paints were made by mixing these materials with blood, milk, egg white, urine or sap.

The San were among the first artists in the world to use the foreshortening technique, which enabled them to depict their subjects in a three-dimensional landscape. They were skillful in conveying the 'essence' of various animals, i.e., the grace of the eland and the bulk of the rhino.

Far from being the naive art of a 'simple' people, San rock paintings are now seen as often complex collections of symbols and metaphors representing the San people's basic philosophical and religious beliefs. Archaeologists and anthropologists now believe that the trance dance, their most important religious ritual, was a fundamental source of their art. In this dance, performed in large groups, rhythmic clapping and singing would induce a state of altered consciousness in shamans in the gathering (up to half the men and a third of the women present).

In this state it was believed shamans could heal the sick, remonstrate with malevolent spirits, have out-of-body experiences and even communicate with God. Researchers now believe it likely that all rock artists were shamans who painted visions of the spirit world and symbols of their supernatural powers after they had returned from the trance state. (While still in this state they would have trembled too much and may have been unconscious.)

It has been suggested that the San ceased living in the northern Drakensberg long before the first whites arrived, because of black expansion. This is indicated by the high proportion of paintings in the north which depict wild rather than domestic animals, and the fact that no 'historical' paintings (i.e., paintings showing encounters with other cultures) are found here. Paintings of horses appear only in southern Drakensberg caves. (Visitors should note that these paintings are extremely fragile and are severely threatened by human encroachment. Many have been destroyed or irreparably damaged by campfire smoke and 'souvenir'

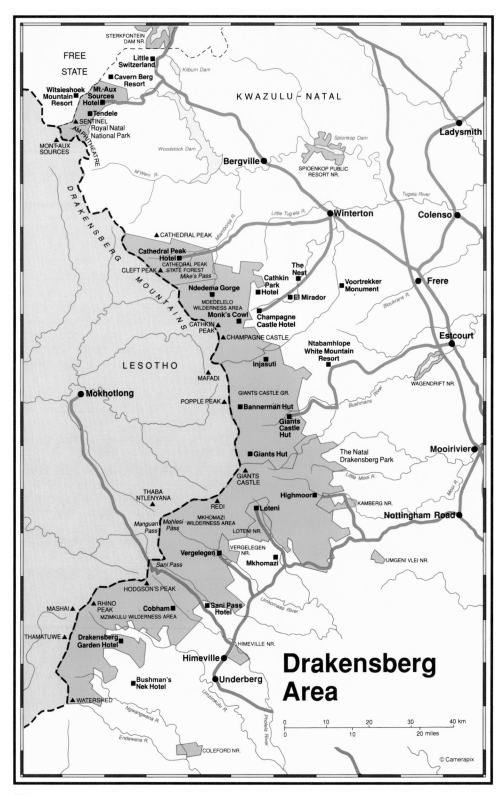

Drakensberg Area

Above: The Tugela River plummets a total of 842 metres (2,763 feet) in a series of falls.

hunters. They should not be touched or interfered with in any way.)

As the traditional hunting grounds of the San disappeared with white and black expansion, they were forced back into the mountains and driven to cattle rustling. To farmers they were a menace, often venturing as far away as Karkloof to steal cattle. They were hunted down and shot as vermin by farmers and, by the beginning of this century, there were no survivors of this ancient culture left in Natal.

Northern Drakensberg

Nowhere is the contrast between basalt 'wall' and river valley greater than in the **Amphitheatre**, the main feature of this northernmost part of the Drakensberg. This commanding wall of rock is about five kilometres (three miles) long and more than 1,500 metres (4,875 feet) high, representing the single greatest altitude drop in southern Africa. Through erosion, a series of towers, pillars and buttresses separated by deep ravines have been carved into its face,

giving it a fluted appearance.

The Tugela River, which has its source on the **Mont-aux-Sources plateau**, plunges over the Amphitheatre's rim, plummeting 842 metres (2,763 feet) in a series of falls. In mid-winter the uppermost cascade freezes into a solid sheet of ice. **Mont-aux-Sources** ('Mountain of Sources'), where another four major rivers begin, was so named by two French missionaries who were the first to ascend it in 1830 while they were exploring Lesotho. There are several climbs that one can do in the vicinity of the Amphitheatre and Mont-aux-Sources, although they are mostly fairly taxing and should only be attempted if you are physically fit and well prepared. There is a popular climb to the top of Mont-aux-Sources which includes passing **Basuto Gate**, a pass which was used by people fleeing Zulu impis during the Mfecane wars of the 1820s, and the **Chain Ladder**, literally a ladder of about thirty metres (98 feet) used to haul oneself up the summit.

From Mont-aux-Sources it is possible to traverse the length of the Amphitheatre, viewing the escarpment and the Tugela

Valley below. It is also possible to continue along the length of the entire escarpment from there, although this would take about two weeks of continual walking. The **Royal Natal National Park** lies in the valley below the Amphitheatre and Witsieshoek, covering an area of 8,000 hectares (19,760 acres). It was proclaimed in 1916 as the Natal National Park, acquiring the 'Royal' prefix when the British royal family visited it in 1947. It is a sanctuary for wildlife including various types of antelope and more than 200 species of bird, although it is popular mainly for its scenic attractions.

The park offers a variety of places to stay, including two superb hotels, the **Royal Natal National Park Hotel** and the **Karos Mont-aux-Sources Hotel**, the **Tendele hutted camp** (where you are assigned a cook to prepare your food) and the **Mahai** and **Rugged Glen camp sites**. Within reach of the Amphitheatre but outside the park are **The Cavern hotel**, a cosy establishment in a lovely setting, **Little Switzerland resort** and the **Witsieshoek Mountain Resort**, which offers chalets and a restaurant.

The **Tugela Gorge walk**, from the car park on the banks of the Tugela River below the Tendele hutted camp, takes one through protea veld and yellowwood forests to the Tugela Gorge where it is possible to see the Tugela Falls cascading down the Amphitheatre wall. In the narrow part of the gorge, watch out for sudden thunderstorms which can bring down a deluge of water and rocks within minutes.

Otto's Walk is a pleasant walk through forest along the Tugela River with views of the Sentinel (3,165 metres, 10,286 feet) and Amphitheatre. It begins at the Natal Parks Board visitor's centre at the Royal Natal National Park Hotel and includes the site of some San paintings.

For more information about walks in this area consult the visitor's centre. Three other San painting sites, as well as Natal's largest trout hatchery are also in this area.

The **Mnweni** ('Place of Fingers') is that area from the Amphitheatre to the

Cathedral range. This is the remotest and most rugged part of the Drakensberg, and is only frequented by the hardiest, most dedicated mountaineers. There are no easy hikes, no accommodation and poor roads in this area. All the hikes begin at the **Isandhlawana Police Post**. Since hikers have been robbed and attacked in this area by local inhabitants, it is wise to be both respectful and cautious.

Two towns which serve the northern and north-central areas are **Bergville** and **Winterton**, in the foothills of the Drakensberg. In the centre of Bergville is a **blockhouse** built by the British during the South African War, which is now a monument and a museum.

The Central Areas

This section of the Drakensberg is covered by a series of reserves and wilderness areas, i.e., the **Mlambonja Wilderness Area**, the **Cathedral Peak State Forest**, the **Mdedelelo Wilderness Area**, the **Giant's Castle Game Reserve** and the **Mkhomazi Wilderness Area**.

The Cathedral Peak area with its numerous free-standing peaks and magnificent scenery is one of the most favoured climbing and hiking areas in the Drakensberg. The Cathedral range, also known as 'AbaMponjwana' or 'Ridge of Horns', juts out from the escarpment for about four kilometres (2.2 miles).

Cathedral Peak at the northern end of the range commands a magnificent view of the Drakensberg from Mont-aux-Sources to Champagne Castle, and is a good spot from which to view the **Mnweni area**. The route to its summit starts at the **Cathedral Peak Hotel**, and takes approximately eight to nine hours. The escarpment in this area, where the peaks are all more than 3,000 metres high, can be reached via a number of passes, the most popular being the **Organ Pipes**, **Camel** and **Thuthumi** passes.

The hotel occupies a unique position — it is completely surrounded by mountains

---

Opposite: Mike's Pass: beckoning lonely peaks of the Drakensberg above a meandering stream.

Above: The magnificent Cathedral Peak offers splendid scenery along with good hiking and climbing trails.

and commands uninterrupted views of Cathedral Peak, **the Bell** and the **two Horns**. The **Tseketseke Campsite** is a four-hour hike from the hotel. From the hotel it is possible to drive to the top of the **Little Berg**, bringing you closer to the Escarpment. Access is via **Mike's Pass**, an eleven-kilometre (seven-mile) jeep track that was built between 1947 and 1949. There is a camp site with washing facilities at **Mike's Pass Gate**, near the forest station. The pass climbs 500 metres (1,625 feet) and ends at the **Arendsig Gate**, the starting point of routes to the **Ndedema Gorge**, the **Organ Pipes** and the escarpment. (The gorge can also be reached by starting at **Emhlawazini Stores**, north-east of Mike's Pass.)

Ndedema Gorge is an extremely valuable rock art area, with more than 3,900 paintings recorded in seventeen shelters. **Sebayeni Cave** is the largest of the painted shelters in the gorge, containing more than 1,100 paintings. A footpath follows the upper edge of the gorge, before descending into the largest natural forest in the Drakensberg. There are two popular caves, **Leopard and Poacher's**, where hikers may

stay overnight. In the vicinity of Cathedral Peak Hotel there are a number of moderate-to-easy walks, including one to **Rainbow Gorge**, which follows the Ndumeni River and has plenty of ferns, lichens and colourful fungi to photograph. There is also a trout hatchery near the hotel.

The **Mdedelelo Wilderness Area** lies between Ndedema Gorge in the north and Giant's Castle in the south. It is one of the most popular and built up parts of the Drakensberg and accommodation is thus varied and plentiful. **Champagne Castle**, **The Nest**, **El Mirador** and **Cathkin Park hotels** all offer solid comforts like hearty meals and cosy log fires.

For more rugged types, camp sites are available at the **Monk's Cowl Forest Station**, **Dragon Peaks Resort** and the **Mountain Splendour Caravan Park**. The **Nkosazana**, **Stable** and **Cowl** caves can also be reserved. The area is dominated by Cathkin peak, a forbidding form which juts out from the escarpment. The Zulu name for this peak is 'Mdedelelo' or 'make room for him', a term used to refer to a bully, because Cathkin Peak seems to push the

Above: Giant's Castle in the Drakensberg.

other peaks around it aside. Cathkin Peak's summit is difficult to reach because it is surrounded by dangerous cliffs.

The main access point to this area is the **Monk's Cowl Forest Station**. The highest point of the headland behind Cathkin Peak is **Champagne Castle** (3,377 metres; 10,975 feet). This peak's name was apparently derived from a bottle of bubbly which failed to survive the ascent made by two Victorian soldiers in 1861. The summit of Champagne Castle is reached via **Gray's Pass** and is a slog rather than a difficult climb. Gray's Pass is only three kilometres (almost two miles) long but you gain 700 metres (2,275 feet) in altitude there. **Nkosazana Cave** at the top of the pass is a good place to spend the night. From the top of the pass Champagne Castle is an easy three kilometres (almost two miles) away. A striking sight is **Gatberg**, a peak with a large hole through its base. The Zulu name for it is *Intunja*, which has been translated as 'the eye of the needle' or 'the hole in the mountain through which the shepherds can creep'.

The contour path which provides access to the south-eastern and north-western parts of the wilderness area is about six kilometres (three-and-a-half miles) from the Monk's Cowl Forest Station. The **Keith Bush Camp**, a beautiful campsite surrounded by cliffs on three sides at the head of the Mhlawazini River is reached via this path. This campsite was named after Keith Bush, a member of a team which opened a new route on the north face of Cathkin Peak in 1955. While descending the peak he fell to his death. Another climber claimed by the treacherous mountains there was Dick Barry, who died during the first attempt to climb Monk's Cowl in 1938. There is a moderate walk of about two-and-a-half hours from the hotel through grass, wattle and forest, which passes his grave.

Eland Cave in the north-western part of **Mdedelelo** has over 1,600 rock paintings. The cave is not on the map and directions must be obtained from the forester at the Monk's Cowl station. The **Drakensberg Boy's Choir School** is on the slopes below Cathkin Peak. This school, founded in the sixties, has three boys' choirs which have acquired an international reputation for excellence.

On a dirt road (D275) off Route 600 which leads to Monk's Cowl station is a farm where **Ardmore Ceramic Studio** is found. **Fee Halstead-Berning** and **Bonnie Ntshalintshali**, two award-winning South African artists, have a studio here along with other artists. Their work is colourful and unique, making a visit to the studio well worthwhile. Open every day except religious holidays.

Injasuti was formerly a private resort called Solitude, before being incorporated into the Giant's Castle Game Reserve in 1980. The name is derived from 'eNjasuthi', given by early Nguni hunters to this valley where game was plentiful and their dogs never went hungry. There are several towering peaks which beckon climbers here, including **Mafadi Peak**, at 3,446 metres (11,200 feet) one of the highest points in South Africa. Accommodation is fairly simple, consisting of bungalows and a camp/caravan site. The Injasuti area also offers three caves which are fairly easy to reach. **Fergy's Cave** is seven kilometres (four miles) from the Injasuthi camp.

Battle Cave, named after a scene painted in red on one of its walls of a battle between two feuding San groups, is nearby. This cave is a national monument and is fenced off. Tours can be arranged.

The **Lower Injasuti Cave** is nine kilometres (five miles) from the main camp and also passes Battle Cave on the way. **Junction Cave** is also nine kilometres (five miles) from the main camp and is the third cave available as overnight shelter. This cave is near **Marble Baths**, a unique spot where the river has polished the sandstone until it is smooth and white. All three of these caves must be booked through the Parks Board.

The **Giant's Castle Reserve** was created in 1903 to preserve the dwindling herds of eland which migrated seasonally from the highveld to the midlands. The reserve is now home to many different types of antelope, baboon and hundreds of different kinds of birds.

The *lammergeier*, or bearded vulture — half vulture, half eagle — is also found here. This magnificent bird was once found from the western Cape to eastern Africa and from the Middle East through China to the Himalayas. Today only the mountains of the Drakensberg and Lesotho provide the conditions necessary for its survival in southern Africa. A special hide has been established for them in the reserve at **Bamboo Hollow**. They are fed every Saturday from May to September, when food is less readily available. From the hide it is possible to watch them eating along with black eagles, jackal buzzards, rock kestrels, lanner falcons and Cape vultures, which also show up to peck the carcasses. The hide is about four kilometres (two miles) north of the Giant's Castle hutted camp and is easily accessible.

Within the Giant's Castle Reserve there are three mountain huts where hikers can stay. **Meander Hut** is almost six kilometres (four miles) from the Giant's Castle main camp. **Giant's Castle Hut**, near Giant's Castle Peak (3,314 metres/10,771 feet), and **Bannerman Hut** are both within about eleven kilometres (seven miles) of the main camp, and are about eighteen kilometres (eleven miles) apart on the same contour path. The path to **Langalibalele Pass** turns off this contour path between the two huts. About six hours should be allowed for the ascent and descent of this pass which rises about 700 metres (2,275 feet).

In 1873 there was a dispute between Chief Langalibalele of the Hlubi tribe and the colonial government of Natal. Langalibalele fled up the pass with his followers pursued by Major Durnford and his forces. Durnford's forces were repulsed and five Natal Carbineers died. A stone cairn at the summit marks their graves.

The Giant's Castle Reserve is another treasure trove of rock paintings, with a total of more than fifty sites containing more than 5,000 paintings found within its borders. At the **Main Caves** near the main camp there are more than 540 paintings, as well as a museum where a recorded commentary on the San's paintings, history and culture is given hourly. There is also a life-size model of a San family depicting their way of life.

The **Hillside Camp** caters for horse-riding enthusiasts, who can either try the two-, three- or four-day horseback trails, led by a ranger and stay overnight in caves, or ride in the vicinity of the camp. Prices are reasonable and, as the trails are popular, bookings should be made well in advance.

The **Mkhomazi Wilderness Area** stretches from Giant's Castle in the north to Sani Pass in the south, and includes the Loteni, Vergelegen and Mzimkhulwana nature reserves. **Kamberg Nature Reserve**, which also lies in this area, is a popular place for trout fishing and also has a unique **wheelchair trail** of about two kilometres along the Mooi River. There is a hutted camp in this and the Vergelegen reserves.

Just outside Kamberg the **Impofana Nature Reserve** has a fine collection of rock art. The **Loteni Nature Reserve** is the most convenient access point to this area for climbers, although **Mkhomazi Forestry Station** is the main control point. The **Loteni** hutted camp area is near peaks such as **The Tent**, **The Hawk** and **Redi**. There is also a campsite at Loteni. The main access routes to the escarpment are via the Hlatimba, Mohlesi, Nhlangeni and Manguan passes. The **Nhlangeni pass** leads to **Thaba Ntlenyana** ('The beautiful little mountain'), at 3,482 metres (11,317 feet) the highest point in southern Africa. As this peak is in Lesotho it is important to take your passport with you.

From this peak it is said that, on a clear day, it is possible to see as far as Mont-aux-Sources and Quachas Nek, 100 kilometres (63 miles) to the north-west and south-west respectively. It is also possible to hike from Giant's Hut at Giant's Castle along the contour path to **Sani Pass**. This is a five-to-six-day hike of about eighty kilometres (50 miles).

There are a number of caves in the Mkhomazi area open for overnight shelter which are within fairly easy reach of the forest station. **Cypress Cave** sleeps six to eight people, and takes about one-and-a-half hours to reach, and **McKenzie's Caves** (there are two which together sleep twenty-four) and **Sinclair's Shelter** (sleeps six) both take three to four hours of hiking

to reach. The **Sani Pass Hotel** is at the bottom of Sani Pass, one of South Africa's most spectacular passes and a traditional route for Basutho traders.

The hotel is an impressive complex, offering a nine-hole golf course, horse riding, trout fishing and a spa. The route was just a path until 1955, when the pass was built which connected Himeville to Mokhotlong in Lesotho. Only four-wheel-drive vehicles are allowed on this road of dizzying bends and dramatic scenery.

Ordinary cars can be driven to the South African border post fifteen kilometres (nine miles) beyond the hotel. From there the hike to the summit takes about three hours. The Lesotho border post and a mountaineer's lodge are situated there.

The Southern Area

The **Mzimkhulu area** is characterized by grasslands, sandstone formations, many rivers and streams and no forests. Apart from the extreme north and south, the escarpment is less spectacular there and there are fewer lofty peaks. It is also less popular than the areas to the north, and hence less crowded.

The wilderness area extends from Sani Pass in the north to Griqualand East in the south. **Cobham Forestry Station** is the best access point to footpaths, and has basic camping facilities. The main holiday area is **Garden Castle** where the **Drakensberg Garden Hotel** is found. This attractive family hotel is set on 348 hectares (860 acres) and has its own golf course and trout dam. **Giant's Cup** at 3,256 metres (10,582 feet) high is the most spectacular formation in the area.

About fourteen kilometres (nine miles) south is **Rhino Peak** (3,051 metres/9,916 feet), which juts out from the escarpment. The peak is reached by following a path from the forestry station at Garden Castle along the Mlambonja River. Along this path is **Pillar Cave**, which can accommodate twelve people. South of Rhino Peak are a number of peaks over 3,000 metres (9,750 feet) — **Wilson's**, **Mashai**, **Walker's**, **Thaba Ngwangwane**,

Thamatuwe and the **Devil's Knuckles**.

South of Garden Castle most of the footpaths are passes leading to the escarpment — Mzimude, Ngwangwane, Thamatuwe, and Knuckle passes. The Mzimkhulu area has many tarns or small lakes, with the area above Cobham Forestry Station being known as the 'Lake District'. Waterfowl, buck and other wildlife are drawn to these lakes, and otters abound in the rivers of this area.

A cave in this area, **Siphongweni Shelter**, has been described as having one of the best displays of rock art in the entire Drakensberg in terms of the number of paintings, their state of preservation and interesting themes. It is believed that the reason for this is that the remoteness of the shelter meant that it was one of the last to be used by the San or discovered by vandals. This area is also popular with trout fishermen. Fishing is good on the **Pholela River** at Cobham and around **Underberg** and **Himeville**, two towns in the foothills nearby.

Himeville has a nature reserve with camping facilities, two lakes and boats for hire, as well as a hotel which is especially welcoming to trout fishermen. There is also a hotel in Underberg and one at **Bushman's Nek**.

Coleford Nature Reserve, twenty-two kilometres (14 miles) south of Underberg is a 1,300-hectare (3,211-acre) area bisected by the Ngwangwana and Ndawana Rivers and is a popular fishing spot. There is accommodation in huts and cottages; other features include antelope, a game-viewing hide and walking and riding trails.

Pietermaritzburg and the KwaZulu-Natal Midlands

One of the most enduring images of Natal is of its rolling green hills, and this is especially true of Pietermaritzburg and the Midlands, which lie between the sub-tropical coastal region and the craggy peaks of the Drakensberg Mountain Range. It is a fertile region which, before the 1830s when the first white settlers arrived and the human population grew exponentially, saw vast herds of eland, hartebeest, gnu (wildebeest), zebra and springbok migrate across its plains each year from the highveld of the Transvaal and the then Orange Free State to graze on its sweet grasses.

San hunters followed the game, some migrating with the herds and others living permanently in the foothills of the Drakensberg. Apart from the San, the region, as with most of Natal, was occupied for an unknown period before about 1820 by various chiefdoms. These were small in area and population, the largest consisting of at most a few thousand people inhabiting an area of a few hundred square kilometres. These chiefdoms were not fixed and homesteads were frequently moved, their owners switching allegiance to another chief. The chiefdoms were linked by similar cultural practices and language, speaking various dialects of an Nguni language now known generally as Zulu.

Pietermaritzburg is a graceful city which, despite the fact that it is Natal's capital, is often overshadowed by its neighbour, Durban. It was founded by Voortrekkers in 1838, who named it after two of their leaders, Piet Retief and Gert Maritz. The city was the seat of government for their Republic of Natalia which lasted until 1843 when the British annexed the territory.

The British influence is strongly evident in the Victorian architecture of the houses and buildings which line the streets of the city centre and are dotted throughout its surrounding suburbs.

Pietermaritzburg has been called a 'city of flowers' because of its profusion of fine gardens and this, combined with the fact that the city centre is surrounded by the tree-covered hills of the 'green belt' adds to its generally relaxed ambience.

The city is a good base from which to explore the rest of the Midlands and appeals especially to outdoor and sporting enthusiasts, with its easy access to rivers,

Opposite: Pietermaritzburg City Hall, a fine example of Victorian architecture.

mountains, forests and open spaces. The Drakensberg Mountain Range is two hours away and offers spectacular terrain for climbing and walking.

There is good trout fishing in rivers throughout the Midlands and, around the city itself, it is possible to walk or cycle undisturbed in the green belt (Consult Publicity House on the corner of Commercial and Longmarket Streets for their map of green belt trails).

When to go

The Midlands climate is pleasant most of the year, although the weather in the summer months is likely to be extremely hot. This is a summer rainfall region, especially in the first half of the season, and the months January to March can be very hot with temperatures of 35–40 degrees Celsius (95–104 degrees Fahrenheit). In winter the days are generally mild to warm, the nights crisp to cold (0 degrees Celsius or 32 degrees Fahrenheit).

Getting there

By road: The N3 highway which links Durban and Johannesburg runs past the city, although the old main road (Route 103) is more scenic. This road runs parallel to the N3 before becoming Route 615 near Frere. Greyhound and Translux coaches, listed in telephone directories, are available from Durban and Johannesburg. The terminus is in Longmarket Street next to Publicity House. Cheetah Coaches, which has an office in the Imperial Hotel, also travels to and from Durban airport and Durban central several times a day (tel: 0331-422673 or 420266).

By rail: Spoornet operates a passenger train service from Pietermaritzburg to most major centres. *By air:* Pietermaritzburg has an airport with daily flights by Link Airways to and from Johannesburg.

To explore the Midlands it is advisable to hire a car, for which there are facilities in Pietermaritzburg and other major cities.

Where to stay

Pietermaritzburg and the Midlands have their share of fine hotels. A number of farms and private homes also provide bed and breakfast throughout the Midlands. Good chalet, lodge and caravan/camping facilities are also available.

Sightseeing in Pietermaritzburg

Publicity House is a good place to start your tour of the city, for a sizeable chunk of its history is contained in this building's immediate vicinity. Here you should collect a copy of the Publicity Association's guide to the city's town trails along with your green belt map. The city is justifiably proud of its red-bricked Victorian buildings. Publicity House itself is a fine example, built in 1884 to house the Borough Police. To the right towards Church Street is the **City Hall**. This was completed in 1900 on the site of the old Voortrekker Raadsaal (meeting hall), and according to Ripley's *Believe it or Not* it is the largest all-brick building in the southern hemisphere. The City Hall also houses one of the largest organs south of the equator. Two blocks away from the City Hall on the corner of Pietermaritz Street and Commercial Road is the **Kine/Capital Towers complex** housing the **Capital Towers Hotel**, four cinemas, restaurants, bars and **The Club** nightclub. Directly across the road from the City Hall is the **Tatham Art Gallery**, in the renovated buildings of the Old Supreme Court. This elegant building is a superb setting for a fine art collection which includes works by European artists (Picasso, Degas, Renoir, Chagall, Henry Moore) and leading South African artists.

At the top of Church Street is the **Pietermaritzburg Station**, another lovely old red-brick building and the place where Mahatma Gandhi was bundled off a train in 1893 because of the colour of his skin. He spent a chilly night in the waiting room there, and later described this as the most important event in his life and the one which inspired him to follow a path of political activism involving non-violence.

St Peter's Church, now partly a museum, was John Colenso's cathedral in the late 19th century. Colenso, first bishop of Natal, was a controversial churchman who was tried for heresy after challenging a number of Anglican beliefs. He is buried in front of the church's altar.

Across Churchill Square is the **Voortrekker Museum**, once the original Church of the Vow. Piet Retief, one of the Voortrekkers after whom the city is named, was among a party of Boers murdered by the Zulu chief Dingaan in 1838. The Boer commando in Pietermaritzburg who avenged his death at the battle of Blood River made a vow to remember December 16 as a day of thanksgiving and to erect a church — which now houses the museum — if their mission was successful. Among the objects on display are an ox-wagon and an ironwood chair carved for Dingaan.

Continuing east from the Voortrekker Museum down Church Street, the ethnic flavour of the city changes. This is a colourful district where shops selling blankets, African 'muti' (medicine), curry spices and bright saris jostle for business. **Popatlall's**, a shop on the right towards the end of Church Street, is worth visiting for its exquisite saris and brass ornaments used by Hindus in prayer.

At the end of Church Street turn right into East Street where you will find the **Nizamia Madressa Islamic School** which features a pair of Islamic-style minarets and fascia over a colonnaded verandah. From East Street turn right into Longmarket Street to the **Sri Siva Soobramoniar** and **Marriamem Hindu temple**, established in 1898. An annual Hindu fire-walking festival is held on Good Friday. The temple is open to visitors on Sunday from 08:00 to 18:00 and Monday to Saturday from 07:00 to 18:00.

The city's warm climate treats plants extremely well. At the end of September each year the city holds the *Natal Witness* Garden Show, where the city's gardeners put on a fine display of exotic and indigenous plants. **Wylie Park** to the north of the city centre in Taunton Road, Wembley, has a fine display of a large variety of azaleas and indigenous plants.

Queen Elizabeth Park, eight kilometres (five miles) north-west of the city covers ninety-three hectares (230 acres) and provides a tranquil setting for the headquarters of the Natal Parks Board. Views of Pietermaritzburg from the park are spectacular and on view are animals including white rhinos and snakes and plants such as aloes and proteas.

Comrades Marathon House in Connaught Road, Scottsville, near Alexandra Park is a restored double-storey Victorian house used as the official headquarters of the Comrades Marathon. This ultra-marathon, run annually over the ninety kilometres (56 miles) between Durban and the city, is one of South Africa's premier road races. The race dates back to 1921, and the museum in the house contains memorabilia of its history.

Sightseeing in the Natal Midlands

South of Pietermaritzburg, the picturesque Route 56 takes you through the farming towns of Richmond and Ixopo. **Richmond** was founded by British settlers in 1850, and their history can be traced at the **Richmond, Byrne and District** museum on the corner of Chilley and Victoria Streets.

From Richmond, the road to **Eastwolds** offers stunning views of the **Umkomaas Valley** and the sandstone cliffs of **Hella Hella**. Twelve kilometres (almost eight miles) outside Ixopo off Route 56 is the **Buddhist Retreat Centre**. Situated on 125 hectares (309 acres), it overlooks one of the great valleys of the Umkomaas River system and offers pleasant walks in scenic surroundings.

Interesting features include a Zen garden and a giant statue of Buddha. It is a pleasant and extremely tranquil place to stop for lunch (vegetarian) or to stay overnight, although guests are asked to respect the centre's rules which include celibacy and no drugs or alcohol.

Ixopo is in the shadow of the southern Drakensberg and serves a dairy farming district. The Zulu word 'ixopo' is an onomatopoeic term which imitates the sound made by cattle squelching through a marsh. Alan Paton's famous novel C*ry, The Beloved Country* begins in this area.

Heading north out of Pietermaritzburg towards Greytown, Route 33 passes **Albert Falls Resort** and **Nature Reserve**, where the Mgeni River tumbles over the falls. The reserve, surrounding the 3,012-hectare (8,132-acre) dam above the falls, is home to a variety of game including oribi, blesbok,

Above: At the dramatic Howick Falls, the Mgeni River pluges a spectacular ninety-five metres (312 feet).

springbok, reedbuck and zebra. Boating and fishing are allowed on the dam.

Greytown is the principal centre of the rich timber-producing area of Umvoti county. During the Bambatha Rebellion of 1906 — a widespread resistance by Africans to the head tax imposed on them by the colonial authorities — Greytown was the centre of military operations. Bambatha, a chief who was one of the ringleaders of the rebellion, was eventually shot and killed and Dinizulu (son of Cetshwayo, king of the Zulus) was banished for life to the Transvaal. There is a hotel in the town and a museum. South of the town is the **Umvoti Vlei Nature Reserve**, a wetland reserve with an impressive array of waterfowl.

At **Muden** there are **orange wineries**. The **Mhlopeni Nature Reserve** at Muden is a conservation success story. Once a badly eroded valley, it has been rehabilitated by the South African Council for Conservation and Anti-Pollution and is used as a valuable educational facility. Features include Iron and Stone Age sites, Zulu kraals dating back to the South African War, and a

variety of game. Accommodation is available in huts and thatched huts.

Weenen ('place of weeping') is one of the oldest towns in Natal. It was established by the Voortrekkers in 1838, who named it to commemorate the deaths of Piet Retief's party at Bloukrans, and subsequent Zulu massacres at Boer laagers nearby. After the murders at Bloukrans, Dingaan gave the order to wipe out the rest of the Voortrekkers in Natal. Five Boer laagers were taken by surprise and altogether 443 people were slaughtered. Three other laagers managed to defend themselves successfully. The dead were buried in a common grave, and the **Bloukrans Monument**, which is signposted near the N3 between Estcourt and Colenso, was erected to honour them.

At Weenen there is also a small museum of Voortrekker relics and a nature reserve which is home to antelope, white rhino and giraffe.

Mooirivier ('beautiful river') lies in a rich stock and dairy farming area. Artists and crafts people living in the area have established the **Midlands Meander**, enabling the public to visit their studios to view (and buy) their works. Check with the Pietermaritzburg or Howick publicity associations for details.

The ruins of **Fort Nottingham**, built in 1856, lie fourteen kilometres (nine miles) from **Nottingham Road**. The fort was built to protect farmers in the area from San raiders, who descended from the Drakensberg to rustle cattle. At Nottingham Road there is a good **hotel** and a quaint **pub** which is a popular watering hole for locals.

Amid the gentle hills of this area there are still a few dramatic sights to be seen. At the **Howick Falls** near Howick the Mgeni River plunges a spectacular ninety-five metres (312 feet). In the days of horses and wagons, the top of the falls was the best place to ford the deep, swift Mgeni River. Even this spot was treacherous though, and many travellers were washed away.

The falls may be admired from a viewing point in the town, or one in the **Umgeni Valley Nature Reserve**, which is reached by a scenic route along the edge of the gorge. The viewing point can also be reached by walking through the reserve.

The reserve is owned by the Wildlife Society of Southern Africa and is used for educational purposes, although accommodation is available there. The **Karkloof Falls**, sixteen kilometres (ten miles) to the east, are 105 metres (341 feet) high.

Trout fishing

In 1890 an enterprising soul brought a few barrels of brown trout spawn to Natal from Scotland. The eggs were hatched at Balgowan, and the fingerlings placed in the Mooi River. Today trout fishing is popular in the Midlands and Drakensberg Rivers. There is a hatchery at the **Kamberg Nature Reserve**, west of Nottingham Road, and various other Parks Board hatcheries keep the rivers well stocked. The trout fishing season for high altitude areas (i.e., most rivers above the Mooi River) runs from 1 September to roughly the end of May. Fishing is permitted all year round in the lower regions and in dams. Temporary fishing licences for controlled areas (valid for eight days) may be obtained at the Parks Board offices or at King's Sports

Shop, Pietermaritz Street, Pietermaritzburg for a nominal fee.

Fishermen can either stay at any number of Parks Board resorts (contact the main office in Queen Elizabeth Park, Pietermaritzburg (tel: 0331-471981), self-catering, privately-owned cottages, or be catered for in the comfort of an upmarket lodge such as the **Trout Bungalow** in the foothills of the Drakensberg (tel: 0333-36417 or 031-286250).

Northern KwaZulu -Natal

This region is often overlooked by visitors, its attractions being fairly modest in comparison with the rest of this spectacular province. Here the undulating landscape of Natal flattens and is characterized by grassy plains interrupted by the odd solitary hill. The towns here — **Dundee**, **Newcastle**, **Ladysmith**, **Vryheid** — are mainly engaged in coal mining and industry. What northern Natal does offer visitors is a wealth of landmarks denoting the rich military history of the area. Here, bitter tensions between Boer, Briton and Zulu erupted in various battles and in the region of the boundary with Zululand, as the three groups struggled to establish a new balance of power.

The first and several subsequent battles of the South African (Anglo-Boer) War, where Britain forced its imperial will on the independent Boer republics of the Transvaal and Orange Free State, were fought on these soils. In the east the **Itala Game Reserve** and the **Ntendeka Wilderness Area** conserve some of the natural beauty of the region.

Getting there

Newcastle has a small airport, with daily flights between Johannesburg and Durban. The roads here are all secondary but tarred and in fairly good condition. There are car hire facilities in larger centres.

When to go

This region enjoys hot summers and mild to crisp winters. Apart from the high summer months of January, February and

March when the heat can be oppressive — and not ideal for tramping around battlefields — Northern Natal is an ideal place to visit all year round.

Where to go

The main towns in this area all have comfortable hotel accommodation. For details of chalet, lodge and caravan/ camping facilities contact Club Caraville Natal Experience, PO Box 139, Sarnia 3615 (tel: Durban 031 701-4156).

Sightseeing

Dundee is the focal point of a tour of northern KwaZulu-Natal battlefields The surrounding districts of this town are literally drenched in the blood of battles from several different wars. To the east lie the Zulu War battlefields of **Rorke's Drift**, **Isandhlwana** and **Ulundi**, discussed in the section on Zululand.

To the north-east is **Blood River**, where a small Boer commando of 470 men, intent on avenging the murder of Piet Retief's party by Dingaan, formed a laager with their ox-wagons, and faced down a Zulu attack. At the end of the day the Zulu force of some 12,000 men had been repulsed, leaving 3,000 dead on the banks of the river. It was said that the river ran red that day, and it was given the name it still carries.

Ladysmith, south-west of Dundee, is most famous for the 115-day siege it withstood from November 1899 to February 1900 during the Boer War. A furious battle occurred here between the Boers and the British in January 1900 with over 2,000 troops dying. The **Spioenkop Nature Reserve** near the battlefield has a dam, game park, chalets and a camping ground. For more information contact the Camp Superintendent, Spioenkop Public Resort, PO Box 140, Winterton, 3340. Phone: 036 - 488 1578

Ntendeka Wilderness Area and **Itala Game Reserve** are east and north-east of Vryheid respectively. Ntendeka covers 5,230 hectares (12,918 acres) of coastal and inland tropical forest and grassland, including the **Ngome Forest** where Cetshwayo hid at the end of the Zulu War. There is an impressive game population featuring wildebeest, giraffe, wart hog, white and black rhino, crocodile, cheetah and leopard. It is possible to walk along a wilderness trail in the reserve led by a game ranger. Participants sleep under canvas for three nights, experiencing life in the heart of the bush.

There is an established tourist route which covers the main sites of historical interest in the area. For details of the Battlefields Route, contact the Dundee, Ladysmith, Newcastle or Vryheid Publicity Associations. There is an good map available of the route, indicating the location of museums and thirty-six different military sites. Taped commentaries, which supplement your tour with information on the various sites (and added sound effects) are also available.

When the road from the north crosses the Great Escarpment at **Van Reenen's Pass**, travellers notice a change; the flat, dry landscape becomes greener and more dramatic, characterized by rolling hills and steep river valleys. This is the beginning of a journey into a land of excesses. Here plants seem to grow more willingly in the favourable climate, the Indian Ocean roars hungrily along its shores and the map is littered with the sites of dozens of bloody battles, from both past and present. For travellers 'more' is better; KwaZulu-Natal offers a wealth of scenic possibilities, from mountains to beaches, game parks to cities.

North and South Coast

The coastal region of Natal is the province's exotic fringe, where rivers come to a lazy end in lagoons before dribbling into the Indian Ocean. Plant life grows furiously, as if threatening to engulf the settlements which have been carved out of the dense bush. The area of the north and south coasts including Durban stretches from Port Edward in the south to the **Tugela River** in the north, a distance of some 257 kilometres (161 miles) of superb holiday country.

The warm Mozambique current offshore ensures very mild winters, while good summer rainfall and plenty of warmth are perfect conditions for luxuriant plant life.

Seasonal changes are minimal here, so that plants are evergreen. A large percentage of KwaZulu-Natal's 4,826 named plant species are found in the dense belt of indigenous bush which hugs the coastline (in some places two kilometres thick).

Rolling fields of sugar cane, which break up the indigenous vegetation and are especially prominent along the north coast to Stanger, are important to the national economy. They yield some twenty-million tons of cane a year, putting South Africa among the world's top five producers.

The south coast stretches from Port Edward to Durban, the north coast from Durban to the Tugela river. These are popular and reasonably well-established holiday areas so the coastline is marked with pockets of fairly intense development at places such as Margate, Amanzimtoti, Umhlanga, Richards Bay and especially Durban, interspersed with numerous small resort towns.

It is possible to have a quiet, un-disturbed holiday in one of these less developed areas, yet still be close to sophisticated pleasures. Most fish found in KwaZulu-Natal waters are migratory, and winter and spring are the months when great shoals move along the coast. In May maasbanker, shad, mackerel, kingfish and barracuda arrive. In June the sardines appear on the south coast pursued by scores of other fish. July to September sees shad and October offers salmon, garrick, galjoen, brass bream and sharks.

Visitors should be aware that the KwaZulu-Natal coastline is particularly dangerous, with seas which are often treacherous. Even on a calm day a sidewash or backwash can make swimming dangerous, and it is unwise to swim outside the demarcated areas, which are watched by lifesavers, on the various beaches. The possibility of being attacked by a shark, although remote, is also a good reason to swim only at protected beaches.

The South Coast

Travelling south along the N2 highway from Durban, the first resort area is **Amanzimtoti** twenty-five kilometres (16 miles) south. This town, with its scores of holiday apartments along the shoreline, receives tens of thousands of holiday-makers each year. Its attractions include beaches protected by shark nets and lifesavers, a lagoon where paddle boats can be hired and taken upstream for a picturesque trip past gardens and coastal bush, two eighteen-hole golf courses, a bird sanctuary and a small nature reserve, **Ilanda Wilds**, which the **Manzimtoti River** passes through.

Between Amanzimtoti and Umnini lies **Aliwal Shoal**, a reef with a minimum depth of only one-and-a-half fathoms (almost three metres, roughly nine feet). This reef has been the downfall of several ships and its wrecks attract many divers. The **Aliwal Cove** is a hotel and dive resort in the area which caters especially for divers wanting to explore this shoal (tel: 0323-31002). A lighthouse erected in 1905 at **Greenpoint** marks the reef. Greenpoint is also renowned internationally as a superb spot for surfing. Four kilometres (almost three miles) north of Scottburgh is **Crocworld**, where crocodiles can be viewed at close quarters. Crocworld also has a wildlife museum, a snake pit, a 'Zulu Village' and nature trails.

Just north-west of **Park Rynie** is the **Vernon Crookes Nature Reserve**, where numerous species of game can be seen on walks through coastal forest and grassland. Accommodation is available in rustic huts. Along this stretch of coast to Port Shepstone there are numerous small towns such as **Pennington**, **Ifafa Beach**, **Hibberdene**, **Banana Beach** and **Bendigo**, where a simple, tranquil seaside holiday can be enjoyed. There it is possible to enjoy uncrowded beaches while still being able to drive to the larger towns for shopping and entertainment. At the hamlet of **Southport** there is a charming restaurant called **Castaways** where the Italian owners serve delightful food, fresh fish and pasta, at reasonable prices (tel: 0391-83105).

Port Shepstone is situated at the mouth of the **Umzimkulu River**, which is navigable by small craft for about eight kilometres (five miles) upstream. The local

Above: The sun sets on a Kudu herd.

economy is centred around sugar, marble and limeworks, timber and subtropical fruits. There is a superb golf course there which is open to visitors. At Umtentweni the N2 swings inland away from the coast. About twenty-five kilometres (12 miles) inland along this road is a turnoff to the area's most striking feature, **Oribi Gorge**. This canyon, carved from layers of sandstone by the **Umzimkulu River**, is twenty-four kilometres (15 miles) long, five kilometres (three miles) wide and 366 metres (1,190 feet) deep.

Viewing points at **Hanging Rock**, **Fairacres Lake**, **Echo Valley**, **the Pulpit**, **Ola's Nose**, **Lehr's Falls**, **Baboon's Castle**, **Horseshoe Bend** and **Oribi Heads** offer some spectacular views. The gorge is set in the **Oribi Gorge Nature Reserve**, which covers 1,837 hectares (4,537 acres) of rugged countryside and is home to some forty species of mammals including baboons and antelope and nearly 270 species of birds. The reserve also offers walking trails, picnic sites, fishing spots (permits required), a hotel and a hutted camp run by the Natal Parks Board.

Between Port Shepstone and Margate the smaller towns of **Shelley Beach**, **St Michaels-on-Sea** and **Uvongo** are found. At Uvongo there is a twenty-three-metre waterfall on the Vungu River and the **Thure Lilliecrone park** above the falls. This twenty-eight-hectare (69-acre) park offers walks through unspoilt coastal forest where 100 different bird species have been sighted. **Margate** is the 'capital' of the lower south coast and the major holiday resort in this area. Among its attractions are an eighteen-hole golf course, bowling greens, shops, speciality restaurants, and an airport.

At **Ramsgate**, four kilometres (almost three miles) south, the **Mbezane Lagoon** is an excellent spot for windsurfing. Two pleasant restaurants offering good food there are the **Bistro** and the **Beefeater**. At **Southbroom** there is an excellent Italian Restaurant — **Trattoria la Terrazza** — which overlooks a tranquil lagoon.

Between Margate and Southbroom the **Riverbend Crocodile Farm** is home to a large assortment of crocodiles — visitors can see the beasts being fed on Sunday afternoons at 15:00.

The **Munster area** comprises a series of small beaches, bays and coves. Port Edward is the last stop before you reach the wide **Umtamvuna River**, which ends in a lagoon surrounded by mangrove swamps. **The Old Ferry Restaurant** is a pleasant place to take the whole family. Overlooking this peaceful town is **Tragedy Hill**, the site of a massacre of the family and followers of the early Natal pioneer Henry Francis Fynn. The killing was the result of a false rumour spread by a discontented Zulu at Port Natal, that the British intended to attack Dingaan's country. The settlers fled south with their possessions, but were attacked by Zulus who thought they were stealing Dingaan's cattle. When Dingaan discovered that the rumour had no substance, he had the man who had started it shot. In the **Umtamvuna Nature Reserve** near here are trees which are not found anywhere else in the world, including the *Syzigium pondoenis*, which was 'lost' for a hundred years. This reserve of forest and gorge is also home to more than 700 species of plant life (including thirty-five types of orchid), Peregrine falcons, crowned eagles and a breeding colony of Cape vultures. San rock paintings have been found in caves here.

The North Coast

There are two routes one can take along the north coast to the Tugela River — along the old north coast road or along the N2, which is closer to the coast. The former follows an old trading route through rolling green canefields. At **Mount Edgecombe** the Huletts Corporation has extensive sugar estates. There is also an interesting national monument there, the small **Ganesh Hindu Temple**, built in 1899.

The largest of the 'sugar towns' is **Tongaat**, where the headquarters of the Tongaat Sugar Group are found. These buildings are built in the Cape Dutch style and are furnished with antiques. Most sugar estates welcome visitors (tour arrangements should be made with the head office).

Stanger is built on the site of the principal kraal of Shaka, kwaDukuza ('the place of the lost person'), so named because of the capital's complex labyrinth of huts. It was here in September 1828 that Shaka was murdered by his two half-brothers, Dingaan and Mhlangana and a bodyguard, Mbopha. After the assassination, Dingaan had kwaDukuza burnt to the ground, and the town of Stanger later grew on the site. A monument erected in 1930 in the centre of town in a small memorial garden marks the spot where Shaka died. The **KwaZulu-Natal North Coast Museum** is in Gledhow Mill Street.

The N2 highway passes through several coastal resort towns. **Umhlanga** is only eighteen kilometres (eleven miles) from Durban and offers holiday-makers a pleasant mix of town and country, with its easy access to the open spaces and relatively uncrowded beaches. It has several fine hotels including the **five-star Beverly Hills** which is famed in South Africa for its luxury. Umhlanga also has excellent shopping and restaurant facilities and a fully protected beach. **Razzmatazz Restaurant** on Beach Road is an award-winning restaurant which dishes up exotic delicacies such as crocodile, hippo and cane rat (tel: (031) 561 5847).

The headquarters of the **KwaZulu-Natal Sharks Board**, which oversees the servicing of hundreds of shark nets along the KwaZulu-Natal coast is found here. Audio-visual presentations are regularly staged for visitors (booking advisable). The **Umhlanga Lagoon Nature Reserve** is a twenty-six-hectare (64-acre) enclosure of dune forest and lagoon, where many different types of bird gather, including the fish eagle and the crested guinea fowl. Antelope are also found there. A shell midden which is estimated to be some 1,400 years old is an interesting historical feature. Picnic sites and a nature trail are other features. Adjacent to this reserve is the larger, privately owned **Hawaan Bush**, which can be explored by arrangement with the Wildlife Society (tel: 031-213126).

Ballitoville, **Shaka's Rock** and **Salt**

Overleaf: Wilderness sunrise.

Above: Crocodiles are a major predator inhabiting many of South Africa's rivers.

Rock are smaller towns which offer attractive recreational facilities in a quieter setting.

The **Harold Johnson Nature Reserve** covers 104 hectares (257 acres) on the south bank of the Tugela River where several skirmishes between the British and Zulus during the Anglo-Zulu War took place. Relics include **Fort Pearson**, built in 1878 by the British when they were preparing to invade what was then Zululand, and the **Ultimatum Tree**, under which, in December 1878, the British presented an ultimatum to the Zulu delegation which made war inevitable. An interesting feature is the **Remedies and Rituals Trail**, which identifies trees used by both white settlers and Zulus for medication. (A booklet is available at the office).

Antelope, bushpig, vervet monkeys and various types of forest birds can be spotted along three self-guided trails which vary from two to seven kilometres (just over one mile to just over four miles). There are also camping and picnic facilities.

The Tugela ('Thukela') River lies between the north coast and Zululand. Its Zulu name — 'something that startles' — undoubtedly refers to the awesome barrier it presented to travellers before the days of a bridge. The **Lower Tugela Drift** was a hazardous crossing point when the water was low — during floods the river was impassable to travellers. The bridge which now spans it was named after John Ross, a boy of fifteen who, in 1827, walked the 900-kilometre (563-mile) return journey from Durban to Lourenço Marques (now Maputo) in the north to obtain medical supplies. The round trip took him forty days.

Zululand

Zululand stretches from the Tugela River to the Mozambique and Swaziland borders, deriving its name from colonial times.

Zululand is called Tongaland here after the Tonga people who have inhabited the area for hundreds of years. This area is far less developed and offers a 'wilder' holiday experience. Sixty million years ago, during the Cretaceous Period, all Tongaland was

Above: The Fish Eagle is fairly common near rivers and lakes.

under the sea. A legacy of this time is the salty, sandy soil, full of shells. Three **large lakes** are found along the coast — **St Lucia**, **Kosi Bay** and **Lake Sibaya**, which is a landlocked, entirely fresh body of water. These lake areas are all protected, and host an assortment of birds and other wildlife, including hundreds of crocodiles. Inland there are a number of impressive **game reserves,** including **Umfolozi** and **Hluhluwe**. Visitors should note that in the far north, from the St Lucia Complex upwards, malaria mosquitoes are prevalent and precautions should be taken.

History of the Zulu kingdom

Apart from its impressive game reserves, Zululand has a particularly rich (and bloody) history. In the early 1800s Zululand was home to some 800 tribes and clans of the Nguni group, which shared common cultural and linguistic features. The Zulus were but a minor part of this social landscape. Relations between clans — barring skirmishes and feuds here and there — had been relatively peaceful until the growing population began to compete for

land and other basic resources. With this competition came greater conflict; smaller clans were forced to enter into alliances with bigger neighbours and centralized systems of authority were formed.

This period also saw the rapid build up of armies. By the early 19th century three major groupings had emerged in what later became known as Zululand: the Ndwandwe under Zwide in the north, the Ngwane under Sobhuza in the far north and the Mthethwa under Dingiswayo in the south.

The Ngwane, forced by the Ndwandwe to flee to what later became Swaziland, defeated many small Sotho and Nguni groups there, thus building what became the Swazi nation. In the south, Dingiswayo was murdered by Zwide and the Mthethwa were driven across the Mfolozi River almost as far south as the Tugela. Dingiswayo's death left the way open for the rise of Shaka, a brilliant soldier and ruthless king whose legend was to acquire mythical proportions.

Shaka spent his early years as an outcast with his mother, the product of a brief alliance between his father, Senzangakona,

151

heir to the throne of the insignificant Zulu chiefdom, and mother Nandi, from the even tinier Langeni clan. When Nandi became pregnant, the Zulu elders at first joked that she had caught 'ushaka', a bug that delayed menstruation. When a baby boy was born, who Nandi named Shaka, the Zulus were forced to accept her and she became a chief's wife.

Things did not go well, however, and after the young Shaka had been blamed for causing the death of a sheep, mother and son were sent packing. They roamed the countryside, finally finding refuge with the Mthethwa. Dingiswayo was impressed with Shaka, and eventually made him a regimental commander. Shaka repaid him by sharing his military genius with him. It was Shaka who was responsible for replacing the throwing spear with the short stabbing spear, and developing brutally efficient new fighting tactics. Soldiers were ordered to remain celibate, so that they could concentrate on fighting, and were drilled mercilessly.

When his father died, Shaka returned to the Zulus and seized the chieftaincy from his half brother. He also assumed control of the small Zulu army.

When Dingiswayo was murdered in 1818 and Shaka assumed the mantle of leader of the Mthethwas, he added thousands of well-trained warriors to his already-feared Zulu army.

And so the bloody wars of the Mfecane began, where thousands of Nguni were either absorbed into the fledgling Zulu state or fled to other regions of southern Africa. Shaka's new kingdom united hundreds of diverse communities under the central authority of the king, but his reign was bloody and short. In 1828 he was murdered by his half-brother Dingaan and another brother. When Shaka first came to power he murdered anyone he considered a threat — except Dingaan, who kept a low profile until he could implement his own plans.

Dingaan was equally ruthless in removing opposition. When his attention turned to his half-brother Mpande, the latter moved his kraal from Mlambonqwenya, near present-day Eshowe, west to Gqikazi. Further tensions between the brothers led to Mpande and 17,000 followers fleeing south across the Tugela. He called on the Boers for assistance to invade Zululand and defeat Dingaan. The trekkers, delighted by this split in the Zulus, responded by proclaiming him 'governing prince of the emigrant Zulus' and assigning a 350-strong white commando to Mpande's invading force. In January 1840 Dingaan fled across the Pongola River to an uncertain fate.

Mpande was proclaimed king of the Zulus by Andries Pretorius and installed as ruler of a vassal state stretching from the Tugela to the Black Umfolozi. When the British annexed Natal soon afterwards, a jittery Mpande signed a treaty whereby the Zulu undertook to stay north of the Tugela and east of its tributary, the Buffalo. Mpande ruled this territory for thirty-two years without any major upheavals, although the British were called in by his son Cetshwayo to mediate in an dispute between himself and his brother as to who would succeed their father. The British ruled in Cetshwayo's favour, although they were to let him down in the future.

With the discovery of diamonds, southern Africa had become an attractive prize for Britain, which sought to consolidate its power in the region. By the end of the 1870s British administrators had decided to do away with an independent Zululand. In 1878 British troops were stationed along the Zululand border in three places and on December 11 Cetshwayo was given an ultimatum which in essence demanded the dismantling of fundamental features of Zulu society within twenty days — a task almost impossible to fulfil. In January 1879 three columns of British infantry, cavalry, artillery and supply wagons crossed the Zululand border and war began.

On 17 January 1879, 20,000 Zulus surprised and overwhelmed 1,200 British soldiers at Isandlwana, south of the present-day town of Nqutu, a decisive victory in an otherwise rather one-sided war. Superior firepower triumphed in the end, and after several horrific battles, including those at Rorke's Drift, Khambula and Gingindhlovu, the morale of Cetshwayo's men was broken.

More VCs, Britain's highest award for valour, were won at the Battle of Rorke's Drift than at any other military engagement. After these military reverses, Cetshwayo went into hiding and was finally captured in the Ngome Forest and sent as a prisoner to Cape Town. With its social and economic life severely disrupted by the war, the back of the Zulu kingdom had been broken. It was carved up into thirteen chiefdoms and finally annexed by the British in 1887.

When to go

Zululand enjoys the hot summers and warm, dry winters of the rest of the KwaZulu-Natal coast, with the exception that in Tongaland the summers tend to be exceptionally hot and humid. At this time mosquitoes are more prevalent, and game in the reserves is harder to see because of wetter conditions, which make it easier for animals to find water away from the main watering holes. Fishing is also not good in summer because rain causes rivers to discolour the sea. Avoid school holiday periods at the more popular resort such as **St Lucia** and **Sodwana**.

How to get there

It is essential to have your own transport in this area, as public transport is poor to non-existent. The N2 highway goes all the way to the Mozambique border, with subsidiary roads mostly either tar or gravel. Some of the most northern reserves are only accessible to four-wheel drives, however, so it is advisable to check on the state of the roads before planning your journey.

Where to stay

There are several luxury lodges in Zululand, as well as many different accommodation options in the region's state game parks and nature reserves.

Contact Bed and Breakfast (tel: (035) 550-0538) for details of accommodation in private homes and farms throughout Zululand.

Sightseeing

Once over the Tugela River bridge **Gingindlovu** beckons. In 1879 the British were victorious in a battle against the Zulus there while on their way to relieve Eshowe. The latter, some seventy-five kilometres (47 miles) north-west of the Tugela River mouth, was established in 1860 by the Zulu king Cetshwayo. The relief of **Eshowe** occurred after some 4,000 British troops had been besieged by Zulus for ten weeks in 1879. The British laager had been established as a base for an advance on the Zulu capital of Ulundi.

The British troops were evacuated and the Zulus burnt the structures they had abandoned. Military entrenchments and an old cemetery remain as relics of that time. At the end of the war the British selected Eshowe as their administrative capital and built a small fort there, which now houses the **Historical Museum**.

The town surrounds a forest known to the Zulus as 'Dlinza', or 'grave-like place of meditation'. In the centre is the **Bishop's Seat**, a clearing where a former bishop of Zululand conducted church services and where occasional services and nativity plays are still held. On the outskirts of town, the **Ocean View Game Park** houses numerous types of antelope and birds.

The **Entumeni Nature Reserve** is sixteen kilometres (ten miles) from Eshowe covering 393 hectares (971 acres) of mistbelt forest. Its attractions are a wide variety of birds, plants and insects.

On the road between Eshowe and Melmouth in the **Nkwaleni Valley** tourists can sample the traditional Zulu lifestyle at one of three different 'living museums'. The biggest of these centres is **Shakaland**, where guests are accommodated in a hotel or in a kraal of 120 beehive huts (with en-suite bathrooms). On offer are Zulu delicacies, dancing, praise singing and displays of the arts of spirit mediums (*sangomas*) and herbalists, as well as basket-weaving, pot-making and hut building. Offering similar attractions on a smaller scale are **Stewarts Far** and **Kwe-Bhekitunga**.

On the secondary road between Eshowe and Empangeni, twenty-seven kilometres (17 miles) from Eshowe is a monument marking the area of **Shaka's principal kraal**, which he named kwaBulawayo (place of the persecuted). This was

Above: A Zulu elder in an animal-skin suit.

apparently in reference to the poor treatment meted out to him by his father. In 1826 one of Shaka's generals, Mzilikazi, broke away from him, formed his own tribe, the Matabele ('the refugees') and established his own kraal called Bulawayo, now the site of the city of the same name in Zimbabwe. Near the site of Shaka's kraal is a tree called **Coward's Bush**, where he apparently tested the courage of those accused of cowardice in battle, killing those who flinched.

On Route 66 past Melmouth is **Ulundi**, once the **capital kraal of Cetshwayo**. Built in 1873 when he was still king, the entire kraal covered sixty hectares (148 acres) on the banks of the White Umfolozi. A few kilometres from the kraal, on 4 July 1879, the Zulus attacked the 5,000-strong advancing British force. The Zulu spears were no match for gunfire and 1,500 were killed. The British burnt the Ulundi kraal to the ground; the original fireplaces and floors, baked hard in the fire, can still be seen. There is a small cemetery for the fifteen British soldiers who died in the battle.

East of Babanango is the valley of the **Mkumbane River**, also known as Emakosini ('the graveyard of the kings') to the Zulu. Much revered by them, this valley is a graveyard for many of the early Zulu rulers. Dingaan built his royal kraal and capital there after he had murdered Shaka, calling it **Mgungundhlovu** ('the swallower of the elephant'), a reference to his successful elimination of the former king. The royal kraal was made up of many rows of round huts in two concentric circles, and up to 200,000 warriors were housed in over 2,000 huts. The entire structure covered an area of sixty hectares (148 acres). It was there at Mgungundhlovu that Dingaan received Afrikaner leader Piet Retief in November 1837 and again in February 1838, when he had him killed after signing a peace treaty. The grave of Piet Retief and his party is in a valley about a kilometre (just over half a mile) from the kraal. When Andries Pretorius reached the kraal after the Battle of Blood River, he found it had been abandoned and burnt to the ground. There are plaques there marking the spots of the Afrikaner graves, Dingaan's kraal,

Above: The Hluhluwe Game Reserve in KwaZulu-Natal features an impressive collection of birdlife.

the site of the signing of the ill-fated treaty and the graves of the Zulu kings.

Fourteen kilometres (almost nine miles) south-west of Nqutu is the battle site of **Isandlwana** and a small museum. Sixteen kilometres (ten miles) west of Isandlwana is **Rorke's Drift**, where a small British garrison of 130 men defended themselves against two Zulu regiments, which had disengaged themselves from the battle at Isandlwana to pursue fugitives. Four hundred Zulu and fifteen British soldiers died in the ensuing battle.

Mtunzini lies north-east of Gingindlovu at the mouth of the Umlalazi River. There is good fishing, boating and the 900-hectare (2,223-acre) **Umlalazi Nature Reserve**, made up of mangrove swamp and sand dune woodland. The reserve offers a trail, picnic spots, log cabins and a camping ground.

Richards Bay is a busy, relatively new, deep-water port which handles mainly bulk materials such as coal, phosphates and fertilizers, pig iron and granite. The coal terminal there is the world's largest, with an annual export capacity of forty-four million tons. Of interest to tourists are the **lagoon** of the **Mhlatuze River** which is a conservation area, the only officially approved safe bathing beach in Zululand and the **Kaffrarian Museum**. **Enseleni Nature Reserve** north-west of Empangeni is home to a variety of animal life, including birds, antelope, hippos and crocodiles. A five kilometre (just over three-mile) **Swamp Walk**, part of which is on a boardwalk, passes through water myrtle trees, mangroves, papyrus beds and a fig forest on the banks of the **Nseleni River**.

The **Windy Ridge Game Park** in the **Nseleni River Valley** some thirty kilometres (almost 19 miles) west of Empangeni stocks larger game, including white rhino, giraffe, leopard, kudu and crocodile. Accommodation is in huts. Other attractions include game-viewing roads and guided drives and walks.

The **St Lucia complex** is made up of a network of separate but closely interrelated ecological components, including river estuary, lake/lagoon, lily-covered pan, woodland, grassland, high dune and sea. The lake is the central feature of this reserve

Above: Dawn breaks over St Lucia Reserve

though, covering 36,000 hectares (88,920 acres), widest in the north where it stretches twenty kilometres (almost thirteen miles) across. The lake was formed sixty million years ago, when the ocean receded to leave a flatland retaining both salt and fresh water. The lake is mostly shallow (about one metre) and home to about 600 hippos, crocodiles and birds which are attracted by the fish, crustaceans and insects which it harbours. Great shoals of mullet, bream, grunter and salmon inhabit these waters, followed by sharks and gamefish, making it an angler's dream. The bird life is rich and varied, including a breeding colony of fish eagles, white pelicans, saddlebills, spoonbills and Caspian terns. A fine way to see this area is on foot. The Natal Parks Board (NPB) offers a **wilderness trail** between April and September which is led by a park ranger. Two nights are spent at the **Bhangazi base** camp next to **Bhangazi Lake** near **Cape Vidal**, and two nights are spent in the **wilderness area**. (For further details contact the NPB.)

St Lucia Village, situated at the mouth of the lake, caters for all the needs of visitors, from accommodation in hotels, self-contained units or campsites to shops, garages, recreational facilities and restaurants. The **Monzi Country Club** welcomes visitors and it is possible to join guided tours to Hluhluwe and neighbouring reserves there. The **mNandi Arts and Crafts Centre** in the main street is a good place to visit for curios. Near the village in the south is the **Crocodile Centre**.

St Lucia Park is a narrow strip of land — about one kilometre wide (just over half a mile) — running along the shores of the lake, covering about 12,500 hectares (30,875 acres) of reedbed, woodland and grassland. There it is possible to see a variety of animals including different types of antelope, bushpig and monkeys. In the park there are log cabins and camping facilities at **Mapelane resort camp** and a hutted camp at **Fanies Island**, eleven kilometres (seven miles) north of **Charters Creek**.

The **Cape Vidal Resort and State Forest** north-east of Lake St Lucia covers 12,000 hectares (29,640 acres) of sand dune forest and marshy grassland. A fine area for bird-watching and game-spotting — watch out for kudu, buffalo, waterbuck and the extremely rare black rhino. At Cape Vidal accommodation is available in log cabins and at the campsite. There is also an eight-bed bush camp open to the public for three months of the year.

South of the Cape Vidal area between the lake and the sea there are a number of other parks. **The Eastern Shores Nature Reserve** covers some 14,000 hectares (34,594 acres) where brown hyena, side-striped jackal and Africa's largest concentration of reedbuck roam. This area made headlines recently when plans were revealed for mining titanium there. The public outcry (over a million signatures were collected against the proposal) caused the plans to be shelved.

The **St Lucia and Maputaland Marine Reserves** extend over 88,000 hectares (217,360 acres), from Cape Vidal to the Mozambique border, stretching out six kilometres (three-and-a-half miles) offshore. Features include the world's southernmost offshore coral reefs, an abundance of game fish and turtle nests on the beaches in the south.

Above: South Africa's coral reefs have been compared to Australia's Great Barrier Reef and are popular with divers and snorkellers.

Dukuduku Forest Reserve is a 6,000-hectare (14,820-acre) expanse of woodland which offers a picnic ground and walking trails. The presence of a large number of insects, in particular butterflies, and the gaboon viper, seldom seen south of the Limpopo, are notable here.

Sodwana Bay is a popular spot for watersports enthusiasts and fishermen. The park covers 400 hectares (988 acres) of lake, marsh and forested sand-dune. Offshore coral reefs have been compared with Australia's Great Barrier Reef, and are popular with divers and snorkellers. Professional guided dives can be booked on arrival at Sodwana and diving equipment can be hired on site. Accommodation abounds in log cabins and chalets at the caravan/campsite, with more upmarket lodgings at the privately run **Sodwana Bay Lodge** on the shores of **Lake Shazibe**. There you can stay in self-contained chalets or time-share units, with the facilities of a central restaurant and pub, swimming pool and a dive pool. Diving and big-game fishing are specialities of the resort.

Just north and slightly inland of Sodwana Bay is **Lake Sibaya**, the country's largest freshwater lake. The clear, blue waters of this lake cover seventy square kilometres (almost 44 square miles) and are thirty metres (98 feet) deep. The lake is presumably fed by underground springs, for no rivers flow into it yet the level remains constant. For game spotters and bird-watchers there are hippo, crocodiles, reedbuck, side-striped jackal and over 250 species of birds. The lake and its surrounds are also a good spot for boating and walking. Accommodation there is in a 'wilderness camp' — with solar-powered hot water. On the coastal side of the headland which separates Sibaya from the sea is **Mabibi Camp**, offering very basic comforts. Caravans and two-wheel-drive vehicles are not recommended.

The **Kosi Bay Nature Reserve** nestles in the far north-eastern corner of Zululand. Its name is a bit of a misnomer, for Kosi is not a bay but a series of four lakes — **Nhlange**, **Mpungwini**, **Sifungwe** and **Amanzimnyama** — separated from the Indian Ocean by a barrier of forested sand-dunes and with only one outlet to the sea. The reserve covers 11,000 hectares (27,170 acres) of lakes and mangrove swamps. The world's largest marine turtle, the leather-back, as well as the smaller loggerhead, nest here. The leatherback can exceed a mass of 500 kilogrammes (1,100 pounds) and a length of two metres (six-and-a-half feet). Hippos, crocodiles, samango and vervet monkeys, antelope and bushpig are also found there.

Swimming is not recommended because of the presence of sharks, crocodiles and bilharzia. **KwaZulu-Natal Bureau of Natural Resources**, which administers the reserve, conducts overnight trails around the lake system with the services of trail guides. Because of the sandy roads four-wheel-drive vehicles are essential.

Slightly inland in this far northern area of Natal there are several impressive **game reserves**. **Hluhluwe** and **Umfolozi** were both proclaimed in 1897, which puts them among the country's oldest game sanctuaries. The Umfolozi covers 47,753 hectares (117,997 acres) of hilly and floodplain country between the Black and White Umfolozi Rivers. This area, which once teemed with game, suffered an ecological disaster when misguided authorities in 1921 tried to wipe out all the game in an attempt to eradicate the tsetse fly. Many thousands of animals were slaughtered before the powers that be came to their senses and began using chemical measures against the fly in 1945.

Today the reserve is a rare breeding ground for white rhino, which number some 1,000 and are often translocated to other reserves. A substantial number of the last surviving black rhino in the world are also found there, as well as a wide variety of other game including buffalo, giraffe, elephant, leopard, cheetah and lion. Accommodation is available in the reserve to suit different needs. There are also a number of trails available including a wilderness trail, where participants hike for three days through the bush in the company of a trail guide and game guard. Accommodation is in tents.

Hluhluwe Game Reserve, Umfolozi's nearest neighbour, covers a variety of terrains including misty mountain forest, grasslands and dense bush and is named after the Hluhluwe River which snakes through its territory (the name actually comes from the lianas or monkey ropes found in the forest). This 23,067-hectare (56,998-acre) reserve is home for many different animals including white and black rhino, elephant, giraffe, zebra, lion and cheetah. Other attractions include a luxury lodge, cottages and huts, walking and auto trails, game viewing guides, a Zulu village, a museum and a shop.

Mkuzi Game Reserve covers 35,000 hectares (86,450 acres) of grassland and forest to the east of the Lebombo Mountains. The **Mkuzi River** and its **Nsumu Pan** attract a large variety of birds including wild geese and duck, pink-backed pelican, fish eagle and squacco heron. Crocodiles lurk in its waters. Other game found there are white and black rhino, giraffe, blue wildebeest, kudu and eland. Thatched hides, trails, camp grounds, huts and bungalows add to Mkuzi's attractions.

Ndumu Game Reserve on the floodplain of the Pongola River offers sanctuary to a wealth of birds (over 461 species have been recorded there), as well as hippo and crocodile. Many East African birds can be sighted there at the southern limit of their travels, and water-birds especially flock to the many pans in the reserve.

Cottages, game-viewing roads and hides are other features. Next to Ndumu is the **Tembe Elephant Park**, covering 29,000 hectares (71,630 acres) of sand forest, woodland, grassland and swampland.

This reserve was proclaimed in 1983 to protect the last remaining herds of free-ranging elephant in South Africa. There are only the basic comforts on offer — accommodation is in safari-style tents — although ablution facilities are provided. The rough roads make a four-wheel-drive vehicle essential.

Opposite: Endangered white rhino.

Cape Province

The Eastern Cape

The Eastern Cape is a long block of territory bordered by the Indian Ocean, stretching from Port Edward at its most northerly point to Nature's Valley in the south. The south-eastern districts of this area are all too often overlooked by tourists in their haste to visit the country's better publicised scenic wonders. Yet it is a region rich in geographical diversity, ranging from the sub-tropical beaches of the Wild Coast and the temperate rainforests of the southern coastal plain, to the mountain grasslands of the southern Drakensberg and the dry scrublands of the eastern Karoo. It is also historically and culturally distinct from the rest of the country.

Whereas the Western Cape is associated principally with the Dutch settlement that goes back to the mid-17th century, the Eastern Cape is more particularly associated with British military conquest and settlement dating from the first quarter of the 19th century. For hundreds of years before either the Dutch or the British arrived on the scene, however, this was the home of the southern Nguni people whose various tribal groupings collectively came to be known as the Xhosa.

Between 1779 — when the Dutch settlers first appropriated Xhosa territory in this part of the country — and 1879, nine bloody frontier wars raged there. Two were fought between the Xhosa and the Dutch, and seven between the Xhosa and the British, who in 1820 imported 4,000 settlers from England to consolidate their stake in the land.

As a result of these wars, most of the Xhosa tribes were pushed back north-east of the Kei River, into territory annexed by the British as the Transkei native reserve and in recent decades became the quasi-independent republic of the same name.

Similarly, a portion of the area south-west of the Kei River, where some Xhosa tribes continued living after the frontier wars, eventually became the nominally independent state of Ciskei. In 1994 both these so-called independent states were re-incorporated into South Africa by the government of National Unity and decreed to be part of the Eastern Cape.

Because of the turbulent frontier past of this region, much that is of historical interest has to do with the British settlers and their clashes with the Xhosa.

A narrow strip of country traditionally known as **Border** lies between the former states of Transkei and Ciskei. It includes the port city of **East London** and towns of military origin, such as **King William's Town**, Stutterheim and Queenstown.

West of the former Ciskei is the area that was settled by the original 1820 settlers and their descendants. It includes the coastal city of Port Elizabeth, the university city of Grahamstown and the industrial centre of Uitenhage. At the coast it is the eastern gateway to the Garden Route.

The climate of the Eastern Cape is as varied as its topography. The warm Indian Ocean makes the beaches of the Wild Coast a perennial holiday attraction, whereas in southern Drakensberg, where there are several ski slopes, one may encounter snow at any time between March and September.

Getting there

Major modern airports at East London and Port Elizabeth are linked by several flights daily to Johannesburg, Durban and Cape Town and are little more than an hour's flying time from any of them.

Transkei Airways also operates flights in smaller passenger aircraft between Umtata , Johannesburg and Durban.

Luxury motor coach companies operate scheduled tours into the area from all the major cities as well as inter-city and scenic tours·within the region. You can, of course, get there by road from anywhere in South Africa.

The sequence of what follows is based on the assumption that you arrived in the

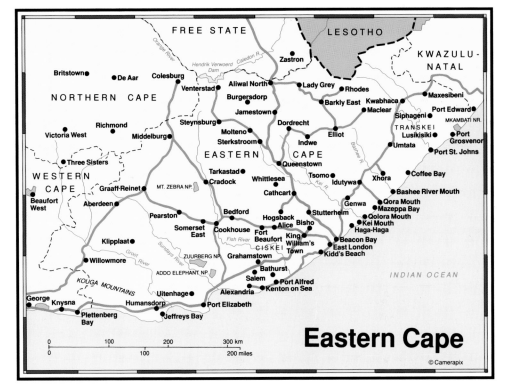

FREE STATE
LESOTHO
KWAZULU-NATAL

Orange River
Hendrik Verwoerd Dam
Caledon R.
Zastron

Britstown
De Aar
Colesburg
Venterstad
Aliwal North
Lady Grey
Rhodes
Maxesibeni

NORTHERN CAPE
Burgersdorp
Barkly East
Kwabhaca
Maclear
Port Edward

Jamestown
Siphageni
MKAMBATI NR.

Richmond
Steynsburg
Dordrecht
TRANSKEI
Lusikisiki
Port Grosvenor

Victoria West
Middelburg
Molteno
Sterkstroom
Elliot
Indwe
Umtata
Port St. Johns

EASTERN CAPE
Queenstown

Three Sisters
Tarkastad
Whittlesea
Tsomo
Idutywa
Xhora
Coffee Bay

WESTERN CAPE
Cradock
Cathcart
Bashee River Mouth

Graaff-Reinet
MT. ZEBRA NP.
Genwa
Qora Mouth
Mazeppa Bay

Beaufort West
Aberdeen
Bedford
Hogsback
Stutterheim
Qolora Mouth
Kei Mouth

Pearston
Alice
Bisho
Haga-Haga

Somerset East
Cookhouse
Fort Beaufort
King William's Town
Beacon Bay
East London

Klipplaat
Fish River
CISKEI
Kidd's Beach

Willowmore
Groot River
ZUURBERG NP.
Grahamstown

Sundays River
ADDO ELEPHANT NP.
Bathurst
Salem
Port Alfred

KOUGA MOUNTAINS
Uitenhage
Alexandria
Kenton on Sea

George
Knysna
Humansdorp
Port Elizabeth

Plettenberg Bay
Jeffreys Bay

INDIAN OCEAN

0 100 200 300 km
0 100 200 miles

Eastern Cape

© Camerapix

country by air at Johannesburg, have visited Durban, and that you are heading south on the N2, intending to take in the Garden Route on your way to Cape Town.

At the Umtamvuna River at Port Edward you cross the border of KwaZulu-Natal into the Eastern Cape.

The Wild Coast

Formerly, the Republic of Transkei, the inhabitants of this region are predominantly members of the southern Nguni tribes, generally known as Xhosa. They, in fact, belong to many southern Nguni tribes, whose leaders trace their lineages back to a common ancestor.

The Pondo occupy the coast and its hinterland from the Umtamvuna River to the Umtata River. South of them are the Bomvana and the Gcaleka. Inland are the Thembu and Mfengu in the south, and the Pondomise, Bhaca, Xesibe, Tlokwa, Hlubi and Kwena in the north.

The traditional tribal character of the country is still predominant as most of the

inhabitants are farmers. Outside the small towns, the land is held by communal tenure and allocated to tribesmen by local headmen. The pattern of occupation created is apparent from the road as you pass through the panorama of rounded grassy hills.

Clusters of thatched round huts made of clay, their doors facing the early morning sun, dot the green slopes of hills that are separated from one another by the deep, tortuous valleys of innumerable streams and rivers. The scene, at least at a distance, is idyllic, despite the rampant soil erosion.

Women, often dressed in the traditional earth-coloured cloth of the Xhosa and adorned with colourful beadwork, cultivate the staple maize and sorghum crops in the adjoining gardens, or gather in groups to do their washing on rocks beside streams. Others may be seen slowly climbing the winding paths to their kraals with pails of water balanced on their heads. For the skilled it is not as precarious as it looks.

Small boys herd the cattle, which are still regarded more as an indicator of wealth and status than a source of sustenance. Their fathers and uncles, if not away

Above: Elephant herds populate game reserves throughout the country.

working in the cities, may gather outside their huts to discuss matters of manly importance over gourds of opaque sorghum beer. This is a a way of life, that tourists are generally only able to glimpse from a distance.

The many small towns, such as Maxesibeni (formerly Mount Ayliff), Kwabhaca (Mount Frere), Siphageni (Flagstaff), Lusikisiki and Gcuwa (Butterworth) are former European enclaves in a tribal society. Even the former capital, Umtata, with its modern university, airport and Holiday Inn, is more a starting point than a destination for tourists.

About sixty kilometres (37 miles) north of Umtata, a turn-off from the N2 towards the coast will take you to one of the Eastern Cape's most celebrated inland beauty spots, the famed **Tsitsa Falls**, on one of the headwaters of the Mzimvubu River.

Most of the major tourist attractions are, however, anything from sixty to 120 kilometres (37 to 75 miles) from the N2 highway, on the celebrated **Wild Coast**, which extends for some 250 kilometres (155 miles) of pristine shoreline.

Poor roads have left great stretches of this coastline, with its wide golden beaches, rocky cliffs and small sandy coves, untamed and undeveloped.

There, it is nearly always warm and often hot and humid, with mean maximum and minimum temperatures of 24 and 15 degrees Celsius (75 and 59 degrees Farenheit). Dune forests crowd down almost to high-water mark.

Although the air is clear at sea level, the wind off the sea turns to mist about the hilltops, providing moisture for dense forests carpeted with lilies, irises and orchids. Above the forest the coastal grassland is splashed with the colours of flame lilies, crane flowers and red hot pokers.

Sepentine rivers wind between the grass and forest-clad hills, to end in sandbarred estuarine lagoons, their tidal reaches often fringed with mangroves.

At resorts situated at the mouths of several of these rivers — **Qolora Mouth**, **Mazeppa Bay**, **Bashee (Mbashe) River Mouth**, **Coffee Bay**, **Umtata Mouth** — there are family hotels, holiday cottages and facilities for campers and caravaners. These

Above: Hole-in-the-Wall, south of Coffee Bay.

serve as bases from which visitors can enjoy the sea and the sand, forest walks and the thrills of superb river, rock, surf and deep-sea game fishing.

At **Port Edward**, in the extreme north, there is the **Wild Coast Sun** a luxury resort complete with an eighteen-hole golf course.

From Umtata the most easily accessible and most popular of the resort towns are **Port St Johns** and **Coffee Bay**.

Port St Johns, at the mouth of the Mzimvubu, is named after a Portuguese galleon, *Sao Joao*, which was wrecked there in 1552. It is about 100 kilometres (60 miles) from Umtata and is reached by a narrow, winding road, the R61, which requires vigilance on the part of the driver. Midway you pass the **Rock of Execution**, rising some 240 metres (800 feet) beside the road, from the top of which offenders received a judicial shove in pre-colonial times.

The picturesque town of Port St Johns is situated on the right bank of the broad estuary, no more than a kilometre from a series of three sheltered beaches.

Four kilometres (two-and-a-half miles) above town you can cross the Mzimvubu

with your car on the **Pondoland Ferry**, and drive northward through forested and grassed hills to **Lusikisiki**, from where a road returns you to the coast at the **Mkambati Nature Reserve**.

The reserve is bounded in the south by the Msikaba River and in the north by the Mtentu River, both of which are lined with Mkambati (Pondo coconut) palms, which bear miniature coconuts, only two centimetres (less than an inch) in diameter and are found nowhere else on earth.

North of Port St Johns there are fewer beaches and more rugged cliffs rising directly out of the sea. On the road to Mkambati there are several turn-offs to places of interest. The first of them leads to the 146-metre (473-foot) **Magwa Falls**; the second to the **Mtihelo Falls** which plummet 160 metres (519 feet) into the ocean, and another to **Waterfall Bluff**, where cliffs dropping sheer into the ocean extend for thirteen kilometres (eight miles), and the Cathedral, a rock stack with tall rocky spires and a wave-cut arch, surrounded by swirling white water. Yet another leads to **Port Grosvenor**, where an ill-fated

Above: The 'Wild Coast' — 250 kilometres (155 miles) of pristine shoreline.

British East Indiaman, the *Grosvenor*, was wrecked near the mouth of the Msikaba River in 1782, reputedly taking to the bottom of the ocean a fortune in gold, diamonds and sapphires.

A different route to the coast from Umtata takes you to the resort at **Umtata Mouth**, and to the south of it **Coffee Bay**, so named because coffee beans from the cargo of a ship that was wrecked there many years ago took root on the shore. A little to the south of Coffee Bay is **Hole-in-the-Wall**, an offshore hill through which waves have made a great hole some four metres (over twelve feet) high.

Continuing south on the N2 highway from Umtata for some forty kilometres (25 miles) you come to the turn-off to Xhora (formerly Elliotdale) which will take you to the **Collywobbles**, a place of great scenic beauty, where the Mbashe (Bashee) River describe great loops through the landscape. Beyond Xhora the road leads to the holiday resort at **Mbashe Mouth** and the **Dwesa Nature Reserve**. Fifty kilometres (30 miles) or so along the N2 highway you come to the town of **Idutywa**, from where you can

drive down to the coast at **Qora Mouth**.

The next town you pass through is **Gcuwa** (formerly Butterworth), founded originally as a Wesleyan mission school in 1827. Places of interest to the sightseer there are the eighty-five-metre (275-foot) **Butterworth River Cascades** and the **Bawa Falls**, another place of execution in pre-colonial times. Roads to the coast from Gcuwa lead to the resorts at **Mazeppa Bay**, **Nxaxo Mouth** and **Qolora Mouth**.

Some fifty kilometres (30 miles) south of Gcuwa you cross the Great Kei River into the Border region.

The Sunshine Coast

South of the Kei to Beacon Bay, also known as Bonza Bay, on the outskirts of the city of East London, the Wild Coast is also known as the Sunshine Coast. Roads running east from the main road to East London lead to several resorts on this stretch of coast.

South of the Kei Bridge, about five kilometres (three miles) past the R63 right turn-off to Komga, a left turn-off, the R349, leads over a distance of some forty-five kilometres (28 miles) to the resorts at **Kei Mouth** and **Morgan's Bay**, both of which have caravan parks and offer a choice of hotels and holiday flats.

The coastal forest there is renowned for its rich bird-life and the beaches are popular with sun-lovers and rock anglers, while lagoons and estuaries provide peaceful waters for boating.

Sixteen kilometres (ten miles) further south on the N2 is the turn-off to **Haga-Haga**, thirty kilometres (18 miles) away at the mouth of a small river, where there is a fine stretch of beach and a hotel and holiday resort built on a shelf of rock that affords excellent fishing.

Thirteen kilometres (eight miles) further down the N2 is the turn-off to **Cintsa Mouth East** and **Cintsa Mouth West**, on opposite ends of a wide beach backed by a lagoon. Here too there are a hotel, holiday resort and caravan park and thatched holiday cabins for hire.

At **Gonubie Mouth**, twenty-five kilometres (15 miles) from East London, there are several hotels and holiday resorts that provide a beautiful base for enjoying the recreations for which this coast is famous. There is also an African medicinal plant garden and a small nature reserve that attracts large numbers of waterfowl.

Beacon Bay (Bonza Bay), bounded by the Nahoon and Quinera Rivers, is only a ten-minute drive from the centre of East London and a favourite weekend retreat for inhabitants of the city.

Kidd's Beach, some thirty-two kilometres (20 miles) south-west of East London, has a sandy bathing beach, rocky ledges from which anglers can catch a wide variety of fish, a tidal pool and a lagoon. There are several hotels and resorts, and sporting facilities include a golf course.

Continuing along the R72, the main coastal road between East London via Port Alfred and Port Elizabeth, you will find the resorts of the **Mpekweni Sun** and neighbouring, more luxurious **Fish River Sun Hotel**, **Country Club and Casino**. The Fish River Sun, one of the few five-star resorts in the area, is 130 kilometres (81 miles) from East London.

East London

South Africa's only river port of consequence, East London was established by the British at the mouth of the Buffalo River 150 years ago as a sheltered harbour for off-loading the troops and equipment they needed to wage frontier wars with the Xhosa.

The city is bounded in the south by the harbour estuary of the Buffalo. To the east of it are the suburbs of Beach and Quigney, which front on the Esplanade, running up the coast from Orient Beach in the south to the mouth of Blind River in the north.

If you arrive in East London by air, you will enter the city from the Schoeman Airport on **Settler's Way**, which crosses the Buffalo and turns east below **Queen's Park** before becoming **Fleet Street**.

The city centre lies north of Fleet Street on three major streets — Buffalo, Oxford and Cambridge — which cut across it at the Queen's Park end. Market Square is at the junction of Fleet and Oxford.

Queen's Park, thirty hectares (74 acres) of indigenous trees and shrubs interspersed with beds of exotic flowers, includes the **Queen's Park Zoo** and **Gately House**, a house museum preserved and furnished in the style of its original owner, John Gately, who was mayor in 1875.

Of interest in the city centre, on Oxford Street (five blocks up from Fleet Street), is the **City Hall**; its clock tower was built to commemorate Queen Victoria's Jubilee and its imposing marble staircase echoes the splendour of that bygone age. The old **Wool Exchange** on Cambridge Street, south of Fleet Street, recalls the importance of wool, which has been East London's principal export since 1837.

St Peter's church in High Street dates from the same period. The **railway station**, on the corner of Fleet Street and Station Street, a block from Cambridge Street, dates from 1877 and is one of East London's oldest buildings.

For an unusual shopping experience you might try the **Lock Street Jail** which is near the station. It used to be a jail; many of the stone cells have been converted into craft, antique and specialized goods shops, but several, including the old gallows chamber, have been preserved as they were when they served their original purpose.

If you plan to stay overnight in East London there is a range of three-star, two-star and one-star hotels as well as holiday flats to choose from.

On Oxford Street, just beyond the M5 intersection, are the 486-seat **Guild Theatre** and the **East London Museum**, probably the best natural history museum in South Africa. Included among the latter's exhibits are the only dodo egg in existence and the coelacanth which, at the time it was netted off East London in 1938, was thought to exist only in the form of fossils dating back fifty million years.

If you continue up Oxford Street and follow the road signs you will return to the N2, where a left turn will set you on the road to King William's Town. The road runs along the former Ciskei border for almost sixty kilometres (37 miles) before it gets there.

King William's Town

King William's Town, on the left bank of the Buffalo River, sixty kilometres (37 miles) from its mouth, is steeped in the turbulent history of the frontier.

In 1835, at the conclusion of the Sixth Frontier War, the town was established on the site of an old mission station by the British governor, Sir Benjamin d'Urban, who moved the frontier from the Fish River to the Kei River and tried to expel the Xhosa from the territory between them.

But the British Government refused to ratify the new border and, in December 1836, when the territory between the Fish and the Kei was returned to the Xhosa, King William's Town was abandoned.

Eleven years later, at the conclusion of the Seventh Frontier War, the then Governor, Sir Harry Smith, again shifted the border and re-established the town as a military centre and capital of British Kaffraria.

At the founding ceremony the Xhosa chiefs in the area were required to kiss Sir Harry's foot as a token of their absolute submission and penitence for their hostility to the British government.

King William's Town has ever since remained part of the Cape Province, and when in recent years the Ciskei was granted a form of independence, the border was drawn to exclude the town, which was the logical capital of the new state, from its territory. Instead, a new town, Bisho, was created alongside King William's Town to serve as the capital of the former independent state of Ciskei.

The **Kaffrarian Museum** in King William's Town houses one of the best collections of African mammals in the world, including a lion shot by Sir Percy FitzPatrick, author of the classic adventure novel *Jock of the Bushveld*.

The **South African Missionary Museum** contains exhibits pertaining to the history of Christian missions in southern Africa. The **Botanical Gardens** are on the left bank of the Buffalo River.

Sailing and watersports facilities are available at the **Rooikrans Dam**, two kilometres from the town, and there is excellent trout fishing on the **Maden Dam**, twenty-three kilometres (14 miles) away.

There are several small hotels and a municipal caravan park in the town. The **Amatola Sun**, a luxury hotel and casino, is five kilometres away from King William's Town, on the road to Bisho.

From the town there is a fine view of the distant **Amatola Mountains**. During the frontier wars the forested ravines of the Amatola were the stronghold from which the British repeatedly tried to dislodge the Xhosa, believing there could be no lasting peace if they did not.

Unless you are in a hurry and wish to proceed directly to Grahamstown on the N2, you may decide to explore the Border region and even the north-east Cape which lies beyond it.

The Border countryside north of King William's town is renowned for its natural beauty. The mountain ranges are covered with indigenous forests and grasslands threaded with streams and rivers that plunge into deep pools over waterfalls that cascade through fern-shaded gorges.

Stutterheim

Some forty kilometres (25 miles) north of King Williams's Town, the timber centre of Stutterheim lies on the Kabousie River at the foot of the eastern slopes of the Amatola. The first **Berlin Mission Station** in the Border region was established there in 1836, and the town was founded in 1857 by soldiers of the British-German Legion.

The grave of Sandile, the Xhosa chief who was the principal adversary of the British in the Eighth Frontier War, is six kilometres (four miles) south of the town.

Of historical interest there is the **Bethel Mission**, built in 1865 on the site of the original mission station.

The river provides excellent boating, fishing and swimming, and there are numerous signposted hikes in the adjoining mountains. Hotels and a caravan park offer a variety of accommodation.

Cathcart

Cathcart, forty-eight kilometres (30 miles) north-west of Stutterheim through the fringes of the **Kologha Forest Reserve**, lies in a sheep farming district.

There you may visit the **Powder Magazine**, built during the Ninth Frontier War, and the **Cathcart Museum**, in which the atmosphere of a rural shop a century ago has been recreated. There are watersports and angling on the nearby **Sam Meyer Dam**.

Hogsback

Should you wish to experience more of the Amatola, you might consider taking the R345 from Cathcart, which runs south-west for some forty kilometres (25 miles) through the most rugged part of the range, to Hogsback. Situated on a spur at the western end of the Amatola, Hogsback is the ideal spot for a quiet holiday where you can fill your lungs with bracing mountain air amid splendid mountain and woodland scenery.

The little village gets its name from the three mountain peaks that together resemble the bristled back of a wild hog.

Hotels and holiday cabins set the mood for visitors seeking the quiet pleasures of leisurely walks and there are breathtaking views.

Queenstown

Queenstown, fifty-eight kilometres (36 miles) north-west of Cathcart, was founded in 1853 to provide for the defence of the north-western left flank of the border. Of cultural interest are the **Queenstown and Frontier Museum** in Shepstone Street, and the **Municipal Art Gallery** in Ebden Street.

Hobbyists should find something of interest to them at the **Queenstown Collectors' Museum**, in Reservoir Road, and in the **Abbot Collection** of old telephones, reputedly the largest in the country.

Outdoor diversions are provided at the **Bongola Dam** and the **L de Lange Game Reserve**. There are several two-star and one-star hotels and a caravan park.

Tarkastad

Beneath the **Martha** and **Mary Mountains**, sixty-four kilometres (40 miles) west of Queenstown, Tarkastad is the centre of a premier hunting area. Bushman painting sites in the area may be visited.

Jamestown

Jamestown lies on the **Stormsberg Plateau** about 100 kilometres (62 miles) north of Queenstown on the direct (R30) route to Aliwal North. About midway between Queenstown and Jamestown the road ascends to the 1,800-metre (3,560-feet) plateau by way of the **Penhoek Pass**.

There is a small museum in the village. A caravan park is the only accommodation for visitors.

Above: Prehistoric 'Bushman' rock art.

Steynsburg

Continue westward from Molteno on the R56 for forty-six kilometres (28 miles) to Steynsburg. The town has a small museum, a hotel and a caravan park.

The only point of interest is at **Teebus Hill**, some twenty kilometres (twelve miles) from the town where you will be able to see the outlet of the **Orange-Fish irrigation tunnel**. Five metres (16.4 feet) in diameter and eighty-three kilometres (52 miles) long, it is reputed to be the longest continuous irrigation tunnel in the world.

Venterstad

The entrance to the irrigation tunnel is near Venterstad, sixty-five kilometres (40 miles) north of Steynsburg on the R390.

Accommodation is provided by holiday chalets and two hotels.

Oviston

A few kilometres from Venterstad is Oviston, on the southern shore of the **Gariep Dam**. The dam, the largest of several on the Orange River, is 100 kilometres (62 miles) long and fifteen kilometres (nine miles) wide at its broadest point. There are facilities for watersports, picnicking, camping and caravaning, and there is a small nature reserve.

Burgersdorp

Burgersdorp, the oldest town in this part of the country, is a little over sixty kilometres (37 miles) east of Venterstad on the R58.

Several national monuments include a **Boer War blockhouse** and the **Language Monument**, which was erected in 1893 to commemorate the introduction of Dutch as an official language in the old Cape Parliament. A 428-hectare (1,057-acre) game reserve adjoins the town. There is a hotel and one caravan park.

Sterkstroom

If you leave the R30 about forty kilometres (34 miles) north of Queenstown and take the R397, you reach Sterkstroom sixteen kilometres (ten miles) further on.

There is a small museum in the village and there are hiking trails and game viewing opportunities in the nearby **Koos Ras Nature Reserve**. There is also good trophy hunting in the area.

There is accommodation in the single hotel or municipal bungalows.

Molteno

Beyond Sterkstroom, the R397 climbs the Boesmanhoek Pass to Molteno, twenty-six kilometres (16 miles) away on the Stormberg Plateau. The **Molteno Museum** has fine collections of old firearms and early photographs.

There are two hotels and one caravan park.

Above: Khoikhoi cave painting.

Aliwal-North

Founded in 1849, three years after Burgersdorp, Aliwal-North lies fifty-eight kilometres (36 miles) to the north-east, on the southern bank of the Orange River.

The town is famed for its **hot springs**, which have been developed into a spa. Of historical interest are a **blockhouse** and **garden of remembrance** for British and colonial soldiers who fell in the Boer War. There is a museum, and a number of buildings dating from the last century have been preserved for posterity. The **Buffelspruit Nature Reserve**, which adjoins the town, maintains breeding populations of antelope indigenous to the area.

There are several hotels, and alternative accommodation is provided in holiday flats and chalets.

Lady Grey

Lady Grey, in the **Witteberg Mountains**, is fifty-three kilometres (33 miles) east of Aliwal-North on the R58.

A small nature reserve surrounds a dam that is stocked with trout. There is a hotel and a boarding house.

Barkly East

At an altitude of almost 2,000 metres (6,500 feet) in the southern Drakensberg, seventy-four kilometres (46 miles) south-east of Lady Grey, Barkly East is one of the highest towns in South Africa.

The cave sandstone of the Karoo geological system that occurs in the surrounding mountains at this elevation allowed for the formation of many caves, many of which contain fine examples of San rock art. There is a museum in the town, and the cemetery has the distinction of being the burial place of Lord Kitchener's war horse.

The rivers and streams in the vicinity were stocked many years ago and teem with wild trout. The vegetation is the natural habitat of the grey wing francolin (partridge). A wild trout and partridge festival in April each year draws fly-fishermen and shotgunners from all over the country. During the winter months, skiers are attracted to the fine ski slopes in the area, including those on the 3,000-metre (9,840-foot) **Ben McDui peak**, the highest mountain in the province.

A hotel, a caravan park and guest farms provide accommodation.

Rhodes

The little village of Rhodes, sixty kilometres (37 miles) from Barkly East, offers all the outdoor attractions of the larger town, but with a greater sense of isolation from the rat race. There is a hotel in the village and holiday flats are available nearby in an old building that was originally designed as a school by the renowned Cape architect Sir Herbert Baker.

Elliot

In a rugged mountain landscape, sixty-four kilometres (40 miles) south-east of Barkly East, Elliot is another place to view San paintings. Interesting rock formations in the area are the **Gatberg**, a peak that appears to have a hole bored through it, and **Giant's Castle**, a natural circle of huge rocks. The eighty-metre (262-foot) high Gilliecullem Falls are eighteen kilometres (eleven miles) from the town.

There are two hotels and one caravan park.

Maclear

Some of the best San painting sites in the country are in caves in the sheep farming district around Maclear, about seventy-five kilometres (46 miles) north-east of Elliot. Also to be seen in the district are the footprints left by dinosaurs millions of years ago.

There are two hotels and one caravan park.

Dordrecht

Westward from Elliot the R56 takes you, by way of Indwe, to Dordrecht, a distance of 106 kilometres (66 miles).

There are some interesting San rock paintings in caves in the area. A hotel and a caravan park provide places to stay overnight in the town.

From Dordrecht you can return on the R392 to Queenstown, seventy-two kilometres (45 miles) away.

Instead of retracing your route all the way from Queenstown to King William's Town, there are several alternative ways of reaching Grahamstown through the former Republic of Ciskei. The Republic consisted of Xhosa territory originally annexed by the British in the 1800s and granted independence by South Africa in 1981.

Its borders were drawn partly by history and partly by the prevailing territorial claims of others. On its south-western side it was separated from the Albany district of Grahamstown by the Great Fish River. Its north-east frontier with the Border region was more arbitrarily defined.

The system of roads was laid out long before Ciskei became independent and so does not form a separate internal grid. The roads that criss-cross the territory are for the most part routes between Cape towns lying on either side of the small state.

This area is unlikely to be your final destination, and you will be passing through it on one of these routes.

When travelling directly from King William's Town to Grahamstown, a distance of 120 kilometres (75 miles) on the N2, you cross Ciskei at one of its former broader points. You enter just outside King William's Town and exit some seventy kilometres (43 miles) further on where the road crosses the Great Fish River at Hunt's Drift.

A little over fifty kilometres (31 miles) from King William's Town you pass through **Peddie**, the only village of any size on this route. During the Frontier Wars British troops were stationed there to defend the Mfengu (Fingoes), an emigrant tribe from Natal who allied themselves to the British in the struggle against the Xhosa. The remnants of the original **Fort Peddie** is the only feature of historical interest. There is a caravan park for overnight stays.

Another route across the former Ciskei is the R63 from King William's Town to Fort Beaufort, a distance of a little under ninety kilometres (56 miles). Twenty-three kilometres (14 miles) before Fort Beaufort the road passes through the town of **Alice**, where the Lovedale mission station was founded by the Scottish Missionary Society in 1824.

Today it is a centre of learning, boasting two academic institutions of historical importance, **Lovedale College** and the **University of Fort Hare**, where many of southern Africa's black leaders received their higher education.

The **Tsorwana Game Reserve** in the far north of the region may be reached by means of secondary roads that link the R344 south-east of Tarkastad and the R67 south of Queenstown.

Above: The town of Grahamstown was established as a military headquarters in 1812 on an old farm.

At Whittlesea the R67 joins the R351. It crosses the Winterberg Mountains at an altitude of 1,612 metres (5,290 feet), and then descends, following the border for sixteen kilometres (ten miles), through the Katberg Pass, completed in 1864.

At the foot of the pass it rejoins the R67, which continues southward along the border for another thirty-six kilometres (22 miles) to Fort Beaufort.

From Fort Beaufort the distance to Grahamstown on the R67 is seventy-one kilometres (44 miles).

Grahamstown

Grahamstown is the cultural heart of the Eastern Cape. Indeed, it is arguably the cultural epicentre of English-speaking South Africa.

Where other cities in the south-east of the country rely for their appeal on their proximity to recreational facilities or their commercial and industrial importance, Grahamstown is principally a city of educational institutions, churches, museums and memorials to the settlement of English-speakers in this part of Africa.

It is pre-eminently a university city, deriving much of its character and sense of cultural continuity from the presence of **Rhodes University**, one of the country's leading English-language academic institutions.

However, the origins of the town were military. It was founded in 1812 on the site of an abandoned farm to be the head-quarters for a series of forts established to defend the frontier with the Xhosa, then deemed by the British to be the Fish River. It was named after its founder, Colonel John Graham.

Grahamstown retained its military role for many years, but after the arrival of the 1820 settlers from Britain it rapidly developed into a market town.

Although in 1820 there were only twelve houses in the town, within ten years it had become the principal town of the Eastern Province, and in the Cape Colony as a whole it was second in importance only to Cape Town.

The natural beauty of its setting, among

green hills almost 550 metres (1,800 feet) above sea level, is matched by the feeling the people of Grahamstown have for their history and preserving their past.

Clusters of cottages built by early settlers — many of them skilled artisans in England before the recession that followed the Napoleonic wars forced them to emigrate — have been restored around **Artificers' Square** and in McDonald Street.

Visitors who find themselves in Grahamstown on Sunday are impressed by the exultation of church bells, which is not surprising, as there are some forty places of worship in this small city, several of them built before 1850.

In Grahamstown's quaintly triangular **Church Square**, the **Cathedral of St Michael and St George** includes some of the oldest examples of Anglican architecture south of the equator

Overlooking the city from the fifty-hectare (123-acre) **Wild Flower Reserve** on Gunfire Hill, is the **1820 Settlers Monument**. Completed in 1974 as a 'living' monument to the contribution to the country by English-speakers.

Today its facilities include a 900-seat theatre and a conference centre that can seat 450 delegates and ninety observers. It is also the headquarters from which the 1820 Settlers Foundation conducts cultural and educational projects.

The major undertaking of the foundation is the **National Festival of the Arts** — music, theatre, dance and art — held in the city for a week in July each year.

Also on **Gunfire Hill** named because for many years a cannon was fired there at noon each day — is **Fort Selwyn**. Built in 1836 as part of the frontier defences, the fort is now one of several buildings that make up the **Albany Museum**, the second oldest museum in South Africa, founded in 1855.

Also part of the Albany Museum are the Provost Prison, the Natural History Museum, the 1820 Settlers Memorial Museum and the Observatory Museum.

The **J L B Smith Institute of Ichthyology**, in Somerset Street, was originally a department of Rhodes University headed by Professor J L B Smith. In 1980 it became a separate cultural institution on the same basis as the National Museums. Although primarily a research institution, it has a small public display section, where two coelacanths are among the exhibits.

Rhodes University has its own museum, off Somerset Street. It is housed in what was formerly the private chapel of the Sisters of the Community of the Resurrection and is devoted to the history of the university and prominent persons connected with it.

Also associated with the university is the **National English Literary Museum**, in Beaufort Street, which grew out of a university project for the Study of English in Africa. The museum has a continually expanding collection of manuscripts by South African English writers and related material such as notebooks, letters, photographs and recordings. The museum's reference library and information retrieval service is available to researchers.

The literary museum also has a department of printing and publishing history, which is lodged in an old building in Anglo African Street.

Here they have reconstructed, complete with old Wharfdales printing press, the offices of Grahamstown's defunct *Eastern Star*, forerunner of the Johannesburg-based *Star*, which is currently South Africa's largest daily newspaper.

In 1837 when Dutch farmers in the Eastern Cape decided to free themselves from British rule by trekking into the interior — the so-called Great Trek — British settlers in Grahamstown presented them with a Bible as a token of their hope that they would remain friends.The incident is commemorated by the **Bible Monument**, also called the Friendship Monument, in Bedford Road.

Letters posted at the post box on the corner of Somerset and Worcester Streets — the oldest in South Africa — are franked with a special post mark.

Apart from the 1820 Wild Flower Reserve on Gunfire Hill, which includes the original **Botanical Garden** established in 1837, there are four nature reserves in the vicinity of Grahamstown.

There are caravan parks where campsites and chalets may be hired. Grahamstown has several bed-and-breakfast establishments and hotels, which include the sedate **Cathcart Arms** and the **Grand**, which offer accommodation in the old colonial style.

The comfort of these establishments make Grahamstown a good base from which to explore towns in the surrounding countryside. The R67 south-east of Grahamstown will take you to Bathurst and Port Alfred.

Bathurst

Bathurst, forty kilometres (26 miles) from Grahamstown, was founded in 1820 and named after the then British Secretary of the Colonies, Earl Bathurst. It was originally intended to be the magistracy for the region, but was superceded by Grahamstown. Bathurst was the centre from which the first 1820 settlers were dispatched to the land allocated to them.

A stone toposcope, inscribed with details of the settler parties, is on the summit of nearby Thornridge, which has an uninterrupted view of the countryside in all directions. It marks the point from which the settlers were directed to their future homes.

A **Powder Magazine**, with a domed ceiling, is all that remains of the military post built in 1821, but a water-driven wool mill built in the same year by Samuel Bradshaw, who was the first to spin wool in South Africa, has been kept in working order. Nearby **Horseshoe Bend Nature Reserve** provides breathtaking views of the bush-covered valley of the Kowie River.

Summerhill Farm, on the outskirts of the town, offers a range of farmyard experiences, bass fishing and a walk through a traditional Xhosa village. On the farm is the much-publicised sixteen-metre (52-foot) **Giant Pineapple** — an idea borrowed from Queensland — in which audio-visual programmes on pineapples are presented.

Port Alfred

Port Alfred, sixteen kilometres (ten miles) from Bathurst, was once a busy port for sailing ships at the mouth of the Kowie

River. It was founded in 1821 as Port Kowie and only given its present name in 1860, in honour of the then Duke of Edinburgh. Although closed to shipping in 1872 because of its treacherous currents, Port Alfred is still a harbour for seagoing yachts and fishing vessels at the mouth of the Kowie River, fifty-eight kilometres (36 miles) from Grahamstown.

In addition to the natural attraction of its golden beaches and warm blue sea, there is now also a marina that extends over five man-made islands.

The 200-hectare (494-acre) Kowie Nature Reserve, some eight kilometres (five miles) north of the town, is perhaps best seen from a boat on the river — a two-day canoe trail takes you twenty-one kilometres (13 miles) upstream — but there is also a hiking trail along the bank.

Several hotels, a guest farm, beach cottages, holiday apartments, caravan parks and camping sites cater for all accommodation preferences.

If the gaming tables add relish to your holiday pleasures, the nearest casino is only twenty-eight kilometres (17 miles) away across the Fish River at the **Fish River Sun Hotel, Country Club and Casino**.

Somewhat quieter, but equally endowed with beaches and rivers are the resorts **Kenton-on-Sea** and **Bushman's River Mouth**, respectively twenty-four and thirty-two kilometres (15 and 20 miles) down the coast from Port Alfred.

Alexandria

Alexandria is about thirty kilometres (19 miles) south-west of Kenton-on-Sea on the R72.

This small town, which boasts several beautifully restored houses, is the centre of a chicory, pineapple and dairy farming area.

On the boundary of the **Alexandria State Forest** is the grave of Nongqause, a young Xhosa girl who in 1856 claimed to be the medium through which ancestral spirits told the Xhosa that if they slaughtered all their cattle and destroyed their crops the dead heroes of the past would arise and drive the English into the sea.

In the following famine, 20,000 people died and 30,000 were forced to find work on white-owned farms to avoid starvation.

There are hiking trails and short forest walks in the Alexandria State Forest, and tours of the **chicory factory**, one of the largest in the world, can be arranged between November and May.

Salem

The village of Salem, twenty-nine kilometres (18 miles) from Alexandria and twenty-five kilometres (15 miles) from Grahamstown, has the charm of an English village, complete with a village green, on which cricket has been regularly played since 1844.

Fort Beaufort

Fort Beaufort is seventy-one kilometres (44 miles) north of Grahamstown on the R67. The original fort from which the town gets its name was built in 1822 to check Xhosa raids on colonial farmers living on the Koonap and Baviaans Rivers. Erected on a peninsula formed by a bend in the Kat River, with steep banks on either side, it was considered one of the most defensible military positions on the frontier.

The history of those turbulent times is reflected in the collections of the **Military History Museum**, housed in the old officer's mess building, and the **Fort Beaufort Historical Museum**.

The **Martello Tower**, preserved as a National Monument, was built to strengthen the town's defences in 1847, according to the design of towers built in England during the Napoleonic wars.

Today Fort Beaufort is the centre of the citrus-producing Kat River Valley.

Adelaide

Thirty-seven kilometres (23 miles) west of Fort Beaufort on the R63 you come to Adelaide, which is also rich in settler

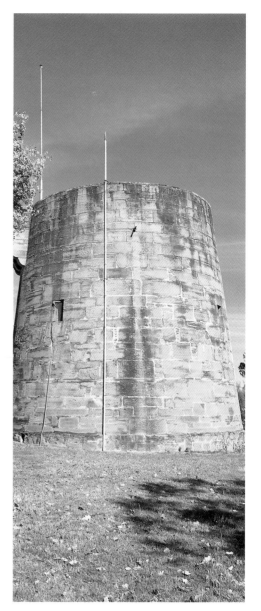

Above: The Martello Tower at Ford Beaufort.

history. Founded in 1849 on the banks of the Koonap River beneath the Winterberg Range, it was named in honour of the wife of King William IV of England.

Our Heritage Museum, which boasts one of the finest porcelain and china collections in the country, is lodged in the old Dutch Reformed Parsonage. There are three hotels and a caravan park.

Bedford

Bedford is about twenty kilometres (twelve miles) further westward on the R63. A hotel provides accommodation.

Of historical interest, near the town is a cave overlooking the Baviaans River in which a Dutch farmer Frederik Bezuidenhout was shot in 1815 by troops sent to arrest him on a relatively minor charge. The shooting sparked rebellion by Dutch farmers against British rule — the *Slagters Nek* Rebellion — for which five of them were publicly hanged.

Twenty kilometres (twelve miles) further on the R63 intersects with the R32, the trunk road running through the eastern Cape Midlands and eastern Karoo, from the N2 fifty-six kilometres outside Port Elizabeth, in the south, to the Orange River (after becoming the R57) in the north. The R63 merges with the R32 for twenty kilometres (twelve miles) until it gets to Cookhouse.

Cookhouse

Cookhouse is a cheese-making centre, with one hotel and a *Slagters Nek* Rebellion Memorial (see Bedford).

Somerset East

Somerset East, on the R63 some twenty-five kilometres (15 miles) west of Cookhouse, lies in the area, known as Agter Bruintjieshoogte at the time, where in 1770 the Dutch farmers expanding eastward first ran into conflict with the Xhosa.

The town was founded there on the banks of the Little Fish River in 1825. Exhibits at the local museum (a former parsonage that has been declared a national monument) illustrate the colourful history of the area.

Another of the town's dozen historical monuments is in the beautiful old house that accommodates the **Walter Battiss Art Gallery**, where there is a permanent exhibition of this remarkable South African artist's work. Other buildings preserved as national monuments are in Paulet Street. The nearby **Bosberg Mountain**, which assures the town of plentiful water, is also a nature reserve, offering spectacular views.

Visitors are catered for by hotels, holiday farms and a caravan park.

Plains of Camdeboo

West of the Bruintjieshoogte, some fourteen kilometres (nine miles) from Somerset East, the R63 begins crossing the northern part of the 'Plains of Camdeboo', made famous by Eve Palmer in her remarkable book of that name.

The *Camdeboo*, meaning 'green hollow' in the language of its early Khoikhoi inhabitants, is the part of the Great Karoo bounded by the **Sneeuberg Mountains** rising to 2,404 metres (7,887 feet) in the north and the Noorsveld in the south.

It continues westward for 110 kilometres (68 miles), through Pearston to Graaff-Reinet, and then another fifty-five kilometres (34 miles) on the R57 to Aberdeen, at the foot of the Camdeboo Mountains.

Pearston

Pearston, Eve Palmer's hometown, has a public museum in the old drostdy (magistrate's residence). **Cranmere Museum**, the private museum of the Palmer family, includes a collection of fossils and Stone Age implements gathered in that part of the Karoo.

Graaff-Reinet

Graaff-Reinet is situated in a loop of the Sundays River among the foothills of the Sneeuberg on the edge of the Camdeboo, and is justly described as the 'gem of the Karoo'.

Surrounded by the 15,000-hectare (37,065-acre) **Karoo Nature Reserve**, the flavour of its cultural past has also been preserved through the restoration as national monuments of some 220 of its old

Above: The klipspringer in the Karoo are uniquely adapted to rocky habitats.

buildings, many of them in the 1.6-kilometre-long (one-mile) **Cradock Street**. Named after Dutch Governor Cornelis Jacob van der Graaff and his wife, whose maiden name was Reinet, Graaff-Reinet was founded in 1886 as the magistracy and administrative centre for the eastern districts.

Built in 1806, the year the British annexed the Cape, the old magistrate's residence, or **Drostdy**, with the adjoining terraces of small houses formerly occupied by emancipated slaves, is now an elegant hotel complex.

Reinet Museum, in the old library building in Church Street, has displays of clothing dating back to 1800, San art, fossils of reptiles that inhabited the Karoo 200 million years ago, and fine 19th-century photographs.

A tarred road winding for fourteen kilometres (almost nine miles) through the mountainous surroundings of the Karoo Nature Reserve affords breathtaking views of the rugged **Valley of Desolation** and the Plains of Camdeboo.

There are four hotels, a guest house, holiday cottages and a caravan park.

Fifty-three kilometres (33 miles) north of Graaff-Reinet is the Karoo village of **Nieu-Bethesda**, which has received wide-spread attention because of its so-called **Owl House**, which was celebrated in a play and a film by South African dramatist Athol Fugard.

The Owl House Museum was the home of naïve artist Helen Martins, who filled its grounds with highly individualistic glass and concrete sculptures.

If you want to go from there to Cape Town by the shortest route, proceed southwest on the R57 for fifty-five kilometres (34 miles) to Aberdeen, and then west on the R61 for 155 kilometres (96 miles) to Beaufort West. From there it is 471 kilometres (293 miles) on the N1 to Cape Town.

However, if you return to Cookhouse and continue travelling northward on the R32 you will have a chance to see the towns of Cradock and Middelburg on your way to Colesburg, which is 632 kilometres (393 miles) from Johannesburg on the N1.

Above: Cape Mountain Zebra in Mountain Zebra National Park.

Cradock

Cradock, on the Great Fish River ninety kilometres (56 miles) north of Cookhouse, though founded initially in 1813 as a military outpost, is a town with literary associations.

It was the home of internationally acclaimed Olive Schreiner, author of the classic novel *The Story of an African Farm*, published in 1883. The single-storey house she lived in, in Cross Street, has been maintained as it was during her lifetime. Her collection of books is preserved in the town's library. Her grave is in the surrounding Sneeuberg Mountains.

The Dutch Reformed Church in Market Square was built in 1868 on the model of London's St Martins-in-the-Field.

The Great Fish River Museum is in High Street. Two hotels, a boarding house and holiday cottages provide accommodation for visitors.

The major natural attraction is the **Mountain Zebra National Park**, west of the town. Established in 1937 to provide a sanctuary for the endangered mountain zebra, it is also a refuge for black wildebeest, red hartebeest, blesbok, eland and ostrich. The Mountain Zebra Hiking Trail extends over three days and two nights.

Middelburg

Founded in 1852, Middelburg, 100 kilometres (62 miles) north of Cradock, is a trypical Karoo town at the centre of a sheep farming area. There are two museums, one of them in a farmhouse that was built in 1827. There are three hotels, a boarding-house, a guest farm and a caravan park.

Port Elizabeth

If instead of exploring the midlands you continue down the N2 from Grahamstown for 130 kilometres (80 miles) you will come to the major city of the region, Port Elizabeth (See Cities. Part 3).

Above: Jeffrey's Bay, just south-west of Port Elizabeth, is a surfer's dream.

Uitenhage

Uitenhage, an industrial and commercial town in the metropolitan area of Port Elizabeth, lies within sight of the **Winterhoek Mountains** on the banks of the Swartkops River thirty-eight kilometres (24 miles) from the coast.

Founded in 1804 to serve the local farming community, it is today a motor manufacturing and wool processing and weaving centre, with a population of almost a quarter of a million people.

Despite its industrial growth, Uitenhage has not lost sight of its rural origins, which are recalled in the many fine buildings that have been preserved, and in its parks and nature reserves. The Old Drostdy, built in 1809, now houses the town's **Africana Museum**.

Cuyler Manor, built in 1814, has been restored and furnished in the style of its time, and is used for demonstrations of traditional crafts, such as soap and candle making, spinning and weaving.

The old railway station, built in 1875, has been restored as a railway museum, where relics of the days of steam, including two vintage locomotives and old coaches, are on permanent display. Other buildings of historical interest include the old Dutch Reformed Church (1843), Victoria Tower (1898) and the Town Hall (1822).

The municipality's 396-hectare (979-acre) **Springs Nature Reserve**, six kilometres north of the town, may be explored on foot or horse-back, and offers accommodation in chalets and a caravan park.

Birdwatching sites owned by the municipality are **Willow Dam** and **Strelitzia Park**, where a wide range of waterfowl may be found. **Groendal Wilderness Area** covers 25,000 hectares

(61,775 acres) of pristine habitat. Parks within the municipal boundaries include Magennis Park and Cannon Hill Park.

Uitenhage is possibly the only town in the world that celebrates the birthday of a steam-engine. **'Little Bess'**, originally used in constructing Lake Mentz on the Sundays River, is one of only two of her kind left in the world. Her birthday is celebrated on the last weekend in July with a street procession and children's beauty contest.

The town has five hotels and a caravan park.

St Francis Bay

About twenty-three kilometres (14 miles) south-west of Uitenhage the R334 joins the N2, which continues westward following the coast of St Francis Bay at a distance of thirty-two kilometres (20 miles) to Humansdorp.

A few kilometres further on, the N2 crosses the Van Stadens River Gorge on a bridge 190 metres (623 feet) above the river. There is a 400-hectare (988-acre) **Wildflower Reserve** overlooking the gorge. Turn-offs towards the coast lead to a number of holiday resorts on St Francis Bay, the largest of which is Jeffrey's Bay.

Jeffrey's Bay

The history of the town dates back to 1852, when Joseph Jeffrey set up a trading store there. It became a village in 1852. Over the years Jeffrey's Bay became popular as a holiday place with farmers and towns-people from adjoining districts, but it remained essentially a fishing village. However, in the 1960s, surfers found that Jeffrey's Bay had the 'perfect wave'. Soon others discovered its unspoilt beach, ideal climate and beautiful mountain setting.

Today Jeffrey's Bay is a fully-fledged municipality, complete with schools, churches, shops, a cinema, a dance club, pool tables and video games and, more recently, a marina.

As a holiday venue it offers excellent surfing, safe swimming and sailing, and good angling for rock, surf and boat fishermen. The surfing spots are known by names which denote the types of waves they produce: Kitchen Windows, Tubes, Supertubes and Magnatubes.

Accommodation is available in a variety of different forms: hotels, bed-and-breakfast establishments, holiday flats and houses, chalets, rooms and caravan parks.

One of Jeffrey's Bay's attractions is the wide range of seashells (now somewhat depleted) that may be found on the beach. A **shell museum**, housed in the public library building, is reputed to be one of the finest in the world.

North of Jeffrey's Bay, the lagoon at the mouth of the Kabeljous River is a marvellous place for watching waterfowl and waders, including flamingoes.

The twenty-nine-hectare (72-acre) **Noorse-kloof** (the Noorsboom is a giant Euphorbia which grows to ten metres) **Nature Reserve** offers a three-kilometre forest walk.

South of Jeffrey's Bay is the **Marina Martinique**, which cultivates a Caribbean ambience. To the south of it is the Seekoei River estuary, with **Aston Bay** holiday resort on its northern shore.

Also on the northern shore, where the estuaries of the Seekoei and Swart Rivers meet, is the **Seekoei River Nature Reserve**.

Paradise Beach, on the southern shore, is one of the most beautiful resorts on this stretch of coast, and also one of the most restful. It provides safe bathing and sailing. The only accommodation is a caravan park.

The resorts at **St Francis Bay** and **Cape St Francis** offer beaches several kilometres long and excellent surfing, angling, sailing and other watersports. There are caravan parks and holiday flats and, at St Francis Bay, there is a two-star hotel.

Humansdorp

Ninety kilometres (56 miles) west of Port Elizabeth on the N2, Humansdorp provides a full range of different types of accommodation — hotel, motel, holiday flats and a caravan park — at the eastern gateway to the Garden Route.

The Garden Route and Little Karoo

The Garden Route, ranked among South Africa's most popular scenic attractions, is a 780-kilometres (485-mile) section of the N2 highway at the south-western corner of the country between Cape Town and Port Elizabeth.

Although sometimes the entire stretch of the highway between these two cities is spoken of as the Garden Route, more precisely it is the 250-kilometre (155-mile) stretch from the Great Brak River, just east of Mossel Bay, to Humansdorp, near Port Elizabeth.

The Garden Route may be approached from either end, but visitors from abroad who travel this route generally arrive in the country at Johannesburg, travel to the coast at Durban, and then head south and west on the N2 via Port Elizabeth to Cape Town. The western approach, at Mossel Bay, exactly mid-way between Port Elizabeth and Cape Town, is reached only after a 390-kilometre (242-mile) drive from Cape Town, whereas the eastern approach, at Humansdorp, is less than ninety kilometres (56 miles) from Port Elizabeth.

The Garden Route runs through the narrow coastal plain of the southern Cape, skirting the foothills of the majestic **Tsitsikamma** and **Outeniqua Mountain** ranges. It traverses the largest natural forest complex in South Africa, crossing yawning river gorges and passing peaceful lakes and tranquil estuarine lagoons. It is seldom more than a few kilometres from the coast, with its rocky wave-cut headlands and kilometre upon kilometre of unspoilt golden beaches.

Of all the natural wonders in which this region abounds, probably nothing is quite as breathtaking as the grandeur of the forests which, though interrupted by farmland and commercial plantations of exotics, extend all the way from Humansdorp to between George and Mossel Bay. These forests, the most southerly outlier of the great high-mountain forests of eastern Africa, derive their diversity and lushness of vegetation from year-round rainfall. Lying between the winter rainfall area of the Western Cape and the summer rainfall area that encompasses most of South Africa, the southern Cape is virtually without seasons.

Mild temperatures prevail throughout the year. Localized onshore breezes, running into the mountain barrier, deposit abundant moisture in the foothills regardless of season, while the low-lying coastal plain remains for the most part warm and dry.

Plettenberg Bay, the playground of the affluent, actually enjoys more hours of sunlight a year than sub-tropical Durban, yet in winter, snow on the highest peaks of the Outeniqua range is visible from the coast. Such seasonal changes as there may be are generally late in coming, and local people consider April and May, when the rest of the country is bracing itself for the onset of winter, to be the best, most peaceful months.

In historical times forest extended all the way from Humansdorp to Mossel Bay and covered thousands of square kilometres. Today, as a result of heavy exploitation, it has been reduced to no more than 70,000 hectares (173,000 acres).

The Dutch settlers at the Cape knew about the forests as early as 1668, but they were unable to exploit them because of the difficulties of transporting the timber over terrain that is deeply incised by many rivers and streams. In 1776, however, the first woodcutting post was established where later the town of George was founded, and Plettenberg Bay was developed as a port from which timber was shipped to Cape Town.

Closed to woodcutters since 1939, the state-owned forests are retained as a valuable asset in the treasure house of the country's natural heritage, a place of peace and wonderment, to be savoured by South Africans and visitors alike.

In sharp contrast with the lush greenery of the Garden Route, only a drive of an hour or so from George, in a broad valley behind the Outeniqua Mountains, you will find a very different world — the Little

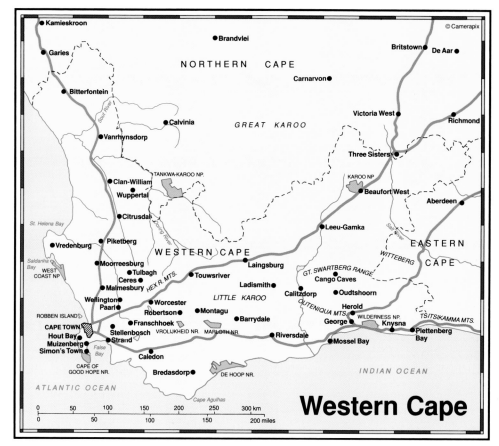

© Camerapix

Western Cape

NORTHERN CAPE

GREAT KAROO

WESTERN CAPE

LITTLE KAROO

EASTERN CAPE

ATLANTIC OCEAN

INDIAN OCEAN

| 0 | 50 | 100 | 150 | 200 | 250 | 300 km |
| 0 | 50 | | 100 | | 150 | 200 miles |

Kamieskroon
Garies
Bitterfontein
Brandvlei
Britstown
De Aar
Carnarvon
Victoria West
Richmond
Calvinia
Vanrhynsdorp
TANKWA-KAROO NP.
Three Sisters
KAROO NP.
Clan-William
Wuppertal
Beaufort West
Aberdeen
Citrusdal
Leeu-Gamka
St. Helena Bay
Piketberg
WITTEBERG
Vredenburg
Saldanha Bay
WEST COAST NP
Moorreesburg
Laingsburg
GT. SWARTBERG RANGE
Tulbagh
Cango Caves
Ceres
Touwsriver
Malmesbury
HEX R. MTS.
Ladismith
Calitzdorp
Oudtshoorn
Wellington
Herold
Paarl
Worcester
OUTENIQUA MTS.
George
WILDERNESS NP.
TSITSIKAMMA MTS.
ROBBEN ISLAND
Robertson
Montagu
Knysna
CAPE TOWN
Franschhoek
Barrydale
Plettenberg Bay
Hout Bay
Stellenbosch
VROLIJKHEID NR.
MARLOTH NR.
Riversdale
Muizenberg
Strand
False Bay
Mossel Bay
Simon's Town
Caledon
CAPE OF GOOD HOPE NR.
Bredasdorp
DE HOOP NR.
Cape Agulhas

Karoo, a name aptly derived from the Khoi word *karee*, meaning 'dry'. Although characterized by the harsher form of beauty that is associated with more arid landscapes, it is a world that in places enterprising farmers have rendered verdant, famed for its ostrich farms and one of the premier unenumerated wonders of the natural world — **the Cango Caves**, of which more later.

Getting there

As previously mentioned, the Garden Route may be entered by road from either end, from Port Elizabeth or Cape Town. But if you are on a flying visit to the country and need to get there fast, you will probably find it best to fly in to George on a scheduled flight from whichever major South African city you may be in.

You will be able to rent a car at George's modern airport, visit the attractions that take your fancy, and then jet off again to wherever you want to be next.

Sightseeing

Approaching the Garden Route via Port Elizabeth from the east, you enter the forest country soon after passing through Humansdorp. Unfortunately, many who travel this route miss the best scenery, because they stay on the new toll freeway constructed about ten years ago to meet the needs of the hasty. The secret here, if you want to get a good feel for the countryside, is to keep to the old road wherever possible.

The new freeway offers some spectacular views from bridges spanning the canyons of the **Bloukrans**, **Groot** and **Bobbejaans Rivers**. Indeed, from the 272-metre (892-foot) main arch of the Bloukrans bridge you gaze down into the amber waters of the river, foaming like beer, 216 metres (708 feet) below.

But much of the freeway runs through pine plantation, and where it does pass through indigenous forest the trees have usually been cut back to a distance from the

Above: Anglican Church in Plettenberg Bay. The town is the retreat of affluent South Africans during holiday periods.

road at which they fail to impress.

On the old road, some ninety kilometres (56 miles) from Humansdorp, you cross the **Storms River** over the Paul Sauer Bridge, which, though less impressive than some of the bridges that bear the freeway, was considered an amazing feat of engineering when it was completed in 1956. A single-span bridge over 200 metres (650 feet) long and spanning a thickly wooded ravine some 130 metres (426 feet) above the water, it was until a few years ago the highest bridge in southern Africa. The largest of four of its design in the world, it was made in two parts, and then lowered from either side to meet in the middle.

The **Bushworkers Museum** at the bridge restaurant, run by the National Parks Board, is worth a visit if you wish to add historical and scientific dimensions to your appreciation of the surrounding **Tsitsikamma** (a Khoi name denoting 'origin of waters') forest.

A few kilometres beyond the bridge there is a signposted turn-off on the right to the **Big Tree**, a giant yellowwood — taller than a ten-storey building, believed to be over 800 years old — at the heart of the 478-hectare (1,181-acre) **Tsitsikamma Forest National Park**.

Continuing westward on the old road for another five kilometres, you come to a turn-off to the left that leads to **Storms River Mouth**, where the offices of the Tsitsikamma National Park are situated. The coastal portion of the park extends for some seventy-five kilometres (47 miles) of wild coastline, from near Humansdorp in the east to Nature's Valley in the west.

Storms River Mouth is the start of the famed **Otter Trail,** a five-day hike down the coast to Nature's Valley, forty-five kilometres (28 miles) away. Unless you have booked well in advance, and set aside five days for the Otter Trail, you will have to be contented with short walks of which the most popular passes through indigenous forest to the river mouth which is spanned by a suspension footbridge.

Continuing westward across the plateau to Nature's Valley, the old road winds through the **Bloukrans Pass**, constructed

Above: The holiday village of Knysna is situated on the northern shore of a large lagoon at the mouth of the Knysna River.

over a century ago, which penetrates the forest with an intimacy that the official freeway route never has. For a distance of seven kilometres, the pass zigzags down 183 metres (600 feet) into the gorge of the Bloukrans River and then climbs back again to the plateau on the far side. On the western side of the gorge is the Bloukrans Forest Station, starting point of a scenic drive, the **Marine Drive**, which takes you to a lookout point from which there is a splendid view over forested hills and along the coast all the way to Plettenberg Bay. Two kilometres down the main road is a turn-off to the north that takes you on a scenic drive through the **Platbos forest**. Another seven kilometres brings you to the **Groot Rivier Pass**, where the road winds down to the river bed, a descent of 222 metres (730 feet), and then ascends again with many twists and turns to the plateau.

The tight loops and bends force you to drive slowly, and you become acutely aware of the forest crowding in on either side, the towering yellowwood trees festooned with old man's beard, and the tangled undergrowth laced with vines. **Nature's Valley**, a seaside settlement of holiday homes, is at the mouth of the Groot Rivier, on a small lagoon and three kilometres of pristine beach. About thirty kilometres (19 miles) further west is the **Keurbooms River** mouth, from which four kilometres of unbroken beach extend eastwards.

The river opens into a broad lagoon that parallels the coast for the next five kilometres and has its outlet to the sea nearer to the town of **Plettenberg Bay**. The lagoon is responsible for the name, Angra dos Alagoas (bay of lagoons), by which Portuguese navigators knew Plettenberg Bay. It was later known to the Dutch as Keurboom Rivier Baai, but in 1778 the Dutch Governor Joachim van Plettenberg officially named it after himself, lest history neglected otherwise to honour him.

Plettenberg Bay was originally a whaling station and afterwards a timber port, but today it is exclusively a pleasure resort. The old whaling station on Beacon Island, which is connected by a causeway, has been replaced by one of South Africa's best known luxury holiday hotels. There is a small, sheltered bathing beach in a cove at the entrance to the lagoon, within which there is excellent fishing. South of the town a long, curving beach extends for about three kilometres to the rocky **Robberg Peninsula**, another superb fishing spot.

As an executive playground, Plettenberg Bay has a Country Club with a championship golf course. Excellent communications, which include a small modern airport, are on hand for those who cannot 'get away from it all' to keep in touch with their interests in the outside world.

Knysna, on the northern shore of a large lagoon at the mouth of the Knysna River, was founded in 1804 by a man of mystery named George Rex, who came to the Cape in 1797 as Marshal of the High Court of the Admiralty, and was believed to be the illegitimate eldest son of the British King George III. Although research in recent years has tended to debunk rather than confirm the belief, many who are romantically inclined still cling to it. Even his descendants are reported to be divided on the issue. So in Knysna you may without knowing it rub shoulders with a pretender to the British throne. Knysna's dependence on the timber industry has in recent decades been overtaken by its importance as a tourist centre. Offshoots of the timber industry, for which Knysna is best known, are furniture making and boat building. The drowned estuary of the Knysna River which forms the sheet of water known as the 'lagoon' is as much an attraction for visitors as the adjoining forests. Its sheltered waters provide ideal conditions for swimming, boating and fishing.

At the narrow mouth of the lagoon, framed by the rocky promontories known as the **Heads,** the sea breaking on a submerged bar is always treacherous. Despite the use of local pilots, many fine ships ended on the rocks in the days when Knysna was a busy timber port. The western Head, which retains its original wild character, is a **private nature reserve** that may be visited only from the sea by arrangement with a charter cruise company. The road from the town to the eastern Head follows the shore, passing the causeway to **Leisure Isle**, a residential suburb, and there is another at the Head itself. The summit of the Head, reached by a footpath, offers the best views.

On the western side of the lagoon two roads lead to the coast, the first to **Brenton-on-Sea**, the second to **Buffalo Bay**, at the mouth of the Goukamma River in the **Goukamma Nature Reserve.**

The Rheenendal turn-off to the right, however, will take you to **Millwood**, the site of a ghost town that owes its origin to the short-lived excitement that attended the discovery of a few gold nuggets in a stream there in 1886. But the deposits were soon worked out, and some foundations are all that remain of what was briefly a town boasting seven hotels, twenty-five shops, three banks, three newspapers and forty mining syndicates.

To get there take the turn-off at Rheenendal to the Goudveld (goldfield) Forestry Station, a distance of under two kilometres to the entrance, from where you pass through nine scenic kilometres to get to the site of the old Millwood diggings, where there is now a forestry settlement. After the diggings were officially closed in 1924, one of the old diggers moved his wood-and-iron cottage to Knysna, where it is preserved as a museum.

From Rheenendal you can take the forest high road all the way to George. The way lies over a plateau some 250 metres (820 feet) above sea-level and is deeply incised by eight rivers, which are crossed by means of the Homtini, Karatara and Hoogekraal passes and the Seven Passes Road. But if you take this route you will miss the lake district and Wilderness.

If you return to the N2 and then continue westward for about seven kilometres (four miles) you will come to the first of the lakes, **Groenvlei**. Originally called Lake Pleasant, Groenvlei is the only freshwater lake of the five and offers some of the best blue-gill and black bass fishing in the country. Lying within the **Goukamma Nature Reserve**, it is immensely popular with birdwatchers. A flock of swans introduced there in 1961 are direct descendants of swans that in the 1880s escaped from a ship taking them to

Australia and came ashore during a storm. According to local legend, beautiful water maids live in the green waters of the lake and can be heard singing as they float on the surface on moonlit nights.

Three kilometres west of Groenvlei you come to the town of **Sedgefield**, on a lagoon that links the largest of the lakes, **Swartvlei**, with the sea, and after another three kilometres the road crosses a two-kilometre section of Swartvlei. Thereafter the road runs south of the linked lakes **Rondevlei**, **Bo Langvlei** and **Onder Langvlei**, which is connected through marshland by the Serpentine to the tidal portion of the Touws River at Ebb and Flow at the head of the Wilderness lagoon.

Wilderness is traditionally a place for honeymooners. The romantic association goes back to the farmer who originally bought the land, and named it to meet the condition set by a young woman who agreed to marry him only if he took her away from civilization 'to live in the wilderness'.

A few kilometres beyond Wilderness the road crosses the estuary of the **Kaaimans River,** which is only about ten kilometres (six miles) from George. Founded in 1811 and named after King George III, **George** was the first new town established after the second British occupation of the Cape in 1806. The oak-lined streets of this 'capital' of the southern Cape date from that time. The Victorian novelist Anthony Trollope, who visited George in the 1870s, described it as the most beautiful village in the world. The old Drostdy (magistrate's residence) at the top of the main street, York Street, houses the George museum. The oldest building is the old Town House, in Market Street. Excellent swimming and fishing are to be enjoyed at Herold's Bay, a cove thirteen kilometres (8 miles) away.

Lying on the southern slopes of the Outeniqua Mountains, George is at the foot of three passes — Outeniqua, Montagu and Cradock's — that cross the range into the Little Karoo.

Although it involves a detour, it would be a pity if, having come this close, you missed the opportunity to make the crossing to **Oudtshoorn** and the **Cango Caves**. The tarred **Outeniqua Pass,** built in the 1950s, crosses the range at an altitude of 800 metres (2,625 feet). A viewpoint on the pass about seven kilometres from George looks out across the valley of the Malgas River to where the two older passes may be clearly seen on the other side.

The gravel surfaced **Montagu Pass**, built in 1848, crosses the range at 736 metres (2,415 feet) above sea level, and is still used as a direct route to the small village of Herold. Visible on the slope above the Montagu Pass, is a line of white stones marking the route of the old Cradock Pass. Pioneered in 1815, it was used by ox-wagons, which took up to three days to cover the hazardous nine kilometres.

Oudtshoorn, some fifty-five kilometres (34 miles) from George, is the chief town of the **Little Karoo**, and is of interest as the only place in the world where ostriches are farmed domestically on a large scale.

These birds have been farmed there for their feathers for over 140 years. A century ago, ostrich feathers were yielding greater profits than any other farm product in the country. The boom peaked in 1913, when ostrich feathers were the fourth largest export after gold, diamonds and wool.

Millionaire Oudtshoorn farmers built themselves mansions — the so-called 'feather palaces' — which are still to be seen, although the bottom suddenly dropped out of the market in 1914, leaving their owners penniless. There were some 750,000 domesticated ostriches on Little Karoo farms in 1914; today there are about a tenth of that number on 200 farms. But today it is not merely the plume feathers of the males, but the whole birds, that are utilized.

Because of the historical and economic importance of the ostrich to Oudtshoorn, a whole hall in the town's C P Nel Museum is devoted to the bird, and there are several ostrich show farms that welcome visitors. Just as the dry Little Karoo is separated from the verdant coastal plain to the south by the Outeniqua Mountains, it is separated from the even drier Great Karoo to the north by the Great Swartberg (black mountain) range.

Thirty kilometres (19 miles) from Oudtshoorn the famed **Cango Caves** penetrate almost two kilometres into a limestone formation in the Swartberg overlooking the **Grobbelaars River**. They were discovered accidentally in 1780 by a farmer named Van Zyl who was looking for a wounded buck while out hunting. Managed by the Oudtshoorn municipality since 1921, the Cango Caves are visited by over 200,000 people each year.

The main caves, which are open to visitors on guided tours, consist of a series of large connected chambers that reach 750 metres (2,460 feet) into the mountain, but require little exertion because the rise and fall is less than sixteen metres (52 feet). The temperature inside is about 18 degrees Celsius and the humidity is about ninety-five per cent. The first and largest chamber, named the **Van Zyl Hall** after its discoverer, has perfect acoustics and has on occasion hosted concerts by full symphony orchestras.

Electrified throughout, the caves present visitors with one of the finest spectacles of limestone formations in the world. Some of the stalactites and stalagmites are reckoned to be 200,000 years old. In the second chamber, known as **Botha's Hall**, can be found the highest column in any known cave, a united stalactite and stalagmite of twelve-and-a-half metres (41 feet), built up at a rate of seven millimetres (about a quarter-of-an-inch) a century by the accrual of minute deposits of lime left by water dripping from the ceiling.

In 1972 the extent of the known caves was more than doubled when speleologists broke through a thin wall and discovered another series of chambers, which they named the **Wonder Caves**, leading on from the first. Entrance to this extension is difficult, however, and the Wonder Caves are not open to the public.

If you are continuing on to Cape Town from Oudtshoorn, you have three choices of route. You can cross the Swartberg into the Great Karoo and link up with the N1 from Johannesburg to Cape Town, you can continue westward through the Little Karoo, or return over the Outeniquas to George and then complete the last leg of the Garden Route to Mossel Bay.

Should you decide to cross into the Great Karoo, you will have to decide between the longer but relatively easy route through **Meiringspoort**, a narrow, precipitous defile that cuts through the Swartberg, and the spectacular, though tortuous, route over the **Swartberg Pass**, which crosses the range at 1,500 metres (4,921 feet).

The two routes join up on the other side at Prince Albert, from where it is forty-five kilometres (28 miles) to the N1 at Prince Albert Road, which is 370 kilometres (230 miles) from Cape Town. Alternatively, if you travel westward through the Little Karoo for 320 kilometres (200 miles) you pass through Calitzdorp, Ladismith, Barrydale, Montagu and Robertson, and link up with the N1 at Worcester, 115 kilometres (71 miles) from Cape Town.

Mossel (mussel) Bay, fifty-four kilometres (34 miles) from George on the N2, has in recent years become the site of a huge refinery for processing natural gas and oil from off-shore wells, although it has long been a popular holiday resort.

It was there that Portuguese explorers first set foot in what was centuries later to become South Africa. Bartolomeu Diaz came ashore there on St Blaize's day in 1487 and, finding a stream of fresh water there, named it the Watering Place of St Blaize. In a milkwood tree beside the stream the leader of a later expedition, Pedro Cabral, placed a navigator's boot with a message and report of his voyage in it.

As South Africa's first 'post office', the **Post Office Tree**, as it is called, now over 500 years old, is a national monument. Although the bay was renamed Mossel Bay in 1602, the lighthouse on the point retains the name St Blaize. From there, there is a magnificent view back across the bay of the Outeniquas as you bid farewell to the Garden Route and start on the 390-kilometre (242-mile) drive on the N2 to Cape Town.

Opposite: The Cango Caves present visitors with one of the finest limestone formations in the world.

Above: The Cape region provides a sanctuary for many birds including penguins.

Exploring the Dry West

North of Cape Town the highway to Namibia (N7) runs for more than 600 kilometres (350 miles) through the plain that lies between the arid West Coast and the mountains of the western escarpment

Leaving the winelands of the Western Cape, the road passes through the country's main wheat-growing area, the Swartland (black land) and the near-desert of Namaqualand, until finally it reaches the Namibian border at Vioolsdrif on the lower Orange River. Most tourists who take this route do so principally for the magnificent display of ephemeral wild flowers that briefly carpet this region at the advent of spring early in September. For the traveller with the time to spare, however, there are many places of perennial interest along the way. To get the best out of it will take at least a week, but you can of course be selective and concentrate on just a few of the many attractions. About a hundred kilometres (62 miles) north of Cape Town you can make a detour to the left to visit the

West Coast National Park, which has as its nucleus the calm turquoise waters of **Langebaan Lagoon,** a popular resort for anglers and watersport enthusiasts.

Although there is an air force base and some resort development on the eastern shore, and the lagoon opens into **Saldanha Bay,** which is now a major iron-ore port, much of the natural beauty has been preserved. Named after the early 16th-century Portuguese explorer Antonio de Saldanha, the bay afforded a safer anchorage than Table Bay and would have been the preferred site for a Dutch East India Company refreshment station had it not lacked fresh water. Mudflats and marshes at the southern end of the lagoon provide sanctuary each year for more than 100,000 migrant wading birds which include curlew sandpipers and several thousand flamingoes. Among endemic species are jackass penguins, cormorants, oyster-catchers, sacred ibis and Cape gannets. The rugged western side of the lagoon — a peninsula between its sheltered waters and the open Atlantic — is roamed freely by springbok, eland and ostrich. The vegetation, though containing elements of the Cape *fynbos*, has more in common with the succulent type of scrub found in drier areas further north.

The road north passes the towns of Malmesbury and Moorreesburg, where there is a **Wheat Industry Museum**, and Piketberg, before crossing from the wheat lands to the orange orchards of the Olifants (elephants) River valley by way of **Piekeniers Pass**. The pass, so named because a troop of lancers sent out in 1675 to 'discipline' a Khoi chief broke off their pursuit here, offers a magnificent elevated view of the Swartland.

Between the pass and the first town, **Citrusdal**, a turn-off to the right leads to natural hot springs, where visitors may relax in comfortable circumstances and enjoy the benefits of taking the waters. From Citrusdal the road continues along the left bank of the **Olifants River** — once the northern boundary of the Cape Colony — to **Clan-William**, where a large dam on the river provides boating, fishing and other freshwater recreations beneath the ragged peaks of the famed Cedarberg mountains.

Rising to 1,900 metres (6,000 feet), the **Cedarberg**, which gets its name from the indigenous Clan-William cedar said to live 1,000 years, is one of the most beautiful natural areas in South Africa. It is a wonderland of spectacular rock formations, honeycombed and carved by the elements into columns and bizarre sculptures. In 1973 some 70,000 hectares (173,000 acres), seventy kilometres (43 miles) from north to south and thirty kilometres (18 miles) across at its widest, was proclaimed a Wilderness Area, to be kept in its natural state, with all traces of civilization removed and access limited to small parties on foot.

Access to the wilderness trails (which has to be arranged well in advance) is from the Algeria forest station, towards the southern end. Entrance by road to the northern end of this rugged mountain land is by way of **Pakhuis Pass**, above Clan-William. By this route you cross the Cedarberg and can take a tortuous mountain road that leads, some eighty kilometres (50 miles) from Clan-William, to

the picturesque village of **Wuppertal**. Contact the State Forester, Cedarberg State Forest, Private Bag X1, Citrusdale 7340. Tel: 02682 - 3440. Here time seems to have stood still since the village was founded in 1830 by Rhenish missionaries, who named it after the German valley in which they received their spiritual training.

The whole Cedarberg area abounds in San rock art, although the San themselves ceased living there long ago. But if you continue from Pakhuis Pass on the road to Ceres you will eventually come to **Kagga Kamma** ('place of the Bushmen') **Nature Reserve,** where a band of San hunter-gatherers has been re-established, and may be visited in their natural surroundings.

Continuing up the N7 from Clan-William, however, you eventually cross the Olifants River 300 kilometres (190 miles) from Cape Town, a little before you reach **Vanrhynsdorp**, the town known as the 'Gateway to Namaqualand'.

At Vanrhynsdorp you may decide to cross the mountains again, and take the R27 (N14) over Vanrhyns Pass, from the summit of which, at an altitude of about 800 metres (2,600 feet), there are breathtaking views back over the plain to the coast. Ten kilometres south of the first town you pass through, **Nieuwoudtville**, is the **Oorlogskloof Nature Reserve**, set in deep ravines incised by the Oorlogskloof River, where there are forty-six kilometres (28 miles) of hiking trails.

Northern Cape

Skirting the south and east of Bushmanland, the R27 (N14) eventually brings you out on the Orange River at **Upington**, some 500 kilometres (310 miles) from Vanrhynsdorp. On the way you pass through Calvinia, at the foot of the Hantam Mountains, Brandvlei, and Kenhardt. Once the hangout of cattle thieves, **Kenhardt**, on the banks of the Hartbees River, lies in the heart of country noted for its many salt-pans, including enormous Verneukpan ('deception pan'), so named for its mirages. There, in 1929, Sir Malcolm Campbell

Above: Diamonds of the purest quality come from the alluvial fields at Kleinsee and Alexander Bay. Alluvial diamonds are often stronger than those mined on land, having survived the buffeting of the sea.

attempted unsuccessfully to break the world land speed record.

There is a giant camelthorn tree in the middle of Kenhardt under which the town was formally founded in 1868. Four kilometres (just over two miles) outside the town, a hiking trail meanders through a forest of *kokerboom* ('quiver trees'), from the bark of which in former times the San made quivers for their arrows.

If you continue north from Vanrhynsdorp on the N7, you enter Namaqualand, land of the Nama people, a Khoi tribe whose descendants still live scattered on farms and mission settlements in the area.

For the next 240 kilometres (140 miles) you drive through undulating arid country characterized by low, succulent scrub vegetation, passing the small towns of Bitterfontein, Garies and Kamieskroon, before arriving, at length, in Springbok.

Until the bottom fell out of the international copper market in recent times, **Springbok** was a thriving mining town. The association of this region with copper mining dates back to the 17th century,

when the Dutch governor, Simon van der Stel sank prospecting shafts, which can still be seen, at nearby Carolusberg. There are many remnants there of the pioneering day of the mines in the form of old mine shafts and smelting furnaces.

South-east of Springbok is the **Goenab Nature Reserve**. Although dry and barren for most of the year, after good winter rains the circular walks thread through a blaze of floral colour.

Particularly deserving of interest are the succulents, many of which, including the *halfmens* ('half human') tree, are found nowhere else. The active copper mining centre today is eight kilometres (five miles) north of Springbok at **Okiep** ('place of salty water'), which was once ranked as the richest copper mine in the world. It is notable for its typically Cornish architecture, a legacy of the Cornish miners who flocked there at the turn of the century.

At **Nababeep** ('place of the rhinoceros'), nineteen kilometres (twelve miles) from Springbok, the history of the area is graphically depicted in displays at the **Mining Museum**. Almost fifty kilometres

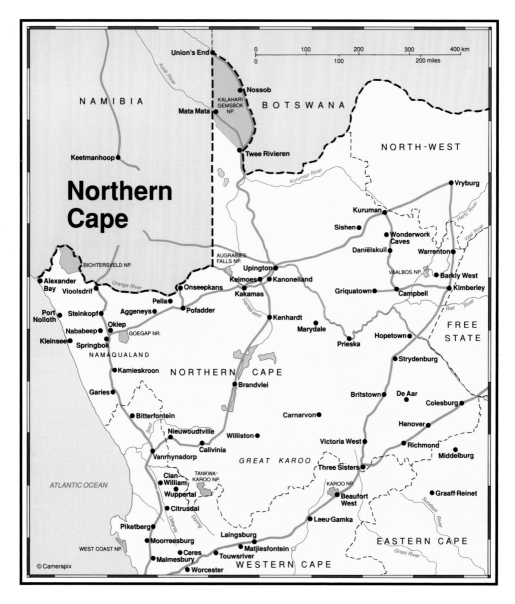

© Camerapix

(30 miles) north of Springbok on the N7 is **Steinkopf**, a mission station, where many of the resident Nama still live in traditional beehive-shaped *matjieshuise* ('mat houses'), though in many cases the traditional reed mats that cover the domed frames have been replaced with hessian.

To the west the R382 leads to **Port Nolloth**, ninety-three kilometres (58 miles) away on the coast. Originally constructed as a port to serve the copper mines, Port Nolloth is today a centre for commercial fishing and coastal alluvial diamond

mining operations.

The alluvial diamond fields at **Kleinsee** and **Alexander Bay**, on the shores of northern Namaqualand, are part of a narrow coastal strip reaching far northward into Namibia, where in bygone days diamonds carried from the interior by the Orange River were deposited on beach terraces by ocean currents. Many diamonds of purest quality come from these mines, because only the best have survived continual abrasion over millenia by sea and wind-driven sand. Kleinsee is

Above: The Augrabies Falls.

also home to one of the world's largest colonies of Cape fur seals.

About seventy-five kilometres (47 miles) north of Springbok the N7 crosses the Orange River into Namibia at Vioolsdrif ('violin ford'). In the great bight of the river to the west is the Richtersveld. The **Richtersveld**, covering some 514,000 hectares (1,270,000 acres), is South Africa's only mountain desert. This remote corner of South Africa was declared the **Richtersveld National Park** in 1991. It is a national park with a difference, however. The 3,000 Nama inhabitants, whose ancestors have herded their sheep and goats there for centuries, continue living there as before and have a say in the administration of the park. Looking at this wild, bleak landscape, where the annual rainfall is fifty–150 millimetres (1.5–4.5 inches), it is difficult to imagine any creature, human or otherwise, being able to sustain itself. Yet in addition to about 5,000 stock kept by the human inhabitants, the region supports a variety of small- to medium-sized mammals. These include herbivores such as grey rhebuck, klipspringer, duiker and steenbok, and predators such as leopard, caracal and jackal. It also has the last wild colony of Hartmann's mountain zebra. Roads within the Richtersveld are few and often impassable, and there are no facilities for visitors.

If at Springbok you turn east on to the N8, however, you traverse northern Bushmanland for about 160 kilometres (100 miles) to Pofadder. The broad, sandy plain of Bushmanland, broken by low mountain chains, is an extension of the Kalahari Desert which lies to the north. Successive turn-offs to the left on this stretch lead to the heavy-metal mines at **Aggeneys** ('place of water'), and to the old Catholic mission station among the mountains at **Pella** close to the Orange River. Pella's church in the wilderness was completed in 1886 and consecrated a cathedral a century later.

Pofadder, often the subject of jokes because the South African puffadder is a rattleless relative of the American rattlesnake, has little to recommend it to the visitor. The puffadder is not particularly prevalent in these parts, however, and the name of the town is the Dutch translation of

Above: Augrabies National Park — a place for the connoisseur of arid environments.

the name of the Khoi chief and notorious stock thief who formerly camped beside the local spring. A few kilometres outside the town, the road to the Orange River crossing at Onseepkans passes through a **Kokerboom Forest**.

Eastward the N8 continues south of the Orange River until about 135 kilometres (88 miles) from Pofadder, near Kakamas ('drinking place'), you come to the turnoff to the **Augrabies Falls National Park**. Above the falls the bed of the Orange River, called the Gariep ('great river') by local Khoi, is braided by islands to a combined width of about three kilometres (a little under two miles). At Augrabies all the channels reunite to direct the entire flow of South Africa's largest river through a channel only a few metres wide into a plunge pool, over fifty-six metres (183 feet) deep, at the bottom of a narrow gorge between smooth vertical cliffs of brownish-red gneiss.

The yellow torrent may be viewed from a railed vantage point close enough to the lip of the falls for you to feel the spray like light rain on your skin. The flow may dwindle to a mere trickle towards the end of winter, but in late summer there may be as many as nineteen separate waterfalls crashing into the gorge from both sides.

From the plunge pool which, according to legend, is diamond-bottomed and inhabited by a giant serpent, the Orange regains its composure as it zigzags for eighteen kilometres (eleven miles) through a narrow gorge incised in grey gneiss and finally emerges into a broad valley with long sandy stretches on either side. The dominant feature of the scenery at Augrabies is bare rock, mottled with deep shadows and painted in a variety of colours by slanting sunlight at different times of the day.

Augrabies, like most of the 'dry west' is a place for the hardened connoisseur of arid environments. The average annual rainfall is less than 130 millimetres (five inches). Temperatures may fall as low as minus four degrees Celsius on a winter's night, but frequently rise to over forty degrees Celsius on a summer's day. On the plus side, the humidity is generally well below thirty per cent,and almost never above forty per cent.

Above: Lion, the largest of Africa's carnivores. Although lion still occur widely, their long-term survival in the wild depends on the continuity of Africa's national parks.

It is forty kilometres (25 miles) on the N8 from Kakamas to **Keimoes** ('great fountain'), a picturesque little town on the north bank of the Orange River. A large water wheel in the main street is an example of many, still in working order, that have been used there (and at Kakamas) since the turn of the century to supply water to an extensive network of irrigation canals.

If you enjoyed the wines of the Western Cape, you may wish to visit the **Wine Cellar** of the Orange River Co-operative in Keimoes. The co-op is the second largest wine co-operative in the world and the largest in South Africa. Grapes are grown extensively on islands and the floodplains of this stretch of the river, and some excellent sweet wines are produced here.

A few kilometres beyond Keimoes is the **Tierberg** (tiger — actually leopard — mountain) **Nature Reserve**, which is noted for its large herd of springbok and great variety of aloes and other succulent plants. It is also a good place from which to get a raised view of the Orange River, broken up there by islands into many streams. The largest island in the river between Keimoes and Upington is **Kanoneiland**, so named because almost 200 years ago Jager Afrikaner, a notorious bandit and outlaw from the Colony, made his hide-out here and mounted a cannon to defend himself against attack from the riverbank. The tangled vegetation that hid him has long since disappeared, however, and today the island is intensively cultivated.

Upington, forty kilometres (25 miles) from Keimoes, is the de facto capital of a region that in former times was South Africa's 'Wild West'. It was renamed towards the end of the last century after the then Prime Minister of the Cape Colony, Sir Thomas Upington. The town's pioneer past is recalled in displays at the **Kalahari Oranje Museum** and life-sized bronze statues of a donkey and a camel and rider, honour the role these animals played in opening up the dry north-west.

The town caters for tourists and holiday-makers, but is also used as a stopover by visitors bound for Augrabies Falls and the Kalahari Gemsbok National Park.

The **Kalahari Gemsbok National Park**, lying almost 300 kilometres (185 miles) away to the north-west of Upington, is reached either by way of dusty dirt roads that provide visitors with an introduction to the **Kalahari Desert**. There is a landing strip for light aircraft near the entrance to the park, but you will need a car to move about inside. At first it does not look at all like a desert; there seem to be trees and grass everywhere, and if your visit follows summer rains it may be surprisingly green. A winter visit provides a stark contrast: the trees are bare, the annual grasses, which have a short lifespan, have disappeared, baring the red sand they covered, and the perennial grasses have withered to straw.

The desert designation is based, not on the absence of vegetation, but on an annual rainfall of less than 120 millimeters (under five inches) and the absence of surface water for all but two or three months a

Above: The upper half of the Auob Valley is one of the best places to see cheetah hunting springbok.

year. Truly the most remote corner of the country, the park occupies 959,103 hectares (2,370,000 acres) in a narrow tongue of South African territory that intrudes between the Botswana border, formed by the Nossob River, and the border with Namibia, on the 20th meridian. As it is abutted on the east bank of the Nossob by Botswana's Gemsbok National Park, the animals are able to roam freely over a combined area of some 2,766,000 hectares (approaching 7,000,000 acres) — one of the largest wildlife sanctuaries in Africa.

The entry point is at **Twee Rivieren** (two rivers), the main rest camp, four kilometres south of the confluence of the Nossob and Auob Rivers, the generally dry beds of which are the principle roads in the park. The much-photographed bare red sand dunes that many people mistakenly think are typical of the Kalahari are confined to the southern end of the park and are largely a result of overgrazing earlier this century, before the park was proclaimed in 1931. Elsewhere the dunes are generally well covered.

Along the riverbeds the most common tree is the camelthorn, which derives its name from the Afrikaans word for giraffe: *kameelperd* ('camel-horse'). Colonies of sociable weavers, numbering hundreds of birds, build communal nests the size of small haystacks in these trees. Sometimes the nests outgrow the strength of the branches that support them and fall to the ground, branches and all.

On the dunes the most prevalent tree is the grey camelthorn. From the fork at the confluence the lefthand road runs up the Auob Valley for 120 kilometres (75 miles) to the small rest camp at **Mata Mata**, on the Namibian border. This valley is probably one of the best places on earth to see cheetahs hunting the springbok that concentrate there to graze in the vicinity of fourteen waterholes scattered along the way. Herds of blue wildebeest are often seen in the lower part of the valley, and Rooibrak, about midway through, is a good place for spotting raptors, such as martial eagle, bateleur and tawny eagle, which prey on snakes and small desert mammals. But the upper half of the valley is usually best for lion and cheetah.

Above: Ostrich display.
Opposite: In the southern section of the confluence of the Nossob and Auob Rivers there are abundant springbok and other plains game.

The road up the Nossob runs through more varied landscapes and is the longer of the two. It extends for just over 300 kilometres (186 miles) to the beacon marking the meeting point of South Africa, Botswana and Namibia at Union's End, which was named before the Union of South Africa became a republic. In the southern section you are likely to see springbok, gemsbok and red hartebeest, and may be privileged to witness a pack of spotted hyena feeding on the proceeds of the previous night's hunt.

Further north, after passing the turn-off to the fifty-five-kilometre (34-mile) road over the dunes to the Auob Valley, you enter good lion country. The rest camp at **Nossob**, 170 kilometres (106 miles) from Twee Rivieren, is a sensible place to stay, because of its proximity to the best game viewing sites.

North of the camp the road passes through grassy plains and savannah scattered with pans, the largest and most accessible of which is **Kwang**, thirty-three kilometres (20 miles) north of Nossob. The pan is visited by large herds of antelope — wildebeest, red hartebeest, gemsbok and springbok — for which reason it is also a favoured haunt of lions. Moving from waterhole to waterhole as you proceed north you enter tree savannah land, until finally you get to Union's End, where there is a pleasant picnic site.

The **Kalahari Gemsbok National Park** is one of South Africa's most rewarding wildlife experiences, but it is an expedition in itself. Approaching it from Cape Town, as we have here in the course of exploring the Dry West, is by no means the shortest route. As a visitor with limited time wanting to visit this part of the country specifically, you will most likely go directly from Johannesburg to Upington, a distance of some 790 kilometres (490 miles) by road.

Upington has a large modern airport and is on scheduled domestic air routes and international routes to Namibia from Johannesburg and Cape Town. So unless you have unlimited time, your best bet is to fly to Upington, and arrange surface transportation from there.

PART THREE: THE CITIES

Above: Cape Town by night. South Africa's southernmost city is famed for its beauty and its wine.
Opposite: Elegant modern lines of the stock exchange building in Johannesburg.

Johannesburg: 'Egoli — the city of gold'

South Africa's largest city, Johannesburg, sprang to life in 1886, following the discovery of the world's richest goldfields on the Witwatersrand — which means 'ridge of white waters'. Today Johannesburg is the gateway to South Africa and forms the centre of the country's mining, financial and commercial industries.

South Africa's visitors generally enter the country via Johannesburg International Airport on the eastern fringe of Johannesburg. Outside the terminal buildings a bustling and vibrant city awaits them. Johannesburg is a modern and exciting city that was literally built on the gold beneath one's feet.

Australian prospector, George Harrison was responsible for the gold rush of 1886 and the frantic development that followed. Harrison arrived in South Africa destitute and homeless after years of prospecting in California and Australia. He was hired as a handyman on a farm called Langlaagte, and it is there that he made his momentous discovery. News of the gold strike spread like wildfire. Within days a great mass of humanity rushed to the new gold fields in search of their fortunes.

By October 1886 nine farms along the Witwatersrand had been declared public diggings and tents and makeshift shelters sprang up alongside them. Today the original township forms the heart of a skyscraper city. A sprawling metropolis of 44,980 hectares (111,146 acres) spreads out from the centre of the city and provides a home for more than two million people.

A magnificent view of Johannesburg and the surrounding area can be appreciated from the top floor of the Carlton Centre in central Johannesburg. The Carlton Centre, one of the largest central city complexes in the world, houses a luxury hotel, a vast shopping centre and an office tower of 50 storeys. Be warned though, the area near the hotel is frequented by muggers.

Johannesburg's central business district is remarkably compact, its growth having been contained by the network of tunnels that have been hollowed out in the gold mines, thousands of metres beneath the earth's surface. This is particularly evident in the south of the city where the line of skyscrapers ends abruptly. Gold mining has rendered the ground unstable in this area and there are few buildings that are more than two or three storeys high; the highway on the southern border of Johannesburg had to be specially designed to deal with this weakness.

As a result of the limited area in which expansion could take place, Johannesburg's development has taken an upward direction. The tightly packed 'flatland' of Hillbrow, on the northern perimeter of the city, houses a vibrant and cosmopolitan community in hundreds of highrise blocks. Beyond the flatlands, Johannesburg spreads out into the northern suburbs, a chain of satellite towns which house the city's more affluent population. The wealthy suburbs of Rosebank, Houghton and Parktown are situated on the ridge where the mining magnates of the past built their first mansions.

To the east, Johannesburg follows the gold bearing reef towards Springs, Brakpan and Germiston. Today these mining communities are cities in their own right, built on gold, and continuing to exist on gold. Closer to the city centre lie the residential suburbs of Edenvale and Bedfordview and the industrial townships which surround them. The western section of Johannesburg houses the city's Indian population; the town of Fordsburg is a lively business and residential community with a number of mosques and a large shopping centre known as the Oriental Plaza.

Johannesburg bears very few reminders of its humble origins as a shanty town. Most of the buildings in the city centre were constructed after 1930, but many of the roads and thoroughfares which brought fortune seekers to early Johannesburg still exist. Jan Smuts Avenue was once the main coach route to Pretoria. Today it winds through the rich northern suburbs. Com-

Top and above: The city built on gold — Johannesburg by night.

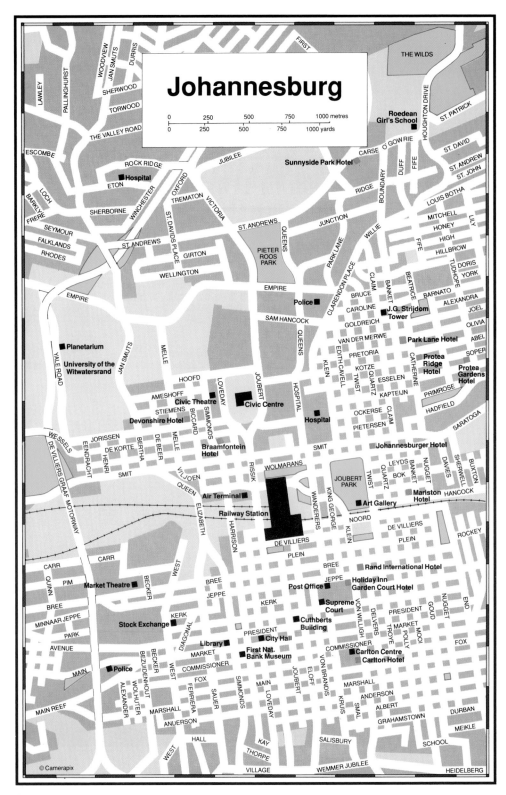

Johannesburg

missioner Street, which flanks the Carlton Centre, was laid in 1886 from wagons laden with stones that travelled up and down the thoroughfare for a whole week. Street names are a constant reminder of the city's gold mining heritage.

There are Quartz, Claim and Nugget Streets, President Street named after Paul Kruger, Pritchard Street, after an early surveyor and the most famous thoroughfare of all, Eloff Street, named after an early mining commissioner, Jan Eloff.

The oldest building in Johannesburg is **St Mary's Anglican Church** in Park Street, Jeppestown. The neo-Gothic structure is thought to have been built in 1889. Closer to the city centre, in Market Street, is the **First National Bank building** which dates to 1890. Today it houses a museum which documents the bank's history since 1838. A guided tour of the museum and an audio visual display are available on request.

The **South African Railway Museum** at the Johannesburg Station is worth a visit. It is housed in a cool, high-ceilinged building and has some interesting relics from the age of steam trains and trolley buses. There is an old steam engine cab that you can climb into, and nearby there is a quiet restaurant where you can enjoy a meal.

Other buildings of historical interest in Johannesburg city include **Victory House** in Commissioner Street, and the **Cuthberts Building** on the corner of Eloff and Pritchard Streets. Victory House was designed in 1897 by W H Stucke, an architect who was responsible for a number of buildings in the city centre. The Cuthberts Building is even older, having been erected in 1893.

In contrast with these remnants from the past, the **Stock Exchange** building in Newtown is a modern and striking building. Situated close to **Diagonal Street**, and bordering on Kerk and West Streets, this building is the financial hub of South Africa.

At the Stock Exchange you can watch the day's trading from the public gallery; at times the stockbroking floor is the scene of frenzied activity. Daily tours of the Stock Exchange building are conducted during the week, at 11:00 and 14:30. There are two

film shows and guides explain how the Stock Exchange works. Audiovisual aids illustrate the exchange and give a brief introduction to the South African economy. Admission is free, but visitors should phone the public relations department on 011-833-6580 prior to their visit. Also housed in the Stock Exchange Building is the South African Hall of Achievement which records South Africa's achievements through the centuries.

Having visited the Stock Exchange, take a walk down Diagonal Street and experience the small entrepreneurs. In this lively and energetic street, dozens of tiny shops of every description spill out on to the street in their eagerness to sell their wares. Here you can buy a bag of raw peanuts or sunflower seeds, some new pots and pans and a variety of new and used clothing.

Some of the most fascinating shops in Diagonal Street are those of the herbalists or traditional healers, cluttered with '*muti*' of every description. One of the better known herbalists can be found at 14 Diagonal Street, in the **African Herbalist shop**. Inside this dark and rather intimidating building you will find animal skins and tree bark hanging from the ceiling and may consult the *inyanga* or *sangoma* on duty for advice on any ailment.

In South Africa traditional healers are commonly referred to as witchdoctors; the term is in no way derogatory, as they are widely consulted and highly respected members of the African community. A word of warning. This area of Johannesburg is also often the hunting ground of muggers. Take care.

Only two minutes walk from Diagonal Street, on the corner of Simmonds and Market Streets is the **Johannesburg City Library**. This rather austere building was erected in 1935. Today it is the centre of the Johannesburg Library network which has more than a 1.5 million volumes and over 200,000 members. The high ceilings and silent corridors of the library house some priceless collections, two of the more interesting being the Africana Library and a press cuttings collection.

Besides its vast collection of books, the

Above: Joubert Park in the city centre is Johannesburg's oldest and best known recreation centre.

Johannesburg Library also houses two large and comprehensive museums — the **Africana Museum of South African history**, and the **Geological Museum**. The Africana Museum occupies the top floor of the building and an entire gallery has been devoted to depicting the rich and dynamic history of Johannesburg. The remaining area illustrates prominent periods of South Africa's past. There is an exhibit of furniture which survived the Great Trek and a special collection of ceramics and glassware from the Dutch East India Company. A selection of drawings and paintings by highly regarded artists such as Thomas Baines and Samuel Daniell are interesting representations of the traditional lives of a number of South Africa's population groups.

The **old Market Building** in Bree Street houses the **Museum Africa**, which forms part of the Newtown Cultural Precinct. It is next door to the world-renowned Market Theatre and a close neighbour to a host of other cultural and entertainment venues. The building itself is of interest; it was built in 1913 and housed Johannesburg's fruit and vegetable market until 1974. The converted building opened as Museum Africa in 1994. Galleries and displays in the museum tell the story of southern Africa from the big bang to the computer age. Museum Africa also houses the Bensusan Museum of photography with its displays of the latest photography, video, digital imaging, photo and multimedia, and the museum of South African Rock Art. The Museum Africa houses a vast ethnological exhibition, representing the different tribes of South Africa. There will be found replicas of huts, displays of beadwork and detailed exhibits of the traditional lifestyles of the various ethnic groups.

The Museum Africa has several branch museums scattered throughout the city. The **Bensusan Museum of Photography** in Empire Road, Parktown, illustrates the history of photography with special reference to South Africa; the **Bernberg Costume Museum** in Forest Town displays costumes and accessories worn in every period of South African history. Another branch is the very popular **James Hall Museum of Transport** at Pioneer Park.

The **Geological Museum** is housed on the first floor of the library buildings. It tells

204

the story of the discovery of gold. There are displays of gold-bearing rock, gemstones and other precious minerals that are mined in South Africa.

Together, the Johannesburg Library and City Hall form **Market Square** — a relaxed and relatively peaceful enclave in the heart of the city. The library gardens form the centre of the square and are a favourite lunchtime haunt for human city dwellers and pigeons alike. Look for the flower stall on the corner of Harrison and Simmonds Streets which adds a splash of colour to the bustling city scene.

Still in the city centre, but situated northeast of Market square is **Joubert Park**, Johannesburg's best known and oldest recreation centre. It features a large open air chessboard with metre-high pieces, a hothouse for tropical plants and an impressive art gallery.

To visit the **Johannesburg Art Gallery and Sculpture Garden**, enter Joubert Park via the Klein Street entrance. There is free parking there. The gallery is housed in a new and attractive building and features collections which are unique to South Africa, including some fine examples of 19th-century art from England, France and Holland. A forty-five-minute tour of the exhibits takes place every Wednesday at 10:30, every Saturday at 15:00 and on the first Sunday of the month at 15:00. Taped tours are available for hire. The art gallery is open every day — bar Monday — from 10:00 to 17:00. During December and January it is also open between 19:00 and 21:00, and you can visit the gallery at this time on Wednesday and Sunday evenings, as well as on public holidays except for Good Friday and Christmas Day.

The **Market Theatre Complex**, situated between Bree, Jeppe and Wolhuter Streets in Newtown is the site of much activity on a Saturday morning. Every weekend the Mary Fitzgerald Square in front of the Market Theatre is transformed into a noisy, vibrant and sometimes chaotic market where you can pick up bargains on everything from curios and clothing to books and records. The market is always busy and it is best to get there early if you want to find parking.

Across the road in the Market Theatre complex, entertainers perform for the crowds. A nearby pub and restaurant, The **Yard of Ale** is a great place to stop for a drink or snack. The theatre complex consists of four theatres, a photographic and art gallery and a bar and restaurant.

Less than a kilometre from the Market Theatre Complex is the **Oriental Plaza** shopping centre, and if you seek bargains this is the place to go. Follow Jeppe Street past Mary Fitzgerald Square and into Fordsburg. The Oriental Plaza is on your left, you cannot miss the building's minaret clock tower. The Oriental Plaza shops have a wide selection of goods which specialize in Indian merchandise including beautiful cotton clothings. There are three restaurants licensed to sell alcohol in the centre.

Johannesburg is a city built on gold mines and one of the biggest attractions of the city is the opportunity to follow the story of gold. **Gold Reef City** (Phone: 011 - 838 8211) at Crown Mines, situated only six kilometres (four miles) from the city centre, is the ideal place to begin your journey. It is best to set aside a whole day to visit Gold Reef City because there is so much to do. Constructed like a Victorian town of the gold rush era it houses a wide variety of gold-related museums, exhibits and demonstrations. At Gold Reef City you can take a trip down a mine shaft to explore the underground workings of a gold mine; you can watch molten gold being poured into bar moulds and enjoy some of the finest mine dancing in South Africa. There are funfair rides for children and a replica steam train which circles the complex.

There are guided tours in several languages, but you are also free to explore the mining village on your own. The first section of the mining village is a representation of the period 1900–1920 and the second section of the museum dates back to 1888. There are exhibits that describe the entire gold mining process with the help of working models or life-sized machinery. A geological exhibition illustrates the characteristics of gold-bearing ore and there are displays of the crafts that used to be associated with mining, such as steel rope-making.

Mine dancers perform at Gold Reef City, twice a day during the week and three times on Saturday and Sunday. This unique style of dance developed on Johannesburg's gold mines with the influx of migrant labourers to the Witwatersrand. Housed in hostels for men only for the duration of their contracts, the miners turned to traditional dances as a release from their gruelling occupation. Because South Africa draws labourers from more than 50 different cultural groups, the variety of dances is phenomenal, one of the most popular being the isicathulo or 'gum boot dance' which is performed in wellington boots. This is said to be a legacy of the days when missionaries banned traditional dancing which they considered to be pagan. African people were taught a more 'civilized' Austrian folk dance which the mine dancers performed in wellington boots, as an act of good humoured defiance.

At Gold Reef City the fun continues after dark in a variety of pubs and restaurants where the gold rush theme prevails. At Rosie O'Grady's you can see can-can girls perform on the bar counter and you can dine in a charming hotel which has been decked out in the decor of the period.

A helicopter flight over Johannesburg and its adjacent city, Soweto, is a fine way to view the city's sights. Helicopters are available for hire from the Gold Reef City heliport. Pleasure flights take place at weekends and on public holidays.

Gold Reef City is open daily from 08:30 to midnight. There is an entrance fee which is halved after 17:00 and on Monday afternoons.

Getting there

Travel south along the **M1 South**. Take the **Xavier Street** offramp (exit 12) and watch for the Gold Reef City signposts which will lead you to the entrance of the complex (tel: 011-496-1600).

The Chamber of Mines arranges tours of a working gold mine but these are not for the faint-hearted. The tours take you deep underground, right to the working face of the rock, and in very confined spaces. Tours must be arranged at least six weeks in advance.

Moving south from the city centre along Rosettenville Road and into the southern suburb of La Rochelle, one encounters the **Rand Stadium** and **Wemmer Pan**, recreation sites which are widely used for soccer matches and watersports. Wemmer Pan is best known for its musical fountains which play every evening except Monday (unless Monday is a public holiday). The multi-coloured fountains are synchronized to 'dance' to popular tunes and they are much loved by children. The show begins at 19:30 in the summer, from September to March, and at 18:30 during the winter months. Each performance takes approximately 90 minutes. At Christmas the fountains dance to Christmas Carols. There are no shows in July and August.

Also in Pioneer Park, on the north-west bank of Wemmer Pan lake is the **Santarama Miniland**. Inspired by the famous miniature city of the Hague in Madurodam, Holland, Miniland is a tiny representation of South African history. It features both working and static models of the past and present South Africa, all on a scale of 1:25. There is a life-sized replica of the *Dromedaris* — the ship in which Dutchman Jan Van Riebeeck sailed to the Cape nearly 350 years ago — and a river boat which takes passengers across Wemmer Pan. A mini passenger train runs guided trips through miniland which also has a restaurant and souvenir shop. The village is open daily from 10:00 and 17:00.

The **James Hall Museum of Transport** at Pioneer Park is a branch of the Africana Museum and one of the most popular in the country. On display in this museum is the oldest car in South Africa, a four horsepower vehicle built by Clement of Paris in 1894. A charming anecdote surrounds this car: it once took part in a demonstration in England to celebrate the removal of the red flag which was required by law to be carried in front of any self-propelled vehicle. Almost every other form of transport ever utilized in southern Africa is on display at the museum including old trams, wagons, bicycles and rickshaws.

Visitors to South Africa who are nostalgic about the days of steam travel, can take advantage of the Railway Museum's restored steam engines which make

Top: A bird's-eye view of Johannesburg, Africa's largest city.
Above: Gold Reef City, based on a gold mining town, is one of Johannesburg's largest theme parks.

Above: The Beautiful Impala lily.

habitat is the latest addition to the zoo. Other special features include a spacious gorilla-camp as well as a cheetah enclosure.

The **Johannesburg Zoo** also houses the first white lion born in captivity. The zoo is open daily from 08:30 to 17:00 and there is an entrance fee (tel: 011-646-2000).

Within the grounds of the Johannesburg Zoo is the **Museum of South African Rock Art**. This open-air museum exhibits pre-historic rock engravings. The pieces are believed to be centuries old and have been collected from the Southern and Eastern Transvaal and Northern Cape areas.

The South African **Museum of Military History**, the most popular museum in Johannesburg, is located within Hermann Eckstein Park and houses momentos from every war that South Africa has fought. There is a fighter plane from World War One suspended from the roof of the main hall as well as some excellent examples of fighter planes from World War Two — including the Hurricane, Messerschmitt and Spitfire. Artillery from the late-19th and early-20th centuries is displayed in the museum's gardens.

Another intriguing exhibit is a German one-man submarine. There are also vast collections of war time memorabilia such as medals, photographs, swords, rifles, handguns and bayonets. The Military Museum is open daily from 10:00 to 13:00 and from 14:00 to 16:00. There is an entrance fee (tel: 011-646-5513).

Across the road from the Zoological gardens is **Zoo Lake**, a large park and recreation area with spacious lawns, a swimming pool, bowling greens and a restaurant that overlooks a picturesque small lake. You can feed the ducks or row on the lake in a hired boat. On the first weekend of the month, an open-air art exhibition called 'Artists Under the Sun' is held in the Zoo Lake grounds, where artists, sculptors and craftsmen exhibit and sell their work. The upmarket Zoo Lake restaurant offers international cuisine.

Another opportunity to purchase works directly from artists is provided on the last Sunday of every month. This is when artists and craftsmen in the Johannesburg area open their studios to visitors between 10:00

regular day trips to the Magaliesburg. The engines and carriages of the Magalies Valley Steamer and the Heidelberg Express date back to 1912 and they have been beautifully restored for tourists who wish to visit some of the loveliest areas around Johannesburg in an authentic steam train. Longer trips are also offered. Further details are available from the Transnet Museum (tel: 011-773-9238).

On the northern fringe of Johannesburg city is an attractive outdoor recreation area called the **Hermann Eckstein Park**. The park covers an area of more than 100 hectares and within its borders are a number of places of interest, including the city's zoo. The park was handed over to the city of Johannesburg by a mining house in 1903 and was named after a senior partner in the firm who had started a private zoo on the land.

Today the zoological gardens cover an area of fifty-five hectares (136 acres). Hermann Eckstein's original menagerie provided the nucleus for the modern zoo which now has over 3,000 varieties of mammals, birds and reptiles. A polar bear

Above: White lion cubs in Johannesburg Zoo.

and 17:00 - **The Studio Route.** The map of the Studio Route is available from the organizers and on the reverse side is a brief description of each artist's work (tel: 011-728-3194 or write to PO Box 2351, Parklands, 2121).

Getting there

You can reach the Hermann Eckstein Park by travelling **north** along the **M1**. Take the **Jan Smuts Avenue** (exit 13) offramp and continue along Jan Smuts (metropolitan Route 27). The main entrance to the zoo is on the right, at the junction of Lower Park Drive. The Zoo Lake grounds are opposite. There is no access to the Military Museum from the Zoological gardens; the main entrance to the museum is from Erlswold Way.

The Randse Afrikaanse Universiteit (RAU) is situated in Johannesburg, directly west of the city centre. Its main campus, which covers fifty-four hectares (133 acres) of land, accommodates residences for students, offices, lecture halls, a library, student cafeteria, laboratories etc. Thirty-two hectares (79 acres) of land nearby provide sports facilities. The medium of instruction at RAU is Afrikaans.

The **University of the Witwatersrand**, or WITS as it is affectionately known by residents of Johannesburg, is the largest University in South Africa. Its campus spreads over thirty-two hectares (79 acres) at Milner Park, slightly north-west of Johannesburg's city centre. A pedestrian bridge links the original campus to the newer buildings of the west campus. On the east side of Yale Road, situated next to the university's entrance is the **Johannesburg Planetarium**. In this domed building, skyshows explore various aspects of the science of astronomy. Relaxing in air-conditioned comfort, and gazing up at the planetarium's sky from an armchair, visitors encounter the wonders of space, travel back in time to the construction of the pyramids and attempt to solve the mystery of the 'Star of Bethlehem'. The night sky programme lasts an hour. English language shows take place on Thursday and Friday at 20:00 and there are matinee shows on Saturday at 15:00 and Sunday at 16:00 — both also in English. Afrikaans shows are

Above: The Wilds — these gardens cover an area of eighteen hectares (44 acres).

on Saturday at 20:00. Tours of the university buildings take place on the first Wednesday of the month at 09:30, from February to November.

Getting there

Follow the **M1 south** and take the **Empire Road** offramp. Turn right at the traffic lights and then left into Yale Road. The Planetarium is situated on the left-hand side of the road, next to the main entrance to the University of the Witwatersrand.

Parks, gardens, trails and resorts

Within the borders of Johannesburg there are a number of open spaces, parks and recreation centres. These are some of the principal areas in Johannesburg for walking, bird watching, sightseeing and relaxing.

George Harrison Park lies in Langlaagte, a few kilometres from the centre of Johannesburg, on the western side of Main Reef Road. The park marks the site of the first discovery of gold on the Witwatersrand and is named after the Australian prospector who made the discovery in 1886.

Within the park is an old battery mill — one of the machines which were used early this century to crush gold. Today the mill is a national monument. An interesting story surrounds George Harrison. He sold his claim for £10 without the slightest idea of what his discovery would lead to and is said to have set off to the Eastern Transvaal. He was never heard of again and historians speculate the luckless prospector was killed by a lion.

Johannesburg's best-known garden is situated only five minutes drive from the flatlands of Hillbrow, one of the most densely populated residential areas in the world. Known simply as **The Wilds** the gardens cover an area of eighteen hectares (44 acres). The Wilds are situated on two rocky ridges which are divided by Houghton Drive.

A number of paths and walkways criss-cross the gardens and there are four special plant houses within the grounds. These provide a sanctuary for a variety of indigenous plants that would otherwise not survive in the Johannesburg climate, including rare cycads from the Eastern

Above: The colourful *Diospyrus*.

Cape and succulents from as far away as Namibia. Unfortunately, The Wilds have been the site of several assaults and visitors to the gardens are cautioned to view the park in groups. Women should never walk alone in The Wilds.

Getting there

Travel north from central Johannesburg, following Rissik Street and then Smit Street into Braamfontein. Turn left into Klein Street which traverses the flatland of Hillbrow. This road becomes Clarendon Street which splits into Houghton Drive and Louis Botha Avenue as you round Clarendon Circle, leaving the Brenthurst Clinic on your left. Follow Houghton drive for a kilometre; The Wilds car park is on the left side of the road next to the playing fields of Roedean School.

Melville-Koppies Nature Reserve

Near the suburbs of Melville and Westdene, on the north-west fringe of Johannesburg is a small nature reserve that incorporates some fascinating archaeological sites. **Melville Koppies Nature Reserve** features

sixty-seven hectares (166 acres) of parkland which is devoted to the cultivation of indigenous flora. There are trails throughout the reserve which lead to places of interest, most notably archaeological sites where the remains of four civilizations have been discovered. Evidence of iron age, middle stone age and earlier stone age civilizations have been found there with some relics dating back 100,000 years. The Witwatersrand Bird Club has identified over 175 species of birds in this inner city haven. Guided tours of the Melville Koppies take place on the third Sunday of the month from September to April between 15:00 and 18:00 (tel: 011-782-7134).

Getting there

Follow Jan Smuts Avenue from the centre of town and turn left into Empire Road. Then turn right into Barry Hertzog and left into Judith Road. The entrance to the nature reserve is in Judith Road.

Melrose Bird Sanctuary

Nature lovers can visit the Melrose Bird Sanctuary in James and Ethel Gray Park,

Melrose. The park features a dam surrounded by extensive reedbeds which provide nests for many birds. Visitors are cautioned to view the park in groups as there have been assaults in the area.

Getting there

The sanctuary is approximately a ten minute drive from Johannesburg on the M1 North. Take the Glenhove offramp and turn left towards Rosebank. Then take the first turning to the right and turn right again into Melrose Avenue. Follow this road for a kilometre, the entrance to the sanctuary is on the left side of the road.

Delta Park

Also of interest to bird watchers is the **Florence Bloom Bird Sanctuary** within Delta Park, a 100-hectare (242-acre) recreation centre in the suburb of Victory Park. Delta Park is the headquarters of the Johannesburg Wildlife Society and features two dams with a large variety of birdlife. Some of the common species that can be seen there are the giant kingfisher and purple heron. The society runs a gift shop in the park in aid of South African wildlife. This is open daily from 08:00 to 16:30.

Getting there

Leave Johannesburg via Jan Smuts Avenue and turn left into Empire Road at the junction. Then turn right into Barry Hertzog and follow this road through the suburb of Victory Park where it becomes Rustenburg Road; it is best to acquire a route map and other details of the trail from the Johannesburg Hiking Club before you set out. Contact the club at PO Box 2254, Johannesburg 2000 (tel: 011-52-8311; alternatively contact the Johannesburg Publicity Association: 011-29-4961 or 337-6650).

Johannesburg Botanical Gardens

The **Johannesburg Botanical Gardens** has an impressive display of exotic trees and flowers in an area of 125 hectares (309 acres). The biggest attractions are a massive rose garden with over 4,000 plants and a herb garden and hedge display. Guided tours of the gardens are conducted on the first Tuesday of every month in summer and there are frequent floral exhibitions at venues in the grounds. Situated in Olifants Road, Emmarentia, the gardens are open daily from sunrise to sunset.

In the vicinity of Johannesburg

Under the policy of apartheid which South African governments adopted from 1948 until 1992, the residential areas of various racial groups in South Africa were separated by law. In the past, the Group Areas Act dictated, strictly on the basis of skin colour, exactly where the citizens of South Africa could and could not live. Although this legislation was scrapped in 1992, many of Johannesburg's (and indeed South Africa's) residential areas are still almost exclusively populated by specific racial groups. There are Indian areas such as Lenasia and Fordsburg, Coloured townships such as Coronationville, and the largest and best known black township of all — Soweto.

South Western Township is the official title for **Soweto**, South Africa's second largest city, and a massive residential area situated on the southern boundary of Johannesburg. Soweto sprang up in the years leading up to World War II following the influx of large numbers of black people to the Witwatersrand and the forced removal of thousands of families from Sophiatown, a once-thriving suburb which was bulldozed to make place for the white working class suburb of Triomf (Triumph). Sophiatown has assumed legendary proportions in black consciousness as its demise spelt the end of a golden era in black culture and commerce.

Thousands of people flocked to the Witwatersrand from the rural areas in search of work and Soweto is where a large majority of them settled. Today Soweto has a population of more than one million people and spreads over an area of ninety-five square kilometres (37 square miles). Many of the original slums in Soweto have been upgraded but there are still poor areas which lack basic facilities.

The gravel roads that dissect Soweto are often litter-strewn and in very bad condition, and certain suburbs are

Above: The Sandton Sun Hotel is situated in the Sandton City luxurious shopping mall.

depressingly dull, featuring row upon row of box-like houses with corrugated iron roofs. Soweto does have affluent suburbs, where the city's prosperous inhabitants have built modern and spacious homes. Township residents refer to these areas as 'Beverly Hills'.

Tours of the townships are arranged to both the poorer and more affluent suburbs of Soweto. It is not a beautiful city and the tours are educational rather than enjoyable; they provide tourists with an insight into how Soweto has been improved over the past few years, and at the same time demonstrate how much work still has to be done. The tourists visit an institution for the handicapped, a creche and a cultural village where traditional dancing can be watched. Tours leave daily from the Carlton Hotel at 09:00 and tourists are returned there by 12:30. The cost is about R50; there are no tours over weekends.

Sandton

On the opposite side of town, and seemingly on the opposite side of the world, lives Johannesburg's wealthy, pre-dominantly white population. Travelling north from the city centre, one reaches the city of **Sandton,** one of the fastest-growing cities in South Africa. It is the heartland of affluent South Africa, bristling with fine restaurants, fancy shopping malls and lavish offices and homes. Sandton City — a luxurious shopping mall, office complex and two five-star hotels — is the spiritual centre of Sandton. It has shopping opportunities on a par with the best in the world in a clean, well designed, safe environment. Here you will also find modern cinemas offering first-run movies from around the world. Among the numerous restaurants in Sandton City are three which are among the best in South Africa — Sant Anna which features Italian cuisine, Villa Moura in the five-star Sandton Sun Hotel — which features Mozambique-accented Portuguese food — and Chapters, also in the Sandton Sun, which offers international cuisine and is one of the few South African restaurants where the wearing of a jacket and tie is mandatory for male diners. For a long time the Sandton Sun was indisputably the best hotel in the

Above: Woodbush Forest Reserve, Mpumalanga.

Johannesburg area, with only the Carlton Hotel in the centre of Johannesburg to challenge it. Now the recently-opened Sandton Towers, linked to the Sandton Sun by an aerial walkway, is challenging for the title. A new shopping mall called Sandton Square, opposite Sandton City, offers a similar mix of shops and restaurants.

Village Walk in Rivonia Road, a few minutes drive — nobody walks in Sandton — from Sandton City, is a smaller shopping mall which has become the weekend mecca for youngsters ranging in age from 12 to 17 and for motor cycle riders who often gather

there on Sunday mornings to show off their gleaming machines and enjoy leisurely breakfasts. Village Walk has two of the best bookshops in South Africa — Exclusive Books and Estoril Books, cinemas, and a number of smart-casual restaurants.

Traditionally Sandton residents tend to live in leafy suburbs in large houses with swimming pools and tennis courts. A drive through the suburbs of Athol, Inanda and Sandhurst will take you past some of the most expensive homes in South Africa and give you a rather chilling illustration of the seriousness of crime in the country —

virtually every home is protected by high walls and razor wire while external walls carry warning signs that the houses are protected by armed response services.

Lately a new trend has appeared in Sandton — small but expensive cluster homes — four or five homes sharing a small piece of land and protected by high levels of security. Demand for apartments and town houses in this area is so high that new complexes are mushrooming — to the fury of long-time residents — encroaching on the spacious older suburbs.

A visit to Sandton is compulsory for any visitor to the Johannesburg area and our advice is that this is the place to shop and stay if personal security is paramount in your mind — places like Sandton City and Village Walk offer almost completely secure environments in a country where muggings and car hijackings are common.

Out on to the less built-up areas of Witkoppen and Fourways. There residents of smallholdings keep horses and other livestock in the relatively open grasslands on the edge of the city. The Fourways Mall is a modern shopping mall on the corner of William Nicol and Witkoppen.

One of the biggest tourist attractions at Fourways is the popular **Lion Park** which provides a sanctuary for a number of antelope species and boasts the highest concentration of lions in the world. There, from the safety of their cars, visitors may appreciate the largest of the big cats at close range. The park is a good place to spend the day as there is a picnic area, restaurant and swimming pool. There is an excellent curio shop within the park which stocks African carvings, baskets, beadwork and jewellery. Children can be amused at 'pet's corner', a special enclosure where they can play with domestic animals. The Lion Park is open every day of the year from 08:00 to 16:30.

Getting there

The Lion Park is situated north of Randburg on the old Pretoria/Krugersdorp road and is an easy drive from anywhere in Gauteng.

Leave Johannesburg via Sauer Street and proceed north into Jan Smuts Avenue (Metropolitan Route 27). Continue through Rosebank and into Hyde Park. After ten kilometres (six miles) turn right into William Nicol Drive (Route 511) which goes through Bryanston to Witkoppen where there is a set of traffic lights at Fourways. Turn left here and travel along Witkoppen Road (Route 564) for 0.5 kilometres (just under half a mile). Then turn right into Cedar Avenue which goes past a drive-in cinema. Continue to the junction of P39-1, nine kilometres (six miles) from the Fourways crossroad. Turn left and the entrance to the Lion Park is situated 1.5 kilometres (just under a mile) along this road.

The **Lipizzaner stallions** are another attraction in the northern suburbs of Johannesburg. A team of white stallions arrived in South Africa from Europe in 1948, and gave their first performance at Kyalami in 1965. Since then, the stallions, which are trained to perform in the style of the Spanish Riding School in Vienna, have been delighting South African audiences. The Lipizzaners gives performances of classical riding set to music every Sunday at 11:00. The indoor arena is situated in Midrand, next to the Kyalami Golf Course.

Johannesburg city does not only spread out to the north but follows the gold-bearing reef west to the satellite towns of **Roodepoort** and **Krugersdorp**. Krugersdorp is the principal town on the West Rand and the country areas that surround the town offer a number of outdoor attractions.

Only five kilometres (three miles) west of Krugersdorp, on the Rustenburg Road is the **Krugersdorp Game Reserve**. A game fence surrounds 1,400 hectares (3,459 acres) of grassland, forest and bushveld that provides a haven for many animals. There are also picnic sites, swimming pools, playgrounds and a small refreshment kiosk. Chalets, caravan and camping sites are available for overnight stays.

Also in the vicinity of Krugersdorp is a **rhino park** which provides visitors with the opportunity to observe the endangered white rhino in its natural surroundings. There are twenty-two other species of game in the rhino park and facilities for day visitors and those who wish to spend the night in the reserve.

Above: Sterkfontein Caves, where Dr Robert Broom discovered many hominid fossils.

Getting there

Take D F Malan Drive and follow this road in a north-westerly direction until you come to the Krugersdorp/Pretoria highway crossing. Two kilometres (just under one mile) after this junction turn left at a rhino park signboard. From there follow the signs to the rhino park entrance.

Situated a little further from the centre of Johannesburg, but still in the Krugersdorp district, are the **Sterkfontein Caves**. The anthropologist Dr Robert Broom described these caves as the anthropological treasure house of the world and it is there that he discovered the famous 'Mrs Ples' skull in 1947. The skull is estimated to be one million years old and is believed to have belonged to a female of the genus *Plesanthropus transvaalensis*. Six large chambers at the site contain fantastic rock and stalactite formations; and the large underground lake within the chambers is the only one of its kind in South Africa. The Sterkfontein Caves are open from 09:00 every day except Monday; experienced guides conduct tours every half hour. **The Robert Broom Museum** at the Sterkfontein Caves houses a number of fossils and prehistoric bird and animal exhibits.

Getting there

The Sterkfontein Caves are situated forty-two kilometres (26 miles) from Johannesburg. Take Empire Road (Route 55) from town and cross the Barry Hertzog Avenue intersection into Stanley Avenue. Turn right at the junction of Metropolitan Route 18 and go along Kingsway Avenue and Perth Road. Then turn right at the junction with Portland Road which bears left.

Continue along Perth Road and then Main Road (Metropolitan Route 18) through the suburb of Newlands to where Ontdekkers Road begins. After following this road for 11.5 kilometres (seven miles) take Hendrik Potgieter Avenue (Route 47) which is on the right of Ontdekkers Road. Follow this route for 38.8 kilometres (24 miles) and then turn right onto route 563. After 1.3 kilometres there is a sign for the Sterkfontein Caves on the right. Take this road, the entrance to the caves is 1.6 kilometres from there.

The **Crocodile River Arts and Crafts Ramble** includes the studios of some of South Africa's top artists, all situated along the picturesque Crocodile River. Artists open their studios to the public on the first weekend of every month, and visitors are welcome to stop by and purchase artwork directly from them, often at a significant saving over gallery prices. There are twenty-one galleries, studios and workshops along the route, as well as eleven restaurants and some scenic hotels which provide overnight accommodation. A map of the route and information brochure is available from **Riverbend Farm Studio** (tel: 011-957-2580 or 957-2793).

Another of Johannesburg's satellite towns which owes its existence to the discovery of gold is the East Rand town of **Germiston**. A travelling Scot called John Jack, who decided to try his hand at prospecting, discovered gold on a farm called Elandsfontein in 1887. Jack and a partner, August Simmer, bought the farm and established a mining company called Simmer and Jack, around which the town of Germiston grew.

The town was declared a municipality in 1903 and elevated to the status of a city in 1950. Today it is the third largest city in the Transvaal and features the world's biggest gold refinery. As a result, Germiston is known as the workshop of the Gauteng.

One of the town's best-known landmarks is an illuminated fountain in the shape of a mine headgear. The industrial city is also home to **Gosforth Park Race Course**, the venue for a number of important horse racing events and head-quarters of the Thoroughbred Breeders Association of South Africa. One of the country's most modern sports complexes, the Hermann Immelman Stadium is situated in Germiston. The stadium's tartan track plays host to national athletics competitions. Two of Germiston's best-known spots are the **Rondebult Bird Sanctuary** and **Germiston Lake**. The bird sanctuary is in Van Dyk road and is open every day from 08:00–17:00. A number of species of bird and waterfowl live in the

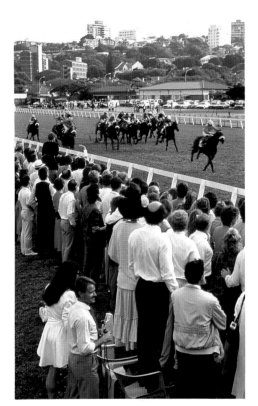

Above: Horse racing is a national sport, drawing large and colourful crowds.

ninety-four-hectare (232-acre) reserve, and guides can be arranged with members of the Witwatersrand Bird Club and Wildlife Society.

Germiston Lake is the largest man-made lake in Gauteng and an excellent place to spend a day outdoors. There are good fishing opportunities, watersports, picnic areas and a restaurant.

Getting there

Leave Johannesburg via the M2 East and take the Geldenhuys Interchange. From there drive until you reach a T-junction where you turn right into Refinery Road which eventually becomes Lake Road and passes the lake.

Further details about Johannesburg and its surrounding areas can be obtained from the city's publicity association. This is situated in the centre of Johannesburg, on the corner of Market and Kruis Streets (tel: 011-29-4961/4).

Pretoria: Jacaranda City

Pretoria, South Africa's administrative capital, lies directly to the north of Johannesburg. It is a city of wide, tree-lined streets and open spaces, and is home to government and provincial offices, two universities and a number of scientific institutes, including the Council for Scientific and Industrial Research (CSIR) and the South African Bureau of Standards (SABS). Pretoria also has a variety of museums, theatres and art galleries.

The ideal time to visit Pretoria is in spring — the months of October and November — when the tens of thousands of jacaranda trees which line the streets of the city are in full bloom. Pretoria's jacaranda trees are famed throughout South Africa and give Pretoria the nickname of 'Jacaranda City'.

Pretoria is spread over an area of 632 square kilometres (244 square miles) and is home to more than 800,000 people. Archaeologists have uncovered evidence indicating that a negroid people lived near Pretoria more than sixteen centuries ago. Whereas Johannesburg was born of a gold rush and developed into a bustling town within a year, Pretoria's growth took place at a more sedate pace with the city gradually evolving from a farming community into a modern metropolis.

In 1854 Pretoria's first Dutch Reformed Church was built in Church Square, and the city grew around the building. Like many other towns in South Africa, Pretoria was built on a grid pattern with the church at its heart. The city was named in 1855 and five years later became the seat of government for Paul Kruger's *Suid Afrikaanse Republiek*. Fifty years later, in 1910, it became the administrative capital of South Africa.

Church Square, at the intersection of Church and Paul Kruger Streets, is the focal point of Pretoria and the ideal place to begin your wanderings. Church Square is off limits to vehicles and even though there is no longer a market place in the square, many of Pretoria's residents still make the plaza their lunchtime meeting place.

A large, stern-faced statue of Paul Kruger dominates Church Square. Kruger is revered by the Afrikaans-speaking people of South Africa, whom he led during the Anglo-Boer war of 1899–1902.

The southern and northern façades of Church Square will be of interest to tourists who are familiar with the European cities of London and Paris. The southern side of Church Square is very similar to London's Trafalgar Square and its northern façade emulates the style of the Place de la Concorde in Paris.

The buildings that surround Church Square are of historical interest, most of them having been built in Kruger's day. On the south side of the square is the old **Raadsaal**, the parliamentary buildings of the *Suid Afrikaanse Republiek*. The Raadsaal was designed by Sytze Wierda, the architect who was also responsible for the Rissik Street Post Office in Johannesburg.

The government building was erected in 1891 in the style of the early Italian Renaissance. Its extravagant architecture is an indication of the wealth the discovery of gold brought to the Transvaal; five years after the gold fields opened on the Witwatersrand there was enough money in Pretoria's coffers to construct this building. The Raadsaal is open to the public by appointment.

On the opposite side of Church Square is the **Palace of Justice** which today houses the Transvaal division of South Africa's Supreme Court. This building, also created by Sytze Wierda, was erected shortly after the Raadsaal and matches its design.

In 1900 The Palace of Justice was used temporarily as a military hospital by British forces who commandeered the building for the duration of the Anglo-Boer war. The room that advocates now use as a dressing room was once used as a mortuary. In some places there are still sawn-off bottle openers lodged in the walls of the building which were used by wounded British soldiers to open soda water bottles when a dysentery epidemic spread through the hospital and

Top: The Union Buildings, erected in 1913, are now the seat of government.
Above: Pretoria is a city of elegant tree-lined streets.

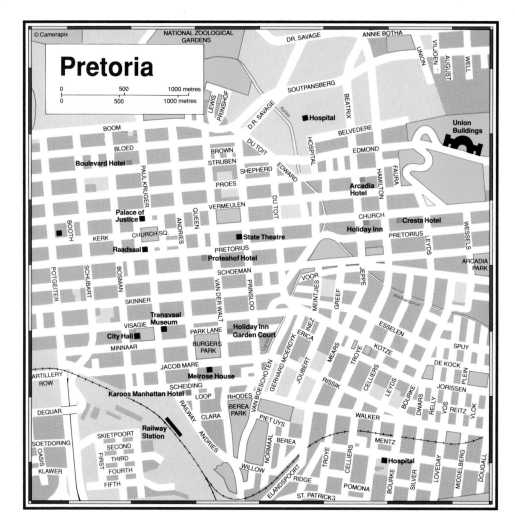

there was no fresh water available.

Close to Church Square, in Pretorius Street, is the **Transvaal Provincial Administration** building, a fine example of modern South African architecture.

Within the administration buildings is a collection of South African art works which may be viewed by appointment. At the entrance to the Nature Conservation division, in Church Street West, there are two fine mosaic panels that represent day and night in the animal world. These were created by South African artist Ernst de Jong and are superbly complemented by a selection of batiks within the building.

Pretoria's **City Hall**, in Paul Kruger Street, has a massive clock tower which contains thirty-two bells. On the lawns in

front of the building is a tympanum which symbolises the growth of the city. The gardens are lovely and have a long colonnade of fountains and fine murals.

Also in Paul Kruger Street is the new **Transvaal Museum**, a natural science museum best known for the Austin Roberts Bird Hall. All of South Africa's 875 species of birds may be seen and heard here — recordings of bird calls allow visitors to identify species by their song.

The museum is an important one and many of South Africa's natural history books have been based on its collections, including Dr Austin Roberts' *Birds of South Africa*, and *Mammals of South Africa*, and Dr V Fitzsimons' *The Snakes of Southern Africa*. Well-known archaeologist, Dr Robert

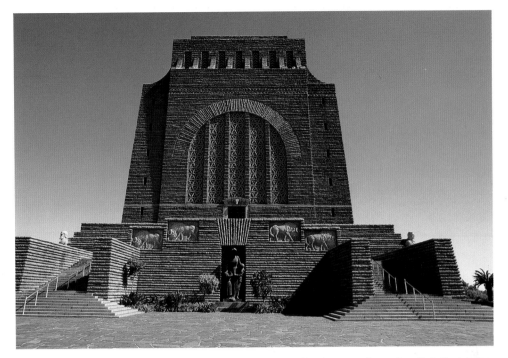

Above: The Voortrekker Monument was built to commemorate the pioneers who ventured into the interior of the country and opened up the South African hinterland.

Broom worked in this museum which has a comprehensive palaeontology display.

Within the building of the Transvaal Museum is the **Museum of the Geological Survey** which houses exhibits of early gold crushers and some interesting murals. Both museums are open daily from 09:00 to 17:00 and on Sunday and public holidays from 11:00 to 17:00.

Pretoria's Church Street is one of the longest straight streets in the world. Its best known feature is **Paul Kruger's house**, to the west of Church Square. The modest home was built for him in 1884 and he lived there until 1900 when he went into exile after his forces lost the Anglo-Boer war.

Kruger's house has been restored and contains some of the president's personal belongings and other relics from the period including one of the first telephones installed in Pretoria. It is open between 07:00 and 16:30 on weekdays and between 11:00 and 16:30 on Saturday, Sunday and public holidays. It is closed on religious holidays.

Proceeding east along Church Street one encounters the administrative headquarters of South Africa in the form of Pretoria's **Union Buildings**. Designed by Sir Herbert Baker in 1910, the buildings and their surrounding gardens nestle against the slopes of Meintjeskop Hill and provide a panoramic view of the city.

Another Pretoria landmark is the **State Theatre**, home of the Performing Arts Council of the Transvaal (PACT). The large square in front of the complex is the site of a bustling Saturday flea market where a large selection of arts, crafts and other good buys are on display. Within the theatre complex are five auditoria which each stage opera, ballet, drama, choir and symphony concerts. There are restaurant facilities and tours of the theatre, including the backstage areas, which are conducted every Wednesday at 09:30 and 14:30 and on Friday at 09:30 (tel: 012-21-9440).

The **Pretoria Art Museum** houses an impressive collection of South African art. Visitors can see works by Pierneef, Frans Oerder, Anton van Wouw and part of the renowned Michaelis Collection of old Dutch and Flemish paintings. The museum is situated in Arcadia Park, off Johann Street and is open from 10:00 to 17:00 from Tuesday to Saturday. On Sunday the museum opens at 13:00 and closes at 18:00 and on Wednesday it is open between the hours of 19:30 and 22:00. It is closed on Monday and public holidays. Library services, lectures and film shows are available (tel: 012-344-1807).

Pretoria is home to two of South Africa's largest universities; **Pretoria University** is the largest residential university in the country and the **University of South Africa** (UNISA) is thought to be the largest correspondence university in the world. Associated with Pretoria University is Onderstepoort, South Africa's only Veterinary Research Institute.

The library of the Transvaal Education Department is housed in the **Staats Model School** building on the corner of Van der Walt and Skinner Streets. The building was used to house prisoners of war during the Anglo-Boer war and it was from there that Winston Churchill — then a war correspondent for the *London Morning Post* — escaped in 1899. He was taken prisoner near Estcourt in KwaZulu-Natal and incarcerated in the school. He escaped by jumping over the perimeter fence and hiding in the bush on the banks of the Apies River. Today an electricity sub-station near this spot is called Winston.

One of the oldest and most beautiful buildings in South Africa is **Melrose House**. It was built in 1886, the year that gold was discovered on the reef, as the home of George Heys, a merchant and stage coach operator. It was there that the treaty of Vereeniging was signed in 1902, bringing an end to the Anglo-Boer war.

The home, now a national monument and museum, is situated opposite **Burgers Park**, in Jacob Mare Street. It is furnished according to the period and has a conservatory, a billiard room, stained glass windows and a verandah with imported iron work. In the garden is one of the stage coaches that made Heys a rich man. The museum is open from Tuesday to Saturday between 10:00 and 17:00 and Sunday from 12:00 to 17:00. There is a small entrance fee.

Located on a hilltop six kilometres (3.7 miles) outside Pretoria is South Africa's most famous monument, a structure which has been elevated to the level of a shrine in the minds of many Afrikaans-speaking people — the massive **Voortrekker Monument** built to commemorate the pioneers who journeyed into the interior and opened up the hinterland of South Africa. The cornerstone of this huge granite building, designed by Gerhard Moerdyk, was laid in 1838 and it was officially opened on 16 December 1949, by the then Prime Minister, Dr D F Malan.

At the entrance to the Voortrekker Monument is a huge bronze sculpture of a Voortrekker mother with her children. The statue was created by Anton van Wouw and depicts the courage and endurance of the trekker women. The wall that surrounds the monument is carved to represent a laager (circular formation) of sixty-four full-sized wagons similar to those used by the Voortrekkers.

There is a spectacular view of Pretoria and the surrounding areas from the roof of the monument and a large museum next door contains a series of wall tapestries and a collection of Voortrekker costumes and antiques. The monument and museum are open from Monday to Saturday between 09:00 and 16:45 and on Sundays and public holidays from 14:00 to 16:45.

Parks, gardens, trails and resorts

Pretoria's parks and gardens have an astonishing display of exotic and indigenous flora. The streets of the city centre alone are lined with over 55,000 trees which gives some indication of the abundance of the capital city's natural heritage.

In the heart of Pretoria lie the **National Zoological Gardens**. Situated on sixty hectares (148 acres) of land, this is one of the largest zoos in the world. Three-thousand-five-hundred animals from 787 species are resident. Two of the biggest attractions are the **Aquarium and Reptile Park**. The Aquarium displays more than 300 marine and freshwater species of fish and several amphibian and invertebrate species such as star fish and anemones. The adjacent Reptile Park houses reptiles from South Africa and around the world.

The beautiful zoo parklands may be viewed from an overhead cableway. During summer the zoo opens at 08:00 and closes at 17:00. In winter (May–August) it closes at 16:30. Group tours are every Saturday morning but must be booked eight weeks in advance. Phone: 012 - 328 3265.

The **Austin Roberts' Bird Sanctuary** in Boshoff Street, New Muckleneuk, was named after the distinguished South African ornithologist who wrote Roberts' *Birds of South Africa* — the country's leading reference work on the bird life of the subcontinent. Within the sanctuary is a superb collection of indigenous birds, all living in a natural environment. An added attraction is an observation hide which allows visitors to closely observe some of the birds. A small display at the entrance gives an idea of what visitors can expect to see at the hide during specific months of the year. The sanctuary is open daily from 08:00 to 17:00 throughout the year.

Fountains Valley is a large park situated approximately three kilometres (2 miles) south of central Pretoria on the banks of the Apies River. The park forms part of the farm Groenkloof, one of the earliest nature reserves established by Paul Kruger and currently the headquarters of the National Parks Board. Fountains Valley has a large variety of indigenous and exotic plants and there are some beautiful examples of the rare white stinkwood (*Celtis africana*) in the valley. The resort has hiking trails and also boasts the ruins of the first house built in Pretoria. There is an open-air theatre, a fine restaurant and sports and camping facilities. This is one of Pretoria's most popular parks and is always very busy over weekends. Its biggest attraction is the wide variety of entertainment that it offers children, including a miniature train which makes trips around the park, a large playground and a swimming pool. Fountains Valley is open daily from 06:00 to midnight (tel: 012-44-7131).

Situated adjacent to the Pretoria suburb of Wonderboom South, in the north of Pretoria, is the unique **Wonderboom Nature Reserve**. The suburbs of Wonderboom take their name from a 1,000-year-old historic fig tree within the reserve — the wonderboom (*Ficus salicifolia*). This tree has such widely spread branches that it appears to consist of a number of trees. The original trunk of this tree has dried out but the branches of the spectacular Wonderboom took root and grew a series of new trees over an area of a hectare. The 450 hectares (1,112 acres) surrounding the tree have been proclaimed a nature reserve which is now home to monkeys, dassies (rock rabbits) and a variety of birds.

The remains of the old **Wonderboom fort** which was designed to protect Pretoria at the end of the 19th century are situated on a hill in the reserve. Wonderboom Nature Reserve has picnic sites and ablution blocks and stays open between 07:00 and 18:00 throughout the year.

Pretoria's **National Botanical Gardens** are situated ten kilometres (six miles) from the city in Cussonia Avenue. Indigenous plants are labelled and grouped together in the gardens according to the regions of South Africa from which they originate. Tours can be arranged for groups of no less than ten people. The tours include a slide show and a visit to a hot-house not usually opened to the public. The gardens are open from 06:00 to 18:00 during the week. Further information can be obtained from the Botanical Research Institute of the Department of Agriculture.

In the vicinity of Pretoria

A little way from Pretoria, near the village of Irene is a farm called **Doornkloof** which was once the home of former South African Prime Minister and statesman, Field Marshall Jan Smuts and his wife Issie. Their eighteen-room home was constructed in 1908 from timber and galvanised iron recovered from the Middelburg military camp after World War One.

The house has been restored and declared a national monument; it contains the family's original modest furniture and some interesting family and state memorabilia. The spacious and shady grounds of Doornkloof farm are a favourite picnic spot for Pretoria residents. Facilities include picnic and braai (barbeque) areas, a tea garden and a camp site. The museum is open daily between 09:00 and 12:00 and from 14:00 to 16:30. It is closed on Christmas Day and Good Friday.

To the east of Pretoria, less than an hour's drive from the city centre, is the quaint village of **Cullinan**, home of the **Premier Diamond Mine**. Although Kimberley is the centre of diamond mining in South Africa, it was at Cullinan that the world famous 3,106 carat Cullinan Diamond was found. The huge diamond, which weighed 0.68 kilos (1lb 6oz) yielded nine major stones, the largest of which now form part of the British Crown Jewels. The volcanic pipe diamond mine at Cullinan has so far produced more than seven tons of diamonds.

Visits may be arranged through the public relations officer at Premier Diamond Mine (tel: 01213-30050) Although you cannot descend the mine shafts, the displays are excellent. Tours are available from Tuesday to Friday at 09:30 and 11:00.

On the road to Cullinan, is the **Roodeplaat Dam and Nature Reserve**, a popular holiday resort that provides good fishing opportunities and watersport activities. There is a restaurant, swimming pool and chalets. The reserve is administered by the Transvaal Nature Conservation division (tel: 012-201-2565 or the Roodeplaat Dam office 012-82-1547).

Thirty kilometres (19 miles) north-west of Pretoria is the district of **Hammanskraal**, which takes its name from a certain Hamman who built a corral there to protect his livestock from lions. Today the area is best known for the **Pretoria Salt-Pan** where mineral salts are extracted from the crater of an extinct volcano. **Papatso** is the name of an Ndebele village situated thirteen kilometres (eight miles) from Hammanskraal, adjacent to the N1 highway to Warmbad. Take the Maubane offramp and follow the signs to the village. A variety of tribal handicrafts are on display and tribal dancing can be arranged.

The village is commercialized but provides an interesting glimpse into the traditional lives of the Ndebele, one of the most colourful tribes of Africa. The tribe's homes are certainly some of the most distinctive in the Transvaal, decorated as they are with colourful designs. Ndebele beadwork is renowned in South Africa and there are good examples of Ndebele craftsmanship for sale at Papatso.

Hartebeespoort Dam is a scenic expanse of water and a popular recreational spot situated to the west of Pretoria in the Magaliesburg mountain range. Originally formed by the damming of the Crocodile River, Hartebeespoort Dam covers an area of twelve square kilometres (seven square miles) when full. The area's warm climate and proximity to both Pretoria and the Witwatersrand make the dam a popular and convenient venue for boating, skiing and fishing. A cableway offers good views of the Magaliesburg/Hartebeespoort Dam area from the highest point of the mountain range. It is open on Wednesday, Thursday and over weekends and public holidays (tel: 01211-30706).

The Magaliesburg mountains stretch from Rustenburg in the west to Pretoria in the east and provide spectacular mountain scenery within easy reach of Johannesburg.

The range was named after Magali, a chief of the Po tribe, and was once the home of large herds of game. Today the Magaliesburg support a range of indigenous fauna and flora and are the setting for a number of private nature reserves and holiday resorts.

The road from Pretoria to the Magaliesburg and Hartebeespoort Dam follows a scenic route and there are beautiful views of the dam and surrounding areas. Motorists cross the dam wall via a small tunnel, on one side of which is an old-fashioned trading store known as *Tan' Malie Se Winkel*. The quaint farmhouse sells traditional South African food and a wide variety of curios, clothes, furniture and pottery. There are also exhibits of historical interest including an old Cape cart and a brandy still. *Tan' Malie's* serves sumptuous teas, has a number of barbeque areas and is open daily from sunrise to sunset (tel: 01211-30188).

On the south-eastern shores of the dam is the **Hartebeespoort Dam Nature Reserve**, also known as **Oberon**. The reserve has a good bird life and a variety of small antelope species. Walking trails wind

Above: Hartebeespoort Dam is a scenic expanse of water situated to the west of Pretoria. The area is a favourite weekend escape for Johannesburg residents.

through thick, indigenous bush and the reserve has good bird life. There are picnic and camping facilities and the nature reserve is open daily between 06:00 and 18:00.

Also on the banks of Hartebeespoort Dam is the **Hartebeespoort Snake and Animal Park** which features a variety of mammals, reptiles and birds. Snake, seal and chimpanzee shows are held on Sunday and public holidays at 12:00 and 15:00. A ferry, which operates daily between 08:30 and 17:00, departs from the park's jetty and takes visitors around Hartebeespoort Dam. A large fresh water aquarium with indigenous and exotic fish is located three kilometres (1.6 miles) from Hartebeespoort Dam. The aquarium has performing seals and aquatic birds and a crocodile enclosure. It is open daily from 08:00 to 18:00 and seal shows take place at 11:00 and 15:00 from Monday to Saturday. On Sunday there are four shows, at 11:00, 13:00, 15:00 and 17:00.

Getting there

The most direct route from Pretoria to Hartebeespoort Dam follows Route 514.

After leaving the city along this route, continue for thirty-one kilometres (19 miles) until the road meets Route 511. From there Route 514 continues west, past the cableway and then joins Route 27 which leads to the Hartebeespoort Dam wall.

From Johannesburg the direct route to the southern side of Hartebeespoort Dam is via Route 512. The route winds through the foothills of the Magaliesburg for fifty-two kilometres (32 miles) and then joins P31-1. The P31-1 goes right, to the south side of the dam and continues east where it joins Route 511, another route from Johannesburg, and Route 27 from Pretoria.

Cape Town: Mother City

Cape Town, the southernmost city in Africa, is often spoken of as South Africa's 'Mother City'. It was there that settlement by people from Europe began some 342 years ago when, in 1652, the Dutch East India Company established a refreshment station to provision its ships on long voyages between Holland and the East Indies.

Both Table Mountain and Table Bay get their names from the flat-topped central massif of the mountain which, viewed from the city, is flanked on the left by Devil's Peak, and on the right by Lion's Head and, in the foreground, Signal Hill. In summer, when the south-easterly (south-east Trade Wind) spreads a 'tablecloth' of cloud over the mountain, local legend has it that the Devil and a mythical Dutchman named Van Hunks are having a smoking contest on Devil's Peak. Devil's Peak, Table Mountain and Lion's Head form a sort of amphitheatre that encloses the city centre and some of the older suburbs. Other older suburbs are on either side of the chain of mountains that runs like a spine through the Cape Peninsula from Table Mountain to Cape Point — the cape from which Cape Town gets its name, situated at the southern tip of the Peninsula, fifty-five kilometres (34 miles) from the city centre. Newer suburbs, residential townships, industrial areas and squatter camps swollen by the process of rapid urbanization, extend over much of the Cape Flats, a generally low-lying sandy plain that links the Peninsula — which millions of years ago was an island — to the 'mainland'.

Navigating the Cape was so perilous for early sailors that they called it the Cape of Storms. In 1486 the Portuguese mariner Bartolomeu Diaz became the first to round the Cape. He was followed eleven years later by a fellow-countryman, Vasco da Gama, who was the first to complete the voyage around Africa to India. It has been known ever since as the Cape of Good Hope. Almost a century later the English seafarer Sir Francis Drake, no doubt influenced by favourable weather, described it as 'the fairest cape in the whole circumference of the earth' — an appraisal that continues to be confirmed by the many thousands of visitors who come each year to enjoy Cape Town. And indeed, it is a city that has much to offer, be it scenic, historical, cultural, culinary or recreational.

From a small settlement in 1652 of 116 able men, some with families, Cape Town has grown into a modern city, with a municipal area of over 300 square kilometres (115 square miles), a metropolitan area of almost 4,000 square kilometres (1,544 square miles), and a rapidly growing population of about three million. The Dutch who settled there in the mid-17th century and the British who annexed the Cape Colony in 1806 left their marks on the cultural traditions and in the form of many splendid buildings in and around the city, just as the East Indians enslaved and exiled there by the Dutch were the creators of traditional Cape cookery.

Cape Town is the legislative capital of South Africa. By seating Parliament there the constitution makers believed — erroneously as it turned out — that the benign climate would produce benign laws, whereas the harsher climate of Pretoria, the administrative capital, was better suited to the requisite temperament for administering the country.

One can understand their reasoning, for Cape Town is perhaps the most kindly of South African cities; a city of public squares and pedestrian malls reminiscent of Buenos Aires, made colourful by buskers, open-air markets, refreshment stalls and the brilliant stands of flower sellers. Shaded public gardens, oak-lined avenues, sunny beaches and a waterfront development boasting many fine restaurants, comparable with San Francisco's Fishermen's Wharf or Sydney's The Rocks, add pleasure to relaxation.

For sportspeople there are race courses and playing fields, yacht clubs, rock, surf and deep-sea fishing opportunities, hiking

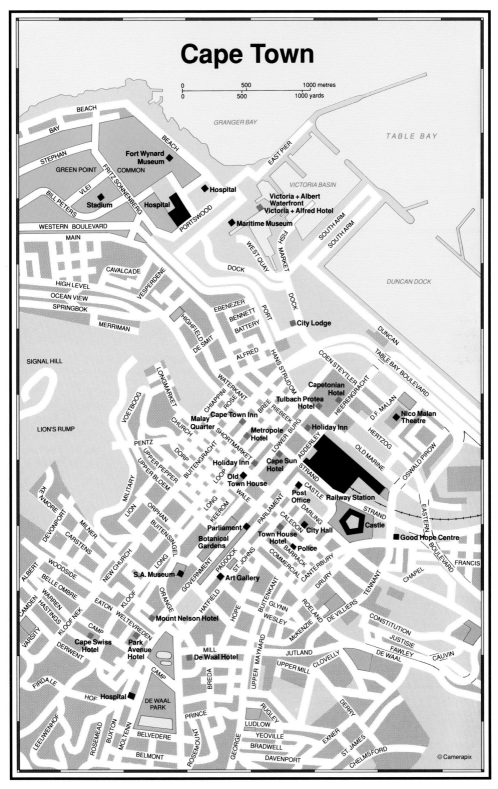

Cape Town

Above: Cape Town's Table Mountain cable car offers spectacular views of the city.

trails and mountains to climb, all within a few minutes of the city centre, while for the more serious-minded there are numerous museums, art galleries and theatres. Comfortable hotels, from economy to luxury, abound in the city centre, on the sea front, throughout the suburbs and nestling in the winelands on the outskirts. Linked to its suburbs by freeways and regular train and bus services, Cape Town is a thoroughly modern city which somehow has managed to retain much of its old-world charm.

When to go

Cape Town has a Mediterranean-type climate with wet, temperate winters and hot dry summers. The season, particularly for those interested in watersports or simply soaking up the sun on the Cape Peninsula's many sandy beaches, is principally at the height of the southern summer, in December and January. The rainy days are rare, daily maximum temperatures average around 26 degrees Celsius and nights are seldom chilly. However, the strong south-easterly wind (the so-called 'Cape Doctor') that often blows at this time of year can be uncomfortable.

Those more interested in sightseeing, hiking and climbing may find the cooler, less windy period from February to April more congenial, although the weather is inclined to be unpredictable.

In winter, minimum temperatures are never lower than several degrees above freezing. Although rain and cold may set in for a few days at a stretch, many winter's days are sunny and pleasant, with daytime temperatures averaging at 17 degrees Celsius.

Getting there

Before the advent of regular air travel, Cape Town was the 'gateway to South Africa' through which visitors arriving by sea entered the country. Today the 'gateway' for most visitors is Johannesburg International Airport near Johannesburg. Some 1,600 kilometres (1,000 miles) from Johannesburg, Cape Town may be reached in about two hours' flying time. Three airlines operate several flights each way between the two cities every day.

There are direct flights between London and Cape Town on South African Airways twice a week, on British Airways three times a week, and between Rio and Cape Town once a week. Lufthansa fly once a week between Cape Town and Frankfurt. Air France fly once a week between Cape Town and Paris. US Africa fly between Washington and Cape Town once a week. Air Malaysia flies between Cape Town and Kuala Lumpur twice a week. Singapore Airlines flies between Singapore and Cape Town once a week.

For those who prefer more leisurely forms of travel between Johannesburg and Cape Town there are luxury inter-city bus services and trains, ranging from the sedate thrice-weekly Blue Train to the daily, less comfortable Trans Karoo Express, both of which cover the distance in about twenty-four hours.

Where to stay

Available accommodation covers the full range from youth hostels to holiday apartments and luxury hotels. Some luxury hotels worth mentioning are the Mount Nelson (Gardens), Cape Sun (City), Bay Hotel (Camps Bay) and the Alphen (Constantia). All of these except the Alphen are five-star hotels. The Alphen is four-star, but hotels are not made on stars alone; this is one of the most pleasant hotels in South Africa and if you book a room in the recently-restored dower house you will have all the luxury of a top five-star hotel at more reasonable prices.

Other four-star hotels include the Capetonian Protea, Town House and Inn on the Square (all City); Newlands Sun and The Vineyard (both Newlands); the Ritz Protea and the Ambassador (both Sea Point) and the Victoria & Alfred, which is part of the Waterfront development.

Three-star accommodation includes the Holiday Inn Garden Court De Waal (Gardens) and the Holiday Inn Garden Court (Newlands).

There are also excellent standard hotels such as the Metropole and City Lodge.

Sightseeing

Few cities in the world can boast the imposing backdrop that Cape Town has in Table Mountain. By whatever means you arrive in Cape Town, the enormous block of quartz sandstone, rising 1,082 metres (3,549 feet) directly behind the city, is the first thing you see on arrival. In summer it is floodlit at night to make sure you don't miss it.

If you arrive by road or rail, the bus terminals and central railway station are in the heart of downtown Cape Town, from where you can take a taxi to your hotel.

Arriving by air, you land at D F Malan Airport, named after a former South African prime minister, twenty kilometres (twelve miles) from the city centre, and travel into town by road. Whether you take a taxi, hire a car or buy a ticket on the airport bus, you travel along **Settlers' Way** with the mountain advancing towards you and eventually towering over you. The broad dual carriageway runs through sub-economic townships, passing the cooling towers of the Athlone power station and rising to the lower slopes of Devil's Peak. The ivy-clad buildings of the **University of Cape Town** are a short distance away on your left. On your right are the **Medical School** and **Groote Schuur Hospital**, where in 1967 the world's first heart-transplant operation was performed by Professor Christiaan Barnard.

Groote Schuur ('Great Barn') gets its name from the old estate, covering most of the lower slopes, and was bequeathed to the nation by the British Empire-builder Cecil John Rhodes. The Rhodes Memorial, resembling a Greek temple made of granite, stands on the slope above the University of Cape Town, and is dedicated to his memory. Behind the hospital, the road divides into De Waal Drive, to the left, and Boulevard East to the right.

De Waal Drive winds along the lower slopes of the mountain and enters the city by way of Roeland Street. On the left you pass the stone facade of the old Roeland Street Jail, now fronting the **State Archives**. Where Roeland Street ends at the top of Plein Street, **St Mary's Cathedral** (Roman Catholic) is on your left, and ahead is a beautiful old building with a white-pillared portico and a row of flagpoles at the gate.

Above: Cape Town is the legislative capital of South Africa.
Opposite: Cape Town's Victoria and Albert waterfront, a multi-purpose development project.

This is **Tuynhuys** ('Garden House'), the office of South Africa's State President. Abutting it on the right are the red-brick **Parliament** buildings. Boulevard East heads down towards Table Bay, passing the **Good Hope Centre** and **Castle of Good Hope** on your left, and brings you out near Cape Town railway station.

City centre

The **Golden Acre,** a multi-storey shopping mall linked to the station by the underground **Strand Street Concourse,** is on the site of the old railway station. A line of black tiles in the floor marks where the shoreline was in Van Riebeeck's time.

Among the many public and commercial buildings on the foreshore is the **Nico Malan Opera House** and theatre complex, where operas, ballets, dramas and musical performances are staged throughout the year. There are several smaller theatres in the city and suburbs.

Strand Street, running back along the western side of the station towards Boulevard East, passes the **Grand Parade**, a large asphalted rectangle, originally a military parade ground and traditionally a venue for political mass meetings, but more commonly used today as a parking area. At the near end, overlooked by the central **Post Office**, are rows of fruit stalls. On the far side, behind a line of palms and a statue of King Edward VII is the apricot-coloured **City Hall.** At the far end is the **Castle of Good Hope.**

The oldest building in South Africa, the **Castle,** was built by the Dutch between 1666 and 1679 in the form of a stylized, five-pointed star. Although still a military headquarters today, parts of the Castle open to the public include the old dungeons and apartments occupied from 1797 to 1802 by the celebrated Lady Anne Barnard. These house the **William Fehr Collection** of Dutch in addition to examples of colonial furniture, paintings and ceramics.

The **City Hall**, completed in 1905, formerly housed the city council and head offices of municipal departments. Today it is the home of the Cape Town Symphony Orchestra and city library.

Offices of Captour, a tourist information service, are in the City Hall, and should be visited to obtain detailed pamphlets on the sights of Cape Town and surrounding districts and on the many sightseeing tours and excursions on offer by private operators. There is also a Captour information office in the Strand Street Concourse.

Strolling up **Adderley Street** you will notice that most of the major shops are concentrated between the middle and the lower end. Turn right into any of the side streets and you will find yourself in **St George's Mall**, running parallel to Adderley Street. St George's Mall, formerly a busy thoroughfare, has been closed to traffic and paved for pedestrians. Several of the big stores in Adderley Street occupy whole blocks and also face onto the mall.

A right-turn from the mall into either Longmarket Street or Shortmarket Street takes you to **Greenmarket Square**. Created in 1710 as a produce market, it seems fitting that it is today a bustling open-air market, where an amazing array of goods are offered at generally fair prices. The two most striking buildings on the square are the **Old Town House**, built in 1755 in the Rococo style, and the **Metropolitan Methodist Church**, built in 1876 in the Gothic Revival style.

The **Old Town House** houses the **Michaelis Collection** of paintings by 17th-century Dutch and Flemish artists, including Frans Hals, Jan Steen, Jacob van Ruysdael, Jan van Goyen, Pieter de Hoogh, Philips de Koningh and David Teniers, and some forty etchings by the great master Rembrandt van Rijn himself.

At the top of Adderley Street the **Cultural History Museum** occupies what was originally the Dutch East India Company's slave lodge, which faced onto Church Square. In the courtyard are the relocated tombstones of Jan van Riebeeck, the first Dutch Commander at the Cape,

and his wife Maria, although their remains are buried where they died in Indonesia. Adderley Street, Wale Street and Government Avenue intersect at the museum.

Wale Street leads up on to the lower slopes of Signal Hill, known as the **Bo-Kaap** ('upper Cape') or old **Malay Quarter**. An extension of the Cultural History Museum, the **Bo-Kaap Museum**, at 71 Wale Street, is lodged in a house built in 1763. Furnished as a typical 19th-century Cape Muslim family home, it is dedicated to showing the influence of the descendants of Muslim slaves and political exiles who the Dutch brought from Indonesia in the 17th and 18th centuries.

The Muslim influence is evident in many mosques which are scattered throughout the suburbs, and the city as a whole lies within a mystical circle of Muslim shrines which are reputed to protect it from natural disasters.

Just beyond the bronze statue of South African statesman **Jan Smuts** outside the museum is the entrance to **Government Avenue**, an oak-lined pedestrian thoroughfare that leads to many other places of interest.

At the foot of the avenue, on the left, are the **Parliament buildings**, then **Tuynhuys**, the State President's office. On the right is **St George's Cathedral** (Anglican), which has been in the process of rebuilding since 1901. Behind the cathedral is the **South African Library**, the oldest public library in the country, which houses collections of rare manuscripts and books, including a copy of Shakespeare's First Folio.

Just past the library is the entrance to the **Company Garden**, originally established in 1652 to cultivate vegetables for supplying the Dutch East India Company ships but is now a public **botanical garden**. Paths shaded by trees collected from all corners of the earth wind among lawns and banks of exotic flowers, sculptures, fountains and an aviary. The paths eventually emerge at an asphalted promenade, which cuts across the avenue and has fish ponds and military relics set on plinths down the centre.

Facing the gardens across the promenade is the **South African Museum,** the oldest and largest natural history museum in the country. Among the wide range of displays, which include some of considerable anthro-pological interest, is a planetarium, and an entire hall devoted to whales. The **South African National Gallery**, at the left hand end of the promenade, has a representative collection of South African as well as international traditional and contemporary art.

Continuing up the avenue, the oldest synagogue in the country, the **Great Syna-gogue**, and **Jewish Museum** are on your left. On your right the avenue carries on past the **Bertram House Museum,** another extension of the Cultural History Museum, restored and furnished in the manner of an affluent early-19th-century English family at the Cape.

Next on your right is the **Hiddingh Hall** campus of the University of Cape Town, which includes the **Michaelis School of Fine Art** and the **Arena theatre,** where drama students stage experimental prod-uctions throughout the academic year. The avenue emerges in **Orange Street,** where on your left across the road are the stone columns of the entrance to one of South Africa's most famous hotels, the stately **Mount Nelson.**

For those who wish to climb the moun-tain there are fifty recognized ascents, ap-proaching the summit from all sides, ranging from easy, though tiring, scram-bles, to rock pitches that require intensive rope work. If you don't have the time, gear or enthusiasm for climbing, you should take the **Cableway** which, wind permitting, continuously shuttles gondola-loads of visi-tors between Kloofnek and the mountain top. In only a few minutes you are hoisted 1,000 metres (3,000 feet) right up to the summit.

The panoramic view from Table Mountain includes Robben Island, which acquired notoriety for being the maximum security prison that held President Nelson Mandela and other political prisoners for many years. Indeed, it has been used for this purpose since the earliest days of European settlement but future plans include turning it into a museum, nature reserve and recreational area.

The most recent addition to the city's attractions is the **Waterfront**. Beautifully restored and re-developed in line with similar dockland developments in other parts of the world, the Waterfront has become immensely popular with local residents and visitors.

A distinctive white-and-blue bus shuttles passengers between lower Adderley Street and the Waterfront. Many of the old buildings and warehouses have been refurbished as restaurants and taverns, specializing in different types of fare and offering the best live music in town. As a result the Waterfront has become the centre of the city's night life, and a daytime mecca for fun-seekers, particularly over weekends. There are craft shops, an explorer's market, a jewellery mall, a theatre and a boutique brewery with fresh ale on tap.

Outdoor entertainment includes boat charters and sunset champagne cruises from the Pier Head. The old **Penny Ferry,** in which dock workers and others have been transported across the entrance to the Alfred Basin since 1914, is still in daily use, although naturally the fare has gone up over the past eighty years. Roads heading north-west from the Waterfront lead on to the suburbs and beaches of the peninsula's Atlantic coast.

Atlantic coast

After passing the **Mouille Point lighthouse**, if you are on Beach Road — or the **Green Point** soccer stadium and athletics and cycling track, if you have taken Main Road — you enter **Sea Point,** one of the most densely populated towns in the country. Here massed apartment buildings tower over streets lined with steakhouses and ethnic restaurants of all kinds.

Unrivalled for its cosmopolitan nightlife before the redevelopment of the Waterfront, **Sea Point** remains as busy as ever after dark. Beyond Sea Point the road winds along the face of precipitous granite cliffs, beneath which the waves surge on the white sands of the peninsula's most fashionable beaches: the four **Clifton beaches** and **Camps Bay.**

The chief attraction at Clifton is that the beaches are sheltered from the summer south-easterly. This makes them a paradise for 'beach-lizards' — edge-to-edge tanned flesh — more than for swimmers, because the water on this coast is usually bitterly cold, owing to the upwelling of Antarctic waters brought by the Benguella current.

Following the scenic drive past the larger, more open beach situated at Camps Bay, you will eventually arrive at **Hout Bay.** But before you arrive there you will pass the approaches to **Sandy Bay,** one of the Peninsula's most beautiful beaches, which has become the unofficial preserve of nudists, who by persistently breaking the law on 'indecent exposure' won for themselves a measure of toleration, though not legality.

Hout Bay ('wood bay'), where Jan van Riebeeck used to send his woodcutters to fell timber, is a picturesque but busy commercial fishing harbour. There are also moorings for pleasure craft, and the sheltered waters of the bay are popular with sailboard sailors and windsurfers. There too you may embark on sightseeing cruises, under sail or power, to view the fur seals on an island in the bay, or to quaff champagne at sunset.

Near the perimeter of the town is the **World of Birds**, a four-hectare (10-acre) bird park which has over 3,000 birds of 450 different species in its spacious walk-through aviaries. From Hout Bay you may either cross to the other side of the Peninsula by the road over **Constantia Nek**, or continue down the Atlantic coast on what is surely one of the most spectacular scenic coastal drives in the world, ending up at the Cape Point Nature Reserve.

East of the mountain

If instead of taking the Atlantic route you leave the city by the same route you took from the airport — either Boulevard East or Roeland Street — you again pass Groote Schuur Hospital. Instead of branching off

on to Settlers' Way, however, you bear right and carry on along the foot of Devil's Peak.

On your right you pass an old whitewashed windmill, **Mostert Mill**, which dates from 1796 and was on the former farm Welgelegen, part of the Rhodes Estate given to the nation. You pass the main campus of the **University of Cape Town** on your right.

A little further on you pass at a distance on your left **Groote Schuur,** the gracious home that Rhodes had built for himself in the Cape Dutch style. Below Groote Schuur is **Westbrooke**, the President's official Cape Town residence.

If you take the next offramp to the left and then turn right under De Waal Drive, you emerge on the road to **Rhodes Memorial.** The broad granite steps, guarded on either side by couchant bronze lions, offer a view over the Cape Flats to the mountains on the other side. Continuing south on De Waal Drive, however, you come to traffic lights, where you should turn right into **Newlands Avenue** to get to the **Kirstenbosch National Botanical Gardens.**

Established in 1913 on ground given to the nation by Cecil Rhodes in 1895, the gardens, which include a natural forest reserve, extend over more than 500 hectares (1,235 acres) on the eastern slopes of Table Mountain. Of historical interest is a section of the hedge of wild almonds planted by Jan van Riebeeck in 1660 to protect what was then the boundary of the small colony.

Beyond Kirstenbosch you come to the traffic circle at Constantia Nek, where you can either turn right to Hout Bay, or left into the **Constantia** valley. Turning down to the left, you eventually come to a board pointing the way to **Groot Constantia,** which in 1685 was granted by the Company to Commander Simon van der Stel as a private wine estate.

This was the home of the first South African wines to find esteem in Europe among such as King Louis Phillipe, Chancellor Bismarck and, while in exile on the island of St Helena, Napoleon Bonaparte. Although still a working estate, producing excellent wines, it is also a

Above: The whitewashed Mostert Mill in Cape Town dates from 1796 and was part of the Rhodes Estate.

showplace for visitors and a satellite of the Cultural History Museum.

On the Cape Flats below Constantia there are several shallow lakes, called *vleis*. The largest, **Zeekoei Vlei** ('hippopotamus lake') is the principal venue for freshwater yachtsmen in the Western Cape. Nearby **Ronde Vlei** ('round lake') is a bird sanctuary, with over 200 avian species and several mammal species, including a small hippo population. The only other *vlei* of interest is **Sand Vlei**, an estuarine system, generally cut off from the sea at **Muizenberg** by a sandbar. The waters are ideal for canoeing and board sailing. At the inland end is an island bird sanctuary, and a marina lines the eastern shore.

To get to Muizenberg from Groot Constantia, continue on down Constantia Road, under the Blue Route freeway (M1), and then turn right on to the onramp signposted 'Muizenberg'. When eventually the freeway ends at a T-junction, a right turn takes you on to the **Ou Kaapseweg** ('old Cape road'), which zigzags up Steenberg mountain to the **Silvermine Nature Reserve**. The reserve, which owes

its name to an unsuccessful mine shaft sunk there in 1687, covers 2,140 hectares (5,288 acres) of some of the most beautiful mountain scenery the Cape Peninsula has to offer. If, however, you turn left at the T-junction at the end of the Blue Route freeway, signposts guide you by way of the old Main Road to Muizenberg. Muizenberg, named after Willem Muys, who early in the 18th century commanded a military post there, is famous among surfers and bathers for its lint-white sandy beach. The strip of sand extends eastward along the coastline of **False Bay**, taking on the names **Strandfontein, Son-wabe, Mnandi, Monwabisi** and **Strand**, before it ends at **Gordon's Bay,** forty kilometres (25 miles) away on the far side of the bay.

Although False Bay is technically still on the Atlantic, its waters are influenced by the warm Indian Ocean currents that flow down the east coast of Africa, and so are more attractive to swimmers than those on the Atlantic coast. Continuing southward along the False Bay coast you pass the old Muizenberg railway station, with its distinctive teak clock tower, built in 1912. A

Above: View of Hout Bay from Silvermine Nature Reserve.

hundred metres or so further, on your right, is the **Post Huys,** built in 1673, the oldest dwelling in the country still standing. Next door is the **South African Police Museum,** consisting of the old police station and court buildings, followed by the Venetian-style **Natale Labia Art Museum,** popularly known as 'The Fort', because it was built on the site of an old British military battery.

This is the start of 'Millionaire's Mile', so named because several of the men who made their fortunes in diamonds and gold at the turn of the century built holiday homes there including the thatched cottage in which Cecil Rhodes died in 1902.

The road continues beside the railway line along this rocky stretch of coast, where there are sheltered tidal bathing pools at **St James** and **Dalebrook,** to **Kalk Bay** ('lime bay'), with its colourful fishing harbour and quaint cobbled lanes and side streets.

A few kilometres further on there is a fine swimming beach at **Fish Hoek** ('fish corner') where, at weekends, the bay is filled with the colourful sails of sailing boats competing in regattas, and a smaller

beach at **Glencairn,** a little before you get to Simon's Town. **Simon's Town,** considered by the Dutch as an alternative port to Cape Town, was formerly the base of the British Royal Navy's South Atlantic Fleet, and the harbour and dockyard were effectively British territory from 1885 until 1957, when by mutual agreement they were handed over to the South African Navy.

Here British influence, evident in the architecture and general character of the town, goes back to the first British occupation of the Cape in 1796, when they built a **Martello Tower** to command the seaward approaches, now a naval museum. Simon's Town is the end of the line for travellers by rail from Cape Town, but for those with road transport there is more to come. Just outside the town are a series of small, cosy beaches — **Seaforth, Boulders, Windmill Beach** and **Froggy Pond** — in coves protected from the open sea by huge granite rocks.

Ten kilometres (six miles) further on the road joins up with the Atlantic coastal road at the entrance to the **Cape Point Nature Reserve.**

Above: Kirstenbosch National Botanical Gardens — one of the world's finest.

Cape Point

The 7,750-hectare (19,150-acre) nature reserve was established in 1939 to conserve the indigenous flora and fauna at the tip of the Peninsula. Within its confines are some 1,100 species of *fynbos* ('fine bush'), the name derived from the fine leaves of the ericas ('heaths') which typify the vegetation of the world's smallest, but richest, floral kingdom, which has some 8,500 species of flowering plants.

The fauna of the reserve is somewhat limited, as *fynbos* is unsuited to large herbivores, but it does support a limited number of eland, bontebok, grey rhebuck, grysbok, springbok and hartebeest, a few zebras and ostriches.

There are several troops of generally troublesome baboons, which have adapted to feeding on marine life. About 160 bird species are found in the reserve, ranging in size from the black eagle to the tiny orange breasted sunbird, which feeds on the nectar of ericas and proteas.

Forty kilometres (24 miles) of coastline in the reserves includes areas set aside for fishing, swimming, boat launching and picnicking, and visitors are allowed to leave their cars and walk anywhere except a few closed areas.

There are monuments commemorating the early Portuguese navigators Bartolomeu Diaz and Vasco da Gama, and the wrecks of many ships which failed to round the Cape litter the coastline.

The Cape Point lighthouse, at the tip of the promontory, is one of the world's most powerful. It can be reached from the parking area up a short but very steep road, either on foot or in a bus known as the Flying Dutchman.

Near the lighthouse you can scramble on to a narrow ledge and gaze down on where the sea tears at the base of the cliffs 200 metres (656 feet) below. Looking out over the ocean, you may realize why this Cape was approached with such trepidation by early mariners.

Although not, as many mistakenly think, the meeting place of the Atlantic and Indian oceans (which is at Cape Agulhas), it is a major landmark in maritime history.

Above: Cape Dutch house in Stellenbosch.
Opposite: Vineyards in the Stellenbosch area. South African wines are cheap yet of very high quality.

Western Cape Countryside

The country areas adjoining Cape Town are dotted with more small towns than you will be able to visit during a short stay in the city, but one of the best and most popular ways of seeing the Western Cape country-side is to follow the **Wine Routes.**

Grapes have been grown in the Cape since the earliest years of European settle-ment. Cape wines have, over the years, acquired a good reputation world-wide and are the principal export of the region.

Numerous operators in Cape Town offer luxury coach tours of the winelands, which enable you to travel in comfort through the green valleys of vines, sample the products of estates along the way and relax over lunch in the shade of ancient oak trees.

There are ten wine routes in all, of which the most accessible is the **Constantia** route, about twenty minutes from the city. The oldest and probably the most interesting is the **Stellenbosch** route, which can be reached easily in forty minutes. Stellenbosch, founded by Commander Simon van der Stel in 1679, is the second oldest town in South Africa, and has preserved more of its earlier charm than any other.

Buildings dating back to the earlier part of the last century have been preserved and restored. Among them the old **Lutheran Church**, built in 1851, houses the **University Art Gallery,** and a townhouse of the period is the home of the **Rembrandt van Rijn Gallery.** Indeed, the urge of private citizens to preserve their cultural heritage is evident everywhere, fostered by the fact that **Stellenbosch University,** established in 1918, is thoroughly intertwined with the life of the town.

The old Dutch East India Company **Kruithuis** ('arsenal'), built in 1777, is maintained as a military museum on **Die Braak,** the lawned town square. The **Village Museum** consists of four restored houses, the oldest dating from 1709, each furnished in the style of a different period.

There is also a **brandy museum** and a **wine museum**, and on the outskirts of the

town at **Oude Libertas** there is a wine centre and open-air theatre, at which operas, ballets, dramas and musical performances are presented during the summer months. Unlikely as it may seem, Stellenbosch found its way into the English language as a verb meaning to supercede a military officer without disgrace by appointing him to an unimportant command. British officers at the Cape were thus 'Stellenbosched' by their superiors.

Other wine routes beyond Stellenbosch take you to **Franschhoek,** where French Huguenot refugees with expertise in wine making were settled in 1689, to **Paarl** (pearl), where KWV, the major wine farmers' co-operative in the Western Cape has its headquarters, and still further afield to the towns of **Wellington** and **Tulbagh**.

Over the mountains are the **Worcester** and **Robertson** routes, and beyond them the **Little Karoo,** which is too distant for a day trip from Cape Town. The **Swartland** and **Olifants River** routes lie inland from the coast north of Cape Town, on the road to the Dry West.

Overleaf: Sunset over Cape Town.

Durban

On Christmas Day of 1497, a Portuguese ship under the command of Vasco da Gama was on its way from Portugal to India when it came across a large natural harbour on the lower east coast of Africa, which the sailors named Rio de Natal. Portuguese influence in Natal did not extend beyond naming it, however, and for the most part the only Portuguese who had anything to do with this territory were the crews of shipwrecked vessels. (British shipwrecks were also frequent, so much so that the Port became known to Dutch sailors as the 'Engelsche Logie' — The Englishman's Inn. Many of these shipwrecked sailors took local wives).

The Port of Natal became valued as a place for ships to weigh anchor, mainly because of the friendliness of the indigenous population. However, for 300 years there were no serious attempts by white people to settle there, until 1824 when Henry Francis Fynn and five others arrived on the *Julia*, to prepare the way for the arrival of Lieutenant Francis George Farewell and a party of twenty-six prospective settlers. Their intention was to set up a trading post and gain a foothold in the lucrative ivory trade in the north. Although most of these original settlers failed to stay, Farewell and Fynn were successful in striking up a friendship with the feared Zulu king Shaka and securing the 'cession' of Port Natal and its environs.

A decade later there were sufficient settlers to form a civic community, which they named D'Urban after Sir Benjamin D'Urban, the governor of the Cape at the time. Durban's growth accelerated around the mid-1800s when Natal was annexed to the Cape Colony. Immigrants streamed in from Britain, and by 1854 the white population stood at 1,200.

South Africa's first railway was built there in 1860, and by the end of the century efforts to dredge the harbour were successful enough to allow it to be opened to ocean-going steamers. These developments allowed the economic base to expand rapidly, and today Durban is a major industrial and commercial centre, with its harbour — the largest in Africa — processing some thirty million tons of cargo each year.

How to get there

Coaches: Coach services link Durban to most major centres.

Shuttle buses: Interport operates a shuttle between Richards Bay and Durban, stopping at Gingindhlovu and Empangeni. The bus leaves Durban at 7:00 and 16:15 daily from St Paul's Church in Pine Street. Their offices are in Empangeni. For further information call tel: 0351-91791.

Margate Mini Coach operates between Durban and Margate, leaving Durban from behind the Royal Hotel in Ulundi Crescent and from the Translux bus terminal and from Louis Both Airport at various times throughout the day, every day. The telephone number from October 1995 is (039) 377 6406.

There is a bus service between Durban and the Wild Coast Sun across the Umtamvuna River at Port Edward. Contact the Durban Publicity Association for details. There is also a bus service linking Durban with Umhlanga (tel: 031-561 1101).

Rail: Inter-city passenger services connect Durban with all major centres. The railway station in Durban is in Umgeni Road. For information on arrivals and departures contact Spoornet. Tel: 011 - 773-5878

Air: Louis Botha Airport, Durban's main airlink with the rest of the country and the world is on the southern freeway. A bus service operates between Durban (leaving corner Smith and Aliwal streets) and the airport. There are also airports at Margate and Richards Bay, with regular flights

Opposite top: The Golden Mile beachfront in Durban is totally geared to leisure activities.
Opposite: Pedestrian Mall in the City of Durban.

Above: Mosque in Natal — nearly 500,000 Muslims live in Natal and the Cape.

arriving from Johannesburg and other parts of KwaZulu-Natal.

Road: Probably the best way to see this area is by car (car hire facilities are easily available in most major centres). The N2 highway, an excellent road, traverses the length of the coast, with the exception of a short stretch near Port Shepstone.

When to go

The coast, like the rest of KwaZulu-Natal, is a summer rainfall region. Summers there are hot and humid, especially in the months January through March. The best time to visit is April through to the end of June, when the weather is near perfect. Winters there are dry and very mild. If possible try to avoid school holidays, especially those of Gauteng schools.

Where to stay

This strip of coastline is one of South Africa's premier holiday destinations and offers a wide selection of accommodation to suit all budgets and needs. There are splendid hotels in Durban offering accommodation which will rival that found anywhere in the world, as well as a number of one-star and ungraded hotels, resorts and caravan/camping facilities.

Sightseeing

The city of Durban sprawls over some 300 square kilometres (188 square miles), and to explore it adequately one needs several days at least. A good place to start, is the **Golden Mile**, six kilometres (four miles) of beachfront totally geared to having a good time. This area stretches from Rutherford Street in the south to North Beach's **Playfair Road**, and includes the streets immediately behind **Marine Parade**.

This is not a place for quiet contemplation, with its bright lights, amusement parks, pavillions, pools, late-night restaurants and nightspots, markets, beaches and walkways past outstanding hotels such as the **Edward**, **Royal**, **Elangeni** and **Maharani**. Behind Marine Parade, situated between **Point Road** and **Gillespie Street** is **the Wheel**, a shopping extravaganza. This multi-storey mall is one of Durban's newest and most colourful theme shopping complexes featuring a

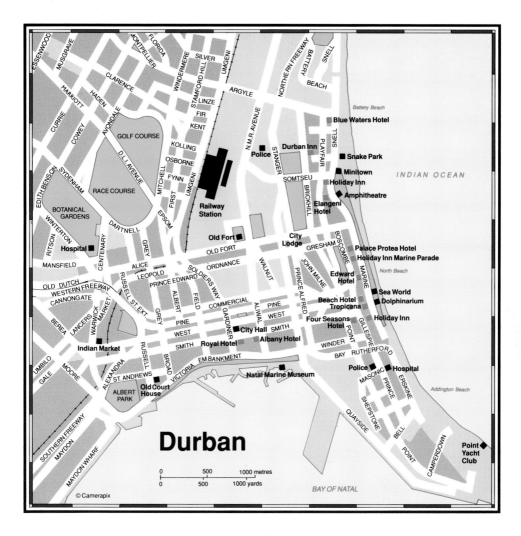

Durban

```
0        500      1000 metres
0        500      1000 yards
```

© Camerapix

dazzling assortment of shops, restaurants, bars and cinemas. Moving to Marine Parade at the lower end of **West Street**, an interesting place to visit is **Seaworld**, made up of an aquarium and dolphinarium of some distinction.

At Seaworld there is an impressive collection of tropical fish, stingrays, turtles, dolphins, seals, penguins, sharks, live corals, ane-nomes, octopus and lobsters. Divers hand-feed sharks in the main tank three times a week, on Monday, Wednesday and Friday. There are also daily shows featuring the dolphins, seals and penguins.

Across from Seaworld are the gaily decorated **rickshaws**, a sight almost synonymous with the city. These light,

human-powered carts were introduced to South Africa in the 1890s by a sugar magnate, and quickly became popular in Pietermaritzburg, Cape Town, Pretoria and Durban, but it was only in the latter that they survived the onslaught of motorized transport, possibly because of their tourist appeal.

Continuing north, there is an advice bureau run by the **Durban Publicity Association**, should you have any queries about the city. **Funworld**, an amusement park which offers an assortment of riotous mechanical rides, lies beyond the tourist office. The **central beach pools** are also there for those who can't be enticed into the sea. Further along is the **Rachel Finlayson salt water pool** where serious swimmers can put in a few good strokes. Towards the end of the Golden Mile is the **Amphitheatre**, where it is possible to find temporary refuge from the surrounding bustle.

This sunken area of lawns, flowers, fountains and pools is also the site of a lively fleamarket every Sunday. Further along is **Minitown**, a miniature replica of a city with its ships and harbour, trains, airport and cars which is sure to entrance children.

Along the **Snell Parade** which runs past Minitown is the city's **Snake Park** — not for the squeamish. Some eighty of South Africa's 157 different species of snake are housed there, along with various other reptiles including crocodiles, leguaans and tortoises. Demonstrations are held four times a day during the tourist season, with snakes being fed publicly on Saturday and Sunday, and crocodiles on Sunday afternoons.

A good place to start a walking tour of the centre of town is in **West Street**, outside the **City Hall**. This impressive building occupies an extensive area, containing a concert hall, municipal offices, the mayoral suite and council chamber, the public library, museum and an art gallery. It took five years to build, being finally opened in 1910, and is a near perfect replica of the Belfast City Hall. The museum occupies several floors of the city hall, and is largely concerned with natural history. The art gallery houses a fine collection of art from South Africa and other countries around the world.

Adjoining the city hall, facing on to **Aliwal Street**, is the **Local History Museum**. This was the first public building to be erected in Durban and was opened in 1866 as the post office and city hall. This museum contains relics relevant to the history of Natal and Durban. Other museums in the city which visitors may find interesting are: the **Killie Campbell Museum** on the corner of **Essenwood and Marriott roads**, housing an Africana library, furniture, Zulu arts and crafts and some 400 'ethnic' paintings; the **Old House Court** at **31 St Andrew's Street**, once the home of Sir John Robinson, Natal's first prime minister; and the **Port Natal**

Maritime Museum at the small craft harbour on the **Victoria embankment**.

Next to the city hall is **Francis Farewell Square**, where life-size statues and glazed-tile plaques tell the story of Durban's history.

Across West Street is the **General Post Office**, officially opened in 1885 as the original city hall. On 23 December 1899 Winston Churchill delivered an historic speech on the front steps, having just escaped as a prisoner of war of the Boer forces. On this block there is another advice bureau of the Durban Publicity Association.

Behind the post office in **Pine Street** are the remnants of the **old Durban Station**. A pedestrian walkway next to this building leads to another theme shopping mall built in the shell of the old railway workshop, the **Workshop**. This upmarket mall has a pleasant 'olde worlde' atmosphere as well as some interesting speciality shops.

Leipoldt's Restaurant in the old station master's house specializes in South African cuisine and **Petit Suisse** is a good place to take a breather from shopping. Enjoy cakes and coffee from an excellent vantage point in the centre of the mall. On the next block from the Workshop, across Aliwal Street, is the **Durban Exhibition Centre**. A lively **fleamarket** is held there in the open-air **South Plaza** every Sunday, where it is possible to shop at a variety of stalls selling unique handcrafted items, bric-a-brac, plants, clothes and food.

The **Old Fort** is situated some distance behind the Workshop and Exhibition Centre, next to **Kingsmead Cricket Ground**. There in 1842 a British Garrison was besieged by Boers for thirty-four days, in defence of the Voortrekker Natalia Republic. On the other side of the city hall, across the road in Smith Street is the **Natal Playhouse**, a popular venue for theatre, ballet, opera, orchestral and popular music.

Legends Restaurant in the complex is a good place to stop for a light meal or coffee after a show. (Other venues for the performing arts in Durban include the **Asoka Theatre** at the **University of Durban-Westville**, the **Elizabeth Sneddon**

Above: The Indian influence is widespread in Durban and has contributed to its multi-cultural society.

theatre at the **University of Natal**, the **Hermit Theatre**, the **Little Abbey Theatre** and the **Nederburg Theatre**.)

The area between **Gardiner**, **Smith**, **West** and **Broad** streets is Durban's premier shopping area, and contains many interesting stores. One which tourists may find especially enjoyable is the **African Art Centre** in the **Guildhall Arcade** off Gardiner Street. This non-profit enterprise exhibits and sells art and craft works from KwaZulu-Natal's rural areas, and has a colourful selection of beadwork, screen-printed fabrics, basket-work, graphics and many other curios on display.

A good place to stop for refreshments while in town is the **Press Club** in **Salisbury House**, on the same block between Smith and West Streets. There you can get good coffee and delicious snacks served in a pleasant 'courtyard' setting.

A tour of Durban would not be complete without a look at its **'Oriental' quarter**. Indian influence is extensive in Durban, and has contributed considerably to its unique flavour.

Indians first arrived in Durban in the 1860s. Desperate to escape the growing impoverishment which was the fate of the rural poor in India, they signed contracts which bound them to working for Natal sugar farmers. Sugar had proved a great success in the hothouse climate of the coastal region but planters were faced with a severe labour problem.

The Zulus, who had intially been earmarked by the whites as the solution to the problem, proved unsuitable. They were reluctant to spend their days cutting down the white planters' cane, and found alternative methods of surviving. The cry among the planters grew for 'coolie' labour.

The people who initially came from India were treated abysmally. While working, 'coolies' were regarded as mere units of labour, and treatment was harsh and living conditions deplorable. After being indentured for five years and working for five years as a 'free worker' they were given the choice of staying in Natal or returning to India. A newspaper declared during this time that 'the only difference between Negro slavery and

247

coolie emigration is that the former was open slavery and the latter is slavery in disguise'.

Many returned home after their contracts came to an end. Those who stayed, however, soon became an indispensible part of the economy. By 1885 Indians were virtually the sole producers of fruit and vegetables for Durban and Pietermaritzburg. Some set up a fishing and fish-curing industry based on Salisbury Island in Durban harbour, while others were involved in coal mining, the railways, domestic work and various trades.

Many also became active in business. Some were ex-labourers who sold to their still-indenture compatriots. Others belonged to a wealthier 'passenger class' who began arriving in the 1870s, mostly from higher castes in the Muslim state of Gujarat. The latter arrived with considerable capital

and were soon doing business with Indians, Africans and whites.

The southern part of town around **Grey Street** (which is an extension of Broad Street) is an exotic shopping district coloured by the predominantly Indian community. Here you can shop in stores filled with the sweet smell of incense, while the wail of the muezzin calling Muslims to prayer at the mosque nearby fills the air. This **mosque** in Grey Street is the largest in the southern hemisphere, and can be visited by contacting the Islamic Propagation Centre (tel: 031-306 0026).

The **Madressa Arcade** next door is an intriguing collection of shops crammed to the ceiling with goods including bronze, brass, wood, silks and satins, jewellery, and other more functional items such as basins and shampoo. Some stores still sell ivory

rants in the city, with the **British Middle East Indian Sporting and Dining Club (Stamford Hill Road)** and the **Ulundi restaurant** at the Royal Hotel among the best.

To complete your 'Eastern experience' you could also visit the **Hare Krishna Temple of Understanding** at the **Chatsworth Centre** south of Durban. Among this lovely temple's features are a golden interior, a moat, beautiful gardens and a vegetarian restaurant. It is open daily for guided tours (tel: 031-435-815/433-384). Other Hindu temples are the **Durban Hindu Temple** in **Somtseu Road** and the **Shree Shiva Subrahmanya Alayam**, in **Sirdar Road, Clairwood**.

Good places to get away from it all are the **Ramakrishna Centre** north of the city, an interdenominational spiritual retreat, and **Phoenix Settlement**, next to the township of KwaMashu. The latter is a place for quiet contemplation, steeped in memories of Mahatma Gandhi, the Indian lawyer and activist who fought tirelessly for justice during his stay in KwaZulu-Natal. Apart from its beaches, Durban has a wealth of parks, gardens and reserves for those who need to escape from city pressures. **Albert Park** is near the city centre in **St Andrew's Street**. Features include a playground, chessboards and a restaurant.

Beachwood Mangroves Nature Reserve is north of Durban, and is the site of one of the area's last remaining mangrove swamps. The **Bluff Nature Reserve** in **Tara Road**, Jacobs, is an excellent spot for birdwatching, covering some forty-five hectares (111 acres) of coastal forest, grassland and wetland. There are marked walks and hides there. Open sunrise to sunset.

The **Botanic Gardens** in **Sydenam Road**, lower Berea, were founded in 1849, and contain indigenous and tropical plants, an orchid house, a herbarium, a cycad collection and a garden for the blind. There is also a tea garden. The **Burman Bush Nature Reserve** in **Morningside** covers forty-five hectares (111 acres) of woodland, and has picnic spots set aside. Also in Morningside is the **Palmiet Nature**

but visitors should note that most countries prohibit its import.

Not to be missed is the **Victoria Street Market**, an extensive area bounded by **Victoria, Russell and Queen Streets** and **Cemetery Lane**. The **old Indian Market**, which supported some 10,000 families, burnt down in 1973 and traders were forced to move to lacklustre premises in Warwick Avenue. The new premises, a colourful, modern complex which features eleven domes, was opened in July 1990. Wander through this bustling centre of shops selling spices, herbs and curries, fish and meat markets and tempting restaurants, and savour the Eastern flavour of Durban.

Something which should definitely be experienced while in Durban is a curry. Curry, a traditional spicy Indian dish, has acquired a taste all of its own in South Africa. There are several good curry restau-

249

Reserve, sixty hectares (148 acres) of thick forest, scrub and grassland where it is possible to see 150 different types of trees and 145 different bird species.

The **Japanese Gardens** in **Tinsley Road, Virginia** is a tranquil place of waterfalls and pagodas, while **Mitchell Park** is a pleasant place for children, with its playgrounds and bird and animal displays. The **Kenneth Stainbank Nature Reserve** in **Yellowwood Park** features game (rhino, giraffe, zebra, various types of antelope) and has self-guided trails and picnic spots.

Birdwatchers will appreciate the **Roosfontein Nature Reserve** in Westville, a sanctuary for birds covering fifty hectares (124 acres) of the **Umbilo Valley**, and the Umgeni River Bird Park, near the Umgeni River, rated one of the finest bird parks in the world.

The **Kranzkloof Nature Reserve** northwest of the city is one of Durban's biggest and most impressive reserves, with its forest, streams and waterfalls. You can do some serious walking here along the reserve's twenty kilometres of pathways.

The Durban department of parks, recreation and beaches has marked out several walks through these green areas. Contact the department (tel: 031-211-303) or the Durban Publicity Association for a map and full descriptions of the trails.

The Publicity Association also organizes a number of city walks which are led by guides. These walks include: the **Durban Architectural Meander**, which reveals some of the city's older and historically significant buildings; the **Feel of Durban Walkabout** takes in the Central Park gardens, the city's oldest cemetery, the Old Fort, the Workshop and the Old House Court; the **Durban Oriental Walkabout** shows you Grey Street and the Victoria Street Market, the Grey Street mosque and a sari emporium; and on the **Durban Historical Walkabout** you will cover a comprehensive list of historical landmarks.

Those visitors with a deeper interest in the country's socio-economic issues may find the **Third Eye** and **Idasa township tours** interesting. The northern route includes KwaMashu, Richmond Farm and Lindelani, Ntuzuma, Inanda Newtown, Phoenix Settlement and the shack community of Bambayi. The southern route takes in Lamontville, Glebe men's hostels and Umlazi.

Visitors with an artistic inclination may be interested in joining the **Berea Meander**, held on the first Sunday of every month, when well-known arts and crafts people open their homes and studios to the public. Refreshments are served and hand-made articles can be purchased. Contact the Publicity Association for a map showing the open studios.

Durban would not be Durban without the sea, and a fine way to spend the day is bobbing off-shore on a charter boat, either deep-sea fishing or just enjoying the sea air and fine views of the city's shoreline. Contact the Publicity Association about fishing charters, or wander down to the jetty at the bay end of Gardiner Street, not far from the Natal Museum, to find out about day cruises. While in this area it is worthwhile taking a stroll along the Victoria Embankment to look at the yachts moored near the **Point Yacht Club** and to the left where the Natal Maritime Museum is situated, at the small-craft harbour.

A spectacular day drive from the city is through the **Valley of a Thousand Hills**. The Umgeni River winds its way through this valley, which begins at **Table Mountain** outside Pietermaritzburg and ends at the Indian Ocean. The views along the way of seemingly endless green hills are breath-taking and should not be missed.

To begin the route take the N3 out of Durban, exiting at **Hillcrest** and **Gillitts**, and get on to **Route 103**. There are a number of stalls selling crafts and produce along the way, and the **Rob Roy Hotel** at **Botha's Hill** is a pleasant place to stop for lunch or tea. Just after the hotel is **Phezulu** and **Assegai Safari Park**. The former is a Zulu 'village' where various aspects of traditional Zulu life, including dancing, traditional medicine, cooking, thatching and beadmaking, are on display. There is also an art gallery, curio shop, nature trail and a restaurant serving light meals. At the safari park there is a Zulu village as well as crocodiles, a museum and a colonial-style restaurant.

Bloemfontein: The City of Roses

Bloemfontein's history can be traced back to 1840 when a Voortrekker named Johannes Brits discovered a natural spring in the hot dry plains of South Africa's interior. He built his home next to the spring and named the area Bloemfontein after an abundance of clover which grew around the water.

Bloemfontein means 'spring of flowers' and the town lives up to its name. It is set among a series of small hills and has spacious parklands and flower gardens. It is home to 250,000 people, has a large, modern university, and all the trappings of a first-world city — shopping malls, theatres and sophisticated sports complexes.

Bloemfontein is regarded as the heart of Afrikanerdom and, not surprisingly, Afrikaans is the most commonly spoken language in the city. However, the city's most prominent landmark, **Naval Hill**, is intimately linked to the British Navy. The flat-topped hill was named after a naval brigade which camped on its slopes during the Boer war and set up their ship's cannon on its summit.

Today Naval Hill forms part of the **Franklin Nature Reserve** which provides a sanctuary for a variety of game including zebra, blesbok, springbok and eland. The shape of a white horse on the slopes of Naval Hill also dates back to the Boer war. It was laid out by the British Wiltshire Regiment as a beacon for British soldiers returning from the plains. Access to Naval Hill is from **Union Avenue**.

Because of its remarkably clear skies, Bloemfontein is internationally recognized as a centre for astronomical observation. The phenomenon of double stars — two suns that revolve around a single axis — is among the heavenly wonders studied from **observatories** constructed near the city centre.

The first of Bloemfontein's observatories was built on Naval Hill in 1925 by Professor Lamont Hussey from the USA's University of Michigan. This observatory was recently converted into a theatre when light pollution from the city made astronomical work impossible. The observatory has now been moved to **Mazelspoort** which is 25 kilometres (15.6 miles) from the city.

Hoffman Square is Bloemfontein's focal point. There are numerous places of historical interest within the city centre. Begin your wanderings at the **Anglican Cathedral** in **George Street**. The cathedral, which dates back to 1850, provides an excellent example of Victorian architecture and features some beautiful stained glass windows.

The **Bloemfontein City Hall** in **President Brand Street** has fine examples of Italian marble and Burmese woodwork.

Bloemfontein is the judicial capital of South Africa; the country's highest court of law, **the appeal court**, is in President Brand Street. The court, built in 1929, has beautifully decorated rooms furnished with stinkwood — a highly treasured indigenous wood.

The **Old Raadsaal**, in **St George Street**, is the oldest building in Bloemfontein and a national monument. Although it is no longer used for parliamentary purposes, it is regarded as the cradle of the Free State government. It is a small, unpre-tentious, thatched structure with a cow dung floor and was originally used as a school and church. Later it became the meeting place for leaders of the (then) Orange Free State Republic.

The present **Raadsaal** is situated in President Brand Street. Exhibits within the building include busts of six Free State presidents and antique furniture. Also in President Brand Street is a stately old Victorian building known as the **Old Presidency**. Built in 1885, the building was home to three presidents of the Free State Republic.

The Presidency has been restored and converted into a museum and is also utilized for art exhibitions, small theatre productions and as a conference venue. **Bloemfontein's Civic Theatre** which is

Above: The Glass Palace — Bloemfontein is South Africa's judicial capital.

decorated with South African works of art, is the city's cultural centre.

There are four museums in Bloemfontein. The **Military Museum** of the Boer Republics in **Monument Road** depicts the story of the Boer forces who took part in the Anglo-Boer War. The museum houses a collection of weapons and domestic items that were used during the war. There is also a display of items made by Boer prisoners of war who were incarcerated in the world's first concentration camps and exhibits depicting the lifestyles in the camps. The personal possessions of former Free State President M T Steyn are on display, as well as those of General Christiaan de Wet, the founder of the Nationalist Party, which introduced apartheid to South Africa. The museum's pride is an extensive research library which has an impressive collection of Africana and war photographs.

Also in Monument Road, on the southern outskirts of Bloemfontein, is the **National Women's Memorial** which commemorates the death of 26,370 Afrikaner women and children who died in concentration camps during the Boer War. The ashes of Emily Hobhouse — an English woman who worked for the welfare of Boer prisoners — are interred at the foot of the monument.

One of the most extensive archaeological displays in South Africa is housed in the **National Museum** in **Aliwal Street**. The fossil remains of the largest known dinosaur from the Triassic period are a big attraction, as is the famous Florisbad skull. It takes its name from the warm spring near which it was found and radio carbon dating suggests that it is between 120,000 to 200,000 years old. The skull was reconstructed from fifteen pieces and the cranium's features are those of an anatomically modern person. The Florisbad skull is significant because it is one of very few human skulls dating back to the Middle Stone Age period.

The **National Afrikaans Literary Museum and Research Centre** houses Afrikaans literary treasures and books and manuscripts that belonged to well-known Afrikaans authors. This museum

Above: Bloemfontein means 'spring of flowers' and the town lives up to its name.

is of cultural importance to the Afrikaans-speaking nation.

The beautiful parklands of **King's Park**, the largest of Bloemfontein's many public gardens, are a riot of colour all year round. The **Bloemfontein Zoo** houses South Africa's largest collection of primates as well as a liger — a cross between a lion and a tiger. One of the zoo's biggest attractions is its night tour which introduces visitors to the behaviour of nocturnal creatures.

At the foot of Naval Hill is a domed **orchid house** which features over 3,000 different species of orchid, cultivated under computer-controlled climatic conditions. The interior of the structure is beautifully landscaped and features waterfalls, pools and bridges, which have been designed to display the orchids to their best advantage. The transparent hothouse roof slides open when conditions permit.

Right: National Women's Memorial.

Port Elizabeth: The Windy City

Port Elizabeth is today one of South Africa's busiest seaports, but for almost 250 years mariners believed that its bay had no merit as an anchorage.

Pieter Timmerman, the Dutch captain sent to survey it in 1690, said it was 'nothing better than an exposed bight' and did not even bother to drop anchor there. Ensign August Beutler, on a similar mission in 1752, felt the roadstead was too exposed to be of any use to shipping.

Yet Algoa Bay, as the British misnamed it on their maps, and Port Elizabeth were to become as important to the development of the Eastern Cape as Table Bay and Cape Town were to the Western Cape.

Dutch farmers first took up farms on the bay in 1772, and in 1799 the British, then occupying the Cape for the first time, built a stone fort overlooking the Baakens River.

In 1820 it was deemed the ideal place for disembarking British settlers. The acting governor, Sir Rufane Donkin, officially awaiting the first shipload of settlers, named the place Port Elizabeth after his recently deceased wife, and ordered the building of a pyramidal stone cenotaph in her memory.

Originally all goods and persons had to be brought ashore through the surf in small boats, but in 1837 local merchants pooled resources to build the first jetty of what has become the modern port that Port Elizabeth is today.

The city, together with nearby Uitenhage, is one of the centres of the motor assembly industry in South Africa, but the city itself and the sea front have a pleasant holiday atmosphere. It lies on a stretch of coast known as the Sunshine Coast, which extends to the north-east all the way to the mouth of the Fish River.

Getting there

The only passenger rail service to Port Elizabeth is from Johannesburg. For visitors coming from other centres, road and air are the usual forms of transport.

The Port Elizabeth Airport is close to the city and handles several flights daily to and from other major South African cities.

There are various inter-city luxury bus services as well as coach tours to this part of the country from other centres.

Assuming you arrive by road from either KwaZulu-Natal via the Eastern Cape on the one side, or the Garden Route on the other side, the N2 skirts the city. At the Creek interchange you will have to select the south-bound lane of the M4, which follows the coast and runs between the city and the harbour.

If you want to get to the downtown area, leave the M4 at the Russell Road Interchange. If you are looking for beach front accommodation, continue on the M4 to Humewood and Summerstrand.

Where to stay

There are a few one-star hotels in the central area. The **Edward Hotel** and **Walmer Gardens** are both 2-star. However, most of the better hotels — among them the four-star **Elizabeth Sun** and the three-star **Holiday Inns, City Lodge**, **Summer Strand Beach** and **Marine** hotels — are in Humewood and Summerstrand.

There is also a choice of holiday apartments and caravan parks in this beach front area.

Sightseeing: City Centre

Almost everything of historical interest in Port Elizabeth is within 500 metres (538 yards) of the cenotaph in the **Donkin Reserve**, which makes it a good place to begin a sightseeing tour of the city.

About 400 metres (438 yards) south on **Belmount Terrace** you will come to **Fort Frederick**, the oldest building in Port Elizabeth.

Built on top of a steep hill to garrison

Opposite: The Donkin Lighthouse, the reserve around is flanked by elegant Victorian terraced houses.

troops during frontier disturbances in 1799, the stone redoubt is twenty-four metres (80 feet) square and its thick walls are almost three metres (nine feet) high. It was never attacked, and was afterwards considered 'completely useless' for defensive purposes.

In **Strand Street**, below **Market Square**, at the entrance to the harbour and the railway station, is Port Elizabeth's most conspicuous landmark: **the Campanile**, a fifty-two-metre (170-foot) red brick tower, with a chiming clock and a twenty-three bell carillon, built to mark the centenary of the 1820 Settlers.

If you are prepared to climb the 204 steps, the viewing platform of the Campanile is an excellent place to get an idea of the layout of the city.

Although Port Elizabeth owes its character largely to the British, it recognizes its debts to others. In **Fleming Square**, between the **City Hall** and the **Post Office**, is a monument to Prester John, the mythical Christian king, in quest of whose African kingdom voyages of discovery were undertaken by the Portuguese.

In **Baakens Street**, directly opposite the City Hall, is the entrance to **Castle Hill**. There you will find **Feather Market Hall**, a huge stone building built in 1885 for auctioning ostrich feathers, but used today for concerts and exhibitions.

Rink Road, running north from the **St George's Park** entrance, intersects with **Cape Road**, where there is the striking **Horse Memorial**, erected in memory of the horses killed on both sides during the Boer War.

Within the city, on the banks of the **Baakens River**, south of **King George VI Park**, is the fifty-four hectare (133 acre) **Settlers Park and Nature Reserve**, where indigenous flora and bird life may be enjoyed in their natural setting.

Sightseeing: Beachfront

Port Elizabeth's recreational and outdoor attractions lie principally on the coast of the point forming the southern arm of the bay, which ends at **Cape Recife**.

To go there, head south on the **M4**, which becomes successively **Humewood Road**, **Beach Road** and **Marine Drive**.

Alternatively, catch the narrow-gauge steam train — **Diaz Express** — from the Campanile to **King's Beach**.

Ocean temperatures are seldom below sixteen degrees Celsius on this coast, and a series of beaches provide facilities for a range of aquatic and other activities.

On Beach Road is the **Port Elizabeth Museum** complex, which includes an oceanarium, a snake park and a tropical house, in which there is a jungle filled with exotic plants and birds.

The oceanarium has daily performances by dolphins and seals, and affords you the opportunity to see sharks, penguins and various fish at close quarters.

The Marine Drive winds along the coast to Cape Recife, where there are facilities in the **Cape Recife Nature Reserve** for picnickers and bird watchers, and the coastline is renowned among surf and rock anglers.

Looking north

The estuarine lagoon of the **Swartkops River**, some ten kilometres (six miles) north of Port Elizabeth, is a must for watersport enthusiasts. Navigable by small craft for eighteen kilometres (eleven miles), the river and its estuary offer protected waters for yachtsmen, power boaters, canoe paddlers, oarsmen and board sailors. It is also popular with anglers.

North of the mouth is the residential area of **Bluewater Bay**, which has one of the best bathing beaches in the area. Further north, turn-offs from the N2 lead to holiday resorts at **St George's Strand**, **King Neptune** and **Sundays River** mouth.

Addo Elephant Park

A visit to **Addo Elephant National Park** is probably one of the most rewarding day trips to be made from Port Elizabeth. About seventy kilometres (43 miles) north of Port Elizabeth on the **R335**, the elephant park occupies 895 hectares (2,212 acres) of dense bush in the **Sundays River valley**.

The succulent bush supports a herd of nearly 200 — more than three times the elephant population density elsewhere. As there are only three or four individuals

further south in the Knysna Forest, the Addo elephant herd is the most southerly in the world.

Other mammals to be seen in the park are black rhino, buffalo, eland, kudu, red hartebeest and several smaller antelope.

The park caters for campers as well as day visitors, and cottages are available for hire on a daily basis.

Apple Express

An exciting way of exploring the hinterland of Port Elizabeth is by steam train. The **Apple Express**, which operates from **Humewood Road Station,** has been travelling the narrow-gauge sixty-one-centimetre (two-foot) line from Port Elizabeth into the fruit-growing parts of the Langkloof since 1906.

The small engine hauls the diminutive green passenger coaches through breath-taking mountain and forest scenery, crossing the **Van Stadens River gorge** on a steel girder bridge 190 metres (623 feet) above the valley floor.

There is a similar service, the **Outeniqua Choo-Tjoe**, on the **Garden Route** between Knysna and George.

Above: Pachyderm playtime in Addo Elephant Park.

Kimberley: Diamond City

Throughout the world the name Kimberley has a lustre it owes to its association with diamonds. It was there that diamonds — hitherto extracted only from river gravels — were found for the first time in a volcanic magma that geologists later named kimberlite.

Today this small provincial city, capital of the dry Northern Cape and head office of the famous De Beers Consolidated Mines Limited, has a drowsy aura which is difficult to reconcile with the fact that it was there that the industrialization of South Africa began.

When the first South African diamond was discovered in 1866 near Hopetown there was no settlement of any kind on the site of the future city of Kimberley — a hill barely nine metres (29 feet) high, called Colesberg Kopje, in a dusty plain covered with low bush.

For the next few years diamond diggers attracted by the find concentrated their activities on alluvial deposits on the Vaal River some forty kilometres (25 miles) away to the north-east.

All this changed in 1869 when the so-called 'dry diggings' were discovered on farms in the vicinity, and 50,000 people flocked there from all corners of the earth to seek their fortunes.

With picks and shovels they began mining Colesberg Kopje in 1871 and over the next forty years converted the hill into the biggest man-made hole in the world: Kimberley mine, now known as Big Hole.

In 1873 the sprawling mining camp called New Rush that had grown up around the mine was renamed Kimberley, in honour of the British Secretary of State for the Colonies, Lord Kimberley.

The fortunes made there in diamonds during the early years were invested in gold mining after the precious metal was discovered on the Witwatersrand, fuelling the powerhouse of the South African economy which, in turn, spawned secondary industry.

However, when it comes to diamonds, Kimberley is now long past its heyday, new mines discovered elsewhere becoming more productive as the reserves of the Kimberley mines have approached exhaustion.

During the Anglo-Boer War of 1899–1902, when the Transvaal and Free State went to war with Britain, Kimberley, with its 30,000 inhabitants, was besieged by the Boers for 124 days.

Kimberley is a modern city, but much that is of interest in and around it is historical. Visitors with a passion for history and an interest in diamonds, will find the city very appealing.

When to visit

Deep inland, some 1,200 metres above sea-level, Kimberley lies within the summer rainfall area although it is, generally, a dry area, situated between the arid Karoo in the south and the Kalahari Desert in the north. The rain — when it comes — is in the form of brief torrential downpours that one associates with thunderstorms.

When the sun is shining, as it does most days of the year, it is hot and dusty, and very hot in summer. On winter nights, however, the temperature often falls below freezing point.

How to get there

Kimberley is linked with all the country's main centres by air, road and rail.

There are several scheduled flights daily between Kimberley and Johannesburg, Bloemfontein and Cape Town.

Daily passenger trains travelling between Cape Town and Johannesburg call there as do several inter-city bus services.

If you are travelling by car between Johannesburg and Cape Town, you can avoid the usual N1 route — which runs

Opposite: Probably the most celebrated of Kimberley's sights is the Big Hole, the largest man-made hole in the world.

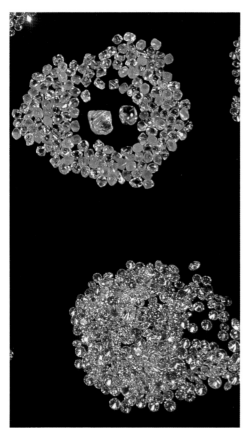

Above: Visitors with a passion for history and an interest in diamonds, will find Kimberley fascinating.

what remains today of the old Kimberley mine. Between 1871 and 1914, when the mine finally closed, thousands of miners, working with picks and shovels, removed some twenty-three million metric tons of earth, leaving a hole 500 metres (1,640 feet) across and 400 metres (1,312 feet) deep.

During its productive life of forty-three years it yielded 2,722 kilograms (almost three tons) or fifteen million carats of diamonds.

Some idea of the flavour of the early days on the diggings can be experienced by visiting the **Kimberley Mine Museum,** in Tucker Street, beside the Big Hole.

There part of the orginal town has been recreated through the restoration of forty-eight old wood-and-iron buildings brought from various parts of the city and re-erected on either side of a cobbled street.

These include cottages, a pub, a diamond buyer's office, blacksmith, haberdashery and the **Boxing Academy** established by Barney Barnato, who was Cecil Rhodes' principal rival over a century ago.

Also preserved there is the private railway coach that was used by early directors of De Beers.

In the city itself there are numerous museums and historical monuments. Among the preserved stately homes of Kimberley that echo the era of the diamond magnates are **Rudd House**, in Loch Road, **Dunluce** in Lodge Road, and the **Africana Library** in Du Toitspan Road.

A peculiar feature of Kimberley is the drive-in pub at the historic **Halfway House Hotel**, which perpetuates a tradition that in the old days permitted horsemen to call in there for a drink or two without having to dismount.

There were many skirmishes between Boer and British forces in the vicinity of Kimberley during the Anglo-Boer War. If you continue **south**, following the **Magersfontein Museum** signs, you will come to the scene of the biggest battle fought in the area.

At **Magersfontein**, thirty-two kilometres (20 miles) south of the city, a pitched battle was fought on 11 December 1899 between some 8,500 Boers under

through Bloemfontein — by taking the alternative R29 route from Johannesburg, which passes through Kimberley and eventually joins the N1 at **Three Sisters**.

Where to stay

There are hotels of varying standards, as well as other forms of accommodation. The most modern hotel in the city is the **Kimberley Holiday Inn**.

Riverton, a pleasure resort on a navigable stretch of the Vaal River sixteen kilometres (ten miles) north-west of the city, offers outdoor activities and holiday accommodation, ranging from luxury chalets to a caravan park and campsites.

Sightseeing

Probably the most celebrated of Kimberley's sights is the **Big Hole**, which is

General Piet Cronje and General Koos de la Rey and a 12,000-strong British force which had been dispatched under Lord Methuen to raise the siege.

It is often said that it was in this engagement that the British received from the Boers their first lesson in the elements of trench warfare that some fifteen years later they practised themselves in World War One.

Thinking the Boers were occupying higher ground, Methuen advanced his troops in close formation to the foot of the hills. There they came under heavy fire from the Boers, who unexpectedly had entrenched themselves. After being pinned down in the hot sun by Boer fire for most of the day, the British troops were eventually forced to withdraw.

The 423-hectare (1,045-acre) battlefield, preserved as a **Field Museum**, includes three cemeteries and six monuments, the principal of which is the pyramidal **Burger Monument** to the Boers who fell there. Other monuments commemorate members of individual British units who died.

Of particular geological interest are the **Nooitgedacht Glacial Pavings** north-west of Kimberley. Take the **R31** leading to **Barkly West** and watch out for the signposted turn-off to the site.

Here the surface rock 'pavement' was scoured some 300 million years ago by stones held in the grip of a slowly moving ice sheet which covered much of the interior of South Africa at that time.

Many millions of years later the lines incised by the stones apparently inspired Stone Age inhabitants of the area to add engravings (petroglyphs) of their own to the scoured surfaces.

Barkly West

A few kilometres further down the R31 after the turn-off is **Barkly West**, formerly Klipdrift, where South Africa's first alluvial diamond diggings were centred in 1869.

There in 1870 a former sailor in the Royal Navy, Stafford Parker, established the tiny diggers' Republic of Klipdrift, with himself as president. His rule ended a year later when Britain annexed the diamond fields.

Nearby **Canteen Kopje**, where Parker owned a 'music salon' bar, is the scene of the actual diggings of that time.

Also an important archaeological site that has yielded the fossil remains of many extinct animals and the artefacts of Stone Age cultures, Canteen Kopje is today maintained as a geological and archaeological reserve. The **Mining Commissioner's Museum** there displays artefacts found by diggers.

There are still a number of private diggers who process the gravels of the Vaal River nearby and bring their finds to the **diamond market** in Barkly West on Saturday mornings.

Campbell and Griquatown

Through the country west of Kimberley ran the main route taken by explorers and missionaries — among them William Burchell, Robert Moffat, John Campbell and Dr David Livingstone — who ventured into the little-known interior to the north over 150 years ago.

Lying respectively 110 kilometres (68 miles) and 158 kilometres (98 miles) west of Kimberley on the **R64**, Campbell and Griquatown were formerly the headquarters of rival Griqua chieftains Adam Kok II and Andries Waterboer.

At Campbell, named after the Rev John Campbell who visited the area on behalf of the London Missionary Society in 1813, is the first church built north of the Orange River.

The Livingstone Church, as it is called, was built in 1831 by the missionary Robert Moffat. It is there that the missionary explorer Dr David Livingstone met his future wife, Mary Moffat.

The house in which Mary Moffat was born, now the **Mary Moffat Museum**, is in Griquatown, which in Griqua times was called Klaarwater. The old Griqua council chamber is still standing, as is the syringa tree from which Waterboer hanged cattle thieves.

A hotel and caravan park accommodate visitors to Griquatown.

Kuruman

Travelling **north** from Campbell on the R385 and then the R31 for a total of eighty-three kilometres (52 miles) you come to **Danielskuil**, the former headquarters of another old Griqua leader, Barend Barends.

The **Wonderwork Caves**, which contain San paintings, lie on the R31 some fifty kilometres (30 miles) north of Danielskuil, and about forty kilometres (25 miles) further on, after passing through the **Kuruman Hills**, is the town of Kuruman itself.

It was there that Robert Moffat of the London Missionary Society baptized the first Tswana converts to Christianity in 1824 and built a mission settlement and church to accommodate 800 people.

There Dr David Livingstone courted and finally married Robert Moffat's daughter Mary in 1845. The press on which Moffat printed the first Setswana translation of the Bible is on display.

Situated at the southern extremity of the Kalahari, the mission and town of Kuruman owe their existence to the **Eye of Kuruman**, a spring draining a vast limestone system of underground streams that delivers some twenty million litres (four million gallons) of water a day.

The spring feeds a pool at the centre of a pleasant recreation area and is the source of the Kuruman River which, when augmented by heavy rains, flows through the desert for about 350 kilometres (217 miles) to the Nossob River, south of the Kalahari Gemsbok National Park.

Hotels and a caravan park provide accommodation at Kuruman.

South-west of Kuruman the **R27** passes at **Sishen** through the world's largest known iron-ore deposits on the way to **Upington,** some 280 kilometres (174 miles) away. About 150 kilometres (93 miles) northeast of Kuruman on the R27 is **Vryburg**, established in 1883 as the capital of the short-lived breakaway Republic of Stellaland. A British expedition ended its independence in 1885, but its flag is preserved in the **Vryburg Museum**.

From Vryburg you can return to Kimberley by heading **south on the R47**. On the 150-kilometre (93-mile) stretch between Vryburg and Warrenton you cross the 40,000-hectare (99,000-acre) Vaalharts Irrigation Scheme, one of the largest irrigation schemes in the southern hemisphere. From Warrenton it is seventy-four kilometres (46 miles) to Kimberley on the R29.

Northern Karoo

Continuing on the **R29 south** of Kimberley you pass through a succession of small towns, all of which have hotels and caravan parks.

The first, **Hopetown,** where the first South African diamond was discovered on the southern bank of the Orange River in 1866, is 130 kilometres (80 miles) south of Kimberley.

Forty-four kilometres (27 miles) on is **Strydenburg,** with **Britstown** another seventy-seven kilometres (48 miles) further. It is 111 kilometres (69 miles) to the next town, **Victoria West**, where there is a 430-hectare (1,062-acre) nature reserve stocked with black wildebeest, eland, gemsbok, springbok and zebra.

There is a garage sixty-three kilometres (39 miles) later where the R29 meets the N1 at **Three Sisters**, which gets its name from three conical Karoo hills. Although a notice advertises 24-hour service at the garage, don't count on it!

If you had been travelling down the N1 from Johannesburg, you would, after crossing from the Free State, have passed through **Colesberg, Hanover** and **Richmond**.

Colesberg, almost exactly halfway between Johannesburg and Cape Town, was founded in 1829 and named after the then Cape governor Sir Lowry Cole. It is principally a sheep-farming area although, also famous for horse breeding, it is dominated by the 1,707-metre (5,600-foot) flat-topped **Coleskop Mountain**.

Seventy-seven kilometres (48 miles) south-west of Three Sisters is **Beaufort West**, the biggest town in the Karoo, where many travellers on the long haul from

Above: Indigenous flora of the Karoo, the great desert of the Northern Cape.

Johannesburg to Cape Town choose to break their journeys.

The **Karoo National Park** in the Nuweveld Mountains west of Beaufort West, preserving some 46,000 hectares (113,620 acres) of typical dry Karoo scrubland, offers hiking trails.

The longest stage of the journey by road between Johannesburg and Cape Town is the 198-kilometre (123-mile) stretch between Beaufort West and Laingsburg, with one petrol station at Leeu Gamka (Lion River), 75 kilometres (47 miles) from Beaufort West.

One hot Sunday afternoon in January 1981 **Laingsburg** was struck by an awesome natural disaster. The town had been built on low ground beside the Buffels River, which was seldom more than a trickle. But that Sunday there were simultaneous cloudbursts in the catchments of three tributaries that fed the river, and without warning a wall of water suddenly swept through the town, carrying homes, livestock, vehicles and several inhabitants with it.

No marks of this calamity remain but as you drive through the town you will notice a post indicating how high the floodwaters rose that day.

Twenty-seven kilometres (17 miles) further **west** is **Matjiesfontein,** a Karoo village that has been restored to its Victorian elegance. There, the **Lord Milner Hotel** is a popular retreat for people from Cape Town who want to escape for a few days, or weeks, to the tranquillity of another era.

The next town, the old railway centre of **Touws River**, is fifty-five kilometres (34 miles) away, and twenty-two kilometres (13 miles) further on you leave the Karoo and cross the Hex River Mountains into the winelands of the Western Cape.

You cross the 112-kilometre-wide (70-mile) valley between the Hex River and Du Toitskloof Mountains, passing the village of **De Doorns** and the town of **Worcester.**

The second range is crossed by way of either a pass over the mountains or a tunnel after which you get your first glimpse of Table Mountain, fifty-seven kilometres (35 miles) away, with the city of Cape Town nestling at its foot.

PART FOUR: SPECIAL FEATURES

Above: Namaqualand Daisies.
Opposite: The majestic Caracal Lynx.

Flora

From the tropical mangrove swamps along the coastline of KwaZulu-Natal, to the dry savannah of Eastern Transvaal and the misty mountain ranges of the Cape Peninsula, the splendour of South African flora is as varied as the land which nourishes it. South Africa boasts 216 of the 400 plant families found in the world.

There are six main types of vegetation in South Africa: desert and semi-desert, Mediterranean, temperate, subtropical coastal, bushveld or savannah, and temperate highveld grasslands. Two distinct varieties of South African flora can be defined: a tropical/subtropical element found in the eastern, central and north-western regions, and a temperate element which is most typical of Cape flora.

Cape Flora

This kind of vegetation occupies the south-western corner of South Africa and a narrow strip within the southern coastline from the Olifants River in the west, to Port Elizabeth in the south-east. This area has been designated one of the world's six floral kingdoms.

Cape flora epitomizes the beauty and variety of vegetation indigenous to South Africa. Former prime minister Jan Smuts said: 'To see the Cape flora in its full glory in spring with all its exquisite variety and colour — is an experience never to be forgotten. And when there is the added song of birds, the hum of insects and the intoxication of scents — the magic of life is seen and felt in a way which would be difficult to match elsewhere.'

The umbrella term for most Cape vegetation is *fynbos* ('fine bush') which is assorted, thick, colourful scrub. The greatest concentration occurs in the Caledon, Paarl, Worcester and Ceres areas. The vegetation is highly resistant to fire, which stimulates certain seeds to germination and prompts bulbs to re-emerge.

Fynbos is an extraordinary family, the largest genus being the Cape heath or Erica which exceeds 100 species. Added to this are seventeen other groups with twenty or more species including oxalis, crassula, disa, helichrysum and gladiolus. Erica forms the biggest single genus in the Cape Peninsula as well as in the entire Cape floral kingdom.

Cape heath has a marvellous array of colours and tones. Lantern heath for example, with its splendid orange and green flowers, can be seen on the slopes of the Langeberg Mountains. During the late spring large patches of dark red heath are visible on the **Apostles Battery**, on the heights above **Llandudno** and on the buttresses above Hout Bay and Constantia Nek. Heath blooms so thickly on the slopes near Blinkwater Gorge that it is clearly visible from Camps Bay beach. Remember that *fynbos* is now protected, and any burning or picking of this seemingly abundant Cape floral feature is strictly prohibited.

The protea, South Africa's national flower, is the most celebrated member of Cape *fynbos*. It is named after Proteus, the Greek god who had the ability to change his shape; in the same way, the protea takes on an infinite variety of forms. These forms vary from tallish trees to small ground creepers.

The orchid is another member of the Cape floral kingdom. Disa, the 'flower of the gods' or 'the pride of Table Mountain' is the emblem of the Cape Province and perhaps the most celebrated member of Cape orchids. This scarlet flower inhabits the summer mist-belt of Table Mountain and it can also be found close to waterfalls and streams.

Another member of the Cape floral

Opposite: Aloes grow abundantly on the hot and hazy highveld.

Above: Vygies (Mesembryanthemacae family) — most intense in colour around midday.

kingdom of particular interest is the chincherinchee. Now a common European houseplant, its stalks make the noise of a beetle when they are rubbed together. More than thirty species bloom between July and October in low-lying areas of the Cape.

Certain topographical and climatic conditions promote this distinctive character; Table Mountain, a national monument and nature reserve, is home to over 1,400 species of flowering plants. These plants thrive on the damp mists that cover the mountain in the dry season. During the winter months vapour-laden clouds condense on Table Mountain, keeping the atmosphere moist.

To view the Cape floral kingdom at its best, visit South Africa's national botanical gardens at **Kirstenbosch**, on the slopes of Table Mountain. The landscape of this magnificent garden devoted entirely to indigenous flora includes flatlands, natural springs, valleys and gorges.

The origins of Cape flora are mysterious; there are two theories. The first is that these particular species of flowering plants were inherent to the southern hemisphere before the ancient land mass of Gondwanaland spilt into the continents as we know them today. The theory is founded on the basis that there are links between the Cape protea family and certain species in Australia, South America and other regions in the southern hemisphere. The second theory is that during the Ice Age, the vegetation of the northern hemisphere migrated downwards, finding harbour in South Africa. When the ice caps retreated, that vegetation was only to be found in the region.

Over the millenia, Cape flora has been threatened by encroaching subtropical plant life. Particular specimens of Cape flora such as proteas and heath occur inland in isolated patches. The natural erosion of the unique flora, combined with human interference, is responsible for endangering the species.

Cape features and landscape are multifarious. The dry semi-desert basin of the Karoo occupies a wide area of the interior and is home to many succulent plants, thorn bushes and those adapted to arid areas such as aloes, stapelias and mesems.

Of all the succulent plants in the Karoo, the lithops or stone plant is particularly interesting. It blends with the dry rocky ground around it and passes unnoticed, except in spring when the very stones of the semi-arid area appear to flower.

Trees are not prolific in this region, and although it is dry and seemingly bleak, a harmonious display of bleached colour and light gives the Karoo a mystical quality unmatched anywhere else.

Visit the **Karoo Botanical Garden** in Worcester which is acclaimed by the International Organization for Succulents as one of the five botanic gardens in the world to display an excellent collection devoted to succulents. There is a strip of land no wider than 125 kilometres (80 miles) along the north-western coast of the Cape Province, which is true desert with little more than red sand dunes and dry river beds.

The **Kalahari Gemsbok National Park** is slightly further to the east in a semi-arid climate. The vegetation includes camel thorn, **vaalkameel, swarthaak**, raisin bush and African blackwood which subsist in the dry river beds of the Nossob and the Auob. The Tsamma melon and wild cucumber are water-retaining plants which provide nutrition for the few animals which inhabit the area. Good spring rains transform this shrivelled-up desert into a wonderland of bright floral colours.

Between Cape Town and **Saldanha Bay** to the north-west, the spring rains bring the sandveld flora into bloom. These fleeting blossoms tantalize flower lovers from all over the world. Sandveld flora is famous for gladioli, daisies, ixias and nemesias. Among the ixias most notable is the Ixia veridiflora with its rare aqua-green petals. The town of **Darling** hosts an annual flower show in the spring where these splendid flowers are on display.

More spectacular than the sandveld flora of the western plains are the celebrated **Namaqualand** daisies. This area is best visited from early August to late September after rains have transformed the dry wasteland into a glorious carpet of pastel hues. Although referred to as daisies, the wild flowers of this inland belt bloom with a magnificent variety. Included in this splendid array are succulents, irises, lilies as well as orange, yellow, blue, cream, red and purple blossoms.

The vegetation of the south-eastern Cape coastline is more lush and tropical than might be expected for its latitude, because of the warming currents and breezes from the Indian Ocean. This is a beautiful stretch of coastline and the dramatic landscape incorporates the glorious heights of the Outeniqua Mountains, the deep gorges such as the **Storms River** mouth and the lush forests of **Knysna** and **Humansdorp**.

The area is most commonly known as the **Garden Route**. Its official boundaries are Mossel Bay in the west and the Storms River mouth in the east. Of South Africa's 22,000 flowering plant species, 3,000 are found along the Garden Route and its surrounding areas. Among them are highly protected plants such as the red lily of George (best known as the Scarborough lily) and more abundant species like the pink watsonia.

Outeniqua is a Khoikhoi word meaning 'men laden with honey'; it is derived from the Stone Age hunters who collected honey in the mountains. **Tsitsikamma** is the Hottentot name for the forest. It means 'clear or abundant water' and aptly describes the moisture on which the sylvan ferns and mosses thrive. There are many spectacular trees in the Tsitsikamma forest; most notable are the yellowwood, stinkwood, and calendarwood trees which are not only famous for the quality of their wood but also for their awesome age and towering size.

Wild orchids and lilies of the Tsitsikamma are a beautiful sight. According to legend, deep in the heart of the forest at the foot of the Outeniqua mountains lies a valley carpeted with scarlet lilies of unsurpassed beauty which bloom only for a short time in late summer. The spot was discovered by a hunter from the village of Knysna. An expedition set out and found the field. Spoor showed that the area was frequented by elephants, so they named the spot The Elephant's Flower Garden. The identity of the flowers was never established, but most botanists speculate they were George lilies.

For a glimpse into the Tsitsikamma

Above: Namaqualand Daisies transform a wasteland into a carpet of gold.

forest, visit **The Garden of Eden**, a short walking trail and picnic spot near the main road between Knysna and Plettenberg Bay. Better still, stay in the coastal chalets of the **Tsitsikamma National Park** or follow the **Otter Trail**, a four day walk along the coastline and through parts of the forest. Any stop along the Garden Route provides an excellent base for exploring the entire Cape floral kingdom.

KwaZulu-Natal flora

The province of **KwaZulu-Natal** is the south-east coastal region bounded on the south-west by the Van Staden's mountains, where the tropical climate and warm breezes of the Indian Ocean strongly determine the nature of the flora.

Many flowering plants, such as the poin-settias, frangipani and bougainvillea found along the coastline, come from abroad as the flora in this area forms a man-made extension of the east African tropical flora. The lush coastline is otherwise dominated by mangrove swamps and true rain forests with palm trees, banana trees and succulent scrub abounding.

Moving inland, sugar cane fields cover most of the interior where the game reserves of **Hluhluwe** and **Umfolozi** are covered with wild thorn, monkey rope, marula and mahogany, and where gardenias and sycamore fig trees can be seen in abundance. The raphia palm is a most beautiful tree with blue-green leaves and dark red mid-ribs. Another spectacular sight is the Anselluia gigantia, a rare orchid found growing on bushveld trees.

The **Nkandla forest** on the edge of the **Tugela River Valley** is a tranquil haven where mists swirl around large ancient trees. **Kranskop** or **Precipice Peak** takes its name from the devilish heights which overlook the southern slopes of the Tugela River Valley. There, among the forests of trees, shrubs and herbs, species of clivia grow.

The **Drakensberg Mountain** range runs roughly parallel to the coast, in a U-shape, but is at its most magnificent in KwaZulu-Natal. The range is a floral paradise containing 800 species of flowering plant and sixty-three species of ground orchid. Particularly noteworthy are the small aquatic plants which float in the many springs and rivers and the beautifully coloured lichens that coat the jagged rocks.

The woodlands of the Drakensberg house yellowwood trees, ferns and proteas. Wild clematis can be seen among the gladioli and orchids that hang from cliffs. Erica or Heath is also predominant in the Drakensberg where the climate is cooler and less humid than along the coastline. The grasslands that lie beneath the craggy heights of the Drakensberg Mountains are famous for species of wild iris and clematis that grow in abundance.

For those not brave enough to venture out on the numerous pathways and walking trails of the Drakensberg Mountains, some of which are specially designed for intrepid botanists, the flora of the KwaZulu-Natal mist belt may be seen in the Pietermaritzburg botanical garden.

Free State flora

The majority of the flat temperate grasslands that cover the Free State are cultivated, taken over for farming maize and wheat. The area is dry and hot, a perfect home for the acacia tree which is spread quite profusely in this area. The karee is another tree native to this area, which shades highveld shrubs and bulbs from the sweltering heat that encloses the plateau. Colourful flowering plants such as the ursinia or the gazania help to brighten up this otherwise khaki-coloured grass–land.

Transvaal flora

The fifth feature of South African vegetation is bushveld or savannah, which occurs mainly in what was the Transvaal. This region has been divided by altitude into highveld and lowveld. The highveld encompasses Gauteng and extends into the North-West and Mpumalanga provinces. Thorn trees and veld (grassland) characterize the hot and hazy highveld from the **Limpopo** River down to the thriving business capital of the country, Johannesburg. The acacia and aloe are found scattered all over this savannah. In late March and early April a profusion of pink and white cosmos flowers provide bright sketches of colour in the veld. In the early summer months, jacaranda trees blossom in brilliant hues of mauve and blue.

Beyond the eastern escarpment lies the town of **Tzaneen**, main centre for the **Magoebaskloof** mountains and the lush valley of the **Great Letaba River**. There the vegetation changes dramatically. Because of its position at the foot of the Mpumalanga plateau with high rainfall and fertile soil, the region is home to citrus, avocado, banana, pawpaw, pecan nut and macadamia nut trees. There are dense forests, most of them under plantation. Fortunately natural forests still exist, including the so-called woodbush, the largest of the area's indigenous forests, where redwoods, ironwoods, cabbage trees, and red stinkwoods occur.

Modjaji, named after northern Transvaal's legendary **Rain Queen** who traditionally brought water to the region, encompasses a beautiful cycad forest where thousands of weird-looking ancient cycads exist.

Seventy kilometres (45 miles) east of Tzaneen at the **Hans Merensky Nature Reserve**, where the descent to the lowveld is almost complete, one finds jackalberry, red bushwillow, weeping boer-bean and the famed lowveld trees, mopane and knobthorn.

Mpumalanga is a truly spectacular region. The mountains there are not as massive as they are in KwaZulu-Natal, but they are breathtakingly beautiful, carved into peaks, ravines and gorges. On the cool higher ground, dense evergreen woodlands and flaming aloes bring colour to the steep slopes. The plains below these mountains are the lowveld savannah where the thorny acacia, lily, ilala palm, wild fig and mopane trees grow. Massive baobab trees are scattered among the mahogany, ebony and ironwood trees, also native to this region.

Wildlife

South African fauna runs over the whole gamut of African wildlife — antelopes, monkeys, big cats, rhino, elephant, crocodile, mongoose, porcupine, jackals and hyena can be found in excellent national parks in the country. Its relatively mild, largely subtropical climate allows the visitor to view these beasts in a cooler environment than in most of the country's northern neighbours.

Big Five

The 'big five' — elephant, rhino, leopard, lion, buffalo — can only be seen in South Africa with any consistency in the eastern area of the **Kruger National Park**, neighbouring private game reserves and the **Pilanesberg National Reserve** next to **Sun City**. But in these areas the chances of seeing these imposing and most sought-after animals are probably higher than anywhere else in Africa.

Elephant

The African elephant is the largest land mammal in the world. It has a complex social structure, with females living in herds with infants and adolescents. Males are usually alone or in bachelor groups. Males have a sort of 'on heat' breeding period during which glands in their cheeks ooze liquid and their penises turn green. This period is called `musth' and it is when two bulls in musth fight over a cow that aggressive and impressive fights can be witnessed by those lucky enough to catch this spectacle.

Ivory can still be bought in South Africa, though it cannot be exported under the current Convention for International Trade of Endangered Species (CITES) ban on the international trade in ivory.

Lion

Lions are also pack animals with prides of up to twenty not being uncommon. The main hunters are the lionesses, who usually hunt in groups of two or three. A group will catch an animal which will be eaten by the whole pride, including those who have stayed to 'babysit' the young. Recent research has shown that lions are predominantly nocturnal; hunting, drinking and playing mostly at night. But they can also be found stalking prey for a kill at first light or dusk. Mature lions will allow adolescent males in their pride until the youngsters reach sexual maturity, at which point they will be forced to leave. A lonester will journey alone or with other bachelors until he either wins a battle to become the head of another, weaker lion's pride, or steals a couple of lionesses from another pride and sets up a harem for himself.

Rhinoceros

Rhinoceros, both white (wide-mouthed) and black (hook-lipped) are found in South Africa. The rhino is one of the most ancient species of animal in the world, and has remained relatively unchanged for some four million years. These tank-like pachyderms are generally solitary animals, meeting infrequently for a short mating period.

The white rhino will mother a calf for approximately two years, until it is fully weaned. A black rhino will chase away its calf when it is about to give birth again, which is usually between two and five years old.

Rhino horns — created from hair — have been prized for centuries leading to a huge poaching industry which has brought the creatures to the brink of extinction. The horns are used in Yemen to make prestigious scabbard handles and, in the Far East, ground horn is mixed into fever-reducing pills.

It is a common fallacy that rhino horn is an aphrodisiac. The misconception may have been caused because of the rhino's extraordinary mating habits — rhino can remain coupled for up to two hours.

The white rhino is, in fact, the same dull

Above: The Cape buffalo — one of the most dangerous animals in the bush

grey colour as the black. The term 'white' is derived from the Afrikaans word *wyd*, meaning wide, because of the subspecies' flat wide mouth. White rhino are grazers, easy to spot on the grassy open veld. Larger than the black, they are the second-largest animal.

Hunting and poaching led to the near extinction of the white rhino. The plight of the animal, even as early as 1895, prompted the establishment of the first nature reserves in South Africa. White rhino had disappeared from all their former habitats except for a small herd in northern KwaZulu-Natal's **Umfolozi National Park**. There the remaining fifty animals were carefully nutured until the population was big enough to sustain the translocation of some animals. There are now some 6,000 white rhino worldwide, almost all of them descended from that small KwaZulu-Natal population.

The extremely endangered black rhino is a browser, picking leaves off shrubs with its pointed, prehensile upper lip. It spends most of its life in thick scrubby bush, making it difficult to spot.

Leopard

Leopard are quite common throughout Africa, despite scares about their potential extinction in the 1970s. This nocturnal big cat is very adaptable, and has even been known to scavenge in suburban dustbins. In South Africa it is mainly confined to mountainous regions and game parks. The leopard relies on its stealth and strength to catch antelope, mainly impala. Its catch is dragged to a tree or cave where it is left to 'hang' and eaten over several days. The leopard's solitary and wary nature, coupled with its chiefly arboreal and nocturnal lifestyle, make this animal difficult to find, unless it allows itself to be seen in one of its bolder moments.

Buffalo

The Cape buffalo is a separate species from the Asian water buffalo. The large bovine animals are among of the most ferocious animals in Africa. Their huge horns, which stretch right across their heads, are made of compressed hair. Usually placidly grazing in large herds, buffalo will stampede when

273

Above: Springbok in the Gemsbok National Park.

alarmed, and those which have been wounded will attack. Buffalo disturbed while sleeping in bush will also attack viciously. Buffalo are often found surrounded by slender white cattle egrets which follow the herds to eat the grasshoppers and other insects stirred up by the passage of the lumbering beasts through the grass. Oxpeckers are often found clinging to the backs, chests and even ears of buffalo as they eat the ticks, mites and other parasites off the animals' skin.

Antelope

A vast variety of antelope can be found in South Africa with four species found exclusively in the country.

Although found elsewhere on the continent, the springbok is commonly associated with South Africa because of its use as the national sporting symbol. A medium-sized antelope about seventy-five centimetres (more than two feet) high, the springbok performs a characteristic 'stotting' leap when agitated. Stotting is when the animal leaps into the air with all four legs off the ground at once, arching its back. A startled springbok will stott several times, alerting the rest of the herd to danger.

Springbok are gregarious, living in large herds on grass plains and are often to be found in mixed herds with wildebeest, hartebeest and even ostrich.

The gemsbok is a beautiful large antelope, similar in size to a horse. A brownish-grey in colour, the animal is highlighted with attractive black and white markings on its face, belly, legs and rump. Gemsbok have very long, prominently ringed, almost straight horns. Their habitat is varied, from grass plains to the bristling heat and drought of semi-arid areas, like that of the **Gemsbok National Park**. In arid areas gemsbok have been known to dig in the sand for water and roots. Usually placid, gemsbok will attack if threatened or wounded. They have been known to spear predators and even humans with their horns.

The klipspringer is just twice the size of a hare. The unique characteristic of this species is that it lives on tiptoe. Klipspringers get all the water they need

Above: Bat Eared Foxes live in dry savannah or semi-desert areas.

from the foliage and fruit they eat. They can stand on their hind legs to browse from bushes. The tiny yellow-brown antelopes live in pairs on rocks near thick bush into which they can run for cover. But they are very agile in their rocky habitat, springing lithely from boulder to boulder. Their specialized hoofs not only provide good footholds, but allow the klipspringer to change direction rapidly. If they see a predator approaching, they cry a warning. The predator will more often than not call off the chase at this point, knowing that the klipspringer has the advantage and, on rocks, can outrun almost anything.

The greater kudu is one of the most elegant antelopes. The male's horns not only corkscrew but spiral two and a half times along their length — which can be up to one metre long (three feet). These large herbivores are a soft brown in colour with stripes of white over their bodies, and black patches on their legs below their front shoulders. Without horns to distract attention, the kudu's very large pale ears are distinctive in the female. The kudu became extinct in South Africa

but has been reintroduced in several parks and is the emblem of the National Parks Board. Other antelope such as impala, eland, waterbuck, tiny duikers and dikdik can all be found in habitats in different parts of South Africa.

Four antelope unique to South Africa: The black wildebeest (white-tailed gnu) had become extinct in the wild, but was still found living basically as in the wild on some large farms. From this stock, and principally from a large farm in the Free State owned by De Beers Consolidated Mines Limited, they have been reintroduced to the wild in reserves around South Africa. The present population is about 3,500. This antelope has a dark brown coat with white tail and mane. Both sexes have horns. Black wildebeest live in open grassland and bushveld habitats, on plains and in hilly regions. The English name for wildebeest, gnu, comes from the male's territorial marking call of 'ge-nu'.

Bontebok and the blesbok are both of the hartebeest family. They are dark brownish-black with white patches on their faces, underside, lower legs and rump. The

Above: Hippo are found in many of the lakes and rivers in South Africa.

blesbok is found in the Cape, Free State, North-West, western KwaZulu-Natal and southern Botswana, but the bontebok is found only in the Cape.

Both species are now unknown in the wild, but can be found in game reserves and on large farms. These herbivores live in open grassland areas in groups led by a dominant male. The male blesbok is often to be seen standing near a large dung heap in the centre of his territory. Young males are seen off the territory as they reach sexual maturity.

The Cape grysbok is a small antelope found in the Cape and KwaZulu-Natal. The coat is a reddish-brown, but it is speckled with individual white hairs which give it its name of 'grey buck.' Grysbok live a solitary life in a mixed habitat, including grass and bush, but prefer bushy river undergrowth.

Conservation

Wildlife protection in South Africa dates back to 1657 when the founder of the Cape colony, Jan van Riebeeck, tried to control hunting. But the traditional Boer view was that everything living on the land was available for them. Some early diarists record that in Gauteng they could shoot at random from their ox-wagons and be sure to hit something good for the pot. Later the addition of trophy hunting led to the extinction of some animals and decimation of others. The extinction of even one species in an ecosystem will set the whole order awry as each niche is affected by the loss.

In South Africa, the indigenous bluebuck was exterminated around 1800. Similar to the roan antelope with a bluish-grey body, it lived on the plains of the Swellendam region of the Cape. A subspecies of lion, the Cape lion is now also extinct.

In 1894 Paul Kruger set aside for posterity a 17,400 hectare (43,000 acre) piece of land in the former Eastern Transvaal. Another piece of land set aside in 1898 provided the beginnings of the vast tract of land now known as the Kruger National Park. Today, over ten per cent of the country's land area is protected, and private landowners are gradually appreciating the importance of maintaining the country's natural heritage.

The Cape mountain zebra is a conservation success story. These slow breeders

Above: Baby Leopard. The leopard is common in South Africa but is nocturnal and thus difficult to find.

had almost disappeared, threat-ened with extinction after years of being shot for the pot. Now their protected numbers are growing. **The Mountain Zebra National Park**, established in 1935 with just five stallions and one mare, now has the largest concentration of the ungulate, with 230 recorded in 1991.

The roan antelope, wild dog, scaly ant eater, cheetah, bald ibis, bearded vulture, Gill's clawed toad, the micro frog and the geometric tortoise are among the animals protected under South African law.

Game hunting is possible in some private parks. Rules vary from province to province. Special permits allow kills of the 'big five' (white rhino only), giraffe, antelope, pangolin and antbear, and of many species of game and fowl.

Introduced species

In the Cape, fallow deer have taken hold, having been introduced to a Cape farm in 1897. The American grey squirrel, which devastated Europe's red squirrel popu-lations when introduced there, is also to be found in the Cape, principally in Cape Town itself. It was introduced to the country by Cecil Rhodes.

The Himalayan thar, a goat-like hairy ruminant, was introduced to a farm in the Cape around 1930. In 1937 a pair escaped to Table Mountain where there is now a wild population of over 100. The European rabbit is also to be found on Robben Island off Cape Town.

Other mammals

Rock dassies are rabbit-like creatures which live on rock faces. Dassies will scamper away shyly over rocks if approached too closely, but can look appealingly nervous as they peer at you through big round eyes from a respectable distance. Dassies can often be found in big colonies — their presence confirmed by 'dassie toilets' where a whole group will leave their small round droppings.

Reptiles

Nile crocodiles are found in the north-east of South Africa. They are very strong and can attack antelope, humans and even buffalo as they come to drink at a ford or river. Crocodiles keep their prey in underwater larders until the meat is tender, then rip it up by clamping their teeth onto a piece of the prey and twisting their bodies until the flesh comes loose.

Crocodiles can stay under water for long periods without coming up for air, and the only indication of their presence is a stream of air bubbles rising to the surface.

The South African Maputaland coast is one of only four known breeding grounds in the world for leatherback turtles. Loggerhead turtles are also found nesting along the KwaZulu-Natal coastline. Leatherback turtles can weigh up to 700 kilogrammes (317 lbs), and hauling their enormous bulk up the beach is a great effort. The female must nest above the spring tide line to ensure her clutch is not swept away. She digs a large hole in the sand in which to lay her eggs. As she covers the hole she urinates to make the sand set hard like concrete to stop other animals digging for the eggs.

Side-necked terrapins pull their heads into one side of their shell. These carnivorous reptiles live in rivers and swamps and can be found basking on logs or rocks. The marsh terrapin falls into this subfamily, and can be found widely throughout South Africa. During severe droughts it will bury itself in the moist soil for the summer and sometimes will migrate to new pastures after rains.

There are four types of land tortoise in South Africa, the greater *padloper*, the Karoo padloper, the speckled *padloper* and the parrot-beaked tortoise. All four are found in the Cape. They are mainly herbivores but will eat snails and millipedes and have even been known to eat hyena droppings for their calcium. The tortoise hibernates in winter, usually underground, and in summer lies in the shade to escape the midday sun.

There are 130 species of snakes recorded in southern Africa. The best time for finding snakes is in spring during the mating season. But snakes in general are elusive, and unless you make an effort you are unlikely to see any. There are thirty-four venomous species of which fourteen have been known to kill people.

The African rock python, Africa's largest snake, is found in the north-east of South Africa. The python can swallow very large prey — antelope such as springbok are eaten live and suffocated. It can take several days for the snake to digest such large meals, during which time it can hardly move and is very vulnerable. Pythons have been known to attack humans in extreme circumstances.

There are five adders which live in South Africa, the puff adder being the most ubiquitous. Arboreal species such as the spotted bush snake have notched tail shields which they hook into crevices in tree trunks to pull up their wide bodies.

South Africa boasts a large number of lizards, from small geckos to the Nile monitor, Africa's largest lizard. Monitor lizards live near water and are great swimmers. They are carnivores, eating fish, shellfish, frogs, crabs, and sometimes even birds or eggs.

Geckos, usually brown, can often be found on the walls and steps of houses Many South Africans believe their presence brings good luck, perhaps because they eat mosquitos and flies. Some lizards are very colourful. The male Cape flat rock lizard has a deep blue head and body with an orange tail.

There are almost ninety species and sub-species of frog in South Africa. Some have wonderful names such as the snoring puddle frogs and the painted reed frog. Reed and lily frogs can change colour in the same way as chameleons. Rain frogs, fat and ugly, are usually only seen after heavy rains. When threatened, rain frogs will blow themselves up into a ball to exaggerate their size.

The banded rubber frog is South Africa's most beautiful frog with its sleek black body with two fawn/orange stripes down the sides and blotches on its legs. Don't be tempted to stroke it however — it secretes a poisonous slime through its skin.

A rare frog, *Capensis microbatrachella,* can be found in the Cape Province. The frog is only one centimetre (just over half an inch) in length and its body varies from a bright metallic green to a deep olive colour with a yellow stripe down its back. The frog was

Above: The puff adder is the most common adder in South Africa. South Africa has more than 130 species of snake.

thought to have been extinct for twenty years when it was rediscovered in a water meadow near Cape Town's Kenilworth racecourse in 1988. These amphibians live in non-perennial marshes, but their habitat is diminishing and is constantly threatened by channelling and draining of marshy areas and pollution.

Spiders and creepy-crawlies

The black widow, or button spider, is the only spider known to have occasionally killed humans in South Africa. Its poison affects the nerves and can result in heart or lung failure. Small scorpions are the most dangerous. Some can squirt their venom long distances — up to one metre (three feet).

There are myriad beetles, moths and insects of every kind which may be attracted to your lights in the evenings, some large enough to look menacing, but none posing any real threat.

In Johannesburg suburbs a large pinkish-brown cricket-like insect surfaces in the summer months. Known as a 'Parktown

Prawn' the creature can grow up to seven centimetres (three inches) long and strike terror into those not used to its presence.

But take heart, the country also boasts 800 species of butterfly.

Freshwater

Barbels resemble catfish and can grow into gigantic predators weighing up to sixty kilogrammes (132 lbs). The barbel catches small fish with its sharp teeth and can also filter small organisms through its wide mouth onto its fine gill rakers. Either a mottled olive green or a uniform grey in colour, the barbel is scaleless. This fish is able to breathe air, allowing it to inhabit water with a very low oxygen content. It can even crawl short distances through wet grass.

Tigerfish, the angler's dream, are found in many inland waterways.

Seals

The Cape fur seal is found around the Cape coast. The seal, over two metres long (six feet), stays close to the shore. Seals will

Above: Cape Fur seals are found around the Cape coast but they are always under threat from those who would use their penises for "aphrodisiacs".

return to their birthplace at sexual maturity to reproduce. A Cape fur seal changes its coat every year in the summer (January-February). New-born seals are black, changing to an olive-green shade and finally to the silver-grey of the adult.

The Cape fur seal was culled annually in South Africa until 1989 when conservationists and a public outcry against the proposed culling of 30,500 seals led to a moratorium on the cull. The culled seals were processed mainly for their genitalia, which were sold to manufacture aphrodisiacs in the Far East. Claims by the fishing industry that the estimated half million seals living along the coast drastically reduce their fish catches have been discredited. Vagrant elephant seals and sub-Antarctic fur seals are sometimes found on South Africa's coast.

South Africa has a large fishing industry, mainly pilchard, mackerel, hake and tuna. Clawless lobster (crayfish), abalone, shrimp, prawn, krill, anchovy, sardines and pilchards are all fished.

At least 2,200 species of fish live or migrate through South Africa's waters. Sea fishing is very popular, from the shore or from boats. Deep-sea anglers can expect billfish, mackerel and tuna. Rock anglers can pick up the odd milk shark.

Most sharks found around the coast are harmless, including the Izak catshark, speckled gully shark and the spiny dogfish. Some can be dangerous to humans such as the blue shark, great white, spotted ragged-tooth, dusky, hammerhead and blunthead. The stingray, infrequently spotted in coastal waters, can sting but the venom is not fatal.

Whales and dolphins

There are thirty-seven cetacean species in southern African waters **Heaviside's** dolphins are small, with a grey cape over their front and white markings beneath. They are often spotted at **Hottentot Bay** and near **Halifax Island**.

Other dolphin species include killer whales, false killer whales, pilot whales and dusky dolphins, common bottlenosed (off KwaZulu-Natal coast) striped, spinner,

Above: Whales are often seen around the coast of South Africa and particularly from the Hermanus shore from August to November.

hump-backed (off KwaZulu-Natal coast), Risso's and the southern right whale dolphin. There are dolphinariums in Durban and Port Elizabeth.

Whaling was carried out off the South African coast from the eighteenth century until 1973. But now South Africa has strict laws conserving whales.

There are eleven species and sub-species of whales, including the sperm and the southern bottlenose. Baleen whales — with large fibrous fronds in their mouths with which they filter fish and plankton — include the southern right whale (no dorsal fin), pygmy right whale, blue, fin, sei, minke and humpback whales.

Whales are often seen from the coast — southern right whales can be seen every year at close quarters near Hermanus from August to November, providing one of the world's best whale-whatching experiences. There is even a whale cryer whose job is to patrol the beaches and sound a horn when he spots whales close to the shore. Whales can also be seen in Plettenberg Bay and off Port Elizabeth.

Marine reserves

There are several marine reserves on the South African coast. The first was Tsitsikamma Coastal National Park, a refuge for the Cape clawless otter, and the beautiful coral gardens offshore.

On the KwaZulu-Natal coast there are several marine reserves, including one at Sodwana Bay where turtles can be found in the colourful coral gardens. At the St Lucia Marine Reserve you can snorkel among the brightly coloured corals, tropical fish and shellfish including cowries. Huge whale sharks, placid yet awesome, swim in the shallows, and turtles are also found there.

Scuba diving is very popular on the reefs.

Birdlife

South Africa is a birdwatcher's paradise. In the country's rich variety of habitats there are over 750 species. This includes thirty-seven which are found exclusively within South Africa's borders.

Whether in the thornveld and savannah of Mpumalanga, the rolling grassland of the central plateau or the arid scrubland and desert to the west, the serious watcher and the casual observer will be rewarded by a rich diversity of avifauna.

City birding

Although the widest variety of birds is found in nature reserves, there is a surprising diversity of bird life in South African cities. A suburban Johannesburg household with a small garden usually boasts an annual bird list of about seventy species, while in some suburbs of Durban more than 100 species can be seen from the front porch.

Johannesburg has three major green areas within the city limits, all of which have a bird list of more than 200 species. **The Melville Koppies Nature Reserve**, the **Delta Park Conservation Area**, and the **Jan van Riebeeck Park** all have a good spread of the more common highveld birds. Some species, like the lesser honeyguide and the Owambo sparrowhawk, are common residents, and the growth in well-wooded gardens has attracted species like the grey lourie and red-billed wood hoopoe which were hardly ever seen within city limits ten years ago.

The most productive birding in the country can be had in **Stainbank Nature Reserve** in Durban. The reserve contains many forest specials, although forest birding requires almost limitless patience and a sense of humour if one is to survive the many half-sightings in dense thickets and tangled undergrowth. Listen for the clear fluting song of the spotted thrush, and the eerie haunting foghorn call of the buffspotted flufftail which is often heard but almost never seen. Look out for grey cuckoo shrike, brown robin, sharp-billed honey-guide and olive and grey sunbirds.

The **Happy Valley Reserve** on the Bluff in Durban, is a comfortable place from which to observe waterbirds. Its main attraction are the heronries in which many species roost. The unique green-backed heron uses bait to catch the small fish on which its feeds. The heron will catch a small insect and throw it onto the surface of the water, then wait motionless for a fish to take the bait.

The **Durban bayhead** is a good area to watch the many resident and migrant waders which gather on the mudflats. Pink-backed pelicans and flamingoes are occasionally present, and it is possible to sight grey and ringed plover, curlew, terek sandpiper and whimbrel among others.

Birding in Cape Town is less productive than in the other two major cities, but the magnificence of the coastline and Table Mountain more than compensate. The Western Cape is home to one of the world's seven plant kingdoms with a staggering variety of species, but the birding is relatively impoverished. Nevertheless, six of the country's seven endemic seabirds — the bank, Cape and crowned cormorants, the Cape gannet, the jackass penguin and Hartlaub's gull — can be easily seen. The endemic black oystercatcher, which is the rarest of the breeding shorebirds, is visible and relatively trusting.

The best place to view the seabirds is from the coastline of the **Cape of Good Hope Nature Reserve**, while a good selection of waders concentrates at the **Strandfontein Sewage Works** and the **Rondevlei Bird Sanctuary**. The prettiest birding on the Cape Peninsula is in the **Kirstenbosch Botanical Gardens** on the slopes of Table Mountain. There is a good selection of natural forest and mountain *fynbos* birds represented. Among them is the Cape sugarbird which, with its northern cousin Gurney's sugarbird, comprises the only bird family unique to South Africa.

You can also see some of the pelagic birds, including four species of albatross, petrels and skuas, on boat trips organized by local bird-watcher groups from Durban and Cape Town.

Kruger National Park

This two-million-hectare (five-million-acre) wonderland in the Eastern Transvaal is justly famous for the magnificence of its game viewing, but the park is also a prime birding destination. Three quarters of South Africa's birds are found there, and many of them are more easily seen in the confines of the park than anywhere else in the country.

Of the species worthy of conservation attention, sixty per cent are found in the Kruger National Park — an indication of the park's vital role in protecting the country's heritage.

For birders, the most productive area of this sprawling wilderness is in the far north. **Punda Maria** and **Shingwedzi** are the two rest camps from which the tourist can best explore this region. The Punda Maria camp is a worthwhile place to begin one's birding as the birds which live near the rest camps have become used to humans.

There is a short walking trail — the paradise flycatcher trail — within the borders of the camp. A fifteen minute walk can produce birds such as the bearded and white-throated robins, African goshawk, yellow-spotted nicator, terrestrial and yellow-bellied bulbul and, of course, the very attractive eponymous paradise flycatcher with its blue-black head and chestnut back and tail.

A drive northwards to the Pafuri River could yield such rarities as Arnot's chat, broad-billed and racket-tailed rollers and Dickinson's kestrel. If you leave the camp early enough you might catch the pennant-winged nightjar. The long trailing streamers which the male displays in flight make this the most easily recognizable example of a nondescript family.

The road to Pafuri runs past the park's only known breeding site of the yellow-billed oxpecker. This species was thought for a long time to be extinct in South Africa, and the recent reappearance in the Kruger National Park is testimony to South African birders' conservation efforts.

Below: Glossy Starling.

Above: Cape Weaver.

283

Above: The Goliath Heron is found mainly in the eastern and northern parts of South Africa.

A team from the S.A. Ornithological Society flew to the Okavango Delta in Botswana where they captured 100 specimens. These were introduced into the Ben Lavin Nature Reserve in Northern Province. The experiment was repeated and the population, which has now stabilized, could have provided the base for the re-establishment of the species in the Kruger National Park.

The yellow and red-billed oxpeckers occur only in Africa and are a fine example of the relationship of interdependence which can exist between different species. They spend their feeding hours on big animals such as buffalo, rhino and giraffe. Not only do they feast merrily while protecting their host from irritation and disease by removing ticks and fleas, they also act as an early warning system for their host. The oxpeckers give a very distinctive alarm call when they sense the approach of a predator.

A drive through the riverine forest on the banks of the Pafuri should produce the aptly named gorgeous bush shrike, the crested guineafowl which looks like a punk rocker with its comical crest, and the long-tailed starling.

Along rivers, hosts of swallows and swifts can be spotted, including the rare Böhms and mottled spinetails, and the three-banded courser can turn up in the dry thornveld. At picnic sites, the wattle-eyed flycatcher, the white crowned plover, the elusive but brilliantly coloured narina trogon and the delicately shaded cinnamon and tamborine doves can all make appearances.

The Pafuri area is also home to most of the country's owl species, including the majestic Pel's fishing owl. The best way to see the owls, and indeed most of the species in the area, is on the **Nyalaland Walking trail**. The Nyalaland is one of seven trails offered throughout the park where, in the company of an armed ranger, one can get almost within touching distance of the park's animal and birdlife.

Although the Pafuri and Punda Maria regions offer the best opportunity of seeing some of the country's rarer avifauna, the entire park is full of birds which will excite and entice the tourist.

Above: The Cape Eagle Owl — *Bubo capensis*.

KwaZulu-Natal

The game reserves of northern KwaZulu-Natal — **Ndumu, Mkuzi, Hluhluwe, Umfolozi** and the **Lake St Lucia** complex are almost as rich in birdlife as the Kruger National Park. But because the Kwa Zulu-Natal reserves are considerably smaller, the tourist in a hurry is able to cover different habitats in a much shorter time.

Ndumu and Mkuzi are highly recommended — the birdwatcher there has the best chance of seeing the subtropical species. Look out for the African broadbill, Rudd's apalis, Stierling's barred warbler, Neergaard's sunbird and pink and green-throated twinspots. Mkuzi has a matchless patch of natural forest through which the tourist is able to walk on a three kilometre (two mile) self-guided trail. Keep an eye and ear out for the scaly-throated honeyguide and white-eared barbet.

A common bird in the forest is the trumpeter hornbill, whose call sounds just like a baby crying. The trumpeter, in common with other hornbills, has an unusual nesting habit. The nest is made in a hole in a tree; the male uses mud to wall the female and her eggs inside, leaving just a tiny slit. When the nestlings are ready to enter the world, they break through the mud.

A bonus in Ndumu and Mkuzi is that the tourist can go for walks in the company of an armed tracker. The local knowledge of these men is encyclopaedic, and their ability to mimic the birds of the area means that one sees much more in their company.

Further south is the **Ngoye Forest**, a magnificent evergreen wonderland which is a relic of a much larger forest of ancient times. The Ngoye is the only place where Woodward's barbet occurs. A similar bird is found only on the Rondo plateau of Tanzania. Ngoye is also a good place to see the shy bronze-naped pigeon.

South of Durban, in the country's most impressive range of mountains, the Drakensberg, is the **Giant's Castle Nature Reserve**. This is a good place to sight Drakensberg siskin and orange-breasted rockjumper.

The main attraction there is the lammergeier hide. *Lammergeier* is the Afrikaans name for the bearded vulture, for whose benefit bones are placed outside the hide throughout the year. The bird picks up large bones in its talons, flies to a height of about eight metres (24 feet), and then lets the bone fall onto a dropping site, usually a flat area of rock. This process is repeated until the vulture is able to manoeuvre the marrow out of the bone with a tongue shaped very like a scoop.

The Dry West

Much of the west of South Africa is covered by vast stretches of harsh and arid semi-desert. Trees are almost as scarce as water, so the species which have settled there have adapted to ground living, and have evolved ways to cope with the scarcity of water. The insectivorous species are able to survive on the moisture that they obtain from their prey. In addition, these birds have super-efficient kidneys and a special salt gland that prevents water loss in the urine.

The Namaqua sandgrouse is one species which needs to drink regularly. It has developed a strong flight ability to cope with the vast distances it travels in search of water. The birds arrive punctually at waterholes, morning and evening. Local lore has it that if you are lost in the desert, follow a sandgrouse and you will be led to water. The chicks are unable to fly but the adult male has special feathers on its belly which become saturated with water as he drinks. Back at the nesting site, the thirsty chicks are drip-fed from their father's wet feathers.

The best place to see the rarer species of this habitat is the **Kalahari Gemsbok Park**. Most of the country's western lark species occur there, and forty-four species of raptors have been recorded. These include the tiny pygmy falcon, the size of a shrike, which has evolved a symbiotic relationship with the sociable weaver.

The weavers build huge communal nest structures with a separate entrance and breeding compartment for each nesting pair. The easy availability of defenceless chicks attracts many predators such as snakes, but these are kept under control by the falcon.

Many large ground birds occur in considerable numbers in the park. Kori and Ludwig's bustards are reasonably common, as are black and red-crested korhaans. The male of the red-crested korhaan has a spectacular display flight — the bird runs along the ground a short distance, takes off almost vertically and flies to a height of thirty metres (100 feet). He then seems to roll himself into a ball, and plummets straight down to earth. Just before hitting the ground, the korhaan opens its wings and glides to a proud landing.

Conserving South Africa's birds

Birds are widely regarded as environmental indicators. A decline in the status of a particular species is often an early warning sign of a looming ecological crisis. Professional and amateur ornithologists began a five year project in the late 1980s to map the distribution and status of all the country's species in order to build up a complete picture of the state of health of the country's bird population.

One species, the Egyptian vulture, has become extinct as a breeding species in South Africa this century. The last confirmed breeding record was in the 1920s. There was great excitement in January 1989, when a pair of Egyptian vultures spent nearly a month in the Langjan Reserve in as far as the North-West but the pair did not fulfil conservationists' hopes that they might settle and start a breeding population.

The African skimmer, which is still relatively common in Botswana and Zimbabwe, last bred in South Africa in 1944. There are plans afoot to reintroduce the species into the Lake St Lucia complex in northern KwaZulu-Natal.

The numbers of black-rumped button-quail have declined sharply because of the destruction of its habitat through over-grazing and excessive burning.

Habitat destruction also threatens the continued South African existence of the wattled crane and blue swallow. At least one of the highveld grassland sites of the blue swallow has been saved after a major timber company shelved plans to afforest the area and pledged to actively promote the existence of the swallow.

Above: Knysna Lourie.

There is one breeding site of the endangered roseate tern — **St Croix Island** off Port Elizabeth. This has been declared a marine reserve and proper management should conserve the roseate tern well into the next century.

Lack of habitat security is the major factor which threatens the seventeen species which are regarded as vulnerable and the forty-two species which are classified as rare. Just on ten per cent of South Africa has been classified as national or provincial nature reserves. But protectionist legislation alone cannot save wildlife. This needs the co-operation of the private landowners who control ninety per cent of the land. Fortunately, increasing interest in bird-watching has alerted many farmers to the economic benefits of encouraging birds to settle on their farms. The best hope for the future of South Africa's birds lies in promoting this enlightened self-interest.

Clubs

South Africa has an extensive network of birding clubs, whose members are always ready to show off their particular treasures.

Any tourist wishing to link into this store of local and regional knowledge should contact the South African Ornithological Society in Johannesburg (tel: 011-888-4147).

Would-be South African birdwatchers also have access to birding literature which is the equal of the best anywhere in the world. The most popular guide is Kenneth Newman's *Field Guide to Southern African Birds*, while Roberts' *Book of Southern African Birds* is a more detailed reference work. There is also a plethora of local and regional guides which tell the enthusiast where to go, and what can be seen.

Cuisine

Traditional South African cooking combines the best of the many cultural cuisines which have co-existed in the country for more than 300 years. The resulting mix has created dishes primarily noted for their robust, down-to-earth qualities.

The earliest South Africans were mainly hunter-gatherers. It was the Bantu settlers who brought agriculture with them. Dishes using maize, sweet potato, gem squash and other vegetables are descended from these folk. The Dutch and English influences have created practical stews and sausages such as bobotie, *potjiekos* and boerewors. Slaves brought from the east — especially Malaysia — and indentured labourers from India added spices and curried flavours to the melting pot as well as fruit to some meat dishes.

The Portuguese, who were the first Europeans to set foot on the South African coast, have always maintained a presence in the country. They added peri-peri and fish dishes to the culinary heritage. Small, but established communities of Chinese, Italians and Greeks have all contributed new flavours to the South African recipe book.

A wide range of restaurants, steakhouses, cafés, fast-food, health-food outlets and coffee shops cater for all tastes. In the larger cities is is possible to find ethnic restaurants specializing in, among others, Chinese, Cajun, Thai, Japanese, Russian, Mexican and Indian dishes.

The position of South Africa as a revictualling post for ships on the spice route between the east and Europe has always made exotic ingredients readily available in the country. South Africa's own climatic regions, ranging from temperate Mediterranean to tropical climes, have provided a rich base of ingredients for a huge variety of recipes. Fruit such as apples which require a cold autumn to 'set' can be easily grown on the coastal belt, while tropical mango, banana and paw paw are grown in the eastern subtropical lowveld.

Vast plains allow grazing for cattle, sheep and many types of game.

Venison from unendangered species can be a rare treat for visitors. Ostrich makes a tender roast; springbok, impala and even crocodile meat can be sampled. Poultry ranging from the common chicken to guinea fowl is readily available. Pigs both wild and domesticated please the palate, and the surrounding oceans provide a wealth of fresh fish and shellfish to enhance the rich variety of South African cooking.

The Braai

The climate of South Africa has contributed to the appeal of the country's favourite national pastime — the braai. This is the South African answer to the barbeque, where meat, fish and sometimes maize, onions and potatoes are cooked over coals outdoors. Almost every suburban garden has a 'braai area', often with a built-in barbeque. Mealie pap (a porridge made from maize) is served along with bread, salads, chutneys and plenty of beer.

Steaks, ribs, and wings may be marinated, and the South African sausage, *boerewors*, ('farmers sausage') is a must. These long, thick sausages are made of any available spiced minced meat. As well as the more normal beef or pork *boerewors* you can try ostrich, impala or giraffe varieties. *Vetkoek*, or deep-fried dough balls are served as a side dish.

Meat dishes

During the days of the ox-wagon trails, trekkers took very few provisions with them on journeys. Meat was hunted along the way. Salt was always carried; sugar, tinned milk and tea or coffee were luxuries. Bush tea, made from the infusion of a strong wild herb, was the usual drink. It was drunk hot round the camp fire and often kept cold in water bottles to drink en route or while out hunting.

One common mode of eating was to make an 'everything' stew called 'hunter's pot'. Hunter's pot was a never-finished

Above: Temptingly colourful, fruits and vegetables from the generous land.

stew made in a three-legged iron pot. As each new animal was shot it was butchered and scraps added to the pot, with the large bones included to thicken and strengthen the brew. Venison ranged from the large eland to the tiny dikdik; poultry such as bustard and guinea fowl went into the pot along with wart hog and bush pig, rabbit and hare. If the travellers were lucky they would have a few vegetables, onions or potatoes, to enhance the flavour of this hotchpotch of ingredients.

Each day when the wagons stopped and the oxen were outspanned for a rest, the pot was placed over a fire and allowed to brew up. Old bones were replaced with new, meat added to replace meat eaten. Hunter's pot could be eaten hot in the evenings and in the mornings, when the fire had died down, enjoyed in a solidified, jellied form.

The hunter's pot has become today's *potjiekos* — in Afrikaans literally 'little iron pot food'. Recipes for *potjiekos* are as numerous as the number of cooks who make it. The basic concept is to put everything for a meal — meat cubes, onions, tomatoes, potatoes, herbs, seasoning, maybe spinach or marrow or squash — into an iron pot with a tight lid and cook it slowly over a small open fire for a long time.

Another distinctly South African stew, or *bredie*, is *waterblommetjiebredie*, which uses as one of its ingredients a flower found on the water meadows, or *vleis*, of the Cape Province. A special way to enjoy game meat is minced and covered with a buttermilk crust made from seasoned buttermilk or yoghurt, eggs and lemon.

Bobotie, a spicy meat loaf, is another traditional dish. Minced meat is cooked with brown sugar, apricots or raisins, almonds, milk-soaked mashed bread and a touch of curry powder. *Wasgoedbondeltjies* ('bundles of washing') are the South African Cornish pasty, spiced meat in a pastry parcel. Sosaties are the local form of kebabs, derived from the Indonesian dish *satay*. Cubes of meat are marinated in a spicy sauce then grilled on skewers.

Tripe is a favourite Boer dish. Well cleaned and cooked in red wine it can be a great delicacy.

Above: Strips of spicy meat are dried in the open air to make biltong.

Dried meat

South Africans love the Voortrekker delicacy biltong, which is the equivalent of
beef jerky — dried and salted strips of
meat. If there was surplus venison, it was
made into biltong to be eaten in leaner
days. Nowadays biltong is enjoyed as a
snack.

To make biltong, venison or beef is cut
along the grain into strips and placed in
layers in an enamel or plastic bowl,
interlayered with salt and vinegar. Sugar,
pepper and coriander may be added to
the salt to add flavour. Bicarbonate of
soda can be added in humid areas, and
saltpetre will impart a bright red colour.
The meat is salted overnight then hung in
a cool, airy place to allow it the curing
process to take place without the risk of
it getting mouldy or too salty.

Other salted foods still enjoyed today
include *soutribbetjie* (salted ribs) which are
useful to take on camping or trekking
holidays because they require no
refrigeration.

Poultry

Chicken is served in many ways, which
owe nothing to South African traditions;
pies, oriental stir-fries and curried recipes.

Vegetables

Maize, known as *mealies*, or sweetcorn, is a
traditional and much-loved staple diet in
South Africa. Simply cooked over coals,
made into mealie bread, creamed or boiled
as corn on the cob, the mealie is a favourite.
Maize meal is the staple diet for many.

Sweet pumpkin is cooked with sugar,
cinnamon and orange. Tiny yellow and
green squashes — called patty pans from
their shape — are delicious steamed or
boiled. Sweet potatoes are cooked with fruit.
Sousboontjies is a dish of dried beans cooked
with sugar, butter and vinegar.

Geelrys, or turmeric rice, has been a
favourite filler in South Africa for many
centuries. Presumably introduced by sailors
returning from the east, or immigrant
Indians, the cheap but substantial dish was
served to travellers before they went on

long journeys. When people travelled long distances to attend auctions or funerals in the 'olden days' *geelrys* was a popular dish to serve the visitors before they set off on their return journey. It is traditionally served with *bobotie*. *Geelrys* is rice dyed yellow with the spice turmeric, then mixed with raisins and sometimes boiled eggs.

Fish

Fish is caught along the Cape southern and western coasts. South African waters are rich in kingklip, snoek, tunny, red roman, mullet, hake, cod, monkfish, angelfish, swordfish, pilchard, haddock and sole.

Trout was introduced to highveld streams early this century, and there is exellent fly fishing and eating to be enjoyed in many areas of South Africa.

As with meat, the braai is a favourite way of cooking fish. Whole fish are braaied, or thick steaks cut from the larger, oily fish.

Fish dishes are frequently made using flavours borrowed from the Malay peoples who came to the Cape as slaves and artisans in the early colonial days. Snoek, a long pike-like fish, is often served with chillis and rice. Kingklip is pickled with curry powder and spices. Fillets are marinated in ginger and lemon juice.

Some linefish, red roman being one, can be caught from the shore; others including kingklip and swordfish are hooked out at sea. Other delicacies harvested from the sea include abalone, oysters, mussels, calamari, shrimps and the South African clawless lobster, the crayfish. Shellfish in South Africa is relatively inexpensive and deliciously fresh. Mussels, for example can be found easily by the amateur on rocky shores. Always ask the locals before eating, however, as these molluscs may be toxic if there has been a 'red tide' of plankton.

Crayfish are best plainly boiled or grilled over coals. South African crayfish are increasingly exported to Europe and America as cheap but tasty lobster equivalents. Abalone (or *perlemoen* in Afrikaans) are cooked on the West coast over an open fire placed between layers of the stalk from large kelp. They can also be cut in slices and fried in oil with lemon.

Above: Harvest of the oceans: choice fish and crustacea.

Puddings

Most desserts include fruit, in the form of salads, tarts or baked puddings. Baked delicacies such as dumplings, bread puddings and soufflés are common.

Fruit from this land of plenty is readily available in many exotic varieties all year round. Pineapples, mangoes, lychees, grapes, apricots, plums, oranges and apples are all grown locally. *Nartjies*, which are large South African mandarines, are available in the winter months.

When in South Africa, eat milk tart (*melktert*). The crust of puff or sour cream pastry is filled with a mix of milk, flour and eggs flavoured with cinnamon sugar and orange to create a quintessentially South African dessert.

South African Wine

Though long ostracized by the international connoisseur's palate, South African wines were among the first 'New World' wines to be widely acclaimed in Europe and are again rising to greatness as the export market reopens.

Over the past fifteen years, South African wine has been surging from strength to strength, with a new generation of young winemakers winning international awards and respect in the world's wine markets.

Wine was one of the first products of the original Dutch Cape colony in the mid-17th century. The hills and valleys behind Cape Town, with their moderately fertile soils, good drainage, hot dry summers and cool wet winters put the region among the best in the world for viticulture. By the 19th

century, Constantia wine from the Cape was very popular in Europe.

Today, both at the superior end of the market and at more down-to-earth levels, South African wines offer excellent quality at reasonable prices.

Wine is grown in several centres, all in the Cape Province. The most famous areas are the original wine regions of Constantia, just south of Table Mountain, and the Stellenbosch/Paarl region in the foothills of the mountains about thirty kilometres (18 miles) east of Cape Town.

Newer regions to the north of Cape Town in the Swartland and along the Olifants River have been put under vines; further to the east, stretching into the Little Karoo mountains, vineyards are scattered across the scenery. All the regions benefit from the Mediterranean climate of the Cape coastal belt. There are now around 5,000 wine growers and 150 cellars in South Africa making mainly white wines.

Cultivars

The most popular cultivar, or variety of grape grown in South Africa is the white Chenin Blanc. This versatile grape can be used to make dry, fruity wines or sweet dessert wines, as well as fortified sherries and ports. Cape Riesling, or South African Riesling, is unique to the country and grown sparingly. Cape Riesling produces the country's top quality dry white wines. The more familiar Riesling, known in South Africa as the Rhine Riesling or the Weisser Riesling, is a more recent import to the country but grows very well.

Other white cultivars include Raisin Blanc, Gewurztraminer, Sauvignon Blanc and Chardonnay. The latter, a very recent import to the country, is producing some excellent new wines in the region.

Of the red varieties, one is exclusive to South Africa. The Pinotage grape is a cross between the Pinot Noir and the Hermitage (now called Cinsaut) cultivars. The grapes make a distinctive mellow red wine. Pinot Noir and Cinsaut are also grown in South

Above: Wine sparkles aplenty, from the fertile valleys of the Cape Province.

Above: One of the picturesque farms you can visit while on the wine route.

Africa, the latter being used to produce the bulk of the cheaper wines. Cabernet Sauvignon, Shiraz and others are also cultivated.

Recently, South African winemakers have taken to producing a sort of Beaujolais nouveau-style wine, and the Gamay Noir grape is gaining favour for this usage. Port, champagne-style sparkling wines and fortified wines are also produced in South Africa — the latter in particular contributing to a great extent to the country's agricultural exports.

Wine routes

Everyone can enjoy the glory of the wine regions. In the older regions of Paarl and Stellenbosch elegant white-gabled Cape Dutch farmhouses rise out of the country-side made richly green by the vines.

Travel through the region, stopping at estates to taste the produce, eating at excellent restaurants where a mixture of fresh seafood, traditional Cape fare and local wines can be enjoyed at their best. The area is one of the most picturesque in South Africa, a delight not to be missed.

Classification

Wines in South Africa are classified according to region, cultivar and sweetness. Seals on every bottle of wine will give the drinker an idea of the type and quality of wine in that bottle.

The 'wine of origin' classification means that the grapes used have come from the area stated on the bottle. The 'cultivar' and 'vintage' stripes on a seal indicate that at least seventy-five per cent of the grapes are of the cultivar/vintage described on the label. All grapes used to make a wine must have come from the same estate to receive the classification 'estate wine'.

A few names for the best wines from the Cape of Good Hope are: Backsberg, Thelema, Talana Hills, Groot Constantia, Hamilton Russell, Louisvale, Klein Constantia, Meerlust, Nederberg, Rosendaal Rustenberg, Simonsig, Stellenryck, Warwick and Zonnebloem.

Despite the excellence of South African wines, the nation's favourite tipple is beer, both lager made from grain and the traditional cloudy sorghum brew.

Art and Craft

Rock painting

This San (Bushman) art dates from between 20,000 to 100 years ago and is thought to have been painted by medicine men in drug-induced trances. The paintings are found on rocks and in caves throughout southern Africa. There are 2,100 known sites of rock paintings or etchings in South Africa with around 150,000 paintings.

Accessible and impressive cave paintings are to be found in the **Giant's Castle Reserve** in KwaZulu-Natal, where several caves offer a vast array of art. **Eland's Cave** in the **Ndedema Gorge** has over 1,500 figures, some of them are beautiful multi-coloured works.

The best museum exhibits are at the **South African Museum** in Cape Town, the **Natal Museum** in Pietermaritzburg and the **McGregor Museum** in Kimberley.

Craft

The craftwork of African tribes is created for four main purposes: ritual, utility, adornment and commercial. Although the most internationally famous African craftwork has until now derived from west Africa, the tribes of southern Africa have long-established skills and beautiful products which are beginning to take their rightful place on the world map.

Grass and straw weavers use their skills to create largely utilitarian objects such as bowls and fishtraps, some with such delicacy and intricacy that they are in themselves works of art. Weaving in mohair and wool is an ancient skill in South Africa and blankets, clothing and wall hangings are produced. Clay workers mainly make vessels, but statuary for ritual purposes is also fashioned, and more recently sculpture has been produced for sale. The carver is one of the most important artisans, using his skills on wood, ivory, bone, horn and stone.

Other products of the regions' craftspeople include painted ostrich eggs which are used to hold milk, leather thongs to make carrier bags and slings, horn to make cups, and leather for clothing and shields. Staves become spears and throwing sticks. Animal hides are used for floor and bed coverings and in costumes.

The diverse mineral wealth of the country has also added its materials to the craftsman's pool. Semi-precious stones such as verdite and azurite, precious metals, copper and iron are all to be found in ceremonial and ritual clothing, jewellery and weaponry.

Pottery

Each tribe has its own distinct pottery style. Older pots were rough and mainly undecorated, kept simply functional because of the frequent need to escape from marauding tribes.

More modern pottery is decorated with traditional designs. In Northern Province, round, ochre-red clay pots are neckless, painted with black and red geometric designs and sometimes bold fishes. Basotho pottery tends to be of simpler design, very round and burnished with black cinders.

Weaving

Baskets, mats, beerstrainers and fishtraps are among the items made from grass of which some are dyed. The Basuto people also weave conical straw hats of a distinctive style.

The creation of the traditional Zulu grass-woven beehive huts is a craft in itself. A knowledge of some forty grasses is needed to weave the huts. The grasses are plaited into long ropes and the ropes are woven together to create the hut structure. The huts are, by necessity, only the height of a man's reach. They take from three weeks to three months to build.

Weaving of fibres is another ancient skill. The Khoikhoi had a type of sheep from very early times, and the Bantu came to South Africa with their sheep and goats. Mohair has long been a product of the country, and woollen blankets and clothing can be found countrywide. Handwoven

Above: Africans are born artisans: handicrafts on sale in Johannesburg.

hangings are also available, mostly of modern design inspired by ancient paintings and decorations. Bed-spreads crocheted from cotton can be found on sale at the side of main roads.

Beading

Beadwork is another traditional craft which has adapted itself to modern materials. Small plastic and glass beads imported in bulk from Czechoslovakia have replaced beads which were homemade or bartered along trade routes in the past.

Zulu women make 'love letters' out of beads to send to boyfriends and husbands who are working hundreds of kilometres away from home in the mines around Johannesburg. The colours and order of beads make up the language of the letter, for example yellow beads stand for eternity, and white for love.

Wood carving

Carving with knives and pokerwork decoration is an integral part of southern African craftwork. Geometric patterns, animals and the human figure are used in decoration. Walking staffs, or staffs of office, have intricate pommels; headrests, pipes, spoons, snuff boxes, clubs, weapons and vessels can all be found with the most beautiful carvings engraved upon them.

Figures

Sculptures of people and animals were not made by many tribes in South Africa, but the tradition is found in peoples living in the northern areas bordering Mozambique and Zimbabwe. The Pedi, Venda and Tsonga tribes use such sculpted figures during the initiation rites whereby young people are instructed in social customs. Figures can also be found in the courts of leaders where they are used in rituals of divination and healing.

Sculptures are usually of pairs of men and women about thirty centimetres (twelve inches) tall, made from clay or polished wood. The figures are usually dressed in cloth, skin or adorned with beading. By the end of the 19th century, such figures came to the attention of Europeans eager to take a token of Africa back with them to Europe. Many sculptures

Above: A pottery shop in Pretoria.

dating from after this time are noticeably different, made especially for the export market. Bases allow the carvings to stand and the clothing is often carved into the wood or clay. These carvings tend to have the gender of the figure toned down, while ethnic features such as hairstyles and weapons are emphasized. Modern sculptors draw frequently upon the human form for their artwork, often creating works with a primitive feel about them. Figures and animals sculpted out of semi-precious stones, wood and soapstone can be bought at most curio shops in South Africa. Although the items can be quite beautiful, they are often of a continent-wide modern day 'African' design, reflecting very little of the traditions of the tribes of South Africa itself.

Voortrekker crafts

As with most pioneering folk, the crafts of the first white settlers are those of basic, functional furniture and housewares. These simple pieces were lovingly crafted from hardwoods and lend a puritan country feel to a room.

Culture-of-poverty items

Ingenious use of rubbish and leftovers have created a whole new art form on the streets of South Africa's townships. Children can be seen playing at the sides of the roads with cars fashioned out of old tin cans and twisted pieces of wire. Rags and wire make little model cyclists.

Western art

Until this century, South Africa's artists almost invariably were educated in Europe; Dutch, English or French influences can be seen in their work. The earliest settlers seemed to have little interest in painting and, prior to the 18th century, the only art to come from the new colony was in the form of line drawings of tribesmen in journals and maps for chronicles.

The first western artists were attracted by the exotic landscapes of South Africa, but their paintings still retain European concepts of structure and more importantly light. It was not until the late 19th century that South African artists grasped and tried to tackle the peculiar and dramatic effects

Above: Pot-painting is an ancient skill.

of 'African light' in their works. Pieter Wenning and Hugo Naude were forerunners who established new conventions for the unfamiliar colours and play of light.

Subjects remained almost exclusively landscapes and colonial depictions of native tribesmen until the 20th century. Irma Stern and Maggie Laubser broke away from the mainstream of South African art by following the violence of the eastern European expressionist movement. Walter Battiss and his New Group in the 1930s tried to incorporate an 'African mystique' into their works, influenced by the continent's ancient art and ruins.

It was not until the 1930s that the works of any black artists came to the fore in South Africa. This was partly due to the differing cultures of the black people. Their tradition was not to have pictures or sculptures adorning their homes, but to fashion beautiful artefacts. By the 1930s, however, urban blacks were being exposed to cosmopolitan culture, and with that the art — often commercial — of the day.

Early artists, such as Gerard Bhengu and George Sekoto, produced watercolours depicting black African lifestyles and customs for predominantly white patrons. In the 1950s Cecil Skotnes founded the Polly Street Art Centre in Johannesburg and trained black artists into the mainstream of western painting methods. The subjects remained African, however, and scenes of township life predominated.

During the '60s black and white artists became interested in depicting Africa as it was, rather than the more romantic visions of Battiss. Under the rigid apartheid of the '60s and '70s, black artists were censored and prevented from exhibiting at many venues. A black art and craft centre opened at Rorke's Drift in KwaZulu-Natal, where the crafts of weaving and pottery became successful with a lot of exports overseas.

The 1980s saw an increase in political awareness in the art world as a whole, with black and white artists refusing to exhibit state-sponsored exhibitions.

Today art is thriving at all levels in South Africa, with more art than ever being exported overseas to eager markets in Europe and America.

Classic Rail

South Africa is a steam buff's dream come true. More than 200 steam engines are still in working order in the country — many of which are unique to southern Africa. They can be viewed in museums or at sidings, experienced on luxury steam safaris or be seen in service pulling goods trains through the beautiful South African countryside.

South Africa was still ordering steam engines — taking possession of its last locomotives in 1956 — when most other countries had switched to diesel. The reason was simple: the country was in a recession and coal was readily available whereas diesel fuel had to be imported.

The first diesel engines were imported in 1958 but steam was still popular with retired engines being restored and reintroduced into the service. At its peak in the early 1960s, South African Railways (SAR) (now known as Spoornet) was running about 5,000 steam engines.

This late introduction to diesel provided South Africa with an insight into the importance of steam travel in the tourism industry. As other countries converted to diesel, enthusiasts from all over the world flocked to South Africa to experience the wonder of the romantic traditional steam locomotives.

In the Cape, the picturesque track from George to Knysna has been identified as a museum line and its traffic is totally steam-hauled. The trains carry mainly timber goods, but the Outeniqua Choo-Tjoe is a quaint passenger train which runs every day except Sunday in the holiday season.

There are also several 0.61 metre (two feet) gauge lines that still use steam. The monthly **Apple Express** runs between Port Elizabeth and Loerie, hauling passengers from the coast into the hinterland over the spectacular **Van Stadens River Bridge** across a deep gorge. The narrow-tracked **Port Shepstone-Harding line** in KwaZulu-Natal carries mainly timber although steam operation continues for tourists.

History

Cecil Rhodes, politician and colonialist, was largely responsible for the development of railways in southern Africa. He had a grand vision of a system linking the whole of Africa from Cape Town to Cairo. His enthusiasm ensured the rapid expansion of rail in southern Africa, and it is possible today to travel by train to Lake Malawi from Cape Town.

To keep costs down, the gauge of the mainline tracks were narrow — only 1.06 metres (3.5 feet) instead of the standard European 1.44 metres (4.75 feet). This gauge became known as the **Cape Gauge**.

In 1860, the first railway track in southern Africa was opened from Durban to Point. In 1862, a line between Cape Town and Wellington was completed. In addition to a system of main and branch line tracks, a further system of very narrow gauge feeder lines was created. This SA narrow gauge — only 0.61 metres (two feet) between the rails — allowed access to the main railway system to territories with no other means of transporting produce, at very little cost.

Now Spoornet has 21,244 kilometres (13,201 miles) of mainline track and 12,847 kilometres (7,983 miles) of branch track. Excluding local commuter facilities, eighty per cent of its traffic is goods. Minerals, iron ore and coal are the main goods transported. The railway is largely containerized.

South Africa's railways also assist Zimbabwe and Zambia. Raw materials from those countries are taken to the ports of Durban, Port Elizabeth and Cape Town while fuel and finished goods are hauled north. Zimbabwe and Zambia's own railway systems rely heavily on South African technology; they have been hiring diesel locomotives from South African rolling stock for more than twenty years.

South Africa's modern block-load trains are the longest in the world. Up to six engines, diesel and electric, are coupled

Above: South Africa is a steam train buff's dream come true.

together to pull one massive train with up to 220 trucks. The trains can be over two kilometres (just over one mile) long and pull a load of more than 100,000 tons.

The technique is perfect for the long distances travelled in South Africa, reducing manning costs both on the trains and at stations and signals.

The steam engines

The oldest engine in running condition is the ZASM (0-4-0), built in 1890 by Emil Kessler in Germany. The antique engine weighs only fourteen tons and is still in perfect running order. It is kept on exhibition in Krugersdorp unless pressed into service for special occasions. All of the engines ordered by South African Railways were built to its own specifications by expert locomotive engineers in Europe.

South African Railways required two main types of engine: one to pull trains long distances along straight, flat track in arid conditions, and one that could haul trucks and carriages up the steep mountains between the coastal plain and the inland plateau, a haul of up to 1,500 metres (5,000 feet) of steep slope. Despite the narrowness of the gauge, South African Railway's steam engines are very large, much bigger than European or Australian standards though still slightly smaller than US stock.

Enthusiasts

The best time of year to photograph South Africa's trains is in the winter between April to October when the sun is low.

Depots and sidings

Spoornet allows visits to locomotive depots, signals, sidings and work shops with prior permission. Apply for a permit to the Transnet Museum, PO Box 3753, Johannesburg, 2000 (tel: 011-773-9238). Local applications take a week to process, applications from abroad take longer.

Museums

The main rolling stock collection is kept in Krugersdorp and the narrow gauge collection at the branch museum in Port Elizabeth.

Above: The Blue Train is generally regarded as one of the great trains of the world.

Steam safari

The **Transnet Museum** organizes fourteen-day safaris at least four times a year. The train, called the **Union Limited**, takes its name and its opulence from a luxury-class boat train that used to run from what was the Transvaal to Cape Town.

The Union Limited travels interesting routes, through picturesque scenery and along unusual tracks. Each route is different — some safaris take in game reserves or journey to Zimbabwe and Zambia, travelling over the rail bridge at the **Victoria Falls**. There are stops for photographic opportunities at particularly spectacular places. The coaching stock dates from the 1920s to the 1950s, with wooden interiors.

Rovos Rail run a separate luxury train on various routes within South Africa. Contact Rovos Rail, Victoria Hotel, PO Box 2837, Pretoria, 0001; tel: 012-323-6052.

Further information

There are several clubs for steam enthusiasts in South Africa. **The Railway Society of South Africa** provides details of events in different regions and the names of different preservation socities in its bi-monthly publication, *SA Rail*. Contact: PO Box 33202, Montclair, 4061.

Sport

South Africans are fanatical about sport. Although soccer, cricket, rugby, boxing and golf are the most popular in the country, many sports have an ardent following.

Many South African sports people and their teams are rated among the best in the world, notably in cricket and rugby. The Springboks — the national sporting emblem and name of the teams — are well known worldwide and associated with outstanding sporting achievements.

The apartheid years allowed for the emergence of talented whites far more easily than that of black sports people. Privileged white schools boasted several games pitches, yet one pitch would be shared among fifty schools in black areas. This kind of disparity is now being addressed, although there is still a long way to go in equalizing opportunities.

During the country's years of isolation, other divides were apparent. Blacks were more interested in soccer and boxing while the major white sports were cricket, rugby and golf. These trends are still noticeable, but interest in all sports is becoming less racially distinct, particularly in athletics which is being encouraged at all levels in schools throughout the country.

South Africa is seeking to host the 2004 Olympics in Cape Town.

Soccer

South Africa is a member of the Federation of International Football Association (FIFA). Clubs such as Kaizer Chiefs and Orlando Pirates draw crowds of 100,000 at big matches.

Rugby

Rugby is a very popular game. The domestic Currie Cup competition attracts regular crowds of up to 50,000. In 1995, South Africa hosted the World Cup, whose final was played at Johannesburg's **Ellis Park Stadium**. South Africa won the prestigious cup, beating the pre-final favourites New Zealand.

Above: Soccer is a national sport.

Cricket

Provincial sides participate in three domestic competitions during the summer months. The national side was re-admitted to international events in 1992 and since then has acquitted itself admirably, frequently beating other cricketing nations.

A development programme, sponsored by the South African Cricket Union, has taken the game to the black townships where a wealth of talent is being encouraged. Local and overseas players conduct 'clinics' in all parts of the country to nurture such talent.

Athletics

Athletics has a big following in South Africa. On an international level there were ten athletes ranked in the world's top thirty in 1994.

Above: Rugby is a very popular game. In 1995, South Africa played host to the World Cup.

One of the most popular sports in the country is road running which is encouraged in schools countrywide. The eighty-nine-kilometre (55-mile) annual **Comrades Marathon** between Durban and Pietermaritzburg is run by more than 14,000 people every year. The fifty-six-kilometre (35-mile) **Two Oceans Marathon** in Cape Town is also a very popular national event.

Boxing

South Africa has had its share of world title holders with Brian Mitchell being one of the finest boxers produced. He retired in 1991, undefeated, as the International Boxing Federation's world junior lightweight champion, a title he won in 1986. At the time of writing Baby Jake Matlala is the world's flyweight champion.

Golf

The scenic beauty and climate combined with excellent courses countrywide make South Africa ideal for golf. **The Sunshine Tour**, a series of tournaments played on world-class courses each year, attracts many young overseas professionals. **The Million Dollar Challenge** which takes place at Sun City, inaugurated in 1980, is one of the richest tournaments in the world, played by the world's top golfers.

Horse racing

South Africa has fourteen race tracks scattered throughout the country. Tracks vary from **Kenilworth** in Cape Town at sea level to **Turffontein** in Johannesburg at 1,828 metres (6,000 feet) above sea level. Because of the changes in altitude, big races are run in seasons across the country to allow horses to acclimatize.

There are almost 10,000 horses in training in the country. Winners can receive up to R1-million in prize money for top races and a sum of over R4-billion is wagered each year.

Surfing

Known as the land of the 'endless summer', South Africa is a surfer's paradise. Its long coastline spans two oceans and two major ocean currents and it is possible to surf all year round. The KwaZulu-Natal coast's surf is generally preferred to that of Cape Town and the west coast because the Indian Ocean is warmer. The sport is hugely popular and international events are hosted annually on the coast.

Hunting

Game-hunting is possible in some private parks, notably **Umfolozi** and the **Pilanesberg National Park**. Rules vary from province to province and special permits are required.

White water rafting

The Vaal provides a thrilling weekend break from Johannesburg with some exciting rapids graded two to three in the low summer months. White water kayaking is also available on this river. **The Tugela River** in Zululand offers wild water again in the summer months with some rapids of grade three and four.

The Orange is the only river in South Africa to guarantee a regular all-year flow. The strong currents allow for an easy ride, except in the rapids which are quite wild. Various sections of this mighty river offer tougher or easier routes, some for canoes, some for inflatable rafts, some passing through desert wilderness, others through deep gorges.

Fishing

It is said that fifteen per cent of the people living on South Africa's coast fish in the sea. Ninety per cent of catches are made up of ten species.

The most popular method is rock and surf angling — simply casting from the shore into the sea. Elf, red roman, red stubnose, bream, kob, hottentot — even sharks such as the dusky milk and sandshark can be caught in this way.

Deep-sea fishing is fast becoming popular for those who can afford it. Fishing is mainly from double-keeled 'ski boats' of which there are more than 4,000 in the country. These vessels take anglers directly through the surf to fishing water. King and queen mackerel, kob and snoek can be caught, but the most desirable are billfish, tuna, shark and kingklip. The billfish (marlin, sailfish, spearfish, swordfish, etc.,)

Above: South Africa boasts many world-class golf courses.
Overleaf: Spring flowers adorn a Natal landscape.

are found most often in east coast waters.

Spearfishing requires a licence in KwaZulu-Natal. This is a good method of catching some otherwise elusive species including the knifejaw and the spadefish.

Inland fishing

Trout farms have been established in the Transvaal and KwaZulu-Natal to stock trout streams. Barbel and tigerfish are also found in some rivers.

Other sports

Kyalami was readmitted as a venue to the Federation Internationale de Sport Automobile's (FISA) grand prix circuit in March 1992.

The Paris-Le-Cap Rally re-appeared on the rallying calendar in 1991.

The **Rapport** cycling tour takes the professional racers round South Africa, while amateurs in their thousands ride the yearly **Argus Tour** around Table Mountain. The **Johannesburg Cycling Association** organizes trips around the city's borders every weekend for amateur enthusiasts.

PART FIVE: BUSINESS IN SOUTH AFRICA

The Economy

The 343 years since Jan van Riebeeck arrived at the Cape of Good Hope in 1652 have seen South Africa progress a long way. The discovery of gold on the Witwatersrand in 1888 proved the turning point in the industrialization of South Africa. Mineral exploitation at the close of the 19th century transformed South Africa to a rapidly industrialized nation.

In terms of the world economy South Africa can be compared with other non-oil developing countries. South Africa is of a similar size to Columbia and Nigeria. By world standards South Africa has a moderate-sized economy, but one still large enough to be significant in world terms. Overall, the performance of South Africa over the last decade places it around the South American and upper African economies in World Bank statistics.

The abundant mineral wealth of South Africa is still the backbone of the economy, although the extent of its influence has fallen to a level of nine per cent of gross domestic product (GDP). The manufacturing industries have grown to be the dominant sector in terms of GDP contribution. The sophistication of South African industry is sometimes overlooked. Similarly, in the financial sector, South African banks and services compare very favourably with foreign banking sectors. Few countries in the world enjoy similar natural beauty. From beaches that would rival any tropical paradise, to game reserves like the Kruger National Park, South Africa has few rivals in the world. It is no surprise that tourism promises to grow significantly during the 'nineties.

South Africa has an infrastructure that ranks above most African countries. An established network of roads and railways transverses the country. South African Airways flies to every continent on the globe and a technologically advanced telecommunication system links the country with all major centres of the world.

With this impressive display of potential, South Africa's continued development becomes all the more important as the hub of sub-Saharan Africa. The Government has committed itself to monetary discipline and fiscal policy has been targeted at social upliftment and should bear fruit for the country in the future. The government encourages foreign investment.

Opportunities

Mining

South Africa has the major proportion of the world reserves of gold, platinum, manganese, chrome, alumino silicates and vanadium. Natural gas has also been found in Mossel Bay — the amounts of which may be commercially exploitable. South African income tax law encourages mineral exploration: rights to natural resources vests in the state, and consequently a lease must be obtained from the government and this is allowable as a deduction for tax purposes.

The major mining areas are the gold fields which range from Gauteng to the Free State. Coal fields are found in the north of KwaZulu-Natal and in Mpumalanga. The Northern Cape mines produce iron ore, copper and diamonds. The famous diamond field of Kimberley affectionately termed the 'Big Hole' is found in the Northern Cape. Various other minerals are mined in the areas around Pretoria. The concentration of mining activities in Gauteng has resulted in the area becoming the economic centre of South Africa.

In the past mining has been a rich source of income for South Africa. Gold in particular has frequently sustained the South African economy. In 1987 three quarters of mineral exports were accounted for by gold. Mining accounted for R24,458 million of gross domestic product in 1994.

Gold is mined on the Reef at very deep levels and this has resulted in a concentration of resources vests in six major mining houses. The six account for the majority of mining ventures in the country. In comparison with the rest of the world, South African gold is contained in low grade ore, and at very deep levels. This has resulted in higher mining costs per ounce than any other regions of the world. South Africa has for many years relied on gold as a major source of its export income and the ensuing tax revenue. This has provided generous amounts of employment, income and foreign exchange, but has made the South African economy dependent on world mineral prices which has accounted for some of the instability in the economy. The challenge to a developing South Africa is to adjust to a world market more interested in its manufacturing capacity than in its raw materials.

Since two-thirds of world gold output is channelled into jewellery production, this could provide a great opportunity for South Africa to benefit from its natural resources. Most jewellery is produced in other countries and development of a growing local industry should be of great value. The lifting of sanctions against South Africa should also see an increase in opportunities for coal exports.

Mining has made a major contribution in developing the employment structure of South Africa because the mining houses have required large numbers of unskilled labour. Hence the industry has been influential in the urbanization of South Africa because a largely black workforce migrated from the rural areas to the mining centres in search of work.

Agriculture

South Africa has a surprisingly diverse agricultural sector. Only twelve per cent of the country is suitable for dry-land crop production, but three quarters of the land is used in agriculture.

The country is divided by the Great Escarpment which runs from the north in a long curve to the west. The central plateau created by the escarpment is suitable for intensive farming but it is often plagued by a lack of water. Two thirds of South Africa receives less than 500mm of rain per annum, so it comes as no surprise that water, or the lack of it, is frequently a crucial factor in determining the success of farming.

About sixty per cent of the land can be classified as 'natural pasture' and is used for grazing of animals. The outcome is that there is a dairy farming sector and a large sheep farming industry, providing wool and mohair. Slaughter stock and sheep farming account for around a quarter of the agricultural production.

Maize is the most common crop grown in South Africa, and this alone accounts for around a quarter of the total agricultural production. It is grown extensively around the country in areas such as the Free State and Northern Province Other small grains are also cultivated.

The tropical climate of KwaZulu-Natal provides ideal conditions for growing sugar cane, now an important crop. Around 389,000 hectares of sugar cane is farmed in the country. In world terms South Africa is a large sugar producer, and the excess not consumed locally is exported to countries such as the United States, Canada and Japan.

The Western Cape enjoys a Mediterranean climate different from the rest of the country — it experiences winter rainfalls. Deciduous fruit producers thrive in this area and crops such as apples, oranges, pears and grapes are grown there with great success. The season runs from November with apricots, peaches, plums and nectarines; and the harvest continues through summer and early autumn when grapes, pears and apples are picked. Large amounts of these crops are exported and the quality is of a very high standard.

The southern hemisphere climate means that fruit can be exported from the Cape when the northern hemisphere consumers are in the middle of a cold winter.

The wine producers of the western Cape are respected worldwide. The industry has grown in stature from the days when the wines of the Groot Constantia estate were enjoyed by Napoleon. South African wines are award winners at international wine festivals, and are currently exported to many parts of the world.

Farming in South Africa is well developed and modernized, but until the repeal of the Land Act in the 1990s, black farmers were prevented from owning land. Consequently the black farming community is far less developed than the white farmers.

The agricultural sector is regulated by the government and there are various control boards which assist with the supply and pricing of most agricultural products. These regulating bodies assist farmers with price regulations and provide financial help.

Manufacturing

Whereas the contribution of mining and agriculture to gross domestic product (GDP) has decreased in the four decades prior to the 1990s, the contribution of the manufacturing and services sector has grown to nearly forty per cent of the GDP. In 1993 manufacturing accounted for R80,963 million of GDP. However, the physical volume of production has shown no real growth in output through the last decade. Partly to blame is the turbulent political situation prevalent in South Africa throughout the 1980s. This disappointing performance of the manufacturing industry has been an underlying cause of the falling growth rate of GDP from 1960 to the current relatively stagnant position which has, however, been improving since the 1994 elections. No real effort has been made to substitute locally manufactured goods for imports and this also provides an opportunity for growth during the 1990s.

Labour problems, resulting in poor productivity, have also hindered manufacturing performance in South Africa.

Notwithstanding all the problems facing South African manufacturers, this sector of the economy managed to produce goods competitive with many from around the globe. South Africa has one of the most sophisticated manufacturing industries in Africa and is therefore a leader in this field in Africa. For example South Africa has one of two BMW motor car manufacturing plants in the world outside Germany.

Tourism

In a country schooled in diversity, it comes as no surprise to find a wealth of different tourist attractions available to the foreign visitor. More than three million people visit the country each year, spending about R6 billion. South Africa is connected by air to every continent, so business in New York is just an overnight flight away.

Tourism falls under the control of the Department of Tourism, a mechanism through which the government assists in encouraging and co-ordinating tourism by means of an international information bureau. Further organization of tourism is undertaken by groups such as the South African Tourist Corporation and the Hotels and Parks Board.

There is no lack of desire to build a growing tourist industry in the country as is demonstrated by the large hotel complex developed by Sun International at Sun City, where investments run into billions of rand.

With an established transport and communications network stretching across the country all areas are accessible. The sophistication of South Africa makes it an ideal country to establish a tourism base for the southern African continent.

The entrepreneur and the informal sector

In the past South Africa's apartheid policy excluded blacks from active participation in the economy. In recent years, the contribution of the black community has begun to be recognized. Frequently, the business of the townships is organized along less structured lines than those in the city centres, which are more familiar to the average business person. Hence this sector of the economy has been termed the informal sector. Various investigations have estimated the contribution of the informal sector to gross domestic product at between ten and twenty per cent, which can be demonstrated by the taxi industry which has overtaken the public bus service as the most popular mode of transport for a large majority of the community.

The poor political situation prevailing during the 1980s induced both a reduction of immigrants and a migration of professionals from South Africa, leaving the labour force critically short of skilled workers. This drain of entrepreneurship has brought with it a stagnation of employment opportunities as unskilled labour has outgrown the number of potential leaders. Poor education has aggravated the problem in generating potential entrepreneurs.

There is thus great potential for the entrepreneurial-minded in the economy during the 1990s, particularly since the new government is committed to a major programme of reconstruction and development.

The workforce

The South African population currently stands at 40,284,634. The years of apartheid have ensured that the majority of skilled labour is drawn from the white population, while the black population makes up the majority of the unskilled labour. The skilled market is characteristically in short supply and paid at rates comparable with overseas countries. In contrast, the unskilled section of the market is characterized by an over - supply, and low education. The population growth in South Africa for the eighties has been around the two-and-a-half per cent mark. This high rate is expected to drop, although to what level is uncertain. This exaggerates unemployment, the level of which is currently at twenty-nine per cent (although some estimates place it as high as thirty-five per cent).

About half the labour force in South Africa is unionized. The largest organization of trade unions is the Congress of South African Trade Unions (Cosatu). The unions are generally organized on the basis of industry or craft. The labour movement in South Africa has been highly politicized and this has added a further complication to industrial relations. There is a formal legal framework, regulated by the Department of Manpower, within which labour relations are conducted and which provides for grievance procedures and unfair labour practices.

Education

The South African education system is in a state of crisis largely as a result of the separate education policies that existed for so long for each racial group. A large discrepancy existed between blacks and whites in the expenditure per pupil and teacher/pupil ratios. This is indicative of the poorer education provided for non-whites during the 'apartheid years'. The government continues to move toward a new education policy. Every effort to redress these differences will have to be made, so that the large mass of under-skilled people may become productive through education.

Tertiary education in South Africa is of a high standard, with world-recognized institutions such as the University of the Witwatersrand in Johannesburg. In 1988, 50,200 degrees, diplomas and certificates were issued by universities and technikons, these contributing to the pool of skilled labour in the market place.

Investment

The private sector

More than half of the expenditure on gross domestic product is accounted for by private consumption expenditure. Capital investment expenditure by the private sector has seen a decrease in the last decade although South African companies tend, on the whole, to be fairly capital intensive.

Private sector ownership is concentrated in a few large conglomerate companies which through various subsidiaries dominate the South African markets. Around seventy-five per cent of GDP is owned by the private sector.

Foreign investment

The South African government welcomes foreign investment and this is demonstrated by the openness of the economy to foreign trade. It should be noted that there is, however, a system of exchange control, but the system of dual exchange rates has been used to encourage foreign investment in recent years.

Over the past decade the largest foreign investors in South Africa have been Europeans (particularly European Community members), followed by North and South Americans. Sanctions introduced by the United States in 1986 were lifted in July 1991.

Various incentives are offered to prospective investors, and there is a growing optimistic view of South Africa's potential to be a major force in sub-Saharan African economics. This should make South Africa an attractive investment opportunity for foreigners.

Exchange control — commercial and Finrand

The extensive exchange controls in use in South Africa serve the purpose of controlling and maintaining the country's foreign reserves. This is performed under the Currency and Exchanges Act No. 9 of 1933. The Reserve Bank administers this Act. Exchange control precludes South African residents from all foreign dealings unless prior approval from the Reserve Bank has been obtained. Any application is considered on the benefit which might accrue from the transaction to South Africa.

Since 1985 South Africa has had a dual currency foreign exchange system which is based on the commercial and financial rand. The commercial rand is used for trade transactions. The financial rand is primarily a vehicle for foreign capital flow into or out of the country. Therefore, a non-resident is able to invest in South Africa at the financial rand exchange rate rather than having to invest at the higher commercial rand rate.

The Reserve Bank also restricts the free distribution of dividends to non-residents. Reserve Bank approval is required before royalties or licence fees may be paid to a non-resident. Income earned in South Africa accrues to a non-resident at the commercial rand rate and may then be transferred to any currency.

Incentives

The Income Tax Act has in recent years been an effective medium through which the government has implemented its economic policy. This is done through the use of tax incentives. For example non-resident investors in government stock are usually exempt from tax on the income.

Exports are encouraged by various means including the following:

- the zero rating of value added tax (VAT) on export sales
- exemption from various customs and excise duties
- the General Export Incentive Scheme which pays out tax free cash subsidies based on export turnover.
- free export promotion is provided by the Department of Trade and Industry

Subsidies are also available for businesses in various regions to encourage higher employment. These are known as 'Regional Industrial Development Incentives'.

Market access

Government policy regarding privatization and deregulation was clarified by a 1987 White Paper. Many areas of the South African economy have been deregulated, including the railways, harbours, airways and post and telecommunications.

On a smaller scale the market is opening up to the general population with considerable speed. The Businesses Act of 1991 makes provision for the abolition of trading licences except in certain instances, and the abolition of restrictions on trading hours with the exception of Sunday. This allows the creation of new businesses with the minimum of legislative interference.

Getting Started

Roman-Dutch Law

The early settlers were from The Netherlands, and introduced Roman-Dutch law to the Cape. This legal system was based on the 17th-century writings of Dutch jurists such as Grotius and Voet. Roman-Dutch law remained the basis of Cape law after the British occupation of 1785, although the influence of English law became noticeable and was particularly influential in company law. Roman-Dutch law was retained as the basis of the common law when the Union of South Africa was established in 1910. It is interesting to note that South African courts will recognize African customary law. Since 1988 any court may take judicial notice of African customary law and apply it to the case at hand where relevant.

Companies and close corporations

The formation, registration, operation and liquidation of close corporations is regulated by the Close Corporation Act #69 of 1984. Companies fall under the ambit of the Companies Act No. 61 of 1973 (as amended) and this act regulates the formation, operation and winding up of all companies. Both Acts are administered by the Registrar of Companies.

A close corporation, introduced in 1984, is a simpler and less expensive corporate form than a company. Many of the formalities of companies have been removed from the requirements for close corporations. Every close corporation must have the letters 'CC' following its name. As with a company, a close corporation has a separate juristic persona. This is a distinct advantage over a partnership or sole proprietorship for small businesses. The number of members is restricted to a maximum of ten. There is no share capital, but the monetary value of the members' interests has no limit.

In South Africa two kinds of companies may be formed: one having a share capital or one limited by guarantee (i.e., not having a share capital). Companies with a share capital are by far in the majority and may be of two different types: private companies whose membership is limited to fifty and whose names are followed by the words '(Proprietary) Limited'; and public companies whose membership is unlimited, who may be listed on the Stock Exchange, and whose names are followed by the word 'Limited'.

Although there is no limit on the maximum value of the share capital in a private company there can be no offer of the share capital to the public. Therefore the transfer of shares in a private company is restricted and always subject to directors' approval.

Public companies must have at least seven members but there is no maximum number of members imposed on them. Only public companies may be listed on the Stock Exchange and the right to transfer shares in a public company is therefore not restricted. A public company may accordingly raise capital from the general public.

Both companies are registered by lodging the required forms with the Registrar of Companies. Each company must file a memorandum and articles of association together with written consents to act as directors and auditors.

Every public or private company is required by law to be audited by a registered member of the Public Accountants and Auditors Association. The memorandum indicates such things as the name of the company, and the amount of share capital. The articles of association describe the nature of the internal regulations in the company.

Directors and shareholders

The shareholders of either a public or a private company elect a board of directors through whom they are represented. Every company must have directors, although they need not be South African residents nor South African nationals. Directors have a fiduciary duty to act with reasonable care in good faith for the benefit of the company. Each year there must be an annual general meeting of shareholders where the annual financial statements are presented and the shareholders elect, or re-elect, the board of directors.

Partnership and sole proprietorship

A small business owned and managed by one person is termed a sole proprietorship. The owner is personally liable for all debts of the business. The income from the business is taxable as the owner's personal income.

Partnerships are commonly found in South Africa among professionals such as accountants, lawyers and doctors. No partnership may have more than twenty members, although the law allows certain exceptions. There are few legislative requirements placed on partnerships. For the most part, partners are personally liable for the obligations of the partnership. The relationships between partners are established by the partners themselves in terms of a partnership agreement.

Requirements for a Stock Exchange listing

The South African Stock Exchange is located in Johannesburg and is regulated by the Stock Exchange Act 1985. Application for a listing must be submitted through a sponsoring broker. The documentation required by the Act includes a pre-listing statement or prospectus. This document will give information on the history, financial position, the type of operations and the future prospects of the company. The articles of association of a company, which regulate the internal relations of that company, must be submitted for approval to the Johannesburg Stock Exchange. The company must offer thirty per cent of the shares to a sponsoring broker who will offer thirty per cent to the broking community, if the listing is on offer to the public.

Subsequent to listing on the Stock Exchange, the company has to comply with certain regulations of the Johannesburg Stock Exchange on an ongoing basis. These requirements extend the duties of the company beyond the requirements of the Companies Act No. 61 of 1973 in such areas as financial reporting, share incentive schemes and the relationship between shareholders and the directors.

Takeovers and mergers

The Securities Regulation Panel and the Code of Takeovers and Mergers was established by the 1991 amendment to the Companies Act. The purpose of the Panel and Code is to protect shareholders in a takeover situation. The Code provides a framework within which takeovers and mergers can be effected, thus creating a fairer climate for these transactions. The Panel does not pass any judgement on the commercial merits of a proposed takeover, but rather concentrates on ensuring a just transaction.

The Code of Takeovers deals with such matters as the conduct of the firm prior to, and during, the making of an offer. For example, negotiations must be conducted in secret, and any subsequent announcement of intention must be published in the press. The Code also compels a company to extend the offer to all shareholders under certain circumstances.

The Code also makes certain requirements of the documentation, ensuring relevant information is disclosed. This documentation must include such details as the reasons for the offer, the intentions of the company making the offer, the terms and the financial effects of the arrangement.

Further requirements are placed on firms intending a takeover deal by the Johannesburg Stock Exchange (JSE), although in many cases the Securities Regulation Panel and the Code on Takeovers and Mergers have superceded these regulations. The JSE extends the duty of the firm beyond that of the Companies Act in matters such as disclosure of information. The nature of the offer and the documentation must be approved by the JSE prior to release and must include similar details to the Takeover Code.

Restrictions on foreign ownership

Foreign companies may set up a place of business in South Africa without incorporating a local company. The branch of a foreign company will, however, need to be registered as an external company. No local board of directors need be appointed, but a resident representative needs to be elected.

Where non-residents control twenty-five per cent of a South African company, the Reserve Bank places restrictions on the level of local financial assistance. Financial assistance would include bank and credit facilities excluding trade creditors. The permissable level is determined through a formula by the Reserve Bank. Current policy is to let a wholly foreign-owned company borrow up to fifty per cent of its shareholders' equity. It is possible to get temporary permission to exceed this level in the interests of expansion and modernization. However, the withdrawals of money by, or dividends paid to non-residents could then be restricted.

Dividends declared to non-residents out of income earned since January 1984 (or the date of acquisition if this is later) are transferred at the commercial rand. In all cases the approval of the Reserve Bank is required before remitting dividends to overseas countries. Directors' fees, management or similar fees are transferable to non-residents subject to certain exchange control regulations largely concerned with ensuring the validity of the fee.

Patents, trademarks and copyrights

The copyright laws of South Africa are regulated by the Copyright Act No. 98 of 1978 and are originally based on the British model. The works falling under the Act include literary works, artistic works, music and sound recording, broadcasts, published editions. Computer works although not expressly mentioned have been held by the court to be literary works and so are protected. The term of copyright is generally fifty years in excess of the author's lifetime. South Africa is a member of the Berne Convention and consequently non-residents can derive benefit from South African copyright.

The Patents Act of 1978 is similar to European patent practice. Patents and designs can be registered at the South African Patents and Designs Office. South Africa is a member of the Paris Convention through which recognition to foreign patents is given. The term of patent is usually twenty years and that of design five years.

The treatment in South Africa of trademarks is similar to that in Britain. Various forms of trademarks are recognized including words, logos, labels, signature and the visual appearance of words. A trademark is registered for ten years, and is renewable for further periods of ten years.

Finance

Financial environment

South Africa has a sophisticated financial system which functions within a modern economy. The financial institutions present in South Africa are on a par with those found in most developed Western countries. However, a gap exists between the mass market which is emerging in a post-apartheid country and the functioning of financial institutions.

There is a growing awareness of the need of the financial organizations to be involved in the development of the community and in the upliftment of the majority of South Africans. The political uncertainty of the last decade has led to significant outflows of capital from the country which the debt standstill of 1985 only served to exaggerate. This has placed an enormous strain on the financial system, but has brought about an introspective awareness of South Africa's own needs rather than those of the international community.

Against this background the financial system can be seen to be in vibrant change, while looking forward to growth within the whole population of South Africa.

The pinnacle of the financial system is the Reserve Bank which, although technically a private body, is in reality an arm of the government. It operates as the central bank for the country and besides controlling the money supply, serves as the banker of the government and other banks.

Johannesburg Stock Exchange

The South African Stock Exchange, the origins of which lie in the discovery of gold on the Witwatersrand, is located in Diagonal Street in Johannesburg. The Johannesburg Stock Exchange (JSE) opened in 1887. The JSE is a creation of legislation and is self-regulating. Trading is done on an open outcry system. There is no jobbing as in the USA, and brokerage firms act on an agency basis.

The brokerage fees range from 1.4 per cent to 0.21 per cent depending on the size of the share deal. There is a high degree of concentration in the market with annual transactions amounting to only five per cent of market capitalization. Similar figures for New York, London and Tokyo are eighty-five per cent, thirty-three per cent and eighty per cent respectively. Shares of the stature of De Beers, Anglo American, and South African Breweries are listed and some are listed in London and New York.

There is also trading in fixed interest securities of a quality high enough to receive a triple A rating from American agencies. Electronic trading is conducted in the money market and for futures and options. However, the foreign exchange market remains underdeveloped largely because of strict exchange control.

Industrial Development Corporation

The Industrial Development Corporation (IDC) has been operating since 1940 and provides financial assistance to developing industries. The IDC has been a part of the government's decentralization programme and is generally an element of government development policy.

Small Business Development Corporation

Since 1981 the Small Business Development Corporation (SBDC) encourages development of small business in various areas. The SBDC provides financial assistance, advisory services, aid in affording and finding business premises, and a public relations function which assists in promoting the small business under its wing.

Taxation

Income Tax is levied in accordance with the provisions of the Income Tax Act No. 58 of 1962 as amended. Each March the Income Tax Act is amended by the Minister of Finance upon presentation by the government of its Annual Budget. Value Added Tax (VAT) is charged at a rate of fourteen per cent and has been in operation since 1 October 1991. Further taxes are imposed by the Customs and Excise Act, Estate Duty Act, Stamp Duties, Regional Services Councils Act and the Transfer Duty Act.

The taxation system falls within the portfolio of the Department of Finance, although the Directorate of Inland Revenue performs the direct administration of taxation through the Commissioner of Inland Revenue. The country is divided into various tax regions which are administered by local Receivers of Revenue.

In cases of uncertainty it is possible for the taxpayer to apply to the commissioner for an advance ruling on a proposed scheme so as to prevent uncertain tax complications.

All taxpayers are required by the commissioner to submit an annual tax return. Individuals pay tax on a progressive system of Pay as You Earn (PAYE) or Standard Income Tax on Employees (SITE). Under PAYE and SITE a part of remuneration paid to employees is withheld by the employer and paid over to the commissioner. Individual tax rates range from a minimum of zero to a maximum rate of forty-three per cent. Companies and close corporations are taxed at a rate of forty-eight per cent and are required to make advance tax payments each year. Partnerships are not considered taxable entities and partners are taxed on profits in their personal capacities.

The Composition of Taxable Income

The tax rates for both companies and individuals are applied to taxable income. In a broad sense, taxable income comprises all income of a revenue nature (as opposed to a capital nature) derived from a source within, or deemed by the commissioner to be within South Africa. Fringe benefits (including motor cars and motor car allowances) derived by an employee from the employer are included in taxable income. Allowances are granted on plant and machinery, mining capital expenditure, research and development, implements and other articles used for the purpose of trade.

The Act regulates the allowable deductions, which generally cover all expenses or losses incurred in South Africa for the purpose of income production. Expenses or losses incurred outside of South Africa are allowable as deductions subject to the approval of the commissioner. Rebates are given to individuals in accordance with their status.

Other taxes of importance

Value Added Tax (VAT) is charged at a rate of fourteen per cent on all transactions. Only a few basic food stuffs, donated goods or services, and the supply of financial services are exempt. Some goods such as exports, gold, petrol subject to the fuel levy, goods supplied to foreign branches of South African enterprises, and services supplied to a non-resident branch, carry a VAT charge of zero per cent. Only those companies enjoying a turnover in excess of R150,000 are compelled to register for VAT under the Act; smaller companies may choose to do so if it is to their benefit.

Gratuitous donations of more than R20,000 per annum are subject to a fifteen per cent donations tax. Estate duty is charged at fifteen per cent of the value in excess of R1-million of the deceased's estate. Stamp duties are payable on a number of legal documents, for example the one per cent transfer duty for shares sales.

South Africa has no established social security, but employers are obliged to pay Workman's Compensation insurance premiums which cover loss of income to employees resulting from injury. Both employees and employers pay Unemployment Insurance which provides benefit for those whose annual income falls below R36,000.

Taxation of non-resident companies

The rates of taxation for non-resident individuals and companies are the same as for South African residents. Companies are divided into either domestic companies or external companies for tax purposes. A domestic company is a company incorporated in South Africa. An external company is defined in the Income Tax Act as any company other than a domestic company. This would encompass foreign, non-resident companies.

If a non-resident company opens a place of business in South Africa, it is obliged to register as an external company. The profits attributed to the external company will be taxed at the standard rate of thirty-five per cent on income sourced from South Africa but profits can be disbursed to the non-resident company without any withholding of taxes.

Alternatively, the non-resident company could establish a locally incorporated subsidiary. Then the locally earned profits will be taxed at the standard rate or thirty-five per cent and dividend payments to the holding company will be subject to a fifteen per cent withholding tax in the form of non-resident shareholders tax.

PART SIX: FACTS AT YOUR FINGERTIPS

Visas and immigration regulations

Visitors require visas except those on holiday visits from the United Kingdom, the U.S.A., the Republic of Ireland, Switzerland, Lichtenstein and Germany. Visitors from Spain, France, Zaire, Lesotho, Botswana, Swaziland and diplomatic passport holders on holiday for two weeks or less are also exempt.

All visas are issued free of charge and should be applied for well in advance of leaving for South Africa from South African missions abroad or direct from the Director General, Home Affairs, Private Bag X114, Pretoria 0001, South Africa.

Multiple-entry and re-entry visas

Prior to entry into South Africa citizens of some countries can apply for a multiple-entry visa if necessary, giving details of their travel itineraries. This type of visa is necessary if you are visiting any neighbouring countries.

Once you are actually in South Africa and want to visit neighbouring territories and then re-enter South Africa, you must get a re-entry visa before leaving by applying in person at any regional Home Affairs department or by mail from Home Affairs, Private Bag X114, Pretoria 0001.

Temporary Residence Permits

Visitors can get a free temporary residence permit — usually for three months — at their entry point to South Africa if they state the purpose and length of their stay. Permits can be extended by applying one month before the expiry date from any Home Affairs department or a police station.

Health requirements

A valid international certificate of vaccination against yellow fever is required from all travellers coming from any part of a country in which yellow fever is endemic except children under the age of one year, who may be subject to medical surveillance on arrival in South Africa.

Malaria is endemic in the Transvaal Lowveld, the Kruger National Park and Zululand in KwaZulu-Natal; visitors are strongly recommended to take anti-malarial tablets before entering these areas.

International flights

The national carrier is South African Airways, which flies to Johannesburg from Amsterdam, Frankfurt, Harare, Hong Kong, Lisbon, London, Madrid, New York, Paris, Rome, Taiwan, Vienna, Windhoek and Zurich. It also services the Indian Ocean Islands of Mauritius, Reunion and the Comores.

Aer Lingus, Aeroflot, Air Afrique, Air Austral, Air France, Air Gabon, Air India, Air Madagascar, Air Malta, Air Mauritius, Air Portugal, Air Seychelles, Air Tanzania, Air UK, Air Zaire, Air Zimbabwe, Austrian Airlines, Alitalia, Atlantic Air, Balkan Bulgarian Airlines, British Airways, Cameroon Airlines, Care Airlines, Cathay Pacific, China Airlines, Egypt Air, El Al, Ethiopian Airlines, Ghana Airways, Gulf Air, Iberia, Inter Air, Japan Airlines, Kenya Airways, KLM, LAM, Lot Polish Airlines, LTU International, Lufthansa, Malaysia Airlines, Olympic, Pakistan Int. Airlines, Qantas, Sabena, Singapore Air, Sudan Airways, Swissair, UTA, Uganda Airlines and Varig international airlines all operate regular scheduled flights to Johannesburg.

In addition, British Airways flies to Cape Town and Durban. KLM flies to Cape Town. Neighbouring territories are served by Air Botswana, Lesotho Airways, Air Malawi, Air Zimbabwe, Sun Air, Linhas Aereas de Mocambique, Air Namibia, Royal Swazi Air, South African Airways, Letaba Airways, Metavia Airlines and Transkei Airways.

Departure tax

Airport tax in included in the price of tickets in South Africa.

Customs

A reasonable amount of personal effects can be imported freely. Visitors are restricted to duty-free items of one litre of spirits, two litres of wine, 50ml of perfumery, 250ml of toilet water, 400 cigarettes, 50 cigars and 250g of tobacco.

Duty is exempt from the first R500 of other new or used goods. Additional items are subject to duty. To speed up your passage through customs you can elect for the first additional R1,000 to be assessed at a flat rate of twenty per cent. Thereafter each item will be assessed individually as to duty and sales tax.

Banned items include automatic weapons, pornographic material and narcotics.

Domestic flights

South African Airways, Sun Air, Air Link, Phoenix

Air and Comair, operate regular flights linking major cities. Smoking is prohibited on SAA domestic services.

Air Cape, Comair, Giyani Airways, Inter Air, Letaba Airways, Air Link, National Airlines, Safair Lines, Theron Airways and Transkei Airways have scheduled flights to smaller airfields.

Charter services can be obtained from all of the above, as well as from Air 2000 (tel: 011-659-2649) and Inter-Air (tel: 011-827-9804).

Driving

A valid national driver's licence issued in any country is accepted in South Africa as long as it has the driver's photograph and signature as an integral part of the licence and is written, or has a certificate of authenticity, in English. International driving permits obtained before arrival in South Africa are also acceptable for a year. Immigrants must apply for a South African licence within six months of being issued a residence permit.

Driving is on the left and the general speed limits are 60 kilometres (37 miles) an hour in town, 100 kilometres (62 miles) on rural roads and 120 kilometres (75 miles) on freeways and major roads.

Visitors who are arriving in South Africa in their own vehicles must have a carnet or triptyque issued by a motoring organisation in their own country.

Taxi services

Normal taxis are metered. Taxis do not cruise — pick one up at a rank or call for one by phone — consult the local yellow pages for phone numbers. Minibus taxis charge a flat rate standard fare for any distance travelled.

Car hire

Licensed car-hire operators hire out a variety of vehicles ranging from small cars to minibuses, either with or without air-conditioning. Rates inclusive or exclusive of mileage are available, and most companies will charge you whichever is cheaper at the end of your hire period.

Large firms will not charge extra if you take a car back to a different office from where it was rented. They will also allow you to travel to Lesotho, Swaziland and Botswana and issue you with a letter of authority to travel across the border. Hiring four-wheel-drive cars is difficult, as they are rarely required in South Africa.

Climate

South Africa is famous for its sunny climate: the capital, Pretoria boasts 3,240 average hours of sunshine yearly comparing favourably with Washington's 2,200; its coastal resorts with 2,750 average hours of sunshine equals southern California or the French Riviera and surpass Hawaii's average of 2,450.

The climate is sunny all year round, with the regions dividing roughly into three. The highveld of central South Africa has a dry winter with frosty nights but clement days. The summer has hot days, warm nights and spectacular afternoon or evening thunderstorms.

The Cape coastal belt is a Mediterranean climate with dry summers and wet winters. In Cape Town the average temperatures in winter are seventeen degrees Celsius in the day and seven degrees Celsius at night and in summer twenty-six degrees Celsius and sixteen degrees Celsius respectively. The eastern coast and lowveld areas have hot summers, warm winters and light rain all year round.

Currency

The South African Rand is divided into 100 cents. Notes are issued in denominations of R10 (green), R20 (brown), R50 (red), R100 (blue) and R200 (orange). The coins are R5, R2, R1, fifty cents, twenty cents, ten cents, five cents, two cents and one cent. The sizes and weights of coins have recently been changed and both old and new coins are currently in circulation.

Currency regulations

There are exchange control regulations in South Africa but you may import or export a maximum of R500 per person in South African bank notes.

Travellers cheques and credit cards

Foreign currency travellers cheques are negotiable only at banks and the hotel in which you are staying. You can get South African Rand travellers cheques from local banks which you can use almost anywhere.

International credit cards are accepted by airlines, many shops and most tour operators and hotels.

Banks

Most banks are open from 09:00–15:30 Monday-Friday and 08:30–11:00 on Saturdays: In some rural areas banks close for lunch between 12:45–14:00. Banks at international airports are open for two hours before international flight departures and two hours after international flight arrivals irrespective of the time of day.

Government

The government of national unity was elected in April 1994. Government departments are usually open from 08:00–16:00 Monday-Friday.

Time

South Africa is two hours ahead of Greenwich Mean Time, one hour ahead of Central European Winter Time and seven hours ahead of American Eastern Standard Winter Time throughout the year.

Daylight

The sun rises at about 06:30 and sets at around 17:30 during the winter, varying slightly depending on the latitude. In the summer the sun rises at about 05:00 and sets at about 19:30.

Business hours

Although business hours are lengthening, shops are usually open from 08:30-17:00 Monday-Friday and from 08:30-13:00 on Saturday, with some supermarkets and pharmacies staying open later. Most shops are closed on a Sunday, although some supermarkets and roadside traders are active on a Sunday morning.

Public Holidays

New Years Day -1 January, Human Rights Day - 21 March, Good Friday - 14 April, Family Day - 17 April, Freedom Day - 27 April, Workers Day - 1 May, Youth Day - 16 June, National Women's - 9 August, Heritage Day - 24 September, Day of Reconcilation - 16 December, Christmas Day - 25 December, Day of Goodwill - 26 December.

Security

Crime is on the increase in South Africa. Do not leave valuables in hotel rooms but use the safety deposit boxes provided. If you leave items in your car, ensure they are out of sight. Do not carry more money or valuables than necessary on city streets.

Communications

The South African Posts and Telecommunications (PTC) and Telkom provide a comprehensive network of postal, telephone, telex and radio services locally and worldwide. International direct dialling is available to most countries. Cellular telephones are available for hire at Johannesburg's International Airport.

Media

All major cities have their own daily newspapers, in Afrikaans and English. *The Citizen* (English), *Cape Times* (English), *Beeld* (Afrikaans), *The Argus* (English), *The Sowetan* (English) and *The Star* (English) are among the daily papers. The *Weekly Mail* (English) and *Sunday Times* are weekly newspapers.

Recent government white papers advocate removing government control of the air waves in favour of an independent broadcasting authority.

The South African Broadcasting Corporation, a government body, runs several commercial radio stations in the country to cater for various tastes from pop to news. The SABC also broadcasts three commercial television stations, TV1 (English and Afrikaans) and CCV and NNTV (all languages) as well as a public broadcasting service, M-Net, an independent pay-TV station with over 750,000 subscribers, broadcasts to Africa from Randburg, north of Johannesburg. Bop TV broadcasts from the North West province on a signal which until recently has been largely restricted to the black residential areas.

Energy

The electricity supply is 220/230 volts (50 cycles per second AC) except in Pretoria (250V) and Port Elizabeth (220/250V). Plugs are three-point, large round-pin.

Medical services and insurance

Visitors are advised to carry medical insurance. They will be liable to pay for all medical services while in South Africa.

The government provides a public health service which caters mainly for lower income groups. Patients pay for treatment on a sliding scale depending on their income. Private medical services, which comprise forty per cent of total health expenditure in the country, are of the highest international standards. Visitors will be treated as private patients, which can be costly.

Names and addresses of doctors and dentists are listed in large cities' telephone directories under 'M' for medical.

Dial 10177 for an emergency ambulance, or look up telephone numbers in the Emergency Services section at the front of all telephone directories. In some towns ambulances are called by telephoning the local fire station.

South Africa has few tropical diseases. Visitors travelling to South Africa should worry only about malaria in Mpumalanga, the Kruger National Park and Zululand in KwaZulu-Natal and are strongly recommended to take anti-malarial tablets before entering these areas.

Water is safe to drink unboiled in cities and most tourist locations.

Chemists/Pharmacies

Medical supplies are readily available and reasonably priced. Pharmacies often stay open late in the evening and on Saturday and Sunday.

Liquor

As well as its world-renowned wines, South Africa also makes fortified wines, beers and spirits. Beer is the most popular drink in the country, made from grain or sorghum.

Alcohol cannot be bought to take away after 18:00 when liquor — or 'bottle' — stores close. Many restaurants are not licensed and will only serve cans of beer or glasses of house wine. To avoid disappointment check before going out to eat and if neccessary purchase your own preferred tipple to take with you.

Tipping

Tips are expected in most service industries. A ten per cent tip is standard.

There are South African branches of all major international clubs including the Rotary Club, Lions, etc. (See Listings)

There is a plethora of sports clubs in the country. (See Listings)

Phrases

English	Afrikaans	Zulu
Hello	Hello	Sawubona
I am well (fine etc)	Dit gaan goed	Kulungile
Thank you	Dankie	Ngiyabonga
Please	Asseblief	Ngiyacela
Goodbye	Totsiens	Salakahle
Hotel	Hotel	Ihotela
Room	Kamer	Ikamelo
Bed	Bed	Umbhede
Food	Kos	Ukudla
Coffee	Koffie	Ikofi
Hot	Warm	Fudumele
Cold	Koud	Makhaza
Water	Water	Amanzi
Tea	Tee	Itiye
Meat	Vleis	Inyama
Fish	Vis	Inhlanzi
Bread	Brood	Isinkwa
Butter	Botter	Ibhotela
Sugar	Suiker	Ushukela
Salt	Sout	Usawoti
Today	Vandag	Namuhle
Tomorrow	Môre	Kusasa
Now	Nou	Manje
Quickly	Vinnig	Ngokushesha
Slowly	Stadig	Totoba
Hospital	Hospitaal	Isibhedlela
Police	Polisie	Amaphoyisa
Mr	Meneer	Mnumzane
Mrs	Mevrou	Nkosikazi
Ms	Mejuvrou	Nkosazana
I	Ek	Mina
You	Jy (polite U)	Wena
You (pl)	Julle (polite U)	Nina-/wena
We	Ons	Thina
They	Hulle	Bona
What?	Wat?	Yini?
Who?	Wie?	Ubani?
Where?	Waar?	Kuphi?
When?	Wanneer?	Nini?
How?	Hoe?	Kanjani?
Why?	Hoekom?	Ngani?
Yes	Ja	Yebo
No	Nee	Cha
To eat	Eet	Yidla
To drink	Drink	Phuza
To sleep	Slaap	Lala
To come	Kom	Woza
To go	Gaan	Hamba
To buy	Koop	Thenga

English	Afrikaans	Zulu
To sell	Verkoop	Thengisa
Street/road	Straat/pad/weg	Umgwaqo
Shop	Winkel	Isitolo
Money	Geld	Imali
One	Een	Ukunye
Two	Twee	Kubili
Three	Drie	Kuthathu
Four	Vier	Okune
Five	Vyf	Kuhlanu
Six	Ses	Isithupha
Seven	Sewe	Isikhombisa
Eight	Agt	Isishiyagalombili
Nine	Nege	Isishiyagalolunye
Ten	Tien	Ishumi
Hundred	Honderd	Ikhulu
Thousand	Duisend	Inkulungwane
Monday	Maandag	Msombuluko
Tuesday	Dinsdag	Lwesibili
Wednesday	Woensdag	Lwesithathu
Thursday	Donnerdag	Lwesine
Friday	Vrydag	Lwesihlanu
Saturday	Saterdag	Umgq(!)ibelo
Sunday	Sondag	Isonto
Where is the hotel?	Waar is die hotel?	Likuphi Ihotela?
Good morning	Goeie Môre	Sawubona
Good afternoon	Goeie Middag	"
Good evening	Goeienaand	"
Come in!	Kom binne!	Ngena
Please sit down	Sit, asseblief	Hlalaphansi
Welcome!	Welkom	Siyakwamukela
Where do you	Waar woon jy? (u)	Uhlalaphi
live? I come from...	Ek kom van .... af	Ngiphuma ....
What is your name?	Wat is jou (u) naam?	Ubani lgama lakho?
My name is ...	My naam is ...	Igama lami Ngingu....
Do you speak (language)	Praat jy (u) ...?	Uyakhuluma ...?
I don't understand	Ek verstaan nie	Angizwa ...
Excuse me (apology)	Verskoon my	Uxolo
What is the time?	Hoe laat is dit?	Yisikhathi sini?
How much does it cost?	Hoeveel kos dit?	Kubiza malini?
Wait a minute, please	Wag asseblief 'n bietjie	Mawulindalinde Kancane

*Note: (!) denotes a click. The 'q' of Umgqibelo (Saturday) and the 'x' of Uxolo (Sorry) have hard click sounds, the 'c' of eg Ngiyacela (Please) has a soft click sound.

English	Sesotho	Xhosa
Hello	Dumela(ng)	Molo/bhota
I am well (fine etc)	Nna ke hantle	Ndi-philile
Thank you	Ke a leboha	Enkosi
Please	(Ka kopo) hle	Nceda
Goodbye	Sala(ng) hantle	Nisale kakuhle
Hotel	Hotele	Ihotele
Room	Kamore	Igumbi
Bed	Bethe	Umandlalo
Food	Dijo	Ukutya

English	Sesotho	Xhosa
Coffee	Kofi	Ikofu
Hot	Tjhesa	Shushu
Cold	Bata	Bandayo
Water	Metsi	Amanzi
Tea	Tee	Iti
Meat	Nama	Inyama
Fish	Tlhapi	Intlanzi
Bread	Borotho	Isonka
Butter	Botoro	Ibhotolo
Sugar	Tswekere	Iswekile
Salt	Letswai	Ityuwa
Today	Kajeno	Namhlanje
Tomorrow	Hosane	Ngomso
Now	Jwale	Ngoku
Quickly	Ka pele	Ngokukhawuleza
Slow	Butle	Cothoza
Hospital	Sepetlele	Isibhedlele
Police	Lepolesa	Ipolisa
I	Ke	Ndi
You	Lona	Nina
You (pl)	Wena	Wena
We	Rona	Thina
They	Bona	Ba
What?	Eng?	Ntoni?
Who?	Mang?	Ubani?
Where?	Kae?	Phi?
When?	Neng?	Ini?
How?	Jwang?	Njani?
Why?	Hobaneng?	Ngokuba?
Yes	E!	Ewe
No	Tjhe	Hayi
To eat	Ja	Tya
To drink	Nwa	Sela
To sleep	Robala	Lala
To come	Tlo	Iza
To go	Ya	Hamba
To buy	Reka	Thenga
To sell	Rekisa	Thengisa
Street/Road	Seterata	Isitalato
Shop	Lebenkele	Ivenkile
Money	Tjhelete	Imali
One	Nngwe	Inye
Two	Pedi	Isibini
Three	Tharo	Ntathu
Four	Nne	Isine
Five	Hlano	Isihlanu
Six	Tshelela	Isithandathu
Seven	Supa	Isixhenxe
Eight	Robedi	Isibhozo
Nine	Robong	Ithoba
Ten	Leshome	Ishumi
Hundred	Lekgolo	Ikhulu
Thousand	Sekete	Iwaka
Monday	Mantaha	UMvulo
Tuesday	Labobedi	UlwesiBini
Wednesday	Laboraro	Ulwesithathu
Thursday	Labone	Ulwesine
Friday	Labohlano	Ulwesi Hlanu

Saturday	Moqebelo	Umgqibelo
Sunday	Sontaha	Icawa
Where is the hotel?	Hotele o haufiufi e kae?	Iphi ihotele yabahambi
Good morning	Dumela(ng)	Molo/bhoto
Good evening	Fonaneng	Molo/bhota
Come in!	Kena	Ngena
Welcome!	Amohela	Amkela
Where do you live?	O dula kae?	Uhlala phi?
I come from ...	Ke tswa ...	Ndivela
What is your name?	O mang na?	Ngubani igama lakho
My name is	Lebitso la ka ke ...	Igama lam ngu ...
Do you speak (language)	Na o a bua ...?	Uyathetha ...?
I don't understand	Ha ke utlwisise	Andiqondi
Excuse me (apology)	Ntshwarele	Uxolo
What is the time?	Ke nako mang?	Ngubani ixesha?
How much money is it?	Ke bokae?	Ixabisa malini?
Wait a minute, please	Ema hanyenyane hle	Khawulinde kancinci

In Brief

South African National Parks and Reserves

South Africa is famed for the outstanding quality of its national parks and game reserves, which are among the finest in Africa.

A variety of government and provincial bodies administer 458 parks and reserves and there are at least 557 nature reserves in private hands or administered by local towns. These parks range in size from a few hectares to the enormous Kruger National Park which covers two million hectares (4,942,000 acres).

The aim of the various semi-government departments which administer the parks is to maintain a natural balance. Management decisions are based on a thorough understanding of the principles of ecology. All the conservation agencies have strong research components and undertake a variety of research with regard to ecosystem management.

Wilderness areas

In 1984, South Africa created a new kind of conservation area in which nature rules without intervention from man. So far eight areas with a total area of 231,966 hectares (635,586 acres) have been designated. Wilderness Areas may not be violated by roads, buildings or mining. Two of the best-known are the Cedarberg, near Clan-William, and extensive areas of the Natal Drakensberg.

Nature areas

These are areas, mainly private with some state-owned properties, which have a high aesthetic and conservation potential. They are managed in terms of the Environmental Conservation Act (Act No. 73 of 1989). Table Mountain and the southern peninsula mountains in the Cape Province and Magaliesberg stretch from Gauteng to the North West Province have been proclaimed as Protected Natural Environments.

Mountain catchment areas

In terms of the Mountain Catchment Areas Act (act No. 63 of 1970), sixteen mountain catchment areas with a total area of 599,598 hectares (1,481,606 acres) were declared on private land in 1985. The intention of this act is to manage these areas in a responsible way according to sound conservation.

Natural Heritage Programme

This programme aims to register and conserve important natural sites in private hands and thus the risk that significant natural life forms or landscapes may be unwittingly degraded or destroyed. The areas which qualify for registration include those with special plant communities, good examples of aquatic habitats, sensitive catchment areas, habitats of threatened species and outstanding natural features.

Safari areas

As one of the most popular hunting regions in the world, South Africa offers a wide variety for trophy hunters during the hunting season. Strict regulations exist regarding the hunting of rhinoceros, black wildebeest, nyala, eland, buffalo and other rare trophies. No hunting is permitted in game parks and therefore dangerous game (lion, leopard, elephant and buffalo) may only be hunted in private game reserves such as Timbavati and Klaserie under a special permit obtained from the Transvaal Directorate for Nature and Environmental Conservation. At both reserves hunting is put up for tender.

For further information write to The Secretary, Timbavati Private Nature Reserve, P O. Box 2001, Tzaneen, 0850. For hunting at Klaserie, write to Mr E Leibnitz, Klaserie Private Nature Reserve, PO Box 150, Hoedspruit, 1380.

Non-landowners may legally hunt most species during the hunting season (1 May to 31 July and in some provinces to the end of August for bird-shooting) provided they are in possession of a valid hunting permit and as long as they have also received the written consent of the landowner.

Game concentrated on farms in the Transvaal and the KwaZulu-Natal bushveld regions include impala, kudu, wildebeest (gnu), zebra, duiker and wart hog, while springbok, blesbok and the rare white-tailed gnu are found in the Northern Province highveld regions, the Free State and the northern Cape.

Sportsmen have organised themselves into hunter's associations and the South African Hunters' and Game Preservation Association is the best known.

The Professional Hunters' Association of South Africa co-ordinates hunting safaris in and around South Africa. Tel: (011) 706-7724.

Botanical reserves

The National Botanic Gardens of South Africa at Kirstenbosch, Cape Town were established in 1913 to cultivate, display, undertake scientific study and preserve native South African flora. The Botanical Society of South Africa was established at the same time to finance and generally assist the gardens. Several regional botanic gardens and reserves have since been established under the control of Kirstenbosch and each is concerned with the native flora of its own ecological area.

Conventions

South Africa is a signatory to various international conventions such as those on wetlands, whaling, endangered species and others concerning conservation. Specifically it is a signatory to the following conventions:

- Convention on International Trade in Endangered Species of Wild Fauna and Flora. CITES CONVENTION
- Convention on Wetlands of International Importance especially as waterfowl habitat. RAMSAR CONVENTION
- Convention on the Conservation of Migratory Species of Wild Animals. BONN CONVENTION

Parks and reserves legislation

Each province administers its own Nature Conservation Ordinance and the National Parks Board administers the National Parks Act.

Advance Bookings

Accomodation in parks under the National Parks Board may be reserved up to one year in advance. To make a reservation contact: Pretoria, National Parks Board PO Box 787, Pretoria 0001; tel: (012) 343-1991. Or: Cape Town National Parks Board, PO Box 7400, Roggebaai 8012; tel: (021) 222-810.

Applications should contain the following information:
(a) Date of the projected visit
(b) Desired camp, or camps in order of preference
(c) Number of persons
(d) Type and number of huts or number of camping sites required.

A deposit is payable, but only on confirmation of the reservation. Proof of confirmation of reservation must be presented on entry to the park concerned. Any cancellation or change is subject to a prescribed fee. Payment may be made in cash, by traveller's cheque or Visa/Mastercard. No pets are allowed into national parks. Speed limits are strictly enforced within the parks for the safety of both visitors and animals.

The gates giving access to and from the national parks normally open and close at sunrise and sunset respectively. Times, however, may vary seasonally and from place to place. Visitors are not permitted to leave their cars and those who break the rule may be required to leave the park, in addition to paying a fine. They may also place themselves in considerable physical danger.

To book accommodation at those parks which fall under the KwaZulu-Natal Parks Board, written applications are accepted up to nine calendar months in advance but accommodation is only allocated six months in advance on a random selection basis. All enquiries should be addressed to: Reservations Officer, PO Box 662, Pietermaritzburg 3200; tel: (0331) 471-981.

The above rules and regulations also apply to users of parks governed by the KwaZulu-Natal Parks Board.

Accommodation specifications

National Parks Board:
The National Parks Board accommodation falls into the following categories:

- Six-bed cottage with kitchenette; two bedrooms, with three beds in each, bathroom, fully equipped kitchenette with fridge.
- Six-bed cottage without kitchenette; two bedrooms with three beds in each, bathroom, toilet and fridge.
- Five-bed cottage with kitchenette; two bedrooms, separate toilet and shower, fully equipped kitchenette.
- Four-bed cottage with kitchenette; one bedroom with two beds plus two beds in lounge. Bathroom, toilet and fully equipped kitchenette with fridge. (Without air-conditioning.)
- Four-bed cottage with kitchenette; one bedroom with two beds plus two beds in lounge. Bathroom, toilet and fully equipped kitchenette with fridge. (Without air-conditioning.)
- Three-bed hut with shower, toilet and kitchenette; one bedroom with three beds, shower and toilet, fridge and fully equipped kitchenette.
- Two-bed hut with shower, toilet and kitchenette; one bedroom with two beds, shower and toilet, fridge and fully equipped kitchenette.
- Hut with shower, toilet, hot plates and sink; one bedroom with three beds (no cooking or eating utensils), fridge.
- Hut with shower and toilet; one room with two or three beds and fridge.
- Ordinary huts
  These huts are available with two, three, four or five beds, hand basin with cold water. Visitors make use of public ablution facilities

Camping and caravan sites

Camping: A maximum of six persons per site. Only one vehicle with caravan per site or tent. All other vehicles to remain in public parking provided. Note: Power points are not provided.

Visitors who bring their own generators must switch them off an hour before sunset and an hour after sunrise. Campers must provide their own camping equipment and bedding.

KwaZulu-Natal Parks Board

The KwaZulu-Natal Parks Board accommodation falls into sixteen categories:

Bungalow: A bungalow is a fully equipped one- or two-bedroomed house with lounge/dining room, bathroom and toilet. Crockery, cutlery, a fridge and linen are provided. Food is prepared by a cook in a central kitchen.

Bush Camps: Bush camps are fully equipped with cutlery, linen, crockery and cooking utensils. Although cooking is usually done over an open fire, a small gas fridge and stove are provided. Visitors do their own cooking.

Cabin: A cabin is a fully-equipped self-contained, serviced dwelling having two bedrooms (one bedroom has a two bunk alcove) a lounge/diningroom, bathroom, toilet and kitchenette. Linen is provided. Visitors do their own cooking.

Caves: Basic toilet facilities only. Cooking may only be done on portable gas cookers which hikers must provide themselves.

Chalet: A chalet is a fully-equipped self-contained, serviced dwelling with one or more bedrooms, lounge/diningroom, bathroom, toilet and kitchenette equipped with cutlery, crockery, stove and fridge. Linen is provided. Visitors do their own cooking.

Cottage: A cottage is a fully-equipped two- or three-bedroomed house with lounge/diningroom, bathroom, toilet and kitchen equipped with cutlery, crockery, stove and fridge). Linen is provided and a cook is in attendance.

Dormitory Cabins: One room with four double bunks (eight beds). Facilities are the same as for cabins (see above).

Leisure Home: The Leisure Home contains two bedrooms (one with a double bed, the other with a double bunk and single bed). Two additional beds for children can be installed. The unit is fully equipped and has a gas fridge, stove, bathroom, toilet and lounge. Visitors do their own cooking and washing up.

Lodge: A lodge contains the same facilities as a cottage (see cottage category) but on a more luxurious scale. Reservations for lodges are only accepted two calendar months in advance.

Log Cabin: A log cabin is a fully equipped two bedroomed building with beds for five or eight people (three or six beds plus one double bunk). It contains a bathroom, toilet and kitchen (equipped with cutlery, crockery, stove and fridge). Linen is provided. Visitors are required to do their own cooking and washing up. Log cabins are serviced each day.

Rest Hut: A rest hut is a fully equipped two- or three-bed rondavel (round-walled, thatched roof dwelling) or square-davel (one room only), provided with cutlery, crockery, a fridge and linen. Communal bathrooms are used. Food is prepared by cooks in a central kitchen.

Rondavel: A rondavel comprises two beds, bathroom, toilet and kitchenette equipped with cutlery, crockery, linen, stove and fridge. Visitors are required to do their own cooking and washing up. Rondavels are cleaned each day.

Rustic Cabin: A rustic cabin is a fully equipped four-bed hut equipped with cutlery, crockery, hot-plate and fridge. The units are served by a communal ablution block. Linen is provided. Visitors are required to do their own cooking and washing up. Rustic cabins are cleaned each day.

Rustic Cottage: Rustic cottages are provided with crockery, cutlery, cooking utensils, a fridge and stove. Visitors do their own cooking and must provide pillowslips, sheets and towels.

Rustic Hut: Rustic hut accommodation is provide with crockery, cutlery and cooking utensils, but contains no fridge or stove. Meals are prepared by visitors over outside open-hearth fires. No linen or towels are provided.

Trail/Mountain Huts: One large room with a divider. Four double bunk beds and mattresses (two at Meander Hut), a two-plate gas cooker, cold water and toilet only are provided. Visitors may have to share the accommodation with other trailers.

Hiking and wilderness trails

From north to south, east to west, in a great diversity of habitats, South Africa is criss-crossed by hiking trails, ranging from physically undemanding to strenuous, lasting from an hour to a week. Some are self-guided, others conducted. In some, only basic overnight huts, caves or tents are available, while on others more sophisticated accommodation is on offer.

More information is available from SATOUR in the booklet *Follow the Footprints*.

Anti-Malarial precautions

Visitors to the Lowveld and to Zululand reserves are strongly advised to take anti-malarial precautions before, during and visiting the area.

Firearms

All firearms must be declared upon arrival at any park and submitted for sealing. Firearms will be unsealed upon departure at the gate.

Fishing

Coastal fishing: No licence is needed to fish in the sea or in estuaries, although it is necessary to get licences for the taking of crayfish, mussels, oysters and other rock life, or the use of nets to take fish. Licences are obtainable on written application to the KwaZulu-Natal Fisheries Licensing Board, Private Bag 15, Congella 4013 or on personal application to the board's offices, Zululand coastal resorts, and to the Development and Services Board offices at Oslo Beach and Park Rynie.

Inland fishing

Licences: Licences are necessary for all inland fishing and obtainable from most magistrates' offices, sports dealers and KwaZulu-Natal Parks Board offices. Separate licences may be bought for trout and for other fishing.

Wildlife Society of South Africa
PO Box 44344
Linden 2104
Tel: (011) 482-1670.

National Parks Board
PO Box 787
Pretoria 0001
Tel: (012) 343-1991

National Botanical Institute
Private Bag X101
Pretoria 0001
Tel: (012) 804-3200

SATOUR
Private Bag X164
Pretoria 0001
Tel: (012) 323-1432

KwaZulu-Natal Parks Board
PO Box 662
Pietermaritzburg 3200
Tel: (0331) 51514

The Professional Hunters' Association
of South Africa
PO Box 770
Cramerview 2060
Tel: (011) 706-7724

World Heritage Sites

The World Heritage Convention was adopted by UNESCO in 1972 in recognition of the obligation of all nations to protect those outstanding natural and cultural areas which are of such unique value that they form part of the heritage of mankind.

Some World Heritage Sites in Africa are:
• Serengeti National Park
• Kilimanjaro National Park
• Ngorongoro Conservation Area
• Great Zimbabwe Ruins

South Africa is currently preparing a list of possible World Heritage Sites and will apply to ratify the convention and list sites as soon as this becomes possible.

Candidate sites for South Africa may include areas such as the Cape Peninsula Mountain Chain and Richtersveld in the Western Cape.

National Parks

Kruger National Park
Size: 2,000,000 hectares (4,942,000 acres)
Province: Mpumalanga and Northern
Geographical location: Lies some 400 kilometres (244 miles) north-east of Johannesburg.
Altitude: The park varies in altitude between 200m (656 feet) in the east and 900m (2,952 feet) at Pretoriuskop in the south-west.
Physical features: It lies in the lowveld/bushveld of what was the Transvaal. The Limpopo (north) and the Crocodile (south) act as its natural boundaries. The Lebombo Mountains in the east, separate it from Mozambique. Summer rains vary between 625 to 750mm (24.6 to 29.5 in) at Pretoriuskop and 375 to 500mm (14.7 to 19.7 in) in the Pafuri-Shingwedzi-Letaba area. Summer temperatures often exceed 40°C and there is seldom frost in the winter.

Vegetation: There are four main areas of plant life in the park:
1. Thorn Trees and Red bush-willow veld. This area lies between the western boundary and roughly the centre of the park south of the Olifants River. Acacia and Red bush-willow (Combretums) predominate.
2. Knob-thorn and Morula veld. This area lies between the western boundary and roughly the centre of the park south of the Olifants River, and the acacia species predominates.
3. Red bush-willow and mopane veld. This area lies in the western half of the park, north of Olifants River.
4. Shrub mopane veld. This covers almost the entire area of the north-western part of the park.
Fauna: There are 137 species of mammals, 49 species of fish and 112 species of reptiles. Mammals are the main feature of interest and there are approximately 7,000 elephant, 30,000 buffalo, 120,000 impala and 30,000 zebra. Antelope species are numerous and giraffe prolific. Predators include lion, leopard, cheetah, jackal and the brown and spotted hyena.
Bird life: Over 493 species recorded. The vulture, the marabou stork, ground hornbill, secretary bird, Cape glossy starling, lilac-breasted roller and the fish eagle are among the most conspicuous.
Visitor facilities: Nineteen rest camps offer comfortable accommodation in the form of thatched huts and bungalows, all equiped with beds, linen, towels and soap. Eight entrance gates give access to the park, three of which have rest camps attached to them. The larger rest camps in the park have restaurant facilities and shops where fresh provisions, tinned foods and curios may be bought.

Camping sites and picnic spots are found throughout the park and petrol, diesel and oil are available at all entrances and gates, except Kruger Gate and Phalaborwa. Eating and cooking utensils are not always available for self-catering, but hot water is.

Pilanesberg National Park

Size: 50,000 hectares (123,000 acres)
Province: North-West province
Geographical location: The reserve is 175 kilometres (105 miles) north-west of Johannesburg, in the Mankwe region and adjoins the Sun City complex.
Physical features: It is located in the crater of a huge, long-extinct volcano which was formed 1,200 million years ago when a massive eruption smashed through the flat bushveld plains.
The crater has weathered down in four concentric rings 700 metres high and 25 kilometres (15 miles) in diameter. Topography is extremely varied, ranging from open plains to thickly-wooded ravines and steep mountain slopes. Summer temperatures can exceed 40°C and winters are mild. A summer rainfall region, the area receives an average of 480 mm annually.
Fauna and flora: There are over 35 species of large mammals, including the big five: Lion, buffalo, leopard, rhino (black and white) and elephant. There are also large herds of giraffe, zebra and antelope to be seen. The park is well known for its bird-life, being home to over 300 species. Birding weekends and wildlife hikes can be arranged through the park's central reservations (011) 465 5423/4.
Visitor facilities: These range from rustic tented camps to comfortable self-catering chalets and a luxury hotel and timeshare development. A luxury tented camp is available for hire by hunting and photographic expeditions. For the ultimate escape, try Tshukudu, an exclusive camp catering for a maximum of twenty-four people. It is notable for its sweeping views, excellent cuisine and service.

Golden Gate Highlands National Park

Size: 11,600 hectares (28,652 acres)
Province: Free State
Geographical location: Among the foothills of the Maluti mountains, it is approximately 360 kilometres (223 miles) south of Johannesburg and about 300 kilometres (186 miles) north east of Bloemfontein.
Altitude: Rises from 1,892 metres (6,207 feet) at its lowest point to a height of 2,770 metres (9,085 feet).
Physical features: Within a summer rainfall region, summer days are pleasantly bracing but temperatures may cool unexpectedly. Waterfalls freeze in winter and snowfalls blanket the grass-covered mountain slopes. Snow may also fall on the plains. This scenically beautiful sanctuary is ringed with massive cliffs - bathed in lights of brilliant blazing gold, a phenomenon that gives the park its name.
Vegetation: Typical highland vegetation is found in the park and consists of sour grasses with a colourful variety of herbs and bulbs. Oldwood

(Leucosidea sericea) and several other species of trees indigenous to the region are found in the ravines. Outcrops of rocks which geologists term the Red Beds and Clarens sandstone formation of the Stormberg Series (part of the Karoo System) dominate the landscape in the form of yellow and red striated cliffs.
Fauna: Black wildebeest, eland, grey rhebuck, oribi, red hartebeest, blesbok and mountain reedbuck thrive as do other animal species such as zebra.
Bird life: The bearded vulture or lammergeier and the black eagle are among the biggest attractions of the park.
Visitor facilities: At the main camp, Brandwag, accommodation is available in the main building in single and double rooms, each with bathroom, telephone, radio and television. Adjoining chalets each contain two single or double beds in the main room and two beds on the enclosed porch. Every chalet is equipped with telephone, television and radio. Barbecue facilities are available, as well as kitchen facilities.

Mountain Zebra National Park

Size: 6,536 hectares (16,150 acres)
Province: Eastern Cape
Geographical location: It is situated twenty-seven kilometres (16 miles) west of Cradock on the northern slopes of the Bankberg range in the Great Karoo.
Altitude: Rises from 1,250 metres (4,100 feet) at its lowest point to a height of 1,981 metres (6,500 feet) above sea level.
Physical features: The rock formations of sandstone, siltstone and mudstone form the lower stage, Beaufort Series of the Karoo System and post-Karoo dolerite intrusions. These have weathered in places to form the characteristic hills which support a great variety of succulents, small animals and reptiles. A dry climate with summer rainfall is characteristic. Summer days are warm, winter days sunny, but the nights cold. Snowfalls are common in the higher regions.
Vegetation: Vegetation differs from the surrounding less-mountainous ares. Thick patches of sweet-thorn (Acacia karoo) occur together with varous karoo species particularly along the Wilgerboom River. Dense groves of wild olive (Olea africana) are found high up in the ravines.
Fauna: As the name suggests, the mountain zebra dominate the park. Large herds of eland, springbok, blesbok and black wildebeest as well as kudu, duiker, steenbok, red hartebeest and mountain reedbuck are also found. Carnivores include caracal, the African wild cat and the vicious little black-footed cat. Others are black-backed jackal, bat-eared fox, Cape fox and aardwolf.
Bird life: Bird life is abundant with 206 species recorded.

Visitor facilities: Twenty-two fully-equipped chalets, a guest house and a caravan park are available for tourists. There is also a laundrette and an á la carte restaurant. A shop is stocked with a variety of goods and petrol can be purchased.

Addo Elephant National Park
Size: 7,735 hectares (19,113 acres)
Province: Eastern Cape
Geographical location: Lies seven kilometres north of Port Elizabeth near the Zuurberg Range in the Sundays River Valley.
Physical features: The climate is warm to temperate with some rain throughout the year.
Vegetation: The Addo bush is a unique tangle of creepers and trees, few of which reach a height of more than 3.6 metres (11.8 feet). It consists mainly of spekboom (Portulacaria afra), sneezewood (Ptaeroxylon obliquum), karroo boer-bean (Schotia afra var. afra) and guarri (Euclea spp.) with a variety of other trees and creepers. Proportionately this vegetation supports three times the number of elephants per area than found in any other nature reserve in Africa.
Fauna: Along with a herd of over 130 elephant are black rhino, buffalo and antelope such as eland, kudu, red hartebeest, bushbuck, grysbok and duiker. Porcupine, antbear and bushpig are found amongst the nocturnal animals.
Bird life: Over 170 species of birds have been identified, including ostriches, hawks, finches, starlings, francolin, dabchick and moorhen. There is an observation point at a dam near the restaurant specifically for birdwatching.
Visitor facilities: Self-contained rondavels and family cottages, with fully equipped kitchens. Camping and picnic sites, an à la carte restaurant, a curio shop and petrol are all available.

Tsitsikamma Forest National Park
Size: 478 hectares (1,181 acres)
Province: Eastern Cape
Geographical location: The park is approximately 100 kilometres (62 miles) east of Knysna and eighty-five kilometres (52 miles) west of Humansdorp.
Physical features: This splendid, deep green natural forest experiences rainfalls throughout the year. May and October are the wettest months, and June and July the driest. The area receives approximately 1,200 mm (472 in) of rain per year. The climate is temperate, allowing for ideal holiday conditions. The name 'Tsitsikamma' derives from the Hottentot word, translated as meaning 'abundant water'.
Vegetation: Within the park are ancient trees of great splendour such as the 'Big Tree' or Outeniqua yellowwood (Podocarpus falcatus). Amongst three different species are the stinkwood (Ocotea bullata), the candlewood (Pterocelastrus

tricuspidatus) and the assegai (Curtisia dentata). Characteristic of the forest is the 'fynbos'. This forms some of the richest scrub vegetation in the world. Because of the perpetual dampness, shrubs, creepers, ferns, msoo and lichen flourish. The richly beautiful Cape protea is another attraction.
Fauna: Bushbuck, bushpig and blue duiker are found within the park.
Bird life: Birdlife is plentiful and rare species such as the Knysna lourie and the Narina trogon can be spotted.
Visitor facilities: Various hiking trails have been established through this maze of vegetation. No accommodation facilities are available, nor are there camping sites in the park.

Tsitsikamma Coastal National Park
Size: A 100-kilometre (62-mile) stretch of southern Cape coast extending on average about five kilometres (three miles) seaward.
Province: Eastern Cape
Geographical location: The marine land lies between the Groot Rivier ('Big River') mouth near Humansdorp to the east and a point near Plettenberg Bay area to the west.
Physical features: The park extends from five kilometres (three miles) seawards off the shoreline, to a narrow coastal plain and its marginal cliffs, so sheer and massive that they screen the rocky shore and its isolated beaches from the interior and the Tsitsikamma Mountains to the north. Here the river cuts through to the sea and everywhere there are streams and pools. The water is a soft brown to amber colour which comes from organic acids caused by vegetable matter. The average rainfall is 880 millimetres per year.
Vegetation: The plant life is rich and varied as a result of the high rainfall. Yellowwoods (Podocarpus falcatus) are fringed by heaths and proteas, one of which is South Africa's national flower - Protea cynaroides. Also abundant are ferns, wild orchids and many species of lily.
Fauna: Although quite elusive, the Cape clawless otter, rock-rabbit, bushbuck, Cape grysbok and blue duiker are found in the park. Baboons and vervet monkeys add life to the forests. Dolphins and whales may be seen beyond the breakers of the Indian Ocean. The fish life is varied and near the camp at the Storms River mouth there are the 'klip' ('stone') fish of the rock pools, starfish, sea-anemones, sponges, sea cucumbers and the incongruously named sea slugs.
Bird life: Plentiful, with 210 species recorded including thirty-five sea birds. The other 175 species are to be found in the wooded areas and 'fynbos'.
Visitor facilities: Self-contained beach cottages and luxury oceanettes are available at Storms River mouth, with all amenities including electricity. A caravan park and camping site is

also established. Fishing is limited to a specific area and bait-collecting and spear-fishing are prohibited. A shop stocks basic necessities and there is a popular à la carte restaurant.

Bontebok National Park
Size: 2,786 hectares (6,884 acres)
Province: Eastern Cape
Geographical location: It lies seven kilometres (four miles) south of Swellendam [just over 200 kilometres (124 miles) east of Cape Town] on the Bree River. The area is 50 kilometres (31 miles) from the coast.
Altitude: Altitude above sea level varies from 60 to 200m (196 to 656 feet).
Physical features: North of the park lies the Langeberg range. The climate is temperate with an average rainfall of 511 mm, (20 in), fifty-nine per cent of which falls in winter.
Vegetation: This area is one of the most prolific botanical areas in the world and more than 470 plant species, including fifty-two species of grass, have been identified in the park. Trees are mostly found on the banks of the Bree River and of these, the Bree River yellowwood (Podocarpus elongatus) is the most important. The wild olive (Olea africana) and white milkwood (Sideroxylon inerme) flourish there. Scattered groves of sweet thorn (Acacia karroo) also occur in the park. Flowering time is late winter/early spring at which time the whole area is a carpet of many colours. There are three species of protea and two leucospermum along with species of erica, gladioli and pelargonium.
Fauna: There are approximately 200 bontebok in the park which cohabit with various species of antelope, including grey rhebuck, Cape grysbok, mountain zebra. A variety of amphibians, fish and reptiles have been identified.
Bird life: To date 184 species of birds have been identified.
Visitor facilities: A camping site can accommodate about twenty-five caravans, with special picnic facilities available for day visitors. Swimming is allowed in the river, but boating is prohibited. There is a shop selling non-perishable goods.

Karoo National Park
Size: 46,000 hectares (113,620 acres)
Province: Western Cape
Geographical location: Near Beaufort West 480 kilometres (298 miles) north-east of Cape Town.
Physical features: It preserves a part of the strangely haunting interior of the South-Western Cape, given to drought and aridity and known as the Great Karoo. The park has an average rainfall of 250mm (9.8 in), which falls mainly in the summer months and compares well with other parts of the Great Karoo. Summer days are hot and while the days are sunny in winter,

temperatures tend to drop at night.
Vegetation: A wide variety of species occurs and much of the plant life is unique to this area. Karoo bush, sweet thorn, wolwedoring (Lycium austrinum), 'ganna' (Salsola spp.), 'skilpadbos' (Zygophyllum spp.) and various species of 'vygie' or Mesembryanthemum are found.
Fauna: Fifty species of mammals exist in the park including mountain zebra, gemsbok, red hartebeest, black wildebeest and springbok.
Visitor facilities: A rest camp offers accommodation for 108 people and restaurant facilities are available.

Augrabies Falls National Park
Size: 9,415,000 hectares (23,264 acres)
Province: Northern Cape
Geographical location: Lies on the Orange River, 120 kilometres (74 miles) west of Upington.
Physical features: The most remarkable feature of the falls is that the river flows over a plateau and drops suddenly over solid granite into a ravine, fifty-six metres (183 feet) deep. The ravine extends for eighteen kilometres (eleven miles) and along its length the river drops a further thirty-five metres (114 feet), giving rise to a series of spectacular rapids. When the river is in flood, a number of secondary falls are formed. A suspension bridge over the main falls gives the visitor the opportunity to view the immense crater-like pool below, and beyond it the extent of the ravine. The area is arid and rainfall is low, occuring mostly during the first four months of the year.
Vegetation: In spite of the meagre rainfall, a rich variety of plant life exists in the area. The tree aloe or 'kokerboom' (Aloe dichotoma) is indigenous to the area. Trees include the camel thorn (Acacia erioloba), white karree (Rhus lancea), wild olive (Olea africana) and karroo boer-bean (Schotia afra var.angustifolia).
Fauna: Baboons and some of the smaller antelope, in particular the dainty klipspringer, inhabit the park. Black rhino and eland were reintroduced in the area in 1985.
Bird life: Abundant in the park.
Visitor facilities: Fully-equipped air-conditioned huts are available, as well as a well-stocked shop and à la carte restaurant. The caravan park is lush and green.

Kalahari Gemsbok National Park
Size: 959,103 hectares (2,369,943 acres)
Province: Northern Cape
Geographical location: Wedged between Namibia to the west and Botswana to the east.
Physical features: This semi-desert region is a facinating place of legend, superstition and contrasts. The San people, who are still found there, are direct descendants of Stone Age man, and their culture dates back 25,000 years. In

summer, day-time temperatures often exceed 40°C. Winter days are bright and sunny, but the temperature during the evening tends to fall below freezing point. A meagre rainfall of approximately 200mm (7.8 in) usually occurs in the first four months of the year.

Vegetation: Twee Rivieren (Two Rivers), the Nossob and the Auob are dry river beds which have a marked influence on the vegetation. Grasses straddle the dunes, with a scattering of trees such as the silver cluster-leaf (Terminalia sericea), the shepherd's tree (Boscia albitrunca) and the grey camel thorn (Acacia haematoxylon) peculiar to the area.

Fauna: Huge herds of blue wildebeest, springbok and eland are to be seen, and there are smaller groups of gemsbok and red hartebeest. Steenbok and duiker occur singly or in pairs. Carnivores are well-represented and besides the distinctive Kalahari lion, there are cheetah, leopard, wild dog, spotted and brown hyena.

Bird life: 215 different bird species have been recorded, including the bateleur, martial and tawny eagles.

Visitors facilities: Rest camps offer fully-equiped cottages and camping facilities. Shops are found at each rest camp.

The Zuurberg National Park

Size: 20,777 hectares (51,339 acres)
Province: Eastern Cape
Geographical location: Twelve kilometres (seven miles) north of the Addo Elephant National Park.
Altitude: The peaks range in height from 600 to 920 metres (1,952 feet) above sea level and the ravines drop to 300 metres (984 feet) above sea level.
Physical features: Undulating landscape with deep valleys and rounded peaks.
Vegetation: There are three veld types found, with the most predominant being fynbos or maccia.
Fauna: Large numbers of grey rhebok, mountain reedbuck, bushbuck and grey duiker and the endangered blue duiker. A selection of carnivores including leopard, caracal, jackal, wild cat and genet is also found.
Bird life: A wide variety of birds includes the black eagles, the Knysna lourie, crowned eagle and black saw-wing swallow.

The Vaalbos National Park

Size: 22,697 hectares (56,084 acres)
Province: Northern Cape
Geographical location: Lies south of the Vaal River, between Kimberley and Barkly West.
Physical features: It is a transitional zone between Karoo, Kalahari and grassveld elements.
Vegetation: The area consists mostly of patches of 'vaalbos' (camphor bush), Trachonanthus camphoratus, surrounded by grassveld.
Fauna: There are established populations of

springbok and red hartebeest, while buffalo and black rhino have been re-established.

Wilderness National Park

Size: 10,000 hectares (24,710 acres)
Province: Western Cape
Geographical location: Lies on the garden route between George and Knysna.. The southern boundary is the Indian Ocean and the northern boundary the Outeniqua Mountains. It encompasses the area between the Touw River in the west and the Goukamma Nature Reserve in the east.
Physical features: The climate is moderate and rainfall is highest in September/October and lowest in February. There are three kinds of lakes — drowned river valleys, drowned low-lying areas and defaltion basins.
Vegetation: The variety of plant communities in the lakes reflects the complexity of the system.
Fauna: No large mammals. Golden moles, Cape clawless otters, variety of bats, rodents and some antelope, make up the mammalian family in this area.
Bird life: Includes marine, estuarine and evergreen forest species such as the Knysna lourie.
Visitor facilities: Two-bedroom chalets are fully-equipped and the caravan park has all the necessary facilities. Shops have been established.

West Coast National Park

Size: 18,000 hectares (44,478 acres)
Province: Western Cape
Geographical location: 100 kilometres (62 miles) north of Cape Town
Physical features: It is made up of Langebaan lagoon, the islands Malgas, Jutten, Marcus, Schaapen and Vondeling. The Postberg Nature Reserve is a contractual national park.
Vegetation: Divided into three main groups: (a) typical Benguela or West Coast marine algae; (b) typical salt-marsh communities; (c) various ground vegetation communities. In spring the veld turns bright green and is dotted with masses of flowers.
Fauna: Renowned for huge numbers of fish.
Bird life: The thousands of birds inhabiting this area include cormorants, gulls, common sandpipers, sanderlings, knots, turnstones.
Visitor facilities: Langebaan lodge offers adequate accommodation and there is an à la carte restaurant available. No visitors are allowed on the islands. However, private guided boat trips around the islands can be arranged. Contact the park for details.

Tankwa Karoo National Park

Size: 27,064 hectares (66,875 acres)
Province: Northern Cape
Geographical location: Lies about ninety kilometres (56 miles) south of Calvinia, 145

kilometres (90 miles) north of Ceres and north of the Tankwa River.

Altitude: 350 to 450m (1,148 feet to 1,476 feet) above sea level

Physical features: Relatively flat in a semi-desert area, it has a few springs and some higher-lying areas such as Leeuberg and Pramberg. The area has a desert climate and average annual rainfall is approximately 50mm 1.97 in).

Vegetation: The vegetation is defined as succulent karoo. It is situated in the inland winter-rainfall area of the Western Cape.

Fauna: There are few animals in the area.

Game and Nature Reserves

Giant's Castle Game Reserve

Size: 34,638 hectares (85,590 acres)

Province: KwaZulu-Natal

Geographical location: It lies sixty-nine kilometres (42 miles) from Estcourt and sixty-four kilometres (39 miles) from Mooirivier.

Physical features: Is situated on the grassy plateaux among the deep valleys below the sheer face of the high Drakensberg.

Fauna: A dozen different species of antelope are known to occur in the reserve. Among them, eland, grey rhebuck, reedbuck, mountain reedbuck, oribi, red hartebeest, and blesbok are often seen in the vicinity of Ijusuti hutted camp. Trout fishing is permitted.

Visitor facilities: There are three camps within the reserve, the main camp, the hillside camp and Injasuti hutted camp. All are self-catering.

Itala Game Reserve

Size: 29,653 hectares (73,272 acres)

Province: KwaZulu-Natal

Geographical location: Located immediately to the north and west of the village of Louwsburg and northwards to the Pongola River.

Vegetation: Almost one-quarter of the reserve consists of open bushveld while the remaining area comprises steep valleys containing streambank vegetation, with grassland on the tops of hills.

Fauna: A variety of mammals are found in the reserve, including black and white rhinoceros, tsessebe, impala, waterbuck, wart hog, reedbuck, giraffe, eland, kudu, baboon and cheetah.

Visitor facilities: Bush camps (one eight-bedded and one four-bedded) are available for hire as well as a campground.

Robberg Nature Reserve

Size: Six kilometres (four miles) in length

Province: Western Cape

Geographical location: In Plettenberg bay which lies 520 kilometres (323 miles) east of Cape Town and 240 kilometres (149 miles) west of Port Elizabeth.

Vegetation: Very rocky peninsula.

Fauna: Small rodents.

Visitor facilities: At 'The Point' the angling club has huts available for hire to fishermen.

Umfolozi Game Reserve

Size: 47,753 hectares (117,997 acres)

Province: KwaZulu-Natal

Geographical location: 270 kilometres (167 miles) from Durban.

Physical features: The climate is temperate in winter and hot in summer, with the average rainfall approximately 750mm (29 in) a year.

Fauna: The reserve boasts a wide variety of large mammals, which include white and black rhinoceros, kudu, zebra, blue wildebeest, buffalo, giraffe, lion, leopard and cheetah. Crocodiles occur in the water and there is an interesting variety of birds within the reserve.

Visitor facilities: Two camps are available for accomodation, Mpila and Masinda camps. Both are self-catering.

Hluhluwe Game Reserve

Size: 23,067 hectares (56,998 acres)

Province: KwaZulu-Natal

Geographical location: 280 kilometres (173 miles) north of Durban.

Fauna: A variety of large mammals inhabit the park — black and white rhinoceros, elephant, nyala, buffalo, zebra and blue wildebeest. Crocodiles and hippos inhabit the rivers.

Bird life: Birds are numerous and varied. Common species spotted are white-backed vultures, bateleur, crested guinea-fowl, green-spotted dove and trumpeter hornbill.

Visitor facilities: A hutted camp offers accomodation for seventy-one people, visitors must provide their own food and drink.

National Botanical Gardens

South Africa's eight National Botanical Gardens cover a wide range of the floral wealth of South Africa — the richest floral region in the world.

Kirstenbosch National Botanical Garden

Size: 528 hectares (1,305 acres)

Province: Western Cape

District: Rhodes Drive, Constantia, Cape Town

Geographic location: Cape Town — below the eastern buttresses of Table Mountain. Approximately twelve kilometres (seven miles) from the centre of Cape Town.

Vegetation: The garden enjoys a spectacular natural setting and supports a rich flora of fynbos and coastal forest vegetation.

The chief features of the gardens are lawns and ponds, a mesembryanthemum garden, compositae and pelargonium gardens, the sandstone koppie, the fern dell, the protea garden, the cycad amphitheatrea and the Mathews rock garden. The best months to see the gardens are from July to October. There is a spring flower show in September and an indigenous plant sale is held during March.

Visitor facilities: A braille trail and a fragrance garden cater for blind visitors. Guided tours are every Tuesday and Saturday at 11:00. No overnight facilities are available within the park.

Harold Porter National Botanical Garden

Size: 188 hectares (466 acres)
Province: Western Cape
District: Clarence Drive, Betty's Bay
Geographic location: This garden, situated amid the magnificent unspoiled and rugged beauty of the mountainous south-western Cape coastal belt, is in the heart of South Africa's fynbos region.
Vegetation: Disas flourish at the waterfall in Disa Gorge and Nerine sarniensis, or the Guernsey lily, is found there in its natural habitat. Best months for disas are December–January, and for proteas from June–October.
Visitor facilities: No accommodation is available.

Karoo National Botanical Garden

Size: 154 hectares (381 acres)
Province: Western Cape
District: Roux Way, Van Riebeeck Park, off National Road, Worcester, Cape.
Geographic location: This garden is set amongst the rocky hillsides above the town.
Vegetation: It concentrates on plants from the drier regions of southern Africa, especially succulents and Karoo vegetation and has a comprehensive collection of international repute. The predominant plants in this area are members of the family Mesembryanthemacae; among these the vygies are particularly prominent and colourful, producing a spectacular show of colour. Best months are April-October for aloes and succulents in flower. Dependent on a favourable season, the last two weeks of September and the first two weeks of October are the best time for a breathtaking display of vygies. The colour is more intense from midday till mid-afternoon when the flowers open fully in response to the sun.
Visitor facilities: There is a braille trail and a kiosk sells beverages drinks, seeds and pamphlets.

Natal National Botanical Garden

Size: 46 hectares (114 acres)
Province: KwaZulu-Natal
District: Mayor's Walk, Pietermaritzburg
Vegetation: The garden has two distinct parts; an exotic section of eighteen hectares (44 acres) and an area of twenty-eight hectares (69 acres) devoted to indigenous flora, which consists mainly of an arboretum of KwaZulu-Natal trees. In spring there is an outstanding display of azaleas and camellias in the international section, which also features a large collection of mature trees. The plane avenue, planted in 1907 and now a national monument, is particularly striking in autumn and spring. The Dorp Spruit, with a newly created dam, runs through the garden.
Visitor facilities: A tea room is open daily (except Tuesday and certain public holidays). No accommodation is available.

Pretoria National Botanical Garden

Size: Seventy-six hectares (188 acres)
Province: Gauteng
District: Cussonia Avenue, Brummeria, Pretoria
Geographic location: Lies in the parallel rocky ridge landscape typical of Pretoria and is an unexpected oasis so close to the bustle of a major city.
Vegetation: It is planted with indigenous flora from the southern African floral region, and adjacent regions such as Madagascar, which are grouped according to major vegetation types (e.g., forest, fynbos, savannah); the habitat for each grouping having been carefully selected to approximate natural climatic conditions. The best months are from September-October for spring flowers, and June-July for aloes.
Visitor facilities: Guided walks are given and a kiosk sells tea, coffee and beverages.

Free State National Botanical Garden

Size: forty-five hectares (111 acres)
Province: Free State
District: Rayton Road, off Dan Pienaar Drive, Bloemfontein.
Vegetation: The principal aim of this highveld garden is the collection, cultivation and display of drought-resistant and frost-hardy plants indigenous to southern Africa. The main displays, in the cultivated central portion of the garden, are primarily of shrubs, succulents, annuals, perennials and bulbs endemic to the Free State and north-western Cape. A major collection of trees of the Rhus genus is being assembled, and there is an attractive dam with an abundance of bird life.
Visitor facilities: A kiosk is open on Sunday and picnic and braai areas are available. No accommodation is available.

Lowveld National Botanical Garden

Size: 150 hectares (371 acres)
Province: Mpumalanga
District: Off White River Road, opposite Sabie intersection, Nelspruit.
Vegetation: The garden boasts the best collection of indigenous trees in South Africa. It also has a tropical rain forest, and an outstanding collection of cycads. About eighteen hectares (43 acres) of the garden is developed, the rest having been left

in its natural state. In the developed garden, most of the plants are grouped either according to their taxonomic relationship or in ecological units. There is an outstanding variety of bird life in the garden.

Visitor facilities: Refreshments are available Wednesday to Sunday and guided walks can be arranged. No accommodation is available.

Witwatersrand National Botanical Garden

Size: 225 hectares (556 acres)
Province: Gauteng
District: Malcolm Road, Poortview, Roodepoort.
Geographic location: Nestled against a rocky outcrop, with a plunging seventy-metre (230-feet) waterfall as a backdrop, this relatively new highveld garden is a well-known beauty spot.
Vegetation: Among the many interesting features are the fern trail at the waterfall, a succulent garden displaying mainly Transvaal aloes and succulents, and a waterside bird hide. The best months are November-April, and July-August for the succulent collection.
Visitor facilities: There is a restaurant and, on Sunday afternoons, guided tours are arranged.

Animal Checklist

Mammals

Insectivores (Insectivora)
South African hedgehog
Long-tailed Forest Shrew
Dark-footed Forest Shrew
Forest Shrew
Greater Dwarf Shrew
Least Dwarf Shrew
Lesser Dwarf Shrew
Greater Musk Shrew
Swamp Musk Shrew
Tiny Musk Shrew
Maquassie Musk Shrew
Reddish-grey Musk Shrew
Lesser Red Musk Shrew
Peter's Musk Shrew
Giant Golden Mole
Rough-haired Golden Mole
Visagie's Golden Mole
De Winton's Golden Mole
Grant's Golden Mole
Van Zyl's Golden Mole
Duthies Golden Mole
Cape Golden Mole
Sclater's Golden Mole
Yellow Golden Mole
Gunning's Golden Mole
Zulu Golden Mole
Hottentot Golden Mole
Juliana's Golden Mole

Elephant Shrew (Macroscelidea)
Four-toed Elephant Shrew
Round-eared Elephant Shrew
Short-snouted Elephant Shrew
Smith's Rock Elephant Shrew
Bushveld Elephant Shrew
Rock Elephant Shrew
Cape Rock Elephant Shrew

Bats (Chiroptera)
Fruit-eating Bats (Megachiroptera)
Egyptian Fruit Bat
Peter's Epauletted Fruit Bat
Wahlberg's Epauletted Fruit Bat
Straw-coloured Fruit Bat

Insect-eating bats (Microchiroptera)
Anchieta's Bat
Banana Bat
Butterfly Bat
Angola Free-tailed Bat

Ansorge's Free-tailed Bat
Large-eared Free-tailed Bat
Natal Free-tailed Bat
Egyptian Free-tailed Bat
Flat-headed Free-tailed Bat
Little Free-tailed Bat
Madagascar Large Free-tailed Bat
Midas Free-tailed Bat
Rufous Hairy Bat
Temminck's Hairy Bat
Angola Hairy Bat
Lesueur's Hairy Bat
Welwitch's Hairy Bat
Bushveld Horseshoe Bat
Darling's Horseshoe Bat
Geoffrey's Horseshoe Bat
Cape Horseshoe Bat
Dent's Horseshoe Bat
Hildebrandt's Horseshoe Bat
Lander's Horseshoe Bat
Peak-saddle Horseshoe Bat
Ruppell's Horseshoe Bat
Swinny's Horseshoe Bat
Yellow House Bat
Lesser Yellow House Bat
Kuhl's Bat
Commerson's Leaf-nosed Bat
Sundevall's Leaf-nosed Bat
Lesser Long-fingered Bat
Schreiber's Long-fingered Bat
Ruppell's Bat
Rusty Bat
Schlieffen's Bat
Somali Serotine Bat
Cape Serotine Bat
Long-tailed Serotine Bat
Melck's Serotine Bat
Common Slit-faced Bat
Wood's Slit-faced Bat
Tomb Bat
Namib Longeared Bat
Short-eared Trident Bat
Damara Woolly Bat
Lesser Woolly Bat

Bushbabies, Baboons and Monkeys (Primates)
South African Lesser Bushbaby
Thick-tailed Bushbaby
Chacma Baboon
Samango Monkey
Vervet Monkey

Pangolins (Pholidota)
Pangolin

Hares and rabbits (Lagomorpha)
Cape Hare
Scrub Hare
Jameson's Red Rock Rabbit
Smith's Red Rock Rabbit
Natal Red Rock Rabbit
Riverine Rabbit

Rodents (Rodentia)
Greater Cane Rat
Dassie Rat
Rock Dormouse
Spectacled Dormouse
Woodland Dormouse
Bushveld Gerbil
Cape Gerbil
Short-tailed Gerbil
Hairy-footed Gerbil
Dune Hairy-footed Gerbil
Brush-tailed Hairy-footed Gerbil
Highveld Gerbil
Common Mole Rat
Cape Dune Mole Rat
Namaqua Dune Mole Rat
Damara Mole Rat
Cape Mole Rat
Chestnut Climbing Mouse
Brant's Climbing Mouse
Grey Climbing Mouse
Nyika Climbing Mouse
Fat Mouse
Tiny Fat Mouse
Krebs's Fat Mouse
House Mouse
Multimammate Mouse
Pygmy Mouse
Desert Pygmy Mouse
Pouched Mouse
Namaqua Rock Mouse
Grant's Rock Mouse
Pygmy Rock Mouse
Barbour's Rock Mouse
Spiny Mouse
Cape Spiny Mouse
Verreaux's Mouse
Striped Mouse
Single-Striped Mouse
Woodland Mouse
Mozambique Woodland Mouse
Porcupine
Giant Rat
House Rat
Brown Rat
Brant's Whistling Rat
Littledale's Whistling Rat

Woosnam's Desert Rat
Red Veld Rat
Vlei Rat
Laminate Vlei Rat
Angoni Vlei Rat
Saunders' Vlei Rat
Karoo Bush Rat
Sloggett's Rat
Tree Rat
Black-tailed Tree Rat
Water Rat
Springhaas
Red Squirrel
Sun Squirrel
Tree Squirrel
Grey Squirrel
Cape Ground Squirrel
Mountain Ground Squirrel

Carnivores (Carnivora)
Aardwolf
Honey Badger
Caracal
African Wild Cat
Small Spotted Cat
Cheetah
African Civet
Wild Dog
Bat-eared Fox
Cape Fox
Large-spotted Genet
Small-spotted Genet
Brown Hyena
Spotted Hyena
Black-backed Jackal
Side-striped Jackal
Leopard
Lion
Banded Mongoose
Dwarf Mongoose
Large Grey Mongoose
Meller's Mongoose
Selous' Mongoose
Slender Mongoose
Small Grey Mongoose
Water Mongoose
White-tailed Mongoose
Yellow Mongoose
Suricate
Cape Clawless Otter
Spotted-necked Otter
Striped Polecat
Serval
African Weasel

Antbears (Tubulidentata)
Aardvark

Elephants (Proboscidea)
African Elephant

Dassies (Hyrax) (Hyracoidea)
Rock Dassie
Tree Dassie
Yellow-spotted Rock Dassie

Odd-toed Ungulates (Perissodactyla)
Black Rhinoceros
White Rhinoceros
Burchell's Zebra
Cape Mountain Zebra

Even-toed Ungulates (Artiodactyla)
African Buffalo
Bushbuck
Bontebok
Blesbok
Bushpig
Blue Duiker
Common Duiker
Red Duiker
Eland
Gemsbok
Giraffe
Grysbok
Sharpe's Grysbok
Red Hartebeest
Hippopotamus
Wart hog
Impala
Klipspringer
Kudu
Nyala
Oribi
Reedbuck
Mountain Reedbuck
Grey Rhebok
Waterbuck
Roan
Sable
Steenbok
Springbok
Suni
Tsessebe
Blue Wildebeest
Black Wildebeest

Birds

Ostrich (Struthionidae)
Ostrich

Penguins (Spheniscidae)
Jackass Penguin
Rockhopper Penguin

Grebes (Podicipedidae)
Dabchick
Black-necked Grebe
Great Crested Grebe

Albatrosses (Diomedeidae)
Wandering Albatross
Shy Albatross
Black-browed Albatross
Grey-headed Albatross
Yellow-nosed Albatross

Petrels, Shearwaters, etc (Procellariidae)
Southern Giant Petrel
Northern Giant Petrel
Antarctic Fulmar
Pintado Petrel
Greatwinged Petrel
Softplumaged Petrel
Atlantic Petrel
Blue Petrel
Broad-billed Prion
Slender-billed Prion
Fairy Prion
White-chinned Petrel
Grey Petrel
Cory's Shearwater
Little Shearwater
Great Shearwater
Flesh-footed Shearwater
Sooty Shearwater
Manx Shearwater

Storm Petrels (Oceanitidae)
European Storm Petrel
Leach's Storm Petrel
Wilson's Storm Petrel
Black-bellied Storm Petrel

Tropicbirds (Phaethontidae)
Red-tailed Tropicbird

Pelicans (Pelecanidae)
Pink-backed Pelican
White Pelican

Gannets (Sulidae)
Cape Gannet

Cormorants (Phalacrocoracidae)
White-breasted Cormorant
Cape Cormorant
Bank Cormorant
Reed Cormorant
Crowned Cormorant

Darters (Anhingidae)
Darter

Bitterns, Egrets and Herons (Ardeidae)
Bittern
Dwarf Bittern
Little Bittern

Black Egret
Great White Egret
Cattle Egret
Little Egret
Yellow-billed Egret
Black-headed Heron
Goliath Heron
Green-backed Heron
Grey Heron
Purple Heron
Rufous-bellied Heron
Black-Crowned Night Heron
White-Backed Night Heron
Rail Heron
Squacco Heron

Hammerkop (Scopidae)
Hammerkop

Storks (Ciconiidae)
Openbilled Stork
Abdim's Stork
Black Stork
Marabou Stork
Saddle-billed Stork
White Stork
Woolly-necked Stork
Yellow-billed Stork

Ibises and Spoonbills
(Plataleidae)
Bald Ibis
Glossy Ibis
Hadada Ibis
Sacred Ibis
African Spoonbill

Flamingoes (Phoenicopteridae)
Greater Flamingo
Lesser Flamingo

Ducks, Geese and Swans
(Anatidae)
African Black Duck
Knob-billed Duck
Moccoa Duck
White-faced Duck
Fulvous Duck
Yellow-billed Duck
White-backed Duck
Garganey
Pygmy Goose
Egyptian Goose
Spurwinged Goose
Southern Pochard
South African Shelduck
Cape Shoveller
Cape Teal
Hottentot Teal
Red-Billed Teal
Mute Swan

Secretarybird (Sagittariidae)
Secretarybird

Raptors (Accipitridae)
Bearded Vulture (Lammergeier)
Cape Vulture
Egyptian Vulture
Hooded Vulture
Lappet-faced Vulture
White-backed Vulture
White-headed Vulture
Palmnut Vulture
Bateleur
Forest Buzzard
Honey Buzzard
Jackal Buzzard
Lizard Buzzard
Steppe Buzzard
Ayres' Eagle
Black Eagle
Booted Eagle
Crowned Eagle
Steppe Eagle
Lesser Spotted Eagle
Long-crested Eagle
Martial Eagle
Tawny Eagle
Wahlberg's Eagle
African Fish Eagle
African Hawk Eagle
Black-breasted Snake Eagle
Brown Snake Eagle
Southern Banded Snake Eagle
African Goshawk
Little Banded Goshawk
Dark Chanting Goshawk
Gabar Goshawk
Pale Chanting Goshawk
Gymnogene
Bat Hawk
Cuckoo Hawk
Black Sparrowhawk
Little Sparrowhawk
Ovambo Sparrowhawk
Red-breasted Sparrowhawk
African Marsh Harrier
Black Harrier
Montagu's Harrier
Pallid Harrier
Black Kite
Black-shouldered Kite
Yellow-billed Kite

Osprey (Pandionidae)
Osprey

Falcons and Kestrels
(Falconidae)
Lanner Falcon
Peregrine Falcon
Pygmy Falcon

Red-necked Falcon
Sooty Falcon
African Hobby Falcon
Hobby Falcon
Dickinson's Kestrel
Greater Kestrel
Lesser Kestrel
Rock Kestrel
Eastern Red-footed Kestrel
Western Red-footed Kestrel

Francolins and Quail
(Phasianidae)
Cape Francolin
Coqui Francolin
Crested Francolin
Greywing Francolin
Natal Francolin
Orange River Francolin
Shelley's Francolin
Red-necked Francolin
Redwing Francolin
Red-billed Francolin
Swainson's Francolin
Blue Quail
Common Quail
Harlequin Quail

Guineafowl (Numididae)
Crested Guineafowl
Helmeted Guineafowl

Buttonquails (Turnicidae)
Black-rumped Buttonquail
Kurrichane Buttonquail

Cranes (Gruidae)
Blue Crane
Crowned Crane
Wattled Crane

Crakes, Gallinules and Rails
(Rallidae)
Red-knobbed Coot
Corn Crake
African Crake
Baillon's Crake
Black Crake
Spotted Crake
Striped Crake
Buff-spotted Flufftail
Red-chested Flufftail
Streaky-breasted Flufftail
Striped Flufftail
White-winged Flufftail
Lesser Gallinule
Purple Gallinule
Moorhen
Lesser Moorhen
African Rail

Finfoots (Heliornithidae)
African Finfoot

**Bustards and Korhaans
(Otididae)**
Kori Bustard
Ludwig's Bustard
Stanley's Bustard
Black Korhaan
Black-bellied Korhaan
Blue Korhaan
Karoo Korhaan
Red-crested Korhaan
White-bellied Korhaan

Jacanas (Jacanidae)
African Jacana
Lesser Jacana

Painted Snipe (Rostratulidae)
Painted Snipe

**Oystercatchers
(Haematopodidae)**
African Black Oystercatcher
European Oystercatcher

Plovers (Charadriidae)
Blacksmith Plover
Black-winged Plover
Lesser Black-winged Plover
Caspian Plover
Crowned Plover
Chestnut-banded Sandplover
Grey Plover
Mongolian Plover
Ringed Plover
Sand Plover
Kittlitz's Plover
Three-banded Plover
Wattled Plover
White-fronted Plover
White-crowned Plover

**Sandpipers, Snipes
(Scolopacidae)**
Turnstone
Greenshank
Redshank
Sanderling
Broad-billed Sandpiper
Common Sandpiper
Curlew Sandpiper
Green Sandpiper
Marsh Sandpiper
Terek Sandpiper
Wood Sandpiper
Ethiopian Snipe
Great Snipe
Little Stint
Whimbrel

Bar-tailed Godwit
Black-tailed Godwit
Curlew
Knot
Ruff
Grey Phalarope
Red-necked Phalarope

**Avocets and Stilts
(Recurvirostridae)**
Avocet
Black-winged Stilt

Dikkops (Burhinidae)
Spotted Dikkop
Water Dikkop

**Coursers and Pratincoles
(Glareolidae)**
Bronze-winged Courser
Burchell's Courser
Double-banded Courser
Temminck's Courser
Three-banded Courser
Black-winged Pratincole
Common Pratincole
Red-winged Pratincole

**Gulls, Terns and Skuas
(Laridae)**
Kelp Gull
Lesser Black-backed Gull
Franklin's Gull
Hartlaub's Gull
Grey-headed Gull
Sabine's Gull
White-winged Black Tern
Caspian Tern
Lesser Crested Tern
Sandwich Tern
Swift Tern
Antarctic Tern
Arctic Tern
Black Tern
Common Tern
Damara Tern
Little Tern
Roseate Tern
Sooty Tern
Whiskered Tern
White-winged Tern

Skimmers (Rynchopidae)
African Skimmer

Sandgrouse (Pteroclidae)
Burchell's Sandgrouse
Double-banded Sandgrouse
Namaqua Sandgrouse
Yellow-throated Sandgrouse

**Doves and Pigeons
(Columbidae)**
Cinnamon Dove
Mourning Dove
Laughing Dove
Namaqua Dove
Red-eyed Dove
Tambourine Dove
Cape Turtle Dove
Blue-spotted Dove
Green-spotted Wood Dove
Green Pigeon
Delegorgue's Pigeon
Feral Pigeon
Rameron Pigeon
Rock Pigeon

**Lovebirds and Parrots
(Psittacidae)**
Rosy-faced Lovebird
Brown-headed Parrot
Cape Parrot
Meyer's Parrot
Rose-ringed Parakeet

**Louries or Touracos
(Musophagidae)**
Knysna Lourie
Grey Lourie
Purple-crested Lourie

Cuckoos, Coucals (Cuculidae)
African Cuckoo
Black Cuckoo
Striped Cuckoo
Didric Cuckoo
Emerald Cuckoo
European Cuckoo
Jacobin Cuckoo
Klaas's Cuckoo
Red-chested Cuckoo
Great Spotted Cuckoo
Thick-billed Cuckoo
Black Coucal
Burchell's Coucal
Coppery-tailed Coucal
Green Coucal

Owls (Tytonidae)
Barn Owl
Grass Owl (Strigidae)
Barred Owl
Cape Eagle Owl
Spotted Eagle Owl
Giant Eagle Owl
Pel's Fishing Owl
Marsh Owl
Pearl-spotted Owl
Scops Owl
White-faced Owl
Wood Owl

Nightjars (Caprimulgidae)
European Nightjar
Fiery-necked Nightjar
Mozambique Nightjar
Natal Nightjar
Pennant-winged Nightjar
Freckled Nightjar
Rufous-cheeked Nightjar

Swifts (Apodidae)
Mottled Spinetail
Bohm's Spinetail
Alpine Swift
Black Swift
Bradfield's Swift
European Swift
Horus Swift
Little Swift
Palm Swift
White-rumped Swift

Mousebirds (Coliidae)
White-backed Mousebird
Speckled Mousebird
Red-faced Mousebird

Trogons (Trogonidae)
Narina Trogon

Kingfishers (Alcedinidae)
Brown-hooded Kingfisher
Grey-hooded Kingfisher
Giant Kingfisher
Half-collared Kingfisher
Malachite Kingfisher
Mangrove Kingfisher
Pied Kingfisher
Pygmy Kingfisher
Woodland Kingfisher
Striped Kingfisher

Bee-eaters (Meropidae)
Blue-cheeked Bee-eater
Carmine Bee-eater
European Bee-eater
Little Bee-eater
Swallow-tailed Bee-eater
White-fronted Bee-eater

Rollers (Coraciidae)
Broad-billed Roller
European Roller
Lilac-breasted Roller
Purple Roller
Racket-tailed Roller

Hoopoe (Upupidae)
Hoopoe

Wood-Hoopoes (Phoeniculidae)
Scimitarbilled Woodhoopoe
Red-billed Woodhoopoe

Hornbills (Bucerotidae)
Crowned Hornbill
Grey Hornbill
Ground Hornbill
Red-billed Hornbill
Silvery-cheeked Hornbill
Trumpeter Hornbill
Yellow-billed Hornbill

Barbets (Capitonidae)
Black-collared Barbet
Crested Barbet
Pied Barbet
Golden-rumped Tinker Barbet
Red-fronted Tinker Barbet
Yellow-fronted Tinker Barbet
White-eared Barbet
Woodward's Barbet

Honeyguides (Indicatoridae)
Greater Honeyguide
Lesser Honeyguide
Scaly-throated Honeyguide
Sharp-billed Honeyguide

Woodpeckers (Picidae)
Bearded Woodpecker
Bennett's Woodpecker
Cardinal Woodpecker
Golden-tailed Woodpecker
Ground Woodpecker
Knysna Woodpecker
Olive Woodpecker

Wrynecks (Jyngidae)
Red-throated Wryneck

Broadbills (Eurylaimidae)
African Broadbill

Pittas (Pittidae)
Angola Pitta

Larks (Alaudidae)
Dusky Lark
Fawn-coloured Lark
Chestnut-backed Finchlark
Grey-backed Finchlark
Black-eared Finchlark
Flappet Lark
Red-capped Lark
Rufous-naped Lark
Sabota Lark
Botha's Lark
Pink-billed Lark
Spike-heeled Lark
Melodious Lark
Monotonous Lark
Clapper Lark
Rudd's Lark
Long-billed Lark

Short-clawed Lark
Karoo Lark
Dune Lark
Red Lark
Sclater's Lark
Stark's Lark
Thick-billed Lark

Martins and Swallows (Hirundinidae)
House Martin
Rock Martin
Banded Martin
Brown-throated Martin
Sand Martin
Blue Swallow
European Swallow
Grey-rumped Swallow
Mosque Swallow
Pearl-breasted Swallow
Greater Striped Swallow
Lesser Striped Swallow
White-throated Swallow
Wire-tailed Swallow
Red-breasted Swallow
South African Cliff Swallow
Black Sawwing Swallow

Cuckooshrikes (Campephagidae)
Black Cuckooshrike
White-breasted Cuckooshrike
Grey Cuckooshrike

Drongos (Dicruridae)
Fork-tailed Drongo
Square-tailed Drongo

Orioles (Oriolidae)
Black-headed Oriole
African Golden Oriole
European Golden Oriole

Crows (Corvidae)
Black Crow
House Cow
Pied Crow
White-necked Raven

Tits (Paridae)
Southern Black Tit
Ashy Tit
Southern Grey Tit

Penduline Tits (Remizidae)
Cape Penduline Tit
Grey Penduline Tit

Babblers (Timaliidae)
Arrow-marked Babbler
Pied Babbler

Bush Blackcap

Bulbuls (Pycnonotidae)
Black-eyed Bulbul
Cape Bulbul
Red-eyed Bulbul
Sombre Bulbul
Terrestrial Bulbul
Yellow-bellied Bulbul
Yellow-streaked Bulbul
Yellow-spotted Nicator

Chats, Robins and Thrushes (Turdidae)
Familiar Chat
Mocking Chat
Stone Chat
Mountain Chat
Buff-streaked Chat
Tractrac Chat
Sickle-winged Chat
Karoo Chat
Arnot's Chat
Anteating Chat
Cape Robin
Heuglin's Robin
Bearded Robin
White-browed Robin
Starred Robin
Chorister Robin
Brown Robin
Natal Robin
White-throated Robin
Karoo Robin
Kalahari Robin
Cape Rockjumper
Orange-breasted Rockjumper
Thrush Nightingale
Capped Wheatear
Collared Palm Thrush
Groundscraper Thrush
Kurrichane Thrush
Cape Rock Thrush
Olive Thrush
Orange Thrush

Warblers, Cisticolas (Sylviidae)
Bar-throated Apalis
Yellow-breasted Apalis
Rudd's Apalis
Black-backed Cisticola
Grey-backed Cisticola
Ayre's Cisticola
Cloud Cisticola
Croaking Cisticola
Desert Cisticola
Fan-tailed Cisticola
Pale-crowned Cisticola
Levaillant's Cisticola
Lazy Cisticola
Rattling Cisticola

Red-faced Cisticola
Tinkling Cisticola
Wailing Cisticola
Titbabbler
Layard's Titbabbler
Long-billed Crombec
Red-faced Crombec
Burnt-necked Eremomela
Green-capped Eremomela
Karoo Eremomela
Yellow-bellied Eremomela
Neddicky
Grassbird
Black-chested Prinia
Tawny-flanked Prinia
Spotted Prinia
Namaqua Prinia
Broad-tailed Warbler
Barred Warbler
Bleating Warbler
Victorin's Warbler
Barratt's Warbler
Knysna Warbler
Stierling's Barred Warbler
Cinnamon-breasted Warbler
Rufous-eared Warbler
Garden Warbler
Icterine Warbler
African Marsh Warbler
European Marsh Warbler
Olive-tree Warbler
Cape Reed Warbler
Great Reed Warbler
River Warbler
Willow Warbler
Yellow Warbler
Yellow-throated Warbler
European Sedge Warbler
African Sedge Warbler
Whitethroat

Flycatchers (Muscicapidae)
Cape Batis
Pririt Batis
Chinspot Batis
Woodward's Batis
Black Flycatcher
Blue-mantled Flycatcher
Dusky Flycatcher
Marico Flycatcher
Pallid Flycatcher
Paradise Flycatcher
Spotted Flycatcher
Wattle-eyed Flycatcher
Blue-grey Flycatcher
Collared Flycatcher
Fan-tailed Flycatcher
Chat Flycatcher
Fiscal Flycatcher
Fairy Flycatcher

Longclaws, Pipits and Wagtails (Motacillidae)
Orange-throated Longclaw
Pink-throated Longclaw
Yellow-throated Longclaw
Buffy Pipit
Bushveld Pipit
Mountain Pipit
Rock Pipit
Short-tailed Pipit
Yellow-breasted Pipit
Richard's Pipit
Long-billed Pipit
Plain-backed Pipit
Striped Pipit
Tree Pipit
Cape Wagtail
Long-tailed Wagtail
African Pied Wagtail
Yellow Wagtail

Shrikes (Laniidae)
Fiscal Shrike
Lesser Grey Shrike
Long-tailed Shrike
Red-backed Shrike

Bush Shrikes (Malaconotidae)
Bokmakierie
Crimson-breasted Boubou
Southern Boubou
Tropical Boubou
Brubru
Puffback
Black-fronted Bush Shrike
Gorgeous Bush Shrike
Grey-headed Bush Shrike
Olive Bush Shrike
Orange-breasted Bush Shrike
Black-crowned Tchagra
Brown-headed Tchagra
Southern Tchagra
Three-streaked Tchragra

Helmetshrikes (Prionopidae)
Chestnut-fronted Helmetshrike
Red-billed Helmetshrike
White Helmetshrike
White-crowned Shrike

Starlings (Sturnidae)
Black-bellied Starling
Greater Blue-eared Starling
Glossy Starling
Long-tailed Starling
Red-winged Starling
European Starling
Indian Myna
Plum-coloured Starling
Burchell's Starling
Pale-winged Starling
Wattled Starling

Oxpeckers (Buphagidae)
Red-billed Oxpecker
Yellow-billed Oxpecker

Sugarbirds (Promeropidae)
Cape Sugarbird
Gurney's Sugarbird

Sunbirds (Nectariniidae)
Black Sunbird
Collared Sunbird
Greater Double-collared Sunbird
Malachite Sunbird
Marico Sunbird
Olive Sunbird
Purple-banded Sunbird
Scarlet-chested Sunbird
White-bellied Sunbird
Yellow-bellied Sunbird
Orange-breasted Sunbird
Neergaard's Sunbird
Lesser Double-collared Sunbird
Dusky Sunbird
Grey Sunbird

White-eyes (Zosteropidae)
Cape White-eye
Yellow White-eye

Sparrows, Weavers, etc (Ploceidae)
Golden Bishop
Red Bishop
Scaly-feathered Finch
Red-headed Quelea
Red-billed Quelea
Cape Sparrow
Brown-throated Weaver
Golden Weaver
Great Sparrow
Grey-headed Sparrow
House Sparrow
Yellow-throated Sparrow
Red-billed Buffalo Weaver
Cuckoo Finch
Masked Weaver
Lesser Masked Weaver
Sociable Weaver
Thick-billed Weaver
Forest Weaver
Cape Weaver
Yellow Weaver
White-browed Sparrow Weaver
Spectacled Weaver
Spotted-backed Weaver
Red-headed Weaver
Red-collared Widow
White-winged Widow
Yellow-rumped Widow
Long-tailed Widow

Waxbills, Firefinches, etc (Estrildidae)
Cut-throat Finch
Melba Finch
Quail Finch
Red-headed Finch
Blue-billed Firefinch
Jameson's Firefinch
Brown-backed Firefinch
Red-billed Firefinch
Bronze Mannikin
Pied Mannikin
Red-backed Mannikin
Pink-throated Twinspot
Green Twinspot
Red-throated Twinspot
Black-cheeked Waxbill
Blue Waxbill
Common Waxbill
Grey Waxbill
Orange-breasted Waxbill
Swee Waxbill
Violet-eared Waxbill

Whydahs and Widowfinches (Viduidae)
Pintailed Whydah
Shaft-tailed Whydah
Paradise Whydah
Broad-tailed Paradise Whydah
Black Widowfinch
Purple Widowfinch
Steel-blue Widowfinch

Buntings, Canaries, (Fringillidae)
Chaffinch
Cape Bunting
Golden-breasted Bunting
Lark-like Bunting
Rock Bunting
Black-throated Canary
Bully Canary
Cape Canary
Lemon-breasted Canary
Streaky-headed Canary
Protea Canary
Forest Canary
Black-headed Canary
Yellow Canary
White-throated Canary
Yellow-eyed Canary
Black-eared Seed-Eater
Streaky-headed Seed-Eater
Cape Siskin
Drakensberg Siskin

Reptiles

Side-necked Terrapins (Pleurodira)
Eastern Hinged Terrapin

Hewitt's Terrapin
Marsh Terrapin
Mashona Hinged Terrapin
Pan Hinged Terrapin
Serrated Hinged Terrapin

Tortoises, Terrapins and Turtles (Cryptodira)
Angulate Tortoise
Bell's Hinged Tortoise
Geometric Tortoise
Greater Padloper
Karoo or Boulenger's Padloper
Leopard Tortoise
Natal Hinged Tortoise
Parrot-beaked Tortoise
Speckled Padloper
Serrated or Kalahari Tent Tortoise
Tent Tortoise
Leatherback Turtle
Green Turtle
Hawksbill Turtle
Olive Ridley Turtle
Loggerhead Turtle
American Red-eared Terrapin

Geckos (Gekkonidae)
African Flat Gecko
Amatola Flat Gecko
Hawequa Flat Gecko
Karoo Flat Gecko
Mountain Flat Gecko
Pondo Flat Gecko
Tembo Flat Gecko
Transvaal Flat Gecko
Giant Ground Gecko
Kalahari Ground Gecko
Moreau's Tropical House Gecko
Wahlberg's Velvet Gecko
Muller's Velvet Gecko
Cape Dwarf Gecko
Bradfield's Dwarf Gecko
Spotted Dwarf Gecko
Stevenson's Dwarf Gecko
Methuen's Dwarf Gecko
Austen's Gecko
Bibron's Gecko
Button-scaled Gecko
Cape Gecko
Western Cape Gecko
Ocellated Gecko
Spotted Gecko
Golden Spotted Gecko
Marico Gecko
Namaqua Gecko
Speckled Gecko
Rough-scaled Gecko
Western-spotted Gecko
Tiger Gecko
Weber's Gecko

Striped Leaf-toed Gecko
Small-scaled Leaf-toed Gecko
Marbled Leaf-toed Gecko
Peringuey's Leaf-toed Gecko
Common Barking Gecko
Namaqua Day Gecko

Agamas (Agamidae)
Ground Agama
Anchieta's Agama
Southern Rock Agama
Spiny Agama
Tree Agama

Chameleons (Chamaeleonidae)
Transkei Dwarf Chameleon
Knysna Dwarf Chameleon
Drakensberg Dwarf Chameleon
Robertson Dwarf Chameleon
Karoo Dwarf Chameleon
Blackheaded Dwarf Chameleon
Cape Dwarf Chameleon
Setaro's Dwarf Chameleon
Smith's Dwarf Chameleon
Natal Midlands Dwarf
Chameleon
Transvaal Dwarf Chameleon
Southern and Namaqua Dwarf
Chameleons
Zululand Dwarf Chameleon
Flap-necked Chameleon
Namaqua Chameleon

Skinks (Scincidae)
Short-headed Legless Skink
Thin-tailed Legless Skink
Striped Legless Skink
Coastal Legless Skink
Cape Legless Skink
Giant Legless Skink
Percival's Legless Skink
Woodbush Legless Skink
Golden Blind Legless Skink
Cregoi's Blind Legless Skink
Lomi's Blind Legless Skink
Striped Blind Legless Skink
Meyer's Blind Legless Skink
Boulenger's Blind Legless Skink
Cuvier's Blind Legless Skink
Gariep Blind Legless Skink
Algoa Dwarf Burrowing Skink
Zululand Dwarf Burrowing
Skink
Western Dwarf Burrowing
Skink
Lowveld Dwarf Burrowing
Skink
Silvery Dwarf Burrowing Skink
Striped Dwarf Burrowing Skink
Hewitt's Dwarf Burrowing
Skink

Cape Dwarf Burrowing Skink
Gronovi's Dwarf Burrowing
Skink
Gunther's Dwarf Burrowing
Skink
Smith's Dwarf Burrowing Skink
Kasner's Dwarf Burrowing
Skink
Limpopo Dwarf Burrowing
Skink
Montane Dwarf Burrowing
Skink
Bouton's Skink
Cape Skink
Sundevall's Writhing Skink
Wedge-snouted Skink
Red-sided Skink
Five-lined or Rainbow Skink
Western Three-striped Skink
Kalahari Tree Skink
Striped Skink
Western Rock Skink
Variable Skink
Variegated Skink
Wahlberg's Snake-eyed Skink

Lizards (Lacertidae)
Bushveld Lizard
Cape Rough-scaled Lizard
Smith's Desert Lizard
Common Rough-scaled Lizard
Southern Rock Lizard
Soutpansberg Rock Lizard
Knox's Desert Lizard
Spotted Desert Lizard
Blue-tailed Sandveld Lizard
Spotted Sandveld Lizard
Delalande's Sandveld Lizard
Ornate Sandveld Lizard
Striped Sandveld Lizard
Burchell's Sand Lizard
Cape Sand Lizard
Spotted Sand Lizard
Namaqua Sand Lizard
Western Sand Lizard
Essex's Mountain Lizard
Cape Mountain Lizard
Cottrell's Mountain Lizard
Common Mountain Lizard
Dwarf Plated Lizard
Rough-scaled Plated Lizard
Yellow-throated Plated Lizard
Black-lined Plated Lizard
Namaqua Plated Lizard
Giant Plated Lizard
Transvaal Grass Lizard
Cape Grass Lizard
Large-scaled Grass Lizard
Armadillo Girdled Lizard
Blue-spotted Girdled Lizard
Cape Girdled Lizard

Giant Girdled Lizard
Lawrence's Girdled Lizard
Dwarf Girdled Lizard
McLachlan's Girdled Lizard
Large-scaled Girdled Lizard
Peers's Girdled Lizard
Karoo Girdled Lizard
Tasman's Girdled Lizard
Warren's Girdled Lizard
Tropical Girdled Lizard
Transvaal Girdled Lizard
Cape Flat Lizard
Fitzsimon's Flat Lizard
Dwarf Flat Lizard
Common Flat Lizard
Relict Flat Lizard
Graceful Crag Lizard
Lang's Crag Lizard
Drakensberg Crag Lizard
Spiny Crag Lizard
Cape Crag Lizard
African Long-tailed Seps
Breyer's Long-tailed Seps
Eastwood's Long-tailed Seps
Short-legged Seps
Common Long-tailed Seps

**Monitors (Leguaans)
(Varanidae)**
Rock Leguaan
Water Leguaan

Worm Lizards (Amphisbaenia)
Langs' Round-headed Worm
Lizard
Violet Round-headed Worm
Lizard
Kalahari Round-headed Worm
Lizard
Cape Spade-snouted Worm
Lizard
Leonhard's Spade-snouted
Worm Lizard
Slender Spade-snouted Worm
Lizard
Blunt-tailed Worm Lizard

**Snakes (Serpentes)
Blind Snakes (Typhlophidae)**
Bibron's Blind Snake
Delalande's Blind Snake
Flower-pot Snake
Fornasini's Blind Snake
Beaked Blind Snake
Schlegel's Blind Snake

**Thread Snakes
(Leptotyphlopidae)**
Long-tailed Thread Snake

Black Thread Snake
Slender Thread Snake
Cape Thread Snake
Peters' Thread Snake
Distant's Thread Snake
Western Thread Snake

Pythons (Boidae)
African Rock Python

Typical Snakes (Colubridae)
Brown House Snake
Olive House Snake
Fisk's House Snake
Spotted House Snake
Aurora House Snake
Yellow-bellied House Snake
Swazi Rock Snake
Cape Wolf Snake
Eastern Wolf Snake
Variegated Wolf Snake
Cape File Snake
Black File Snake
Common Slug Eater
Variegated or Spotted Slug Eater
Mole Snake
Forest Marsh Snake
Many-spotted Snake
Sundevall's Shovel-snout
Mozambique Shovel-snout
Two-striped Shovel-snout
South-western Shovel-snout
East African Shovel-snout
Bark or Mopane Snake
Rufous Beaked Snake
Dwarf Beaked Snake
Spotted or Rhombic *Skaapsteker*
Striped *Skaapsteker*

Western Sand Snake
Jalla's Sand Snake
Stripe-bellied Sand Snake
Karoo Sand Snake or Whip Snake
Cape, Namib and Fork-marked Sand Snakes
Dwarf Sand Snake
Leopard and Short-snouted Grass Snakes
Olive Grass Snake
Cross-marked or Montane Grass Snake
Southern or Bibron's Burrowing Asp
Reticulated Centipede Eater
Duerden's Burrowing Asp
Cape Centipede Eater
Natal Black Snake
Natal Purple-glossed snake
Common Purple-glossed snake
Eastern Purple-glossed or white-lipped snake
Spotted Harlequin Snake
Striped Harlequin Snake
Bicoloured Quill-snouted Snake
Transvaal Quill-snouted Snake
Spotted Bush Snake
Dusky-bellied Water Snake
Common Brown Water Snake
Whyte's Water Snake
Green Water Snake
Natal Green Snake
Western Green Snake
Common or Rhombic Egg Eater
Southern Brown Egg Eater
Herald or Red-lipped Snake
Eastern Tiger Snake

Namib Tiger Snake
Cross-barred or Marbled Tree Snake
Boomslang / Tree Snake
Bird or Twig Snake

Cobras, Mambas (Elapidae)
Coral Snake
Shield-nose Snake
Sundevall's Garter Snake
Angolan and Boulenger's Garter Snakes
Forest Cobra
Egyptian Cobra
Cape Cobra
Black-necked Spitting Cobra
Mozambique Spitting Cobra
Black Mamba
Green Mamba
Rinkhals
Yellow-bellied Sea Snake

Adders and Vipers (Viperidae)
Common or Rhombic Night Adder
Snouted Night Adder
Puff Adder
Berg Adder
Gaboon Adder
Horned Adder
Many-horned Adder
Desert Mountain Adder
Plain Mountain Adder
Namaqua Dwarf Adder

Crocodiles (Crocodylia)
Nile Crocodile

Wildlife Profile

Elephant, *Loxodonta africana*: Wide habitat tolerance and distributed throughout all major wildlife areas.

Black rhinoceros, *Diceros bicornis*: Browser, now confined to major wildlife areas and subjected to heavy poaching pressure.

White rhinoceros, *Ceratotherium simum*: Grazer, mainly confined to smaller wildlife areas. Re-introduced.

Burchell's zebra, *Equus burchelli*: Common in grasslands and open savannah woodlands.

Buffalo, *Syncerus caffer*: Widely distributed throughout major wildlife areas.

Blue wildebeest, *Connochaetes taurinus*: Found in wildlife areas.

Lichtenstein's hartebeest, *Sigmoceros lichtensteinii*: Small population.

Red hartebeest, *Alcelaphus bucelaphus*: Confined to open grasslands and dry savannah.

Tsessebe, *Damaliscus lunatus*: Now being re-introduced into many wildlife areas.

Blue duiker, *Philantomba monticola*: Confined to forests.

Common (Grey) duiker, *Sylvicapra grimmia*: Widely distributed throughout the country.

Suni, *Neotragus moschatus:* A very small antelope confined to thickets in dry woodland.

Steenbok, *Raphicerus campestris:* Mainly on open grasslands with cover nearby.

Klipspringer, *Oreotragus oreotragus:* Widely distributed but confined to rocky habitats, to which it is uniquely adapted.

Waterbuck, *Kobus ellipsiprymnus:* Inhabits areas near rivers and marshes and is never far from water.

Reedbuck, *Redunca arundinum:* Associated with reed beds, vleis, and stands of tall grass close to water throughout wildlife and farming areas.

Impala, *Aepyceros melampus:* Common and prolific throughout most of the country.

Sable, *Hippotragus niger:* Widespread and fairly common in many wildlife areas.

Roan, *Hippotragus equinus:* Endangered species. Inhabits open woodland near water.

Eland, *Taurotragus oryx:* Africa's largest antelope found throughout major wildlife areas and on many farms and ranches.

Bushbuck, *Tragelaphus scriptus:* Habitat includes riverine bush and other dense vegetation, usually close to water.

Kudu, *Tragelaphus strepsiceros:* Located throughout savannah woodlands in most major wildlife areas.

Giraffe, *Giraffa camelopardalis:* Endemic to several wildlife areas.

Bushpig, *Potamochoerus porcus:* Common and widespread, but nocturnal in habits.

Wart hog, *Phacochoerus aethiopicus:* Prefers open grasslands,vleis, and floodplains. Unmistakable in appearance.

Hippopotamus, *Hippopotamus amphibius:* Found throughout South Africa's rivers and lakes.

Lion, *Panthera leo:* Stable populations in most major wildlife areas, but virtually exterminated in farming and other regions.

Leopard, *Panthera pardus:* Found in wildlife and other areas; mainly nocturnal.

African wildcat, *Felis lybica:* Widespread but interbreeding with feral domestic cats in areas.

Cheetah, *Acinonyx jubatus:* Endangered species. Found in specific wildlife areas where open woodland and savannah occur.

Serval, *Felis serval:* Although similar to a young cheetah in appearance, it prefers thicker, more humid woodlands.

Spotted hyena, *Crocuta crocuta:* Inhabits most major wildlife areas.

Brown hyena, *Hyaena brunnea:* A shy, nocturnal species, inhabiting dry woodland areas.

Aardwolf, *Proteles cristatus:* Smaller member of the hyena family; feeds mainly on termites and other insects.

Cape clawless otter, *Aonyx capensis:* Found in most water bodies — both fresh and marine water. Has been known to raid poultry and ornamental ponds.

Honey badger, *Mellivora capensis:* Occurs widely throughout the country, raids wild beehives and is notorious for its aggressive nature.

Black-backed jackal, *Canis mesomelas:* Usually in open terrain.

Side-striped jackal, *Canis adustus:* Nocturnal, shy and seldom seen.

Wild dog, *Lycaon pictus:* Resides in several wildlife areas, but nowhere common and may be endangered.

Bat-eared fox, *Otocyon megalotis:* Largely limited to open areas in dry savannah or semi-desert areas.

Mongooses, *Viverridae:* Ten species, of which the slender mongoose is probably the most often sighted.

African civet, *Civettictis civetta:* This mainly nocturnal species thrives in a wide range of habitats.

Lesser bushbaby, *Galago senegalensis:* This small, nocturnal animal is arboreal and seldom touches the ground.

Thicktailed bushbaby, *Galago crassicaudatus:* Commonly found in well-developed woodlands and forests.

Vervet monkey, *Cercopithecus aethiops:* widespread throughout much of the country.

Samango monkey, *Cercopithecus mitis:* These shy diurnal primates inhabit mountains, riverine, dry and coastal forests.

Chacma baboon, *Papio ursinus:* Can occupy virtually any habitat except desert.

Birdlife Profile

In South Africa, the most diverse conditions of environment for birds are found, with tropical, temperate, winter and summer rainfall areas.

Ostrich, *Struthio camelus:* These, the world's largest birds, are commonly found in grasslands and lightly wooded areas, both in the wild and domesticated on farms.

Pelicans: The white pelican, *Pelecanus onocrotalus,* and the pink-backed pelican, *Pelecanus rufescens,* both very large birds, can be found near pools and stretches of water.

Cormorants: White-breasted cormorants, *Phalacrocorax carbo,* are the largest cormorants and are found throughout South Africa, while Cape cormorants, *Phalacrocorax capensis,* are found along the entire South African coast. Reed cormorants, *Phalacrocorax africanus,* and Darters, *Anhinga melanogaster,* are widely distributed throughout South Africa.

Herons: Herons are medium to very large wading birds with long, straight bills. Grey herons, *Ardea cinerea,* and black-headed herons, *Ardea melanocephala,* are found throughout South Africa as are purple herons, *Ardea purpurea;* Goliath herons, *Ardea goliath,* are the largest herons and are found mainly in the eastern and northern parts of South Africa.

Egrets: Cattle egrets, *Bubulcus ibis,* can be found throughout the country. Great white egrets, *Egretta albus,* are found in all parts of South Africa, but rarely in the Cape. The black egret, *Egretta ardesiaca,* is located in the eastern and northern part of the country and is easily identified by the distinctive way it forms a canopy with its wings while fishing.

Storks: The yellow-billed stork, *Mycteria ibis,* migrates to South Africa from the northern tropics of Africa and Malagasy — rarely sighted in the south-western Cape. Black storks, *Ciconia nigra,* are seen throughout South Africa during the northern hemisphere winter. The white stork, *Ciconia ciconia,* is a common summer visitor to the dry Karoo and grass veld of the Free State and Transvaal.

Ibises: The sacred ibis, *Threskiornis aethiopicus,* is a common resident except in the drier western regions. The hadada ibis, *Bostrychia hagedash,* is very common along the southern and eastern moist belt, Northern Province and upper Vaal river. The African spoonbill, *Platalea alba,* is widespread except in the dry west.

Flamingoes: The greater flamingo, *Phoenicopterus ruber,* is found all around South Africa. The lesser flamingo, *Phoenicopterus minor,* found over most of South Africa, is smaller and haspinker, more even colouration than the previous species.

Ducks and geese: Egyptian geese, *Alopochen aegyptiacus,* are found throughout South Africa, while the spur-winged goose, *Plectropterus gambenis,* can usually be seen along the larger rivers. The South African shelduck, *Tadorna cana,* can be seen mainly in the highveld and semi-arid regions. Cape shovellers, *Anas smithii,* are common in the southwest Cape and on the highveld and African black ducks, *Anas sparsa,* are widespread throughout most of South Africa. Perhaps South Africa's best-known duck is the yellow-billed duck, *Anas undulata,* which is located throughout most of South Africa as are the red-billed teal, *Anas erythrorhyncha,* the Cape teal, *Anas capensis,* and the Maccoa duck, *Oxyura maccoa.*

Secretary birds, *Sagittarius serpentarius,* are found all over South Africa except in mountainous and forested regions.

Vultures: The Cape vulture, *Gyps coprotheres,* is widely distributed throughout South Africa and is the commonest in the Republic, even though its numbers have been drastically reduced. The white-backed vulture, *Gyps africanus,* is the common vulture of the tropical savanna and bushveld. The lappet-faced vulture, *Torgos tracheliotus,* is a much larger bird and is widely dispersed except in the Cape. The Egyptian vulture, *Neophron percnopterus,* is very rare in the Republic. The Lammergeier (bearded vulture) may be seen in the Giant's Castle Nature Reserve.

Kites and buzzards: The black-shouldered kite, *Elanus caeruleus,* is probably South Africa's most widespread raptor. Both the yellow-billed kite, *Milvus migrans parasitus,* and the black kite, *Milvus migrans migrans,* are common summer migrants. Of the buzzard species, the steppe buzzard, *Buteo buteo,* is the most widespread, while the jackal buzzard, *Buteo rufofuscus,* is common in mountainous country.

Eagles: The black eagle, *Aquila verreauxi,* is fairly common throughout the country. The tawny eagle, *Aquila rapax,* is a species of the dry bushveld thorn country. The martial eagle, *Polemaetus bellicosus,* is the country's largest eagle and is found throughout South Africa, except in the south-west Cape. The African fish eagle, *Haliaeetus vocifer,* is a beautiful and distinctive bird which is fairly common near rivers and lakes.

Sparrowhawks and goshawks: Five goshawk species and four sparrowhawk species are found in South Africa. The gabar goshawk, *Micronisus gabar*, is a common species of woodland areas, while the African goshawk, *Accipiter tachiro*, is a common species in forested areas of the northern, eastern and southern areas of South Africa. All sparrowhawk species tend to be fairly uncommon.

Harriers: Four species of harrier, long-legged raptors with long wings and tails, are found in South Africa. The African marsh harrier, *Circus ranivorus*, is the most common species. The gymnogene, *Polyboroides typus*, can be found clambering about tree trunks searching for insects and lizards.

Guineafowl: The helmeted guineafowl, *Numida meleagris*, is a very common ground-bird in most wildlife areas and on farmlands; the crested guineafowl, *Guttera pucherani*, is much rarer and is confined to the north-eastern regions of South Africa.

Francolins: The coqui francolin, *Francolinus coqui*, is common in woodlands. The redwing francolin, *Francolinus levaillantii*, is a fairly common inhabitant of moister grasslands and is found in the southern Cape, KwaZulu-Natal, and northwards to the Soutspansberg.

Quails: The common quail, *Coturnix coturnix*, and the harlequin quail, *Coturnix delegorguei*, are both fairly widespread. The blue quail, *Coturnix adansoni*, migrates from North Africa to the eastern Cape Province, KwaZulu-Natal and Northern Province and Mpumalanga.

Rails: South Africa has eighteen species of rails, crakes and gallinules. The African rail, *Rallus caerulescens*, occurs fairly commonly in marshy areas. The black crake, *Amaurornis flavirostris*, is often seen in the moister northern, eastern and southern areas of the country near rivers and streams, as are the purple gallinule, *Porphyrio porphyrio*. The moorhen, *Gallinula chloropus*, is a common resident known worldwide.

Cranes: The wattled crane, *Grus carunculatus*, an uncommon but conspicuous resident, is found in South Africa, except in the Western Cape and in drier areas. The blue crane, *Anthropoides paradisea*, is seen mainly in the Karoo and grassveld areas of South Africa.

Bustards: The kori bustard, *Ardeotis kori*, is the heaviest flying bird in the world, sometimes weighing up to twenty kilograms (44lb). It occurs throughout the country, except the coastal lowlands of the southwest Cape and KwaZulu-Natal. The Karoo korhaan, *Eupodotis vigorsii*, is

common to the Karoo area and the black korhaan, *Eupodotis afra*, is commonly widespread across the country except east of the Drakensburg.

Jacanas: The African jacana, *Actophilornis africanus*, sometimes called the 'lily-trotter' is frequently seen on most dams, rivers and wetlands in the northern and eastern parts of the country. The lesser jacana, *Microparra capensis*, is an inconspicuous and rarely observed species.

Plovers: The crowned plover, *Vanellus coronatus*, widespread and common all over South Africa, is gregarious and flocks can number up to forty birds. The blacksmith plover, *Vanellus armatus*, is also widespread and easily identified by its distinctive 'klink-klink' call.

Coursers: Burchell's courser, *Cursorius rufus*, is found inland on grassy or barren flats over most of South Africa except along the eastern coastal belt to George. The double-banded courser, *Rhinoptilus africanus*, lives mainly on open grasslands in the western part of the country. The country's two pratincole species are both migrants.

Gulls: There are four common gull species along South Africa's coast, inland waters and lakes. The grey-headed gull, *Larus cirrocephalus*, is common along South Africa's entire coast as well as on Transvaal and Free State dams and pans.

Sandgrouse: Four species of sandgrouse occur in South Africa. The most prevalent is the Namaqua sandgrouse, *Pterocles namaqua*, which is usually found in flocks in open desert and semi-desert.

Pigeons and doves: There are fourteen species of pigeons and doves in South Africa. The rock pigeon, *Columba guinea*, is a common species wherever there are rocks or artificial structures. The Cape turtle dove, *Streptopelia capicola*, is probably the commonest dove in South Africa and is found almost anywhere, as is the laughing dove, *Streptopelia senegalensis*, which is found in gardens. The Namaqua dove, *Oena capensis*, is another common species in the drier areas of the country.

Cuckoos: Many cuckoos are brood parasites, laying their eggs in other birds' nests, while coucals build their own. Most cuckoos are migrants including the European cuckoo, *Cuculus canorus*, which is similar to the African cuckoo, *Cuculus gularis*. The Burchell's coucal, *Centropus superciliosus*, is the commonest and best-known in South Africa. The Didrik cuckoo, *Chrysococcyx caprius*, is the commonest of the glossy cuckoos and is found mainly in the thornveld and stands of exotic trees such as gums.

Parrots: South Africa has three species of parrot — the brown-headed, the Cape and the Meyer's —

one species of parakeet and one lovebird. The brown-headed parrot, *Poicephalus cryptoxanthus*, is a quite common species attracting attention by its noisy behaviour. Found predominantly in Zululand and Mpumalanga, Meyer's *Poicephalus meyeri* is common in dry thornveld. The rosy-faced lovebird, *Agapornis roseicollis*, is found in flocks around lower Orange River and northwards to Angola.

Louries: The Knysna lourie, *Tauraco corythaix*, is fairly common in forested areas, from George eastwards to KwaZulu Natal and Mpumalanga. The purple-crested lourie, *Tauraco porphyreolophus*, is a fairly common species which also inhabits well-wooded areas in the eastern parts of South Africa. The grey lourie, *Corythaixoides concolor*, is also common and is well-known for its 'go-away' call.

Owls: The barn owl, *Tyto alba*, has become a city dweller and occurs throughout South Africa. The giant eagle owl, *Bubo lacteus*, is the largest owl and is common in woodland and savannah areas. The wood owl, *Strix woodfordii*, the marsh owl, *Asio capensis*, and the scops owl, *Otus senegalensis*, are all fairly common. Pel's fishing owl, *Scotopelia peli*, is an uncommon and very large species found along larger rivers and lakes.

Nightjars: The fiery-necked nightjar, *Caprimulgus pectoralis*, is common and easily identified by its call, 'Good-Lord-deliver-us'. While the freckled nightjar, *Caprimulgus tristigma*, and the Mozambique nightjar, *Caprimulgus fossii*, are local residents, the European nightjar, *Caprimulgus europaeus*, is a summer migrant.

Swifts: The European swift, *Apus apus*, is a fairly common migrant which is found in large flocks. The palm swift, *Cypsiurus parvus*, uses saliva to glue its nest to the underside of palm fronds and is a common resident.

Mousebirds: There are three species of mousebirds in South Africa: the red-faced mousebird, *Colius indicus*, speckled mousebird, *Colius striatus*, and white-backed mousebird, *Colius colius*.

Trogons: The Narina trogon, *Apaloderma narina*, is a beautiful bird which inhabits the forests of Knysna and along the eastern part of the country, in fairly open coastal bush.

Kingfishers: The pied kingfisher, *Ceryle rudis*, is common to all waters, while the giant kingfisher, *Ceryle maxima*, is the largest kingfisher in South Africa and is found around permanent water. The tiny but beautifully coloured malachite kingfisher, *Alcedo cristata*, is a resident fishing species, while the similar pygmy kingfisher, *Ispidina picta*, is an African migrant found mainly in woodlands.

Bee-eaters: European bee-eaters, *Merops apeaster*, migrants to South Africa as far south as Cape Town. The white-fronted bee-eater, *Merops bullockoides*, the little bee-eater, *Merops pusillus*, and the swallow-tailed bee-eater, *Merops hirundineus*, are all local residents.

Rollers: The lilac-breasted roller, *Coracias caudata*, is popularly named 'blue-jay' because its blue wings are particularly beautiful in flight. It is fairly common in the thornveld savannas as is the purple roller, *Coracias naevia*.

Hoopoes: The hoopoe, *Upupa epops*, is a common and well-known species, usually found in the savannah veld but also in towns and domestic gardens, where it can be seen walking about and probing the ground with its long, thin bill. Both the red-billed woodhoopoe, *Phoeniculus purpureus*, and the scimitar-billed woodhoopoe, *Phoeniculus cyanomelas*, are widespread and found in small flocks.

Hornbills: All these species are characterized by raucous calls and huge bills. The grey hornbill, *Tockus nasutus*, is found in highveld woodlands, while the red-billed hornbill, *Tockus erythrorhynchus*, is common in the lowveld. The most distinctive species is the ground hornbill, *Bucorvus leadbeateri*, a large bird with a deep, booming call.

Barbets: The pied barbet, *Lybius leucomelas*, is common and widely distributed, as is the black-collared barbet, *Lybius torquatus*, which is widely distributed in any woodland and even in well wooded suburbia. Another conspicuous species is the crested barbet, *Trachyphonus vaillantii*, which has become quite tame in large gardens in Pretoria and Johannesburg.

Honeyguides: The greater honeyguide, *Indicator indicator*, and the lesser honeyguide, *Indicator minor*, are both widespread in South Africa. Both the scaly-throated honeyguide, *Indicator variegatus*, and the sharp-billed honeyguide, *Prodotiscus regulus*, are fairly rare.

Woodpeckers: The ground woodpecker, *Geocolaptes olivaceus*, is unique to South Africa. The cardinal woodpecker, *Dendropicos fuscescens*, is South Africa's most common woodpecker, found wherever there are trees, but not in forests. The bearded woodpecker, *Thripias namaquus*, is also a fairly common species which is found in drier areas.

Passerines: A great variety of this group is found, including starlings, shrikes, sunbirds, weavers, whydahs and finches. Several of the local species of weaver build distinctive nests in a variety of shapes and designs.

Plant Profile

ACANTHACEA (barleria)
A prolific and varied family that contains herbs, shrubs, some trees, and woody climbers. Many species have conspicuous flowers and some are used as garden shrubs or perennials.

AMARANTHACEAE (pigweed and amaranth)
Most members of this family are herbs; some are shrubs or climbers. Some species are found where extreme desert conditions prevail in the west of the Republic.

AMARYLLIDACEAE (vlei lily and daffodil)
This family contains nine species of vlei lily, with showy pink and white flowers that appear in December. The veld fan or windball is also a member of this family and is often widespread in woodlands and grasslands, particularly in the eastern grassveld and in the southwest.

ANACARDIACEAE (mango and marula)
The best-known member of this family is the marula, *Sclerocarya birrea*, which is widespread at medium to low altitudes and has a fruit that is much sought after by both people and wildlife.

ANONNACEAE (custard apple)
The custard apple family includes trees, shrubs, and lianas. Many species have edible fruit, often growing in colourful clusters that may be eaten by monkeys and other wildlife.

APOCYNACEAE (oleander)
The wild rubber tree, *Diplorhynchus condylocarpon*, is part of this family. Several ornamental members of the family, including frangipani and the Madagascar periwinkle, are grown in gardens. The beautiful Save star (Desert Rose), *Adenium obesum*, is a member of this family.

ARECACEAE (palm)
The raphia palm, *Raphia farinefera*, is part of this family. Another member is the ilala palm and is widespread at lower altitudes. The South African Arecaceae, like the majority of the subtropical members of the family, are swamp plants.

ASCLEPIADACEAE (milkwood and stapeliad)
A large number have adapted to grassland conditions, and the most highly specialized of all, *Stapelieae*, are especially characteristic of the Karoo and drier area of the western side of South Africa. Perennial herbs and erect or climbing shrubs form the majority of this large family.

ASTERACEAE (sunflower)
This large family includes sunflowers, ragworts, marigolds, African and Barberton daisies, and chamomiles as well as lettuce and chicory. Many species have been introduced from various parts of the world.

BIGNONIACEAE (sausage-tree)
The best-known member of this family is the sausage-tree, *Kigelia africana*, which is found at lower altitudes and grows large, distinctive, sausage-shaped fruits. Most other members are lianas, adapted to climbing in forests.

BOMBACEAE (baobab)
The baobab is an unmistakable feature of South Africa's lower-lying areas. It stores water in its thick trunk. The flowers — which last less than a day — are pollinated by bats. Baobabs provide a range of useful products including water, bark, and seeds rich in tartaric acid.

BORAGINACEAE (borage)
Besides borage, which is often grown in gardens, this family includes the *Cordia* genus of which *Cordia abyssinica*, with its conspicuous white flowers, is the most spectacular and best known.

BRASSICACEAE (cabbage)
Most species, such as rape, cabbage, kale, kohlrabi, brussel sprouts, and cauliflower, are introduced. However, several indigenous species related to the watercress can be found near water.

CANNABACEAE (hemp and dagga)
Tha cannabis subspecies, *cannabis sativa indica*, sometimes grown illegally among maize crops or in bush clearings.

CAPPARACEAE (caper)
The family includes trees, shrubs, and herbs. Capers themselves, *Capparis spinosa*, were introduced from the Mediterranean, but some indigenous species scramble into the crowns of low-altitude trees.

CELASTRACEAE (catha)
This family consists largely of trees and shrubs. The two largest South African genera are *Maytenus* and *Hippocratea*; the confetti tree, *Maytenus senegalensis*, grows to eight metres (27 feet) and has sweetly scented cream flowers.

COMBRETACEAE (combretum)
Many *Combretum* and *Terminalia* species occur in South Africa that are ecologically important. The so-called 'jesse bush' of lower-lying areas is composed largely of *Combretum* species, while the flame-bush, *Combretum microphyllum*, flowers spectacularly in August and September.

CONVOLVULACEAE (morning-glory)
Ipomoea, South Africa's most common genus, is composed mainly of succulents with purple or white flowers. The tubers of some species are eaten raw or cooked, and one species, the Save morning-glory, *Ipomoea plebia*, has become a problem in irrigated lands.

CORNACEAE (dagwood and assegai tree)
The assegai tree, *Curtisia dentata*, occurs in the Nyanga area.

EBENACEAE (ebony)
Several *Diaspyros* and *Euclea* species occur in South Africa; however, none produce timber of economic significance, although the wood is sometimes used for furniture or carvings. *Diaspyros mespiliformis* is sometimes seen overhanging low-veld pans.

FABACEAE (pea and bean)
This is South Africa's largest family of flowering plants. It includes such apparently diverse species as the highveld msasa and mnondo and the mopanes of the lowveld. All the Acacias are included which is the great subtropical genus which is usually thorny.

FLACOURTIACEAE (flacourtia)
One species, *Oncoba spinosa*, has large, scented fruit used by traditional dancers to make ankle rattlers. Another, *Bivinia jalbertii*, is specially protected because of its rarity.

GESNERIACEAE (African violet)
The most spectacular is *Streptocarpus eylesii*, found on rock faces and stream banks in granite areas.

MALVACEAE (cotton and hibiscus)
Cotton grown in South Africa comes from cultures of American species, *Gossypium hirsutum*. Indigenous members of the family include okra, which is cooked and eaten as a vegetable, and the *Hibiscus* genus, of which some are commonly used as garden shrubs or hedge plants.

MORACEAE (fig and mulberry)
Figs genus *Ficus* of several species are widespread and commom. The strangler fig, *Ficus thonningi*, often begins as an epiphyte and then destroys its host. The mulberry is cultivated in many South African gardens.

OCHNACEAE (ochna)
Members of this family occur widely in diverse habitats and include *Ochna pulchra*, a graceful woodland tree with peeling bark that reveals a creamy-white under-bark.

POLYGALACEAE (milkwort)
Twenty-eight milkworts of the genus *Polygala* occur in South Africa, and were so named because cows that ate the plant were said to increase their milk yield.

POLYGONACEAE (rhubarb and buckwheat)
Most South African members of this family are berberidaceous. Ten species of *Polygonum*, which usually have pink or white flowers, occur along stream banks and in other moist habitats.

PROTEACEAE (protea)
South Africa's national flower. An outlying population of *Protea dracomontana*, is found in the Drakensberg Mountains.

RANUNCULACEAE (buttercup)
This family includes the genus *Clematis*, or old man's beard, of which five species are found in South Africa.

RASSULACEAE (crassula and kalanchoe)
All members of this family are succulents. The genus crassula is the largest with at least sixty species.

RHAMNACEAE (buffalo thorn)
The buffalo thorn, *Ziziphus mucronata*, is common in open woodlands and often grows on termite mounds. One naturalized member of this genus, *Ziziphus mauritania* is prized for its edible fruit.

STERCULIACEAE (cocoa)
Many exotics of this family are grown in South Africa.

THYMELAECEAE (daphne and dias)
Gnidia kraussiana, which flowers in the wake of grass fires, is familiar. One species, *Dias cotinifolea*, occurs on forest edges, but is often cultivated as an ornamental shrub.

TILIACEAE (jute)
The genus *Corchorus*, from which jute is made, is represented by twelve species in South Africa. *Corchorus kirkii* is a shrub found among granite boulders, while *Corchorus olitorius* is grown as a relish and for its fibre.

TURNERACEAE (pimpernel)
All the South African members of this family are perennial herbs or annuals. One perennial, *Piriqueta capensis*, has a single golden flower and is only found in the Beitbridge area. The most common is the *Tricliceral longipedunculatum*. It is strongly cyanogenic.

VITACEAE (grape)
Members of this family are perennial herbs, climbing shrubs and, occasionally, trees. The wing grape, *Vitis vinifera*, is widely grown in South Africa. None of the wild genera produce particularly palatable fruit.

Demographic Profile

The population of South Africa is 39 million. The poorer, less educated people tend to have larger families. With greater urbanization and higher standards of living, a decline in the birth rate is expected. At present, the population is increasing by three per cent a year.

Language

Languages spoken in South Africa include English, Afrikaans, Zulu, Xhosa, North/South Sotho and Tswana. Other languages spoken are Swazi, South/North Ndebele, Shangaan/Tsonga, Venda, Tamil, Hindi, Dutch, German, Greek, Portuguese and Italian.

Religious affiliation of the South African population

Religious grouping	Nos in 000s	%
African indigenous churches	7,006	22.75
Nederduitse Gereformeerde churches (NGK)	4,299	13.96
Roman Catholic church	2,963	9.62
Methodist church	2,747	8.92
Anglican churches	2,026	6.58
Lutheran churches	1,093	3.55
Presbyterian churches	758	2.46
Congregational church	607	1.97
Nederduitse Hervormde churches	357	1.16
Apostolic Faith Mission	351	1.14
Baptist churches	317	1.03
Gereformeerde churches (GK)	243	0.79
Full Gospel churches	228	0.74
Assemblies of God	179	0.58
Seventh Day Adventists	102	0.33
Other Christian churches	773	2.51
Total Christian churches	**24,049**	**78.09**
Hindus	650	2.11
Muslims	434	1.41
Judaists	148	0.48
Other non-Christians	5,513	17.90
Total non-Christians	**6,745**	**21.90**
Total population	**30,794**	**100.00**

(Taken from the latest religious census of 1980 and are assumed not to have changed significantly.)

Gazetteer

All towns/cities listed have hopitals, police stations, petrol stations and hotel accommodation available. Contact local tourist information offices for the relevant telephone numbers and addresses.

(second line indicates kilometre distance from major towns)

Beaufort West
Bloemfontein 537, Cape Town 471, Colesberg 318, Durban 1,185, East London 599, George 258, Grahamstown 527, Johannesburg 961, Kimberley 504, Ladysmith 947, Mafikeng 884, Port Elizabeth 478, Pretoria 1,019, Welkom 688.

Bloemfontein
Cape Town 1,008, Colesberg 219, Durban 648, East London 586, George 673, Grahamstown 590, Johannesburg 424, Kimberley 177, Ladysmith 410, Mafikeng 472, Port Elizabeth 670, Pretoria 482, Welkom 151.

Britstown
Bloemfontein 414, Cape Town 722, Colesberg 195, Durban 1062, East London 611, George 509, Grahamstown 539, Johannesburg 725, Kimberley 253, Ladysmith 824, Mafikeng 633, Port Elizabeth 572, Pretoria 783, Welkom 565.

Cape Town
Bloemfontein 1,008, Colesberg 789, Durban 1,656, East London 1,102, George 647, Grahamstown 920, Johannesburg 1,432, Kimberley 975, Ladysmith 1,418, Mafikeng 1,355, Port Elizabeth 790, Pretoria 1,490, Welkom 1,159.

Colesberg
Bloemfontein 219, Cape Town 789, Durban 867, East London 490, George 576, Grahamstown 418, Johannesburg 643, Kimberley 266, Ladysmith 629, Mafikeng 646, Port Elizabeth 451, Pretoria 701, Welkom 370.

De Aar
Bloemfontein 362, Cape Town 774, Colesberg 143, Durban 1,010, East London 559, Grahamstown 444, Johannesburg, 786, Kimberley 305, Ladysmith 772, Mafikeng 685, Port Elizabeth 520, Pretoria 844, Welkom 513.

Durban
Bloemfontein 648, Cape Town 1,656, Colesberg 867, East London 676, George 1,323, Grahamstown 858, Johannesburg 601, Kimberley 825, Ladysmith 238, Mafikeng 883, Port Elizabeth 988, Pretoria 659, Welkom 578.

East London
Bloemfontein 586, Cape Town 1,102, Colesberg 490, Durban 676, George 647, Grahamstown 182, Johannesburg 1,010, Kimberley 763, Ladysmith 752, Mafikeng 1,058, Port Elizabeth 312, Pretoria 1,068, Welkom 737.

George
Bloemfontein 673, Cape Town 447, Colesberg 576, Durban 1,323, East London 647, Grahamstown 465, Johannesburg 1,097, Kimberley 762, Ladysmith 1,083, Mafikeng 1,142, Port Elizabeth 343, Pretoria 1,155, Welkom 824.

Grahamstown
Bloemfontein 590, Cape Town 920, Colesberg 418, Durban 858, East London 182, George 465, Johannesburg 1,014, Kimberley 594, Ladysmith 934, Mafikeng 1,062, Port Elizabeth 130, Pretoria 1,072, Welkom 741.

Harrismith
Bloemfontein 328, Cape Town 1,336, Colesberg 547, Durban 320, East London 834, George 1,001, Grahamstown 947, Johannesburg 281, Kimberley 505, Ladysmith 82, Mafikeng 568, Port Elizabeth 1,077, Pretoria 339, Welkom 264.

Johannesburg
Bloemfontein 424, Cape Town 1,432, Colesberg 643, Durban 601, East London 1,010, George 1,097, Grahamstown 1,014, Kimberley 472, Ladysmith 363, Mafikeng 280, Port Elizabeth 1,094, Pretoria 58, Welkom 278.

Keetmanshoop
Bloemfontein 1,085, Cape Town 995, Colesberg 1,063, Durban 1,733, East London 1,479, George 1,377, Grahamstown 1,364, Johannesburg 1,380, Kimberley 908, Ladysmith 1,495, Mafikeng 1,066, Port Elizabeth 1,440, Pretoria 1,404, Welkom 1,236.

Kimberley
Bloemfontein 177, Cape Town 975, Colesberg 266, Durban 825, East London 763, George 762, Grahamstown 594, Johannesburg 472, Ladysmith 587, Mafikeng 380, Port Elizabeth 717, Pretoria 530, Welkom 294.

Klerksdorp
Bloemfontein 296, Cape Town 1,304, Colesberg 515, Durban 707, East London 882, George 969, Grahamstown 886, Johannesburg 164, Kimberley 308, Ladysmith 469, Mafikeng 176, Port Elizabeth 966, Pretoria 222, Welkom 145.

Kroonstad
Bloemfontein 211, Cape Town 1,219, Colesberg 430, Durban 551, East London 797, George 884, Grahamstown 801, Johannesburg 213, Kimberley

388, Ladysmith 313, Mafikeng 297, Port Elizabeth 881, Pretoria 271, Welkom 65.

Ladysmith
Bloemfontein 410, Cape Town 1,418, Colesberg 629, Durban 238, East London 1,058, George 1,142, Grahamstown 1,062, Johannesburg 280, Kimberley 380, Ladysmith 645, Port Elizabeth 1,097, Pretoria 338, Welkom 321.

Mafikeng
Bloemfontein 472, Cape Town 1,355, Colesberg 646, Durban 883, East London 1,058, George 1,142, Grahamstown 1,062, Johannesburg 280, Kimberley 380, Ladysmith 645, Port Elizabeth 1,097, Pretoria 338, Welkom 321.

Messina
Bloemfontein 965, Cape Town 1,355, Colesberg 646, Durban 1,088, East London 1,151, George 1,638, Grahamstown 1,555, Johannesburg 541, Kimberley 1,013, Ladysmith 850, Mafikeng 821, Port Elizabeth 1,635, Pretoria 483, Welkom 819.

Nelspruit
Bloemfontein 792, Cape Town 1,800, Colesberg 1,011, Durban 708, East London 1,222, George 1,554, Grahamstown 1,404, Johannesburg 368, Kimberley 840, Ladysmith 470, Mafikeng 648, Port Elizabeth 1,462, Pretoria 330, Welkom 646.

Oudtshoorn
Bloemfontein 736, Cape Town 506, Colesberg 517, Durban 1,382, East London 706, George 59, Grahamstown 524, Johannesburg 1,160, Kimberley 703, Ladysmith 1,142, Mafikeng 1,083, Port Elizabeth 394, Pretoria 1,218, Welkom 887.

Pietermaritzburg
Bloemfontein 567, Cape Town 1,575, Colesberg 786, Durban 81, East London 595, George 1,240, Grahamstown 777, Johannesburg 520, Kimberley 744, Ladysmith 157, Mafikeng 807, Port Elizabeth 907, Pretoria 578, Welkom 497.

Pietersburg
Bloemfontein 754, Cape Town 1,762, Colesberg 973, Durban 931, East London 1,340, George 1,427, Grahamstown 1,344, Johannesburg 330, Kimberley 802, Ladysmith 693, Mafikeng 610, Port Elizabeth 1,424, Pretoria 272, Welkom 608.

Port Elizabeth
Bloemfontein 670, Cape Town 790, Colesberg 451, Durban 988, East London 312, George 343, Grahamstown 130, Johannesburg 1,094, Kimberley 717, Ladysmith 1,064, Mafikeng 1,097, Pretoria 1,152, Welkom 821.

Pretoria
Bloemfontein 482, Cape Town 1,490, Colesberg

701, Durban 659, East London 1,068, George 1,155, Grahamstown 1,072, Johannesburg 58, Kimberley 530, Ladysmith 421, Mafikeng 338, Port Elizabeth 1,152, Welkom 336.

Queenstown
Bloemfontein 377, Cape Town 1,133, Colesberg 233, Durban 678, East London 209, George 678, Grahamstown 213, Johannesburg 801, Kimberley 554, Ladysmith 754, Mafikeng 849, Port Elizabeth 343, Pretoria 859, Welkom 528.

Upington
Bloemfontein 590, Cape Town 886, Colesberg 568, Durban 1,238, East London 984, George 882, Grahamstown 869, Johannesburg 885, Kimberley 413, Ladysmith 1,000, Mafikeng 571, Port Elizabeth 945, Pretoria 909, Welkom 741.

Welkom
Bloemfontein 151, Cape Town 1,159, Colesberg 370, Durban 578, East London 737, George 824, Grahamstown 741, Johannesburg 278, Kimberley 294, Ladysmith 340, Mafikeng 321, Port Elizabeth 821, Pretoria 336.

National Museums and Historical Sites

Museums

CAPE PROVINCE

The Castle of Good Hope
Province: Western Cape
District: Cape Town
Features: The Castle, which was built in 1666, is one of the oldest European structures in South Africa. It is located in Darling Street and houses the William Fehr collection of Africana, as well as a Maritime and Military Museum.

The South African Museum
Province: Western Cape
District: Cape Town
Features: Located in Government Avenue, near to the Botanic Gardens, it is dedicated to the study of natural history. It is the oldest establishment of its kind in southern Africa.

The Cultural History Museum
Province: Western Cape
District: Cape Town
Features: Located at the top of Adderley Street in the city centre, this building was once the Old Supreme Court, and is itself of historic importance. It houses art and other exhibits from ancient Egypt, Greece, imperial Rome, the Far East, and other civilizations. More modern exhibits include early Cape furniture, silver, glass and stamps. There is also a fine collection of objects dating from the Dutch East India Company period of rule.

The Jewish Museum
Province: Western Cape
District: Cape Town
Features: Housed in South Africa's oldest synagogue, in the Gardens, it contains a collection of ceremonial silver, antiquities, books and documents relating to South African Jewish history.

Groot Constantia
Province: Western Cape
District: Constantia
Features: This beautiful example of Cape Dutch architecture is nestled in the Constantia Valley near Cape Town. It was the home of Governor Simon van der Stel from 1699 until his death in 1712. Today a museum, the manor house is furnished with fine antiques and paintings of this period, and portrays life on the farm in the 1800s. There is a wine museum which has wine drinking and storage vessels in glass, silver, copper and stoneware from 500 BC to the nineteenth century

Hout Bay Museum
Province: Western Cape
District: Hout Bay
Features: Exhibits of life in Hout Bay over the ages.

Kronendal
Province: Western Cape
District: Hout Bay
Features: Today this fine example of an H-shaped Cape Dutch House is an historical monument. It dates back to 1677 and houses a restaurant, antique shop and gift shop.

Simon's Town Museum
Province: Western Cape
District: Simon's Town
Features: This museum has a large number of exhibits which depict the history of Simon's Town and its involvement with the naval port and docklands.

Martello Tower Naval Museum
Province: Cape Province
District: Simon's Town
Features: The museum is devoted to naval history and, in particular, South Africa's natural history.

The Warrior Toy Museum
Province: Western Cape
District: Simon's Town
Features: This museum holds a permanent exhibition of Dinky toys, dolls, Meccano, model cars, boats, trains and other toys.

Irma Stern Museum
Province: Western Cape
District: Rosebank
Features: A collection of works by this South African artist, antique furniture, art treasures from 600 BC and Congolese artefacts.

Rust-en-Vrede
Province: Western Cape
District: Durbanville
Features: Set in a beautiful landscaped garden, is an old Cape Dutch complex dating back to 1850. On exhibition, among others, are examples of contemporary works by South African ceramicists such as Bosch, Walford, Gerling and Saalberg as well as the Oude Meester collection, Lynnware and ethnic pottery

Village Museum
Province: Western Cape
District: Stellenbosch
Features: Comprises approximately 5,000 square metres of the oldest part of the town. Original houses depicting various period styles from Stellenbosch's history have been restored.

Cango Caves
Province: Western Cape
District: Oudtshoorn
Features: These caves are among the most beautiful calcite caves in the world. They are open all year round and tours are conducted daily.

Old St George's Church
Province: Western Cape
District: Knysna
Features: Built of local stone, the church was consecrated by Bishop Gray on 3 October 1855. It has been declared a national monument.

The Drostdy Museum
Province: Western Cape
District: George
Features: It has the largest selection of mechanical musical instruments in South Africa and a display depicting the history of wood in the area.

St Mark's Cathedral
Province: Western Cape
District: George
Features: Built in 1850, this is the smallest cathedral in South Africa and contains beautiful stained-glass windows.

St Peter and St Paul's Church
Province: Western Cape
District: George
Features: Built in 1843, it is the oldest Catholic church in South Africa. Permission must be obtained to visit the church.

Historical Museum
Province: Eastern Cape
District: Port Elizabeth
Features: One of the oldest surviving private dwelling houses in Port Elizabeth, built in 1827. Today it exhibits period furniture and contemporary items of domestic equipment.

Cuyler Manor
Province: Eastern Cape
District: Uitenhage
Features: This, the first Landdrost of Uitenhage, has been restored to its former elegance and forms an interesting cultural museum.

Ann Bryant Art Gallery
Province: Eastern Cape
District: East London
Features: This fine example of late-Victorian architecture houses a valuable art collection, all bequeathed to the city by the late Ann Bryant.

Gately House
Province: Eastern Cape
District: East London
Features: Built in 1878, this is a good example of a town house of this period, and virtually every item on display was acquired by the original owners over the years.

The Albany Museum
Province: Eastern Cape
District: Grahamstown
Features: The museum comprises the Natural History Museum, the 1820 Memorial Museum, the Observatory Museum, Fort Selwyn, and the Provost.

Fort Selwyn
Province: Eastern Cape
District: Grahamstown
Features: The fort ceased to be used by the army in 1870 and it fell into disrepair until 1925 when restoration began. In 1936 it was declared a National Monument. There is a pleasant tea room within the monument.

The Provost
Province: Eastern Cape
District: Grahamstown
Features: This was built as a military prison in the Drostdy gounds by the British Royal Engineers. It was proclaimed a National Monument in 1937 and restored. There is a delightful crafts shop within the monument.

The Alexander McGregor Memorial Museum
Province: Northern Cape
District: Kimberley
Features: This museum has a fine collection of San skeletons, weapons and implements.

Kimberley Mine Museum and Big Hole
Province: Northern Cape
District: Kimberley
Features: A cultural history museum re-creating the way of life of Kimberley's pioneers through original and carefully reconstructed buildings of historic and architectural importance.

FREE STATE

Military Museum
Province: Free State
District: Bloemfontein, Monument Road
Features: Weapons and domestic items used by Boer forces in the Anglo-Boer War.

National Museum
Province: Free State
District: Bloemfontein, Aliwal Street
Features: Fossil dinosaur remains from the Triassic period and the famous Florisbad skull.

GAUTENG & MPUMALANGA

The Africana Museum
Province: Gauteng
District: Johannesburg
Features: This museum is housed in the Johannesburg Public Library on Market Square and has displays dealing with the history of South Africa.

The Adler Museum
Province: Gauteng
District: Johannesburg
Features: Sited in the grounds of the South African Institute for Medical Research at the University of the Witwatersrand, Hospital Hill, Johannesburg. It features the history of medicine in general and of South Africa in particular. It houses special exhibits on pharmacy, a doctor's surgery, a dental museum, hospital, optometry, as well as an authentic reconstruction of an African herbalist's shop.

First National Bank Museum
Province: Gauteng
District: Johannesburg, Market Street
Features: Houses documents on the bank's history since 1838. Audiovisual display available.

Gold Reef City
Province: Gauteng
District: Johannesburg
Features: Visitors are taken back to the rumbustious days of the 'gold rush' in a typical, period mining town. See gold pouring, mine dancing and go down the old mine shaft.

South African Railway Museum
Province: Gauteng
District: Johannesburg
Features: Relics from the age of steam trains and trolley buses.

Pretoria Art Museum
Province: Gauteng
District: Pretoria, Arcadia Park
Features: Contains part of the Michaelis Collection of old Dutch and Flemish paintings.

The Voortrekker Monument Museum
Province: Gauteng
District: Pretoria
Features: Located below the Voortrekker Monument, the museum has exhibits depicting the social lives of the Voortrekkers (pioneers) during the years of the 'Great Trek'.

The Transvaal Museum of Natural History
Province: Gauteng
District: Pretoria, Paul Kruger Street
Features: It houses a 'Life's Genesis' exhibition, reflecting an integrated story of life throughout the animal kingdom. The Austin Roberts' Bird Hall contains a comprehensive collection of South African birds and offers an audio-visual display.

Melrose House
Province: Gauteng
District: Pretoria, Jacob Mare Street
Features: Located opposite Burgers Park, this is an historical museum which commemorates the signing of the peace treaty which ended the Anglo-Boer War in 1902.

The Pierneef Museum
Province: Gauteng
District: Pretoria, Vermeulen Street
Features: A collection of paintings reflecting the various periods in Pierneef's artistic career, is displayed in this museum which is found in the Eureka Building on Vermeulen Street.

National Cultural History and Open-Air Museum
Province: Gauteng
District: Pretoria, Boom Street
Features: Displays of rock engravings, ethnology and silverware, as well as an archaeological room are housed here.

Kruger House
Province: Gauteng
District: Pretoria
Features: Some of the modest personal belongings of President Paul Kruger are to be found there.

Block House
Province: Mpumalanga
District: Barberton
Features: Dating back to 1901, this was the earliest type of block house erected in South Africa. It was used as a position of defence against the Boer forces at the time of the British occupation of Barberton, during the Anglo-Boer War.

KWAZULU-NATAL

The Durban Museum
Province: KwaZulu-Natal
District: Durban
Features: This museum is housed in the City Hall, Durban. It contains natural history exhibits and marine, archaeological, numismatic and philatelic collections.

The Killie Campbell Museum
Province: KwaZulu-Natal
District: Durban, 22 Marriott Road
Features: The William Campbell furniture collection, an Africana library and the Mashu Ethnology collection featuring Zulu art and crafts are part of this important museum.

Local History Museum
Province: KwaZulu-Natal
District: Durban
Features: Located in the Old Court House, this museum houses a fine collection of exhibits depicting Natal's colonial past.

Natal Museum
Province: KwaZulu-Natal
District: Pietermaritzburg
Features: From dinosaurs to warfare to birdlife, the Natal museum has a diverse range of exhibits.

Macrorie House
Province: KwaZulu-Natal
District: Pietermaritzburg
Features: Once the home of Bishop William Macrorie, it is a fine example of the kind of gracious living some enjoyed during the 1860s.

Tatham Art Gallery
Province: KwaZulu-Natal
District: Pietermaritzburg
Features: It houses one of the finest art collections in the country, including works by Degas, Renoir, Sisley, Sickert and the Bloomsbury group.

Comrades Marathon House
Province: KwaZulu-Natal
District: Pietermaritzburg
Features: This museum tells the story of the annual 100-kilometre race and consists of honours boards, trophies, and an excellent collection of photographs, and memorabilia.

Vootrekker Museum
Province: KwaZulu-Natal
District: Pietermaritzburg
Features: Within the oldest double-storey house in Pietermaritzburg, many handmade articles form part of the collection representing Voortrekker life. Included in the museum is the house that belonged to Andries Pretorius, which was reconstructed on the museum site.

Caves

NELSPRUIT CAVES

Sudwala Caves
Province: Mpumalanga
District: Nelspruit
Features: Accommodation is available as well as caravan and camping sites. An adjacent outdoor museum features life-size exhibits of prehistoric animals.

KRUGERSDORF CAVES

Sterkfontein Caves
Province: North-West Province
District: Krugersdorp
Features: This is a treasure house of fossil remains. Guided tours throughout the year are run by the University of the Witswatersrand and may be undertaken daily from Tuesday to Sunday.

Monuments

CAPE PROVINCE

Cape Town
City Hall and Library (historical), city
Martin Melck House (historical), city
SA Library (historical), city
Bokaap Museum (historical), city
Cape Education Museum (historical), city
Cape Medical Museum (historical), city
Fort Wynyard (historical), Green Point
Herring Bequest Institute (historical), Green Point
Leewenhof (historical), Kuilsrivier
Michaelis (Old Town House), city
Natale Labia Museum (historical), Muizenberg
The Post Huys (historical), False Bay
Rhodes Memorial (historical), Rondebosch
Round House (historical), Camps Bay
Rugby Museum (historical), Newlands
SA Air Force Museum (historical), Ysterplaat Airforce Base
SA Maritime Museum (historical), Table Bay Harbour

Sendinggestig Museum (historical), city
Stal Plein (historical), city centre
Stem Pastorie Museum (historical), Simon's Town
Valkenberg Manor House (historical), Observatory
Victorian Clock Tower (historical), Table Bay
Harbour

Stellenbosch
De Witt House (historical), town centre
The Town Hall (historical), town centre
Devonshire House (architectural), town centre
Moederkerk (architectural), town centre
Kerkhuis (architectural), town centre
Morkelhuis (architectural), town centre
Saxonhof (architectural), town centre
Oude Pastorie (architectural), town centre
Libertas Parva Cellar (historical), town centre
Libertas Parva (historical), town centre
Rhenish Complex (architectural), town centre
VOC Kruithuis (historical), town centre

Grahamstown
Cathedral of St Michael and St George
(architectural), town centre
City Hall, Settler Memorial Tower (architectural),
town centre
Commemoration Church (architectural), town
centre
The Drostdy Gate (architectural), town centre
The Observatory Museum (historical), town
centre
The Priest's House (historical), town centre
St Patrick's Church (architectural), town centre
The Shaw Hall (architectural), town centre

East London
Queens Park (natural), town centre
Cuthbert's Building (architectural), town centre
City Hall (architectural), town centre
Old Library (architectural), town centre
The Wool Exchange (historical), town centre
Old Standard Bank Building (architectural), town
centre
Fort Glamorgan (historical), town centre
Needs Camp (natural), town centre
St Peter's Church (architectural), West Bank
John Baillie Memorial, Signal Hill (historical),
Signal Hill
Railway Station (historical), East Bank
Lock Street Goal (architectural), town centre

King William's Town
Victorian Drill Hall (historical)
Sutton House (historical)
Old Military Hospital (historical)
Kaffrarian Museum (historical)
Old Methodist Church (architectural)

Fort Beaufort
Fort Brown (historical)
Martello Tower (historical)

Victoria Bridge (historical)
Officers' Quarters (historical)
Officers' Mess (historical)

Queenstown
The Hexagon (architectural)
Portions of Queen's College (architectural)
The Museum (architectural)
Town Hall Façade (architectural)

Uitenhage
The Old Railway Station (historical)
King George V1 Coronation Tower (historical)

Port Elizabeth
Campanile (historical), Docks
Cora Terrace (historical), city centre
Donkin Reserve (historical), city centre
Fort Frederick (historical), city centre
Horse Memorial (historical), city centre
Market Square (historical), city centre
Old Grey Institute (historical), city centre
Concentration Camp (historical), city centre
Piet Retief Monument (historical), Summerstrand
Reserve Bank (architectural), city centre
Public Library (historical), city centre
St Mary's Collegiate Church (historical), city
centre
White House (historical), city centre

Kimberley
Duggan Cronin Bantu Gallery (art), city centre
McGregor Museum and Old Museum (historical),
city centre
Magersfontein Battle and Field Museum
(historical), outside centre
Mini War Museum (historical), city centre
Dutch Reformed Church (historical), city centre
Dunluce (historical), city centre

FREE STATE

Bloemfontein
Appeal Court (architectural), city centre
Supreme Court (architectural), city centre
City Hall (architectural), city centre
Fourth Raadsaal (architectural), city centre
Twin-Spired Church (architectural), city centre
Anglican Cathedral (architectural), city centre
Waldorf Building (architectural), city centre
Railway Station Building (architectural), city
centre
Jubileum Building (architectural), city centre
Jubileum Hall (architectural), city centre

KWAZULU-NATAL

Pietermaritzburg
Fine Victorian House (historical), city centre
Voortrekker House (architectural), city centre
Pooles's Building (architectural), city centre

Clark House (architectural), city centre
Old Presbyterian Church (architectural), city centre
City Hall (architectural), city centre
St George's Garrison Church (architectural), city centre
First National Bank (architectural), city centre
J.H. Isaacs Building (architectural), city centre
Reid's Building (architectural), city centre

GAUTENG

Johannesburg
Melville Koppies (archaeological), Melville
Windybrow (architectural), Hillbrow
City Hall Complex (architectural), city centre
Old Crown Mines (historical), Ormonde
Jeppe Boys High School (architectural), Kensington
St Margaret's House (architectural), Parktown
Cuthbert's Building (architectural), city centre

Pretoria
Skanskop Fort (historical), Groenkloof
The Union Buildings (architectural), city centre
General Smut's House (historical), Doornkloof
Pretoria High School for Girls/Boys (architectural), city centre
Voortrekker Monument (6km from the city)

MPUMALANGA

Barberton
De Kaap Stock Exchange (architectural), town centre
Globe Tavern (historical), town centre
Stopforth House (historical), town centre
Belhaven House Museum (historical), town centre
Fernlea House (historical), town centre
Masonic Temple (architectural), town centre
Lewis and Marks Building (architectural), town centre

Lydenburg
Echo Caves (archaeological), Lydenburg district
Remains of Voortrekker Fort (archaeological), Lydenburg district

Middleburg
Mapoch's Caves (archaeological), Middleburg district

Pilgrim's Rest
The town of Pilgrim's Rest (historical).

NORTHERN PROVINCE

Phalaborwa
Kgopolwe, Iron Age Site (archaeological), Phalaborwa
Sealeng, Iron Age Site (archaeological), Schiettocht

Pietersburg
British Fort (historical), Pietersburg district
Irish House (historical), town centre

Potgietersrus
Makapan Caves (archaeological), Potgietersrus district

Soutpansberg
Machemma Ruins (archaeological), Soutpansberg district
Stonehenge (archaeological), Soutpansberg district

Listings

Airlines

AER LINGUS
Nedbank Mall
145 Commissioner St
Johannesburg
PO Box 52851
Saxonwold 2132
Tel: (011) 880 4854
Fax: (011) 788 0890

AEROFLOT
PO Box 782
Auckland Park
2006
Tel: (011) 726 8070
Fax: (011) 726 2553

AIR AFRIQUE
The Courtyard,
Cnr Oxford and
Tyrwitt Ave
Rosebank
Johannesburg
PO Box 1807
Rivonia 2128
Tel: (011) 880 8537
Fax: (011) 880 8425

AIR AUSTRAL
Oxford Manor
Cnr Oxford and
Chaplin Road
Illovo 2196
PO Box 41022
Craighall 2024
Tel: (011)880 8055
Fax: (011) 880 7774

AIR BOTSWANA
257 Oxford Road
Block 1, Fedlife
Building
Illovo 2196
Tel: (011) 447 6078
Fax: (011) 447 4163

AIR FRANCE
Oxford Manor
Cnr Oxford and
Chaplin Road
Illovo 2196
PO Box 41022
Craighall 2024
Tel: (011) 880 8055
Fax: (011) 880 7774

PO Box 1722
Durban 4000
Tel: (031) 305 5416
Fax: (031) 304 6128

19th Floor, Golden
Acre
Cape Town 8001
Tel: (021) 21 4760
Fax: (021) 21 7061

AIR GABON
PO Box 1834
Kempton Park
1620
Tel: (011) 394 2566
Fax: (011) 975 4634

AIR INDIA
2nd Floor, Block
D, Oxford Manor
Cnr Oxford and
Chaplin Road
Illovo 2196
Tel: (011) 442 4421
Fax: (011) 442 4105

AIR LINK
Bonaero Park
Bonaero Drive
Johannesburg
PO Box 7529
Bonaero Park
1622
Tel: (011) 394
2430/1/5
Fax: (011) 394 2649

**AIR
MADAGASCAR**
PO Box 1834
Kempton Park
1620
Tel: (011) 394 1997
Fax: (011) 975 4634

AIR MALAWI
Colosseum
Building
Cnr Fox and Kruis
Streets
Johannesburg 2001
PO Box 10424
Johannesburg 2000
Tel: (011) 331 7627/8
Fax: (011) 331 7629

AIR MAURITIUS
7th Floor
Carlton Towers
Commissioner
Street
Johannesburg
2001
PO Box 9732
Johannesburg
2000
Tel: (011) 331 1918
Fax: (011) 331 1954
Telex: 486668

PO Box 4783
Durban 4000
Tel: (031) 3/4 6681
Fax: (031) 306 2709
Telex: 628609

11th Floor
Strand Towers
66 Strand Street
Cape Town 8001
Tel: (021) 21 6294
Fax: (021) 21 7371

AIR NAMIBIA
1st Floor
Dunkeld Place
12 North Road
Dunkeld West
PO Box 1795
Pinegowrie 2123
Tel: (011) 442 4461
Fax: (011) 442 4111

4 Shell House
Waterkant Street
Cape Town
PO Box 739
Cape Town 8000
Tel: (021) 21 6685
Fax: (021) 21 5840

AIR NEVADA
3rd Floor
Varig Centre
134 Fox Street
Johannesburg
PO Box 6287
Johannesburg
2000
Tel: (011) 331 2911
Fax: (011) 331 2648
Telex: 488196

AIR PORTUGAL
21st Floor
Sanlam Centre
Jeppe Street
Johannesburg 2001
PO Box 10008
Johannesburg 2000
Tel: (011) 337 1660
Fax: (011) 29 4207
Telex: 485050

PO Box 837
Durban 4000
Tel: (031) 304 9311
Telex: 622412

PO Box 788
Cape Town 8000
Tel: (021) 21 7224
Fax: (021) 21 7861
Telex: 526031

AIR SEYCHELLES
Suite 113
Time Square
Entrance B
Raleigh Street
Johannesburg
PO Box 27755
Yeoville 2143
Tel: (011) 487 3556
Fax: (011) 487 3635

AIR TANZANIA
PO Box 10424
Johannesburg
2000
Tel: (011) 331 7627
Fax: (011) 331 7629

AIR UK
PO Box 536
Randburg 2125
Johannesburg
Tel: (011) 787 1045
Fax: (011) 787 0406

PO Box 5579
Durban 4000
Tel: (031) 304 6235
Fax: (031) 307 5880

PO Box 3189
Cape Town 8000
Tel: (021) 23 1310
Fax: (021) 23 0007

AIR ZAIRE
PO Box 1641
Joubert Park 2044
Johannesburg
Tel: (011) 838 4933
Fax: (011) 838 6508

AIR ZIMBABWE
Upper Shopping
Level
Carlton Centre
Commissioner
Street
Johannesburg
PO Box 9398
Johannesburg 2000
Tel: (011) 331 1541
Fax: (011) 331 6970
Telex: 488561

PO Box 1689
Durban 4000
Tel: (031) 301 2671
Fax: (031) 301 0271
Telex: 621444

ALITALIA
1st Floor,
Oxford Manor
Cnr Oxford and
Chaplin Road
Illovo 2196
PO Box 937
Northlands 2116
Tel: (011) 880 9259
Fax: (011) 880 9277

PO Box 392
Durban 4000
Tel: (031) 301 8581
Fax: (031) 304 0526
Telex: 628436

PO Box 4768
Cape Town 8000
Tel: (021) 21 6335
Fax: (021) 25 1209
Telex: 527775

ALPHA AIR
247 Old Pretoria
Road
Midrand 1685
PO Box 1980
Halfway House 1685
Tel: (011) 315 1002
Fax: (011) 315 1645

AMERICAN AIRLINES
Dunkeld Crescent North
Albury Road
Hyde Park
Johannesburg
PO Box 41805
Craighall 2024
Tel: (011) 880 6370
Fax: (011) 880 6228

AMERICA WEST
Liberty Life Gardens
Cnr Broadway and Marcia Streets
Bruma
Johannesburg
Tel: (011) 616 7680
Fax: (011) 622 3565

ANSETT
Everite House
20 De Korte Street
Braamfontein
Johannesburg
PO Box 9874
Johannesburg 2000
Tel: (011) 339 4865
Fax: (011) 339 2474
Telex: 421740

AUSTRIAN AIRLINES
Atrium House
41 Stanley Avenue
Auckland Park
Johannesburg
PO Box 91998
Auckland Park 2006
Tel: (011) 482 3670
Fax: (011) 726 5871

PO Box 37739
Overport 6067
Durban
Tel: (031) 29 1663
Fax: (031) 28 3523

AUSTRALIAN AIRLINES
Village Walk
Maude Street and Rivonia Road
Sandton
PO Box 651350
Benmore 2010
Tel: (011) 884 5300
Fax: (011) 884 5312

PO Box 51182
Durban 4000
Tel: (031) 21 6061
Fax: (031) 21 7809

PO Box 3189
Cape Town 8000
Tel: (021) 419 9382
Fax: (021) 419 5208

BALKAN BULGARIAN AIRWAYS
PO Box 4509
Rivonia 2128
Tel: (011) 883 0957
Fax: (011) 883 0959

BOP AIR
Bonaero Drive
Bonaero Park
Johannesburg
PO Box Jan Smuts 1627
Tel: (011) 395 2500
Fax: (011) 395 2512
Telex: 747337

BRITISH AIRWAYS
158 Jan Smuts Avenue
Rosebank
Johannesburg
PO Box 535
Parklands 2121
Tel: (011) 441 8600
Fax: (011) 880 5784

PO Box 4756
Durban 4000
Tel: (031) 304 4741
Fax: (031) 305 7118
Telex: 622221

PO Box 976
Cape Town 8000
Tel: (021) 25 2970
Fax: (021) 418 2673
Telex: 527764

BRITISH MIDLAND
4th Floor,
Petrob House
343 Surrey Ave
Randburg 2615
PO Box 2140
Randburg 2125
Tel: (011) 789 6706/8/9
Fax: (011) 787 3800

CAMEROON AIRLINES
Tel: (011) 784 1161

CATHAY PACIFIC
1st Floor, Norwich Life Towers
Cnr Fredman Drive & Bute Lane
Sandton
Private Bag 14
Benmore 2010
Tel: (011) 883 9226
Fax: (011) 883 9073

1305 Kingsfield Place
30 Field Street
Durban 4000
Tel: (031) 306 4257/8
Fax: (031) 306 4259

PO Box 36317
Glosderry 7702
Cape Town
Tel: (021) 683 2106
Fax: (021) 683 1296
Telex: 521241

CHINA AIRLINES
President Place
1 Hood Avenue
Rosebank
Johannesburg
PO Box 1028
Parklands 2121
Tel: (011) 880 7125
Fax: (011) 880 7197

COMAIR
Bonaero Drive
Jan Smuts Airport
Johannesburg
PO Box 7015
Bonaero Park 1622
Tel: (011) 973 2911
Fax: (011) 973 1659
Telex: 746738

CONTINENTAL AIRLINES
7th Floor,
Everite House
20 De Korte Street
Braamfontein
Johannesburg
PO Box 9874
Johannesburg 2000
Tel: (011) 339 4865
Fax: (011) 339 2474
Telex: 421740

DELTA AIRLINES
2nd Floor
North City House
28 Melle Street
Braamfontein
Johannesburg
PO Box 4779
Johannesburg 2000
Tel: (011) 403 5702
Fax: (011) 339 3804
Telex: 420171

DRAGONFLY HELICOPTER ADVENTURES
PO Box 1042
White River 1240
Tel: (01311) 50 565
Fax: (01311) 51 061

EGYPT AIR
PO Box 55349
Northlands 2116
Tel: (011) 880 4126
Fax: (011) 880 4360

EL AL
5th Floor
South Wing
Nedbank Gardens
33 Bath Avenue
Rosebank 2196
Johannesburg
PO Box 52879
Saxonwold 2132
Tel: (011) 880 3232
Fax: (011) 447 3690
Telex: 421506

11th Floor
Saambou Building
45 Castle Street
Cape Town 8001
Tel: (021) 24 1273
Telex: 526472

ETHIOPIAN AIRLINES
PO Box 30693
Braamfontein 2017
Tel: (011) 880 3232
Fax: (011) 339 6348

GULF AIR
PO Box 6353
Johannesburg 2000
Tel: (011) 622 3524
Fax: (011) 622 3565

IBERIA
55 Padstow Street
Raceview Alberton
Johannesburg
PO Box 611
Alberton 1450
Tel: (011) 907 1632
Fax: (011) 907 2246

INTERAIR
Tel: (011) 397-1467
Fax: (011) 397-1468

JAPAN AIRLINES
Park Gallery
84 Corlett Drive
Melrose North
Northlands
PO Box 55524
Northlands 2116
Tel: (011) 442 8015
Fax: (011) 442 5745

KENYA AIRWAYS
PO Box 5946
Johannesburg 2000
Tel: (011) 337 8620
Fax: (011) 337 3670

KLM
Sable Place
1a Stan Road
Morningside
Johannesburg
PO Box 8624
Johannesburg 2000
Tel: (011) 881 9696
Fax: (011) 881 9691

PO Box 2732
Durban 4000
Tel: (031) 304 5701
Fax: (031) 307 1313
Telex: 620710

PO Box 3741
Cape Town 8000
Tel: (021) 21 1870
Fax: (021) 418 2712
Telex: 522843

KOREAN AIR
Everite House
20 De Korte Street
Braamfontein
Johannesburg
PO Box 9874
Johannesburg 2000
Tel: (011) 339 4865
Fax: (011) 339 2474
Telex: 421741

KWAZULU
NATIONAL
AIRLINES
Virginia Airport
Durban
PO Box 20096
Durban North 4016
Tel: (0358) 22254
Fax: (0358) 700 204

LAM
14th Floor,
Kine Centre
Commissioner St
Johannesburg
PO Box 7827
Johannesburg 2000
Tel: (011) 331 6081
Fax: (011) 331 7795

LESOTHO
AIRWAYS
PO Box 7049
Bonaero Park 1622
Johannesburg
Tel: (011) 970 1046
Telex: 747768

LETABA AIRWAYS
International
Arrival Hall
Jan Smuts Airport
PO Box 304
Lanseria 1748
Johannesburg
Tel: (011) 970 1511
Fax: (011) 394 0809
Telex: 746638

LTU INTERNAT.
AIRLINES
PO Box 2443
Parklands 2121
Tel: (011) 880 7684
Fax: (011) 880 7419

LUFTHANSA
1st Floor,
11 Wellington Road
Parktown
Johannesburg
PO Box 1083
Johannesburg 2000
Tel: (011) 484 4711
Fax: (011) 484 2750

PO Box 2410
Durban 4000
Tel: (031) 305 4262
Fax: (031) 307 3295
Telex: 620502

PO Box 3699
Cape Town 8000
Tel: (021) 25 1490
Fax: (021) 25 1420
Telex: 527554

MALAYSIA AIR
PO Box 47369
Parklands 2194
Tel: (011) 880 9614
Fax: (011) 880 9615

METAVIA
AIRLINES
Terminal C
PO Jan Smuts
Airport
Johannesburg 1627
Tel: (011) 394 3780
Fax: (011) 394 3726

PO Box 1082
Nelspruit 1200
Tel: (01311) 43141/2
Fax: (01311) 41266

NATIONAL
AIRLINES
PO Box 4598
Randburg 2125
Johannesburg
Tel: (011) 659 2506
Fax: (011) 659 1120

PO DF Malan
Airport 7525
Cape Town
Tel: (021) 934 0350
Fax: (021) 934 3373
Telex: 527814

NORTHWEST
AIRLINES
2nd Floor,
132 Jan Smuts
Avenue, Parkwood
Johannesburg
PO Box 447
Parklands 2121
Tel: (011) 880 4222
Fax: (011) 880 3015

OLYMPIC
AIRWAYS
4th Floor, JHI House
11 Cradock Ave
Johannesburg
PO Box 47224
Parklands 2121
Tel: (011) 880 4120
Fax: (011) 880 7075

28th Floor,
Suite 2802
320 West Street
Durban 4001
Tel: (031) 307 7788
Telex: 622850

PO Box 1328
Cape Town 8000
Tel: (021) 23 0260
Fax: (021) 24 4166
Telex: 527909

PAKISTAN (PIA)
2nd Floor,
Liberty Life Bldg
Cnr Broadway and
Marcia Street
Bruma 2198
Johannesburg
Tel: (011) 6229310

PROGRESS AIR
Office No 10,
Lanseria Airport
Johannesburg
PO Box 75
Lanseria 1748
Tel: (011) 659 2745
Fax: (011) 659 1726
Telex: 431031

QANTAS
3rd Floor,
Petrob House
Maude Street and
Rivonia Road

Sandton
PO Box 651350
Benmore 2010
Tel: (011) 884 5300
Fax: (011) 884 5312

PO Box 51182
Durban 4000
Tel: (031) 21 6061
Fax: (031) 21 7809

PO Box 3189
Cape Town 8000
Tel: (021) 419 9382
Fax: (021) 419 5208

ROYAL SWAZI AIR
2nd Floor, Finance
House, Ernst
Oppenheimer Drive
Bruma Office
Park 2198
Tel: (011) 616 7323
Fax: (011) 616 7757

SABENA
25th Floor,
Carlton Towers
Commissioner Str
CC Box 99/133
Johannesburg 2001
Tel: (011) 331 8166
Fax: (011) 331 6937
Telex: 487464

PO Box 5144
Durban 4000
Tel: (031) 304 4034
Fax: (031) 304 7238
Telex: 622367

PO Box 6600
Roggebaai 8012
Cape Town
Tel: (021) 21 7957
Fax: (021) 419 5713
Telex: 527594

SAFAIR LINES
PO Box DF Malan
Airport 7525
Cape Town
Tel: (021) 973 1921
Fax: (021) 934 0728
Telex: 520246

SCENIC AIRLINES
Everite House
20 De Korte Street
Braamfontein
PO Box 9874
Johannesburg 2000
Tel: (011) 339 4865
Fax: (011) 339 2474
Telex: 421740

SHABAIR
PO Box 59201
Kengray 2100
Tel: (011) 331 9584
Fax: (011) 331 9316

SINGAPORE
AIRLINES
257 Oxford Road
Illovo 2196
PO Box 997
Johannesburg 2100
Tel: (011) 880 8560
Fax: (011) 880 8792

PO Box 4337
Durban 4000
Tel: (031) 301 4250
Fax: (031) 304 2488
Telex: 620784

PO Box 1400
Cape Town 8000
Tel: (021) 419 0495
Fax: (021) 419 6226

SOUTH AFRICAN
AIRWAYS (SAA)
PO Box 7778
Johannesburg 2000
Tel: (011) 333 6504
Fax: (011)333 8132

SWISSAIR
Swisspark
10 Queen Road
Parktown
Johannesburg
PO Box 3866
Johannesburg 2000
Tel: (011) 484 1980
Fax: (011) 484 1999
Telex: 423662

PO Box 1012
Durban 4000
Tel: (031) 304 0653
Fax: (031) 304 1039
Telex: 622944

PO Box 3352
Cape Town 8000
Tel: (021) 21 4938
Fax: (021) 21 4754
Telex: 527499

THERON
AIRWAYS
Office No 19,
Lanseria Airport
PO Box 40
Lanseria 1748
Tel: (011) 659 2738
Fax: (011) 659 2690
Telex: 428026

TRANSKEI
AIRWAYS
Office 43, Intl
Departure Lounge
Jan Smuts Airport
Johannesburg
PO Jan Smuts
Airport 1627
Tel: (011) 970 2057
Fax: (011) 973 3752
Telex: 747537

PO Box 773
Umtata, Transkei
Tel: (0471) 24638
Fax: (0471) 23368
Telex: 0968727

TWA
7th Floor, Regent House
87 Market Street
PO Box 9564
Johannesburg 2000
Tel: (011) 333 4028
Fax: (011) 333 0074

UGANDA AIRLINES
PO Box 11298
Johannesburg 2000
Tel: (011) 616 4672
Fax: (011) 616 4620

UNITED AIRLINES
Sandton Terrace
137c Eleventh Street
Parkmore
Johannesburg
PO Box 650052
Benmore 2010
Tel: (011) 884 6767
Fax: (011) 884 2442
Telex: 430071

UTA (AIR FRANCE)
1st floor, Oxford Manor
Cnr Oxford and Chaplin
Road
Illovo 2196
PO Box 41022
Graighall 2024
Tel: (011) 880 8040
Fax: (011) 880 7772

VARIG
Varig Centre
134 Fox Street
PO Box 4142
Johannesburg 2000
Tel: (011) 331 2471
Fax: (011) 331 9803
Telex: 485350

PO Box 7397
Roggebaai 8012
Cape Town
Tel: (021) 21 1850
Fax: (021) 419 8338
Telex: 520147

VIRGIN ATLANTIC
AIRWAYS
Petrob House
343 Surrey Avenue
Randburg 2125
Johannesburg
PO Box 2140
Randburg 2125
Tel: (011) 886 6121
Fax: (011) 886 0250
Telex: 420810

Musgrave Road
PO Box 51182
Durban 4062
Tel: (031) 21 6061
Fax: (031) 21 7809

1502 Sanlam
Golden Acre
PO Box 3189
Cape Town 8000
Tel: (021) 419 9382
Fax: (021) 419 5208

ZAMBIA AIRWAYS
PO Box 88
Cyrildene 2026
Tel: (011) 622 7281
Fax: (011) 622 6239

Air Charter

AIR 2000
Terminal Building
PO Box 120
Lanseria 1748
Tel: (011) 659 2649
Fax: (011) 659 2931
Telex: 430229

AIRNET AVIATION
PO Box 224
Lanseria 1748
Tel: (011) 659 1420
Fax: (011) 659 1373
Telex: 430029

ATAIR EXECUTIVE JET
CHARTER
PO Box 169
Lanseria 1748
Tel: (011) 659 2528
Fax: (011) 659 2403

COURT HELICOPTERS
PO Box 18115
Rand Airport 1419
Tel: (011) 827 8907
Fax: (011) 824 1660

HELIQUIP (PTY) LTD
PO Box 5526
Halfway House 1685
Tel: (011) 315 0001
Fax: (011) 805 3409

INTER-AIR (PTY) LTD
PO Box 18046
Rand Airport
Tel: (011) 827 9804
Fax: (011) 827 9805
Telex: 749418

PO Box 259
Lanseria Airport 1748
Tel: (011) 659 1574
Fax: (011) 659 2498
Telex: 4233550

K-AIR
Main Terminal Building
Rand Airport
PO Box 18072
Rand Airport 1419
Tel: (011) 827 5488
Fax: (011) 827 5489

KWENA AIR (SA) (PTY)
Honeywood Park
Cnr Humber / Morris Str
Woodmead Sandtdon
PO Box 4565
Rivonia 2128
Tel: (011) 803 4921
Fax: (011) 803 4566
Telex: 421002

NATIONAL AIRWAYS
CORP (PTY) LTD
PO Box 18016
Rand Airport 1419
Tel: (011) 827 0504
Fax: (011) 824 2678

PO Box 293
Lanseria 1748
Tel: (011) 659 2630
Fax: (011) 659 1120
Telex: 423015

ROSSAIR
PO Box 482
Lanseria 1748
Tel: (011) 659 2980
Fax: (011) 659 1389
Telex: 421331

PO Box 4711
Halfway House 1685
Tel: (011) 315 5888
Fax: (011) 315 5896

SAFAIR
PO D.F. Malan 7525
Cape Town
Tel: (021) 934 0572
Fax: (021) 934 8796
Telex: 520246

PO Box 938
Kempton Park 1620
Tel: (011) 973 1921
Fax: (011) 973 4620
Telex: 742242

SAFARI SERVICES
PO Box 1405
Nelspruit 1200
Tel: (01311) 26259
Fax: (01311) 28146

SPEED AIR (PTY) LTD
Terminal Building
Lanseria
PO Box 641
Jukskei Park
Tel: (011) 659-2885
Fax: (011) 659-1775

STREAMLINE AIR
CHARTER
PO Box 18152
Rand Airport
Germiston 1419
Tel: (011) 824 1650/1/2
Fax: (011) 824 1757

Airports

D.F. Malan Airport
International Airport
Cape Town
Tel: (021) 934 0452

Louis Botha Airport
International Airport
Durban
Tel: (031) 426156

Jan Smuts Airport
International Airport
Johannesburg
Tel: (011) 975 1185

H.F. Verwoed Airport
Port Elizabeth
Tel: (041) 5077204

B.J. Voster Airport
Kimberley
Tel: (0531) 8511241

Ben Schoeman Airport
East London
Tel: (0431) 460211

P W Botha Airport
George
Tel: (0441) 769310

Pierre van Ryneveld
Upington
Tel: (054) 311364

Lanseria Airport
Randburg (North
of Johannesburg)
Tel: (011) 659 2750

Rand Airport
Germiston
Tel: (011) 827 8884

Grand Central
Airport
Half-way House
(North of
Johannesburg)
Tel: (011) 805 3166

**South African
Airways Offices in
South Africa**

Bloemfontein
Liberty Building
Cnr Andrew &
Kerk Streets
Tel: (051) 473 811

Cape Town
Southern Life
Building
Cnr Lower Burg St
& Riebeck Streets
Tel: (021) 25 4610

Durban
Shell House
Cnr Smith &
Aliwal Streets
Tel: (031) 305 6491

East London
Terminus Street
Tel: (0431) 44 5299

George
Elsa le Roux
Building
Van der Stel Plain
Tel: (0441) 738 448

Johannesburg
Airways Towers
Cnr Wolmarans
and Rissik Streets
Tel: (011) 333 6504

Pietermaritzburg
Shell House
Cnr Smith &
Aliwal Street
Tel: (0331) 958 2546

Port Elizabeth
69 Greenacres
Shopping Centre
Tel: (041) 34 4444

Pretoria
De Bruyn Park
Building
Cnr Vermeulen &
Andries Streets
Tel: (012) 328 3215

Stellenbosch
85 Andringa Street
Tel: (021) 886 6383

Foreign Diplomatic Missions

Please note that
most missions are
in the
Johannesburg-
Pretoria area, but
that missions
transfer their
political staff to
Cape Town during
the Parliamentary
Sessions held in
that city during the
first six months of
the year. Many
embassies also
have consulates in
Johannesburg,
phone numbers
given for details.

ANGOLA
2nd and 3rd floor,
400 Struktura
Building
533 Church Street
Arcardia, 0083
Tel: (012) 443643/4
(3rd floor)
3416999/3 (2nd
floor)
Fax: (012) 443645

ARGENTINA
Embassy
200 Standard Plaza
440 Hilda Street
Hatfield 0083
Pretoria
Tel: (012) 433527
Fax: (012) 433521

Consulate
26 Ameshoff Street
Braamfontein
Johannesburg 2001
PO Box 31909
Braamfontein 2017
Tel: (011) 3392382
Telex: (011) 428302

AUSTRALIA
Embassy
292 Orient Street
(Cnr Schoeman Str)
Arcadia 0083
Private Bag X150
Pretoria 0001
Tel: (012) 3423740
Fax: (012) 3424222
Visa section: (012)
3423750-3

AUSTRIA
Embassy
1109 Duncan Street
Brooklyn 0011
PO Box 851
Pretoria 0001
Tel: (012) 462483
Fax: (012) 461151

BELGIUM
Embassy
275 Pomona Street
Muckleneuk
Pretoria 0002
Tel: (012) 443201/2
Fax: (012) 443216

BOTSWANA
Representative
Office
Infotec Building
1090 Arcadia Street
Arcadia 0083
Pretoria
PO Box 57035
Arcadia 0007
Tel: (012) 3424760

BRAZIL
Embassy
Sanlam Building
353 Festival Street
(Cnr Arcadia Str)
Arcadia 0083
Pretoria
PO Box 3269
Pretoria 0001
Tel: (012) 435559
Fax: (012) 3421419

BULGARIA
Embassy
Techno Plaza East
305 Brooks Street
Menlo Park 0081
Pretoria
Tel: (012) 3423720
Fax: (012) 34237121

CANADA
Embassy
Nedbank Plaza
Cnr Church &
Beatrix Streets
Arcadia 0083
Pretoria
PO Box 26006
Arcadia 0007
Tel: (012) 3243970
Fax: (012) 3231564
Telex: 322112
(CANDOM)

Visa Office
4th Floor,
Nedbank Plaza
9 Cnr Church &
Beatrix Streets
PO Box 26016
Arcadia 0007
Tel: (012) 3243976/7

CHILE
Embassy
5th Floor,
Campus Centre
Burnett Street
Hatfield 0083
PO Box 2073
Pretoria 0001
Tel: (012) 3421511
Fax: (012) 3421658

CHINA(REPUBLIC)
Embassy
1147 Schoeman Str
Hatfield 0083
Pretoria
PO Box 649
Pretoria 0001
Tel: (012) 436071-3
Fax: (012) 435816

CHINA (PEOPLES
REPUBLIC)
972 Pretorius Street
Arcadia 0083
Pretoria
Tel: (012) 3424194
Fax: (012) 3424244
Visa: (012)3424244

CZECH REPUBLIC
Embassy
936 Pretorious Street
Arcadia 0083
PO Box 3326
Tel: (012) 3423477
Fax: (012) 432033

DENMARK
Embassy
8th Floor,
Sanlam Centre
Cnr Andries and
Pretorius Streets
PO Box 2942
Pretoria 0001
Tel: (012) 3220595
Fax: (012) 3220596

FINLAND
Embassy
628 Leyds Street
Muckleneuk
Pretoria
PO Box 443
Pretoria 0001
Tel: (012) 3430275
Fax: (012) 3433095

FRANCE
Embassy
807 George Avenue
Arcadia 0083
Pretoria
Tel: (012) 435564/5
Fax: (012) 433481

GABON
Holiday Inn
Garden Court
Cnr Van der Walt
and Minaar Streets
Pretoria
PO Box 2301
Tel: (012) 3227500
ext 402-404
Fax: (012) 3229429

GERMANY
Embassy
180 Blackwood
Street Arcadia
Pretoria
PO Box 2023
Pretoria 0001
Tel: (012) 3443854-9
Fax: (012) 3439401
Telex: 321386 AA
PRE
(DIPLOGERMA
PRETORIA)

GREECE
Embassy
995 Pretorius
Street
Arcadia
Pretoria 0083
Tel: (012) 437351-3
Fax: (012) 434313
Telex: 320520
(GREEK EMBASSY)

GUATELMALA
Consulate
16th Floor
2 Long Street
Cape Town 8001
PO Box 1661
Cape Town 8000
Tel: (021) 4182020
Fax: (021) 4181280
Telex: 522266

745 Saddle Drive
(Cnr Woodmead
Drive and van
Reenen Avenue)
Woodmead Park
Woodmead,
Sandton 2199
PO Box 783551
Sandton 2146
Tel: (011) 8045080
Fax: (011) 8044844

HUNGARY
Embassy
959 Arcadia Street
Hatfield 0083
PO Box 27077
Sunnyside 0132
Tel: (012) 433020/30
Fax: (012) 433029

Commercial Section
2 Valley Road
Benmore Gardens
Sandton
PO Box 78640
Sandton 2146
Tel: (011) 8845759
Fax: (011) 8845904

Consulate-General
301 Rygersdal
44 Camp Ground
Road
PO Box 555
Rondebosch 7700
Tel: (021) 6861502
Fax: (021) 6861502

ICELAND
Consulate
15 Landsborough Rd
Robertsham
Southdale 2135
PO Box 82298
Southdale 2135
Tel: (011) 4333730
Fax: (011) 6803766

INDIA
Johannesburg 2000
2011 Sanlam Centre
Jeppe Street
Johannesburg 2001
Tel: (011) 3331525
Fax: (011) 330690

IRAN
See Switzerland

IRELAND
Consulate
8/9/10 London Hse
21 Loveday Street
Johannesburg 2001
Tel: (011) 8365869

ISRAEL
Embassy
Dashing Centre
339 Hilda Street
Hatfield 0083
Pretoria
PO Box 3726
Pretoria 0001
Tel: (012) 4212222
Fax: (012) 3421442
Telex: 322168
MEMISRAEL
PRETORIA

ITALY
Embassy
796 George Av
Arcadia 0083
Pretoria
Tel: (012) 435541-4
Fax: (012) 435547
Telex: 321397
(ITAL DIP)

JAPAN
Embassy
Sanlam Building
353 Festival Street
Hatfield 0083
Pretoria
PO Box 11434
Brooklyn 0011
Tel: (012) 3422100/5
Fax: (012) 433922

KOREA
Embassy
Suite 103
Infotech Building
1090 Arcadia Street
Hatfield 0083
PO Box 11056
Brooklyn 0011
Tel: (012) 3423401/2
Fax: (012) 3424675

LEBANON
7-16th Avenue
Lower Houghton
Johannesburg 2198
Tel: (011) 4831106/7
Fax: (011) 4831810

LESOTHO
Embassy
6th Floor,
West Tower
Momentum Centre
343 Pretorius Street
Pretoria
PO Box 55817
Arcadia 0007
Tel: (012) 3226090-2
Fax: (012) 3220376
Telex: 482985

LIECHTENSTEIN
See Switzerland

LUXEMBOURG
Consulate
Suite 72,
Heerengracht
87 De Korte Street
Braamfontein
Johannesburg
PO Box 31558
Braamfontein 2017
Tel: (011) 4033852/3
Fax: (011) 3391885
Telex: 427739 SA

MALAWI
Embassy
1st Floor,
Delta Building
471 Monica Road
Lynnwood
Pretoria 0081
PO Box 11172
Brooklyn 0011
Tel: (012) 477827
Fax: (012) 3484649
Telex: 322017
MALAWIAN-
PRETORIA

Consulate-General
1st floor, Sable
Centre House
41 De Korte Street
Braamfontein
PO Box 31752
Braamfontein 2017
Tel: (011) 3391569
Fax: (011) 3396926

MAURITIUS
Consulate-General
4th Floor,
Infotech Building
1090 Arcadia Street
Hatfield 0083
Pretoria
Tel: (012) 3421283/4

MONACO
Consulate
Credit Lyonnais,
Suite 4315,
Carlton Centre
Commissioner
Street
Johannesburg 2001
PO Box 99300
Johannesburg 2000
Tel: (011) 8830600
Fax:(011) 3317578

MOROCCO
799 Schoeman
Street
(Cnr Farenden
Street)
Arcadia 0083
Pretoria
Tel:(012) 3430230
Fax: (012) 3430613

MOZAMBIQUE
Embassy
199 Beckett Street
Arcadia
PO Box 40750
Arcadia 0083
Tel: (012) 3437840
Fax: (012) 3430959
Telex: 484842 SA

Trade Mission
2nd Floor,
Glencairn Building
73 Market Street
PO Box 4635
Johannesburg 2000
Tel: (011) 3334807
Fax: (001) 3334918

NAMIBIA
Suite 2, Eikendal,
Tulbach Park
1234 Church Street
Colbyn 0083
Pretoria
PO Box 29806
Sunnyside 0132
Tel: (012) 3423520
Fax: (012) 3423565

**THE
NETHERLANDS**
Embassy
825 Arcadia Street
Arcadia 0083
PO Box 117
Pretoria 0001
Tel: (012) 3443910-5
Fax: (012) 3439950
Telex: 321332
NETH SA
(HOLLANDIA)

NORWAY
Embassy
7th Floor,
Sancardia
524 Church Street
Arcadia 0084
PO Box 9843
Pretoria 0001
Tel: (012) 3234790-3
Fax: (012) 3234789

PAKISTAN
Liason Office
35 Marais Street
Brooklyn 0181
Pretoria
Tel: (012) 461080
Fax: (012) 455470

**PAPAU NEW
GUINEA**
See Australia

PARAGUAY
Embassy
189 Strelitzia Road
Waterkloof
Heights
Pretoria 0181
PO Box 95774,
Waterkloof 0145
Tel: (012) 451081/2
Fax: (012) 451083

PERU
See Brazil

POLAND
Embassy
14 Amos Street
Colbyn 0083
Pretoria
Tel: (012) 43261-3
Fax: (012) 342608

Commercial
56 Sixth Street
Houghton 2198
PO Box 1547
Houghton 2041
Tel: (011) 4552127
Fax: (011) 4425359

PORTUGAL
Embassy
599 Leyds Street
Muckleneuk 0002
Pretoria
PO Box 27102
Sunnyside 0132
Tel: (012) 3412340-2
Fax: (012) 3413975

Consular
701 Van Erkom Bdg
217 Pretorius Street
Pretoria
Tel: (012) 262141/
3235554

ROMANIA
Embassy
117 Charles Street
Brooklyn 0181
Pretoria
PO Box 11295
Brooklyn 0011
Tel: (012) 466941
Fax: (012) 466947

Consulate-General
16 Breda Street
Gardens
Cape Town 8001
Tel: (021) 4614860
Fax: (021) 4612485

RUSSIA
Embassy
First National Bank
Plaza
1105 Park Street
(Cnr Hilda Street)
Hatfield 0083
Pretoria
PO Box 6743
Pretoria 0001
Tel: (012) 432731/2
Fax: (012) 432842

360

Consular Office
135 Bourke Street
Sunnyside 0002
Tel: (012) 3438636

Consulate-General
8 Riebeck Street
Cape Town 8001
Tel: (021) 6861907

RWANDA
Consulate-General
Suite 113,
Infotech Building
Hatfield 0083
Pretoria
PO Box 55224
Arcadia 0007
Tel: (012) 3421740/1
Fax: (012) 3421743

SINGAPORE
Consulate
Village Walk Offices
(Cnr Rivonia Road
and Maude Street)
Sandown 2146
Johannesburg
PO Box 1597
Parklands 2121
Tel: (011) 8831422
Fax: (011) 8832766

SLOVACK
REPUBLIC
103 Matroosberg Rd
Waterkloof Heights
Pretoria 0181
Tel: (012) 3463650
Fax: (012) 460226

SPAIN
Embassy
169 Pine Street
Arcadia 0083
PO Box 1633
Pretoria 0001
Tel: (012) 3443875
Fax: (012) 3434891

SURINAM
See The
Netherlands

SWAZILAND
Trade Mission
915 Rand Central
165 Jeppe Street
Johannesburg
PO Box 8030
Johannesburg 2000
Tel: (011) 299776-8
Fax: (011) 299763

SWEDEN
Legation
Old Mutual Centre
167 Andries Street
Pretoria 0002
PO Box 1664
Pretoria 0001
Tel: (012) 211050
Fax: (012) 3232776
Telex: 321193
SWEDE SA

SWITZERLAND
Embassy
818 George Avenue
Arcadia 0083
PO Box 2289
Pretoria 0001
Tel: (012) 436707
Fax: (012) 436771
Telex: SA 322106

THAILAND
Consulate-General
7th Floor,
JHI House
11 Cradock Ave
Rosebank 2196
Johannesburg
PO Box 78786
Sandton 2146
Tel: (011) 8803999
Fax: (011) 4473892

TURKEY
Consulate -General
Sandown 2196
PO Box 650931
Benmore 2010
Tel: (011) 8849060-3
Fax: (011) 8849064

UNITED
KINGDOM
Embassy
Greystoke
225 Hill Street
Arcadia 0083
Pretoria
Tel: (012) 433121
Fax: (012) 433207

UNITED STATES
OF AMERICA
Embassy
877 Pretorius Street
Arcadia 0083
PO Box 9536
Pretoria 0001
Tel: (012) 3421048
Fax: (012)3422299/
44

URUGUAY
Embassy
1st Floor,
Tulbagh Park
Delheim Suite
1234 Church Street
Colbyn 0083
PO Box 3247
Pretoria 0001
Tel: (012) 432829/31
Fax: (012) 432833

8th Floor,
Vogue House
Thibault Square
Cape Town
PO Box 4774
Cape Town 8000
Tel: (021) 251847
Fax: (021) 253308
Telex: 524176
(URUSUD)

VENDA
Embassy
821 Arcadia Street
Arcadia
PO Box 4664
Pretoria 0001
Tel: (012) 3443950/3
Fax: (012) 3445615

YUGOSLAVIA
1st Floor,
Window and Door
Centre Building
275 Struben Street
PO Box 7753
Pretoria 0001
Tel: (012) 216114
Fax: (012) 216114

ZAMBIA
353 Sanlam Centre
Festival Street
Hatfield 0083
Pretoria
Tel: (012) 452838

ZIMBABWE
Trade Mission
6th Floor, Bank of
Lisbon Building
37 Sauer Street
Johannesburg
2000
PO Box 61736
Marshalltown 2107
Tel: (011) 8382156-
9

SA Missions Abroad

ANGOLA
South African
Embassy
Rua Manuel
Fernandes
Caldeira 6B
(Postal address)
Caixa Postal 6212
Luanda
Tel: (09-2442)
39-7391

ARGENTINA
South African
Embassy
Avenida Marcelo T
de Alvear
590-8 Piso
Bueno Aires 1058
Tel: (0954-1)
311-8991-8

Comodoro
Rivadavia
Carrero
Patagonico 2915
9000 Comodoro
Rivadavia
Chubut
Tel: (0967) 26195
28671

AUSTRALIA
South African
High Commission
Rhodes Place
State Circle
Yarralumla
Canberra ACT 2600
Tel: (0961-6)
273-2424

AUSTRIA
South African
Embassy
Sandgasse 33
Vienna A-1190
Tel: (0943-1)
32-6493

Graz
13/2
Villefortgrasse
Tel: (0943) 316-37671

Innsbruck
Adamgasse 15
Tel: (0943-512)
577-333

BAHRAIN
South African
Embassy
Villa No 1520
Road 7329
Al-Qadim
New Tubli
Manama
PO Box 15574
Adliya
Tel: (09937) 78-6699

BELGIUM
South African
Embassy
26 Rue de la Loi B
7/8
Brussels 1040
Tel: (0932-2)
230-6845

Antwerp
9 Eiken Street
Tel: (0932-3)
31-4960

Liege
Quai du Condroz
21/011
Tel: (09324) 42-8084

BOLIVIA
La Paz
Rosendo Gutierrez
No 482
Tel: (09591-2)
367-754

BOTSWANA
South African
High Commission
IGI House
The Mall
Private Bag 0042
Gaberone
Tel: (09267)
30-4800-3

BRAZIL
South African
Embassy
Avenida das Nacoes
Lote 6
Brasilia DF 70406-
900
Tel: (0955-61)
223-4873

South Africa
Consulate-General
1754 Avenida
Paulista
12th Floor,
Sao Paulo SP
01310-920
Tel: (0955-11)
285-0433

Rio de Janeiro
Rua Lauuro Muller
116/1107
Botafogo 22299
Rio de Janeiro
22270
Tel: (0955-21)
533-0158

BULGARIA
South African
Embassy
3 Vasil Aprilov
Street
Sofia 1540
Tel: (09359-2)
44-2916

CANADA
South African
High Commission
15 Sussex Drive
Ottawa, Ontario
K1M 1MB
Tel: (091-613)
744-0330

South Africa
Consulate-General
Suite 2615
1 Place Ville Marie
Montreal
Tel: (091-514)
878-9231-2

South Africa
Consulate-General
Stock Exchange
Tower
Suite 2300
2 First Canadian
Place
Cnr York and King
Street West
PO Box 424
Toronto
Ontario M5X 1E3
Tel: (091-416)
364-0314

CHILE
South African
Embassy
Avda 11 de
Septiembre 2353
Piso 16
Providencia
(Postal address)
Casilla 16189
Santiago 9
Tel: (0956-2)
231-3361

CHINA (BEIJING)
South African
Office C801
Beijing Lufthansa
Centre
50 Liangmaqiao Rd
Chaoyang District
Beijing 100016 PRC
Tel: (0986-1)
465-1941

CHINA(TAIWAN)
South African
Embassy
Bank Tower
205 Tun Hwa
North Road
PO Box 540
Taipei, Taiwan, ROC
Tel: (09886-2)
715-3251/4

COLUMBIA
Calle 17, nr 10-16
Oficina 502
Bogota
Tel: (0957-1)
241-1291

**CZECH
REPUBLIC**
South African
Embassy
65 Ruska Street
PO Box 133
100-00 Prague 10
Tel: (0942-2)
6731-1114

DENMARK
South African
Embassy
Gammel Vartov
Vej 8
PO Box 128
DK-2900 Hellerup
Copenhagen
Tel: (0945-31) 18-
0155

EGYPT
South African
Embassy
18th Floor,
Nile Tower Bldg
21/23 Giza Street
Cairo
Tel: (09202)
571-7238/9

ETHIOPIA
South African
Embassy
PO Box 1091
Addis Ababa
Tel: (09251-1)
711-330

FINLAND
South African
Embassy
Rahapajankatu 1A5
00160 Helsinki 16
Tel: (09358-0)
65-8288

FRANCE
South African
Embassy
59 Quai d'Orsay
75343 Paris
Cedex 07
Tel: (0933-1)
4555-9237

South Africa
Consulate-General
408 Avenue du
Prado
(Postal address)
Boite Postale 105
13008 Marseilles
Tel: (0933-91)
22-6633

Le Havre
Tel: (0933-35)
228-181

Lille
104 Rue Nationale
Tel: (0933-20)
575-473
Telex: (0933-20)
120-112

Reunion
St Denis
2 Rue de la Dique
Tel: (09262) 210-
619

GABON
South African
Embassy
2nd Floor
Les Arcades
Building
(Postal address)
Boite Postal 4063
Libreville
Tel: (09241)
77-4530/1

GERMANY
South African
Embassy
Auf der Hostert 3
5300 Bonn 2
Tel: (0949-228)
8-2010

South African
Interest Office
Douglasstrasse 9
14193 Berlin
Tel: (0949-30)
82-5011

South Africa
Consulate-General
20149 Hamburg
Tel: (0949-40)
450-1200

South Africa
Consulate-General
18th Floor
37-39 Ulmenstrasse
60325 Frankfurt
Tel: (0949-69)
719-1130

Bremen
Tel: (0949-421)
467-7081

Hanover
Tel: (0949-511)
57021

Lubeck
Tel: (0949-451)
57021

Düsseldorf
Tel: (0949-211)
43-4068

Kiel
Tel: (0949 431)
68921

South Africa
Consulate-General
Sendlinger-Tor-
Platz 5
80336 Munich
Tel: (0949-89)
231-1630

GREECE
South African
Embassy
60 Kiffisias
Avenue
Marousi 15125
PO Box 14281
GR 115-10 Athens
Tel: (0930-1)
680-6645

HONG KONG
South Africa
Consulate-General
27th Floor
Sunning Plaza
10 Hysan Avenue
Causeway Bay
Tel: (09852)
2577-3279

HUNGARY
South African
Embassy
Rakoczi ut 1-3
1088 Budapest
(Postal address)
Budapest PF 295
H-1364 Hungary
Tel: (0936 1)
266-2148

ICELAND
South Africa
Consulate-General
Hafnarstraeti 7
IS-101 Reykjavik
PO Box 462
IS-121 Reykjavik
Tel: (09354-1)
562-9522

INDIA
South Africa
Consulate-General
Room 602
Hotel President
Cuffy Parade
Bombay 400 005
Tel: (09-9122)
215-0808

South Africa High
Commission
B-18 Vasant Marg
Vasant Vihar
New Delhi 110057
Tel: (09-9111)
611-9411

INDONESIA
South African
Embassy
Borobudur
Intercontinental
Hotel
Sumatra Room 28
Jalan Lapangan
Ban Teng Selatan
Jakarta
Tel: (0962-21)
350-0176

IRELAND
Dublin
SA Embassy
Trafalgar Square
London WC2N
5DP
Tel: (0944-71)
930-4488

ISRAEL
South African
Embassy
Top Tower
16th Floor
Dizengoff Street
Tel Aviv 54734
PO Box 7138
Tel Aviv 61071
Tel: (09972-3)
525-2566

ITALY
South African
Embassy
Via Tanaro 14
Rome 00198
Tel: (0939 6)
841-9794

South Africa
Consulate-General
Vicolo San Giovanni
Sul Muro 4
(Postal address)
Casella Postale 1468
Milan 20101
Tel: (0939-2)
80-9030

Naples
Tel: (0939-81)
551-7519

Florence
Tel: (0939-55)
21-0237

Venice
Tel: (0939-41)
524-4735

IVORY COAST
South African
Embassy
Villa Marc Andre
Rue Monsignor
Renee Kouassi
Cocody
President
(Postal address)
Boite Postal 1806
Abidjan
Tel: (09225) 44-5963

JAPAN
South African
Embassy
414 Zenkyoran
Building
7-9 Hirakawa-cho
2-Chome
Chiyoda-ku
Tokyo 102
Tel: (0981-3)
3265-3366

JORDAN
South African
Embassy
Mohammad al-
Mahdi Street
North West
Abdoun
PO Box 851508
Sweifiyyia 11185
Amman
Tel: (09-626)
81-1194

KENYA
South African
High Commission
17th Floor,
Lonrho House
Standard Street
Nairobi
Tel: (09254-2)
21-5616

KOREA (South)
South African
Embassy
1-37, Hannam-
dong
Yongsan-ku
140-210 Seoul
Tel: (0982-2)
792-4855

LESOTHO
South African
High Commission
10th Floor,
Consular section
8th Floor,
Lesotho Bank Centre
Private Bag A266
Maseru 0100
Tel: (09266) 31-5758

LUXEMBOURG
South African
Embassy
26 Rue de la Loi
B7/8
1040 Brussels
Belgium
Tel: (0932-2)
230-6845

MADAGASCAR
South African
Embassy
Lot 11 J 169 Ivandry
(Postal address)
Boite Postal 4417
101 Antananarivo
Tel: (09261-2) 42494

MALAWI
South African
High Commission
Mpico Building
City Centre
PO Box 30043
Lilongwe 3
Tel: (09265) 78-3722

MALAYSIA
South African
High Commission
29th Floor
Empire Tower
Jalan Tun Razak
50400 Kuala
Lumpur
Tel: (0960-3)
264-2653

MAURITIUS
South African High
Commission
4th Floor,
British American
Insurance Building
Pope Hennessy
Street
PO Box 908
Port Louis
Tel: (09230)
212-6925
Fax: (09230) 212
6935

MEXICO
South African
Embassy
Andres Bello 10
9th Floor,
Forum Building
Colonia Polanco
CP 11560
(Postal address)
Embajada de
Sudafrica
Apartado Postal
105-219
Colonia Polanca
CP 11581
Mexico City
Tel: (09525) 282-
9260

MONACO
30 BD Princesse
Charlotte
Monte Carlo
Tel: (0933-93)
25-2426

MOROCCO
South African
Embassy
34 Rue des
Saadiens
Rabat
Tel: (09212-7)
70-6760

MOZAMBIQUE
South African
Embassy
Avenue Julius
Nyerere 745
(Postal address)
Caixa Postal 1120
Maputo
Tel: (092581)
49-1614

NAMIBIA
South African High
Commission
RSA House
Cnr Jan Jonker and
Nelson Mandela
PO Box 23100
Windhoek
Tel: (09264-61)
22-9765/6

South Africa
Consulate-General
M & Z Building
8th Street
Private Bag X 5003
Walvis Bay
Tel: (09264)
642-7771-4

THE
NETHERLANDS
South African
Embassy
40 Wassenaarsweg
CJ 2596 The Hague
PO Box 90638
LP 2509 The Hague
Tel: (0931-70)
392-4501-4

NIGERIA
South African High
Commission
177B Ligale
Ayorinde Street
Victoria Island
Lagos
Tel: (09-234-1)
61-5000

NORWAY
South African
Embassy
Drammensveien 88C
0271 Oslo
PO Box 7588
Skillebek 0205
Oslo 2
Tel: (0947)
2244-7910

PAKISTAN
South African
High Commission
House No 48
Margalla Road
Khayaban-e-Iqbal
Sector F-8/2
Islamabad
Tel: (09-9251)
25-0318

PARAGUAY
South African
Embassy
Edificio Banco
Sudameris
4 Piso
Independencia
Nacional
(Postal address)
Casilla de Correo
1832
Asuncion
Tel: (09595-21)
44-4331/2

POLAND
South African
Embassy
IPC Business
Centre
U1 Koszykowa 54
00-675 Warsaw
Tel: (0948-2)
625-6228

PORTUGAL
South African
Embassy
Avenida Luis
Bivar 10
1097 Lisbon Codex
Tel: (09351-1)
353-5041

Madeira
South Africa
Consulate-General
Rua Pimenta Aguiar
Lote C-3 Andar
9000 Funchal
Tel: (09351-91)
74-2825-7

ROMANIA
South African
Embassy
Grigore
Alexandrescu Street
Sector 1
71129 Bucharest 22
Tel: (0940-1)
312-0346/8

RUSSIA
South African
Embassy
Bolshoi
Strochenovsky
Per. 22/25
Moscow 113054
Tel: (097-095)
230-6869/72

South Africa
Consulate-General
Naberezhnaya
Reki Moiki 11
191065 St Petersburg
Tel: (097-812)
119-6363

SAUDI ARABIA
South African
Embassy
Riyadh
Intercontinetal Hotel
PO Box 3636
Riyadh 11481
Tel: (09-9661)
4-65-5000
Ext 521/523

South Africa
Consulate-General
Jamloom Centre
Jeddah
Tel: (09-9661)
661-2000

SENEGAL
South African
Embassy
Hotel Teranga
Suite 916
Tel: (09-221)
21-4840

SINGAPORE
South African
High Commission
No 15/01-06
Odeon Towers
331 North Bridge Rd
Singapore 0718
Tel: (0965) 339-
3319

SLOVAKIA
South African
Embassy
Jancov U1 8 B1/5
Bratislava 811 02
Tel: (0942-7)
31-1582

SPAIN
South African
Embassy
Edificio Lista
Calle Claudio
Coello 91
Cnr J Ortega Y Gasset
Madrid 28006
Tel: (0934-1)
435-6688

Las Palmas
Tel: (0934-28)
33-3394

Bilbao
Tel: (0934-4)
210-0498

SWAZILAND
South African
High Commission
Standard Bank
Pension Fund Bldg
Allister Miller Str
PO Box 2507
Mbabane
Tel: (09268) 44651-4

SWEDEN
South African
Embassy
Linnegatan 76
115 23 Stockholm
Tel: (0946-8) 24-3950

SWITZERLAND
South African
Embassy
Jungfraustrasse 1
3005 Berne
Tel: (0941-31)
352-2011

South Africa
Consulate-General
65 Rue du Rhône
1204 Geneva
Tel: (0941-22)
849-5454

South Africa
Consulate-General
Basteiplatz 7
8001 Zürich
Tel: (0941-1)
221-1188

TANZANIA
South African
High Commission
Hotel Oyster Bay
Dar es Salaam
Tel: (09255-51)
68-062/4

THAILAND
South African
Embassy
The Park Place
231 Siu Sarasin
Bangkok 10330
Tel: (0966-2)
253-8473-6

TRANSKEI
Private Bag X5022
Umtata 5100
Tel: (0471) 31-2191

TUNISIA
South African
Embassy
7 Rue Acthart
Nord Hilton
Boite Postale 251
1082 Cite
Mahrajene
Tunis
Tel: (09216-1)
80-0311

TURKEY
South African
Embassy
Filistin Caddessi 27
Gaziosmanpasa
Ankara 06700
Tel: (0990-312)
446-4056

South Africa
Consulate- General
Serbecti is Merkezi
Kat 15
Buyukdere
Caddesi 106
80280 Esentepe
Istanbul
PO Box 65
80622 Levent
Tel: (0990-212)
275-4793

UKRAINE
South African
Embassy
6 Maculan Complex
9/2
Chervonoarmiyska
Street
PO Box 7
Central Post Office
252001 Kiev
Tel: (09-9744)
227-7172

UNITED ARAB
EMIRATES
South African
Embassy
Intercontinental
Suite 426
PO Box 4171
Abu Dhabi
Tel: (09971-2)
654604

UNITED
KINGDOM OF
GREAT BRITAIN
AND NORTHERN
IRELAND
South African
High Commission
South Africa House
Trafalgar Square
London WC2N 5DP
Tel: (0944-71)
930-4488

135 Edmund Street
Birmingham B3 2HS
Tel: (0944-21)
236-7471

USA
South African
Embassy
3051 Massachusetts
Avenue NW
Washington DC
20008
Tel: (091-202)
232-4400

South Africa
Consulate-General
333 East 38th Street
New York 10016
Tel: (091-212)
213-4880

South Africa
Consulate-General
200 South
Michigan Avenue
Chicago Illinois
60604
Tel: (091-312)
939-7929/32

South Africa
Consulate-General
Suite 300
50 North La
Cienega Boulevard
Beverly Hills CA
90211
Tel: (091-310)
657-9200-8

URUGUAY
South African
Embassy
Dr Prudencio de
Pena 2483
Montevideo
Tel: (09598-2)
79-0411

ZAIRE
South African
Embassy
(Postal address)
Boite Postal 7829
Kinshasa
Tel: (09243) 3-4676

ZAMBIA
South African
High Commission
4th and 5th Floor,
Bata House
Cairo Road
Private Bag W369
Lusaka
Tel: (09260-1)
22-8443

ZIMBABWE
South African
High Commission
Temple Bar
House
Cnr Baker Avenue
and Angwa Street
Harare
Tel: (09263-4)
75-3147

South African Tourist (SATOUR) Offices

BLOEMFONTEIN
Shop No 9,
Sanlam Parkade
Charles St
PO Box 3515
Bloemfontein
9300
Tel: (051) 47 1362
Fax: (051) 47 0862

CAPE TOWN
Shop 16,
Piazza Level 3
Golden Acre
Adderley St
Private Bag
X9108
Cape Town 8000
Tel: (021) 21 6274
Fax: (021) 419 4875
Telex: 524592 SA

DURBAN
Shop 104
(Information)
Suite 520
(Marketing and
Standards)
320 West St
PO Box 2516
Durban 4000
Tel: (031) 304 7144
Fax: (031) 305 6693
Telex: 621205 SA

JAN SMUTS
INTERNATIONAL
AIRPORT
International
Arrivals Hall
Jan Smuts Airport
1627
Tel: (011) 970 1669
Fax: (011) 394 1508

JOHANNESBURG
Suite 4305
Carlton Centre
PO Box 1094
Johannesburg 2000
Tel: (011) 331 5241
Fax: (011) 331 5420

KIMBERLEY
Room 620
Slaxley House
Du Toitspan Rd
Private Bag X5017
Kimberley 8300
Tel: (0531) 3 1434/
2 2657
Fax: (0531) 81 2937

NELSPRUIT
Tarentaal Trading
Post Building
Cnr Kaapschehoop
Rd & N4 Highway
PO Box 679
Nelspruit 1200
Tel: (01311) 44405/6
Fax: (01311) 44509

PIETERSBURG
Cnr Vorster and
Landdros Mare St
PO Box 2814
Pietersburg 0700
Tel: (01521) 3025/
2829
Fax: (01521)
912 654

PORT ELIZABETH
Satour House
21/3 Donkin St
PO Box 1161
Port Elizabeth 6000
Tel: (041) 55 7761
Fax: (041) 55 4975

PRETORIA
Shop 153
Nedbank Plaza
Beatrix St
PO Box 26500
Arcadia 0007
Tel: (012) 28 7154/
5/87
Fax: (012) 28 7154/
5/87 x229

HEAD OFFICE
Private Bag X164
Pretoria 0001
Tel: (012) 347 0600
Fax: (012) 45 4768
Telex: 3204575 SA

SATOUR offices abroad

AUSTRIA
Stefan-Zweig-Platz
11
A-1170
Vienna
Tel: (222) 4704 5110
Fax: (222) 4704
5114

CHINA
(REPUBLIC OF),
TAIWAN, HONG
KONG
Room 1204
12th Floor,
Bank Tower Bldg
205 Tun Hau
North Road
Taipei
Tel: (2) 717 4238
Fax: (2) 717 1146

FRANCE
98 Avenue de
Villiers
75017 Paris
Tel: (14) 4227 4020
Fax: (14) 267 8015
Telex: 651730

GERMANY
D-6 Frankfurt/
Main 1
Alemannia-Haus
An der
Hauptwache 11
Postfach 101940
6000 Frankfurt
Tel: (69) 2 0656
Fax: (69) 28 0950
Telex: 4189252

ISRAEL
14th Floor,
Century Towers
124 Ibn Gvirol
Street
PO Box 3388
Tel Aviv
Tel: (3) 527 2950/
2351/2352
Fax: (3) 527 1958

ITALY
Via M Gonzaga 3
Milan 20123
Tel: (2) 869 3847/
56
Fax: (2) 869 3508
Telex: 313307

JAPAN
2nd Floor,
Akasaka Lions
Building,
1-1-2 Moto
Akasaka
Minatoku
Tokyo 107
Tel: (3) 3478 7601
Fax: (3) 3478 7605

NETHERLANDS,
BELGIUM AND
SCANDINAVIA
Parnassustoren
7E Locatellikade 1
1076 AZ
Amsterdam
Tel: (20) 664 6201
Fax: (20) 662 9761

SWITZERLAND
Seestrasse 42
8802 Kilchberg
Tel: (1) 715 1815/16/
17
Fax: (1) 715 1889
Telex: 826572

UK AND EIRE
No 5&6 Alt Grove
London SW19 4DZ
Tel: (81) 944 6646
Fax: (81) 944 6705

USA, EASTERN
20th Floor,
747 Third Avenue
New York
NY 10017
Tel: (212) 838 8841/
(800) 822 5368
Fax: (212) 826 6928

USA, WESTERN
Suite No 1524
9841 Airport
Boulevard
Los Angeles
California 90045
Tel: (213) 641 8444
Fax: (213) 641 5812

ZIMBABWE
4th Floor,
Mercury House
George Silundika Av
PO Box 1343
Harare
Tel: (4) 70 7766/7
Fax: (4) 70 7767

Hotels

Johannesburg

ASCOT HOTEL
(two stars)
59 Grant Avenue
Norwood
PO Box 37138
Birnam Park 2015
Tel & Fax: 483 1211

CAPRI HOTEL
(three stars)
27 Aintree Avenue
Savoy Estates
PO Box 39605
Tel: 786 2250/1
Fax: 887 2286

THE CARLTON
COURT
(five stars)
Main Street
PO Box 7709
Tel: 331 8911
Fax: 331 3555

THE CARLTON
HOTEL
(five stars)
Cnr Main & Kruis
Street
PO Box 7709, 2000
Tel: 331 8911
Fax: 331 3555

THE DEVONSHIRE
HOTEL
(three stars)
Cnr Jorissen &
Melle Streets
PO Box 31197
Braamfontein 2017
Tel: 339 5611
Fax: 403 2495

HOLIDAY INN
GARDEN COURT
(three stars)
Auckland Park
PO Box 31556
Braamfontein 2017
Tel: 726 5100
Fax: 726 8615

HOLIDAY INN
GARDEN COURT
(three stars)
84 Smal Street
PO Box 535, 2000
Tel: 29 7011
Fax: 29 0515

KAROS
JOHANNESBURGER
HOTEL
(three stars)
Cnr Twist &
Wolmerans Streets
PO Box 23566
Joubert Park 2044
Tel: 725 3753
Fax: 725 6309

LINDEN HOTEL
(three stars)
Cnr 7th Str & 4th
Ave Linden, 2195
Tel & Fax: 782 4905

MARISTON
HOTEL
(three stars)
Cnr Claim & Koch
Streets
PO Box 23013
Joubert Park 2044
Tel: 725 4130
Fax: 725 2921

THE
PARKTONIAN
(four stars)
120 De Korte Street
PO Box 32278
Braamfontein 2017
Tel: 403 5740
Fax: 339 7440

PROTEA
GARDENS
HOTEL
(three stars)
35 O'Reilly Rd Berea
PO Box 688
Houghton 2041
Tel: 643 6610/1
Fax: 484 2622

PROTEA RIDGE
HOTEL
(three stars)
8 Able Road
Berea 2198
Tel: 643 4911
Fax: 643 1070
PO Box 17145
Hillbrow 2038

ROBERTSHAM
HOTEL
(two stars)
Cnr Harry & De
Lamere Streets
Robertsham
PO Box 82784
Southdale 2135
Tel & Fax: 680 5387

ROSEBANK HOTEL
(four stars)
Cnr Tyrwhitt &
Sturdee Avenue
PO Box 52025
Saxonwold 2132
Tel: 447 2700
Fax: 447 3276

SPRINGBOK
HOTEL
(two stars)
73 Joubert Street 2001
Tel: 337 8336
Fax: 337 8396

SUNNINGDALES
HOTEL
(two stars)
88 Corlett Drive
PO Box 37138
Birnam Park 2015
Tel: 887 6810/5
Fax: 887 6816

SUNNYSIDE
PARK HOTEL
(four stars)
2 York Road
PO Box 31256
Braamfontein 2017
Tel: 643 7226
Fax: 642 0019

Eastern Cape

Addo

ZUURBERG INN
(one star)
Zuurberg Pass
PO Box 12
Addo 6105
Tel & Fax: 40 0583

Aliwal North

THATCHER'S SPA
HOTEL
(two stars)
Dan Pienaar
Avenue
PO Box 297
5530
Tel: 2772
Fax: 42008

UMTALI MOTEL
(two stars)
Dan Pienaar
Avenue
PO Box 102
5530
Tel & Fax: 2400

Craddock

NEW MASONIC
HOTEL
(two stars)
Stockenstroom
Street
PO Box 44
5880
Tel: 3115/2114
Fax: 4402

East London

DOLPHIN HOTEL
(two stars)
85 Harewood Drive
Nahoon
PO Box 8010
5210
Tel: 35 1435
Fax: 35 4649

ESPLANADE
HOTEL
(two stars)
Beachfront
PO Box 18041
Quigney 5211
Tel: 2 2518
Fax: 2 3679

HOLIDAY INN
GARDEN COURT
(three stars)
Cnr John Baillie &
Moore Streets
PO Box 1255, 5200
Tel: 2 7260
Fax: 43 7360

HOTEL MAJESTIC
(two stars)
21 Orient Road
PO Box 18027
Quigney 5211
Tel & Fax: 43 7477

HOTEL OSNER
(three stars)
Esplanade
PO Box 334, 5200
Tel & Fax: 43 3433

KENNAWAY
PROTEA HOTEL
(three stars)
Esplanade
PO Box 583, 5200
Tel: 2 5531
Fax: 2 1326

KING DAVID
HOTEL AND
CONFERENCE
CENTRE
(three stars)
25 Inverleith
Terrace
Quigney
PO Box 1582
5200
Tel: 2 3174/5
Fax: 43 6939

Fort Beaufort

SAVOY HOTEL
(two stars)
53 Durban Street
PO Box 46
Fort Beaufort 5720
Tel: 3 1146
Fax: 3 2082

Gonubie

GONUBIE HOTEL
(two stars)
141 Main Road
PO Box 115, 5256
Tel: 40 4010/11
Fax: 40 4012

Graaff-Reinet

DROSTDY HOTEL
(three stars)
30 Church Street
PO Box 400, 6280
Tel: 2 2161
Fax: 2 4582

Grahamstown

CATHCART
ARMS HOTEL
(two stars)
5 West Street
PO Box 6043, 6140
Tel & Fax: 2 7111

GRAHAM
PROTEA HOTEL
(two stars)
123 High Street
PO Box 316, 6140
Tel: 2 2324
Fax: 2 2424

SETTLERS INN
(three stars)
N2 Highway
PO Box 219, 6140
Tel: 2 7313
Fax: 2 4951

Hogsback

HOGSBACK INN
(two stars)
Main Road
PO Box 63
Hogsback 5721
Tel: (045 642)
Ask 6
Fax: Ask 15

Jeffreys Bay

SAVOY PROTEA
HOTEL
(three stars)
16 Da Gama Road
PO Box 36
6330
Tel: 93 1106/7
Fax: 93 2445

Kei Mouth

KEI MOUTH
BEACH HOTEL
(two stars)
Beach Road
PO Box 8, 5260
Tel & Fax: 88 0088

King Williams Town

GROSVENOR
LODGE
(three stars)
48 Taylor Street
PO Box 61, 5600
Tel: 2 1440
Fax: 2 4772

Middelburg

COUNTRY
PROTEA INN
(two stars)
Cnr Meintjies and
Loop Streets
PO Box 8
Cape 5900
Tel: 2 1126/2 1187
Fax: 2 1681

HOTEL
MIDDELBURG
LODGE
(two stars)
Meintjies Street
PO Box 343
Cape 5900
Tel: 2 1100
Fax: 2 1681

Morgan's Bay

MORGAN BAY
HOTEL
(one star)
Morgan's Bay
PO Box Morgan's
Bay 5292
Tel & Fax: 62

Paterson

SANDFLATS
HOTEL
(one star)
2 Bruton Street
PO Box 31
Paterson 6130
Tel: 851 1012
Fax: 851 1176

Port Alfred

THE FERRYMANS
HOTEL
(one star)
Beach Road
PO Box 177
Port Alfred 6170
Tel & Fax: 4 1122

KOWIE GRAND
HOTEL
(two stars)
Cnr Grand and
Princes Avenues
PO Box 1
Kowie West 6170
Tel: 4 1150
Fax: 4 3769

VICTORIA
PROTEA HOTEL
(three stars)
7 Albany Road
PO Box 2, 6170
Tel & Fax: 4 1133

Port Elizabeth

THE BEACH
HOTEL
(three stars)
Marine Drive
Summerstrand
PO Box 319
6000
Tel & Fax: 53 2161

CITY LODGE
PORT ELIZABETH
(three stars)
Cnr Beach & Lodge
Roads
Summerstrand
PO Box 13352
Humewood 6013
Tel: 56 3322
Fax: 56 3374

THE EDWARD
HOTEL
(two stars)
Belmont Terrace
PO Box 319
6000
Tel & Fax: 56 2056

ELIZABETH SUN
(three stars)
PO Box 13100
Humewood 6000
Tel: 041 523720
Fax: 041 555754

HOLIDAY INN GARDEN COURT KINGS BEACH

(three stars)
La Roche Drive
Humewood
PO Box 13100
6013
Tel: 52 3720
Fax: 55 5754

HOLIDAY INN
GARDEN COURT
(SUMMERSTRAND)
(three stars)
Marine Drive
Summerstrand
PO Box 204
6000
Tel: 53 3131
Fax: 53 2505

THE HUMEWOOD
HOTEL
(two stars)
33 Beach Road
Humewood
PO Box 13023
6013
Tel & Fax: 55 8961

MARINE PROTEA
HOTEL
(three stars)
Marine Drive
Summerstrand
PO Box 501
6000
Tel: 53 2101
Fax: 53 2076

WALMER
GARDENS
HOTEL
(two stars)
10th Avenue
Walmer
PO Box 5108
6065
Tel & Fax: 51 4322

Queenstown

GRAND HOTEL
(two stars)
41 Cathcart Road
PO Box 712
5320
Tel & Fax: 3017

HEXAGON HOTEL

(two stars)
Cathcart Road
PO Box 116, 5320
Tel: 3015
Fax: 8 1428

JEANTEL HOTEL
(two stars)
2 Shepston Street
PO Box 116, 5320
Tel: 3016
Fax: 8 1428

Rhodes

RHODES HOTEL
(one star)
Miller Street
PO Box 21, 5582
Tel & Fax:(04 542)
Ask for 21

Storms River

TSITSIKAMMA
LODGE
(two stars)
N2 National Road
Tsitsikamma
PO Box 10, 6308
Tel: 802
Fax: 702

TSITSIKAMMA
FOREST INN
(two stars)
Darnell Street
PO Box Storms
River 6308
Tel: 541 1711
Fax: 541 1669

Venterstad

UNION HOTEL
(two stars)
Kruger Street
PO Box 128, 5990
Tel: 4 0045

Eastern Transvaal

Belfast

BELFAST HOTEL
(one star)
103 Vermooten Str
PO Box 14
1100
Tel & Fax: 3 0461

Dullstroom

CRITCHLEY
HACKLE LODGE
(three stars)
Teding van
Berkhout Street
PO Box 141, 1110
Tel: 4 0415
Fax: 4 0262

THEDULLSTROOM
INN
(two stars)
Cnr Teding van
Berkhout &
Nassau Streets
PO Box 44, 1110
Tel: 4 0071/2
Fax: 4 0278

WALKERSONS
COUNTRY
MANOR
(four stars)
Waboomkop Farm
Dullstroom/
Lydenburg Road
PO Box 185, 1110
Tel: 4 0246
Fax: 4 0260

Evander

HIGHVELD
PROTEA INN
(three stars)
Cnr Rotterdam &
Stanford Streets
PO Box 611, 2280
Tel: 2 4611
Fax: 62 4405

Groblersdal

GROBLERSDAL
HOTEL
(two stars)
1 Hereford Street
PO Box 786
0470
Tel: 2057/8
Fax: 2058

Hazyview

BöHMS
ZEEDERBERG
(three stars)
District Hazyview
PO Box 94
Sabie 1260
Tel: 6 8101
Fax: 6 8193

**HAZYVIEW
PROTEA HOTEL**
(three stars)
Burgers Hall
PO Box 105, 1242
Tel: 6 7332
Fax: 6 7335

KAROS LODGE
(four stars)
Sabie River
Kruger Gate
PO Box 54
Skukuza 1350
Tel: 6 5671
Fax: 6 5676

HOTEL NUMBI
(three stars)
Hazyview
PO Box 6, 1242
Tel & Fax: 6 7301

SABI RIVER SUN
(four stars)
Main Sabi Road
PO Box 13
1242
Tel: 6 7311
Fax: 6 7314

Kiepersol

THE FARMHOUSE
COUNTRY LODGE
(four stars)
R40 Road to
Hazyview
PO Box 40, 1241
Tel: 6 8780
Fax: 6 8783

Komatipoort

BORDER
COUNTRY INN
(three stars)
N4 Farm
Lebombo
PO Box 197, 1340
Tel: 5 0328
Fax: 5 0100

Lydenburg

MORGAN'S
HOTEL
(two stars)
14 Voortrekker Str
PO Box 11, 1120
Tel: 2165/6

Malelane

MALELANE SUN
LODGE
(four stars)
Riverside Farm
PO Box 392
1320
Tel: 3 0331
Fax: 3 0145

Middelburg

MIDWAY INN
(three stars)
Jan van Riebeeck Str.
PO Box 1240
1050
Tel: 46 2081
Fax: 46 1172

Nelspruit

CROCODILE
COUNTRY INN
(three stars)
Schagen
PO Box 496
1200
Tel: 6 3040
Fax: 6 4171

HOTEL
PROMENADE
(three stars)
Louis Trichardt Str.
PO Box 4355
1200
Tel: 5 3000
Fax: 2 5533

TOWN LODGE
NELSPRUIT
(one star)
Cnr Gen Dan
Pienaar &
Koorsboom Streets
PO Box 5555
1200
Tel: 4 1444
Fax: 4 2258

Pilgrim's Rest

MOUNT SHEBA
HOTEL
(four stars)
District Pilgrim's
Rest
PO Box 100
1290
Tel & Fax: 8 1241

Volksrust

TRANSVAAL
HOTEL
(two stars)
57 Joubert Street
PO Box 303, 2470
Tel: 2078/2088
Fax: 2314

Waterval Onder

BERGWATERS
LODGE
(three stars)
PO Box 71
Waterval Boven,
1195
Tel: 103

MALAGA HOTEL
(three stars)
N4 Sycamore
PO Box 136
Waterval Boven
1195
Tel & Fax: 431

White River

CYBELE FOREST
LODGE
(four stars)
PO Box 346, 1240
Tel: 5 0511
Fax: 3 2839

GLORY HILL
GUEST LODGE
(three stars)
R358
Numbi Road
PO Box 24
1240
Tel: 3 3217/8

HOTEL THE/DIE
WINKLER
(four stars)
Old Numbi Road
(R538)
PO Box 12
1240
Tel: 3 2317/8/9
Fax: 3 1393

HULALA
LAKESIDE LODGE
(three stars)
R40
PO Box 1382
1240
Tel & Fax: 5 1710

KARULA HOTEL
(two stars)
Old Plaston Road
PO Box 279
1240
Tel: 3 2277/8/9
Fax: 5 0413

Kwazulu/Natal

Bergville

LITTLE
SWITZERLAND
RESORT
(three stars)
District Bergville
Private Bag X1661
3350
Tel & Fax: 438 6220

Botha's Hill

ROB ROY HOTEL
(three stars)
Rob Roy Crescent
PO Box 10
3660
Tel: 777 1305
Fax: 777 1364

Dargle

LANDHAUS
KARIN
(two stars)
Sub 42
Middelbosch
No 897
PO Box 4
3265
Tel & Fax: 4274

Durban

CITY LODGE
DURBAN
(three stars)
Cnr Brickhill & Old
Fort Roads
PO Box 10842
Marine Parade
4056
Tel: 32 1447
Fax: 32 1483

DRAKENSBERG
GARDEN HOTEL
(three star)
Marine Parade 4056
Tel: (033) 7011 355
Fax: (033) 7011 355

ELANGENI SUN
(four stars)
63 Snell Parade
PO Box 4094, 4000
Tel: 37 1321
Fax: 32 5527

HOLIDAY INN
GARDEN COURT
- NORTH BEACH
(three stars)
83/91 Snell Parade
PO Box 10592
Marine Parade
4056
Tel: 32 7361
Fax: 37 4058

HOLIDAY INN
GARDEN COURT
- SOUTH BEACH
(three stars)
73 Marine Parade
PO Box 10199, 4056
Tel: 37 2231
Fax: 37 4640

HOLIDAY INN
MARINE PARADE
(four stars)
167 Marine Parade
PO Box 10809
4056
Tel: 37 3341
Fax: 32 9885

KAROS EDWARD
HOTEL
(four stars)
Marine Parade
PO Box 105
4000
Tel: 37 3681
Fax: 32 1692

THE PALACE
PROTEA HOTEL
(three stars)
211 Marine Parade
PO Box 10539
4056
Tel: 32 8351
Fax: 32 8307

ROYAL HOTEL
(five stars)
267 Smith Street
PO Box 1041
4000
Tel: 304 0331
Fax: 307 6884

Hilton

CROSSWAYS
COUNTRY INN
(two stars)
2 Old Howick
Road
PO Box 16
3245
Tel & Fax: 3 3267

HILTON HOTEL
(three stars)
Hilton Road
PO Box 35
3245
Tel: 3 3311
Fax: 3 3722

Himeville

HIMEVILLE
ARMS
(two stars)
Arbuckle Street
PO Box 105
4585
Tel & Fax: 702 1305

SANI PASS
HOTEL &
LEISURE RESORT
(three stars)
Sani Pass Road
PO Box 44
4585
Tel & Fax: 701
1435/6

Howick

OLD HALLIWELL
COUNTRY INN
(four stars)
Currys Post
PO Box 201
3290
Tel: 30 2602
Fax: 30 3430

Illovo Beach

KARRIDENE
PROTEA HOTEL
(three stars)
Old Main
South Coast Road
PO Box 20
4155
Tel: 96 3332
Fax: 96 4093

Kokstad

MOUNT CURRIE
INN
(two stars)
PO Box 27, 4700
Tel & Fax: 727 2178

Ladysmith

ROYAL HOTEL
(three stars)
140 Murchison
Street
PO Box 12, 3370
Tel & Fax: 2 2167

Margate

BEACH LODGE
HOTEL
(two stars)
Marine Drive
PO Box 109, 4275
Tel: 2 1483/4
Fax: 7 1232

PALM RIDGE
GUEST HOUSE
(two stars)
20 Ridge Road
PO Box 1931, 4275
Tel: 7 1347

Mkuze

GHOST
MOUNTAIN INN
(two stars)
Old Main Road
PO Box 18, 3695
Tel & Fax: 573
1025/7

Mont-aux-Sources

KAROS MONT-
AUX-SOURCES
HOTEL
Private Bag XI
3353
Tel & Fax: 438 6230

Mtunzini

TRADE WINDS
HOTEL
(two stars)
Hely
Hutchinson Street
PO Box 100, 3867
Tel: 40 1411/2
Fax: 40 1629

Newcastle

HOLIDAY INN
GARDEN COURT
- NEWCASTLE
(three stars)
Cnr Victoria and
Hunter Streets
PO Box 778
2940
Tel: 2 8151
Fax: 2 4142

Nottingham Road

NOTTINGHAM
ROAD HOTEL
(two stars)
PO Box 26
3280
Tel: 3 6151
Fax: 3 6167

RAWDONS
HOTEL
(three stars)
(R103)
PO Box 7
3280
Tel: 3 6044/5
Fax: 3 6142

Pietermaritzburg

IMPERIAL HOTEL
(three stars)
224 Loop Street
PO Box 140
Natal 3200
Tel: 42 6551
Fax: 42 9796

Richards Bay

KAROS
BAYSHORE INN
(two stars)
The Gulley
PO Box 51
3900
Tel: 3 1246
Fax: 3 2335

KAROS RICHARDS
HOTEL
(three stars)
Hibberd Drive
PO Box 242
3900
Tel: 3 1301
Fax: 3 2334

Tongaat

WESTBROOK
BEACH HOTEL
(two stars)
82 North Beach
Road
Westbrook Beach
PO Box 48
4400
Tel & Fax: 42021

Tweedie

FERN HILL HOTEL
(three stars)
R103 Midmar
PO Box 5
3255
Tel & Fax: 30 5071

Umhlali

SHORTENS
COUNTRY HOUSE
(four stars)
Compensation Rd
PO Box 499
4390
Tel: 71140
Fax: 71144

Umhlanga Rocks

BEVERLY HILLS
SUN
(five stars)
54 Lighthouse Rd
PO Box 71
4320
Tel: 561 2211
Fax: 561 3711

OYSTER BOX
HOTEL
(three stars)
2 Lighthouse Road
PO Box 22
4320
Tel: 561 2233
Fax: 561 4072

Umzumbe

PUMULA HOTEL
(two stars)
67 Steve Pitts Road
PO Box 17
4225
Tel: 84 6717
Fax: 84 6303

Uvongo

BRACKENMOOR
HOTEL
(three stars)
Lot 2013
PO Box 518
St Michael's on the
Sea 4265
Tel: 5 0065/7 5165
Fax: 75109

Vryheid

STILWATER
PROTEA HOTEL
(two stars)
Dundee Road
Private Bag X9332
3100
Tel: 6181
Fax: 80 8846

VILLA PRINCE
IMPERIAL
(two stars)
201 Deputation
Street 3100
Tel & Fax: 80 2610

Wartburg

WARTBURGER
HOF COUNTRY
HOTEL
(three stars)
53 Noodsberg Road
PO Box 147, 3450
Tel & Fax: 503 1482

Westville

THE WESTVILLE
(three stars)
124 Jan Hofmeyer Rd
PO Box 145, 3630
Tel & Fax: 86 6326

Winterton

CATHEDRAL
PEAK HOTEL
(three stars)
PO Box Winterton
3340
Tel & Fax: 488 1888

CAYLEY LODGE
(three stars)
Bergvlei
PO Box 241, 3340
Tel & Fax: 468 1222

**CHAMPAGNE
CASTLE**
Private Bag X8
Winterton 3340
Tel: (036) 468 1036

DRAKENSBERG
SUN
(four stars)
Cathkin Park
PO Box 335, 3340
Tel: 468 1000
Fax: 468 1224

THE NEST
Private Bag X14
Winterton 3340
Tel: (036) 468 1068
Fax: (036) 468 1390

Northern Cape

Colesburg

MERINO INN
MOTEL
(three stars)
N1 Bypass
PO Box 10, 5980
Tel: 0781/2/3/4
Fax: 0615

SPES BONA
(one star)
22 President
Kruger Street 5980
Tel: 0210

VAN ZYLSVLEI
(two stars)
Philippolis Road
PO Box 50, 5980
Tel: 0589

Groblershoop

GROOT RIVIER
HOTEL
(two stars)
15 Main Street
PO Box 1, 8850
Tel: (05 472)
Ask for 14
Kakamas

WATERWIEL
PROTEA HOTEL
(three stars)
Voortrekker Street
PO Box 250
8870
Tel: 431 0838
Fax: 431 0836

Kamieskroon

KAMIESKROON
HOTEL
(two stars)
Old National Road
PO Box 19, 8241
Tel: 614
Fax: 675

Kimberley

COLINTON
HOTEL
(two stars)
14 Thompson
Street
PO Box 400, 8300
Tel & Fax: 3 1471

DIAMOND
PROTEA LODGE
(two stars)
124 Du Toitspan
Road
PO Box 2068, 8300
Tel & Fax: 81 1281

HOLIDAY INN
GARDEN COURT
(three stars)
120 Du Toitspan
Road
PO Box 635, 8300
Tel: 3 1751
Fax: 2 1814

HOTEL
KIMBERLITE
(three stars)
162 George Street
8301
Tel: 81 1967/8
Fax: Ext 237

KIMBERLEY
HOLIDAY INN
(three stars)
PO Box 635, 8300
Tel: 0531 31751
Fax: 0531 21814

Kuruman

ELDORADO
MOTEL
(three stars)
Main Street
PO Box 313
8460
Tel: 2 2191/2/3
Fax: 2 2191

Nababeep

NABABEEP
HOTEL
(one star)
Main Street
Private Bag X18
8265
Tel: 3 8151
Fax: 2 2257

Postmasburg

POSTMASBURG
HOTEL
(two stars)
37 Main Street
PO Box 6
8420
Tel & Fax: 7 1166/7

Springbok

KOKERBOOM
MOTEL
(two stars)
PO Box 340
8240
Tel: 2 2685
Fax: 2 2257

Upington

OASIS PROTEA
LODGE
(two stars)
26 Schroeder Street
PO Box 1981
8800
Tel & Fax: 31 1125

Victoria West

MELTON WOLD
VAKANSIEPLAAS
(three stars)
PO Box 162
7070
Tel: (02 042)
Ask for 1430

Williston

WILLISTON
HOTEL
(one star)
Lutz Street
PO Box 5
7040
Tel: 5

Northern Transvaal

Duiwelskloof

IMP INN HOTEL
(one star)
Botha Street
PO Box 17, 0835
Tel: 9253/4
Fax: 9892

Louis Trichardt

BERGWATER
HOTEL
(three stars)
5 Rissik Street
PO Box 503, 0920
Tel: 2262/3/4
Fax: 2262

CLOUDS END
HOTEL
(three stars)
Private Bag X2409
0920
Tel: 9621
Fax: 9787

INGWE RANCH
MOTEL
(three stars)
PO Box 433, 0920
Tel: 9687/9703
Fax: 9722

Magoebaskloof

GLENSHIEL
COUNTRY
LODGE
(four stars)
PO Box 1
Haenertsburg
0730
Tel & Fax: 4335

MAGOEBASKLOOF
HOTEL
(three stars)
Road R71
PO Magoebaskloof
0731
Tel: 4276
Fax: 4280

TROUTWATERS
INN
(two stars)
Road R71
PO Magoebaskloof
0731
Tel & Fax: 4245/6

Messina

KATES HOPE
RIVER LODGE
(three stars)
Kates Hope
Farm Mt 21
District Messina
PO Box 2720
Cresta 2118
Tel: 476 6217
Fax: 678 0732

Nylstroom

SHANGRI LA
COUNTRY LODGE
(three stars)
Eersbewoond Str
PO Box 262
0510
Tel & Fax: 2381/2071

Phalaborwa

IMPALA INN
HOTEL
(three stars)
52 Essenhout Street
PO Box 139
1390
Tel: 5681
Fax: 8 5234

Pietersburg

HOLIDAY INN
GARDEN COURT
PIETERSBURG
(three stars)
Vorster Street
PO Box 784
0700
Tel:291 2030
Fax: 291 3150

THE RANCH
(three stars)
N1
PO Box 77
0700
Tel: 293 7180
Fax: 293 7188

Potgietersrus

OASIS LODGE
(two stars)
1 Voortrekker
Road
PO Box 810
0600
Tel & Fax: 4124/5/6

PROTEA PARK
HOTEL
(three stars)
1 Beitel Street
PO Box 1551, 0600
Tel: 3101/2
Fax: 6842

Tzaneen

COACH HOUSE
HOTEL
(five stars)
Old Coach Road
Agatha
PO Box 544, 0850
Tel: 307 3641
Fax: 307 1466

KAROS
TZANEEN HOTEL
(three stars)
1 Danie Joubert Str
PO Box 1
0850
Tel & Fax: 307 3140

Vaalwater

LA RIVE HOTEL
(two stars)
Farm Bergsig
District Vaalwater
PO Box 436, 0530
Tel: Bulgerivier 311

Warmbad

MABULA GAME
LODGE
(three stars)
Private Bag X1665
0480
Tel: 616/717
Fax: 733

Private Bag X22
Bryanston 2021
Tel: 463 4217
Fax: 463 4299

North-West

Boshoek

SUNDOWN
RANCH HOTEL
(three stars)
Rustenburg/
Boshoek
PO Box 139, 0301
Tel: 73 3121
Fax: 73 3114

Potchefstroom

ELGRO HOTEL
(three stars)
60 Wolmarans
Street
PO Box 1111
2520
Tel & Fax: 297 5411

Rooigrond

SEHUBA PROTEA
INN
(two stars)
Mafikeng/
Lichtenburg Road
PO Box 54
2743
Tel: 644/651
Fax: 775

Rustenburg

BELVEDERE
HOTEL
(three stars)
Rhenosterfontein
PO Box 1298
0300
Tel: 9 2121
Fax: 9 2519

KAROS SAFARI
HOTEL
(three stars)
Kloof Road
PO Box 687
0300
Tel: 97 1361
Fax: 97 1220

OLIFANTSNEK
COUNTRY
HOTEL
(two stars)
184 Machol Street
PO Box 545
0300
Tel: 9 2208
Fax: 9 2100

SPARKLING
WATERS
HOLIDAY HOTEL
(three stars)
Rietfontein Farm
PO Box 208
0300
Tel: 75 0151
Fax: 75 0190

THE WIGWAM
HOLIDAY HOTEL
(two stars)
Modderfontein
PO Box 269, 0300
Tel: 9 2147
Fax: 9 2164

WESTWINDS
COUNTRY
HOUSE
(three stars)
Westwinds Farm
Zuurplaat
PO Box 56
Kroondal 0350
Tel: 75 0560
Fax: 75 0032

Sun City

THE CASCADES
PO Box 7
Sun City 0316
Tel: 01465 21000
Fax: 01465 7545

THE PALACE
PO Box 308
Sun City 0316
Tel: 01465 73000
Fax: 01465 7311

SUN CITY
CABANAS
PO Box 3
Sun City 0316
Tel: 01465 21000
Fax: 01465 21590

SUN CITY HOTEL
PO Box 2
Sun City 0316
Tel: 01465 21000
Fax: 01465 21470

Vryburg

INTERNATIONAL
HOTEL
(two stars)
43 Market Street
PO Box 38, 8600
Tel: 2235/6/7
Fax: 2235

ABJATERSKOP
HOTEL
(three stars)
Rustenburg Road
PO Box 390
2865
Tel & Fax: 2 2008

Free State

Bethlehem

PARK HOTEL
(two stars)
23 Muller Street
PO Box 8
9700
Tel & Fax: 303 5191

Bloemfontein

BLOEMFONTEIN
INN
(two stars)
17 Edison Street
Hospital Park
PO Box 7589
9300
Tel: 22 6284
Fax: 22 6223

CITY LODGE
BLOEMFONTEIN
(two stars)
Cnr Voortrekker
Street & Parfitt
Avenue
PO Box 3552
9300
Tel: 47 9888
Fax: 47 5669

DIE HERBERG
(two stars)
12 Barne Street
PO Box 12165
Brandhof 9324
Tel: 30 7500
Fax: 30 4494

HOLIDAY INN
GARDEN COURT
(three stars)
Cnr Zastron Street
& Melville Drive
PO Box 12015
Brandhof 9324
Tel: 47 0310
Fax: 30 5678

HOLIDAY INN
GARDEN COURT
- NAVAL HILL
(three stars)
1 Union Avenue
PO Box 1851
9300
Tel: 30 1111
Fax: 30 4141

Boshof

BOSHOF HOTEL
(two stars)
Jacob Street
PO Box 13
8340
Tel: (053 232)
Ask for 91
Fax: Ask for 451

Bothaville

HOTEL ENKEL
DEN
(two stars)
13 President Street
PO Box 48
9660
Tel: 4341/2/3
Fax: 4344

Edenburg

EDENBURG
HOTEL
(two stars)
2 Church Street
PO Box 168
9908

Ficksburg

FRANSHOEK
MOUNTAIN
LODGE
(two stars)
PO Box 603
9730
Tel: 3938/2828
Fax: 3938

NEBO HOLIDAY
FARM
(three stars)
Nebo Farm
PO Box 178
9730
Tel & Fax: 3947/3281

Fouriesburg

FOURIESBURG
HOTEL
(two stars)
17 Reitz Street
PO Box 114
9725
Tel: (058 222)
Ask for 30
Fax: Ask for 284

Frankfort

LODGE 1896
(two stars)
55°A Brand Street
PO Box 77
9830
Tel: 3 1080

**Hendrik
Verwoerd Dam**

VERWOERDDAM
MOTEL
(three stars)
2 Aasvoël Avenue
PO Box 20
Hendrik 9922
Tel: (052 172)
Ask for 60/61/62
Fax: Ask for 268

Ladybrand

TRAVELLERS
INN
(two stars)
23 a Kolbe street
PO Box 458
9745
Tel: 4 0191/3
Fax: 4 0193

Reddersberg

HOTEL SARIE
MARAIS
(one star)
22 Van Riebeeck Str
PO Box 6
9904
Tel: (052 122)
Ask 138

Sasolburg

INDABA HOTEL
(two stars)
47 Fichardt Street
PO Box 103
9570
Tel: 76 0600
Fax: 76 1938

Thaba Nchu

THABANCHUSUN
PO Box 114
Thaba Nchu 9780
Tel: 051871 2161
Fax: 051871 2521

Trompsburg

BEAU VISTA
MOTEL
(two stars)
Louw Street
PO Box 65, 9913

Vrede

LANGBERG
HOTEL
(two stars)
Marina Dam
PO Box 166, 2455
Tel: 3 2080

Welkom

WELKOM HOTEL
(three stars)
283 Koppie
Alleen road
PO Box 973, 9460
Tel & Fax: 5 1411

WELKOM INN
(three stars)
Cnr Tempest &
Stateway Roads
PO Box 887, 9460
Tel: 357 3361
Fax: 352 1458

Zastron

MALUTI HOTEL
(three stars)
22 Hoofd Street
PO Box 2, 9950
Tel: 107
Fax: 379

**Pretoria
Bronkhorstspruit**

PARK HOTEL
(two stars)
18 Church Street
PO Box 64, 1020
Tel: 2 3105
Fax: 2 5687

Edenvale

CITY LODGE JAN
SMUTS AIRPORT
(two stars)
Sandvale Road
PO Box 448
Isando 1600
Tel: 392 1750
Fax: 392 2644

Germiston

TOWN LODGE
JAN SMUTS
AIRPORT
(one star)
Herman Road
Germiston
PO Box 600
Isando 1600
Tel: 974 5202
Fax: 974 5490

**Pretoria
Kempton Park**

HOLIDAY INN
GARDEN COURT
(JOHANNESBURG
AIRPORT)
(three stars)
6 Hulley Road
Isando
Private Bag 5
Jan Smuts Airport
1627
Tel: 392 1062
Fax: 974 8097

HOLIDAY INN
JAN SMUTS
AIRPORT
(four stars)
Pretoria Highway
PO Box 388
1620
Tel: 975 1121
Fax: 975 5846

Krugersdorp

AUBERGE
AURORA
(three stars)
Off Pappegaai Str
Rant En Dal
PO Box 145
1740
Tel: 956 6307/8
Fax: 956 6089

Magaliesburg

MAGALIESBURG
COUNTY HOTEL
(three stars)
41 Main
Rustenburg Road
PO Box 4
2805
Tel & Fax: 77 1109

MOUNT GRACE
COUNTRY
HOUSE HOTEL
(four stars)
PO Box 251, 2805
Tel & Fax: 77 1350

VALLEY LODGE
(four stars)
Jenning Street
PO Box 13, 2805
Tel: 77 1301
Fax: 77 1306

Midrand

CONSTANTIA
LODGE
(two stars)
239 Old Pretoria Rd
PO Box 84
Irene 1675
Tel: 315 0530
Fax: 315 1466

MIDRAND
PROTEA HOTEL
(four stars)
14th Street
Noordwyk Ext.20
PO Box 1840, 1685
Tel: 318 1868
Fax: 318 2429

TOWN LODGE
MIDRAND
(one star)
Cnr Bekker Road &
Le Roux Avenue
Waterfall Park
Vorna Valley
PO Box 5622
Tel: 315 6047
Fax: 315 6004

Muldersdrift

ALOE RIDGE
HOTEL
(three stars)
Swartkop
PO Box 3040
Honeydew 2040
Tel & Fax: 957 2070

HEIA SAFARI
RANCH
(three stars)
Swartkop
PO Box 1387
Honeydew 2040
Tel: 659 0605
Fax: 659 0709

Pretoria Akasia

BENTLEYS
COUNTRY
LODGE
(three stars)
Cnr Main Street
& 4th Avenue
Heatherdale
PO Box 16665
Pretoria North 0116
Tel: 542 1751
Fax: 542 3487

Pretoria Arcadia

ARCADIA HOTEL
(three stars)
515 Proes Street
PO Box 26104
Arcadia 0007
Tel: 326 9311
Fax: 326 1067

CRESTA
PRETORIA
HOTEL
(three stars)
230 Hamilton
Street
PO Box 40663, 0007
Tel: 341 3473
Fax: 44 2258

HOLIDAY INN
PRETORIA
(four stars)
Cnr Church &
Beatrix Streets
PO Box 40694, 0007
Tel: 341 1571
Fax: 44 7534

KAROS
MANHATTAN
HOTEL
(three stars)
247 Scheiding Str
PO Box 26212, 0007
Tel: 322 7635
Fax: 320 1252

Pretoria Central

HOLIDAY INN
GARDEN COURT
PRETORIA
(three stars)
Cnr Van Der Walt
& Minnaar Streets
PO Box 2301, 0001
Tel: 322 7500
Fax: 322 9429

THE FARM INN
(three stars)
Lynwood Rd East
PO Box 71702
Die Wilgers 0041
Tel: 807 0081
Fax: 807 0088

LA MAISON
(four stars)
235 Hilda Street
Hatfield 0083
Tel: 43 4341
Fax: 342 1531

BATISS HOUSE
(three stars)
92-20th Streets
PO Box 35869
Menlo Park 0102
Tel: 46 7318

Randburg

FLEET STREET
GUEST HOUSE
(two stars)
101 Fleet Street
PO Box 464
Ferndale 2160
Tel: 886 0790
Fax: 789 6601

Sandton

BALALAIKA
PROTEA HOTEL
(four stars)
20 Maud Street
Sandown
PO Box 783372, 2146
Tel: 884 1400
Fax: 844 1463

CITY LODGE
RANDBURG
(two stars)
Cnr Main Road
& Peter Place
Bryanston West
PO Box 423, 2060
Tel: 706 7800
Fax: 706 7819

CITY LODGE
SANDTON
KATHERINESTR
(three stars)
Cnr Katherine Str
& Graystone Drive
PO Box 781643, 2146
Tel: 444 5300
Fax: 444 5315

CITY LODGE
SANDTON
MORNINGSIDE
(three stars)
Cnr Hill & Rivonia
Roads
PO Box 784617
2146
Tel: 884 9500
Fax: 884 9440

HOLIDAY INN
GARDEN COURT
SANDTON
(three stars)
Cnr Katherine &
Rivonia Roads
PO Box 783394
2146
Tel: 884 5660
Fax: 783 2004

HOLIDAY INN
SANDTON
(four stars)
Cnr Graystone
Drive & Rivonia Rd
PO Box 781743
2146
Tel: 783 5262
Fax: 783 5289

KAROS INDABA
HOTEL
(four stars)
Hartebeespoort
Dam Road
Wiltkoppen
Fourways
PO Box 67129
Bryanston 2021
Tel: 465 1400
Fax: 705 1709

SANDTON SUN
(five stars)
Cnr Alice and 5th
Streets
PO Box 784902
2146
Tel: 780 5000
Fax: 780 5002

SANDTON SUN
TOWERS
(five stars)
Cnr 5th and Alice
Streets
PO Box 784902
2146
Tel: 780 5000
Fax: 780 5002

Springs

HOTEL DROSTDY
(two stars)
52 -4th Ave
Geduld
PO Box 58, 1560
Tel: 815 1471
Fax: 815 3041

Vereeniging

RIVIERA
INTERNATIONAL
HOTEL AND
COUNTRY CLUB
(four stars)
Mario Milani Drive
PO Box 64, 1930
Tel: 22 2861
Fax: 21 2908

Verwoerdburg

CENTURION
LAKE HOTEL
(four stars)
1001 Lenchen
Avenue North
PO Box 7331
Hennopsmeer,
0046
Tel: 663 1825
Fax: 663 2555

Western Cape

Albertinia

ALBERTINIA
HOTEL
(two stars)
61 Main Street
PO Box 85, 6795
Tel: 5 1030
Fax: 5 1495

Beaufort West

OASIS HOTEL
(two stars)
66 Donkin Street
PO Box 115, 6970
Tel: 3221
Fax: 3221

Bellville

BELLVILLE INN
(three stars)
Cross Street
PO Box 233, 7530
Tel: 948 8111
Fax: 946 4425

THE LODGE
BELLVILLE
(one star)
Cnr Willie Van
Schoor Avenue &
Mispel Road
PO Box 3587
Tygerpark 7536
Tel: 948 7990
Fax: 948 8805

Bonnievale

AVALON
BONNIEVALE
HOTEL
(one star)
87 Main Road
PO Box 63, 6730
Tel: 2155/6/7
Fax: 3046

Brackenfell

CAPE
RENDEZVOUS
PROTEA HOTEL &
CONFERENCE
CENTRE
(three stars)
Brackenfell
Boulevard
PO Box 16, 7560
Tel: 981 2171
Fax: 981 2267

Brandvlei

BRANDVLEI
HOTEL
(one star)
Main Street
PO Box 2, 7020
Tel: 2

Bredasdorp

ARNISTON
HOTEL
(three stars)
Beach Road
Waenhuiskrans
PO Box 126, 7280
Tel: 5 9000
Fax: 5 9633

HOTEL VICTORIA
(two stars)
10 Church Street
PO Box 11, 7280
Tel: 4 1159
Fax: 4 1140

STANDARD
HOTEL
(one star)
31 Long Street
PO Box 47
7280
Tel: 4 1140
Fax: 4 1141

Brenton-on-Sea

BRENTON ON
SEA HOTEL
(two stars)
Agapanthus Avenue
Brenton-on-Sea
PO Box 36
Knysna 6570
Tel & Fax: 81 0081

Caledon

ALEXANDRIA
HOTEL
(two stars)
Market Square
PO Box 3
7230
Tel: 2 3052
Fax: 4 1102

THE OVERBERGER
COUNTRY HOTEL
& SPA
(three stars)
Nerina Avenue
PO Box 480
7230
Tel: 4 1271
Fax: 4 1270

Cape Town

AMBASSADOR BY
THE SEA
(four stars)
34 Victoria Road
Bantry Bay
PO Box 83
Sea Point 8060
Tel: 439 6170
Fax: 439 6336

THE BAY HOTEL
(five stars)
Victoria Road
PO Box 32021
Camps Bay 8040
Tel: 438 4444
Fax: 438 4455

CAPE SUN HOTEL
(five stars)
Strand Street
PO Box 4532
8000
Tel: 23 8844
Fax: 23 8875

CAPETONIAN
PROTEA HOTEL
(four stars)
Pier Place
Heerengracht
PO Box 6856
Roggebaai 8012
Tel: 21 1150
Fax: 25 2215

CARLTON
HEIGHTS HOTEL
(two stars)
88 Queen Victoria
Street 8001
Tel: 23 1260
Fax: 23 2088

HOLIDAY INN
GARDEN COURT
- GREENMARKET
SQUARE
(three stars)
10 Greenmarket
Square
PO Box 3775
8000
Tel: 23 2040
Fax: 23 3664

HOLIDAY INN
GARDEN COURT
- ST GEORGES
MALL
(three stars)
Trustbank
Building
St Georges Mall
PO Box 5616
8000
Tel: 419 0808
Fax: 419 7010

METROPOLE
HOTEL
(two stars)
38 Lond Street
PO Box 3086
8000
Tel: 23 6363
Fax: 23 6370

PLEINPARK
TRAVEL LODGE
(two stars)
9 Barrack Street
PO Box 16488
Vlaeberg 8018
Tel: 45 7563
Fax: 45 7005

TOWN HOUSE
HOTEL
(four stars)
60 Corporation
Street
PO Box 5053, 8000
Tel: 45 7050
Fax: 45 3891

TUDOR HOTEL
(two stars)
153 Longmarket
Street 8001
Tel: 24 1335
Fax: 23 1198

TULBAGH
PROTEA HOTEL
(three stars)
9 Ryk Tulbagh Sq
PO Box 2891, 8000
Tel: 21 5140
Fax: 21 4648

ALPHEN HOTEL
(four stars)
Alphen Drive
PO Box 35
Constantia 7848
Tel: 794 5011
Fax: 794 5710

THE CELLARS -
HOHENORT
COUNTRY
HOUSE HOTEL
(five stars)
15 Hohenort Ave
PO Box 270
Constantia 7848
Tel: 794 2137/8
Fax: 794 2149

CAPE SWISS
HOTEL
(three stars)
1 Nicol Street
Gardens
PO Box 21516
Kloof Street
Gardens 8000
Tel: 23 8190
Fax: 26 1795

HELMSLEY HOTEL
(three stars)
16 Hof Street
Gardens 8001
Tel: 23 7200
Fax: 23 1533

HOLIDAY INN
GARDEN COURT
-DE WAAL
(three stars)
Mill Street
PO Box 2793
Gardens 8000
Tel: 45 1311
Fax: 461 6648

MOUNT NELSON
HOTEL
(five stars)
76 Orange Street
PO Box 2608
Gardens 8000
Tel: 23 1000
Fax: 24 7472

CITY LODGE
MOWBRAY GOLF
PARK
(three stars)
Off Raapenburg Rd
Mowbray
PO Box 124
Howard Place 7450
Tel: 685 7944
Fax: 685 7997

HOLIDAY INN
GARDEN COURT
- NEWLANDS
(three stars)
Main Road
Newlands 7700
Tel: 61 1105
Fax: 64 1241

THE VINEYARD
HOTEL
(four stars)
Colinton Road
PO Box 151
Newlands 7725
Tel: 64 2107
Fax: 683 3365

KAROS
ARTHUR'S SEAT
HOTEL
(four stars)
Arthur's Road
Sea Point 8001
Tel: 434 1187
Fax: 434 9768

THE CENTURION
ALL-SUITE
HOTEL
(three stars)
275 Main Road
PO Box 17188
Sea Point 8061
Tel: 434 0006
Fax: 434 0051

WINCHESTER
MANSIONS
HOTEL
(three stars)
221 Beach Road
Sea Point 8001
Tel: 434 2351
Fax: 434 0215

MIJLOF MANOR
HOTEL
(three stars)
5 Military Road
Tamboerskloof
8001
Tel: 26 1476
Fax: 22 2046

CITY LODGE
(two stars)
Cnr Dock & Alfred
Roads
Victoria and Albert
Waterfront
PO Box 6025
Roggebaai 8012
Tel: 419 9450
Fax: 419 0460

VICTORIA AND
ALFRED HOTEL
(four stars)
Waterfront
PO Box 50050
8002
Tel: 419 6677
Fax: 419 8955

HOLIDAY INN
GARDEN COURT
- EASTERN
BOULEVARD
(three stars)
Cnr Melbourne &
Coronation Streets
PO Box 2979
Woodstock 8000
Tel: 448 4123
Fax: 47 8338

Citrusdal

CEDARBERG
HOTEL
(two stars)
Voortrekker Street
PO Box 37
7340
Tel: 921 2221
Fax: 921 2704

Clan-William

CLANWILLIAM
HOTEL
(two stars)
Main Street
PO Box 4
8135
Tel: 482 1101
Fax: 482 2228

Franschhoek

HUGUENOT
HOTEL
(two stars)
Huguenot Road
PO Box 27
7690
Tel: 2092

George

FAR HILLS
PROTEA HOTEL
(three stars)
N2 National Road
PO Box 10
6530
Tel: 71 1295
Fax: 71 1951

HAWTHORNDENE
HOTEL
(two stars)
Morning Glory Lane
PO Box 1
6530
Tel & Fax: 74 4160

Gordon's Bay

VAN RIEBEECK
HOTEL
(three stars)
67 Beach Road
PO Box 10
7150
Tel: 56 1441
Fax: 56 1572

Grabouw

HOUW HOEK
INN
(two stars)
Off N2
off Grabouw / Bot
River
PO Box 95, 7160
Tel: 4 9646
Fax: 4 9112

Greyton

THE GREYTON
(two stars)
36 Main Road
PO Box 7, 7233
Tel & Fax: 254 9892

Hermanus

MOUNTAIN
DRIVE GUEST
HOUSE
(two stars)
66 Mountain Drive
PO Box 785, 7200
Tel: 2 4452

THE MARINE
HOTEL
(three stars)
Main Road
PO Box 9
7200
Tel: 2 1112
Fax: 2 1533

Hout Bay

HOUT BAY
MANOR
(two stars)
Main Road
PO Box 27035
7872
Tel: 790 5960
Fax: 790 4952

Keurboomstrand

KEURBOOMS
HOTEL
(two stars)
Keurbooms Road
PO Box 889
Plettenberg Bay
6600
Tel: 9311 / 2
Fax: 9362

Kleinmond

THE BEACH
HOUSE
(three stars)
13 Beach Road
PO Box 199
Kleinmond 7195
Tel: 3130
Fax: 4022

Knysna

KNYSNA
PROTEA HOTEL
(three stars)
51 Main Street
PO Box 33, 6570
Tel: 2 2127
Fax: 2 3568

Laingsburg

GRAND HOTEL
(two stars)
Station Street
PO Box 8, 6900
Tel: 38

LAINGSBURG
COUNTRY
HOTEL
(two stars)
Voortrekker Street
PO Box 53, 6900
Tel: 9 / 185
Fax: (02 372) 62

Lambert's Bay

MARINE PROTEA
HOTEL
(three stars)
Voortrekker Street
PO Box 249, 8130
Tel: 432 1126
Fax: 432 1036

RASTON
GASTHAUS
(three stars)
24 Riedeman Street
PO Box 20, 8130
Tel: 432 2431
Fax: 432 2422

Matjiesfontein

LORD MILNER
HOTEL
(two stars)
Logan Road 6901
Tel: Ask for 5203
Fax: Ask for 5802

Montagu

AVALON
SPRINGS HOTEL
(three stars)
Uitvlucht Street
PO Box 110, 6720
Tel: 4 1150
Fax: 4 1906

MONTAGU
HOTEL
(two stars)
Bath Street
PO Box 338, 6720
Tel: 4 1115
Fax: 4 1905

Moorreesburg

SAMOA HOTEL
(two stars)
Central Street
PO Box 16, 7310
Tel: 3 1201
Fax: 3 2031

Mossel Bay

EIGHT BELLS
MOUNTAIN AIR
(three stars)
Ruitersbosch
District
PO Box 436, 6500
Tel & Fax: 95 1544/5

ROSE & CROWN
HOTEL
(three stars)
3 Matfield Street
PO Box 302
6500
Tel: 91 1069
Fax: 91 1426

SANTOS PROTEA
HOTEL
(three stars)
Santos Road
PO Box 203
6500
Tel: 7103
Fax: 91 1945

Muizenberg

SHRIMPTON
MANOR
(two stars)
19 Alexander Road
7945
Tel: 788 1128/9
Fax: 788 5225

Oudtshoorn

CAVES MOTEL
(two stars)
Baron Van Reede Str
PO Box 125, 6620
Tel & Fax: 22 2511

HOLIDAY INN
GARDEN COURT
- OUDTSHOORN
(three stars)
Baron Van Reede
Street
PO Box 52, 6620
Tel: 22 2201
Fax: 22 3003

KANGO PROTEA
HOTEL
(three stars)
Baron Van Reeds
Street
PO Box 370, 6620
Tel: 22 6161
Fax: 22 6772

THE FEATHER
INN
(two stars)
218 High Street
PO Box 165, 6620
Tel & Fax: 29 1727

QUEENS HOTEL
(two stars)
Baron Van Reede
Street
PO Box 19
6620
Tel: 22 2101
Fax: 22 2104

Paarl

GRANDE ROCHE
HOTEL
(five stars)
Plantasie Street
PO Box 6038
7620
Tel: 63 2727
Fax: 63 2220

ZOMERLUST
GASTEHUIS
(four stars)
193 Main Street
PO Box 92
7620
Tel: 2 2117
Fax: 2 8312

Plettenberg Bay

FORMOSA INN
COUNTRY
HOTEL
(three stars)
N2 National Road
PO Box 121, 6600
Tel: 3 2060
Fax: 3 3343

HUNTERS
COUNTRY HOUSE
(four stars)
Pear Tree Farm
PO Box 454, 6600
Tel & Fax: 7818

STROMBOLIS INN
(two stars)
N2
PO Box 116, 6600
Tel: 7710
Fax: 7823

THE ARCHES
HOTEL
(two stars)
Marine Way
PO Box 155, 6600
Tel: 3 2118
Fax: 3 3884

THE
PLETTENBERG
(four stars)
40 Church Street
PO Box 719, 6600
Tel: 3 2030
Fax: 3 2074

Prince Alfred Hamlet

HAMLET HOTEL
(two stars)
Voortrekker Road
6840
Tel: 3070
Fax: 3682

Robertson

AVALON GRAND
HOTEL
(two stars)
68 Barry Street
PO Box 171
6705
Tel: 3272
Fax: 6 1158

Saldanha Bay

HOEDJIESBAAI
HOTEL
(two stars)
Main Road
PO Box 149, 7395
Tel: 4 1271
Fax: 4 1677

SALDANHA BAY
PROTEA HOTEL
(three stars)
51B Main Street
PO Box 70, 7395
Tel: 4 1264
Fax: 4 4093

Sedgefield

LAKE PLEASANT
HOTEL
(three stars)
Groenvlei
PO Box 2
6573
Tel: 3 1313
Fax: 3 2040

Simon's Town

THE LORD
NELSON INN
(three stars)
58 St Georges
Street 7995
Tel: 786 1386
Fax: 786 1009

Somerset West

LORD CHARLES
HOTEL
(five stars)
Cnr Stellenbosch
and Faure Roads
PO Box 5151
Helderberg 7135
Tel: 55 1040
Fax: 55 1107

Stellenbosch

DEVON VALLEY
PROTEA HOTEL
(three stars)
Devon Valley Road
PO Box 68
7600
Tel: 882 2012
Fax: 882 2610

D OUWE WERF HERBERG
(three stars)
30 Church Street
PO Box 3200
Coetzenburg 7602
Tel: 887 4608
Fax: 887 4626

GUEST HOUSE 110 DORP STREET
(three stars)
110 Dorp Street
7600
Tel: 883 3555
Fax: 883 8174

LANZERAC
HOTEL
(four stars)
Lanzerac Road
PO Box 4, 7599
Tel: 887 1182
Fax: 887 2310

Swellendam

SWELLENGREBEL
HOTEL
(three stars)
91 Voortrek Street
PO Box 9, 6470
Tel: 4 1144
Fax: 4 2453

Vredendal

MASKAM HOTEL
(one star)
Cnr Church Street
& Van Riebeeck Av
PO Box 100, 8160
Tel: 3 1336
Fax: 3 2715

VREDENDAL
HOTEL
(two stars)
11 Voortrekker Str
PO Box 17, 8160
Tel: 3 1064
Fax: 3 1003

Wellington

KLEIN
RHEBOKSKLOOF
(two stars)
Rhebokskloof Farm
Blouvlei
PO Box 270, 7655
Tel & Fax: 3 4115

Wilderness

FAIRY KNOWE
HOTEL
(two stars)
Dumbleton Road
PO Box 28, 6560
Tel: 9 1100
Fax: 9 0364

HOLIDAY INN
GARDEN COURT
- WILDERNESS
(three stars)
N2
National Garden
Route Highway
PO Box 26, 6560
Tel: 9 1104
Fax: 9 1134

KAROS
WILDERNESS
HOTEL
(four stars)
N2 National Road
PO Box 6, 6560
Tel: 9 1110
Fax: 9 0600

Witsand/Port Beaufort

BREEDE RIVER
LODGE
(two stars)
Port Beaufort
PO Witsand, 6761
Tel: 631
Fax: 650

Worcester

CUMBERLAND
HOTEL
(three stars)
2 Stockenstroom
Street
PO Box 8, 6850
Tel: 7 2641
Fax: 7 3613

Casinos

Sun International
Casino & Slots
Locations

Northwest

Sun City
Tel: (014651) 21000

The Carousel
Tel: (01464) 77777

Mmabatho Sun
Tel: (0140) 21142/4

Molopo Sun
Tel: (0140) 24184

Morula Sun
Tel: (0146) 23320

Taung Sun
Tel: (01405) 41820

Thaba'Nchu
Tel: (05265) 2161

Tlhabane Sun
Tel: (01466) 56543/5

Botswana

Gaborone Sun
Tel: (0923) 51111

Eastern Cape

Amatola Sun
Tel: (0410) 91111

Fish River Sun
Tel: (0403) 612101

Mdantsane Sun
Tel: (0403) 612126

Mpekweni Sun
Tel: (0403) 613126

Wild Coast Sun
Tel: (0471) 59111

Umtata Holiday Inn
Tel: (0471) 22181

Umtata Imperial
Hotel
Tel: (0471) 24295

Butterworth Hotel
Tel: (0474) 4589

Lesotho

Lesotho Sun
Tel: (050) 31311

Maseru Sun
Cabanas
Tel: (050) 312434

Swaziland

Royal Swazi Sun
Tel: (09268) 61001

Nhlangano Sun
Tel: (09268) 78211

**Northern
Transvaal**

Venda Sun
Tel: (015581)
21011/2

**Central
Reservations:**

Sandton 011 783
8660

Cape Town 021 418
1465/6

Durban 031 304
9237

**Protea Hotels &
Casino**

Protea Piggs Peak
Hotel & Casino
PO Box 385
SWAZILAND
Tel: (09268)
71104/5

National
Parks &
Reserves

All camps in all the
National Parks are
open throughout
the year.
Accomodation
may be reserved
up to one year in
advance.

Pretoria

PO Box 787
Pretoria 0001
Tel: (012) 343 1991

Cape Town

PO Box 7400
Roggebaai 8012
Tel: (021) 222810

George

PO Box 774
George 6530
Tel: (0441) 74
6924/5

**Northern and
Eastern Transvaal**

Kruger National
Park
Private Bag X402
Skukuza 1350
Tel: (01311) 65611

Emaweni Game
Lodge
Tel: (012) 21 1778

MalaMala Rattray
Reserve
PO Box 2575
Randburg 2125
Tel: (011) 789 2577

Mabula Lodge
Private Bag 1665
Warmbad 0480
Tel: (015334) 616/
717

Inyati Game Lodge
PO Box 38838
Booysens 2016
Tel: (011) 493 0755

Sabi Sabi
PO Box 52665
Saxonwold 2132
Tel: (011) 880 4840

Londolozi Game
Reserve
PO Box 1211
Sunninghill 2157
Tel: (011) 803 8421

Matumi Game
Ranch
PO Box 57
Klaserie 1381
Tel: (0020) and to
book call 4313

Mfuli Game Ranch
PO Box 17
Nkwalini 3816
Tel: (03546) 620

Mkambati Game Res
PO Box 574
Kokstad 4700
Tel: (0372) 3101

Motswari — M'Bali
Game Lodges
PO Box 67865
Bryanston 2021
Tel: 463 1990

Ngala Game Lodge
PO Box 4068
Rivonia 2128
Tel: (011) 803 7400

North-West

Kwa Maritane
(Pilanesburg
National Park)
PO Box 39
Sun City 0136
Tel: (014651) 21820

Free State

Golden Gate
Highlands
National Park
PO Box Golden
Gate 9708
Tel: (014326) No.
711

Willem Pretorius
Game Reserve
Private Bag X07
Ventersburg
9450
Tel: Ventersburg
4168

Erfenis Dam
Nature Reserve
PO Box 131
Theunissen 9410
Tel: Theunissen
9410

Rustfontein Nature
Reserve
PO Box 517
Bloemfontein 9300
Tel: (051) 470511 x
2290

Tussen-die-Riviere
Game Farm
PO Box 16
Bethulie 9992
Tel: Bethulie 2803

Soetdoring Nature
Reserve
PO Box 517
Bloemfontein 9300
Tel: (051) 331011

Sandveld Nature
Reserve
PO Box 414
Bloemhof 2660
Tel: Bloemhof 1103

Sterkfontein Dam
Nature Reserve
PO Box 24
Harrismith 9880
Tel: Harrismith
23520

Mount Everest
Game Reserve
PO Box 471
Harrismith 9880
Tel: (01436) 23493/
22353

Caledon Nature
Reserve
PO Box 84
Wepener 9944
Tel: Weldam 32

Kalkfontein Dam
Nature Reserve
PO Box 78
Fauresmith 9978
Tel: Fauresmith 1422

Koppies Dam
Nature Reserve
PO Box 151
Koppies 9540
Tel: Koppies 2640

Gariep Dam
Nature Reserve
Private Bag X10
Hendrik Verwoerd
Dam 9922
Tel: Hendrik
Verwoerd Dam 45

Cape Province

Mountain Zebra
National Park
Private Bag X66
Cradock 5880
Tel: (0481) 2427

Addo Elephant
National Park
PO Box 52
Addo 6105
Tel: (0426) 400556

Tsitsikamma Forest
National Park
PO Box Storms
River 6308

Bontebok National
Park
PO Box 149
Swellendam 6740
Tel: (0291) 42735

Karoo National Park
PO Box 316
Beaufort West 6970
Tel: (0201) 52828/
9

Wilderness
National Park
Private Bag X6528
George 6560
Tel: (04455) 31302

West Coast
National Park
PO Box 25
Langebaan 7357
Tel: (02287) 22144

Augrabies Falls
National Park
Private Bag X1
Augrabies 8874
Tel: Augrabies
Falls No.4

Kalahari Gemsbok
National Park
Private Bag X5890
Gemsbok Park 8815
Tel: Gemsbok Park
901

Kagga Kamma
Nature Reserve
PO Box 7143
North Paarl 7623
Tel: (02211) 638355

**KwaZulu-Natal
Parks Board**

The following
camps are booked
through the
following:

False Bay Park
Officer-in-Charge
False Bay Park
PO Box 222
Hluhluwe 3690
Tel: Hluhluwe
03562 ask for 2911

Harold Johnson
Nature Reserve
PO Box 148
Darnall 4480
Tel: Darnall (0324)
61574

Himeville Nature
Reserve
Officer-in-Charge
PO Box 115
Himeville 4585
Tel: Himeville
(033) 702 1036

Klipfontein Public
Resort Nature
Reserve
Officer-in-Charge
PO Box 1774
Vryheid 3100
Tel: Vryheid (0381)
4383

Loteni Nature
Reserve Camp
Superintendent
PO Box 14
Himeville 4585
Tel: 033722 ask for
1540

Mkuzi Game
Reserve Camp
Superintendent
PO Box Mkuze, 3965
Tel: Mkuze Reserve
Call Office

Sodwana Bay
National Park
Officer-in-Charge
Private Bag 310
Mbazwana 3974
Tel: Jozini 1102

Spioenkop Public
Resort Nature
Reserve Camp
Superintendent
PO Box 140
Winterton 3350
Tel: Winterton
03682 as for 78

St Lucia Resort
Officer-in-Charge
Private Bag St
Lucia Estuary 3936
Telephone: St Lucia
(03592) 20

Umfolozi Game
Reserve
Reservations Officer
PO Box 662
Pietermaritzburg
3200

Umlazi Nature
Reserve
Officer-in-Charge
PO Box 234
Mtunzini
3867
Tel: Mtunzini
035322

Vernon Crookes
Nature Reserve
Officer-in-Charge
Tel: Umzinto
(03231) 42222

Wagendrift Public
Resort Nature
Reserve
Officer-in-Charge
PO Box 316
Estcourt
3310
Tel: Estcourt
(03631) 22550

Weenen Nature
Reserve
Officer-in-Charge
PO Box 122
Weenen 3325
Tel: Weenen
(03632) 809

The following
reserves fall under
the Transvaal
Provincial
Administration:

Rustenburg Nature
Reserve
Officer-in-Charge
PO Box 511
Rustenburg
0300
Tel: (0142)31050

Suikerbosrand
Nature Reserve
Officer-in-Charge
Private Bag H616
Heidelberg
2400
Tel: (0151) 2181/2/3

Blyderivierspoort
Nature Reserve
Officer-in-Charge
PO Bourke's Luck
1272
Tel: (0020) 15

Loskop Dam
Nature Reserve
Officer-in-Charge
Private Bag X606
Groblersdal 0470
Tel: (01202) 4184

Messina Nature
Reserve
PO Box 78
Messina 0900
Tel: (01553) 3235

Car Rental

Avis (Head Office)
PO Box 221
Isando 1600
Tel: Domestic Res.
(Toll free) 0809 41
3333
Inter. Res (Toll
free) 0800 03 4444

Avis - Airport
Johannesburg
Tel: (011) 788 5435

Durban
Tel: (031) 42 3282

Cape Town
Tel: (021) 934 0330

Avis Chauffeur
Drive
Johannesburg
Tel: (011) 788 5435
Cape Town
Tel: (021) 689 5971

Budget
PO Box 1777
Kempton Park 1620
Tel: Toll Free
0800016622

Budget — Airports
Johannesburg
Tel: (011) 394 2905
Port Elizabeth
Tel: (041) 51 4242
East London
Tel: (0431) 46 2634
Cape Town
Tel: (021) 934 0216
Durban
Tel: (031) 42 3809
Bloemfontein
Tel: (051) 33 1178

Campers Corner
(Camper &
Motorhome Rental)
PO Box 48191
Roosevelt Park 2129
Tel: (011) 789 2327

Protea Car Hire
PO Box 16736
Doornfontein
Johannesburg 2028
Tel: (011) 402 6328

Imperial Car Hire
(Head Office)
PO Box 260177
Excom 2023
Tel: Toll Free
0800110157

Imperial — Airport
Johannesburg
Tel: (011) 394 4020
Cape Town
Tel: (021) 934 0243
Durban
Tel: (031) 42 4648
Bloemfontein
Tel: (051) 33 3511
Port Elizabeth
Tel: (041) 51 1268

Knysna Camper
Hire
PO Box 1222
Knysna 6570
Tel: (0445) 22 444

Leisuremobiles
PO Box 48928
Roosevelt Park
2129
Tel: (011) 447 2374

Prime Car Leasing
(Formerly Hertz)
PO Box 1590
Bedfordview 2008
Johannesburg
Tel: (011) 453 7277
Pretoria
Tel: (012) 323 4504
Cape Town
Tel: (021) 234 100

Rolls Royce Hiring
PO Box 464
Constantia 7848
Tel: (021) 785 3100

Sabonazi 4x4 Cross
Country Rentals
PO Box 48191
Roosevelt Park 2129
Tel: (011) 789 2327

Bus Companies

Connex (Plusbus)
Johannesburg
Tel: (011) 774 2021
Durban
Tel: (031) 361 3363
Cape Town
Tel: (021) 218 2181
East London
Tel: (0431) 23 952
Bloemfontein
Tel: (051) 47 6352
Port Elizabeth
Tel: (041) 520 3105

Inter-Cape
PO Box 618
Bellville 7530
Tel: (021) 934 4400

Leopard Express
PO Box 307
Grahamstown 6140
Tel: (0461) 24589

Margate Mini-
Coach
PO Box 117
Margate 4275
Tel: (03931) 21406

Translux
Cape Town
Tel: (021) 405 3333
Durban
Tel: (031) 361 8333
Johannesburg
Tel: (011) 774 3333
Port Elizabeth
Tel: (041) 520 2400
Bloemfontein
Tel: (051) 408 3242
East London
Tel: (0431) 44 2333

Greyhound
Express Cityliner
Johannesburg
Tel: (011) 333 2130
Cape Town
Tel: (021) 418 4312
Durban
Tel: (031) 361 774
Bloemfontein
Tel: (051) 30 2361

Taxis

Johannesburg

City Taxis cc
PO Box 10982
Johannesburg 2000
Tel: (011) 29 5213-6

Jan Smuts Taxi
Bureau
Tel: (011) 979 2222

Maxi Taxi Cabs
Tel: (011) 648 1212

Rose Radio Taxis
Tel: (011)
725 3333 / 725 1111

Serviceable Sisters
37a Keyes Ave
Rosebank
Tel: (011) 788 9302

Taxi Bureau
Tel: (011) 337 5858/9

Cape Town

Marine Taxi & Car
Hire
Tel: (021) 434 0434

Peninsula Taxis
Service
Tel: (021) 434 4444

Casanova's
Simonstown
Tel: (021) 786 3930

Delhouzie Taxis
Tel: (021) 994 659

Durban

Aussies Taxis
Tel: (031) 37 2345

Fast Get-abouts
Between beaches
and south of Berea
Tel: (031) 307 3503
Port Elizabeth
Hunters Radio Cabs
Tel: (041) 55 7344

Taxi Ranks

Victoria Quay
Fleming St
Tel: (041) 55 3296
Railway Station
Tel: (041) 55 268

Trains

The Blue Train
Johannesburg
Tel: (011) 774
4469 / 774 4470
Cape Town
Tel: (021) 405 2672
Pretoria
Tel: (012) 315 2436
Durban
Tel: (031) 361 7550

Spoornet
Johannesburg
Tel: (011) 773 2944 /
5/6/7
Pretoria
Tel: (012) 315 2401 / 6
Cape Town
Tel: (021) 405 3071 /
3581
Durban
Tel: (031) 361 7621
Port Elizabeth
Tel: (041) 520
2400 / 520 2662
East London
Tel: (0431) 44
2719 / 44 2769
Bloemfontein
Tel: (051) 408 2941
Pietermaritzburg
Tel: (0331) 55
2006 / 55 2390

Major Hospitals

Cape Town

Groote Schuur
Hospital
Tel: (021) 404 9111

Medic-Alert C.T.
61 7328 / 25 4835

Tygerberg Hospital
Tel: (021) 938 4911

Johannesburg

Johannesburg
General Hospital
Tel: (011) 488 4911

Mulpark Hospital
PO Box 91155
Auckland Park 2006
Tel: 726-3124

Park Lane Clinic
12 Junction Av
Parktown
Tel: 642-7311

Morningside Clinic
Private Bag X6
Bryanston 2021
Tel: 783-8901

Rosebank Clinic
PO Box 52230
Saxonworld 2132
Tel: 788-1980

Sandton Clinic
Private Bag X1
Bryanston 2021
Tel: 709-2000

Kenridge Hospital
21 Eton Road
Parktown
Tel: 726-5331

J.G. Strijom
Hospital
Auckland Park
Johannesburg
Tel: (011) 726 5128

Hillbrow Hospital
Joubert Park
Johannesburg
Tel: (011) 720 1121

Baragwanath
Hospital
Tel: (011) 933 1100

South Rand
Hospital
Tel: (011) 435 0022

Edenvale Hospital
Tel: (011) 882 2400

Durban

Addington
Hospital
South Beach
Tel: (013) 322111

Entabeni Hospital
148 South Ridge Rd
Tel: (031) 811344

Parklands Hospital
Hopelands Road
Tel: (031) 288181

St Augustine's
Hospital
107 Chelmsford Rd
Tel: (031) 211221

Wentworth
Hospital
Oceanview Road
Bluff
Tel: (031) 484311

Westville Hospital
Spine Road
Tel: (031) 867053

Banks

ABSA Bank
28th Floor,
Sanlam Centre
(Cnr Jeppe and
Van Wielligh
Street)
Johannesburg
PO Box 1190
Johannesburg 2000
Tel: (011) 330 3111
Fax: (011) 330 3513/
4
Telex: 4 82483

African Bank
Limited
56 Marshall Street
Johannesburg 2001
PO Box 61352
Marshalltown 2107
Tel: (011) 836 2331
Fax: (011) 838 2845
Telex: 4 83089

Cape of Good Hope
Cape of Good Hope
Bank Building
117 St George's Mall
Cape Town 8001
PO Box 2125
Cape Town 8000
Tel: (021) 480 5000
Fax: (021) 26 1453

Development Bank
of Southern Africa
Headway Hill
Midrand
PO Box 1234
Halfway House
1685
Tel: (011) 313 3911
Fax:(011) 313 3086

First National Bank
of Southern Africa
4th Floor
4 First Place Bank
City
(Cnr Simmonds
and Pritchard Str)
Johannesburg
2001
PO Box 7791
Johannesburg
2000
Tel: (011) 371 9111
Fax: (011) 371 2202
Telex: 4 88565

Habib Overseas
Bank Limited
2nd Floor
Standard Bank
Centre
78 Fox Street
PO Box 10098
Johannesburg 2000
Tel: (011) 834 8410
Fax: (011) 834 7446

Mercantile Bank
Limited
2nd Floor
9 St David's Place
Parktown 2193
PO Box 32917
Braamfontein
2017
Tel: (011) 484 3500
Fax: (011) 484 1244

Rand Merchant
Bank Limited
25 Fredman Drive
Sandton 2196
PO Box 786273
Sandton 2146
Tel: (011) 883 3650
Fax: (011) 783 0715
Telex: 4 27796

Santambank
40 De Ville Street
Langlaagte
Johannesburg
2001
Tel: (011) 837 9675

South African
Reserve Bank
PO Box 427
Pretoria 0001
Tel: (012) 313 9111

Standard Bank of
South Africa
5 Simmonds Street
Marshaltown
Johannesburg
2001
PO Box 4425
Johannesburg
2000
Tel: (011) 636 9112
Fax: (011) 636 6816

The Trust Bank of
Africa
Trust Bank Centre
56 Eloff Street
PO Box 4854
Johannesburg
2000
Tel: (011) 331 4411

Volkskas
230 van der Walt
Street
PO Box 578
Pretoria 0001
Tel: (012) 295911

Financial Organisations

Central Economic
Advisory Service
HSRC Building
5th Floor
134 Pretorius Street
Private Bag x455
Pretoria 0001
Tel: (012) 325 1545
Fax: (012) 325 1569

Financial Services
Board
446 Rigel Avenue
Erasmusrand
Pretoria 0181
PO Box 35655
Menlo Park 0102
Tel: (012) 347 0660
Fax: (012) 347 0221

Johannesburg Stock
Exchange (JSE)
Cnr Pritchard and
Diagonal Streets
PO Box 1740
Johannesburg 2000
Tel: (011) 377 2200
Fax: (011) 834 7402

South African
Chamber of Business
(SACOB)
JCC House
3rd Floor, (Cnr
Empire and Owl
Streets
Auckland Park
Johannesburg 2092
PO Box 91267
Auckland Park 2006
Tel: (011) 482 2524
Fax: (011) 726 1344

Witwatersrand
Chamber of
Commerce and
Industry
JCC House
6th Floor, Cnr
Empire and Owl Str
Auckland Park
Johannesburg 2092
Private Bag 34
Auckland Park
2006
Tel: (011) 726 5300
Fax: (011) 726 8421

Night Spots

Durban
Music:
Edward Hotel
(live music)
Marine Parade
Tel: (031) 37 3681

Elarish
(dinner & dance)
Southway Mall
Tel: (031) 4659577

Genesis
(Restaurant, jazz
club & disco)
Central
Tel: (031) 37 9756

Octagon
(jazz & reggae club)
Central
Tel: (031) 304 8921

Palladium
(cabaret)
Isipingo
Tel: (031) 92 4870/
4320

Select 21
(supper club)
City Centre
Tel: (031) 37 2435/

Pubs
Keg and Thistle
140 Florida Road
Tel: (031) 235 315

Cape Town
Music:
City Hall
(Cape Town
Symphony
Orchestra)
Tel: (021) 462 1250

Victoria & Alfred
Waterfront
V&A Basins, Table
Bay Harbour
Tel: (021) 418 2369
*Found at the
Waterfront:*
Bertie's Landing
(pub)
Quay Four
(live music)
The Pumphouse
(live music)
Ferrymans's (pub)
Dock Rd Cafe
(theatre & jazz)
The Green Dolphin
(live music, jazz)
Arena (dancing)

Pubs
Keg and Grouse
Shop 40 Riverside
Centre
Rondebosch 7700

Keg and Carriage
77 Old Dock Road
Foreshore
Tel: (021) 419 6484

Artie's Cellar Pub
34 Riebeeck St
City Centre
Tel: (021) 419 3366

Barristers
Newlands
Tel: (021) 64 1792

Boer 'n Brit
Alphen Hotel
Constantia
Tel: (021) 794 5011

Brass Bell
Kalk Bay Station
Tel: (021) 788 5455

The Crowbar Pub
43 Waterkant
Street
City Centre
Tel: (021) 419 3660

Dias Tavern
15 Harrington
Street
City Centre
Tel: (021) 45 7547

Emily's
Lord Nelson Hotel
Simonstown
Tel: (021) 786 1386

Feathers
Royal Standard
Hotel
Mowbray
Tel: (021) 689 2001

Fireman's Arms
25 Mechau Street
City Centre
Tel: (021) 419 1513

Flags
Caledon Street
City Centre
Tel: (021) 462 4455

The George
32 Waterkant Str
City Centre
Tel: (021) 25 3636

Jug 'n Jar
Metropole Hotel
38 Long Street
City Centre
Tel: (021) 23 6363

Queen's
Dock Road
City Centre
Tel: (021) 25 2201

On the Rocks
Ambassador Hotel
Bantry Bay
Tel: (021) 439 6170

Seagulls
Fritz Sonnenberg Rd
Green Point
Tel: (021) 419 0295

The Stag's Head
71 Hope Street
City Centre
Tel: (021) 45 4918

Vasco da Gama
Tavern
3 Alfred Street
City Centre
Tel: (021) 25 2157

Johannesburg

**Pubs and Wine
Bars**

Keg and Crown
192 Oxford Street
Illovo 2196
Tel: (011) 880 3143

Keg and Lion
Shop 4, Grosvenor
Crossing
Cnr William Nicol
& Main Road
Bryanston
Tel: (011) 463 5818

Radium Beer Hall
282 Louis Botha Av
Orange Grove
Tel: (011) 728 3866

Theme Bars

Milpark Holiday Inn
Auckland Park
Tel: (011) 726 5100

**Dinner Dance/
Supper Clubs**

Caesar's Palace
Cnr Jorissen/
Simmonds St
Braamfontein
Tel: (011) 403 2420

Capri Hotel
off Louis Botha Av
Savoy Estate
Tel: (011) 786 2250

Jaggers
Mutual Square
Oxford Road
Rosebank
Tel: (011) 786 1718

The Huntsman
Mariston Hotel
Cnr Claim/Koch
Streets

The Villa Moura
Sandton Sun Hotel
Sandton
Tel: (011) 783 8701

Late Night Venues

Late-Nite Al's
Empire Road,
Auckland Park
Tel: (011) 482 2055

Fisherman's Village
Bruma Lake
Tel: (011) 616 2206

The First,
Rosebank
Tel: (011) 880-3980
D.F. Malan Drive,
Blackheath
Tel: (011) 678-7815

Hard Rock Cafe
204 Oxford Road
Illovo 2196
Tel: (011) 447 2583/
788 5505

Cabaret
58 Pretoria Street
Hillbrow
Tel: (011) 642 1644

**Live Music
Venues**

Kippie's at the
Market Theatre

Roxy Rhythm Bar
Melville Hotel
Tel: (011) 726 6019

Sunnyside Hotel
2 York Road
Parktown
Tel: (011) 643 7226

Foxy's
Old Rivonia Road
Tel: (011) 803 2202

Cinemas

Cape Town
Cine 1,2,3
4th Floor,
Golden Acre
Adderley Str
Tel: (021) 25 2720

Labia: Orange
Street, Gardens
Tel: (021) 24 5927

Nu-Metro:
Stuttafords Town
Square,
Adderley Street
Tel: (021) 26 1818

Monte Carlo 1 & 2
Monte Carlo
Building
Rua Vasco da Gama
Tel: (021) 25 3052

Durban
The Wheel
Gillespie Street
Durban
Tel: (031) 324324

Sanlam Centre
Pinetown

Ster Kinekor
Tel: (031) 379 331

Johannesburg
Computicket
Tel: (011) 331 9991
(Booking Agency)

Ster-Kinekor
Tel: (011) 331 4944

Nu-Metro Theatres
Tel: (011) 880 7040

Mini Cine,
Hillbrow
Tel: (011) 642 8915

Port Elizabeth
Kine Park Complex
Rink Street
City Centre

Cine 1,2,3,4
Hotel Elizabeth
City Centre

Theatres

Cape Town
UCT Arena
Orange Street
Tel: (021) 24 2340

Baxter Theatre
Complex
Main Rd, Rosebank
Tel: (021) 685 7880

Herschel Theatre
21 Herschel Road
Claremont
Tel: (021) 64 4010

Little Theatre
Orange Street
Tel: (021) 24 2340

Masque Theatre
(Amateur)
Main Rd
Muizenberg
Tel: (021) 788 1898

Milnerton
Playhouse
Pienaar Road
Milnerton
Tel: (021) 557 3206

Nico Malan
Theatre Complex
DF Malan Street
Tel: (021) 21 5470

The Theatre on the
Bay
1A Link Street
Camps Bay
Tel: (021) 438 3301

Durban
Natal Playhouse
Smith Street
City Centre
Tel: (031) 304 3631

Elizabeth Sneddon
Theatre
Tel: (031) 814 544

Johannesburg
The Market Theatre
Bree Street
Newtown
Tel: (011) 832 1634

State Theatre
Pretoria
Tel: (012) 322 1665

Windybrow Theatre
Nugget Street
Hillbrow
Tel: (011) 720 7009

Alhambra Theatre
109 Sivewright Av
Doornfontein
Tel: (011) 402 6174

Alexandra Theatre
36 Stiemens Street
Braamfontein
Tel: (011) 339 3461

Port Elizabeth

Opera House
Whites Road
City Centre

The City Hall
On the square
City Centre

Manneville
St George's Park
Cnr Park Drive
and Rink Street
City Centre

The Savoy Club
Cnr Stirk and
Collett Streets
Parsons Hill

Ford Little Theatre
The Athenaeum
Belmont Terrace
City Centre

Bloemfontein
Sand Du Plessis
Theatre
St Andrew Street
Bloemfontein

Art
Galleries

Cape Town
Michaelis
Green Market Sq
City Centre
Tel: (021) 24 6367

Rust-en Vreugd
78 Buitenkant St
City Centre
Tel: (021) 45 3628

SA National Art
Gallery
Off Government
Avenue, Gardens
City Centre
Tel: (021) 45 1628

William Fehr
Cape of Good
Hope Castle
City Centre
Tel: (021) 408 7911

Durban

Africa Gallery
Shop 11b
Granada Centre
Umhlanga Rocks

African Art Centre
Guildhall Arcade
Gardiner Street

Big Ben Art Gallery
Cnr 7th Ave &
Argyle Rds
Tel: (031) 328441

Durban Art Gallery
City Hall
Smith Street
Tel: (031) 3006911

NSA Gallery
Overport City
Ridge Road
Tel: (031) 294934

Peter van
Blommestein
Elangeni Hotel
Marine Parade
Tel: (031) 371 321

Maharani Art
Gallery
Maharani Hotel
Tel: (031) 327 361

Royal Hotel Gallery
Smith Street
Marine Parade
Tel: (031) 304 0331

Johannesburg
Artist's Market
Zoo Lake
Tel: (011) 432 1482

Johannesburg Art
Gallery
Joubert Park
Tel: (011) 725 3130

Everard ReadGallery
6 Jellicoe Avenue
Rosebank
Tel: (011) 788 4805

Totem Meneghelli
Primitive Arts &
Antiques
Shop U 17A
Sandton City
Tel: (011) 884 6300

Primitive Art and
Antiquities
34 Mutual Square
169 Oxford Road
Rosebank
Tel: (011) 447 1409

Soweto Art Gallery
Victory House
2nd Floor,
Cnr Commissioner
and Harrison Street
Tel: (011) 836 0252

Gallery 21
3rd Floor,
Victory House
34 Harrison Street
Johannesburg
Tel: (011) 838 6630

Unisa Art Gallery
Pretoria
Tel: (012) 429 6621

Wits University
Art Gallery
University Campus
Braamfontein
Tel: (011) 716 3162

Katlehong Art
Centre
Zicelele Ihlombe
Gallery
Germiston
Tel: (011) 825 3235
ext 342

Fuba Gallery
Market Theatre
Johannesburg
Tel: (011) 834 7139

Zalah Wildlife
Gallery
21 Barnacle Road
Forest Hill
Tel: (011) 683 7254

Johannesburg
Studio Route
Tel: (011) 646 1170

The Photo
Workshop
Market Theatre
Cnr Bree &
Wolhunter Streets
Newtown
Tel: (011) 832 1641

Natalie Knight
Gallery
8 Lower Mall
Hyde Park Corner
Hyde Park
Tel: (011) 880 2212

Pretoria Art
Museum
Cnr Wessels &
Schoeman Street
Arcadia
Tel: (012) 344 1807

Port Elizabeth

King George VI Art
Gallery
St Georges Park
City Centre

Anthony Adler
Gallery
164 Russell Road
Tel: (041) 561 353

Atelier Galerie
Pearson Street
City Centre

Bloemfontein

Oliewenhuis Art
Gallery
Harry Smith Road
Arboretum
Bloemfontein

SA Media Directory

Magazines

Getaway
3rd Floor, Sandton
City Centre
Sandton
Tel: (011) 783 7030

Finance Week
171 Katherine
Street
Sandton 2146
Tel: (011) 444 0555

Cosmopolitan &
Femina Magazine
Rio Tinto House
122 Pybus Road
Werda Valley
PO Box 781416
Sandton
Tel: (011) 883 5212

Fair Lady &
Woman' Value
Eton Norwich Park
Sandown
Tel: (011) 884 4940/
(021) 406 2205

Style
368 Jan Smuts Ave
Craighall Park
Tel: (011) 889 0600

Drum
Eton Norwich Park
Sandown
PO Box 785266
Sandton
Tel: (011) 783 7227

You and
Huisgehoot
40 Iterengracht Str
Cape Town
Tel: (021) 4062209
Fax: (021) 4062925

People
368 Jan Smuts Av
Craighall Park
Tel: 011 889-0600

Signature
368 Jan Smuts Av
Craighall Park
Tel: 011 889-0631

Pace
368 Jan Smuts Av
Craighall Park
Tel: (011) 889 0600

Black Enterprise
Dysart House
Winchester Road
Parktown
Tel: (011) 726-2497

Picture Libraries

Shooting Star
Caxton House
368 Jan Smuts Av
Craighall Park

Newspapers

Business Day
PO Box 1138
Johannesburg 2000
Tel: (011) 497 2711

The Citizen
28 Height Street
Doornfontein 2094
Tel: (011) 402 2900

The Sowetan
61 Commando Rd
Industria West 2042
Tel: (011) 474 0128

The Star
47 Sauer Street
Johannesburg 2001
Tel: (011) 633 2411

Beeld
23 Miller Street
New Doornfontein
2094
Tel: (011) 402 1460

The Argus
PO Box 56
Cape Town 8000
Tel: (021) 488 4911

The Cape Times
PO Box 11
Cape Town 8000
Tel: (021) 488 4911

The Daily News
PO Box 47549
Greyville 4023
Tel: (031) 308 2911

Financial Mail
11 Diagonal Street
PO Box 9959
Johannesburg 2000
Tel: (011) 497 2711

The Natal Mercury
PO Box 950
Durban 4000
Tel: (031) 308 2300

The Sunday Times
First National House
11 Diagonal Street
Johannesburg 2001
Tel: (011) 497 2711

Weekly Mail
139 Smit Street
Braamfontein 2001
Tel: (011) 403 7111

Radio

Radio 702
135 Rivonia Road
Rivonia
Johannesburg 2128
Tel: (011) 884 8488

SABC Radio
Henley Road
Auckland Park
Tel: (011) 714 2566

Television

BOP-TV
Tel: (0140) 897 240

M-Net Television
137 Hendrik
Verwoek Drive
PO Box 4950
Randburg
Tel: (011) 889 1911

SABC Television
Henley Road
Auckland Park PBX1
Auckland Park
Tel: (011) 714 3287

International News Services

Agence France-
Presse (AFP)
Atrium Building
41 Stanley Avenue
Auckland Park
Johannesburg 2092
Tel: (011) 482
2170/1/2/5

American
Broadcasting
Company (ABC)
Richmond Square
15 Napier Road
Richmond 2092
Tel: (011) 482 2065

ANSA News Agency
9 Maori Road
Llandudno 7800
Tel: (021) 790 3911

ARD-TV
Richmond Square
15 Napier Road
Richmond 2092
Tel: (011) 726 4304

Associated Press (AP)
Richmond Square
15 Napier Road
Richmond
2092
Tel: (011) 726 7022

BBC World Service
1 Park Road
3rd Floor,
Richmond 2092
Tel: (011) 482 2305

CBC News
1 Park Road
Richmond 2092
Tel: (011) 482 1036

CBS News
7th Floor,
Royal St Mary's
85 Eloff Street
Johannesburg 2000
Tel: (011) 299146

Central News
Agency (CNA)
Kine Centre
1st Floor,
141 Commissioner
Street
Johannesburg 2001
Tel: (011) 331 6654

CNN
Richmond Square
15 Napier Road
Richmond 2092
Tel: (011) 726 4251/6

DPA
96 Jorissen Street
Room 201
Nedbank Corner
Building
Johannesburg
2001
Tel: (011) 339 1148

ITAR-TASS
1261 Park Street
Hatfield 0083
Pretoria
Tel: (012) 436 677

ITN
Richmond Square
15 Napier Road
Richmond 2092
Tel: (011) 726 4305/6

KYODO News
Service
Royal St Mary's Bdg
4th Floor,
85 Eloff Street
Johannesburg 2001
Tel: (011) 33 4207

LUSA News
Agency
Royal St Mary's Bdg
4th Floor,
85 Eloff Street
Johannesburg 2001
Tel: (011) 336 8881

Mainichi Shimbun
141 North Road
Sandown ext 24
Sandton 2146
Tel: (011) 844 4062

NBC News
3rd Floor,
1 Park Road
Richmond 2092
Tel: (011) 726 2501

Reuters
1 Park Road
Richmond 2092
Tel: (011) 482 1003

Sky News
1 Park Road
Richmond 2092
Tel: (011) 482 2313
(News)
726 7200 (TV)

South African
Press Association
(SAPA)
Kine Centre
141 Commissioner
Street
Johannesburg 2001
Tel: (011) 331 0661/7

UPI
Nedbank Corner
Building
96 Jorissen Street
Johannesburg 2001
Tel: (011) 403 3910

US News and
World Report
1 Second Street
Parkhurst
Johannesburg 2193
Tel: (011) 880 8596/7

Visnews
Sunnyside Centre
13 Frost Avenue
Auckland Park 2092
Tel: (011) 726 1711

Voice of America
Royal St Mary's
Building
85 Eloff Street
Johannesburg 2001
Tel: (011) 333 3811

WTN
Richmond Square
15 Napier Road
Richmond 2092
Tel: (011) 726 6302

ZDF TV
1 Park Road
Richmond 2092
Tel: (011) 726 4221

Cultural Centres, Libraries & Museums

Johannesburg
Africana Museum
121 Bree Street
Newtown
Johannesburg
Tel: (011) 833 5624

First National Bank
Museum
90 Market Street
Johannesburg
Tel: (011) 836 5887

Bensusan Museum
of Photography
Empire Road
Parktown
Tel: (011) 403 1067

Bernberg Costume
Museum
Tel: (011) 646 0716

Chris Lessing
Boxing Museum
11th Floor,
Old Mutual Centre
29 Kerk Street
Tel: (011) 834 3088

Die Ou Kaaphuis
Museum
120 Main Street
Sandown
Tel: (011) 884 2322

Geological Museum
Johannesburg
Public Library
Market Street
Tel: (011) 836 3787

Haenggi
Foundation Inc
Victory House
34 Harrison St
Johannesburg
Tel: (011) 838 6630

James Hall
Transport Museum
Pioneer Park
Tel: (011) 435 9718

Jewish Museum
Sheffield House
Kruis & Main Str
Johannesburg
Tel: (011) 331 0331

Johannesburg
Library
Market Street
Johannesburg
Tel: (011) 836 3787

Railway Society of
SA Preservation
Centre
Near Krugersdorp
Game Park
Tel: (011) 888 1154

South African
Airforce Museum
Lanseria Airport
Tel: (011) 659 2750

South African
National Museum
of Military History
Adjoining
Zoological Gardens
Earslwold Way
Saxonwold
Tel: (011) 646 5513

South African
Transport Service
Museum
Johannesburg
Station Complex
Tel: (011) 773 9114

Pretoria
Transvaal Museum
Paul Kruger Street
Pretoria
Tel: (012) 322 7632

Voortrekker
Monument Museum
Pretoria
Tel: (012) 323 0682

Cape Town
Bertram House
Goverment Av
City Centre
Tel: (021) 24 9381

Bokaap Museum
71 Wale Street
City Centre
Tel: (021) 24 3846

Cape Education
Museum
9 Aliwal Road
Wynberg
Tel: (021) 762 1622

Cape Medical
Museum
Heighton House
30 Kloof Street
City Centre
Tel: (021) 23 6172

Castle of Good
Hope
Buitenkant Street
City Centre
Tel: (021) 469 1111

Cultural History
Museum
Upper Adderley Str
City Centre
Tel: (021) 461 8280

Eskom Information
Centre
Ground Floor,
Main Tower
Standard Bank
Centre
Heerengracht
Cape Town
Tel: (021) 25 1979

False Bay Fire
Museum
48 Clovelly Rd
Clovelly
Tel: (021) 782 1387

The Fisheries Centre
Tel: (021) 418 2312

Fort Wynyard
Museum
Fort Wynyard
Street
Green Point
Tel: (021)419 1765

Herring Bequest
Institute
3 Antrim Road
Green Point
Tel: (021) 434 1216

Houses of
Parliament
Parliament Street
City Centre
Tel: (021) 403 2911

Hout Bay Museum
4 St Andrews
Road
Hout Bay
Tel: (021) 790 3270

Irma Stern Museum
Cecil Road
Rosebank
Tel: (021) 685 5686

Libraries

The City Library
Darling Street
City Centre
Tel: (021) 462 4400

The South African
Library
Botanical Gardens
Victoria Street
Tel: (021) 24 6321

Museums

SAP Musuem
Main Road
Muizenberg
Tel: (021) 788 7035

Natale Labia
Museum
Main Road
Muizenberg
Tel: (021) 788 4106

Rugby Museum
Boundary Road
Newlands
Tel: (021) 686 4532

SA Airforce
Museum
Ysterplaat Base
Piet Grobler Street
Brooklyn
Tel: (021) 508 6911

SA Maritime
Museum
Dock Road
Table Bay Harbour
Tel: (021) 419 2506

SA Museum
Queen Victoria Str
City Centre
Tel: (021) 24 3330

Sendinggestig
Museum
40 Long Street
City Centre
Tel: (021) 23 6755

Simon's Town

Simon's Town
Museum
The Residency
Court Road
Simon's Town
Tel: (021) 786 3046

Stem Pastorie
Museum
2 Church Street
Simon's Town
Tel: (021) 786 3226

The Warrior Toy
Museum
St George's Street
Simon's Town
Tel: (021) 786 1395

Worcester

Beck House
Baring Street
Worcester

Afrikaner Museum
75 Church Street
Worcester

Stofberg House
23 Baring Street
Worcester

Kleinplasie Living
Open Air Museum
Corner of Grewe
and Traub Str
Worcester

Hugo Naude
House
113 Russell Street
Worcester

Durban

Durban Library
West Street
City Centre
Tel: (031) 300 6911

Natural Science
Museum
City Hall
Smith Street
Tel: (031) 300 6214

Local History
Museum
Aliwal Street
City Centre
Tel: (031) 300 6244

Natal Maritime
Museum
Tugboat JR More at
small crafts basin
Tel: (031) 306 1092

Durban Museum
and Art Gallery
Smith Street,
City Hall
City Centre
Tel: (031) 300 6234

Killie Campbell
Africana Museum
220 Marriott Road
Durban

Whysall's Camera
Museum
33 Brickhill Road
Durban
Tel: (031) 371431

Port Elizabeth

Port Elizabeth
Museum
Beach Road
Humewood
Tel: (041) 561051

Historical Museum
No. 7 Castle Hill
City Centre

PE Military
Museum
Donkin Reserve
City Centre

Bloemfontein

The National
Museum
Aliwal Street
Bloemfontein
Tel: (051) 479609

Freshford House
Museum
Cnr Markgraaff
and Kellner
Street
Bloemfontein
Tel: (051) 479609

Queen's Fort —
Military Museum
Church Street
Bloemfontein
Tel: (051) 475478

National Women's
Memorial & War
Museum
Monument Road
Bloemfontein
Tel: (051) 473447

Hertzog House
Museum
Goddard Road
Bloemfontein
Tel: (051) 477301

Presidency
President Brand
Street
Bloemfontein
Tel: (051) 80949

The First
Raadsaal
St George Street
Bloemfontein
Tel: (051) 479610

National Afrikaans
Literary Museum
& Research Centre
President Brand
Street
Bloemfontein
Tel: (051) 4054911

Public Library
West Burger Street
Bloemfontein
Tel: (015) 83636 x 250

Business Associations

Armaments
Development &
Production
Corporation of
South Africa
(ARMSCOR)
Krygkor Building
Visagie Street
Pretoria 0002
Tel: (012) 292 9111

Association of
Chambers of
Commerce and
Industry
PO Box 784055
Sandton 2146
Tel: (011) 726 5309

Association of
Southern African
Travel Agents
(ASATA)
PO Box 5032
Johannesburg
2000
Tel: (011)403 2923/33

Atomic Energy
Corporation of
South Africa
PO Box 582
Pretoria 0001
Tel: (012) 324 2811

Cape Tourism
Authority
(CAPTOUR)
PO Box 1403
Cape Town 8000
Tel: (021) 418 5202

Council for
Nuclear Safety
PO Box 7106
Hennopsmeer
0046
Tel: (012) 663 5500

Phalabora Mining
Company
Unicorn House
70 Marshall Street
Johannesburg
2000
Tel: Phalaborwa
1390

SASOL
PO Box 5486
Johannesburg 2000
Tel: (011) 441 3111

Southern African
Regional Tourism
Council (SARTOC)
PO Box 600
Parklands 2121
Tel: (011) 788 0742

South African
Tourism Board
(SATOUR)
Private Bag X164
Pretoria 0001
Tel: (012) 347 0600

Union Steel
Corporation
General Hertzog Rd
PO Box 48
Vereeniging

Chamber of Mines
Chamber of Mines
Building
5 Hollard Street
PO Box 61809
Marshalltown
Johannesburg
Tel: (011) 838 8211

Clubs & Societies

Durban

Lions
Tel: (031) 305 5735

Rotary
International
Tel: (031) 52 3923

Round Table
Tel: (031) 705 3375

Toastmasters
International
Tel: (031) 28-2739

Freemasons:
English
Tel: (0331) 965203
Scottish
Tel: (031) 219702
Irish
Tel: (031) 217244
South African
Tel: (0931)424815

Cape Town

Lions International
Tel: (021) 45 7215

Rotary
International
Tel: (021) 61 9107

Round Table
Tel: (021) 434 8537

Toastmasters
International
Tel: (021) 531 7052

Freemasons:
English
Tel: (021) 531 6192
Irish
Tel: (021) 686 3144
Scottish
Tel: (021) 531 3627
South African
Tel: (021) 461 5400

Johannesburg

Lions Club
International
Tel: (011) 838 1537

Rotary
International
Tel: (011) 834 7909

Round Table
Tel: (011) 976 4529

Wildlife
Conservation &
Preservation
Society
Tel: (011) 867 3839

Freemasons Hall
Tel: (011) 643 3311

Country Clubs

Durban

Amanzimtoti
Country Club
Tel: (031) 283 069

Beachwook
Fairway
Durban North
Tel: (031) 838 8318

Durban Country
Club
Snell Parade
Tel: (031) 238 282

Kloof Country
Club
Tel: (031) 764 0555

Royal Durban
Country Club
Mitchell Crescent
Tel: (031) 309 1373

Windsor Country
Club
Athlone Drive
Durban North
Tel: (031) 232245

Umbogintwini
Country Club
Tel: (031) 941224

Huletts Country
Club
Tel: (031) 595330

Royal Health and
Squash Centre
Tel: (031) 3040331

Jewish Club
Old Fort Road
Tel: (031) 372 581

Umhlanga Country
Club
Umhlanga Rocks
Tel: (031) 5613779

Point Yacht Club
Yacht Mole
Tel: (031) 301 5425

Royal Natal
Yacht Mole
Tel: (031) 301 5425

Cape

Golf Clubs:
Mowbray Golf Club
PO Box 3
Pinelands 7430

Royal Cape Golf
Club
Ottery Rd Wynberg

Paarl Golf Club
PO Box 305
Paarl 7620

Stellenbosch Golf
Club
PO Box 277
Stellenbosch 7600

Hermanus Golf
Club
Main Road
Hermanus 7200

Worcester Golf
Club
PO Box 162
Worcester 6850

Western Province
Sports Club
Kelvin Grove
Campground Road
Newlands
Tel: (021) 689 8775

Belville Golf Club
Kommandeur Str
Welgemoed
Tel: (021) 913 3100

Durbanville Golf
Club
De Villiers Street
Durbanville
Tel: (021) 96 8121

Swimming Pools

Long Street
Swimming Pool
Long Street
City Centre
Tel: (021) 400 3302

Newlands
Swimming Pool
Corner of Main and
Sans Souci Rd
Newlands
Tel: (021) 644 197

Muizenberg
Seawater
Swimming Pool
Muizenberg Beach
Front
Muizenberg
Tel: (021) 788 7881

Sea Point
Swimming Pool
Beach Road
Sea Point
Tel: (021) 434 3341

Johannesburg

Country Clubs:
Royal Johannesburg
Golf Club
Fairway Ave
Linksfield North
Tel: (011) 640 3021

Houghton Golf Club
2nd Avenue
Lower Houghton
Tel: (011) 728 7337

The Bryanston
Country Club
Bryanston Drive
Bryanston
Tel: (011) 706 1361

Kyalami Country
Club
PO Box 1050
Sunninghill
Tel: (011) 702 1610

Parkview Golf Club
Emmarentia Ave
Parkview
Tel: (011) 646 5400

Bedfordview Health
and Country Club
1 Harpur Road
Bedfordview
Tel: (011) 455 1870

Benoni Country
Club
Morris Ave, Morehill
Benoni
Tel: (011) 849 5211

Sandton Health &
Raquet Club
4 Helen Road
Strathoven
Tel: (011) 883 4633

Horse Racing

Durban

Greyville
Racecourse
Mitchell Crescent
Durban
Tel: (031) 309 4545

Clairwood
Racecourse
Southern Freeway
Durban
Tel: (031) 425332

Pietermaritzberg
Scottsville
Racecourse
Pietermaritzburg
Tel: (0331) 453405

Cape Town
Kenilworth
Racecourse
Lansdowne Road
Kenilworth
Tel: (021) 797 5140

Western Province
Racing
Racecourse Road
Milnerton
Tel: (021) 551 2110

Johannesburg
Turffontein
Racecourse
Turf Club Street
Turffontein
Johannesburg
Tel: (011) 683 9330

Gosforth Park
Racecourse
Airport Road
Germiston
Tel: (011) 873 1000

Travel, Tour & Safari Operators

U Tours
PO Box 1746
Durban 4000
Tel: (031) 368 2848

Springbok Atlas
George
PO Box 3063
George Industria
6536
Tel: (0441) 74 1710

Holidays for Africa
PO Box 40802
Arcadia 0007
Tel: (012) 833 981

Hylton Ross
PO Box 32154
Camps Bay 8040
Tel: (021) 438 1500

Rand Coach Tours
PO Box 81240
Parkhurst 2120
Tel: (011) 339 1658

Springbok Atlas
Johannesburg:
PO Box 10902
Johannesburg 2000
Tel: (011) 493 3780

Durban:
PO Box 1085
Durban 4000
Tel: (031) 304 7938

Cape Town:
PO Box 819
Cape Town 8000
Tel: (021) 448 6545

Port Elizabeth:
PO Box 225
Port Elizabeth 6000
Tel: (041) 35 1038
Tel: (011) 403 2562

Tourlink
PO Box 169
Cresta 2194
Tel: (011) 404 2617

Tours d' Excellence
PO Box 120
Lanseria 1748
Tel: (011) 659 2930

Welcome Tours &
Safaris
PO Box 2191
Parklands 2121
Tel: (011) 833 7030

Outeniqua Choo-
Tjoe
Station Manager
PO Box 850
George 6530
Tel: (0441) 73 8202

African Fishing
Safaris
PO Box 124
Bergvliet 7945
Tel: (021) 48 5201

Bushveld
Breakaways
PO Box 926
White River 1240
Tel: (01311) 51998

Orange River
Adventures
5 Matapan Road
Rondebosch
Cape Town
Tel: (021) 685 4475

River Rafters
PO Box 1198
Roosevelt Park 2129
Tel: (011) 888 2084

Zululand Safaris
PO Box 79
Hluhluwe 3960
Tel: (035562) 0144

Lawson's
Birdwatching,
Wildlife &
Photographic
Tours
PO Box 507
Nelspruit 1200
Tel: (01311) 552147

Comair Wings of
the Wild
Tel: (011) 973 2911

Rail Tours
Port Shepstone &
Alfred Country
Railway Banana
Express
PO Box 572
Port Shepstone
4240
Tel: (03931) 76443

Rovos Rail
PO Box 2837
Pretoria 0001
Tel: (012) 323 6052

Travel Agents

Johannesburg
American Express
Travel Service
PO Box 1655
Johannesburg 2000
Tel: (011) 331 2378

Associated Tour
Operators
PO Box 6266
Johannesburg 2000
Tel: (011) 786 5160

Concorde Travel
PO Box 7053
Johannesburg 2000
Tel: (011) 486 1850

Cosmopolitan
Travel
PO Box 7525
Johannesburg 2000
Tel: (011) 836 0781

Delta Travel
Delta House
Kingfisher Drive
Fourways
Tel: (011) 465 8660

Endless Vacation
Travel
PO Box 783940
Sandton
Tel: (011) 783 7204

Funorama Tours &
Travel
Shop 102
Banking Mall
East Rand Mall
Boksburg
Tel: (011) 826 1511

Gundelfinger
Travel
PO Box 785620
Sandton 2146
Tel: (011) 883 9332

Miller Weedon
Travel
Head Office
Miller Weedon
House
44 Twist Street
Joubert Park
Johannesburg
Tel: (011) 720 3200

Rennies Travel
(Thomas Cook
Travel Agency)
Safren House
19 Ameshoff Street
Braamfontein
Tel: (011) 407 3211

Rosebank Travel
Service
PO Box 52394
Saxonwold
Tel: (011) 880 5954

Transnet
8 Hillside Road
Parktown
Johannesburg
2193
Tel: (011) 488 7012

World Travel
Agency
PO Box 4568
Johannesburg
2000
Tel: (011) 403 2606

World Travel
Agency (Pty)Ltd
African Life
Centre
Eloff Street
Johannesburg
Tel: (011) 29 7234

Durban
Rennies Travel
(Thomas Cook
Travel Agency)
333 Smith Street
Durban
Tel: (031) 304 9971

Club Caraville
Natal Experience
PO Box 139
Sarnia 3615
Tel: (031) 701 4156/
(011) 622 4628

Bed & Breakfast
(organize
accommodation in
private homes)
Durban & District
Tel: (031) 561 1638
South Coast
Tel: (03931) 2 2322
North Coast
Tel: (035) 550 0538
Pietermaritzburg
Tel: (0332) 303 343
Northern Natal
Tel: (03431) 51915

Underberg
Hideaways
Tel: (0331) 443505

Cape Town

Rennies Travel
(Thomas Cook
Travel Agency)
Belville
Tel: (021) 945 4000
Cape Town
Tel: (021) 25 2370
Claremont
Tel: (021) 64 2027

Miller Weedon
Travel
PO Box 1983
Belville 7535
Tel: (021) 946 1137

Trigon Travel
Old Mutual Bldg
Strand Street
Cape Town
Tel: (021) 25 1186

Fullerton's Travel
Cape Town
Tel: (021) 685 3048

Youth Hostels

Cape Town

National Office
PO Box 4402
Cape Town 8000
Tel: (021) 419 1853

Room 606
Boston House
Strand Street
Cape Town 8001

Northern Cape

Kimberley Youth
Hostel
Bloemfontein Road
Kimberley 8301
Tel: (0531) 28577

Cape Peninsula

Stans Halt Youth
Hostel
The Glen
Camps Bay 8001
Tel: (021) 4389037

Abe Bailey Youth
Hostel
11 Maynard Road
Muizenberg 7951
Tel: (021) 788 2301

Lutheran Youth
Hostel
Cnr 8th Ave &
Adventist Street
Belgravia Estate
Athlone 7760
Tel: (021) 696 6612

Cape Coastal
George Youth
Hostel
29 York Street
George 6530
Tel: (0441) 747807

Port Elizabeth
Youth Hostel
7 Prospect Hill
Port Elizabeth 6001
Tel: (041) 560697

East London Youth
Hostel
128 Moore Street
East London 5201
Tel: (0431) 23423

Transvaal
Fairview Youth
Hostel
4 College Street
Fairview 2094
Tel: (011) 618 2048

Kew Youth Hostel
5 Johannesburg
Road
Kew 2090
Tel: (011) 887 9072

Eastern Transvaal
Kruger Park Youth
Hostel
Hazyview
Tel: (01317) 67465

KwaZulu-Natal
Club Tropicana
Between
Hibberdene & Port
Shepstone
Natal South Coast
Tel: (0391) 83545

Durban Youth
Hostel
167 Ninth Avenue
Morningside 4001
Tel: (031) 303 1433

Durban Beach
Youth Hostel
19 Smith Street
Durban 4001
Tel: (031) 324945

All pictures taken by **Mohamed Amin** and **Duncan Willetts** except the following:

Gerald Cubitt: Page: 211.

G. Glass: Pages: 14 (top left), 16, 20, 22, 26, 55, 56, 199, 236, 238, 239, 281, 293 and 299.

Gerry Nelson: Page: 105.

HPH Photography: Pages: 93 and 177.

Lex Hes: Pages: 67, 154, 270, 273, 277, 287 and 302.

Marek Patzer: Pages: 14 (top right and bottom) 62, 63, 64, 65, 71, 117, 124, 139, 163, 164, 186, 192 and 264.

Mike Tamlin: Pages: 2/3, 8/9 and 188.

Nigel Dennis: Pages: 5, 25, 27, 57, 86, 95, 102, 106, 114-115, 118, 121, 123, 133, 142, 150, 151, 155, 176, 195, 197, 237, 240/241, 267, 276, 283, 284 and 285.

Walter Knirr: Pages: 73, 77, 79, 174, 208 and 214.

Peter Lillie: Pages: 59, 81, 84, 101, 108, 193, 263, 265, 268, 274, 275 and 279.

SAA: Pages: 18 and 53.

Salim Amin: Pages: 194, 257 and 303.

SATO: Pages: 30, 32, 43, 70, 88, 98, 104, 107, 110, 111, 131, 134, 156, 171, 182, 183, 198, 204, 207, 209, 225, 228, 235, 243, 247, 253, 289 and 300.

Shane Doyle: Page: 94.

Wendy Dennis: Pages: 96 and 135.